Citizens and E-Government: Evaluating Policy and Management

Christopher G. Reddick
The University of Texas at San Antonio, USA

Information Science REFERENCE

INFORMATION SCIENCE REFERENCE
Hershey · New York

Director of Editorial Content: Kristin Klinger
Director of Book Publications: Julia Mosemann
Acquisitions Editor: Lindsay Johnson
Development Editor: Elizabeth Arder
Typesetter: Gregory Snader
Quality control: Jamie Snavely
Cover Design: Lisa Tosheff
Printed at: Yurchak Printing Inc.

Published in the United States of America by
Information Science Reference (an imprint of IGI Global)
701 E. Chocolate Avenue
Hershey PA 17033
Tel: 717-533-8845
Fax: 717-533-8661
E-mail: cust@igi-global.com
Web site: http://www.igi-global.com/reference

Library of Congress Cataloging-in-Publication Data

Citizens and E-government : evaluating policy and management / Christopher Reddick, editor.
p. cm.
Includes bibliographical references and index.
Summary: "This book examines the role that citizens play in the development of electronic government or e-government, specifically focusing on the impact of e-government and citizens, exploring issues of policy and management in government"--Provided by publisher. ISBN 978-1-61520-931-6 (hardcover) -- ISBN 978-1-61520-932-3 (ebook) 1. Internet in public administration. 2. Electronic government information. 3. Electronic public records. 4. Government Web sites. 5. Political participation--Technological innovations. I. Reddick, Christopher G. JF1525.A8C57 2010
352.3'80285--dc22

2009039787

British Cataloguing in Publication Data
A Cataloguing in Publication record for this book is available from the British Library.

Table of Contents

Detailed Table of Contents

Section I examines some of the theoretical and conceptual issues on the policy and management of citizens and e-government. The collection of chapters in this section covers user-centered e-government, service delivery, and democratic governance. After reading this section the reader should be very familiar with some of the more important theories and conceptual models of citizens and e-government.

Jaeger and Bertot examine the design for and evaluation of research about user-centered e-government and its implications for policy and management. They argue that an often neglected area of e-government research is how e-government is meeting the needs of users. These authors believe that the goal of improving user-oriented e-government and more efficient government can be problematic because it is always more costly taking into account the users' perspectives. Jaeger and Bertot offer several strategies for designing citizen-centered e-government. One important conclusion of this chapter is that developing successful citizen-centered e-government can be labor-intensive and costly, requiring a range of research methods and ability to understand what citizens desire from e-government.

Verdegem and Huattekeete make the case that in e-government research the user is often neglected. These authors argue that in developing e-government policies there is a need to shift from government centric e-government to user-centric e-government. In addition, e-government research needs to move from the focus on efficiency towards effectiveness. This requires a cultural shift from a government orientation to a citizen orientation in the development of e-government. Currently the uptake of e-government adoption and use in most countries is rather low; this is most likely due to the focus of the research on its government orientation rather than citizen focus. These authors conclude that e-government research as a result should take a more holistic perspective than what it currently does.

Huang and Lee conducted a citizen survey of e-government users and nonusers in Taiwan and found that e-government had a significant impact on citizens regarding their time savings, perception of information credibility, and satisfaction with government. In Taiwan the most important impact of e-government on citizens was the savings in time that citizens received from e-government services. However, their results did not find that trust in government was enhanced as a result of e-government use.

Park examines the effectiveness of delivering e-government services and how citizens value and are satisfied with these services. Through an empirical study this author found that 38 items grouped into eight major categories influencing the effectiveness of e-government services. Essentially, the work by Park shows that the success of e-government is related to citizens' willingness to use these services. Therefore, it is critical to understand the effectiveness of e-government services, whether they are perceived to be better than conventional methods of contacting government.

Fitsilis, Anthopoulos, and Gerogiannis provide an evaluation framework for e-government projects as a way of measuring the success of e-government projects in achieving targets and user satisfaction. A key component of their framework is the inclusion of citizens in project management. Citizen satisfaction with e-government is a key measure that these authors incorporate in their framework.

Jensen shows that the content of most e-government websites reveals that they are almost universally communicating in a consumer mode of interactions rather than a participatory mode of interactions. This author's study examines both consumer and participatory interactions of citizens through an examination of 24 local government websites in the United States. The findings of the empirical analysis reveal that local government websites are generally more consumer rather than participatory oriented. Political information on a website is generally less accessible and useful than other forms of more consumer information.

Anttiroiko explores Web 2.0 technologies and their application to government. This chapter provides an overview of this technology and demonstrates some important issues that public administrators should know when adopting this technology. Web 2.0 technologies refer to users' networks and user generated content that provide a social dimension and social networking opportunities on the Web. While Government 2.0 are those technologies that give users a new role in public service and governance through social networking and content sharing activities. For example, YouTube and Facebook are able to disseminate information and services to a large audience of citizen on their government. Anttiroiko believes that Government 1.0 is hierarchical, single channel, and input-oriented, while Government 2.0 is collaborative, multi-channel, and outcome-driven.

Rosa, Rovira, Beer, and Montaner examine information and referral services through a comparative case study of Greenwich, Massachusetts, in the United States and Terrassa, Catalonia, Europe. The results of their study reveal that when comparing phone and online approaches to citizen contact, online referral services helped to reduce the required manned telephones by a third, with an increase in the number of phone calls. These information and referral services can help agencies collect data regarding the number and nature of enquiries that they received, and these statistics could be used to better serve citizens.

Section 2
Issues and Challenges

Section II examines some of the common issues and challenges faced in citizens and e-government. Some important issues covered are e-government and transparency and accountability, e-government and individual rights and responsibilities, and channel choice and e-government. After reading this section readers should be very familiar with some of the most important challenges that governments face in the implementation of e-government.

Pérez, Bolivar, and Hernández examine the degree of online transparency in Latin-American capital cities. Specifically, they examine whether capital cities are using the Internet to enhance citizens' access to public sector information. The disclosure of government information online is a significant factor in improving governance and public accountability. The empirical results of their study indicate that Latin-American capital cities are still not fully aware of the potential importance of the Internet to increase transparency.

Hamner, Taha, and Brahimi found that human factors appear to play the greatest role in the success or failure of e-government initiatives rather than more technical factors in developing countries. These authors note that one should understand the intention of use for e-government technology before its implemented. These authors believe an approach that takes into account systems engineering, determining the requirements of key stakeholders in e-government development, especially for developing countries, is critical. This chapter notes that one of the key stakeholders is citizens and their input is critically important for e-government development.

Wolf and Korosec believe that there are few e-government studies that examine security, individual rights, and government responsibility. With more governments placing information online there is an increased potential for misuse and abuse of data collected, managed and stored online. One central component to this question is the issue of privacy of citizens' information. These authors argue that governments should be more proactive in creating comprehensive legislation to protect individuals from potential intrusions on their personal lives.

Miller, Higgins, and Lopez argue that cybercrime is an unavoidable by product of greater use of the Internet. Their chapter examines the scope of cybercrime in the United States as a way to determine what future research program in this important area should address. These authors indentify the most common cybercrimes such as identify theft, online child pornography, and electronic copyright theft. Their conclusions indicate that we know very little in the fields of criminal justice and e-government on this important area of inquiry and they advocate a research program as a result.

Halperin and Backhouse examines the issue of digital indentify management of citizens in the UK as a proposed government policy. Their empirical results indicated that a number of citizens in the UK were deeply nervous about how electronic identity management might usher in a degree of risk never encountered before for citizens and government. The issues that citizens commented upon were technology failure, public authority competence and integrity, lack of control over personal data, and overpowering the state with information. Halperin and Backhouse believe that governments should understand these implications before they embark upon creating a national identity management system.

Pieterson provides an overview of channel choice and public sector service delivery. The author found that the choice of service channel such as phone and website is dependent upon the task at hand. Research shows that traditional service channels such as visiting a government office or calling the agency on the phone are still more popular than going online. The author argues that an integrated strategy, where channels are seamlessly connected, is the best in terms of serving the needs of citizens and an example of this technology is New York City's 311 customer relationship management system.

Reddick discusses the role of channel choice examining public opinion data in the United States. The results of this empirical study indicate that e-government is just one of many possible service channels for citizen-initiated contacts with their government, with the phone being the most popular contact channel. The results also indicate that when citizens need information they are more likely to want to go online, when they have a problem they will turn to the phone. The results of this chapter indicate that the task at hand drives service channel choice.

Warner and Chun show that social tagging technology can support citizen information and service requirements by facilitating discovery of needed information, services, and knowledge. Social tags act as a filter that narrows the range of potential sources that might be of interest to the researcher. This has an advantage over the traditional search engine because it makes use of knowledge and expertise of human taggers, which can be especially helpful when searching for government information online.

Section 3
Case Studies

Section III, the final section of this book, examines some selected case studies on the implementation of e-government in relationship to citizens. Some of the chapters in this section explore empirically e-government and citizens in, Malaysia, Taiwan, USA, China, and Australia. After reading this section, the reader should have a solid grasp of some of the impacts of e-governments on citizens in different countries throughout of world.

Cassell and Hoornbeek examine three models of citizen engagement, namely electronic bureaucracy, information management, and populist models. These authors perform a content analysis of municipal government websites, in a region of the United States, looking for these three features. The empirical results indicate that information management was the dominate model of developing municipal government websites. There was little evidence of municipal websites providing a populist intervention, with less than 3% having this feature. Therefore, websites have not fully accounted for democratic governance in their design and are mostly information management tools.

Kaliannan, Raman, and Dorasamy examine the reasons why citizens intend to use e-filing systems in income tax submissions in Malaysia. The purpose of e-filing systems is to encourage taxpayers to submit their income tax online, thus reducing the paper based version of income tax return filing. The results of their empirical study indicated that the intention of citizens to use e-filing systems was related to the perceived usefulness and perceived readiness of this system.

Lean, Zailani, Ramayah, and Fernando examine the factors that influence the use of e-government services in Malaysia. These authors use a survey of e-government service use and their empirical results show that trust was one of the biggest factors that decreased use of e-government services by citizens. Their findings imply that government should look into ways of enhancing trust in e-government services among citizens, as this is directly related to a higher volume of service transactions over the Internet.

Lollar conducted an analysis of 31 provincial and metropolitan websites in China to examine e-government adoption. There are two sides, as noted by this author, for increased web utilization of e-government. On the one hand, the web can be used to bring greater transparency and efficiency to its citizens. On the other hand, the web can be used to monitor and control citizens by the Chinese government. One of the important findings of this study is that Chinese e-government shows an effort to reach out to citizens and respond to their needs. Overall, e-government has played a greater role in providing public information and improving transparency and citizen outreach, while playing less of a significant role in delivering efficient services and including citizens in the decision making process of government.

Hu, Chen, and Tseng conducted a case study of an e-governance scenario workshop in Taiwan in 2008 on citizens and their views of e-government. The results of this case study indicate that current e-government initiatives are insufficient in Taiwan since they lack participatory planning for citizens or users. Citizens have little intention of using the services because they were not involved in the development. These authors recommend a model where citizens are much more involved in the development of e-government, indicating a needed move from government being technocratic driven to citizen-centric.

Yeh and Chu examine the electronic complaint system in Taiwan as a way of providing outreach to its citizens through e-government. Through a survey of users of the electronic complaint system, these authors found that service quality impacted satisfaction with e-government. The authors argue that the e-complaint system has the potential to help meet citizens' needs for better service quality and focuses on citizens' demands for e-government.

Shackleton examines the progress in local e-government in the State of Victoria, Australia, in utilizing the Internet to deliver traditional services and improve governance. This chapter does a comparative case study analysis of four local councils. This author found that adoption was related to external factors such as technology, digital divide, and higher levels of government. There were also internal factors such as funding and innovation and change that influenced e-government adoption in Australia. Therefore, differences in council should be related to priories placed on citizen involvement in their government.

Preface

This book examines the role that citizens play in the development of electronic government or e-government. This book specifically focuses on the impact of e-government and citizens, exploring issues of policy and management in government. What is unique about this book is that many of the chapters actually focus on the effectiveness of e-government, as a way of improving citizen access and engagement with their government. This book does not just focus on the adoption of e-government and its impact on citizens, but it also discusses the effectiveness this technology for governance. The primacy audiences for this book are scholars and practitioners in the area of e-government, but secondary audiences exist with those interested in the importance of citizens in information technology adoption and development.

There are twenty four chapters in this book divided into the sections of theoretical and conceptual issues, issues and challenges, and case studies. The theoretical and conceptual issues section covers some of the leading edge theories in the development of e-government and citizens. Some of the chapters in this section include: e-government creating a more user-centered government, trust and e-government use, effectiveness of e-government services, evaluation of e-government projects, images of citizens through e-government, Web 2.0 technologies and government, and online referral systems. After reading the first section the reader should have a thorough grasp of some of the major theoretical research in e-government and citizens. Most of the chapters in this section come to the conclusion that there is a need to study theoretical and conceptual reasons why citizens engage in e-government, in order to further enhance its effectiveness.

The second section of the book examines the issues and challenges, showing some of the most important problems that countries have faced in the adoption of e-government and its influence on citizens. Some of the topics discussed in this section include online transparency, human factors and e-government initiatives, security, individual rights, and government responsibility, cybercrime, electronic identity management, channel choice, and social tagging and e-government. After reading this section the reader will understand some of the most important dimensions of how e-government impacts citizens and their behavior.

The final section of this book examines case studies on the adoption of e-government and its influence on citizens. Some of the issues covered are citizen engagement and the Internet, e-filing income taxes, and citizen use of e-government services. This section also covers the development of e-government and citizens in various countries such as China, Taiwan, Australia, and India. After reading the third section the reader will have a very thorough grasp of the application of citizens and e-government in several different countries and the benefits and costs of its implementation. The following sections provide a summary of the key contributions of each of the chapters in this book to the research on citizens and e-government.

THEORETICAL AND CONCEPTUAL ISSUES

Jaeger and Bertot in Chapter 1 examine the design for and evaluation of research about user-centered e-government and its implications for policy and management. They argue that an often neglected area of e-government research is how e-government is meeting the needs of users. These authors believe that the goal of improving user-oriented e-government and more efficient government can be problematic because it is always more costly taking into account the users' perspectives. Jaeger and Bertot offer several strategies for designing citizen-centered e-government. One important conclusion of this chapter is that developing successful citizen-centered e-government can be labor-intensive and costly, requiring a range of research methods and ability to understand what citizens desire from e-government.

Verdegem and Huattekeete in Chapter 2 make the case that in e-government research the user is often neglected. These authors argue that in developing e-government policies there is a need to shift from government centric e-government to user-centric e-government. In addition, e-government research needs to move from the focus on efficiency towards effectiveness. This requires a cultural shift from a government orientation to a citizen orientation in the development of e-government. Currently the uptake of e-government adoption and use in most countries is rather low; this is most likely due to the focus of the research on its government orientation rather than citizen focus. These authors conclude that e-government research as a result should take a more holistic perspective than what it currently does.

In Chapter 3 Huang and Lee administered a citizen survey of e-government users and nonusers in Taiwan and found that e-government had a significant impact on citizens regarding their time savings, perception of information credibility, and satisfaction with government. In Taiwan the most important impact of e-government on citizens was the savings in time that citizens received from e-government services. However, their results did not find that trust in government was enhanced as a result of e-government use.

Park in Chapter 4 examines the effectiveness of delivering e-government services and how citizens value and are satisfied with these services. Through an empirical study this author found that 38 items grouped into eight major categories influenced the effectiveness of e-government services. Essentially, the work by Park showed that the success of e-government was related to citizens' willingness to use these services. Therefore, it is critical to understand the effectiveness of e-government services, whether they are perceived to be better than conventional methods of contacting government.

Fitsilis, Anthopoulos, and Gerogiannis in Chapter 5 examine an evaluation framework for e-government projects as a way of measuring the success of e-government projects in achieving their targets and user satisfaction. A key component of their framework is the inclusion of citizens in project management. Citizen satisfaction with e-government is a key measure that these authors incorporate in the framework.

Jensen in Chapter 6 showed that the content of most e-government websites revealed that they were almost universally communicating in a consumer mode rather than a participatory mode of interactions with citizens. This author's study examined both consumer and participatory interactions of citizens through an examination of 24 local government websites in the United States. The findings of the empirical analysis revealed that local government websites were generally more consumer rather than participatory oriented. Political information on a website was generally less accessible and useful than other forms of more consumer information.

Anttiroiko in Chapter 7 explored Web 2.0 technologies and their application to government. This chapter provided an overview of this technology and demonstrated some important issues that public administrators should know when adopting this technology. Web 2.0 technologies refer to users' networks and user generated content that provide a social dimension and social networking opportunities on the Web,. Wwhile Government 2.0 areis technologies that give users a new role in public service and governance through social networking and content sharing activities. For example, YouTube and Facebook are able to disseminate information and services to a large audience of citizen about their government. Anttiroiko chapter showed that Government 1.0 is hierarchical, single channel, and input-oriented, while Government 2.0 is collaborative, multi-channel, and outcome-driven.

In Chapter 8 Rosa, Rovira, Beer, and Montaner examinesexamine information and referral services through a comparative case study of Greenwich, Massachusetts, in the United States and Terrassa, Catalonia, Europe. The results of their study reveal that when comparing phone and online approaches to citizen contact, online referral services helped to reduce the required manned telephones by a third with an increase in the number of phone calls. These information and referral services can help agencies collect data regarding the number and nature of enquiries that they received and governments can use these statistics to better serve their citizens. The next section provides chapters that demonstrate some of the issues and challenges in the adoption of e-government and citizens.

ISSUES AND CHALLENGES

In Chapter 9 Perez, Bolivar, and Hernandez examine the degree of online transparency in Latin-American capital cities. Specifically, they examine whether capital cities are using the Internet to enhance citizens' access to public sector information. The disclosure of government information online is a significant factor in improving governance and public accountability. The empirical results of their study indicate that Latin-American capital cities are still not fully aware of the potential importance of the Internet to increase transparency.

Hamner, Taha, and Brahimi in Chapter 10 found that human factors appeared to play the greatest role in the success or failure of e-government initiatives rather than more technical factors in developing countries. These authors note that one should understand the intention of use for e-government technology before it is implemented. These authors present an approach that takes into account systems engineering, determining the requirements of key stakeholders in e-government development, especially for developing countries is critical to their model. This chapter notes that one of the key stakeholders is citizens and their input is crucially important for e-government development in developing countries.

Wolf and Korosec in Chapter 11 argue that there are few e-government studies that examine security, individual rights, and government responsibility. With more governments placing information online, there is an increased potential for misuse and abuse of data collected, managed and stored online. One central component to this question is the issue of privacy of citizens' information. These authors believe that governments should be more proactive in creating comprehensive legislation to protect individuals from potential intrusions on their personal lives.

Miller, Higgins, and Lopez in Chapter 12 argue that cybercrime is an unavoidable by product of greater use of the Internet. Their chapter examines the scope of cybercrime in the United States as a way to determine what future research program in this important area should address. These authors indentify the most common cybercrimes such as identify theft, online child pornography, and electronic copyright theft. Their conclusions are that we know little in the fields of criminal justice and e-government on this important area of inquiry and they advocated a research program as a result.

Halperin and Backhouse in Chapter 13 examines the issue of digital indentify management of citizens in the United Kingdom, a proposed government policy. Their empirical results indicated that a number of citizens in the UK were deeply nervous about how electronic identity management might usher in a degree of risk never encountered for citizens and government. The issues that citizens' commented upon were technology failure, public authority competence and integrity, lack of control over personal data, and overpowering the state with information. Halperin and Backhouse believe that governments should understand these implications before they embark upon creating a national identity management system.

In Chapter 14 Pieterson provides an overview of channel choice and public sector service delivery. The author found that the choice of service channel such as phone and website is dependent upon the task at hand. Research shows that traditional service channels such as visiting a government office or calling the agency on the phone are still more popular than going online. The author argues that an integrated strategy, where channels are seamlessly connected, is the best in terms of serving the needs of citizens. An example of this technology is New York City's, in the U.S. 311 system customer relationship management system.

Reddick in Chapter 15 also discusses the role of channel choice examining public opinion data in the United States. The results of this empirical study indicated that e-government was just one of many possible service channels for citizen-initiated contacts with their government, with the phone being the most popular contact channel. The results also indicated that when citizens need information they were more likely to want to go online, when they had a problem they turned to the phone. The results of this empirical study are similar to the previous chapter arguing that task at hand drives service channel choice.

In Chapter 16 Warner and Chun showed that social tagging technology can support citizen information and service requirements by facilitating discovery of needed information, services, and knowledge. Social tags act as a filter that narrows the range of potential sources that might be of interest to the researcher. This has an advantage over the traditional search engine because it makes use of knowledge and expertise of human taggers, which can be especially helpful when searching for government information online for citizens to get access to. The following section provides case studies of citizens and e-government focusing on its development and effectiveness in a diverse range of countries throughout the world.

CASE STUDIES

Chapter 17 by Cassell and Hoornbeek examine three models of citizen engagement, namely electronic bureaucracy, information management, and populist models. These authors performed a content analysis of municipal government websites and looked for these three features. Their empirical results indicated that information management was the dominate model of developing municipal government websites. There was little evidence of municipal websites providing a populist intervention, with less than 3% of them having this feature. Therefore, websites have not fully accounted for democratic governance in their design and are mostly information management tools for governments.

In Chapter 18 Kaliannan, Raman, and Dorasamy examines the reasons why citizen intend to use e-filing systems in income tax submissions in Malaysia. The purpose of e-filing systems is to encourage taxpayers to submit their income tax online thus reducing the paper based version of income tax return filing. The results of their empirical study indicated that the intention of citizens to use e-filing systems was related to the perceived usefulness and perceived readiness to use e-filing.

In Chapter 19 Lean, Zailani, Ramayah, and Fernando examined the factors that influenced the use of e-government services in Malaysia. Using a survey of e-government service users, the empirical results showed that trust was one of the biggest factors that decreased use of e-government services by citizens. Their findings imply that government should look into ways of enhancing trust in e-government services among citizens, as this was directly related to a higher volume of transactions over the Internet.

In Chapter 20 Lollar conducted a comprehensive analysis of 31 provincial and metropolitan websites in China to examine e-government adoption. There are two views as noted by this author for increased web utilization of e-government. On the one hand, the web can be used to bring greater transparency, accountability, and efficiency to its citizens in China. On the other hand, the web can be used to monitor and control citizens in China. One of the important findings of this study is that Chinese e-government shows an effort to reach out to citizens and respond to their needs. Overall, e-government has played a greater role in providing public information and improving transparency and citizen outreach, while playing less of a significant role in delivering efficient services and including citizens in the decision making process of government.

Hu, Chen, and Tseng in Chapter 21 conducted a case study of an e-governance scenario workshop in Taiwan in 2008 on citizens and their views of e-government. The results of this case study indicated that current e-government initiatives were insufficient in Taiwan since they lacked participatory planning for citizens or users. Citizens had little intention of using the services because they were not involved in its development. These authors recommended a model where citizens were much more involved in the development of e-government, indicating a needed move from government being technocratic driven to citizen-centric.

In another case study of Taiwan, Yeh and Chu in Chapter 22 examined the electronic complaint system in Taiwan as a way of providing outreach to its citizens through e-government. Through a survey of users of the electronic complaint system these authors found that service quality impacted satisfaction with e-government. The authors argued that the e-complaint system had the potential to help meet citizens' needs for better service quality and focuses on citizens' demands for e-government.

Shackleton in Chapter 23 examined the progress in local e-government in the State of Victoria, Australia in utilizing the Internet to deliver traditional services and improve governance. This chapter conducted a case study of four local councils and found that adoption was related to external factors such as technology, digital divide, and higher levels of government. There were also internal factors such as funding and innovation and change that influenced e-government adoption in Australia. This chapter concluded that differences in councils might be related to priories placed on citizen involvement in their government.

The final chapter by Arlikatti, Wachira, and Gregory examined community policing and e-governance using a case study of India. This chapter indicates that the use of e-governance for policing has made it easier to measure the time required to respond to critical incidents and complaints, monitor citizen satisfaction with police response, and to obtain input from citizens when citizens are dissatisfied with the response. In several case studies of an electronic community policing system these authors found that increased transparency, trustworthiness, and efficiency in policy administration in India was enhanced through e-government.

Acknowledgment

I would like to thank the authors of this book who have made tireless efforts to get me, on time, their first drafts and revised chapters. I am also especially grateful to the peer reviewers of this book and their thorough comments on the draft chapters. I am very thankful for the editorial advisory board of the book; they were a good source of advice and inspiration. I am very much appreciative of the help that the staff at IGI Global provided to me for the development of this book; special thanks goes to Ms. Elizabeth Ardner. On a personal note, I would like to thank my wife Cathy and my two daughters Rachel Olivia and Abigail Sophia for their support during this book project.

Section 1
Theoretical and Conceptual Issues

Chapter 1
Designing, Implementing, and Evaluating User-Centered and Citizen-Centered E-Government

Paul T. Jaeger
University of Maryland, USA

John Carlo Bertot
University of Maryland, USA

ABSTRACT

The effectiveness of user interactions and engagement with e-government hinges on the extent to which the information and services being offered are user-centered, and in particular citizen-centered. E-government is not effectively serving users if they cannot find the information and services that they seek due to organizational, educational, policy, or management issues; do not have the skills to properly interact with e-government; do not understand the results that they get; or do not trust the information that they receive. As such, user-centered design and evaluation must be a key consideration in the development and management of e-government. Building on a range of previous research by the authors, this chapter will examine the issues of the designing for, evaluation of, and research about user-centered e-government and implications for e-government policy and management.

DOI: 10.4018/978-1-61520-931-6.ch001

INTRODUCTION: USERS AND E-GOVERNMENT

E-government includes a wide-range of functions such as e-voting, e-procurement, data collection, management and analysis, inter-agency collaboration, intra- and inter-agency communication, e-learning, for agency staff, and human resource management. A key focus of e-government development in many nations is on interactions between the government and users and many government agencies view e-government as their primary method for interacting with users (Bertot & Jaeger, 2006, 2008; Ebbers, Pieterson, & Noordman, 2008; Steib & Navarro, 2006). Since the early days of e-government, there have been many predictions that e-government will revolutionize democratic participation and the delivery of government services for users (Borins, 2002; Browning, 2002; Noveck, 2003; Prins, 2001; Toregas, 2001). Users of e-government include citizens, other types of residents, businesses, government employees, other government agencies, those looking to immigrate, and those looking to visit, creating a wide range of user groups to consider in the design, implementation, and evaluation of e-government. And within these user communities there is a wide range of technical, language, and other expertise – or lack thereof – that creates a number of challenges regarding the interaction with and use of e-government services and resources (Bertot, 2003). As such, it is important for e-government research to focus on the issues of how e-government is meeting the needs of users and the ways in which it is possible to improve user-centered e-government.

Designing e-government initiatives and evaluating the results through a citizen-centered lens is essential if e-government is to meet the practical expectations of delivering government information and services more efficiently and effectively and the social expectations of increasing civic engagement and government literacy. Some aspects of application development already have established methodologies for design and evaluation (e.g., functionality, usability, and accessibility), while other aspects of e-government (e.g., service preferences, performance measurement, and outcomes-based evaluation) do not have established methodologies. However, these issues will not be sufficiently addressed if considered in isolation – there is a need to focus e-government design and evaluation on these interrelated issues as the mosaic of user-centered concerns.

Many users look to e-government as a valuable source of information, considering e-government sites to be "objective authoritative sources" (Anderson, 2002, p. 1). Currently, the primary reason that people use e-government is to gather information (Reddick, 2005). In the United States, 58% of Internet users in the United States believe e-government to be the best source for government information and 65% of Americans expect that information they are seeking will be on a government site, with 26 million Americans seeking political information online everyday (Horrigan, 2006; Horrigan & Lee, 2002). Public satisfaction with the e-government services available, however, is limited.

As commercial sites are developing faster and provide more innovative services than e-government sites, public satisfaction with government websites is declining (Barr, 2007). Public confidence in government websites has also declined as much of the public policy related to e-government since 9/11 has emphasized the reduction of access to information through e-government (Feinberg, 2004; Halchin, 2004; Kirtley, 2006; Relyea & Halchin, 2003). The types of information that have been affected include many forms of socially useful information from scientific information to public safety information to information about government activities (Jaeger, 2007).

For these and other reasons, the majority of users seeking government information and services, even those with a high speed Internet connection at home, prefer to speak to a person directly in their contacts with the government (Horrigan, 2004).

Users still show a strong preference for phone-based or in person interactions with government representatives when they have questions or are seeking services, though individuals with higher levels of education are typically more open to using online interactions with government (Ebbers, Pieterson, & Noordman, 2008; Ebbers & van Dijk, 2007; Steib & Navarro, 2006; van Dijk, J.A.G.M., Peters, & Ebbers, 2007).

Even for technology-savvy users, e-government services generally are limited by difficulties in searching for and locating the desired information, as well as lack of availability of computers, Internet access, or even basic electrical and telecommunications infrastructure for many segments of the general population (Singh & Sahu, 2008; Bertot, et al, 2006). Such problems are exacerbated by a general lack of familiarity with the structure of government, lack of education about the value of e-government, language barriers, and attitudes toward technology and government among many users (Jaeger & Thompson, 2003, 2004). Also, as many e-government sites give more emphasis to presenting political or agency agendas rather than promoting democratic participation, users are less trusting of the sites themselves (Jaeger, 2005, 2007). Some studies have suggested that trust in e-government can be built through increased responsiveness to user needs and inquiries and through increased transparency, but such efforts are thus far limited (Cullier & Piotrowski, 2009; Gauld, Gray, & McComb, 2009; Hung, Tang, Chang, & Ke, 2009; Tolbert & Moss, 2006).

Further complications arise from ambivalence on the part of government agencies and officials toward direct user participation in the political process, and studies of political process behind e-government have been infrequent (Ho & Ni, 2004; Jaeger & Matteson, 2009; Roberts, 2004; Tsai, Choi, & Perry, 2009). While many governments emphasize the transformative effect of e-government, it is still primarily used as a way to make information available, provide forms and electronic filing, create an electronic face of government, and distribute the viewpoints of government agencies (Chadwick, 2001; Chadwick & May, 2003; Jaeger, 2005; Mahler & Regan, 2006). The potential transformative effects of e-government have likely also been hampered by the lack of understandings of the technologies and their potential by many political leaders, with some early efforts at direct connecting between politicians and users being undermined by the politicians' inability to use the technologies (Coleman, 2004; Graff, 2007; Jaeger, Paquette, & Simmons, 2010).

As a result of these tensions between policy, implementation, and public perception, e-government exists as an option, but not the preferred option, of a number of users. While there is a range of reasons that may deter some users – infrequent need for the sites, lack of interactivity, lack of availability of services or information that people really want, limited technological literacy – a key part of the problem is that e-government websites are not being designed to be centered on the needs of users.

BACKGROUND: EVALUATING FOR USER-CENTERED E-GOVERNMENT

E-government is a dynamic socio-technical system encompassing issues of governance, societal trends, technological change, information management, interaction, and human factors (Dawes, 2009). As a result, there have been numerous suggestions of specific methodologies that could be used to evaluate e-government websites for different purposes or from different perspectives. An early suggestion for evaluating e-government websites was in terms of compliance with laws related to security, privacy, and freedom of information (Eschenfelder et al., 1997; Smith, Fraser, & McClure, 2000). Eschenfelder et al. (1997) provide an extensive list of more than sixty evaluation criteria in two major categories – information content criteria and ease of use criteria. This methodology was originally proposed for United States federal government websites, but has since been extended to other national e-governments, such as New Zealand (Smith, 2001).

Huang and Chao (2001) assert that e-government websites should be evaluated based on usability principles, specifically that websites should employ a user-centered design that allows users of e-government websites to effectively reach the information they seek. Holliday (2002) created a set of evaluation criteria for the level of usefulness of e-government websites, including factors such as amount of information about the government, contact information, feedback options, search capabilities, and related links. The Value Measuring Methodology encourages evaluation of e-government websites based on cost/benefit, social, and political factors (Mechling & Booz Allen Hamilton, 2002). Gupta and Jana (2003) suggest evaluating e-government sites in terms of the tangible and intangible economic benefits the sites produce, while Dragulenscu (2002) suggested focusing on the quality of the services provided.

Some of these methods for evaluating e-government websites were created with specific populations in mind. Ritchie and Blanck (2003) indicate that e-government websites should be evaluated in relation to the users of human services that are provided on the site, such as everyday life information, referral services, peer counseling, and advocacy. Fenton (2004), in examining e-government websites of adoption agencies, also focuses on the evaluation factors that impact users of human services provided through e-government. While the evaluation of e-government websites in terms of users can be approached from many directions, a particularly robust approach is user-centered evaluation, which focuses on the implementation of the website from the perspective of the user (Bertot & Jaeger, 2006; Bertot, Snead, Jaeger, & McClure, 2006).

Users of e-government comprise a number of groups – citizens employing government information and services; residents and immigrants seeking information about their new country; government employees using e-government in their job functions; people in other countries wishing to know more about a nation; and on and on. Typically, "top-down" or systems-based e-government design fails to adequately consider user information needs. To be truly user-centric, e-government development must consider a series of issues that go far beyond technology: desire to use e-government, the presence of sufficient skills and technical resources among users, the means to access e-government at home, at work, or in public, and confidence in e-government (Hamner & Al-Qahtani, 2009).

For all of these different methods for designing and evaluating e-government, however, there is a need to focus on the ways in which e-government connects with citizens, as citizens constitute perhaps the most significant user groups for e-government information and services. If e-government is to be truly transformative of government in terms of citizen participation and engagement, then e-government must be citizen-centered in its development and implementation.

ISSUES: CONSIDERATIONS FOR CITIZEN-CENTERED E-GOVERNMENT

The promise of e-government is often presented as being either to engage citizenry in government in a user-centered manner or to develop quality government services and delivery systems that are efficient and effective (Bertot & Jaeger, 2008). The former suggests that governments will provide services and resources tailored to the actual service and resource needs of users, including citizens, residents, government employees, and others. The latter suggests that governments will gain economies of scale, reduce costs, and provide technology-enabled user services. However, the development of citizen-centered e-government services that achieve cost savings implies that governments know what citizens want from e-government, want to meet these identified citizen expectations and needs, and actively seek to discover what citizens want from e-government on an ongoing basis. Information collection efforts such as these by governments are, perhaps not surprisingly, rare at best (Bertot, Jaeger, & McClure, 2008; Heeks & Bailur, 2007; Yildiz, 2007).

While few governments would openly object to the concept of citizen-centered e-government, there are key barriers to creating it. Most importantly, developing citizen-centered e-government requires a number of planning and design processes to be successful. But such planning and design includes various time, effort, and financial costs that ultimately increase the costs of providing e-government services. Thus, the degree to which both goals of improved user-oriented e-government and more efficient (reduced costs of) government services can be accomplished simultaneously through e-government may be problematic.

Paralleling the need for more focus on citizen-centered design of e-government sites is the need for a stronger focus on the means of educating a more e-government aware citizenry. These services will only meet their potential for governments and for citizens if the citizens are educated about the information and services available through e-government and the clear benefits in using e-government. Governments need to find ways to increase awareness of e-government, knowledge about the ways to use e-government, and trust in e-government as a part of the overall efforts to build citizen-centered e-government through educational efforts (Jaeger & Thompson, 2003).

Ultimately, any attempt to create citizen-centered e-government must account for a number of essential elements. These range from basic issues related to the ability to use e-government to issues of building trust and tying e-government to established social institutions:

- *Access needs.* Increasingly, e-government functions rely on a high-end Internet connection. However, about half of the residents of the United States do not have access to broadband services on which e-government services rely (Horrigan, 2008). Without sufficient home access, many citizens must turn to other sources of access, either places of work or social institutions, primarily public libraries. With Internet penetration in public libraries at nearly 100%, in almost 75% of communities in United States the only free public Internet access is that which is provided by public libraries (Bertot, McClure, & Jaeger, 2008). As a result, Internet access in public libraries serves as the guarantor of access to e-government for those with no other access, those with insufficient access, and those who need assistance using e-government (Bertot, Jaeger, Langa, & McClure, 2006a, 2006b). Among patrons using e-government in libraries, 52.4% do not own a computer, 42.4% lack access both at home and at work, 40% are there because access is free, and 38.1% rely on the assistance of librarians (Gibson, Bertot, & McClure, 2009).
- *Information and service needs.* There is a need to systematically determine the actual government information and service needs for citizens. For example, in seeking information on health care services, what are the kinds of questions that users need answered? How best could such information needs be addressed through e-government services? Where are citizens most likely to turn first to try to meet these information needs?
- *Technology needs.* Governments cannot assume that having access to a computer and an Internet connection is sufficient to engage e-government. Governments need to understand the technologies by which

citizens prefer to receive their e-government services. Many government agencies view e-government websites as their primary method for interacting with citizens (Ebbers, Pieterson, & Noordman, 2008; Steib & Navarro, 2006). However, citizens may wish to receive their services through multiple technologies – computer, mobile phone, or PDA – depending on familiarity, service, and need (Van Dijk, Peters, & Ebbers, 2007). Moreover, governments need to understand the types of computing workstations, software, and telecommunications that are available to citizens to maximize access to e-government services.

- *Information and technology literacy*. A key aspect of e-government service delivery and availability is the ability of citizens to successfully use e-government services. It is not the case that all citizens are familiar with computing and Internet-based technologies (Bertot, 2003). Skills at issue can be so fundamental as to be easily missed in service development, such as the ability to use a mouse, a word processing program, a browser, a hyperlink, or a dropdown menu (Cilan, Bolat, & Coskun, 2009; van Deuesen & van Dijk, 2009). Further, underlying issues of language differences and reading literacy are significant barriers to use of e-government services for certain users. To what degree do governments have responsibilities in the area of user e-government training?
- *Government literacy*. How users interact with e-government will depend greatly on how well they understand the structure of the government. By typically arranging content by agency, governments assume users will know what agencies to check for the services they need. This approach also assumes that the name of the agency is a valid indicator of the information they have or provide. Portals alone will not solve this problem as typically, users need information that cuts across multiple agencies. A recent study found that 77.4% of United States citizens seeking e-government information check Google or a similar search engine, while only 16.5% check the main portal of U.S. e-government (www.usa.gov) (Burroughs, 2009).
- *Availability of appropriate content and services*. Once it is clear what types of services and information are needed by citizens, the government must determine the degree to which they can provide or create these services. Governments that "push" services and content that are not needed or will not be used simply encourage the non-use or distrust of e-government.
- *Usability and functionality*. Prior to the full-scale development of e-government delivery systems, there is a need to engage in an iterative design process that encompasses user assessment throughout the service's development processes (Lazar, 2005). Waiting to the end of a project, if at all, to engage in usability and functionality testing is too late. There is a wide body knowledge available to assist governments in using usability guidelines in the design of services and conducting usability testing to assess the degree to which the service meets accepted usability guidelines, such as the widely respected www.usability.gov site and the World Wide Web Consortium (www.w3c.org). Further, researchers continue to develop new approaches to more effective usability and functionality testing of e-government (e.g., Baker, 2009; Schedler & Summermatter, 2007; van den Haak, de Jong, & Schellens, 2009), meaning that government agencies could learn a great deal from research in this area.
- *Accessibility*. Although some consider accessibility testing a subset of usability, it is presented here separately as increasingly

aging populations and other populations have a range of challenges in skills to use e-government services successfully. The full range of physical and cognitive impairments presents different challenges and requires various kinds of design requirements and compatibility with assistive technologies (Jaeger, 2006, 2008). As a majority of persons with disabilities acquire them later in life, the aging of the baby boom population will swell the numbers of persons with disabilities, making universal accessibility an increasingly urgent issue in e-government (Jaeger & Xie, 2009).

- *Meeting user expectations*. For most governments, consistency between sites and services or of the materials provided has not been a high priority. However, users tend to develop expectations of what will be available and where it will be located on a site. To meet user expectations, e-government services need to be coherently presented in terms of design, organization, and intuitiveness to the user to the greatest extent possible to promote usability and consistency.
- *Information concerns*. Many e-government services – including tax filing, social services, and health services – require users to provide a great deal personally identifiable information. The privacy, anonymity, and security of information of citizens' personal information will be of significant concern to most users (Horst, Kuttschreuter, & Gutteling, 2007). Given the public attention received by lapses in privacy and security by various government agencies in handling personal information, creating true protections for these concerns and making sure citizens understand these protections is a significant challenge.
- *Social institutions providing access to e-government*. The development process also needs to account for the social institutions through which many citizens access e-government. For example, many citizens access e-government through their local public library because they lack other means of access, do not have sufficient connectivity, or need help using the services (Bertot et al, 2006a, 2006b; Gibson, Bertot, & McClure, 2009; Jaeger, Langa, McClure, & Bertot, 2007). As a result, much of the support for e-government is now provided not by the government agencies, but by library staff; some government agencies even direct citizens to go to the nearest public library if they need help using the site (McClure, Jaeger, & Bertot, 2007). These realities must be accounted for in the development of e-government services, including soliciting the input of the library professionals who are now expected to provide e-government instruction and support.
- *Trust*. The development of trust of e-government services requires engendering a perception among citizens that the information and services they receive will be accurate and current, while the information they provide will be handled properly. Such concerns are difficult to quantify and operationalize in the development process, yet are vital to the creation of truly citizen-centered e-government (Kaye & Johnson, 2006; Scott, 2006; Tolbert & Moss, 2006). One potential road to success in building trust in e-government can be seen through the reliance of many citizens on public libraries for their e-government access. Because citizens have a strong sense of trust of the library as a social institution, the e-government services they access in the library gain a higher level of trust among citizens (Jaeger & Fleischmann, 2007; Quinn & Ramasubramanian, 2007).
- *E-government 2.0*. Many agencies are moving to incorporate social networking and other Web 2.0 technologies – such as

blogs, wikis, RSS feeds, chat rooms, and twitter feeds – into the information and services they provide (Chang & Kannan, 2008). Some governments and government agencies are even creating virtual government spaces within Second Life (Laris, 2009). Such tools present the opportunity to encourage participation, engagement, and new means for disseminating government information. The Obama administration's revised www.whitehouse.gov site is a successful example of an e-government site that promotes engagement.

- *Lifelong e-government usage*. If e-government is to become socially engrained as the primary means for citizens to interact with government, more work needs to be put into developing meaningful and engaging content for children. Thus far, most kids' pages of e-government sites include facts, vaguely-educational games, and an attempt at a cute mascot, but not much in the way of the initiating a lifelong engagement with e-government. While a few sites do an excellent job of engaging children as citizens, such as the Ben's Guide to the Government from the Government Printing Office (www.bensguide.gpo.gov) or the NASA sites designed to encourage interest in science conducted by the government (www.nasa.gov), this is an area where a great deal more effort is needed to meet the potential of e-government.
- *Understanding how users actually use e-government*. Once the information, service, technology, and other user needs are better understood as a part of e-government service development, there is a need to iteratively explore how users actually use developed e-government services. A range of on-going evaluation efforts, such as outcomes assessment (Gouscos, et al., 2007), can provide information to monitor and improve e-government services. Development work does not end upon the launch of an e-government service.

These considerations are essential to the development, implementation, and continual improvement of citizen-centered e-government. Depending on the level of impact and the number of users who experience the impact, failures in any of the above areas have the potential result of not attracting new users or driving current users away, with many of these disenchanted users perhaps never intending to use e-government again.

In developing evaluation strategies to research, measure, and assess any of these elements, the use of multi-method approaches that collect data using a number of methods from the range of stakeholders of an issue is likely to provide the fullest picture of the problem and clearest path to potential solutions (McClure & Jaeger, 2008). For example, a project designed to understand the reasons for the different levels of accessibility for persons with disabilities among federal government agency websites included a policy analysis of the requirements and their intents, a survey of the web developers for the sites, user testing of the sites by persons with disabilities, expert testing of the sites by web design professionals, and analysis of the management structures of the agencies (Jaeger, 2006, 2008; Jaeger & Matteson, 2009). The appropriate data collection and evaluation methods will vary by the issue being studied and goal of such evaluation (Bertot & Jaeger, 2006; McClure & Jaeger, 2008), but the example above demonstrates the breadth and depth of information that can be central to assessing e-government and devising strategies for improving e-government services.

SOLUTIONS: STRATEGIES FOR DEVELOPING CITIZEN-CENTERED E-GOVERNMENT

Based on these elements of citizen-centered e-government, it is possible to envision a range of integrated and coordinated methods, approaches, and strategies to better incorporate citizens into the development and implementation of e-government services. The majority of these strategies are neither complicated nor difficult to implement. They may, however, result in additional costs and effort in the development, implementation, and refinement of e-government services.

Below are seven strategies for citizen-centered design that can benefit the development and implementation of e-government services and resources. The discussion at hand focuses on the major issues and the reasons these issues are important. These issues are primarily discussed at a general level to ensure the issues are as portable as possible between contexts. However, the reality is also that there is the need for a great deal more research to be conducted in the area of user-centered e-government (Bertot & Jaeger, 2006). As more research develops around these issues, there will be further studies from which to draw lessons and create references for the specific strategies that best fit the issues being studied.

Comprehensive Planning for Citizen-centered Design

A comprehensive plan for citizen-centered e-government services would minimally include identifying the:

- Goals of that service;
- Ways in which the service supports other agency/government goals;
- Managerial structure for the development of the service;
- Target audience(s) of the service;
- Information needs of citizens that the service addresses;
- Resources available for the development of that service; and
- Timeline describing key tasks and responsibilities for the development, implementation, and evaluation of that service.

Most importantly, the plan would describe the specific citizen-centered strategies – such as those detailed above – to be incorporated in the design and operation of the e-government service under development. Developing e-government services without such a plan is likely to result in poor quality services with limited capacity to meet citizen information needs, though such a service may meet agency goals of cost reduction.

Citizen Information Needs Assessments

Before the design and development of an e-government service, governments need to understand how citizens:

- Seek information on a particular topic or issue (strategy);
- Acquire information on a topic or issue (acquisition);
- Solicit expertise (source); and
- Use of that information (application).

Such knowledge enables governments to know how citizens find and use information, as well as the sources they use. Equally important is understanding the ways in which the information will be used and the specific types of problems the citizen intends to address with the information. This helps in not only an overall understanding of citizens' information behavior, but also identifies potential community partners to assist in e-government service delivery and adoption strategies.

Information and Communication Technology Availability, Expertise, and Preference

Developing a Web-based e-government service that requires a broadband connection, high-end computer, and advanced technology competencies will immediately exclude a segment, or multiple segments, of the intended service population. For example, the Department of Children and Families in Florida, through its services (food stamps, medicare, financial assistance) gateway application Access Florida (http://www.myflorida.com/accessflorida/), requires that its clients complete the application online. Yet, those who qualify for these services are the least likely to own a computer, have access to the Internet, or be conversant in computing and Internet technologies (Pew Internet and American Life Project, 2007).

The tension between system developers and designers and citizen ability to use high-end computing and telecommunications is critical to resolve. A too complex system may not be used at all; a system that resides on technologies to which the citizen does not have access will also guaranty failure. By understanding the technology access and capabilities of the various segments of citizens, governments can develop systems that better meet the needs of citizens, but also understand the types of training and support citizens may need for successful engagement of e-government.

Citizen Engagement

Top-down, systems-oriented e-government services can result in elegantly designed and technically sophisticated e-government systems that completely miss the intended citizens' needs. The top down approach is often less costly than conducting a range of needs assessments and other strategies as outlined in this chapter. The products and services that can result from top-down or systems based design can include, for example, lengthy forms that collect unneeded data; services that defy logic in their use and/or access; complicated instructions that simply cannot be accommodated by online applications; and excessive personal data for which the user has not been reassured of privacy and security concerns (to name but a few). All of these types of problems can be identified and corrected by engaging users in the actual design of the service.

There are a range of tools and techniques in which governments can engage to develop successful e-government services:

- Focus groups and interviews (with experts and users);
- Usability, functionality, and accessibility testing throughout the design and development process;
- Encouraging real-time comments and suggestions about the services being used;
- Log file and transaction log analysis;
- Providing interactive help screens or 1-800 assistance; and
- Developing and adhering to measures and standards of service quality.

There are other strategies and approaches, but the key is to include user feedback during the e-government service development and design phases as well as while the service is in operation – not as an afterthought.

Iterative Evaluation for Continual Improvement

Because an e-government service is launched does not mean that feedback should discontinue. Governments need to incorporate ongoing evaluation practices regarding their e-government services to continually improve and enhance their services. This type of evaluation is known as formative evaluation – ongoing evaluation that monitors program activities with the goal of modifying and improving the program on a regular basis. Such program evaluation cannot occur without significant and ongoing user input that is collected in a systematic and regular process. Governments can implement various strategies to do this – online surveys (brief pop-up surveys or more detailed surveys); focus groups and interviews with service users; log file analysis; and continued usability testing, for example.

Community-Based Partnerships

Related to many of the above, the development and launch of e-government services can benefit from the inclusion of community-based organizations such as public libraries and community technology and other centers. In the United States, users of e-government services are increasingly seeking assistance with e-government services from public libraries (Bertot et al, 2006a, 2006b), though governments do not necessarily view public libraries as agents of e-government. As trusted community centers with information and technology professionals and providers of public access computer and Internet access, citizens find their way to public libraries for help in accessing, understanding, and using e-government services (Bertot et al, 2006a, 2006b; Jaeger & Fleischmann, 2007). This is particularly true in times of disaster, as witnessed during the multiple hurricanes that struck the U.S between 2004 and 2006 (Jaeger, et al, 2006).

By working with community partners, governments can increase the chances of success and use of e-government by helping the partners understand the e-government programs, services, and service requirements. The key word here, however, is "partnership." The perspective of the government "off-loading" e-government services, instruction, and support to community organizations without coordinating, training, and involvement is not likely to improve citizen-oriented services. Moreover, governments and community partners can collaborate in preparing a range of training and support material to facilitate citizen interaction with a range of e-government services.

Politically-Based Content and Design

Governments are inherently political and operate in an environment in which politics often drive service and other decisions, frequently resulting in e-government websites that are politically motivated or inherently partisan (Chadwick, 2003; Jaeger, 2005, 2007). Citizen-based e-government services meet the needs of citizens as a *first* consideration rather than first meeting the political needs of a government official or agency. Citizens will never trust e-government fully if they see it as a primary means for disseminating the partisan views of leaders of the government. Further, a significant barrier to citizen-centered e-government are political concerns from government officials who do not want to know (or let it be made public) about problems with e-government services not serving the needs of the citizens. Strategies outlined in this paper ensure input from citizens as a means of improving those services, even if some of this input may not be the input that designers want to hear.

Strategies to reduce politically-based design and implementation considerations in e-government may be complicated and difficult to implement, though the key goal is to avoid intermingling purely partisan content with unbiased government information and services. One approach is to make certain that potential political impacts from e-government services are anticipated prior to implementing the service and steps to mitigate possible problems have been considered. A second strategy is to keep the broader community of government officials informed about the development and design of individual e-government services. But the best approach may be for the service designers to have done their homework by including citizens in services design so that unanticipated political impacts can be minimized before the e-government services are implemented.

FUTURE RESEARCH PATHS AND OPPORTUNITIES

The above strategies are not comprehensive, but they suggest a mosaic of the issues involved in developing successful citizen-centered e-government. In short, successful citizen-centered e-government can be labor-intensive and costly, requiring a range of expertise in research methods, qualitative and quantitative data analysis techniques, technologies, systems and application design, a fundamental understanding of what citizens want from e-government, and an ability to elicit from users their needs from e-government.

The trade-offs between successful citizen-centered e-government services (as described above) and the drive for reduced costs in the delivery of government services offers a broad range of research opportunities that have yet to be addressed include:

- What value does citizen-centered design and implementation add to e-government?
- How can citizen-centered design and implementation be employed to increase usage of e-government?
- How do citizen-centered e-government services accommodate the needs of different segments the population?
- Are there generalizable strategies and best practices for improving citizen-centered e-government services among state, local, and federal governments?
- How can usability, functionality, and accessibility testing be incorporated into the design and operation of e-government to promote citizen-centered services?
- What are appropriate measures of high quality citizen-centered e-government services and what are comparable measures across different types of governments?
- What approaches are most successful in increasing trust of e-government?
- How do different managerial styles and organizational structures affect the development of citizen-centered e-government services?
- What types of knowledge, skills, and attitudes are most important for the successful design and operation of citizen-centered e-government services?
- How important are government developed/sponsored user training sessions for the success of citizen-centered e-government services?
- What organizational factors – such as cost, effort, time, and understanding of technology – mitigate against the inclusion of user-centered design strategies in the development of citizen-centered e-government services?
- How would the minimization of politically partisan content in e-government affect usage of e-government?

These represent a subset of the important research topics that deserve greater attention to further the development and implementation of citizen-centered e-government.

CONCLUSION: SUCCESSFUL CITIZEN-CENTERED E-GOVERNMENT SERVICES

In very diverse, multicultural societies, simply accounting for the needs of different groups of citizens can be difficult, given the unique needs of older adults, youths, persons with disabilities, the economically disadvantaged, gay/lesbian/bisexual/transgender persons, and other populations (Jaeger & Thompson, 2003, 2004). Different countries are trying very different approaches to reach diverse populations through e-government, using varying approaches and divergent views of what constitute diverse populations (Hoffman, 2007). While it can be daunting to try to envision creating e-government that meets the needs and expectations such diverse groups of citizens, it is essential to consider the breadth and scope of the citizenry. One potential way to reach many different groups of citizens was revealed in the U.S. government's response to the salmonella outbreak in 2008-2009 from tainted peanut butter. A number of federal government health agencies worked together to disseminate information about the health emergency through websites, widgets, blogs, wikis, Twitter, podcasts, mobile technologies, and online videos, as well as in partnership with individual bloggers, to reach as many different segments of the population as possible at the same time (Nagesh, 2009).

Ultimately, citizen-centered e-government does not just benefit citizens. Users who are visitors, residents, or people in other countries interested in learning about the nation will all be better served by citizen-centered services. Further, government employees and companies that work with the government are also significant users of e-government information and services in the course of their jobs. An inability to find or use the content they need can be problematic, particularly for government employees trying to act in pressure situations. Among the many significant information problems at all levels of government in the response to Hurricane Katrina in 2005 related to government employees having difficulty accessing and using e-government. For example, the inadequate instructions regarding how states should write their formal requests for assistance from the federal government led to significant delays in support being sent to Louisiana, even after the storm (Brinkley, 2006; Cooper & Block, 2006). At the same time, New Orleans' city government was failing to follow their disaster plan for hurricanes, apparently unable to locate it on the city website (Brinkley, 2006). Even in less extreme circumstances, citizen-centered e-government will benefit citizens, residents, and government employees in the use of e-government services.

Provision of citizen-centered e-government is an iterative process, requiring an ongoing commitment; a desire to measure service quality and constantly look for opportunities to determine the degree to which the services meet user needs; and a willingness to implement the lessons learned from the various needs assessment. In short, citizen-centered e-government is costly and likely requires a cultural shift in governments – from an efficiency orientation to a user orientation. But the citizen-oriented approach is more likely to improve the use of e-government services, increase the impact of those services, and increase user interaction with government (Jaeger & Thompson, 2004).

Citizen-centered e-government contrasts directly to e-government as a means to reduce the cost of government service provision and as a means to simply provide the same service on a different platform. A service that does not meet the needs of the citizen or one that is difficult for the citizen to use is a service that will not be used widely. An unused or under-used service is a costly mistake that will require greater investments to correct, if it is ever corrected at all. While the promise of citizen-centered e-government may revolutionize government-user interaction in the long-term, it will require substantial investment and change in the short-term. Not making these investments, however, minimizes the benefits of including users in the design, development, and implementation of e-government services – and will limit the overall success of e-government.

As the United States federal e-government begins to evolve under the Obama Administration, it will be headed by a president whose campaign was defined by its creative use of new technologies – including websites, social networking, and multimedia – to engage citizens, raise money, mobilize volunteers, and coordinate voter turnout (Google, 2008; Pariser, 2008; Vargas, 2008). Whether this ability with technology as a campaign tool translates into more citizen-centered e-government, however, remains an open question at the time of this writing in 2009. The Obama

Administration has changed the federal approach to technology by creating the positions of Chief Information Officer and Chief Technology Officer, which are intended to better coordinate applications and planning across government agencies and increase technology-based outreach to citizens. The administration has also worked to make government websites more interactive and encouraged agencies to use social networking technologies to improve direct communication with and engagement of citizens. While these early efforts demonstrate a better understanding of the power of technology in governance than previous administrations, the extent to which these efforts lead to a more citizen-centered e-government will be a major issue through the course of the administration. This is a particularly salient issue given that the current dialogue between the administration and citizens involves those who are connected and interacting with a range of technologies and thus potentially leaving the nearly 50% of U.S. residents without adequate access to computing and broadband technologies – the minimum requirement to participate in e-government services and resources – out of the conversation.

REFERENCES

Anderson. (2002). *A usability analysis of selected federal government web sites*. Washington DC: Author.

Baker, D. L. (2009). Advancing e-government performance in the United States through enhanced usability benchmarks. *Government Information Quarterly, 26*, 75–81. doi:10.1016/j.giq.2008.01.004

Barr, S. (2007). Public less satisfied with government websites. *Washington Post*. Retrieved from http://www.washingtonpost.com/wp-dyn/content/article/2007/03/20/AR2007032001338.html.

Bertot, J. C. (2003). The multiple dimensions of the digital divide: more than the technology 'haves' and 'have nots.'. *Government Information Quarterly, 20*(2), 185–191. doi:10.1016/S0740-624X(03)00036-4

Bertot, J. C., & Jaeger, P. T. (2006). User-centered e-government: Challenges and benefits for government Web sites. *Government Information Quarterly, 23*, 163–168. doi:10.1016/j.giq.2006.02.001

Bertot, J. C., & Jaeger, P. T. (2008). The e-government paradox: Better customer service doesn't necessarily cost less. *Government Information Quarterly, 25*, 149–154. doi:10.1016/j.giq.2007.10.002

Bertot, J. C., Jaeger, P. T., Langa, L. A., & McClure, C. R. (2006a). Public access computing and Internet access in public libraries: The role of public libraries in e-government and emergency situations. *First Monday, 11*(9). Retrieved from http://www.firstmonday.org/issues/issue11_9/bertot/index.html.

Bertot, J. C., Jaeger, P. T., Langa, L. A., & McClure, C. R. (2006b). Drafted: I want you to deliver e-government. *Library Journal, 131*(13), 34–39.

Bertot, J. C., Jaeger, P. T., & McClure, C. R. (2008). *User-centered e-government services: Benefits, costs, and research needs.* Paper presented at the 9th Annual International Conference on Digital Government Research.

Bertot, J. C., Snead, J. T., Jaeger, P. T., & McClure, C. R. (2006). Functionality, usability and accessibility: Iterative user-centered assessment strategies for digital libraries. *Performance Measurement and Metrics, 7*(1), 17–28. doi:10.1108/14678040610654828

Borins, I. (2002). On the frontiers of electronic governance: A report on the United States and Canada. *International Review of Administrative Sciences, 68*, 199–211. doi:10.1177/0020852302682003

Brinkley, D. (2006). *The great deluge: Hurricane Katrina, New Orleans, and the Mississippi Gulf Coast*. New York: Harper Perennial.

Browning, G. (2002). *Electronic democracy: Using the Internet to transform American politics* (2nd ed.). Medford, NJ: Cyberage Books/ Information Today.

Burroughs, J. M. (2009). What users want: Assessing government information preferences to drive information services. *Government Information Quarterly*, *26*, 203–218. doi:10.1016/j.giq.2008.06.003

Chadwick, A. (2001). The electronic face of government in the Internet age: Borrowing from Murray Edelman. *Information Communication and Society*, *4*(3), 435–457.

Chadwick, A., & May, C. (2003). Interaction between states and citizens in the age of the Internet: E-government in the United States, Britain, and the European Union. *Governance*, *16*(2), 271–300. doi:10.1111/1468-0491.00216

Chang, A., & Kannan, P. K. (2008). *Leveraging Web 2.0 in government*. New York: IBM Business of Government Foundation. Retrieved from http://www.businessofgovernment.org/main/publications/bog/chang_fall08.pdf

Cilan, C. A., Bolat, B. A., & Coskun, E. (2009). Analyzing digital divide within and between member and candidate countries of European Union. *Government Information Quarterly*, *26*, 98–107. doi:10.1016/j.giq.2007.11.002

Coleman, S. (2004). Connecting Parliament to the public via the Internet. *Information Communication and Society*, *7*(1), 1–22. doi:10.1080/1369118042000208870

Cooper, C., & Block, R. *Disaster: Hurricane Katrina and the failure of homeland security*. New York: Times Books.

Cullier, D., & Piotrowski, S. J. (2009). Internet information-seeking and its relation to support for access to government records. *Government Information Quarterly*, *26*, 441–449. doi:10.1016/j.giq.2009.03.001

Dawes, S. S. (2009). Governance in the digital age: A research and action framework for an uncertain future. *Government Information Quarterly*, *26*, 257–264. doi:10.1016/j.giq.2008.12.003

Dragulanescu, N.-G. (2002). Website quality evaluations: Criteria and tools. *The International Information & Library Review*, *34*, 247–254. doi:10.1006/iilr.2002.0205

Ebbers, W. E., Pieterson, W. J., & Noordman, H. N. (2008). Electronic government: Rethinking channel management strategies. *Government Information Quarterly*, *25*, 181–201. doi:10.1016/j.giq.2006.11.003

Ebbers, W. E., & van Dijk, J. A. G. M. (2007). Resistance and support to electronic government, building a model of innovation. *Government Information Quarterly*, *24*, 554–575. doi:10.1016/j.giq.2006.09.008

Eschenfelder, K. R., Beachboard, J. C., McClure, C. R., & Wyman, S. K. (1997). Assessing US federal government websites. *Government Information Quarterly*, *14*, 173–189. doi:10.1016/S0740-624X(97)90018-6

Feinberg, L. E. (2004). FOIA, federal information policy, and information availability in a post-9/11 world. *Government Information Quarterly*, *21*, 439–460. doi:10.1016/j.giq.2004.08.004

Fenton, R. (2004). United Kingdom adoption agency Web sites. *First Monday*, *9*(2). Retrieved from http://www.firstmonday.org/issues/issue9_2/fenton/index.html.

Gauld, R., Gray, A., & McComb, S. (2009). How responsive is e-government? Evidence from Australia and New Zealand. *Government Information Quarterly*, *26*, 69–74. doi:10.1016/j.giq.2008.02.002

Gibson, A. N., Bertot, J. C., & McClure, C. R. (2009). *Emerging roles of public libraries as e-government providers.* Paper presented at the 42nd Hawaii International Conference on Systems Sciences.

Google. (2008). *Lessons learned from the 2008 campaign trail.* Washington, DC: Author.

Gouscos, D., Kalikakis, M., Legal, M., & Papadopoulou, S. (2007). A general model of performance and quality for one-stop e-government service offerings. *Government Information Quarterly*, *22*(4), 860–885. doi:10.1016/j.giq.2006.07.016

Graff, G. M. (December 2, 2007). Don't know their Yahoo from their YouTube. *Washington Post.*

Gupta, M. P., & Jana, D. (2003). E-government evaluation: A framework and case study. *Government Information Quarterly*, *20*, 365–387. doi:10.1016/j.giq.2003.08.002

Halchin, L. E. (2004). Electronic government: Government capability or terrorist resource. *Government Information Quarterly*, *21*, 406–419. doi:10.1016/j.giq.2004.08.002

Hamner, M., & Al-Qahtani, R. (2009). Enhancing the case for electronic government in developing nations: A people-centric study focused in Saudi Arabia. *Government Information Quarterly*, *26*, 118–127. doi:10.1016/j.giq.2007.08.008

Heeks, R., & Bailur, S. (2007). Analyzing e-government research: Perspectives, philosophies, theories, methods, and practice. *Government Information Quarterly*, *24*(2), 243–265. doi:10.1016/j.giq.2006.06.005

Ho, A. T.-K., & Ni, A. Y. (2004). Explaining the adoption of e-government features: A case study of Iowa County Treasurers' offices. *American Review of Public Administration*, *34*, 164–180. doi:10.1177/0275074004264355

Hoffman, K. M. (2007). *Government websites for special populations: Toward content-based evaluation.* Unpublished Master's Thesis: University of Maryland.

Horrigan, J. (2008). *Home broadband 2008.* Washington, DC: Pew Internet & American Life Project.

Horrigan, J. B. (2004). *How Americans get in touch with government.* Washington, DC: Pew Internet & American Life Project.

Horrigan, J. B. (2006). *Politics online.* Washington, DC: Pew Internet & American Life Project.

Horrigan, J. B., & Rainie, L. (2002). *Counting on the Internet.* Washington, DC: Pew Internet & American Life Project.

Horst, M., Kuttschreuter, M., & Gutteling, J. M. (2007). Perceived usefulness, personal experiences, risk perception and trust as determinants of adoption of e-government services in The Netherlands. *Computers in Human Behavior*, *23*(4), 1838–1852. doi:10.1016/j.chb.2005.11.003

Huang, C. J., & Chao, M.-H. (2001). Managing WWW in public administration: Uses and misuses. *Government Information Quarterly*, *18*, 357–373. doi:10.1016/S0740-624X(01)00085-5

Hung, S.-Y., Tnag, K.-Z., Chang, C.-M., & Ke, C.-D. (2009). User acceptance of intergovernmental services: An example of electronic document management system. *Government Information Quarterly*, *26*, 387–397. doi:10.1016/j.giq.2008.07.003

Jaeger, P. T. (2005). Deliberative democracy and the conceptual foundations of electronic government. *Government Information Quarterly*, *22*, 702–719. doi:10.1016/j.giq.2006.01.012

Jaeger, P. T. (2006). Assessing Section 508 compliance on federal e-government websites: A multi-method, user-centered evaluation of accessibility for persons with disabilities. *Government Information Quarterly*, *23*(2), 169–190. doi:10.1016/j.giq.2006.03.002

Jaeger, P. T. (2007). Information policy, information access, and democratic participation: The national and international implications of the Bush administration's information politics. *Government Information Quarterly*, *24*, 840–859. doi:10.1016/j.giq.2007.01.004

Jaeger, P. T. (2008). User-centered policy evaluations of Section 508 of the Rehabilitation Act: Evaluating e-government websites for accessibility. *Journal of Disability Policy Studies*, *19*(1), 24–33. doi:10.1177/1044207308315274

Jaeger, P. T., & Fleischmann, K. R. (2007). Public libraries, values, trust, and e-government. *Information Technology and Libraries*, *26*(4), 35–43.

Jaeger, P. T., Langa, L. A., McClure, C. R., & Bertot, J. C. (2007). The 2004 and 2005 Gulf Coast hurricanes: Evolving roles and lessons learned for public libraries in disaster preparedness and community services. *Public Library Quarterly*, *25*(3/4), 199–214. doi:10.1300/J118v25n03_17

Jaeger, P. T., & Matteson, M. (2009). E-government and technology acceptance: The implementation of Section 508 guidelines for e-government websites. *Electronic Journal of E-Government*, *7*(1), 87-98. Retrieved from http://www.ejeg.com/volume-7/vol7-iss1/v7-i1-art8.htm

Jaeger, P. T., Paquette, S., & Simmons, S. N. (2010). Information policy in national political campaigns: A comparison of the 2008 campaigns for President of the United States and Prime Minister of Canada. *Journal of Information Technology & Politics*, *7*, 1–16. doi:10.1080/19331680903316700

Jaeger, P. T., & Thompson, K. M. (2003). E-government around the world: Lessons, challenges, and new directions. *Government Information Quarterly*, *20*(4), 389–394. doi:10.1016/j.giq.2003.08.001

Jaeger, P. T., & Thompson, K. M. (2004). Social information behavior and the democratic process: Information poverty, normative behavior, and electronic government in the United States. *Library & Information Science Research*, *26*(1), 94–107. doi:10.1016/j.lisr.2003.11.006

Jaeger, P. T., & Xie, B. (2009). Developing online community accessibility guidelines for persons with disabilities and older adults. *Journal of Disability Policy Studies*, *20*, 55–63. doi:10.1177/1044207308325997

Kaye, B. K., & Johnson, J. (2002). Online and in the know: Uses and gratification of the Web for political information. *Journal of Broadcasting & Electronic Media*, *46*, 54–71. doi:10.1207/s15506878jobem4601_4

Kirtley, J. E. (2006). Transparency and accountability in a time of terror: The bush administration's assault on freedom of information. *Communication Law and Policy*, *11*, 479–509. doi:10.1207/s15326926clp1104_2

Laris, M. (January 4, 2009). O brave new world that has such avatars in it. *Washington Post.*

Lazar, J. (2005). *Web usability: A user-centered design approach*. Boston, MA: Addison-Wesley.

Mahler, J., & Regan, P. M. (2006). Crafting the message: Controlling content on agency Web sites. *Government Information Quarterly*, *24*, 505–521. doi:10.1016/j.giq.2006.06.008

McClure, C. R., Jaeger, P. T., & Bertot, J. C. (2007). The looming infrastructure plateau?: Space, funding, connection speed, and the ability of public libraries to meet the demand for free Internet access. *First Monday*, *12*(12). Retrieved from http://www.uic.edu/htbin/cgiwrap/bin/ojs/index.php/fm/article/view/2017/1907.

Mechling, J., & Booz Allen Hamilton. (2002). *Building a methodology for measuring the value of e-services*. Washington, DC: Booz Allen Hamilton.

Nagesh, G. (2009). Agencies used social media to manage salmonella outbreak. *Nextgov*. Retrieved from http://www.nextgov.com

Noveck, B. S. (2003). Designing deliberative democracy in cyberspace: The role of the cyber-lawyer. *Boston University Journal of Science and Technology*, *9*, 1–91.

Pariser, E. (2008). Will he bring change.gov we can believe in? *Washington Post* (December 28, 2008), B04.

Pew Internet and American Life Project. (2007). *Latest trends*. Last accessed December 17, 2007 at http://www.pewinternet.org/trends.asp.

Quinn, A. C., & Ramasubramanian, L. (2007). Information technologies and civic engagement: Perspectives from librarianship and planning. *Government Information Quarterly*, *24*, 595–610. doi:10.1016/j.giq.2006.08.005

Reddick, C. G. (2005). Citizen interaction with e-government: From the streets to servers? *Government Information Quarterly*, *22*, 38–57. doi:10.1016/j.giq.2004.10.003

Relyea, H. C., & Halchin, L. E. (2003). Homeland security and information management. In Bogart, D. (Ed.), *The Bowker annual: Library and trade almanac 2003*. Medford, NJ: Information Today.

Ritchie, H., & Blanck, P. (2003). The promise of the Internet for disability: A study of online services and website accessibility at centers for independent living. *Behavioral Sciences & the Law*, *21*, 5–26. doi:10.1002/bsl.520

Roberts, N. (2004). Public deliberation in an age of direct citizen participation. *American Review of Public Administration*, *34*, 315–353. doi:10.1177/0275074004269288

Schedler, K., & Summermatter, L. (2007). Customer orientation in electronic government: Motives and effects. *Government Information Quarterly*, *24*, 291–311. doi:10.1016/j.giq.2006.05.005

Scott, J. K. (2006). E the people: Do US municipal government websites support public involvement? *Public Administration Review*, *66*(3), 341–353. doi:10.1111/j.1540-6210.2006.00593.x

Singh, A. K., & Sahu, R. (2008). Integrating Internet, telephones, and call centers for delivering better quality e-governance to all citizens. *Government Information Quarterly*, *25*, 477–490. doi:10.1016/j.giq.2007.01.001

Smith, B., Fraser, B. T., & McClure, C. R. (2000). Federal information policy and access to We-based information. *Journal of Academic Librarianship*, *26*, 274–281. doi:10.1016/S0099-1333(00)00128-2

Streib, G., & Navarro, I. (2006). Citizen demand for interactive e-government: The case of Georgia consumer services. *American Review of Public Administration*, *36*, 288–300. doi:10.1177/0275074005283371

Tolbert, C. J., & Mossberger, K. (2006). The effects of e-government on trust and confidence in government. *Public Administration Review*, *66*(3), 354–369. doi:10.1111/j.1540-6210.2006.00594.x

Toregas, C. (2001). The politics of e-gov: The upcoming struggle for redefining civic engagement. *National Civic Review*, *90*(3), 235–240. doi:10.1002/ncr.90304

Tsai, N., Choi, B., & Perry, M. (2009). Improving the process of e-government initiative: An in-depth case study of web-based GIS implementation. *Government Information Quarterly*, *26*, 368–376. doi:10.1016/j.giq.2008.11.007

van den Haak, M. J., de Jong, M. D. T., & Schellens, P. J. (2009). Evaluating municipal websites: A methodological comparison of think-aloud variants. *Government Information Quarterly*, *26*, 193–202. doi:10.1016/j.giq.2007.11.003

van Deursen, A. J. A. M., & van Dijk, J. A. G. M. (2009). Improving digital skills for the use of online public information and services. *Government Information Quarterly*, *26*, 333–340. doi:10.1016/j.giq.2008.11.002

van Dijk, J. A. G. M., Peters, O., & Ebbers, W. (2007). Explaining the acceptance and use of government Internet services: A Multivariate analysis of 2006 survey data in the Netherlands. *Government Information Quarterly*, *24*, 148–164.

Vargas, J. A. (2008). Politics is no longer local: It's viral. *Washington Post* (December 28, 2008), B01.

Yildiz, M. (2007). E-government research: Reviewing the literature, limitations, and ways forward. *Government Information Quarterly*, *24*, 646–665. doi:10.1016/j.giq.2007.01.002

KEY TERMS AND DEFINITIONS

Accessibility: The provision of equal or equivalent access to all users of a technology, including those with physical or cognitive challenges and those who employ assistive technologies.

Citizen-Centered E-Government: The design and implementation of e-government based on identified citizen expectations and needs.

E-Government: The provision of government information, services, and engagement via electronic means for communications, interactions, and transactions between citizens, businesses, and government agencies.

Functionality: The degree to which a technology operates as it is intended and provides the results that are intended.

Public Policy: The set of government directives intended to shape decisions and actions of individuals, organizations, and government agencies through legislation, executive orders, judicial rulings, guidelines and regulations, rulemaking, agency memos, signing statements, agency circulars, and other types of official statements.

Trust: The reliance on the integrity and/or reputation of an institution.

Usability: The level of ease by which a user can interact with a technology, including how users react to, understand, and interact with a technology.

User-Centered E-Government: The design and implementation of e-government based on identified expectations and needs of all users, including citizens, residents of other jurisdictions, government employees.

This work was previously published in International Journal of Electronic Government Research, edited by Vishanth Weerakkody, pp. 1-17, copyright 2010 by IGI Publishing (an imprint of IGI Global).

Chapter 2
A User-Centric Approach in E-Governmant Policies:
The Path to Effectiveness?

Pieter Verdegem
Ghent University, Belgium

Laurence Hauttekeete
Ghent University, Belgium

ABSTRACT

E-government is given a central role in the modernization debate of the public sector. Despite large-scale investments the electronic public services do not (yet) seem to come up to the promising expectations. As a result, consensus seems to exist that e-government policies require a rethinking. In this chapter the origins and objectives of the electronic service delivery are discussed. The authors state that the development of e-government suffers from deterministic conceptions. Consequently, the user seems to be neglected and minor attention is given to the impact of the electronic services on the customer. As a contribution to the theoretical discussion of e-government, the authors explain why a two-fold paradigm shift is needed. The user-oriented rethinking comprises both the development of e-government services as the evaluation of its policies. At the end of this chapter, the theoretical considerations are linked to daily-based activities by presenting briefly some Belgian e-government practices.

INTRODUCTION

In today's information society, the production, management and consumption of information and knowledge are increasingly seen as prerequisites for societal development and economic productivity. In this perspective, new information and communication technologies (ICT) continuously foster the further development of this so-called knowledge economy, valuable for different kinds of stakeholders (Castells, 2000; Freeman & Soete, 1997).

Also governmental organizations can and should profit from these new possibilities created by ICTs in providing better services for constituents[1] and rethink their ways of working (Bekkers & Homburg, 2007; Heeks, 1999; Prins, 2001). This way, government will be able to meet the (new) needs and demands of its customers in an environment which is strongly mediated by reduced budgets (Bertot & Jaeger, 2008). At the same time, e-government is

DOI: 10.4018/978-1-61520-931-6.ch002

given a central role in the modernisation debate as being pushed forward by New Public Management and Reinventing Government views. Nevertheless, large-scale investments in electronic public services do not (yet) seem to come up to the promising expectations.

Different e-government strategies have been profoundly examined and questioned (Jaeger & Thompson, 2003; Heeks & Bailur, 2007; Titah & Barki, 2006). The criticism towards the current e-government policies is mainly influenced by the relatively low uptake of electronic public services (in most countries) by larger parts of the population. Experts claim that the development of these services is too much guided by supply-side factors, in which users needs regarding design or functionality have often been neglected (van Dijk, Peters, & Ebbers, 2008; Kunstelj, Jukic, & Vintar, 2007; Gareis, Cullen, & Korte, 2004). Consequently, in scholarly discussions as well as among e-government practitioners consensus seems to exist that the electronic service delivery – as part of larger e-strategies – requires a fundamental rethinking.

Indeed, both in theoretical and empirical research relatively little attention is given to the impact of electronic services on constituents (Bertot & Jaeger, 2006; Jaeger, 2003; Reddick, 2005a). However, a user-centric approach is essential when rethinking e-government strategies, especially in response of the criticism that too much attention is given to technology in e-government provision as well as that its development too often starts from a supply-side point of view. In response of this, the concept of 'user-centered e-government' gained in importance in developing e-government policies. Furthermore, attention is gradually shifting from efficiency (value for government) to effectiveness (value for constituents) when evaluating the impact of e-government services.

This chapter aims to provide a contribution to the theoretical discussion of e-government policy, by focusing on mindsets that could inspire both researchers and practitioners in rethinking public e-services development. In first instance, a brief overview is given of the context wherein e-government has been initiated and its several promises are scrutinized. Furthermore, the authors thoroughly discuss the criticism on e-government, pointing at new ways of thinking to make e-government more user-centric and, consequently, to focus also on the effectiveness of these services for customers and businesses. Lastly, some recommendations derived from the analysis of Belgian e-government practices are be presented, illustrating how to (try to) ensure a more user-centric e-government policy.

THE ORIGINS OF ELECTRONIC GOVERNMENT

Back to the Roots

A Public Sector in Crisis?

The e-government notion can be seen as a buzzword rather than a scholarly concept. It has a variety of interpretations, dependent on the applied framework or perspective. There are many definitions of e-government and the term itself is not universally used. The differences are not merely semantic and may reflect priorities in government strategies (Heeks & Bailur, 2007; Yildiz, 2007; Relyea, 2002; Evans & Yen, 2006).

The concept has its origins in the late eighties - early nineties, a period in which the public policy was subjected to great pressure. A public sector reform became loudly applauded, due to a climate crisis and ideological changes (Heeks, 1999; Osborne & Gaebler, 1992). The crisis in the public service sector has a long but steady evolution. From the seventies onwards, certain perception problems arose towards public service delivery, resulting in some countries to a crisis in the public sector. Especially the input (rising costs), output (results) and processes (way of working) were scrutinized (Heeks, 1999).

At the same time, the ideological climate changed: the neoliberal thinking "*market good, government bad*" (Heeks, 1999, p. 11) challenged the – rather dominant – bureaucratic government model (Kernaghan, Marson, & Sandford, 2002). The economic efficiency of the market became accentuated, strongly recognizing the large potential of competition and the decision power of the individual. The Thatcher regime was undoubtedly one of the most famous neoliberal examples.

Due to this 'public reform' movement, two paradigms became of great importance: 'New Public Management' and 'Reinventing Government'. In general, New Public Management is a concept with different interpretations (Hammerschmid & Meyer, 2005): a movement striving for a diminished role of the public sector in society, a reform of government administrations and a fundamental change in the management of public sector organizations (Bevir, Rhodes, & Weller, 2003; McLaughlin, Osborne, & Ferlie, 2002; Kernaghan et al., 2002). Over time, these interpretations became more concrete. New Public Management believers are convinced that democracy can only survive by offering better and more efficient public services, either by using a market oriented approach or fundamentally reforming the public service delivery (Homburg & Bekkers, 2005; Margetts, 2009). This way, the New Public Management school ambitions the rethinking of 'old' or 'more conservative' bureaucratic and hierarchical ideas about public service delivery, towards a more transparent, effective, efficient and result oriented public sector (Pollit & Bouckaert, 2004; McLaughlin et al., 2002). More specific, this implies the adoption of private sector ideas and techniques into a public sector (Zussman, 2002; Sindane, 2004; Hammerschmid & Meyer, 2005). From this perspective, the focus is on the introduction of new management techniques, targeting a greater efficiency and saving costs.

Related to the New Public Management paradigm, is the concept of 'Reinventing Government' in which several reform initiatives for government organizations are defined. The first ideas about Reinventing Government expressed a rather normative and pejorative attitude towards government, illustrated by phrases such as: "*steering rather than rowing, empowering rather than serving, from hierarchy to participation and teamwork" and "from meeting the needs of the customer, not the bureaucracy*" (Osborne & Gaebler, 1992), all indicating a strong need for more private oriented procedures. Over time, the several ideas on Reinventing Government received a more positive interpretation, accentuating a belief in radical change and new ways of working. Heeks (1999) summarizes these main ideas of public reform in five action items: (1) an increase of efficiency, (2) decentralization, (3) more accountability of the personnel, (4) an amelioration in the allocation of resources, and (5) a clear marketization. The Reinventing Government was also one of the forerunners of user-centered thinking, as they made a plea for a shift from an 'inward-looking approach' (starting from the public sector itself) to an outward-looking approach' (starting from the citizens) (Ho, 2002).

To conclude, the New Public Management and Reinventing Government paradigms stimulated a rethinking of the broad area of public service delivery. By introducing modern business management methods, a plea was made for the increased use of information technology (IT) instead of paper-based channels. Nonetheless, according to Margetts (2009) this pro-IT theme was not really a distinctive feature of the paradigms, partly because public sector organizations were meanwhile using gradually more IT in their processes. The rise of the digital government era especially took place with the widespread use of computers combined with the development of networks.

The Rise of ICTs: Governments Online

Although governments have already used different kinds of information technologies for many years, the emergence of e-government actually started with the Internet in the second half of the 1990s (Milward & Snyder, 1996). While information systems were mainly implemented for back-office processes, the Internet emerged as a new channel for offering services to citizens and businesses (Margetts, 2009).

The World Wide Web rapidly grew in the nineties. The liberalization of the telecom industry and the reduced prices of personal computers spread the Internet into the households (van Dijk, 1999). Once more, the private sector set the example: the industry discovered the advantages of the new medium and soon the first e-commerce applications started. Companies (shops, banks and travel agents in particular) started to interact with their customers via the Internet.

As Internet penetration was increasing in the developed countries, more citizens expected the same possibilities in the public sector. Indeed, governments could not lag behind and started to perceive the potential of Internet for new forms of government-citizen interaction (Reddick, 2005a; West, 2004; Bekkers & Homburg, 2007). Consequently, ICTs were no longer a matter of back-office and attention was increasingly given to front-office activities (Margetts, 2009). The constituents, at their turn, commenced by expecting a higher degree of flexibility within the public service sector: they wanted to use the services anytime, anywhere and anyhow (Wimmer, 2002). On top of it, the new possibilities in the information society constantly created new user preferences.

The first e-government services can be conceptualized as so-called 'self service websites' (Dugdale, Daly, Papandrea, & Maley, 2005). These online services were a simple copy of their offline equivalent, without taking into account the preference of the users, nor the specific characteristics of the new channel. The idea was that the constituents would be autonomously able to apply the services, without any intervention of the government. In addition, government authorities were convinced that this would lead to more efficiency. Simultaneously, it was expected that a growing amount of online services (together with increasing Internet penetration) would spontaneously lead to a large-scale use of the e-government services (OECD, 2005).

Summarizing, the hype of e-government is clearly pushed forward by the connection of the two phenomena that have been described above: the rethinking of the public sector on the one hand and the rise of ICTs on the other hand. They found each other on a special point. New Public Management and Reinventing Government share the vision that the organization of the public sector (as well as its service delivery) should be radically reshaped. So especially in that era, the rise of new communication technologies, with also promising expectations, came in time. So-called 'hypermodernists' (Margetts, 1999) were convinced that ICTs would rapidly become ubiquitous and as a result the objectives of both a rethinking of the public sector as well as e-government itself would become reality.

E-Government and Its Objectives

What is e-government about? And what are the main promises of e-government? There is no universally accepted definition of e-government. Some prefer to speak about 'e-government' while other refer to 'digital government' or 'virtual state' (Fountain, 2001). The definitions and terms adopted by individual countries have shifted, as priorities have changed and as progress has been made towards particular objectives (Evans & Yen, 2006; Jaeger, 2003). This is as it should be: the area is a dynamic one and policies, as well as definitions, need to remain relevant an up-to-date. The definitions are also closely related to the perceived goals of e-government. It is no surprise that there are differences in its philosophical underpinnings. Jaeger (2003, p. 324-325) distinguishes two perspectives: (1) the focus on the practical efficiencies and cost reductions of e-government ("*the application of the tools and techniques of e-Commerce to the work of government*") and (2) the focus on initiatives that will bring interaction between government and citizens to new levels ("*to improve democratic participation*" and "*to overcome political alienation*").

Definitions of e-government frequently refer to the 'reform potentiality' ("*tremendous administrative potential*" [Yildiz, 2007, p. 650]) of e-government. High expectations exist as e-government will be the driving force for change. According to the United Nations e-government is defined as following:

"We put the 'e' in front of 'government' to recognize that a public administration is in the process of transforming its internal and external relationships with the use of modern Information and Communication Technology (ICT)" (United Nations, 2003, p. 1)

Similarly, the Organisations for Economic Co-Operation and Development (OECD) defines e-government as:

"The use of information and communication technologies, and particularly the Internet, as a tool to achieve better government" (OECD, 2003, p. 23)

Both definitions emphasize the belief (or hope) that the deployment of new communication technologies will result in a better government. Summarizing, the outcome opportunities are stressed.

So, what are the objectives of the electronic government? First of all, e-government is seen as a powerful tool to make the public sector more efficient. Information technologies have a clear potential for transforming administrative tasks and procedures by which a reduction in costs would become possible. The increase in efficiency thus would strengthen the ambition to achieve more effective outcomes in key policy areas (Relyea, 2002; Margetts, 2009; Eyob, 2004). Closely related to this is the expectation that e-government would also push the reform agenda (the modernization of the administrations) and simultaneously promote economic policy objectives (Dunleavy, Margetts, Bastow, & Tinkler, 2006; Fountain, 2009; Cordella, 2007). Another important objective of e-government is to make the government and its policies more effective: by providing citizens with better access to government information, and enabling citizens to use interactive services in a more personal, flexible and cost-effective manner (Bekkers & Zouridis, 1999; Heeks, 1999; Prins, 2001). ICTs have the advantage that public services will be available constantly, in profit of the citizens. In addition, the electronic public service delivery would also lead to an improved relationship between government and citizens or businesses. In other words, this will enhance better accountability (Millard, 2003; Heeks, 1999; Ghere & Young, 1998). Finally, e-government is perceived as having the potential to fortify democracy and reducing the distance between citizens and government. By doing so, a better transparency of the public sector would become possible (Macintosh, Robson, Smith, & Whyte, 2003; Welch, Hinnant, & Moon, 2005; Netchaeva, 2002).

E-GOVERNMENT: DOES IT FULFILL ITS PROMISES?

After the Internet boom, most developed countries have waged efforts to implement their e-strategies, resulting in electronic services with increasing levels of sophistication. The provision of services varies across different countries. Each country can be situated differently on a specific level in the stages model of Layne & Lee (2001): some are offering only basic information (catalogue), while others have developed full online transaction and electronic case handling (transaction). In addition, there are also countries who are working on more advanced systems wherein back-offices get linked or integrated across different functions (vertical and horizontal integration). And while most attention is still given to the Internet as the preferred channel for offering e-government, a few countries are experimenting with new channels such as digital television or mobile applications (Ebbers, Pieterson, & Noordman, 2008; Verdegem & Hauttekeete, 2008). To conclude, the future of e-government looks bright. Or not?

In other words, the question whether e-government today is fulfilling the promising expectations remains very pertinent. A thorough analysis of the impact of the service delivery, both from the viewpoint of the government (supply) and that of the constituents (demand) is therefore necessary. One way to examine the impact of e-government is focusing on the actual usage of the services. And using this criterion to evaluate e-government progress, one could say that e-government is missing its goal. Many sources state that there exists a low uptake of electronic public services in most Western countries, both when it comes to adoption and usage (van Deursen, van Dijk, & Ebbers, 2006; van Dijk et al., 2008; Kunstelj et al., 2007). Although the acceptance of e-government services is only one part of the story (demand oriented), it certainly entails some major consequences. More specifically, low uptake becomes problematic as greater efficiency and return on investment are only possible with a widespread use of the electronic services (Norris & Moon, 2005; Jaeger, 2003).

Criticism Toward the E-Strategies of Governments

The current e-government strategies are increasingly the target of scholarly research as well as criticism. As an explanation of the relatively low user uptake, government centricity and technological determinism are often mentioned. The first refers to the observation that electronic public services have often been primarily guided by supply-side factors (Bertot & Jaeger, 2006; Reddick, 2005a; Kunstelj et al., 2007). In this approach, governments often commence by enlarging their portfolio of services by creating an electronic version of their existing (offline) services (van Dijk et al., 2008; Lee-Kelley & Kolsaker, 2004). The latter (technological determinism) is also put central when it comes to critically reviewing the current e-government strategies. Many authors state that the design of online public services has all too often been driven by technological possibilities rather than user needs and expectations, neglecting this way the fact that technological readiness does not naturally equal some kind of user readiness (Ebbers et al., 2008; Pieterson & Ebbers, 2008; Reddick, 2005b).

More on a meta-level, Bekkers and Homburg (2007) perfectly unravel and synthesize the existing criticism towards the several e-government initiatives, based on an analysis of e-government reforms (period 1994-2006) in different countries. To underpin their arguments, they use four myths: '*new and better government*', '*technological progress and instrumentality*', '*e-government as rational information planning*' and '*citizen as empowered consumer*'. With the first myth of a new and better government, Bekkers and Homberg (2007) carefully criticize the idea that ICTs play a decisive role in creating a better government, ignoring this way the tremendous problems that arise when trying to integrate the back-offices and also not taking into account the necessity of organizational restructuring. Related to this, the myth of technological progress and instrumentality denotes that there is too much belief and confidence in the potential of ICTs, which is a clear example of technological determinism. Contextual political, socio-economical and institutional situations should thus be considered. Furthermore, the authors point at the myth of e-government as rational information planning, whereas in reality most e-government projects are not the result of top-down strategic and standardized planning methods. Of main importance in the light of this article is the last myth of citizen as empowered consumer, with which Bekkers and Homburg (2007, p. 380) argue that "*a focus on service delivery (and a focus on the consumer rather than on the citizen) narrows the multidimensionality of citizenship and public administration and may therefore decrease legitimacy*".

It' s All About Government and Technology

When reviewing the origins of e-government and evaluating the criticism formulated towards its development, one can state that there exists a twofold deterministic proposition.

First, following the movement of rethinking the public sector, sole attention was given to government itself. The main focus was on how to develop strategies to make the public service delivery better than in the past. We could formulate this as a government-centric approach which is perfectly illustrated in the frequently cited stages model of Layne & Lee (2001). This model describes e-government development only from a policy point of view. To some extent, the former can be seen as a deterministic vision, indicating that reinventing the public sector and its service delivery would automatically lead to better informed citizens or citizens being more satisfied with the proposed service provision. As a consequence, only little attention was given to citizens' needs when it comes to the development of e-government services (Lee-Kelley & Kolsaker, 2004; Reddick, 2005a). In a nutshell, the government-centric approach is a first example of deterministic thinking.

Second, the technological developments are often seen as the driving forces of modernization and, as a result, leading to new and better services for the citizens. Although ICTs indeed offer some particular advantages (such as the anywhere/anyplace character, the ability to deliver services faster and cheaper, etc.) it is a misunderstanding to see the new technologies as a solution for all kinds of problems. The rhetoric of the new information society runs the risk to be too optimistic when it comes to the potential of new ICTs. Consequently, in this vision it is assumed that the technology mediated service delivery would automatically be evaluated as better than the traditional services (Heeks & Bailur, 2007). Moreover, this technological deterministic viewpoint also neglects the user: in this discourse there is no space for people who, for example, prefer personal contact instead of faster delivery or who are just refusing to employ new technology. The first e-government policies were clearly technological deterministic (Aldrich, Bertot, & McClure, 2002) leading to the dominance of a techno-centric approach.

A TWO-FOLD PARADIGM SHIFT

To answer the criticism, the authors state that e-government policies must be the subject of reconsideration. In addition, responding to the deterministic viewpoints, it is our opinion that a twofold paradigm shift is needed. First, when it comes to developing e-government policies the authors make a plea for a shift from 'government centric e-government' to 'user-centered e-government'. Second, regarding e-government measurement and policy evaluation, we are convinced that there is a need to shift from 'efficiency' towards 'effectiveness'. After all, it is not sufficient to rethink the strategies for realizing an electronic service provision that better responds to constituents' needs (in terms of the design of electronic services or channel strategies). The evaluation of the policies also needs to be revised.

Thus, a strong plea is made for a holistic approach wherein the user – comprising of citizens, businesses and other constituents – receives the attention he or she deserves. The authors are convinced that a good implementation of these ideas is a first but important step to evolve to a fully-developed e-government. Moreover, taking this into account may be useful to create the large potential of governmental e-strategies, both when it comes to uptake and impact of the services. In the next paragraphs, these theoretical mindsets are explained more in detail.

The User at the Centre of the Design of E-Government Services

Starting from a government point of view, the first e-government policies mainly dealt with the technical and practical dimensions of getting information and services online. The constituents (both citizens and businesses) were the target group, although they were not at the centre of the developments. Also in scholarly research, a number of studies have examined who is and who is not using e-government, amongst other subjects related to the modernization of the public sector (Yildiz, 2007; Heeks & Bailur, 2007). Nevertheless, special attention given to constituents' needs and expectations seems to be relatively scarce (Bertot & Jaeger, 2006). Again, the private sector set the example: new concepts such as 'user-centered design' or 'user experience' gained in importance. The e-government research community adopted this shift in attention resulting in the user-centered e-government paradigm (Bertot & Jaeger, 2006; Bertot & Jaeger, 2008; OECD, 2005). Governments are slowly following by putting this user-oriented thinking in their policy documents. Nonetheless, bringing these promising intentions into practice does not seem to be easy. In the next paragraphs, we seek to understand what lies behind the concept and we provide some guidelines how to implement this in the public sector e-strategies.

It is important to take into account the needs of the users. As Bertot & Jaeger (2006, p. 164) state: "*While users may appreciate the cost savings to agencies for any number of reasons, their primary interest is in their ability to interact with e-government services with ease.*" Therefore, governments should deal with the dilemma to develop citizen-centered e-government services that achieve good budget spending and, simultaneously, to know or discover what citizens expect from electronic public services. According to Bertot & Jaeger (2008) it requires iterative and integrated design processes to engage citizenry in e-government. More precisely, this entails (1) a thorough needs assessment, (2) attention to literacy, and an (3) in-depth understanding of access and use of (electronic) public services. First, policymakers should pay attention to information and service needs assessment as well as technology needs assessment. The first refers to asking citizens how they (want to) fulfill their expectations towards public information and services. The latter deals with the preferences of citizens towards technology use. Second, the issue of literacy may not be neglected. It refers not only to the ability to successfully using electronic public services, but also to the degree of knowledge about government and its structure. With regard to the actual use of e-government services, government must take into account issues such as functionality, usability and accessibility (Bertot & Jaeger, 2006). Functionality is about the evaluation that the service is suitable to meet the goals of its underlying policy. Usability refers to intuitively accessing and employing the service (e.g. satisfaction, value, helpfulness, frustration, etc.). And last but not least, policymakers may not neglect that a growing portion of citizens suffers with disabilities, which implies that – without appropriate measures – the electronic public services will not be usable for some parts of the population.

There exist a lot of methods and strategies to better incorporate citizens in the development of e-government services. Via qualitative (focus group interviews, personal interviews) or quantitative research a lot of empirical evidence can be gathered, in order to broaden or deepen the existing knowledge. Scholarly projects have studied themes such as e-government adoption (e.g. van Dijk et al., 2008; Norris & Moon, 2005; Dimitrova & Chen, 2006), user expectations (Reddick, 2005a; Kunstelj et al., 2007), channel preferences (e.g. Ebbers et al., 2008; Reddick, 2005b; Pieterson

& Ebbers, 2008), user satisfaction (e.g. Gupta & Jana, 2003; Verdegem & Verleye, 2009). Some countries have already implemented this kind of initiatives in their daily-based activities. Interesting examples in this field are the Canadian 'Citizens First Surveys' (Roy, 2006), the 'Use of and Satisfaction with E-Government Services' studies from the Australian government (2005) or the 'E-Government Trendbarometer' carried out in Switserland (Berner Fachhochschule & Unisys, 2005). It is important, however, to stress that this user-centric approach should be an integral part of governmental e-strategies. The continuous inquiry of electronic public services' customers is a must as both users (and their expectations) and services are changing permanently, especially in the world of ICTs where new innovations pass on in a rapid succession.

Although governments often see e-government mainly as a cost saving evolution, they should be aware that the above mentioned activities are worth taking into consideration. It requires commitment and thus a cultural shift: from a government orientation to a citizen orientation. As Bertot & Jaeger (2008, p. 153) state: "*The danger of not doing so, however, far outweighs not incorporating citizens in the design, development, and implementation of e-government services. A service that is difficult to use is a service that is not used – and that is a costly mistake that will require greater investments to correct, if at all.*"

The User at the Centre of E-Government Policy Evaluation

As policy makers increasingly use electronic channels to deliver a wide range of information, interaction and transaction services at a growing level of sophistication, the measurement of the progress of e-government development has become a hot topic (Kunstelj & Vintar, 2004; McLaughlin et al., 2002; Peters, Janssen & van Engers, 2005; Heeks, 2006). In line with the traditional definitions of electronic service delivery, e-government policy (especially in Europe) has focused several years on bringing a variety of online electronic public services and on benchmarking their availability and sophistication. This benchmarking offers valuable data, but – as stated above – it should also be accompanied with more user-centric strategies. Closely related to the shift from a government orientation to a citizen orientation is the paradigm shift from efficiency to effectiveness. The latter refers to objectives of government policy in general and e-government in particular. Millard (2008) distinguishes three types of goals concerning public policy: (1) Efficiency, that can be seen as the search for savings. Consequently, efficiency mainly deals with value for government. (2) Effectiveness has more to do with the search for quality services and, as a result, the emphasis is on the value for the constituents. (3) Governance, more in general, is about the search for good governance, in which value for society is the key word.

The paradigm shift (namely equal attention for efficiency and effectiveness) has originated from the rethinking of e-government as such as well as from the strategies concerning the evaluation of e-government (i.e. measurement activities). Not only the supply-oriented approaches were scrutinized, critiques also exist towards the so-called supply side benchmarking (Bannister, 2007; Janssen, Rotthier, & Snijkers, 2004; Peters et al., 2005). Codagnone & Undheim (2008) summarize the main lines of this criticism: the overall relevance and validity of purely supply side approaches and the reliability, comparability and transparency of the methodologies used are questioned. More specifically, both the model of stages of Layne and Lee (2001) and the measurement of a basic list of online public services no longer seem to be sufficient for accurately evaluating e-government progress.

It is beyond dispute that the electronic service delivery as well as the underlying business processes are quite complex, whereby it is difficult for governments to determine adequate measures for evaluating the efficiency and effectiveness of their spending (Kunstelj & Vintar, 2004; Peters et al., 2005). Measurement for knowledge – an adage that rises in importance – is an important but difficult to achieve challenge and, therefore, it needs to be based on a holistic framework (Norris & Moon, 2005). In this perspective, the traditional e-government value chain – comprising the elements input, output and outcomes (Codagnone & Undheim, 2008) – must be reconsidered. While efficiency mainly deals with the input-output ratio, attention also should be given to effectiveness. More precisely, effectiveness is perceived to focus on the outcomes and impact of e-government services on behalf of the users. This entails investigations of the actual use as well as the added value and consequences of electronic public services. Possible examples of the impact of e-government are increased user satisfaction, reduced administrative burden, more inclusive public services, better transparency, accountability, etc. Thus, the impact of e-government is a topic that urgently needs further research, which must be holistic and therefore not limited to the impact of the government (e.g. cost savings, reduced number of staff, etc.).

Summarizing, fully developed e-government strategies would benefit from a more elaborated framework to evaluate the current policies. It is our conviction that these evaluation activities should focus simultaneously on efficiency (benefits for government) as well as on effectiveness (benefits for constituents). By doing so, the twofold paradigm shift towards user-oriented e-government policies can be realized: first, the development of policies should be more citizen-centric and, second, the assessment and evaluation of the policies should incorporate both elements of efficiency and effectiveness. Bringing this into practice is not an easy task but policy makers are invited to do so when they are pursuing successful e-government policies in the long term.

BELGIAN E-GOVERNMENT: STEP BY STEP

Elaborating briefly on the development of e-government in Belgium, gives the opportunity to link the theoretical knowledge regarding the rethinking of e-government to the daily-based practices. Existing ways of working or initiatives can be reviewed and, consequently, guidelines can be deduced that may be interesting to share with both the community of researchers and practitioners.

Belgium started to prioritize e-government at the end of the 1990s, responding to the rapid development of the Internet and the increase in the usage of ICTs. Since the beginning of its history in Belgium, e-government was mainly seen as a crucial driver for public modernization. Simultaneously, the focus has primarily been on the technical aspects of e-government. In Belgium, the intergovernmental co-operation management strategies of integrated e-government (regarding the complex state structure[2]) is an important point of attention, next to a reduction of the digital divide. Belgium has a relatively low Internet and computer penetration in households and for individuals, compared to for example the Scandinavian countries or The Netherlands (OECD, 2008). Other challenges are, amongst others, dealing with legislative/regulatory issues and budgetary challenges. In what follows, we would like to focus on the emerging common priorities for the development of user-oriented strategies, and to initiatives to increase the user uptake of e-government services.

In the OECD Peer Review Report of Belgium (OECD, 2008, p. 19) it is stated that: "*Belgian governments could consider acquiring a systematic basis on knowledge of user needs and channel this knowledge into the design and development of targeted e-government services, with the purpose of making these services more attractive to users and more adapted to their true needs.*" This is a clear call for more user-centric strategies. Belgian governments have a tradition – like other countries – to start in most cases from a government centric orientation. A focus on the supply side was thus the dominant principle of developing e-government strategies, concretized by putting more services online. Nonetheless, research discovered that this does not correspond to the demands of most citizens (Kampen, Snijkers, & Bouckaert, 2005). At the same time, a comprehensive framework for measuring e-government progress in Belgium is lacking. Policy evaluation activities mainly consist of the participation of consultancy firms to benchmarking studies and other initiatives such as OECD or UN.

Since 2004 the Belgian federal government has set up an action plan to overcome this situation. Fed-e-View is an initiative of Fedict (Federal Public Service for Information and Communication Technology) and consists out of a threefold approach (OECD, 2008). First, Fed-e-View/Administration[3] aimed at measuring the level of computerization of the public agencies of the Federal government. For instance, the ICT budget, the number of ICT employees or the common use of e-government technical components were mapped out. Alternatively, Fed-e-View/Citizen[4] measured user needs in 2005 and 2006. This research concerning user demand, user needs and user satisfaction revealed that priorities for Belgian citizens are: (1) rapidity and flexibility (in terms of location and time of access), (2) user-friendliness (citizens are willing to use electronic services if they provide an easier alternative to traditional channels and (3) personalized services (the Belgian citizen is more interested in accessing relevant, personalized services online than having to go through the complexities of the government to gain access to services). Lastly, a specific study focusing on business' needs towards e-government is planned for the next period and is called 'Fed-e-View/Business'.

The Fed-e-View studies are good initiatives to respond to the call for governmental rethinking. However, a systematic framework for integrating initiatives that supports the development and the monitoring of e-government – especially in the long term – is still lacking. As OECD (2008, p. 181) states: "*The absence of systematic consideration of knowledge of user needs in the development of e-government services has left Belgian government with limited possibilities for developing customized e-services for their users.*" As a result, instead of once-only studies, a plea should be made for long-term projects. And this asks for robust methodologies that are flexible regarding new trends.

To conclude, the authors encourage the Belgian government to continue their efforts to build a holistic framework which should serve a double goal: on the one hand it should support the development of (more) user-centric e-government services, and, on the other hand, it should enable an adequate measurement or policy evaluation by paying attention to both efficiency and effectiveness.

REFLECTIONS

E-government services boomed in a period of techno-optimism, fortified by the idea that technological readiness will automatically lead to user readiness. Unfortunately, the reality is more disappointing. The uptake of e-government services – both in terms of adoption and use – remains in most countries rather low, leading to different debates about who's to blame. After all, without customers, no return on investment. In general, we discovered that this low uptake has been caused by a too government centric and technological deterministic way of working, resulting in the creation of e-services which neglect the user. Consequently, this chapter strongly encourages the use of a more holistic framework with a twofold paradigm shift towards user-oriented e-government policies, whereby user centricity and effectiveness are the key words.

This mindset of putting the user at the centre of the development of e-government services and making some clear reflections about the technological deterministic way of thinking, confronts us immediately with a more fundamental problem underlying the low uptake of public e-services: the digital divide.

Research about digital inequalities is often limited to the divide between people who have access to ICT and others who have not, the so-called 'divide between the haves and the have-nots'. In this reasoning, ensuring that every individual possesses the necessary ICTs to make use of e-government services will automatically lead to the adoption of these e-services. The problem of the digital divide is in this perspective narrowed to a problem of access. The reality, however, shows a far more complex picture. Bridging the digital divide(s) may require attention not only to access to ICT infrastructure, but also to motivations/attitudes towards the technology as well as skills to master the devices (van Dijk, 2005). To some extent, the same goes for e-government acceptance. It is not sufficient to offer access to electronic public services. Particularly, governmental measures should also focus on raising the awareness with regard to the added value of e-government services. In addition, literacy and the capabilities to use the e-services (regarding the technology itself but also, for instance, concerning the structure of government) could be of major importance. Therefore, in order to convey people to use e-government services, all these parameters must be taken into account and the user must be studied multidimensional.

As a result, related to the debate of the digital divide and the impact of e-government services on its constituents and thus society, we should not be blind for the different dangers which are hidden in the too enthusiastic creation of e-government services. Government authorities must be aware of the 'too much-too soon'-danger, in which they overload the customer with new services that do not fit directly in their everyday lives because of different reasons. Moreover, we should not neglect that some customers of e-government services may be excluded or resisting, as studies reveal that many users still prefer the counter as channel for dealing with government services (Ebbers et al., 2008; Verdegem & Hauttekeete, 2008). To this end, the authors believe that the successful realization of a better (e-)government in the future must be based on the multichannel government principle, in which different channels (counter, phone, postal services and internet, mobile, digital television, etc.) for service delivery exist, combining integrated offline and online platforms.

To conclude, the creation and adoption of e-government services demands a long term, structural and holistic process, which is not always that straightforward. It calls for deeper insights in the social and even emotional dimensions or longings of human nature, as these humans are the ones to be favored.

REFERENCES

Aldrich, D., Bertot, J. C., & McClure, C. R. (2002). E-government: initiatives, development, and issues. *Government Information Quarterly*, *19*(4), 349–355. doi:10.1016/S0740-624X(02)00130-2

Australian Government. (2005). *Australians' use of and satisfaction with e-government services*. Barton, Australia: Commonwealth of Australia.

Bannister, F. (2007). The curse of the benchmark: an assessment of the validity and value of e-government comparisons. *International Review of Administrative Sciences*, *73*(2), 171–188. doi:10.1177/0020852307077959

Bekkers, V. J. J. M., & Homburg, V. M. F. (2007). The myths of e-government: looking beyond the assumptions of a new and better government. *The Information Society*, *23*(5), 373–382. doi:10.1080/01972240701572913

Bekkers, V. J. J. M., & Zouridis, S. (1999). Electronic service delivery in public administration: some trends and issues. *International Review of Administrative Sciences*, *65*(2), 183–196. doi:10.1177/0020852399652004

Berner Fachhochschule & Unisys. (2005). E-government trendbarometer. Thalwil: Unisys (Schweiz, AG).

Bertot, J. C., & Jaeger, P. T. (2006). User-centered e-government: challenges and benefits for government web sites. *Government Information Quarterly*, *23*(2), 163–168. doi:10.1016/j.giq.2006.02.001

Bertot, J. C., & Jaeger, P. T. (2008). The e-government paradox: better customer services doesn't necessarily cost less. *Government Information Quarterly*, *25*(2), 149–154. doi:10.1016/j.giq.2007.10.002

Bevir, M., Rhodes, R. A. W., & Weller, P. (2003). Traditions of governance: interpreting the changing role of the public sector. *Public Administration Review*, *81*(1), 1–17. doi:10.1111/1467-9299.00334

Brown, D. (2005). Electronic government and public administration. *International Review of Administrative Sciences*, *71*(2), 241–254. doi:10.1177/0020852305053883

Castells, M. (2000). *The rise of the network society: Economy, society and culture*. Oxford: Blackwell Publishing.

Codagnone, C., & Undheim, T. A. (2008 August). Benchmarking eGovernment: tools, theory and practice. *European Journal of ePractice*, 4. Retrieved April 19, 2009, from http://www.epracticejournal.eu/document/4970.

Cordella, A. (2007). E-government: towards the e-bureaucratic form? *Journal of Information Technology*, *22*, 265–274. doi:10.1057/palgrave.jit.2000105

Dimitrova, D. V., & Chen, Y.-C. (2006). Profiling the adopters of e-government information and services. *Social Science Computer Review*, *24*(2), 172–188. doi:10.1177/0894439305281517

Dugdale, A., Daly, A., Papandrea, F., & Maley, M. (2005). Accessing e-government: challenges for citizens and organizations. *International Review of Administrative Sciences*, *71*(1), 109–188. doi:10.1177/0020852305051687

Dunleavy, P., Margetts, H., Bastow, S., & Tinkler, J. (2006). *Digital era governance*. Oxford, UK: Oxford University Press.

Ebbers, W. E., Pieterson, W. J., & Noordman, H. N. (2008). Electronic government: rethinking channel management strategies. *Government Information Quarterly*, *25*(2), 181–201. doi:10.1016/j.giq.2006.11.003

Evans, D., & Yen, D. C. (2006). E-government: evolving relationship of citizens and government, domestic, and international development. *Government Information Quarterly*, *23*(2), 207–235. doi:10.1016/j.giq.2005.11.004

Eyob, E. (2004). E-government: breaking the frontiers of inefficiencies in the public sector. *Electronic Government, an International Journal*, *1*(1), 107-114.

Fountain, J. E. (2001). *Building the virtual state: information technology and institutional change*. Washington, DC: Brooking Institution Press.

Fountain, J. E. (2009). Bureaucratic reform and e-government in the United States. An institutional perspective. In Chadwick, A., & Howard, P. N. (Eds.), *Routledge handbook of Internet politics* (pp. 99–113). London, New York: Routledge.

Freeman, C., & Soete, L. (1997). *The economics of industrial innovation*. London: Continuum.

Gareis, K., Cullen, K., & Korte, W. (2004). Putting the user at the center. Implications for the provision of online public services. In P. Cunningham & M, Cunningham (Eds.), eAdoption and the knowledge economy. Issues, applications, case studies (pp. 611-618). Amsterdam: IOS Press.

Ghere, R.K., & Young, B.A. (1998). The cyber-management environment: where technology and ingenuity meet public purpose and accountability. *Public Administration and Management: An Interactive Journal*, 3(1).

Gupta, M. P., & Jana, D. (2003). E-government evaluation: a framework and case study. *Government Information Quarterly*, *20*(4), 365–387. doi:10.1016/j.giq.2003.08.002

Hammerschmid, G., & Meyer, R. E. (2005). New public management in Austria: local variation on a global theme. *Public Administration*, *83*(3), 709–733. doi:10.1111/j.0033-3298.2005.00471.x

Heeks, R. (1999). *Reinventing government in the information age. International practise in IT-enabled public sector reform*. London: Routledge.

Heeks, R. (2006). *Understanding and measuring eGovernment: international benchmarking studies*. Paper presented at the UNDESA Workshop, E-participation and E-government: Understanding the present and creating the future, Budapest, Hungary, 12-28 July 2006.

Heeks, R., & Bailur, S. (2007). Analyzing E-Government research: perspectives, philosophies, theories, methods, and practice. *Government Information Quarterly*, *24*(2), 243–265. doi:10.1016/j.giq.2006.06.005

Ho, A. T.-K. (2002). Reinventing local governments and the e-government initiative. *Public Administration Review*, *62*(4), 434–444. doi:10.1111/0033-3352.00197

Homburg, V. M. F., & Bekkers, V. J. J. M. (2005). E-government and NPM: a perfect marriage? In Bekkers, V. J. J. M., & Homburg, V. M. F. (Eds.), *The information ecology of e-government*. Amsterdam: IOS Press.

Jaeger, P. T. (2003). The endless wire: e-government as global phenomenon. *Government Information Quarterly*, *20*(4), 323–331. doi:10.1016/j.giq.2003.08.003

Jaeger, P. T., & Thompson, K. M. (2003). E-government around the world: lessons, challenges, and future directions. *Government Information Quarterly*, *20*(4), 389–394. doi:10.1016/j.giq.2003.08.001

Janssen, D., Rotthier, S., & Snijkers, K. (2004). If you measure it they will score: an assessment of international eGovernment benchmarking. *Information Polity*, *9*(3-4), 121–130.

Kampen, J. K., Snijkers, K., & Bouckaert, G. (2005). Public priorities concerning the development of e-government in Flanders. *Social Science Computer Review*, *23*(1), 136–139. doi:10.1177/0894439304271557

Kernaghan, K., Marson, B., & Sandford, B. (2002). *The new public organization*. Toronto: Institute of Public Administration of Canada.

Kunstelj, M., Jukic, T., & Vintar, M. (2007). Analysing the demand side of E-Government: what can we learn from Slovenian users? *Lecture Notes in Computer Science*, *4656*, 305–317. doi:10.1007/978-3-540-74444-3_26

Kunstelj, M., & Vintar, M. (2004). Evaluating the progress of e-government development: a critical analysis. *Information Polity*, *9*(3-4), 131–148.

Layne, K., & Lee, J. (2001). Developing fully functional e-government: a four stage model. *Government Information Quarterly*, *18*(2), 122–136. doi:10.1016/S0740-624X(01)00066-1

Lee-Kelley, L., & Kolsaker, A. (2004). E-Government: the fit between supply assumptions and usage drivers. *Electronic Government, an International Journal, 1*(2), 130-140.

Macintosh, A., Robson, E., Smith, E., & Whyte, A. (2003). Electronic Democracy and Young People. *Social Science Computer Review, 21*(1), 43–54. doi:10.1177/0894439302238970

Margetts, H. (1999). *Information technology in government: Britain and America*. London: Routledge.

Margetts, H. (2009). Public management change and e-government. The emergence of digital-era governance. In Chadwick, A., & Howard, P. N. (Eds.), *Routledge handbook of Internet politics* (pp. 114–127). London, New York: Routledge.

McLaughlin, K., Osborne, S., & Ferlie, E. (2002). *New public management: current trends and future prospects*. London, New York: Routledge.

Millard, J. (2003). *ePublic services in Europe: past, present and future. Research findings and new challenges*. Final draft-paper prepared for IPTS, not published.

Millard, J. (2008 August). eGovernment measurement for policy makers. *European Journal of ePractice*, 4. Retrieved April 19, 2009 from http://www.epracticejournal.eu/document/4971

Milward, H. B., & Snyder, O. (1996). Electronic government: linking citizens to public organizations through technology. *Journal of Public Administration: Research and Theory, 6*(2), 261–275.

Moore, T., & Flynn, P. (2004). *Future challenges for E-Government. The changing role of multi-channel service delivery*. Discussion Paper n° 4. Australian Government Information Management Office. 2004. Retrieved September 6, 2008 from: http://www.finance.gov.au/Publications/future-challenges-for-egovernment/docs/AGIMO-FC-no4.pdf

Netchaeva, I. (2002). E-government and e-democracy. A comparison of opportunities in the North and South. *Gazette: the International Journal for Communication Studies, 64*(5), 467–477. doi:10.1177/17480485020640050601

Norris, D. F., & Moon, M. J. (2005). Advancing e-government at the grassroots: tortoise of hare? *Public Administration Review, 65*(1), 64–75. doi:10.1111/j.1540-6210.2005.00431.x

OECD. (2003). The E-Government imperative. Paris: OECD E-government Studies.

OECD. (2005). E-Government for better government. Paris: OECD E-government Studies.

OECD. (2008). Belgium: OECD country report. Paris OECD E-government Studies.

Osborne, D., & Gaebler, T. (1992). *Reinventing government: how the entrepreneurial spirit is transforming the public sector*. Reading, MA: Addison-Wesley.

Peters, R., Janssen, M., & van Engers, T. (2005). Measuring e-government impact: existing practices and shortcomings. In *Proceedings of the 6th International Conference on Electronic Commerce, session: eGovernment services and policy track* (Copenhagen, August 22-26, 2005) (pp. 480-489). New York: ACM Press.

Pieterson, W., & Ebbers, W. (2008). The use of service channels by citizens in the Netherlands: implications for multi-channel management. *International Review of Administrative Sciences, 74*(1), 95–110. doi:10.1177/0020852307085736

Pollit, C., & Bouckaert, G. (2004). *Public management reform: a comparative analysis*. Oxford, UK: Oxford University Press.

Prins, J. E. (2001). *Designing e-government. On the crossroads of technological innovation and institutional change*. The Hague: Kluwer Law International.

Reddick, C. G. (2005a). Citizen interaction with e-government: from the streets to servers? *Government Information Quarterly*, *22*(1), 38–57. doi:10.1016/j.giq.2004.10.003

Reddick, C. G. (2005b). Citizen-initiated contacts with government: comparing phones and websites. *Journal of E-Government*, *2*(1), 27–53. doi:10.1300/J399v02n01_03

Relyea, H. C. (2002). E-gov: introduction and overview. *Government Information Quarterly*, *19*(1), 9–35. doi:10.1016/S0740-624X(01)00096-X

Roy, R. (2006). E-service delivery and new governance capacities: 'Service Canada' as a case study. *International Journal of Services Technology and Management*, *7*(3), 253–271.

Sindane, A. M. (2004). Public administration versus public management: parallels, divergences, convergences and who benefits? *International Review of Administrative Sciences*, *70*(4), 665–672. doi:10.1177/0020852304048454

Titah, R., & Barki, H. (2006). E-Government adoption and acceptance: a literature review. *International Journal of Electronic Government Research*, *2*(3), 23–57.

United Nations. (2002). *E-government at the crossroads. World Public Sector Report 2003*. New York: United Nations.

van Deursen, A., van Dijk, J., & Ebbers, W. (2006). Why E-Government usage lags behind: explaining the gap between potential and actual usage of electronic public services in the Netherlands. *Lecture Notes in Computer Science*, *4084*, 269–280. doi:10.1007/11823100_24

van Dijk, J. (1999). *The network society: social aspects of new media*. London: Sage.

van Dijk, J. (2005). *The deepening divide: inequality in the information Society*. London: Sage.

van Dijk, J., Peters, O., & Ebbers, W. (2008). Explaining the acceptance and use of government internet services: a multivariate analysis of 2006 survey data in the Netherlands. *Government Information Quarterly*, *25*(3), 379–399. doi:10.1016/j.giq.2007.09.006

Verdegem, P., & Hauttekeete, L. (2008). The user at the centre of the development of one-stop government. [IJEG]. *International Journal of Electronic Governance*, *1*(3), 28–274. doi:10.1504/IJEG.2008.020449

Verdegem, P., & Verleye, G. (2009). User-centered e-government in practice: a comprehensive model for measuring user satisfaction. *Government Information Quarterly*, *26*(3), 487–497. doi:10.1016/j.giq.2009.03.005

Welch, E. W., Hinnant, C. C., & Moon, M. J. (2005). Linking citizen satisfaction with e-government and trust in government. *Journal of Public Administration: Research and Theory*, *15*(3), 371–391. doi:10.1093/jopart/mui021

West, D. M. (2004). E-government and the transformation of service delivery and citizen attitudes. *Public Administration Review*, *64*(1), 15–27. doi:10.1111/j.1540-6210.2004.00343.x

Wimmer, M. (2002). A European perspective towards online one-stop government: the eGov project. *Electronic Commerce Research and Applications*, *1*, 92–103. doi:10.1016/S1567-4223(02)00008-X

Yildiz, M. (2007). E-government research: reviewing the literature, limitations, and ways forward. *Government Information Quarterly*, *24*(3), 646–665. doi:10.1016/j.giq.2007.01.002

Zussman, D. (2002). Alternative service delivery. In Dunn, C. (Ed.), *The handbook of Canadian public administration*. Oxford: Oxford University Press.

ENDNOTES

1 'Constituents' is used as collective term instead of the more common term 'users' of e-government services. With constituents we refer to both citizens, businesses and public servants. Consequently, it comprises all groups in society that are served or supported by public service activities.

2 The Belgian public governance structure (federal government versus the regional level) limits interference of governments in each others' sovereign areas of responsibility, limiting opportunities for cooperation and collaboration across governments; this also holds true for e-government (OECD, 2008).

3 More information can be found via: http://www.epractice.eu/en/cases/fedeviewa

4 More information can be found via: http://www.epractice.eu/en/cases/fedeviewc

Chapter 3
Evaluating the Impact of E-Government on Citizens:
Cost-Benefit Analysis

Tong-yi Huang
National Cheng-chi University, Taiwan

Chung-pin Lee
National Cheng-chi University, Taiwan

ABSTRACT

Since the early 1990s, the trend of e-government has attracted scholarly attention to the issue of how governments apply the information and communication technologies (the ICTs) in different services. While most studies focus on "what" and "how" questions of e-government, relatively little literature addresses the issue of "to what effect" it has on citizens. To fill this void, from user-centric perspective, this study examines Taiwan's e-government performance, which has been ranked by international institutions as one of the top performers worldwide. The authors use a telephone interview data set from a survey conducted in 2007 with a random sample of 2000 respondents to analyze what impact the ICTs applications in administrative service and democracy improvement have on citizens in terms of cost and benefit. The authors' findings show that e-government has had a significant, positive impact on citizens regarding their time saving, perception of information credibility, and satisfaction with the government. The results also suggest that the ICTs facilitate broader distribution of political information, a key to the success of e-democracy. The authors conclude this chapter by proposing suggestions for further strategic planning and critical research issues.

INTRODUCTION

With the advent of new information and communication technologies (ICTs), e-government has been one of the important innovations that have greatly reshaped public administration since last decade. Owing to the belief that the ICTs can significantly improve the efficiency and effectiveness of public services, e-government has brought many new issues, models, debates, and theories into public administration research. Among these newly emerged areas, one important but relatively unexplored topic is the effects of e-government. What is the e-government impact on stakeholders? Have

DOI: 10.4018/978-1-61520-931-6.ch003

e-government users received better service quality than traditional government service users?

With regard to these questions, existing research provides insufficient evidence-based answers. This void is partly attributed to the fact that previous academic research lacked a linkage with practices and lacked attention in considering the impact on e-government stakeholders (Heeks and Bailur, 2007). It is also because the focus of most research is mainly placed on e-government providers (Reddick, 2005) rather than service receivers. A tech-centric e-government initiative would fail since its policy process would ignore the perspective from citizens (Saxena, 2005). In order to ensure that e-government efforts are indeed invested in the right places and direction, this chapter argues that the citizen-centric e-government impact should be continuously and precisely assessed. Only a responsive and customer-oriented e-government policy can play a permanent role in society.

The purpose of this chapter is to display the e-government impact on citizens through a citizen-centric perspective. We examine the case of Taiwan's e-government service by analyzing telephone survey data conducted in 2007 on e-government users and non-users. Taiwan has been ranked as one of the top performers in e-government in the new millennium.[1] The findings on this benchmark case should have implications for other countries and for policy makers in Taiwan in developing next-step strategy. This chapter uses Taiwan's case by comparing e-government service users and traditional government service users and aims to investigate what citizens have received from e-government and what its impact is on citizens. This is not a top-down e-government evaluation, but an assessment of citizens' gains from e-government usage. In the next section, we review earlier studies about e-government evaluations to illustrate the achievements and gaps in this field. Based on this review, Section III constructs an analytical framework and elaborates the measurement and data collection. Sections IV and V present our results and discuss our findings, respectively. The last section concludes our study by proposing a further research agenda.

LITERATURE REVIEW

Based on the perception that the ICTs can be a powerful tool to enhance the efficiency and effectiveness of public services and to improve the quality of public participation, modern democratic nations have been recognizing them as an important part of public governance since the early 1990s. In particular, "e-government" is the most significant innovation during this period of time both in academia and in the practical arena. The emergence of e-government could be traced to the accompanying report of the National Performance Review, which was called "Reengineering through Information Technology" in the Clinton Administration (Lenk & Traunmuller, 2002). Since citizens are the principal service receivers of e-government, citizens' perspective regarding what the e-government services bring to citizens' life should be important. There have been highly recommended qualifications that e-government has to satisfy users' needs (Horan et al., 2006). This argument brings the first significance of assessing the impact of e-government on citizens. Unfortunately, most existing e-government research focused on the perspective from the supply side (Reddick, 2005), not the (user-centric) demand side. Whether there is a gap between the perspectives of citizens and bureaucrats is unknown (Moon and Welch, 2005), and the bureaucrats may not be aware of whether e-government achievements have already met citizens' expectations.

The need for an e-government impact assessment could also be found in the process of the e-government value chain (EVC, Figure 1). EVC refers to a model that illustrates how e-government turns inputs into outcomes (Heeks, 2006).

A well-developed e-government research field is supposed to cover all of the components in

Figure 1. E-government value chain. Source: Adapted from Heeks(2006).

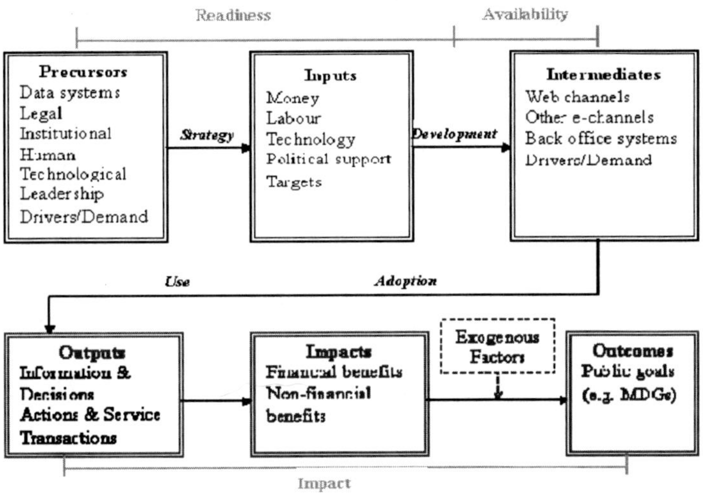

the EVC model. Early articles in e-government research, however, focused mainly on system evaluation and system adoption, such as the e-government website evaluation research that was conducted by the United Nations and Brown University, as well as the technology acceptance model, which applies to the reasoned action theory developed by Davis (1989). This body of research only covers the first half of the EVC model. Few studies have discussed the benefit of e-government to the users or its individual-level impact. As Bhatnagar (2007) points out, while an increasing number of governments are investing in ICTs, evidence to date on the outcomes of ICTs investment in the public sector has not been fully established.

The research gap mentioned above exhibits urgent needs for further examination of e-government implementation and evaluation. To fill this gap, this chapter aims to construct an impact assessment framework and empirically analyze the created value of e-government. The rest of this section discusses two topics. The first one is the major functions regarding what e-government has provided to users; the second is what e-government users may receive from these functions.

The Functions of E-Government

Much of the literature argued that the early concept of e-government is too ambiguous and should be divided into distinct parts (6, 2004). It should be realigned into two categories: e-government and e-democracy. In other words, e-government is a term that not only denotes the service delivery that we called e-government, but also covers so-called e-democracy, which implies the transformation of political systems through the ICTs (Mahrer and Krimmer, 2005; Bishop and Anderson, 2004).

Backus (2001) uses "e-governance" to represent the overall context of IT implication in the public sector. He sees e-governance as an aggregate of two electronic means. The first one is the interaction between government and citizens and government and businesses–the e-democracy; the second one is internal government operations to simplify and improve the democratic, government and business aspects of governance–the e-government. This explanation is very similar to Chadwick (2003) and Lenihan's (2005) statements. Chadwick (2003) argues that the IT application in the public sector is a convergence of "e-democracy" and "e-government." This convergence can provide a broader understanding of how IT is reshaping public governance; Lenihan (2005) also provides an idea through the use of three aspects to clarify a complete concept of e-government: service delivery improvement, information, and e-democracy. These parts of e-government are intertwined, as research has demonstrated that delivering public service via the internet will also alter the nature of democracy (Bishop and Anderson, 2004). That is, the e-government's functions cover not only the improvement of administrative services, but also the reformation of democratic quality. In this study, we broadly divide e-government into e-government (administration) and e-democracy. Under these two functions, we further develop dimensions from the perspective of a cost-benefit analysis.

The Impact of E-Government on Citizens: a Cost-Benefit Analysis Approach

Drawing from a review of 180 studies, DeLone and McLean (1992) defined the impact of an information system as the influence on its recipients, and they believe that the "impact" is the most difficult dimension to measure. The OECD report, *E-government For Better Government* (OECD, 2005a), used a cost-benefit analysis perspective to construct an e-government impact framework. It sees the e-government project as a private business case and lays out the reasons why e-government should be estimated with cost and benefit indicators. Based on this report, the OECD (2005b) indentifies three types of costs and benefits to consider and two types of beneficiaries to whom these costs and benefits will accrue. These two types of beneficiaries refer to internal and external customers/users of e-government (Figure 2).

The first impact dimension in this report, direct financial costs and benefits, refers to the most immediate and easily quantified return on e-government investments. For a citizen and business (the external customers), it can be the form of time and money saved in finding online information and using online public service. The second impact dimension, direct non-financial costs and benefits, is the form of service quality, access to information, and confidence. These may be displayed as user satisfaction and trust in government. The final category, indirect costs and benefits, implies a broader impact on gross environment, such as the economy and political institutions. (OECD, 2006b)

In a similar vein, several scholars have not only suggested perspectives in line with the dimensions proposed by the OECD cost-benefit analysis framework, but also conducted empirical research. Among these studies, Thompson et al. (2005) found that small firms' information technology capabilities are positively associated with the use of e-government services. Gilbert et al. (2004) argued that trust, finance, time, and information quality are all important drivers for e-government use behaviors. Furthermore, Welch et al. (2005) analyzed survey data and found that government website usage is positively associated with e-government satisfaction, and that e-government satisfaction is positively associated with trust in government. They attributed this association to the fact that e-government strategies such as transaction, transparency and interactivity can affect citizens' perceptions of government. The research done by Parent et al. (2004) also showed that e-government usage could significantly improve citizens' trust and political efficacy. There is an abundance of studies arguing that citizens' trust in government will rise and fall with respondents' economic status (Lawrence, 1997). Following this logic, Parent et al. (2005) believe that the

Figure 2. E-government benefit. Source: Adapted from OECD (2005b).

Benefits \ Beneficiaries	Internal Customers (Government)	External Customers (Citizens & Business)
Direct Financial Cost and Benefit	**Reducing Cost**: freeing resources for public and private innovation; increasing the value of products and services	**Reducing the Burden**: administrative simplification; providing higher valued and faster public services; saving time and money and improving equity
Direct Non-Financial Cost and Benefit	**Capturing the Total Benefit of Investment:** achieving synergies across service delivery channels; enabling the sharing and reuse of data for more proactive service delivery; promoting access as part of a channel management strategy	**Increasing User Satisfaction and trust:** better service; improving personalization and service quality; improving access and equity; addressing security and privacy concerns; transparency and choice
Indirect Cost and Benefit	**Supporting Legitimacy**: supporting security and trust at an aggregate level; modernization and transformation of the public sector; ensuring equity; increasing responsiveness, accountability and participation	**Supporting Growth:** improving the business environment; creating an quality information society; establishing an infrastructure for secure and reliable transactions

government had a significantly positive impact on people's trust. Tolbert and Mossberger (2006) find that local government website visits enhance citizens' trust in local government, controlling for other attitudinal and demographic factors.

A cost-benefit analysis can be a good start for e-government impact assessment research. Although most indicators are not yet clear nor mutually exclusive (OECD, 2005b), this framework undoubtedly brings a user-centric perspective to e-government research. The work we need to do now is to accumulate more data that are empirical to consolidate and to modify this cost-benefit framework. However, it is difficult to estimate the so-called 'impact' without longitudinal data. In the case of e-government impact, the 'impact' generally means the difference between before e-government use and after. Due to the cost and scarcity of panel data, a quasi-experiment design comparing users and non-users of e-government was designed instead to detect the impact of e-government.

FRAMEWORK AND MEASUREMENT

Founded on the OECD's cost-benefit framework, this chapter further divides the cost/benefit into e-government and e-democracy functions. The former is substantiated by "administrative service" and the latter by "democracy function." Figure 3 shows the trajectories of functions and dimensions and all the comparative questions we used. To assess the impact on citizens by comparing two service channels, the survey asked e-government users about their online experiences and asked non e-government users about their experience with traditional government contacts. These questions are framed according to the cost-benefit analysis framework from OECD reports (Figure 2), and they are also the basis of our statistical analysis.

The survey items in Figure 3 are instruments for a telephone interview that was sponsored by the Research, Development and Evaluation Commission (RDEC) of the Executive Yuan of Taiwan's central government. This interview was conducted by the Chinese Association of National Competitiveness (CANC) in 2007. From March 3 to 10, 2007, the telephone survey randomly interviewed 1,034 non e-government users who had never visited government websites, and 982 e-government users who had online experience in looking for information or seeking service from government websites. The sampling error is ±2.18% with a 95% confidence level.

A profile (Figure 4) of e-government users shows that 46.6% are men, 66.5% are younger than 40 years of age, 21.8% are between 40 and 49 years, 11.6% are older than 50 years, 63.1% have bachelor degree, and 9.1% have a Master's or Ph.D. degree. The characteristics of the non e-government users have some differences from the e-government users. More than 54.6% of non e-government users are older than 50 years. In addition, 45.8% (10%+18.3%+17.5%) of non e-government users have never enrolled in high school or higher education. These statistics show that e-government users, in general, are younger and have higher education than the non e-government users.

Based on the analysis of this data set, the following section will display the e-government impact on its users by presenting the costs and benefits to citizens of using various traditional government or e-government services.

Costs and Benefits of E-Government Users and Non-Users

The analysis of this section will follow the framework elaborated above. We will first demonstrate the direct financial and non-financial cost of administrative service and then the direct non-financial cost and benefit of the e-democracy function.

Administrative Service Delivery

The first widely recognized function of e-governance is e-service delivery. The primary incentive for government to invest in e-government is to enhance efficiency in internal management and providing services to citizens. From a citizen-centric perspective, e-services constitute a major part of their perception in e-government because these applications are closely related to their everyday life. We propose the direct financial and non-financial cost-benefit indicators in Figure 3 with the following results.

Direct Financial Cost and Benefit—Time and Money

We first describe the time saved in using an e-service, searching for information and contacting government officials. It is followed by the money saved in getting government service by e-government users and non-users. Figure 5 shows that 96.6% (52.3%+44.3%) of e-government users agree that they spent less time in e-service than in traditional public service. There are 24.2% traditional service users who remarked that they have to spend a lot of time in contacting governments for services, while 75.8% disagreed with this statement. Figure 5 presents the differences between the two channels users about their time spent in government service delivery.

In addition to service delivery, information search is another function of e-service. As Figure 6 demonstrates, 94.9% of e-government users agree online means saved time in searching for information; 89.8% of non e-government users agree that getting government information by traditional means can be done quickly.

Figure 7 reports the difference in time spent in contacting public servants. Regardless of whether they were e-government users or traditional means users (such as telephone, letter, face-to-face contact), most people who had contact with public servants agreed that they could receive a quick response from the public servant (78.4% and 80.1%). To a certain extent, this means that online communication, such as providing an e-mail address, is not an urgent need from the user's perspective.

In addition to time, money saving is another consideration of cost and benefit. Figure 8 shows that 80.6% of e-government users agree that e-channel usage has saved them money. However,

Figure 3. The research framework and measurement for the impact of e-government. Note: This survey does not include relevant questions regarding this category. Source: the authors.

Government functions and impact		E-government service Users	Traditional public serving channel users
Administrative service	Direct Financial Cost and Benefit	Q.22. Do you agree that online service delivery channels cost you less time to get public services than traditional service channels?	Q67. Do you agree that getting a public service costs a lot of time?
		Q23. Do you agree that online service delivery channels cost you less money to get public service than traditional service channels?	Q68. Do you agree that getting public services costs a lot of money?
		Q33. Do you agree that online interactive channels make it easier to receive quick responses from public servants?	Q62. Do you agree that you usually can receive a quick response when you try to contact public servants?
		Q17. Do you agree that the government's websites cost you less time to get information than traditional information searching channels?	Q57. Do you agree that citizens are usually able to get governmental information from agencies quickly?
	Direct Non-Financial Cost and Benefit	Q14. Do you agree that most information on government websites is credible?	Q53. Do you agree that most information released from governments is credible ?
		Q.20. In general, are you satisfied with the information on government websites?	Q58. In general, are you satisfied with the government information search channels?
		Q27. In general, are you satisfied with online public service?	Q69. In general, are you satisfied with public service procedures?
		Q81 Do you trust the central government?	Q81 Do you trust the central government?
		Q82. Do you trust the local government?	Q82. Do you trust the local government?
	Indirect Cost and Benefit: "Good Governance"	*	*
Democracy function	Direct Financial Cost and Benefit	*	*
	Direct Non-Financial Cost and Benefit	Q45. Do you agree that sufficient information on the Internet facilitates citizens' understanding of politics?	Q80. Do you agree that politics is too complicated to understand?
		Q44. Do you agree that public servants will not pay attention to the comments posted on the online policy forum?	Q79. Do you agree that public servants will not care about citizens' opinion at all?
		40. Do you agree that posting your comments on the government websites can distribute them to more people?	Q76. Do you agree that you can distribute your comments regarding public policy to many people by speaking up?
	Indirect Cost and Benefit: "Good Governance"	*	*

most traditional channel users (92.7%) disagree that contact with the government to get public service via traditional channels cost too much money.

Comparing money saving with time saving, we can infer that citizens have more interest in efficient e-public service. Most of them do not care about the transaction cost in the traditional

Figure 4. Characteristics of the respondents. Source: the authors.

Gender		Male	Female	Total
E-gov users	N	457	524	981
	%	(46.6%)	(53.4%)	(100.0%)
Non e-gov users	N	554	480	1034
	%	(53.6%)	(46.4%)	(100.0%)

Age		18-29	30-39	40-49	50-59	60--	Total
E-gov users	N	349	291	210	88	24	962
	%	(36.3%)	(30.2%)	(21.8%)	(9.1%)	(2.5%)	(100.0%)
Non e-gov users	N	134	115	202	230	312	993
	%	(13.5%)	(11.6%)	(20.3%)	(23.2%)	(31.4%)	(100.0%)

Education		None	Elementary school	Junior High School	High school	Bachelor	Master and Ph.D.	Total
E-gov users	N	0	4	25	244	619	89	981
	%	(.0%)	(.4%)	(2.5%)	(24.9%)	(63.1%)	(9.1%)	(100.0%)
Non e-gov users	N	102	188	179	367	178	11	1025
	%	(10.0%)	(18.3%)	(17.5%)	(35.8%)	(17.4%)	(1.1%)	(100.0%)

channel, but they do care about whether they can get a "quick" response regarding their request.

Direct Non-Financial Cost and Benefit: Information Credibility, Satisfaction and Trust in Government

Regarding the direct non-financial cost and benefit, this study estimates the differences in information credibility, users' satisfaction, and trust in government. Figure 9 shows that 91.7% of e-government users agree that the information on government websites is credible. In contrast, only 53.8% of non e-government users deem credible most information released by the government.

Citizen satisfaction is a typical form of measuring government performance, especially in micro-level impact assessments. According to Figure 10, 86.6% of e-government users are satisfied with online government information, and 70.5% of traditional means users expressed their satisfaction with government information.

Another pair of satisfaction comparisons refers to citizens' perception of channels. In Figure 11, 91.3% of e-government users are satisfied with online service. There are 82.1% of non e-government users who are satisfied with the traditional channel they are using.

As previous literature (Welch et al., 2004; Tolbert and Mossberger, 2006) suggests, e-government usage and satisfaction would strengthen citizens' trust in local government, controlling for other attitudinal and demographic factors. However, our results show that non e-government users have slightly higher trust in both local and central governments. Figures 12 and 13 illustrate that 43.7% and 68.7% of non e-government users expressed their trust in central and local government, respectively, while the percentage of e-government users is 41.9% and 65.6%. Such results are not congruent with Welch et al. (2004) and Tolbert and Mossberger (2006) and deserve further exploration.

DEMOCRATIC FUNCTION

In the evaluation framework we laid out in the previous section, democratic function includes direct and indirect cost and benefit. Constrained by a lack of appropriate survey questions, this chapter only reports the direct non-financial cost and benefit of e-government users and non-users. In this study, we examine the spread of information perceived by our respondents and the political efficacy of e-government users and non-users.

One of the widely recognized characteristics of the ICTs is their capacity to distribute information in cyberspace, transcending distance and time. Figure 14 shows that 82.5% of e-government users experienced the ICTs' power in spreading personal ideas. This is much better than traditional channels. Only 59.5% of non-users agree that they could broadcast their own opinions usefully to other people by speaking up.

Another dimension of democratic function is political efficacy. Figure 15 shows that 39.6% of e-government users have higher external political efficacy than traditional means users (31.5%). This may be caused by the advantage of the ICTs on information distribution (Figure 15).

For internal efficacy, 31.3% of e-government users agree that government websites have facilitated their understanding of politics. However, only 21% of non e-government users agree that they are able to understand politics.

SUMMARY

To sum up the above analysis, Figure 16 demonstrates that the most significant impacts of e-government on citizens are related to administrative services. Among these impacts, time saving is one of the most significant returns that citizens have received from e-government service. In addition, increasing citizens' perceived credibility of the information released by the government and citizen satisfaction are also important impacts of e-government on citizens. Interestingly, our data exhibit that there is no significant difference between e-government users and non-users regarding trust in government. Contrary to previous studies, trust in government of non-users is even slightly higher than that of e-government users.

In the democratic function, the most significant improvement is the diffusion effect of political advocacy or personal ideas. The online channel can spread political comments rapidly, extensively and efficiently. Although political efficacy is an important target in the e-government's democratic function, its effects are not as good as expected thus far.

DISCUSSION

With the emergence of the ICT application in the public sector, the assessment of the ICT's impact has become a big issue in e-government research. In general, it is very difficult to measure the policy impact without longitudinal data, regardless of whether one is studying the micro or macro level. In an explorative attempt offset by a data constraint, this chapter uses a quasi-experimental arrangement to present key dimensions of the cost and benefit of e-government to users and non-users. To a certain extent, we believe this method can show not only the needs of non e-government users in their interaction with the government, but also show what the e-government has done in these respects.

Taiwan's e-government has been ranked one of the top performers by different world-renowned e-government research institutions, such as Brown University and the World Economic Forum. The e-government impact is supposed to be significantly positive in Taiwan. The findings regarding the assessment of the impact of Taiwan's e-government should be an important reference for future policy planning.

Based on the findings we report above, we conclude that Taiwan's e-government has significantly saved user time spent in contacting the government and in receiving public service delivery. It further enhances users' perception in the government's information credibility. We

Figure 5. Time spent for two channel users. Source: the authors.

Users	Items	Strongly agree	Agree	Disagree	Strongly disagree	Total
E-gov. users	Q.22. Do you agree that online service delivery channels cost you less time to get public services than traditional service channels?	156 (52.3%)	132 (44.3%)	9 (3.0%)	1 (.3%)	298 (100%)
Non e-gov. users	Q67. Do you agree that getting public service costs a lot of time?	36 (5.9%)	112 (18.3%)	341 (55.6%)	124 (20.2%)	613 (100%)

Figure 6. Time spent on information search. Source: the authors.

Users	Items	Strongly agree	Agree	Disagree	Strongly disagree	Total
E-gov. users	Q17. Do you agree that the government's websites cost you less time to get information from than traditional information searching channels?	380 (45.1%)	420 (49.8%)	42 (5.0%)	1 (.1%)	843 (100.0%)
Non e-gov. users	Q57. Do you agree that citizens usually are able to get governmental information from agencies quickly?	30 (30.6%)	58 (59.2%)	6 (6.1%)	4 (4.1%)	98 (100.0%)

attribute time saving to the strength of the ICTs that transcend time and space. We suggest that the increase in the credibility of government information is derived from a decreased information asymmetry between bureaucrats and citizens. From our preliminary assessment, it seems that several scenarios of e-dreams have been realized, except for the positive impact on citizens' trust. Even though many technology optimists believe that ICT will enhance citizens' trust by increasing public service efficiency and government transparency, our data show that this expectation has yet to be proved.

These results remind us that there are at least several critical issues that need to be systematically addressed in the future. First, our data show online e-government users receive a positive impact on administrative services. However, most traditional channels also have "not bad" performances in information search or service delivery. We believe that this is due to the fact that the non e-government users have not had any experience on the Internet for comparison. This is a typical phenomenon of the digital divide and the information gap between ICTs haves and haves-not. This is also a big alarm for ICT policy. The difference between e-government users and non-users is growing. Therefore, the government has to invest more resources in the marketing of e-government initiatives. By doing so, the government can show the advantages of the e-government to the information poor.

Second, our findings suggest that information credibility is one of the significant impacts on citizens. This phenomenon clarifies the reason why some researchers found that e-government usage improves government transparency. While applauding the disclosure of government information by the ICTs, we should not neglect the privacy issues. In addition, the problem of administrative accountability also needs to be paid close attention to. Public servants must be accountable for website usability, website accessibility, data updates, data accuracy, and data arrangement.

The third issue we need to deal with is the relatively few applications of the ICTs in e-democracy. According to our findings, both e-government users and non-users have low political efficacy. Although institutional, political, and psychological factors are important drivers to enhance political efficacy, we believe that technology should be able to facilitate efficacy if there is a good e-democracy design (Wright and Street, 2007). According to the UN e-participation survey, most countries do not perform well in this dimension. Most countries lack the design for e-consulting and e-decision making (UN, 2006). In short, e-government needs more mechanisms to invite people into the public policy decision making process, to let people know that their participation can have an impact.

The final issue is the academic research agenda for the e-government. Although this chapter has attempted to measure the impact of e-government on citizens, its generalizability has been constrained by the features of cross-sectional data. We absolutely need a longitudinal data set to detect the causal relationship between e-government usage and the possible impact it has on users. This will be not only a big help for academic e-government research, but also a key to link practice and academia.

CONCLUSION

Policy impact assessment is invariably an important issue in public administration, especially the assessment on a new policy. Since e-government investment has become a substantial part of the public budget, its impact should be continuously and accurately evaluated. It is difficult to precisely measure the degree of change without longitudinal observations. This chapter goes a step toward addressing this limitation by using a quasi-experimental comparison that measures the differences between e-government users and traditional means users.

Our findings show that e-government has had a significant positive impact on citizens in terms of time saved, increased credibility of government information, and citizens' satisfaction with service delivery. In their democratic function, the ICTs lead to a faster and wider diffusion of political opinions. This diffusion of information can improve the feasibility of e-democracy. However, we did not see significant evidence that supports the proposition that e-government use will increase the level of trust. The association between ICT use and citizens' trust in government needs further testing.

Academically, this chapter is not only an exploratory attempt of citizen-centric e-government assessment but also a practice of cost-benefit analysis of e-governance. For e-government policy-makers, the results of this study offer an evidence-based reference for planning and implementing in the future. It suggests that the e-government designer should put more resources into the mechanisms that are supposed to cause a positive impact but are not yet in existence.

There are several limitations to this study. Due to the fact that the survey data mainly focus on individual level variables, macro impact measurements such as indirect non-financial benefit and cost are not covered in this chapter. Moreover, the limited variables constrain the ability to construct an optimal model to explain the differences. Finally, the causality is difficult to justify without a longitudinal panel data. We suggest several critical topics for future research: first, a more complete and precise evaluation of e-government impact including not only subjective individual-level assessment but also macro and meso-level analysis; second, increased understanding of the attributes of non-users and the reason why they do not use e-government; third, a longitudinal data collection mechanism that includes panel data to detect the impact of e-government.

Figure 7. Time spent in public servant contact. Source: the authors.

Users	Items	Strongly agree	Agree	Disagree	Strongly disagree	Total
E-gov. users	Q33.Do you agree that online interactive channels make it easier to receive quick responses from public servants?	69 (28.0%)	124 (50.4%)	38 (15.4%)	15 (6.1%)	246 (100.0%)
Non e-gov. users	Q62. Do you agree that you can usually receive a quick response when you try to contact public servants?	53 (27.7%)	100 (52.4%)	27 (14.1%)	11 (5.8%)	191 (100.0%)

Figure 8. Money spent between two channel users. Source: the authors.

Users	Items	Strongly agree	Agree	Disagree	Strongly disagree	Total
E-gov. users	Q23. Do you agree that online service delivery channels cost you less money to get public service from than traditional service channels?	82 (27.9%)	155 (52.7%)	53 (18.0%)	4 (1.4%)	294 (100.0%)
Non e-gov. users	Q68. Do you agree that getting public services costs a lot of money?	11 (1.8%)	34 (5.5%)	353 (57.2%)	219 (35.5%)	617 (100.0%)

Figure 9. Perception of information credibility. Source: the authors.

Users	Items	Absolutely credible	Credible	Incredible	Absolutely incredible	Total
E-gov. users	Q14.Do you agree that most information on government websites is credible?	143 (15.3%)	716 (76.4%)	70 (7.5%)	8 (.9%)	937 (100.0%)
Non e-gov. users	Q53. Do you agree that most information released by the government is credible ?	41 (6.5%)	298 (47.3%)	225 (35.7%)	66 (10.5%)	630 (100.0%)

Figure 10. Satisfaction with government information. Source: the authors.

Users	Items	Very unsatisfied	Unsatisfied	Satisfied	Very satisfied	Total
E-gov. users	Q.20. In general, are you satisfied with the information on government websites?	15 (1.8%)	98 (11.7%)	619 (73.6%)	109 (13.0%)	841 (100.0%)
Non e-gov. users	Q58. In general, are you satisfied with government information search channels?	3 (3.2%)	25 (26.3%)	61 (64.2%)	6 (6.3%)	95 (100.0%)

Figure 11. Satisfaction with government information. Source: the authors.

Users	Items	Very unsatisfied	Unsatisfied	Satisfied	Very Satisfied	Total
E-gov. users	Q27. In general, are you satisfied with online public service?	1 (.3%)	25 (8.4%)	219 (73.5%)	53 (17.8%)	298 (100%)
Non e-gov. users	Q69. In general, are you satisfied with public service procedures?	26 (4.3%)	83 (13.7%)	411 (67.6%)	88 (14.5%)	608 (100%)

Figure 12. Trust in central government. Source: the authors.

Users	Items	Not at all	Very little	Quite a bit	Very much	Total
E-gov. users	Q81. Do you trust the central government?	221 (23.8%)	320 (34.4%)	367 (39.5%)	22 (2.4%)	930 (100.0%)
Non e-gov. users	Q81. Do you trust the central government?	181 (21.1%)	293 (34.2%)	298 (34.8%)	85 (9.9%)	857 (100.0%)

Figure 13. Trust in local government. Source: the authors.

Users	Items	Not at all	Very little	Quite a bit	Very much	Total
E-gov. users	Q82. Do you trust the local government?	75 (8.0%)	248 (26.4%)	571 (60.9%)	44 (4.7%)	938 (100.0%)
Non e-gov. users	Q82. Do you trust the local government?	80 (9.4%)	188 (22.0%)	510 (59.7%)	76 (8.9%)	854 (100.0%)

Figure 14. Effectiveness of information distribution. Source: the authors.

Users	Items	Strongly agree	Agree	Disagree	Strongly disagree	Total
E-gov. users	Q40. Do you agree that posting your comments on government websites can distribute them to more people?	11 (19.3%)	36 (63.2%)	6 (10.5%)	4 (7.0%)	57 (100%)
Non e-gov. users	Q76. Do you agree that you can distribute your comments regarding public policy to many people by speaking up?	124 (12.9%)	437 (45.5%)	295 (30.7%)	104 (10.8%)	960 (100%)

Figure 15. Political efficacy. Source: the authors.

	Users	Items	Strongly agree	Agree	Disagree	Strongly disagree	Total
External Efficacy	E-gov. users	Q44. Do you agree that public servants will not pay attention to the comments posted on the online policy forum?	189 (20.9%)	358 (39.5%)	327 (36.1%)	32 (3.5%)	906 (100%)
	Non e-gov. users	Q79. Do you agree that public servants will not care about citizens' opinions at all?	253 (30.4%)	297 (35.7%)	226 (27.2%)	55 (6.6%)	831 (100%)
Internal Efficacy	E-gov. users	Q45. Do you agree that sufficient information on the Internet facilitates citizens' understanding of politics?	142 (15.2%)	499 (53.3%)	226 (24.1%)	69 (7.4%)	936 (100%)
	Non e-gov. users	Q80. Do you agree that politics is too complicated to understand?	303 (34.2%)	397 (44.8%)	132 (14.9%)	54 (6.1%)	886 (100%)

Figure 16. Summary of results of e-government impact on citizens. Source: the authors.

Beneficiaries / Impact		Items	E-government Users	Traditional channel users
Administrative service	Direct Financial Cost and Benefit	Time spent on service delivery	Good (96.6%)	Fair (75.8%)
		Money spent on service delivery	Good (80.6%)	Good (92.7% positive perception)
		Time spent on public servant contact	Fair (78.4%)	Fair (80.1% positive perception)
		Time spent on information search	Good (94.9%)	Good (89.8% positive perception)
	Direct Non-Financial Cost and Benefit	Information credibility	Good (91.7%)	Bad (53.8% positive perception)
		Satisfaction with government information	Good (86.6%)	Fair (70% positive perception)
		Satisfaction with service channels	Good (91.3%)	Fair (82.1% positive perception)
		Trust in government	No significant difference in trust between users and non-users	
Democratic Function	Direct Non-Financial Cost and Benefit	Internal Political Efficacy	Fair (31.5%)	Bad (21%)
		External Political Efficacy	Fair (39.6%)	Bad (31.5%)
		Diffusion effect	Good (82.5%)	Bad (58.5% positive perception)

REFERENCES

Backus, M. (2001). *E-Governance and developing countries-introduction and examples*. IICD Research Report No. 3. Retrieved from http://www.ftpiicd.org/files/research/reports/report3.doc

Bhatnagar, S. (2007). *Impact Assessment Study of Computerized Services Delivery Projects from India and Chile*. IT@WEB Staff working Papers. Retrieved April 28, 2009, from http://www.iimahd.ernet.in/egov/documents/impact-assessment-study-wbr.pdf

Bishop, P., & Anderson, L. (2004). *E-government to e-democracy: 'High Tech' solutions to 'No Tech' problems*. A paper prepared for the Australian Electronic Governance Conference. Centre for Public Policy, University of Melbourne, Melbourne Victoria, 14th and 15th April, 2004.

Chadwick, A. (2003). Bring E-Democracy Back In Why It matters for Future Research on E-governance. *Social Science Computer Review*, *21*(4), 443–455. doi:10.1177/0894439303256372

Davis, F. D. (1989). Perceived Usefulness, Perceived Ease of Use and User Acceptance of Information Technology. *Management Information Systems Quarterly*, *13*(3), 318–339. doi:10.2307/249008

DeLone, W. H., & McLean, E. R. (1992). Information System Success: The Quest for the Dependent Variable. *Information Systems Research*, *3*(1), 60–95. doi:10.1287/isre.3.1.60

Gilbert, D., Balestrini, P., & Littleboy, D. (2004). Barriers and Benefits in the adoption of E-government. *International Journal of Public Sector Management*, *17*(4/5), 286–301. doi:10.1108/09513550410539794

Heeks, R. (2006). *Benchmarking eGovernment: Improving the National and International Measurement, Evaluation and Comparison of eGovernment*. iGovernment Working Paper No. 18. Manchester, UK: University of Manchester.

Heeks, R., & Bailur, S. (2007). Analyzing e-government research: Perspectives, philosophies, theories, methods, and practice. *Government Information Quarterly*, *24*, 243–265. doi:10.1016/j.giq.2006.06.005

Horan, T. A., Abhichandani, T., & Rayalu, R. (2006). Assessing User Satisfaction of E-Government Services: Development and Testing of Quality-in-Use Satisfaction with Advanced Traveler Information. In *Proceedings of the 39th Hawaii International Conference on System Sciences*.

Lawrence, R. Z. (1997). Is it really the economy stupid? In Nye, J. S. (Ed.), *Why people don't trust government* (pp. 111–132). Cambridge, MA: Harvard University Press.

Lenihan, D. G. (2005). Realigning Governance: From E-Government to E-democracy. In Khosrow-Pour, M. (Ed.), *Practicing e-Government: A Global Perspective*. Hershey, PA: Idea Group Publishing.

Lenk, K., & Traunmüller, R. (2002). Electronic Government: Where are we Heading? In Lenk, K., & Traunmüller, R. (Eds.), *Electronic government: first international conference, EGOV2002*. New York: Springer.

Mahrer, H., & Krimmer, R. (2005). Towards the enhancement of e-democracy: identifying the notion of the middleman paradox. *Information Systems Journal*, *15*(1), 27–42. doi:10.1111/j.1365-2575.2005.00184.x

Moon, M. J., & Welch, E. W. (2005). Same Bed, Different Dreams? A Comparative Analysis of Citizen and Bureaucrat Perspective on E-Government. *Review of Public Personnel Administration*, *25*(3), 243–264. doi:10.1177/0734371X05275508

OECD. (2005a). *E-government for Better Government*. OECD publishing.

OECD. (2005b). *Proposed outline for Accessing E-government Benefits*. OECD publishing. Retrieved February 18, 2008, from http://webdomino1.oecd.org/COMNET/PUM/egovproweb.nsf/viewHtml/index/$FILE/GOV.PGC.EGOV.2006.1.doc

Parent, M., Vandebeek, C. A., & Gemino, A. C. (2004). *Building Citizen Trust Through e-Government*. Paper presented at the 37th Hawaii International Conference on System Sciences. Retrieved February 18, 2008, from http://csdl2.computer.org/comp/proceedings/hicss/2004/2056/05/205650119a.pdf

6Perri. 2004. *E-Governance*. New York: Palgrave.

Reddick, C. G. (2005). Citizen Interaction with E-government: From the streets to servers? *Government Information Quarterly*, *22*, 38–57. doi:10.1016/j.giq.2004.10.003

Saxena, K. B. C. (2005). Towards excellence in e-governance. *International Journal of Public Sector Management*, *18*(6), 498–513. doi:10.1108/09513550510616733

Thompson, D. V., Rust, R. T., & Rhoda, J. (2005). The business value of e-government for small firms. *International Journal of Service Industry Management*, *16*(4), 385–407. doi:10.1108/09564230510614022

Tolbert, C. J., & Mossberger, K. (2006). The Effects of E-Government on Trust and Confidence in Government. *Public Administration Review*, *66*(3), 354–369. doi:10.1111/j.1540-6210.2006.00594.x

UN. (2006). Global E-government Readiness Report 2005. New York: UN.

Welch, E. W., Hinnant, C. C., & Moon, M. J. (2005). Linking Citizen Satisfaction with E-Government and Trust in Government. *Journal of Public Administration: Research and Theory*, *15*(3), 371–391. doi:10.1093/jopart/mui021

ENDNOTE

1 According to Brown University's e-government Survey, Taiwan has ranked in the top five since 2002 and ranked first in 2002, 2004 and 2005. According to World Economic Forum Network Readiness Index, Taiwan has ranked as one of the ten top performers since 2003.

Chapter 4
Effectiveness of E-Government in Delivering Services

Ronnie Park
Nova Southeastern University, USA

ABSTRACT

This chapter examines the effectiveness of delivering e-government services in terms of how citizens value the service and how e-government has changed citizens' expectation of contacting government by digital means. This chapter articulates the following issues as they are related to the effectiveness of e-government services. It starts by addressing e-government strategies in developing and developed countries throughout the world, then discusses the inherited nature of e-government from e-commerce and the differences between them. Next, it considers various barriers to the success of e-government and how to overcome those barriers. The chapter concludes with a list of the value items collected from an empirical study, and explores how they might improve e-government's effectiveness in delivering services.

INTRODUCTION

Government agencies have been exploring better ways to provide new and improved services to the public through the use of emerging technology. In the 1990s, the proliferation of network-based Information Systems (IS) represented a turning point in the strategic direction for government agencies to achieve their objectives through its use (Kalakota & Whinton, 1997; West, 2004). Given that more government entities invest heavily in e-government, e-government has become an evolving and important research area (Chen, Chen, Huang, & Ching, 2006).

The success of e-government depends on how governments entice citizens to use its online services (Dwivedi, Weerakkody, & Williams, 2009). Citizens are likely to use these services if they feel that they provide better value than conventional government services, as values are the basic principles that guide actions and preferences (Keeney, 1992). E-government values are largely derived

DOI: 10.4018/978-1-61520-931-6.ch004

from enhanced information dissemination, expended use of transactions online, and increased citizen participation. Values might be economic, personal, or social. Economic value could include cost and time savings; personal value could mean convenience or security; social value could be protection of the environment or participation in decision making. A common value is economic. Largely, citizens would like the benefits of using e-government services to be reflected in terms of cost and time savings (Wang & Liao, 2008). E-government value is an important construct for academics and professionals studying e-government (Chang, Torkzadeh, & Dhillon, 2004).

While e-government and e-commerce share technical and functional characteristics, the differences are mainly in the inherited nature of public administration and governance. E-government links people not just to each other and the e-commerce marketplace, but also to the public marketplace of ideas, debate, priorities, initiatives, innovation, services, transactions, and results (Council for Excellence in Government, 2001). It is profoundly changing the way society communicates, works, and learns (Council for Excellence in government, 2001). To explore how citizens value e-government service and how it changed citizens' expectations of government, a case study of service users was conducted. The study resulted in a list of 38 value items that would contribute to the effectiveness of delivering e-government services. The objectives of this chapter are to increase the reader's knowledge, and to propose areas for future research into e-government phenomena.

BACKGROUND

E-government is narrowly defined as "the delivery of government information and services online thorough the Internet or other digital means" (West, 2004, p.2). The principles of e-government include building services around citizens' choices, improving accessibility to government and its services, facilitating social inclusion, presenting information responsibly, and using government resources effectively and efficiently (Office of the e-Envoy, 2008). The e-government framework can be characterized as (a) transformation areas – internal and external; (b) users, customers, actors and their interrelationships – citizens, businesses, government organizations, employees; (c) e-government application domains – e-services, e-democracy, e-administration (Ndou, 2004).

E-government can be viewed as (a) transformation of the business of government, i.e., improving service and renewing administrative processes, and (b) transformation of governance itself, i.e., re-examining the functioning of administrative practices and processes (Aichholzer & Schmitzer, 2000). E-government can be thought of as a conceptual lens through which the changing role and shape of government in the 21st century can be examined. This era is expected to be more digital, knowledge-intensive, driven by innovation, and interdependent than any previous time (Roy, 2003).

As e-government is pervasive at all levels of government, becoming a global phenomenon (Schuppan, 2009), strategies vary because each vision is driven by its own unique set of political, social, economic, and environmental factors. A key factor driving the achievement of any e-government program is the vision of e-government, articulated and adopted by a government administration (Grant & Chau, 2005).

The mission that emanates from these e-government visions varies by different countries. Some countries focus on service delivery while others are weighted towards transparency or economic development by administrative reform (Ma, Chung, & Thorson, 2005). The following examples illustrate various e-government strategies for the different regions of the world (Grant & Chau, 2005; U.S. Office of Management and Budget, 2002; Ma et al, 2005; National Computerization Agency, 2002; Ciborra & Navarra, 2005).

Box 1.

E-government strategy	Country
Increase transparency and efficiency	Brazil
Attempts to bring economic development through administrative reform	China
Tends to balance several strategic objectives	England
Introduces new technologies to facilitate inter and intra-agency communication	Jordan
Enhances the national competitiveness by increasing productivity and transparency	Korea (South)
Concentrates on the exposure and outreach area	Malaysia
Heavily weighted towards service delivery	South Africa
Focus on service delivery and on increasing cross-functional efficiencies	United States

The performance of e-government can be measured in various ways. Identifying e-government measurement criteria clarifies the current state of knowledge and the effectiveness of e-government's evolution, and contributes to understanding the e-government phenomena that are an integral part of modern IS research. Gupta and Jana (2003) stated that the importance of measuring the performance of e-government cannot be overemphasized.

Based on the DeLone and McLean's IS success model (2003), Wang and Liao (2008) proposed a multidimensional model (see Figure 1) of e-government systems success that includes six success variables: information quality, system quality, service quality, use, user satisfaction, and perceived net benefit. High-quality information, system, and service would encourage the increased use of the e-government system and also would result in user satisfaction. Use and user satisfaction are closely related as positive experience with "use" leading to greater "user satisfaction." And because of "use" of convenient e-government services and the realized "user satisfaction," a certain net benefit will occur. The link in the model reflects the relationship of these variables.

One of the most popular measuring criteria is to assess the progress of e-government implementation. A four-stage format (Layne & Lee, 2001) reflects the growth model that assesses the breadth and width of the implementation of e-government initiatives.

1. Cataloging (online presence, catalogue presentation, downloadable forms): Provides basic information through a one-way interface. The information is provided on the basis of functions or departments as opposed to service access points.

Figure 1. E-government success model (Wang & Liao, 2008)

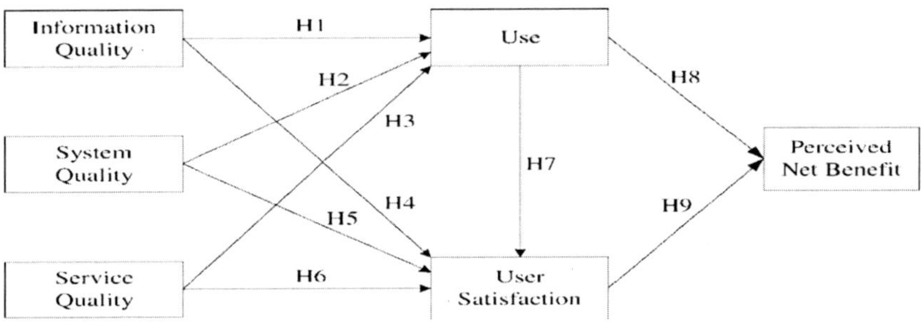

2. Transaction (interactive online transactions and services): Empowers citizens to interface with their governments online to save time and cost. Applying permits and filing taxes online are the beginning of such transaction-based services.
3. Vertical Integration (linking local to higher-level governments): Enables access to services at a higher level than the municipal portal as the local systems are connected to the upper-level systems directly or indirectly.
4. Horizontal Integration (integrating across different functions, one-stop shopping):

Facilitates one-stop shopping for the citizens that provides one portal for all government services, using IS to achieve greater efficiency and effectiveness. Each organization may have to give up some power to move to this stage.

Research into determining whether e-government systems deliver according to public expectations may borrow from the SERVQUAL model used in the marking discipline, which is a good predictor of overall service quality (Fisk, Brown, & Bitner, 1993). The model uses gap analysis to identify and measure five different types of gaps that may exist between customers' expectations and perceptions of service. The five gaps are (Jain & Patnayakuni, 2003):

1. Service gap: between public expectations for e-government services and the perception of service delivered.
2. Understanding gap: between public expectations and management perceptions of what these public expectations are.
3. Design gap: between management's understanding of public expectations and the design and specification of service quality.
4. Delivery gap: between the specification of service quality and the actual quality of the service delivered.
5. Communication gap: between what is promised and what is actually delivered.

Steyaert (2004) proposed a marketing model to be used to improve the content and value of e-government services. Five marking indicators were used:

1. Consumer awareness: deals with the number of visitors to a site.
2. Popularity: refers to the ranking of the site.
3. Contact efficiency: indicates site usability and content.
4. Conversion: refers to customer satisfaction, transaction, and time spent on the site.
5. Retention: deals with customer loyalty.

The United Nations (2008) conducted a survey to assess readiness for e-government based on the conceptual question, "How ready are Member States to take advantage of the opportunity provided by advances in information technology?" The readiness is assessed by the three indexes:

1. Web measure index – the presence or absence of specific electronic facilities and services.
2. Telecommunication infrastructure index – a country's infrastructure capacity as it relates to the delivery of e-government services, such as available telephone lines, PCs, and broadband.
3. Human capital index – Adult literacy rate and the combined primary, secondary and tertiary gross enrollment ratio.

The lifeblood of government is information, and the digital revolution has allowed government organizations to more effectively and efficiently store, analyze, and retrieve information (Bretschneider, 2003). At present, access to information is one of the most popular features of e-government services. Increasingly, governments are creating a presence on the Internet through the use of a Web page or site where a variety of information is offered to the public. While searches may retrieve a great number of items, the best-matched items from the search query are placed at the top of the results list. Result ranking in information retrieval has a major impact on the effectiveness of e-government services in terms of users' success in retrieving relevant documents. Result ranking is judged by three criteria (Courtois & Berry, 1999):

1. All terms: Does the document contain at least one occurrence of all search items?
2. Proximity: Is there at least one occurrence of all search terms appearing as a contiguous phrase?
3. Location: Is there at least one occurrence of all search terms appearing within the title, headers, or metatags?

THE INHERITED NATURE OF E-GOVERNMENT FROM E-COMMERCE AND THE DIFFERENCES BETWEEN THE TWO

One of the most significant innovations in IS has been the creation and ongoing development of the Internet. The Internet increases communication flexibility while reducing communication costs by permitting the instantaneous exchange of large amounts of information regardless of geographic distance and time. Similar to the dramatic changes in e-commerce, the e-government revolution offers the potential to reshape the public sector and remake the relationship between citizens and government (West, 2000).

The major inherited nature of e-government from Internet technology is the ability to facilitate access by reaching far beyond the traditional constraints of region and time. Thus, a U.S. taxpayer living in Africa could file a federal income tax return online with the Internal Revenue Service; a tour company in Asia could access up-to-date sightseeing information in New York via the New York City Web site; and an exporting company in Europe could inquire about marketing opportunities in California for its products using California's state Web sites. And reaching beyond traditional business hours frees citizens to seek information at their own convenience 24 hours a day, seven days a week, not just when a government office is open (West, 2004).

Just as public administration's managerial concepts and practices, such as TQM, strategic management, and participative management were influenced by the private sector's development of those concepts and practices, the idea of e-government followed private-sector adoption of e-commerce (Moon, 2002). E-government and e-commerce (also referred to as Internet commerce) are similar in nature in that e-commerce models can be used to study electronic services in the public sector (Carter & Belanger, 2004). E-government is based on Internet technology designed to facilitate the exchange of goods, services, and information between two or more parties (Carter & Belanger, 2004) by sharing the same characteristics: paperless, timeless, and borderless (Schubert & Hausler, 2001).

Governments provide goods and services to citizens the same way e-commerce provides those things for them as consumers; thus e-commerce may provide a useful role model for e-government. In general, there are two types of e-commerce: business-to-consumer (B2C), and business-to-business (B2B). In B2C transactions, online transactions are made between businesses and individual consumers, such as when airlines sell tickets to travelers, whereas in B2B transactions, businesses make online transactions with other businesses, such as when businesses purchase parts, fuel, or services online (King, Lee, Warkentin, & Chung, 2002). Comparable categories for e-government services are government-to-citizen (G2C), government-to-business (G2B), and government-to-government (G2G). G2C and G2B are similar to B2C because citizens and businesses are the public consumers of e-government services, and G2G is similar to B2B because the interaction between government and government operates much like the interaction between business and business. Analogous to what the private market has seen in the new economy with the diffusion of e-business in almost all forms, e-government has been conceived as a tool to define and manage relationships between citizens and the government, and among governments (Fugini & Mezzazanica, 2004).

While the similarities between e-government and e-commerce are largely in the technical and functional arenas, the differences are mainly in the inherited nature of public administration and governance. There are three salient distinctions between e-government and e-commerce: access, structure, and accountability (Jorgensen & Cable, 2002). To provide access, business has the luxury of domain choice flexibility, meaning the ability to choose its customers, which government cannot do because government services must be made accessible to all citizens (Elmagarmid & Mcler, 2001). Eliminating the digital divide that limits opportunities for certain groups, such as the poor and the elderly, and access issues related to persons with disabilities has been a priority for e-government (Jaeger & Matteson, 2009). The structure of government creates a number of concerns not relevant to the business sector. Decision-making authority is much more dispersed in the public sector than the private, and the lines of authority are often not as direct. Dispersed authority could become a challenge for the implementation of e-government since each authority has the independent capacity to set priorities. In addition, concerns arise in relation to standardizing format and procedures, encouraging innovation, and managing processes and progress (Jorgensen & Cable, 2002). The accountability can be derived from the nature of democratic government addressed in fiscal performance and political responsiveness. Compared to e-business, e-government usually takes longer to implement and costs more. This less efficient fiscal performance could result from citizens' expectations that the latest technology will be made available for public service, which can conflict with the government's continued attempt to use emerging technology that requires significant commitments of both time and money and is often a trial-and-error process. A good example is the e-vote, through which citizens can vote online. A further problem is that acquiring IS resources, such as hardware, software, and peopleware, requires more time-consuming and restricted procurement processes than in the private sector, due to regulations. Careful supervision by political bodies could result in micro-management in order to assure accountability. Thus, there is the likelihood that the timely implementation of emerging technology can prove challenging, and that e-government performance can be compromised.

Another significant difference between e-government and e-commerce is the aspect of user participation via interactive dialogs. Though e-commerce users interact with vendors and other pertinent parties, the magnitude of citizen participation in e-government is much greater in the context of promoting e-democracy. As e-government must rest on and support democratic principles (Gronlund, 2003), e-democracy aims at active participation and influence in democratic processes via the Internet, such as e-town halls and e-forums, through which citizens, political organizations, and lawmakers interact with each other. The Public Electronic Network (PEN) in the City of Santa Monica is one of the most innovative attempts to provide e-forums. It helps citizens to take advantage of the interactive strengths of the Internet, through which democratic responsiveness and leadership accountability can be boosted (West, 2004).

Despite similar reliance on Internet technologies and a shared need to progress along the information-communication-transaction-transformation continuum, e-government faces some issues uniquely different from those of e-commerce (Chen, 2002). Since governmental institutions take part in marketing and sales activities, e-commerce is not the heart of e-government.

The core task of government is governance, the job of regulating society, not marketing and sales. In modern democracies, responsibility and power for regulation is divided up and shared among the legislative, executive, and judicial branches of government. E-government is about moving forward with the work of all of these branches, not just public administration in the narrow sense (Gorden, 2002).

BARRIERS TO THE SUCCESS OF E-GOVERNMENT, AND ACTIONS FOR OVERCOMING THEM

E-government initiatives must overcome numerous barriers before they can bear fruit. These barriers may be technical, organizational, managerial, social, socio-economical, cultural, and psychological in nature (Dwivedi et al, 2009, Kappelman, Koh, Prybutok & Sanchez, 2003). Examples of the barriers are articulated in this section.

Traditionally, government agencies have been developing information systems within the boundaries of a single business process without considering the need for interoperability with other functional areas, which has resulted in each agency having its own heterogeneous type of system (Janssen et al., 2006). Because of this fragmented nature, a single government service, such as issuing a building license, is performed by multiple agencies (Janssen et al., 2006); this ineffectiveness causes the citizens inconvenience. As the proliferation of Web services increases, the technological threshold for creating interoperable systems that facilitate collaborative efforts between agencies performing the cross-agency process has been lowered (Lim & Wen, 2003).

The Government Information Quarterly (Gupta & Jana, 2003) was concerned about the digital divide. The "digital divide" refers to concerns about inequities between citizens who do not have access to the Internet, and those who do. The likelihood of a person owning a PC with Internet access varies significantly by household income, education level, age, and region. A thoughtful response by governments to shrink these disparities to promote an information-rich society will be a major factor in e-government effectiveness.

The U. S. Office of Management and Budget (2002) identified five key barriers that may prevent the successful implementation of e-government initiatives. Table 1 lists these barriers and actions for overcoming them. As the actions (mitigations) are solutions to the problems (barriers), implementing the solutions would contribute to the success of e-government initiatives.

Ndou (2004) presented various barriers and solutions in terms of delivering better e-government services in developing countries, including the Philippines, China, India, Brazil, Columbia, and Guatemala, after conducting case studies. The common barriers include strategy, leadership role, infrastructure, policy issues, and human capital. A clear strategy has to be established to overcome the barriers to implementing e-government. It requires a holistic vision and long-term focus to better serve citizens. This includes providing greater access to information, as well as better and more equitably distributed services, and improved government processes. Leadership is the main driving force for new and innovative initiatives, and the e-government initiative is not an exception. Leadership involvement is critical to overcoming organizations' natural resistance to change, allocating appropriate resources, and building and maintaining the commitment to new ways of providing government services (McClure, 2001). Infrastructure is one of the main technical challenges for e-government. Internetworking enables sharing of information and opens up channels for delivering e-government services. In addition, architecture is needed to guide a set of principles, models, and standards. Policy issues encompass new rules, policies, and laws to provide secured online activities, protect intellectual properties, and foster freedom of information. Human capital is essential to providing e-government services.

Table 1.

Barriers to the Success of E-government Initiatives and Actions for Overcoming Them	
Barrier	**Mitigation**
Agency Culture	Sustain high level of leadership and commitment.
	Establish interagency governance structure.
	Give priority to cross-agency work.
	Engage interagency user/stakeholder groups, including communities of practice.
Lack of Architecture	Lead government-side business and data-architecture rationalization.
	Sponsor architecture development for cross-agency projects.
	The home page will be the primary online delivery portal for G2C and G2B interactions.
Trust	Through e-authentication e-government initiatives, establish secure transactions and identify authentications that will be used by all e-government initiatives.
	Incorporate security and privacy protections into each business plan.
	Provide public training and promotion.
Mitigation Resources	Move resources to programs with the greatest return and citizen impact.
	Set measures up front and monitor implementation.
	Provide online training to create new expertise among employees and contractors.
Stakeholder Resistance	Create comprehensive strategy for engaging authorities.
	Have multiple agency members argue collectively for initiatives.
	Tie performance evaluations to cross-agency success.
	Communicate strategy to stakeholders.

The availability of appropriate skills is central to this endeavor. This includes technical skills for implementing the infrastructure, and management skills for overseeing online processes, functions, and stakeholders.

Developing countries often lack financial resources and government stability and structure, which tends to hinder the growth of e-government and e-democracy. Government officials in developing countries, compared with developed nations, are sometimes less willing to allocate already scarce resources toward something they are not familiar with, especially since return on investment is not immediate and seemingly unapparent. Lack of sufficient capital to build up infrastructure causes difficulties in facilitating citizens' participation in government issues, which results in lower levels of political involvement, thereby inhibiting the promotion of e-politics, as elements of e-democracy (Chen, Chen, Huang, & Ching, 2006). Another major barrier is low-performing public administration, characterized by an often rigid centralism that is perceived as inefficient and ineffective to the extent that the implementation of political will is barely possible. As the e-government concept originated in the public administrations of developed countries, for e-government to be successful in developing countries, it has to overcome a range of barriers in diverse administrative environments (Schuppan, 2009).

One of the major e-government challenges for the European Union (EU) is deploying innovative e-health services in order to meet ever-increasing demand. As the EU has a worldwide lead in the deployment of regional/national health information networks, providing adequate health care management can be a priority for most of its countries. The EU must address the economic challenges of providing e-health services in OECD countries where health spending is increasing faster than GDP and is expected to reach 16% of GDP by 2020 as the population ages and requires long-term health care. The e-health initiative to effectively manage this situation focuses on providing specialized services such as e-prescriptions, electronic health records, telemonitoring, and homecare (European Commission, 2008).

Cortes, Espinosa, and Tari (2008) presented three barrier factors and facilitating factors from their e-government case study in Spain. The barriers are institutional, infrastructural, and social. Institutional barrier factors include lack of political will, lack of knowledge of e-government benefits, and decisions being made by politicians instead of IT professionals. The infrastructural barriers encompass scarcity of financial resources, scarcity of qualified human resources, and cost of IT infrastructure availability. The social barriers are complexity of public work processes and bureaucracy, employee resistance to change due to lack of knowledge, low citizen demand for e-services, and unsuitable legislation. The facilitating factors are political leadership and commitment, qualified human resources, usability of Web site, availability of financial resources, acknowledgement of e-government benefits by political statements, e-government explicit strategic planning, IT infrastructure availability, designation of a formal project manager, quality management models application, and changes toward less bureaucratic decision-making processes.

EMPIRICAL STUDY OF E-GOVERNMENT VALUE ITEMS THAT MIGHT IMPROVE THE EFFECTIVENESS OF E-GOVERNMENT

An empirical study of e-government effectiveness was conducted that focused on collecting the value items citizens assign to e-government services. The study first generated a list of e-government objectives from the published research pool. Then the survey instruments were developed based on this list and a survey of e-government users was conducted, measuring how they evaluated the items on the list. Once all the data were collected, data reduction and analysis were performed using factor analysis. The outcome of the study was a list of 38 items that affect the effectiveness of e-government services.

An instrument valid in content is one that has drawn representative questions from a universal pool (Straub, 1989). E-government value items for this research were extracted from the broad research pool published mostly in the leading refereed literatures covering the 7-year period from 2000 to 2006, using the list from the Keeney study in Internet commerce (Keeney, 1999) as the base. A total of 76 items were generated for the survey questionnaires. Using the Keeney approach, these items were grouped into two types: means and fundamental objectives.[1] *Fundamental objectives* are those that are important to citizens; *means objectives* are those that help government achieve the fundamental objectives. Thus, the total of 76 questionnaire items was grouped into 48 for the means and 28 for the fundamental objective types. The list of items reflected the benefits and costs of what e-government offers to citizens in terms of information, products, and services, and how these offerings can be better than what is currently available through conventional means.

The next step was to perform a quantitative empirical study to explore the list of e-government value items by developing instruments and conducting a survey. The instruments were tested for validity and reliability. The case study was conducted with the following framework (Sekaran, 2000):

1. Type of investigation – Correlational
2. Extent of researcher interference – Minimal
3. Measurement – Scaling (Likert-type in 1 to 5 scale, 5 being most relevant)
4. Instrument validation – Validity and reliability
5. Data collection – Probability sampling and Web survey
6. Time horizon – One shot (cross sectional)
7. Unit of analysis – Individual

Working professionals in the United States who had experience in using e-government services formed the population. The samples were recruited from various professional sources, such as university alumni, bankers, lawyers, travel agents, accountants, engineers, and architects from metropolitan areas, such as New York City, Los Angeles, and Seattle. The sample size with the survey responses was 210. As the study involved in human subjects, the design and conduct of research followed the guidelines to ensure their protection provided by the National Research Act Public Law 99-158 and the Health Research Extension Act of 1985.

All 76 items were perceived to be relevant because the mean values for all items were closer to 4 and over. The use of descriptive statistics analysis revealed the most and least important items that related to the effectiveness of e-government services. The most important items of the means objective type (those with the highest mean, of 4.69) were related to security, while the most important items of the fundamental objective type (those with the highest mean, of 4.47) were related to ease of finding and usefulness:

1. Security – "I like to discourage hacking," "I am concerned about identity theft," and "I am concerned about the safeguarding of personal information."
2. Ease of finding – "It's important to find information and services easily."
3. Usefulness – "It's important that information and services are useful."

The least important item of the means objective type (with the lowest mean, of 3.68) was related to the foreign language option, while the least important item of the fundamental objective type (with the lowest mean, of 3.56) was related to using e-government as a social event:

1. Foreign language options – "I like to have a variety of foreign language options available to people."
2. Social event – "It is important to make using e-government a social event."

For the means objective type items, the construct validity was provided by the item purification process, which resulted in removing nine items. Eight items were removed because the correlation coefficients were low (below 0.050) and another item was removed because the correlation coefficient was high (greater than 0.90). Then, the dimensionality of the remaining constructs was examined. The Barlett's test of sphericity being 0.000 and the KMO measure of 0.925 suggested that factor analysis was appropriate. The exploratory factor analysis using principal component analysis identified outliers and four components (factors) while reducing the number of variables. Twelve cases of outliers were identified using the regression equation with factor scores wither greater than 3.0 or smaller than -3.0, thus, the remaining 198 cases were used to extract components. To extract the principle components, the Varimax rotation with Kaiser normalization method was used. A factor analysis removed 28 items and the results suggested a four-factor 20-

item model with eigenvalues greater than one. The reliability was evidenced by the high Cronbach's Alpha of 0.734 to 0.919, which implied the internal consistency of the scale variables. The four components accounted for 64.738% of the total variances where the first accounted for 37.421%, the second 14.7215, the third 6.809%, and the fourth 5.788%.

For the fundamental objective type items, the construct validity was provided by the item purification process, which resulted in retaining all 28 items for which all the correlation coefficients were greater than 0.05 and smaller than 0.90. The Barlett's test of sphericity being 0.000 and the KMO measure of 0.929 suggested that the factor solution generated would be reliable. The exploratory factor analysis using principal component analysis identified outliers and four components (factors) while reducing the number of variables. Eight cases of outliers were identified using the regression equation with factor scores wither greater than 3.0 or smaller than -3.0; thus, the remaining 202 cases were used to extract components. To extract the principle components, the Varimax rotation with Kaiser normalization method was used. A factor analysis retained removed 10 items, and the results suggested a four-factor 18-item model with eigenvalues greater than one. The reliability was evidenced by the high Cronbach's Alpha of 0.799 to 0.931 that implied the internal consistency of the scale variables. The four components accounted for 67.298% of the total variances where the first accounted for 37.421%, the second 14.7215, the third 6.809%, and the fourth 5.788%.

To address the relation, the cross-relations among factors were examined. Subscales of means objective type items were correlated more closely with the overall 20-item means objective type times than with the subscales of the fundamental objective type items and vice versa, indicated by the ranges of 0.777 to 0.792 for means objective type items that are greater than the ranges of 0.551 to 0.652 for others.

Table 2 lists the resulting 38 valid items, which are grouped into eight major categories (factors) in two groups (means and fundamental objective types) that influence the effectiveness of e-government services. The eight categories include public trust, information access, public accessibility, and quality of service (for the means objective types); and time savings, efficiency of services, service to citizens, and social awareness (for the fundamental objective types).

FUTURE RESEARCH DIRECTIONS

In the postindustrial setting, scholars contend that the implications for information technology lie in the nature of work, productivity, and economic growth (Torkzadeh & Dhillon, 2002). IS could potentially create new ideas, increase values, and more effectively satisfy customer needs. The instrument developed in this research can be used as a tool to assess this potential.

As providing value to citizens is the ultimate goal of e-government, the list of e-government value items provided can be used to develop and improve e-government effectiveness. The e-government value and the instrument to be introduced in this study should be beneficial for academics and practitioners for a number of reasons. First, they can be used by practitioners to improve the development of the e-government services. Second, they can be used to further develop the instrument for measuring success of e-government initiatives to serve as a base for the appropriate IS measures. Third, the model to be developed in this study will provide researchers with a basis for guiding future research.

CONCLUSION

Governments are employing network-based IS in the expectation that it will be cheaper, faster, and more convenient than traditional means of

Table 2.

Value Items for the Effectiveness of E-government Services	
Category	**Item**
Public trust	I am concerned about identity theft.
	I am concerned about the safeguarding of personal information.
	I am concerned about privacy risks.
	I am concerned about misuse of my credit card.
	I am concerned about transaction security.
	I am concerned about sharing of personal information.
Information access	I like to get as much information about services as possible.
	I like to have information on demand.
	I like to have a great amount of information.
	I like to have search criteria.
	I like the opportunity for two-way interaction.
	I like to minimize the risk of skipping or missing information.
	I like to have up-to-date information.
Public accessibility	I feel accessibility for individuals with special needs (e.g.,disabilities)should be maximized.
	I would like to minimize the digital divide demarcated by wealth, age, language, culture, geographical location, etc.
	I would like to promote public outreach.
	I feel that new services should be made as convenient as possible utilizing various devices, such as cell phones, PDA, etc.
Quality of service	I am concerned about the quality of the information and services delivered.
	I am concerned about reliable delivery of information and services.
	I am concerned about accuracy of transaction.
Time savings	It is important to minimize payment time.
	It is important to minimize search time.
	It is important to minimize overall communication time.
	It is important to minimize processing time.
	It is important to minimize the time it takes to select information and services.
	It is important to minimize dispatch time.
	It is important to minimize shipping time.
Efficiency of service	It is important that information and services are useful.
	It is important to find information and services easily.
	It is important to make communication cost efficient.
Service to citizen	It is important to make using e-government a social event.
	It is important to inspire citizens to use e-government online services.
	It is important to bring government services closer to citizens.
	It is important to avoid giving citizens cause to regret using e-government online services.

Table 2. continued on following page

Table 2. continued

	It is important to minimize unnecessary driving through the advantages of having services accessible from home (e.g., parking, accident, etc.).
Social awareness	It is important to minimize pollution.
	It is important to minimize environmental impact.
	It is important to always consider the overall good of society.

delivering products and services (McNeal, Tolbert, Mossberger, & Dotterweich, 2003). Having invested an enormous amount of resources in e-government (Peter, Jansen, Enger, 2004), governments strive to succeed in this endeavor. The success of e-government initiatives is contingent upon citizens' willingness to use these services (Carter & Belanger, 2004; Devadoss, Pan, & Huang, 2002). Therefore, to further the success of e-government, it is critical to understand the effectiveness of e-government services in terms of how citizens value such services, and whether they are perceived to offer better value than conventional government services.

The focus of science is theory. A scientific theory consists of analytic and empirical components. The analytic component reflects the linkage of reasoning that follows logical rules without empirical content whereas the empirical component reflects the linking of empirical data for a theory to apply to reality (Rummel, 1970). The empirical component connects the analytic component to the facts.

This research linked empirical data (e-government value items) to theory (e-government effectiveness).

It is anticipated that many governments will be implementing changes and improvements during this study. Therefore, the result of this study will only reflect the time period of the research. Continued studies are needed to examine the progress and effectiveness of e-government in delivering services and facilitating citizens' political participation (Moon, 2002). The value items developed in this research might need to be changed over time. For example, the public trust related items need to address new risks arising from the use of emerging technology, and the public accessibility related items need to consider the impact of new devices (e.g., wireless). The items such as time savings and social awareness remain relatively the same, as they are less likely to be affected by changes. The value items developed in this research are bound to evolve over time; thus, they need to be refined to satisfy future research requirements. As little research on e-government in the public sector is currently being published in scholarly journals (Melitski, 2003), this research will contribute to this gap in the context of studying the e-government value to users.

REFERENCES

Aichholzer, G., & Schmitzer, R. (2000). Organizational challenges to the development of electronic government. In *Proceedings from 11th International Workshop on Database and Expert Systems Applications*, London, England (pp. 379-383).

Bretschneider, S. (2003). Information technology, e-government, and institutional change. *Public Administration Review*, *63*(6), 738–741. doi:10.1111/1540-6210.00337

Carter, L., & Belanger, F. (2004). Citizen adoption of electronic government initiatives. In *Proceedings of the 37th Hawaii International Conference on Systems Sciences,* Honolulu, HI (pp. 1-10).

Chang, J., Torkzadeh, G., & Dhillon, G. (2004). Re-examining the measurement models of success for Internet commerce. *Information & Management*, *41*(4), 577–584. doi:10.1016/S0378-7206(03)00091-0

Chen, H. (2002). Digital government: technologies and practices. *Decision Support Systems*, *34*, 223–227. doi:10.1016/S0167-9236(02)00118-5

Chen, H., Chen, Y., Huang, W., & Ching, R. (2006). E-government strategies in developed and developing countries: an implementation framework and case study. *Journal of Global Information Management*, *14*(1), 23–24.

Ciborra, C., & Navarra, D. (2005). Good governance, development theory, and aid policy: risks and challenges of e-government in Jordan. *Information Technology for Development*, *11*(2), 141–150. doi:10.1002/itdj.20008

Cortes, E., Espinosa, S., & Tari, J. (2009). E-government challenges: barriers and facilitators in Spanish City Councils. In *Connectivity and Knowledge Management in Virtual Organizations* (pp. 205–220). Hershey, PA: IGI Global.

Council for Excellence in Government. (2001). *E-government: the next American revolution*. Washington, DC: Author.

Courtois, M. P., & Berry, M. W. (1999). Results ranking in Web search engines. *Online*, *23*(3), 39–44.

DeLone, W. H., & McLean, E. R. (2003). The DeLone and McLean model of information systems success: A tenyear update. *Journal of Management Information Systems*, *19*(4), 9–30.

Devadoss, P. R., Pan, S. L., & Huang, J. C. (2002). Structurational analysis of e-government initiatives: a case study of SCO. *Decision Support Systems*, *34*(3), 253–269. doi:10.1016/S0167-9236(02)00120-3

Doctor, R., & Ankem, K. (March, 1996). *An information need and services taxonomy: For evaluating Computerized Community Information Systems.* Presented at Community Networking 96: "Bringing People Together." Retrieved February 24, 2009, from http://www.laplaza.org/about_lap/archives/cn96/doctor1.html

Dwivedi, Y. K., Weerakkody, V., & Williams, M. D. (2009). Guest editorial: From implementation to adoption: Challenges to successful e-government diffusion. *Government Information Quarterly*, *26*(1), 3–4. doi:10.1016/j.giq.2008.09.001

Elmagarmid, A. K., & McIver, W. J. (2001, February). The ongoing march toward digital government. *Computer*, 32–38. doi:10.1109/2.901165

European Commission. (2008). Preparing Europe's Digital [*Mid-Term Review.* Luxembourg.]. *Future*, 2010.

Fisk, R. P., Brown, S. W., & Bitner, M. J. (1993). Tracking the evolution of the services marketing literature. *Journal of Retailing*, *69*(1), 61–103. doi:10.1016/S0022-4359(05)80004-1

Fugini, M., & Mezzanzanica, A. (2004). *An application within the plan for e-government: the workfare portal*. Hershey, PA: Idea Group Inc.

Gorden, T. F. (2002). E-government–Introduction. *ERCIM News, Special Theme: E-government, European Research Consortium for Information and Mathematics.* Retrieved on March 4, 2009, from http://www.ercim.org/publication/Ercim_News/enw48/intro.html

Grant, G., & Chau, D. (2005). Developing a generic framework for e-government. *Journal of Global Information Management*, *13*(1), 1–30.

Gronlund, A. (2003). Emerging electronic infrastructures: exploring democratic components. *Social Science Computer Review*, *21*(1), 55–72. doi:10.1177/0894439302238971

Gupta, M. P., & Jana, D. (2003). E-government evaluation: a framework and case study. *Government Information Quarterly*, *20*(3), 365–387. doi:10.1016/j.giq.2003.08.002

Jaeger, P., & Matteson, M. (2009). e-Government and technology acceptance: the case of the implementation of section 508 guidelines for websites. *Electronic. Journal of E-Government*, *7*(1), 87–98.

Jain, A., & Patnayakuni, R. (2003). Public expectations and public scrutiny: an agenda for research in the context of e-government. In *Ninth Americas Conference on Information Systems,* Tampa, FL (pp. 811-820).

Janssen, M., Gortmaker, J., & Wagenaar, R. W. (2006). Web service orchestration in public administration: challenges, roles, and growth stages. *Information Systems Management*, *23*(2), 44–55. doi:10.1201/1078.10580530/45925.23.2.20060301/92673.6

Jorgensen, D., & Cable, S. (2002). Facing the challenges of e-government: a case study of the city of Corpus Christi, Texas. *S.A.M. Advanced Management Journal*, *67*(1), 34–45.

Kalakota, R., & Whinston, A. B. (1997). *Electronic Commerce*. Reading, MA: Addison-Wesley.

Kappelman, L. A., Koh, C. E., Prybutok, V. R., & Sanchez, A. D. (2003). The relationship between IT for communication and e-government barriers. In *Ninth Americas Conference on Information Systems*, Tampa, FL.

Keeney, R. L. (1992). *Value-Focused Thinking: A Path to Creative Decision Making*. Cambridge, MA: Harvard University Press.

Keeney, R. L. (1999). The value of Internet commerce to the customer. *Management Science*, *45*(4), 533–542. doi:10.1287/mnsc.45.4.533

King, D., Lee, J., Warkentin, M., & Chung, H. M. (2002). *Electronic Commerce a Managerial Perspective*. Upper Saddle River, NJ: Prentice Hall.

Layne, K., & Lee, J. (2001). Developing fully functional e-government: a four-stage model. *Government Information Quarterly*, *18*(2), 122–136. doi:10.1016/S0740-624X(01)00066-1

Lim, B., & Wen, H. (2003). Web services: An analysis of the technology, its benefits and implementation difficulties. *Information Systems Management*, *20*(2), 49–57. doi:10.1201/1078/43204.20.2.20030301/41470.8

Ma, L., Chung, J., & Thorson, S. (2005). E-government in China: Bringing economic development through administrative reform. *Government Information Quarterly*, *22*(2), 20–37. doi:10.1016/j.giq.2004.10.001

Marchionini, G., Samet, H., & Brandt, L. (2003). Digital government. *Communications of the ACM*, *46*(1), 25–27.

McClure, D. L. (2001). *Electronic government: Challenges must me addressed with effective leadership and management*. U.S. General Accounting Office. Retrieved March 30, 2009, from http://www.gao.gov/new.items/d01959t.pdf

McNeal, R. S., Tolbert, C. J., Mossberger, K., & Dotterweich, L. J. (2003). Innovating in digital government in the American states. *Social Science Quarterly*, *84*(1), 52–70. doi:10.1111/1540-6237.00140

Melitski, J. (2003). Capacity and e-government performance. *Public Performance & Management Review*, *26*(4), 376–390. doi:10.1177/1530957603026004005

Moon, M. (2002, Jul/Aug). The evolution of e-government among municipalities: rhetoric or reality? *Public Administration Review*, *62*(4), 424–433. doi:10.1111/0033-3352.00196

National Academy of Sciences. (2002). *Information Technology, Research, Innovation and E-government*. Washington, DC: National Academy Press.

National Computerization Agency. (2002). *E-government in Korea*. Seoul: Republic of Korea.

Ndou, V. (2004). E-government for developing countries: opportunities and challenges. *Electronic Journal on Information systems in Developing countries, 18*(1), 1-24.

Office of the e-Envoy. (2008). *Modernizing government: Benchmarking electronic service delivery.* Retrieved December 2, 2008, from http://egov.alentejodigital.pt/Benchmarks/BenchmarkingESD.pdf

Peristeras, V., & Tarabanis, K. (2000). Towards an enterprise architecture for public administration using a top-down approach. *European Journal of Information Systems, 9*(4), 252–260. doi:10.1057/palgrave/ejis/3000378

Peters, R., Jansen, M., & Engers, T. (2004). Measuring e-government impact: existing practices. *Sixth International Conference on Electronic Commerce*, Delft, Netherlands (pp. 480-488).

Roy, J. (2003). Introduction e-government. *Social Science Computer Review, 21*(1), 3–5. doi:10.1177/0894439302238966

Rummel, R. (1970). *Understanding factor analysis*. University of Hawaii. Retrieved March 14, 2009 from http://www.hawaii.edu/powerkills/UFA.HTM

Schubert, P., & Hausler, U. (2001). E-government meets e-business: a portal site for startup companies in Switzerland. In *Proceedings of the 34th Hawaii International Conference on System Sciences,* Big Island, HI.

Schuppan, T. (2009). E-government in developing countries: Experiences from sub-Saharan Africa. *Government Information Quarterly, 26*(1), 118–127. doi:10.1016/j.giq.2008.01.006

Sekaran, U. (2000). *Research Methods for Business*. New York: John Wiley & Sons, Inc.

Straub, D. (1989). Validating instruments in MIS research. *Management Information Systems Quarterly, 13*(2), 147–170. doi:10.2307/248922

Swartz, N. (2004). E-government around the world. *Information Management Journal, 38*(1), 12–15.

Torkzadeh, G., & Dhillon, G. (2002). Measuring factors that influence the success of Internet commerce. *Information Systems Research, 13*(2), 187–204. doi:10.1287/isre.13.2.187.87

United Nations. (2008). *UN E-government survey 2008: From e-government to connected governance. Division for Public Administration and Development Management*. New York: United Nations.

U.S. Office of Management and Budget. (2002). *E-government strategy: Simplified delivery of services to citizens*. Washington, DC: U.S. Government Printing Office.

Wang, Y., & Liao, Y. (2008). Assessing eGovernment systems success: A validation of the DeLone and McLean model of information systems success. *Government Information Quarterly, 25*(7), 717–733. doi:10.1016/j.giq.2007.06.002

West, D. M. (2004). E-government and the transformation of service delivery and citizen attitudes. *Public Administration Review, 64*(1), 15–26. doi:10.1111/j.1540-6210.2004.00343.x

ENDNOTE

1 To explore the categorization of means and fundamental objectives, refer to Keeney's publication (Keeney, 1992 & 1999).

Chapter 5
An Evaluation Framework for E-Government Projects

Panos Fitsilis
TEI Larissa, Greece

Leonidas Anthopoulos
TEI Larissa, Greece

Vassilis C. Gerogiannis
TEI Larissa, Greece

ABSTRACT

E-government progress is being evaluated by multiple surveys, carried out by international and supra-national organizations national observatories and individual parties. All surveys evaluate e-government progress using different methods, indices and perspectives. E-government progress evaluation is complex, since e-government projects vary from infrastructural, to software and to political ones. In this chapter, an evaluation framework for e-government software projects' progress and results is introduced. The framework consists of indices extracted from e-government related literature and from the project management field of knowledge. Major benchmarking approaches -from the Information Society Directorate General, United Nations, World Bank etc. - were analyzed for the purposes of this framework. The approach results in the development of an "e-government balanced scorecard", able to measure facets such as product and process issues, as well as project management processes. Each facet of the scorecard has a set of objectives and utilizes a set of measurements to evaluate e-government projects from various perspectives, interrelated to strategic planning, such as product, process and project management as well as service quality management.

INTRODUCTION

Central Governments worldwide have developed strategic plans for e-government and Information and Communication Technologies (ICT) investments. Major strategic plans such as the US Federal Government's (US Federal Government, 2002), the European (European Commission, 2002), the UK's *Modernizing Government* plan (UK Cabinet Office, 2000), the German *Bund Online* 2005 strategic plan (German Federal Government, 2003) and the Canadian "*Government on-Line* (GOL)" (Treasury

DOI: 10.4018/978-1-61520-931-6.ch005

Table 1. Common targets of major e-government strategies

Strategic plan	Primary targets
"Expanding e-government" (US)	1. Citizen centered, results-oriented, market-based Public Administration. 2. Federal and State Agencies interconnected in a one-stop portal. 3. Guidelines and standards for all unique initiatives, performed by state or local Agencies.
"Modernizing Government" (UK)	1. Knowledge economy revolution. 2. Transformation of Business, Government, People. 3. Citizen-focused Government. 4. Better services for citizens and businesses. 5. Application of e-business methods in public sector. 6. All key services available online by 2008.
"Bund Online 2005" (Germany)	1. Define and deliver online Federal Public services. 2. Client-orientation services. 3. Transparency and faster processing for federal services. 4. Quality and security of public services.
"eEurope 2005" (European Committee)	1. Citizen centered Public Administration. 2. Encourage participation. 3. 25 primary digital public services for all European member countries. 4. Multilingual one-stop shop. 5. Telecommunication's costs reduction. 6. Pan-European network of Public Administrations (IDA) of member-countries.

Board Secretariat, 2001) define common targets for e-government, such as "time and cost savings for citizens and Public Agencies" (Cap Gemini Ernst & Young, 2005) and "the development of a citizen centered, results oriented and market based Public Administration" (Federal Enterprise Architecture, 2002). Moreover, technological standards such as "openness, usability, customization and transparency for public portals" (Gant & Gant, 2002) and "interoperability between e-government systems" (UK Cabinet Office, 2002) guide the implementation of e-government projects. Table 1 summarizes the major targets of these strategic plans (Anthopoulos, Siozos & Tsoukalas, 2007).

All above strategies are implemented by multiple programmes and projects, concerning investments on infrastructures (e.g. broadband networks and information systems); on software platforms (e.g. public portals, digital public services and back-office applications); on initiatives encouraging social participation (e.g. public access points, e-Democracy portals and campaigns).

The evaluation of the above projects' progress indirectly measures e-government progress and it is a difficult and complex procedure, due to projects' variety, scope and range. However, evaluation is necessary since significant financial resources have been invested. The evaluation results are used to support the reviewing procedure of the strategic plans. Further, the improvement of citizen satisfaction, which is measured systematically, from digital public services and e-government software products, establishes trust between citizens and political leadership, and can strengthen social participation.

Current evaluations are executed by multiple organizations and observatories, which use a variety of models and perspectives. The achievement of strategic goals and sources of the project funding are critical parameters for the definition of an e-government scoreboard. In European Commission, for instance, Information Society Directorate General (DG) offered e-Europe 2003, e-Europe 2005, i2010 action plans on which funding of ICT programmes and projects by Member Countries were based. The same organization,

Information Society DG, evaluates how European funding succeeds in achieving e-Europe targets, and measures ICT progress at a supranational level. Simultaneously, European Member Countries have installed observatory organizations, which investigate ICT progress at national levels, according to e-Europe targets. Survey results are used for ICT management at national levels and they are forwarded to the Information Society DG, at European Union level, as far as results concern European funding.

On the other hand, the United Nations (UN) (United Nations, 2008) and the World Bank carry out international investigations and publish their results regarding e-government programmes. They consider e-government progress from different perspectives: UN is emphasizing on interconnected Government and evaluates national projects and strategic plans respectively, while the World Bank considers e-government progress related to national economic growth and political rationalization. Alternatively, organizations such as the American Customer Satisfaction Index (ACSI) and the Accenture carry out unique surveys. Their investigations examine user and citizen satisfaction from digital service execution on e-government portals. All of the above investigations examine e-government regarding achieving general, economic and strategic targets, and they measure its progress at international, supranational and national levels. However, all of these surveys do not follow common methods and they lack of measuring unique project success.

In this chapter, we analyze the current evaluation models, in order to examine their perspectives and their targets. Moreover, we introduce an "evaluation framework for e-government projects" as a survey tool for measuring the success of e-government projects in achieving their targets and user satisfaction. The proposed framework consists of indices extracted from the above approaches and from the project management field of knowledge. The framework can be applied at national e-government initiatives and in individual projects; it focuses on software project progress measurement, since software applications structure the interfaces between e-government stakeholders (citizens, enterprises, back-office users and public organizations) and platforms. Moreover, software applications offer and execute digital public services, accessed by citizens and enterprises and, by this point of view, the proposed framework can assess software quality and citizen satisfaction. Even tough, this framework is mainly developed for software or ICT projects its applicability is wider and it can be used with small modifications/adoptions in other domains, such as construction or service projects.

The development of the framework is mainly an exercise of measurement, simply because in order to evaluate, compare, predict and control effectively, measurements are required. Unfortunately, measurement -particularly in a software project- is not always a straight forward procedure. There are many attributes of software and software projects to be considered, such as size, complexity, reliability, quality, adherence to process, and portability (Project Management Institute Standard Committee, 2004). The quality attributes that we propose, deal indirectly with citizen satisfaction.

The approach that we have followed was the development of a balanced scorecard, able to measure the various facets of the product, process and project management process and service quality, as well. Each facet of the scorecard has a set of objectives and utilizes a set of measurements.

BACKGROUND

Project Management Background

The practice of project management has evolved over half a century and permeates all industries, institutions and governments throughout the world. In response to the perceived need to organize thinking about project management, a number of frameworks have been produced. Three kinds of frameworks are broadly identifiable, all of which have sought to model the subject area by presenting only what is "generally" agreed. Knowledge of these frameworks is mandatory in order to study e-government projects:

- *Software Life-Cycle models.* A software life cycle model is a high level description of phases or activities of a software project from conception until the product is retired. It specifies the relationships between project phases, including transition criteria, feedback mechanisms, milestones, baselines, reviews, and deliverables. A large number of software life-cycle models have been proposed in the literature. Even though the complete list is exhaustive, Waterfall model, V-model, Spiral Model, Unified Process, Extreme Programming are some of the most well known models (Pressman R, 2009).
- *Maturity models.* Common examples include the ISO series (especially BS ISO10006:2003 (British Standards Institution, 2003)), "Project Excellence Model" by the Association of UK Project Managers (International Project Management Association, 2009), "Project Management Maturity Model" (Programme Management Maturity Model, 2009), "Projects In Controlled Environments 2 (PRINCE 2)" (Office of Government Commerce, 2005), the family of Software Engineering Institute "Capability Maturity Models" (Carnegie Mellon University, 2002), etc.
- *Bodies of Knowledge.* They provide the standards and knowledge framework for understanding the elements that comprise project management. In these areas we notice APM Body of Knowledge, PMI Guide to the Project Management Body of Knowledge (Project Management Institute Standard Committee, 2004), BSI BS6079 Guide to Project Management (British Standards Institution, 2002), etc. At the same time, there are numerous project management methodologies for software development.

Project success is a topic that is frequently discussed and yet rarely agreed upon (Liu and Walker, 1998) Achieving project success is concerned with the project's external effectiveness, while PM success is measured in terms of cost-time-quality can be viewed as "internal measures of efficiency" (Shenhar, Levy and Dvir, 1997). Despite the fact that very often success and failure is seen as "black and white", projects may not always be seen as completely successful or complete failure" (Wateridge, 1998).

More than 80% of software projects are either cancelled before completion, don't deliver what was intended, or run significantly over budget or schedule. (Vandersluis, 2002) According to a survey conducted by the Standish Group, the track record of software engineering industry is rather disappointing (Standish, 2001):

- A full 23% of all software projects are cancelled before completion.
- Regarding the completed projects, only 28% were delivered on time, within budget, and with all originally specified features.
- The remaining 49% of the projects are challenged (completed but failed to achieve all objectives).

There are many reasons why a project can fail; the key in order to avoid these causes of failure is the use of effective and experienced PM. Research and surveys on failed projects indicate that there are common themes in every doomed project and in the top of the list occurs "Bad Project Management" (Kelly and Stalnaker, 2002). It must be noted that "Good project management" can contribute toward project success but is unlikely to be able to prevent project failure.

The discipline of project management includes nine project management knowledge areas which are: Project Integration Management, Project Scope Management, Project Time Management, Project Cost Management, Project Quality Management, Project Human Resource Management, Project Communications Management, Project Risk Management and Project Procurement Management (Project Management Institute Standard Committee, 2004).

E-Government Evaluation Models

E-Government evaluation is currently based on surveys carried out at international, supranational and national levels. Surveys focus on the achievement of the targets of major e-government strategic plans (Anthopoulos et. al., 2007). For the purposes of this chapter, we present the most important evaluation models that are used to measure e-government progress.

The World Bank (www.worldbank.org) analyzes e-government into five axes of precedence: a) Better Service Delivery to Citizens, b) Improved Services for Businesses, c) Empowerment through Information, d) Transparency and Anti-Corruption and e) Efficient Government Purchasing. World Bank surveys deliver useful data regarding e-government, when combining Public Sector Governance (Kaufmann, Daniel, Kraay, Aart, Mastruzzi & Massimo, 2008) with ICT topics (Zhen-Wei Qiang, Lanvin, Minges, Swanson, Wellenius, Clarke, Halewood, Adamali, Coffey & Safdar, 2006). World Bank surveys examine e-government as part of countries' e-strategies and evaluate the growth of public service offering from national e-government portals (G2C, G2B, G2G), together with e-government interventions (in process reform, IT standards, government networks, training, promotion and private financing). World Bank evaluates also, the existence of central government web portals, together with the percentage of basic public services available online, and with the most desirable digital public services. Moreover, government annual investments in ICT are measured, which can be combined to governance effectiveness (Kaufmann, Daniel, Kraay, Aart, Mastruzzi &Massimo, 2008).

The United Nations (United Nations, 2008) provides an e-government assessment model in order to evaluate countries' migration to Connected Governance. Connected Governance is the UN vision for e-government, where public administration efficiency and public service delivery will be established. Some major advantages with Connected Governance are considered to be the avoidance of duplication; the reduction of operation costs; service transparency, efficiency and faster delivery; information sharing and security; citizen empowerment and participation etc. UN model contains indices that measure existing e-government approaches: e-government readiness, e-service provision, e-service stages and e-participation indices. The UN e-government readiness index is a composite index comprising the web measure index, the telecommunication infrastructure index and the human capital index.

Moreover, UN examines the maturity for the migration to Connected Governance with the following indices: central initiatives, dynamic structure of portals, and the overall progress and performance. The first index measures whether the e-government initiative is centrally defined and managed. The portals index evaluates government web sites for their dynamic structure. The final index evaluates the affordability in infrastructure and network integration, the public administration transformation efforts (integration, service transformation and efficiency, service innovation, service delivery, document control, staff training) and the social networks existence.

The Information Society DG investigates e-government progress in Europe, by evaluating e-Europe 2003 and e-Europe 2005 targets with specific benchmarking methods (Cap Gemini Ernst & Young, 2005). The indices used for e-government progress evaluation (Council of the European Union, 2003) emphasized on the achievement of e-Europe political targets and on new member countries progress. The main metrics of e-Europe benchmarking deal with: a) Internet indicators (Internet access, usage and cost by citizens and enterprises), b) modern online public services (offering the 20 basic services defined by the Internal/Market/ Consumer/Tourism Council, digital public service usage by individuals and enterprises, e-Learning and e-Health services), c) a dynamic e-business environment (e-commerce online transactions by individuals and enterprises, e-business readiness, use of ICT by business), d) a secure information infrastructure (security problems encountered by individuals and enterprises), e) broadband (penetration to households and enterprises). The final benchmarking (Cap Gemini Ernst & Young, 2005) considered e-government as an integrated model, which was evaluated with the following indices: a) structural landscape (dealing with existing politics, society, demography and economy), b) readiness (meaning the existence of policies, funding and capability for e-government), c) quality of service (examining the access channels for public services), d) back-office fulfilment (evaluating infrastructures, integration and process improvement), e) service adoption and use (by citizens and businesses) and f) service impact (regarding economic, social and democratic values).

Today the i2010 policy framework for the ICT followed up e-Europe and it is currently in progress (http://ec.europa.eu/information_society/eeurope/i2010/index_en.htm). Information Society DG evaluates i2010 progress with a new benchmarking framework (Information Society DG, 2006). The new framework uses indices that evolved from e-Europe ones, and conform with i2010 priorities and guidelines: a) developments of broadband (coverage, usage, performance and prices, multiplatform services), b) advanced services (availability and usage of online services), c) security, d) impact (ICT sector growth, market transformation), e) investment in ICT research, f) adoption of ICT by businesses (basic connectivity, ICT and open source usage, e-commerce and e-business growth), g) impact of adoption of ICT by business (investments by business, individuals and government, productivity increase, employment and skills), h) inclusion (ICT use by households, public access points, accessibility, digital literacy), i) public services (e-government availability and usage). The benchmark framework presented above, has many similarities to the e-Europe's ones, and evaluates e-government with multiple indices, which examine government investments and readiness in Europe.

The Greek Information Society Observatory (www.observatory.gr) is presented as a national evaluation model case. The observatory carries out multiple surveys, using different perspectives to assess Information Society diffusion in Greece. Most of the perspectives conform to e-Europe benchmarking framework, since most initiatives in Greece are funded by the European Commission sources. The Greek Observatory evaluates e-government with the following indices (Greek Information Society Observatory, 2008): a) number of public services available online (availability and sophistication), complying to e-Europe framework, b) individuals and enterprises transacting with Government online, c) number of digital public services with back office readiness, d) e-procurement services and f) public agencies using open source software.

Moreover, the Greek Observatory examines the efficiency of ICT investments in public sector. The methodology used for this investigation adopted international best practices and applied Multiple Criteria Decision Making (MCDM) methods (National Technical University of Athens, 2008). This particular study concluded that ICT investment in public sector is not always efficiency-driven, and by that sense the parameters that influence an investment decision should be analyzed (e.g. investments driven by a framework program). The study investigated e-government users (public servants, tax-payers, consumers and voters) and mentioned three areas of efficiency in public sector: a) internal organizational and economic improvement, b) social implications of ICT investments (better services and chances for citizens and enterprises), c) external political implications (reliable and transparent public administration). The indices defined in the study concern the following axes of precedence (National Technical University of Athens (2), 2008): a) direct economic benefits, b) indirect economic benefits, c) ICT contribution to quality of citizen life and d) ICT contribution to competitiveness. All the above data resulted in an evaluation model (National Technical University of Athens (3), 2008) consisting of a) financial indices, b) direct profit indices, c) performance indices, d) satisfaction indices and e) staff training indices.

The American Customer Satisfaction Index (ACSI) (www.theacsi.org) is one of the leading customer satisfaction indices in the world. ACSI was developed by the National Quality Research Centre (NQRC) at the Stephen M. Ross Business School at the University of Michigan. The ACSI helps to determine how satisfied consumers in the US are, so that consumer behaviour can be understood. The ACSI uses customer interviews as input to a multi-equation econometric model developed at the University of Michigan's Ross School of Business. The ACSI model is a cause-and-effect model with indices for drivers of satisfaction on the left side (customer expectations, perceived quality, and perceived value), satisfaction (ACSI) in the centre, and outcomes of satisfaction on the right side (customer complaints and customer loyalty, including customer retention and price tolerance). ACSI personnel question around 80,000 Americans per year regarding how satisfied they feel about any products and services they may have used for that year. The satisfaction of the public with e-government services is rated by the ACSI and concerns citizen satisfaction with US federal government websites (news & information, portals, search engines and digital public services). Citizen satisfaction shows how well e-government initiatives go, and how much traffic is driven to the web channel. Latest surveys using the ACSI, show that investment in the online channel will pay itself off and result in increased efficiency and happy citizens.

Accenture (Accenture (2), 2005) evaluates e-government regarding the performance the public sector achieves from the citizen perspective. According to Accenture research, high performers in the public sector base the value they create on two criteria: a) the outcomes they deliver, meaning that they provide relentlessly citizen-centred services and b) the cost-effectiveness they achieve, meaning that they hold themselves accountable and they make their operations and results transparent to all. Moreover, Accenture (Accenture, 2005)) defines the notion of shared services in the public sector, as "the consolidation of administrative or support functions (such as human resources, finance, information technology and procurement) from several departments or agencies into a single, stand-alone organizational entity whose only mission is to provide services as efficiently and effectively as possible". From shared services point of view, each public agency behaves as part of a larger system, and it works in open and collaborative ways.

Accenture methods consist of quantitative and qualitative components, and both are applied over interviewing procedures carried out on public sector senior executives. The Quantitative method displays survey sizes such as the number of countries, public agencies and civil servants where the interviews are carried out. On the other hand, the qualitative method traces the efficiency targets, and demands for improved services and cost pressures, which governments face.

E-Government Evaluation Frameworks

Recent studies give significant approaches to e-government evaluation. They all realise e-government projects' complexity and define dif-

Table 2. Key findings from existing evaluation frameworks

Author(s)	Approach	Key findings
Wang and Liao (Wang and Liao, 2008)	Framework for evaluating G2C projects, based on Delone- McLean model	- data are collected from direct surveys - some project management evaluation dimensions are not included in the framework
Van Der Westhuizen and Edmond (Van Der Westhuizen & Edmond, 2005)	Evaluation framework based on Delone-McLean model	- project and product dimensions are included - no social or economic implications of e-government projects are considered - organizational or political strategy is not considered
Braclay (Barclay, 2008)	Evaluation framework for ICT project performance	- it is ICT general and not focused on e-government projects - it uses a balanced scoreboard methodology - it uses SERVQUAL project management perspectives - useful for single project assessment - lacks in multi-project evaluation capability
Victor et. al. (Victor, Panikar & Kanhere, 2007	Post completion evaluation model	- provides useful information for the improvement of forthcoming projects - based on COBIT and CMM process maturity frameworks - it does not consider existing major e-government evaluation models - specific metrics and indices are not defined
Liu et. al. (Liu, Derzsi, Raus & Kipp, 2008)	Evaluation model defining KPAs and KPIs for e-government stakeholders	- stakeholders dimension is very important in e-government - it contains a dimension for Strategy - indices of all dimensions should be affected or measure strategy
Esteves and Joseph (Esteves & Joseph, 2008)	Evaluation model	- it uses dimensions concerning organization's maturity and stakeholders - it does not define specific indices or targets
Batini et. al. (Batini, Viscusi and Cherubini, 2009)	GOVQual e-government project selection tool	- multi-layered framework - associates project quality with social context - it does not examine strategy

ferent perspectives and methods of assessment. This section presents some of them, describing in short their strengths and weaknesses (Table 2). Wang and Liao (Wang and Liao, 2008) use the evaluation model of DeLone and McLean for assessing e-government success, and they define an evaluation framework for measuring the success of Government-to-Citizen information systems. Although their framework is useful and provides important evaluation perspectives, data are collected from direct surveys, while some important project management evaluation dimensions (e.g. project organisation and project processes) are not included in the framework.

Van Der Westhuizen and Edmond (Van Der Westhuizen & Edmond, 2005) provide an alternative approach, again based on DeLone and McLean evaluation model: they include project and product dimensions for assessing e-government projects, but they do not emphasize on the social or on the economic implications of e-government projects. Moreover, the proposed model does not associate the e-government projects under evaluation with the applied organization or political strategy.

Moreover, Braclay (Barclay, 2008) presents a framework for evaluating and measuring ICT project performance, which is not focused on e-government area. The proposed framework also uses a balanced scoreboard methodology as an evaluation tool combined with other project management perspectives, as they are defined in SERVQUAL, and it is useful for single project assessment. However, it lacks in multi-project evaluation capability, especially in e-government cases where strategy guides project design and implementation.

Victor et. al. (Victor, Panikar & Kanhere, 2007) define the importance of post-completion project evaluation in e-government. The authors consider that conclusions and information extracted from post-completion evaluation, can provide useful information for the improvement of forthcoming projects. The proposed model is based on COBIT (Boonen & Brand, 2008) and CMM (Dymond, 2005) process maturity frameworks, but it does not consider existing major e-government evaluation models presented in this chapter. Additionally, the study does not define specific metrics and indices for the evaluation model.

Liu et. al. (Liu, Derzsi, Raus & Kipp, 2008) provide Key Performance Areas (KPAs) and Key Performance Indicators (KPIs) for different e-government stakeholders. Their framework considers the e-government strategy as an evaluation dimension and they examine project success according to strategic requirements. However, all evaluation dimensions of an e-government model or framework must contain indices and criteria affected by or concerning either the organizational or the national strategy, because e-government projects have to align totally to strategic planning objectives and characteristics.

Esteves and Joseph (Esteves & Joseph, 2008) present an alternative assessment model of e-government projects. Their model defines the assessment dimensions, which are related to the organization's maturity and to the e-government stakeholders. However, this model cannot be considered as an evaluation framework, since it does not provide specific measurement indices and targets.

Finally, Batini et. al. (Batini, Viscusi and Cherubini, 2009) propose a framework for e-government project selection that is called GovQual. It is a multi-layered framework that measures project quality with respect to an organization's environment (social context) and specific targets for service quality. However, this framework does not examine strategy and strategic targets for quality measurement.

All the above approaches are based on existing evaluation tools (e.g., SERVQUAL, Balanced Scoreboard, COBIT etc.) to provide evaluation frameworks for e-government project progress, success and quality. The approaches focus on multiple e-government stakeholders and on their different points of view for project quality. Moreover, the presented approaches recognize strategic goals as important parameters for project evaluations, but only one of them (Barclay, 2008) incorporates strategy in all evaluation dimensions. (Victor, et. al., 2007) approach can be used as a project post-completion selection tool, giving the selection dimension in e-government evaluation scope.

MAIN FOCUS OF THE CHAPTER

In the previous sections we provide a detailed literature review concerning existing e-government evaluation frameworks and models. All of them provide useful results to their audiences, but they all have strong and weak points. This chapter aims to provide an evaluation model that succeeds in both combining major e-government approaches –structured and applied by significant organizations-, and measuring user satisfaction from an e-government software project. Additionally, we aim to provide a common tool that is able to succeed in measuring e-government software projects, which can be utilized by unique organizations, and which can be applied in local initiatives.

We focus on software projects because, e-government software applications are the final product of e-government, and they compose the transaction interface amongst e-government stakeholders. Moreover, we consider that no common framework is able to assess all kinds of e-government projects, because they vary from infrastructural to software and to campaign activities, meaning that their targets, their scope, their complexity and their audience are different and they demand different evaluation approaches.

The method that we have followed in order to develop the framework has been inspired from the SERVQUAL instrument (Asubonteng, McCleary & Swan, 1996; Van Iwaarden, Van der Wiele, Ball & Millen, 2003). The SERVQUAL instrument defines five generic dimensions (factors) to measure customer satisfaction: a) tangibles, b) reliability, c) responsiveness, d) assurance and e) empathy. However, indices have to be identified for each of the above factors of the SERVQUAL, which focus on the individual evaluation requirements.

Initially, we exploited existing evaluation frameworks and models for identifying generic perspectives (factors). These perspectives result in a balanced scoreboard that comprises the existing maturity of e-government evaluation. Then, we defined and assigned indices in each of the generic factors. These indices can evaluate even single e-government projects, and they can measure citizen satisfaction.

The Identification of Generic Factors

Models and frameworks presented above use different standards and perspectives to evaluate e-government progress. E-Government models focus in the evaluation of multiple indices: a) *quantitative indices* that measure usage, infrastructure and information growth, and b) *qualitative indices* that measure service quality, citizen satisfaction and participation in e-government initiatives. The quantitative indices are all direct, while some of the qualitative are indirect. For instance, citizen satisfaction can be indirectly measured with number of users that access the services. However, satisfaction concerning digital services, which citizens are obliged to access (e.g. tax services) cannot be measured indirectly, and ACSI seems to be appropriate for this measure.

In (Table 3) and (Table 4) we tried to group the indices from the presented benchmarking models, as a first step to comprise an evaluation model that can succeed in a more effective and global measurement of e-government software projects.

Many similarities and common targets can be identified in Table 2. We used these similarities in order to proceed in the development of four groups of indices (Table 4), which measure the political targets of a strategic plan. *Online Availability* is a factor that displays how well Governments are moving towards e-government and e-Democracy in the front-office stages. The factor shows the number of portals and services available online, and the ongoing efforts for improvement of the online mechanisms. *E-Government readiness* measures the back-office maturity and improvement, in delivering better services to the citizens and in simplifying internal procedures in the public sector. *Prosperous External Environment* is an index that indirectly measures e-government efficiency. In societies, where investments are made on broadband and ICT, citizens and enterprises are more prepared to transact with the public sector online, and participate in decision making. *Citizen satisfaction* is a qualitative index, which can be measured both directly and indirectly: the number of digital service stages and the citizen applications for online transactions can display citizen satisfaction indirectly. Indirect measurements cannot investigate citizen satisfaction from services to which they are obliged to apply, such as the tax services. However, only ACSI can directly investigate how well the online services perform concerning citizen needs and expectations. In this group, we also assigned indices that influence citizen satisfaction: citizens expect transparency and cost savings from e-government initiatives,

Table 3. Indices from existing e-government benchmarking models

Index target	Index name	Benchmarking model
Growth of public service offering	Online availability growth	The World Bank (WB)
Public web portals existence, together with the percentage of basic public services available online	Online availability	-//-
Process reform, IT standards, government networks, training, promotion and private financing	e-government implications	-//-
Annual investments in ICT by Governments	Public investments on e-government	-//-
Public web portals offering most desirable public services	Citizen Satisfaction	-//-
Public portals, broadband networks and trained staff in the public sector	e-government readiness	The United Nations (UN)
Public services available online	e-Service Provision	-//-
Digital channels offering public services	e-service stages	-//-
e-Democracy portals, number of themes put under requests for comments	e-Participation	-//-
Whether the e-government initiative is centrally defined and managed	Central initiatives	-//-
Evaluates government web sites for their dynamic structure	Portals	-//-
The affordability in infrastructure and network integration, the public administration transformation efforts and the social networks existence	Progress and Performance	-//-
Internet access, usage and cost by citizens and enterprises	Internet indicators	Information Society DG (InfoSoc)
Offering the 20 basic European services	modern online public services	-//-
e-commerce online transactions by individuals and enterprises, e-business readiness, use of ICT by business	a dynamic e-business environment	-//-
Security problems encountered by individuals and enterprises	a secure information infrastructure	-//-
Penetration to households and enterprises	Broadband	-//-
Percentage of skilled civil servants, number of interconnected public agencies, interoperability among different agencies	internal organizational and economic improvement	Greek Information Society Observatory (Greek InfoSoc)
Number of services available online, improved services	social implications of ICT investments	-//-
Reliable and transparent public administration (number of digital transactions versus the traditional ones)	External political implications	-//-
Citizen satisfaction	ACSI	The ACSI
Number of available public services	e-government Outcomes	Accenture
Accountable public sector, transparent operations and results	Cost effectiveness	-//-

Table 4. Groups of indices from e-government benchmarking models

Index group name	Indices grouped
Online Availability	online availability growth (WB), online availability (WB), e-Service Provision (UN), Portals (UN), e-Participation (UN), modern online public services (InfoSoc), social implications of ICT investments (Greek InfoSoc), e-government Outcomes (Accenture).
e-government readiness	e-government implications (WB), e-government readiness (UN), central initiatives (UN), progress and Performance (UN), secure information infrastructure (InfoSoc), internal organizational and economic improvement (Greek InfoSoc).
Prosperous external environment	public investments on e-government (WB), broadband (InfoSoc), internet indicators (InfoSoc), dynamic e-business environment (InfoSoc).
Citizen Satisfaction	citizen satisfaction (WB), e-service stages (UN), external political implications (InfoSoc), cost effectiveness (Accenture), The ACSI.

parameters that make them satisfied, even if they have never transacted with online services.

The Identification of Software Measurement Indices

It is clear that current e-government evaluation frameworks do not proceed to software project evaluation, although software is the interface amongst e-government stakeholders and systems. The proposed framework consists of indices that focus on software quality measurement. The main objectives for the identification of these indices deal with: a) the establishment of a measurement system for software projects, and b) the development of a software project knowledge management system able to store, organize, and possibly reuse project knowledge.

The framework aims to provide a more holistic approach to e-government software projects' assessment. It comprises a set of metrics aiming to measure all aspects of an e-government software project. Traditionally software metrics are classified as (Fenton & Pfleeger, 1997): a) *process metrics* concern the software development activities and processes (usually such metrics are measuring defects per testing hour, time, number of people, etc.) b) *Product metrics* that evaluate the software product and c) *Resources metrics* refer to the development process inputs (e.g. people and methods). These types of metrics are not always sufficient to measure the results or the process of a project, due to project complexity. Complexity is based on technical, on financial, on organizational, and on environmental reasons.

Software evaluation methods measure software complexity and performance. However, e-government software -such as portals, digital public services, web services for interoperability etc.- influences citizen interaction with the public sector and digital transactions amongst e-government stakeholders. This perspective forces to measure the impact of the project deliverables to the citizens. Only external indices can be used to evaluate software impact, which measure software interaction with its environment (i.e. behaviour and impact).

The combination of metrics in a measurement system can be done with balanced scorecards. Kaplan and Norton (Kaplan & Norton, 1999) developed a framework that helps top management to select a set of metrics that provide an integrated look at an organization. They originally suggested *four* groups of indices. Originally, in the balanced scorecard proposed by Kaplan and Norton, the customer scorecard usually deals with the question "*how do customers see us?*" The proposed framework focuses on the "citizen" and the "enterprise" and therefore we attempt to measure and monitor how the development of the IT system affects the digital public services.

The Proposed Framework

An e-government software project is both a part of the strategic vision of an organization or of the public sector in general, and a standalone project that delivers products and services to the customers (the e-government stakeholders in this case). The existing evaluation models that we described, evaluate the vision progress and not projects' progress. However, the implementation of a common framework for e-government project is a complex procedure. Multiple approaches deliver different assessment models, as described.

The framework that we developed and proposed focuses on the following objectives: a) to evaluate the conformation of a project to the strategic vision of the organization and probably to the general strategic plan, which fund the project. The results of the evaluation have to provide data for e-government progress evaluation, with means common to existing evaluation models. b) To analyze project financial data, in order to measure cost-benefit and return of investment (although cost-benefit criteria are not always part of public investments). c) To investigate the project environment in order to manage necessary organization changes, and to predict and handle risks during project implementation. d) To assess project deliverables, in order to measure their conformation to the contract, their quality and customer satisfaction.

Understanding the above points of view, we used the *balanced scoreboard material* (Kaplan & Norton, 1999) in order to identify the required perspectives and the generic groups of the framework. According to Kaplan and Norton (Kaplan & Norton, 1999) the balanced scoreboard uses the following perspectives:

- *The Learning & Growth Perspective*: includes employee training and corporate cultural attitudes related to both individual and corporate self-improvement.
- *The Business Process Perspective*: refers to internal business processes. Metrics based on this perspective allow the managers to know how well their business is running, and whether its products and services conform to customer requirements (the mission).
- *The Customer Perspective*: contains indices that measure customer satisfaction, via analyzing customers in groups, and via assigning business processes to products and services delivered to these groups.
- *The Financial Perspective*: refers to financial indices, which evaluate funding and cost-benefit results.

Our objective for the proposed balanced scoreboard was the identification of the proper perspectives for the evaluation of an e-government project. According to (Anthopoulos, Siozos, Nanopoulos & Tsoukalas, 2006) a development methodology of an e-government software project considers five perspectives:

- *The organizational perspective* that deals with the internal administrative characteristics of a public agency and of the public sector in general.

Figure 1. The proposed evaluation framework's perspectives

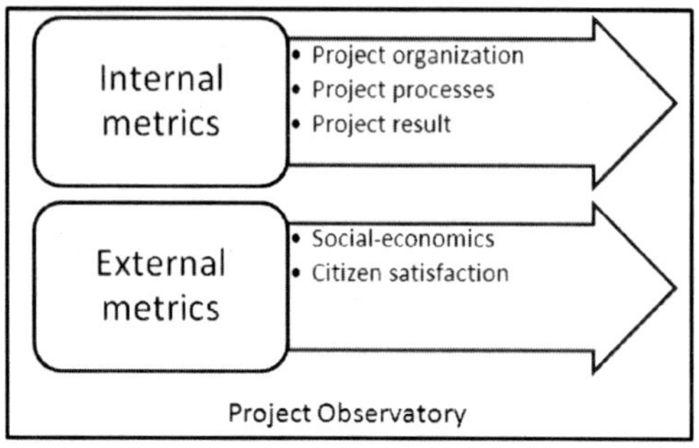

- *The technical perspective* that analyzes the necessary components and the architecture for the project deliverables, the standards that these components conform to, and the case studies used for the development of the deliverables.
- *The informational perspective*, which handles data and their structure that will be used or be produced by project deliverables, capacity demands, and security and privacy aspects regarding this data.
- *The e-government perspective*, considering how the project conforms with the strategic planning and with the e-government principles in general.
- *The ethical perspective,* dealing with stakeholders' ambitions and with their contribution during and after project implementation.

Other studies such as (Anthopoulos & Tsoukalas, 2005) emphasize on the *financial* and the *social* perspectives usage, for e-government projects' design and implementation. The financial perspective demands costs minimization of the project deliverables' operation and maintenance, while the social perspective examines how the project deliverables support the 'close' of the digital divide. All of the above models were combined and used in our study, for the identification of the perspectives (Figure 1) for the proposed balanced scoreboard, since the framework needs to measure most of the issues that existing models do. However, the main purpose of the framework is the evaluation of the progress of unique e-government software projects.

These concepts resulted in a balanced scoreboard model (Figure 2), in the middle of which is the organization vision and strategy, together with e-government principles. The scoreboard measures the following perspectives that focus on project management issues:

- *Project organization perspective* examines the organizational and operational environment, where the project will be implemented and the deliverables will be installed. Organization perspective matches organization's readiness (infrastructure, experience, maturity and willingness etc.) concerning project management and ICT. Moreover, the organization's perspective considers a lot of managerial aspects for the project (time and cost attributes etc.). Furthermore, this perspective measures aspects regarding the *e-government readiness* and the *prosperous external environment* perspectives (Table 4), while it considers the *learning and growth* perspective from the balanced scoreboard. The proposed indices are analyzed in a) *direct cost* indices that size existing and

Figure 2. The proposed evaluation framework

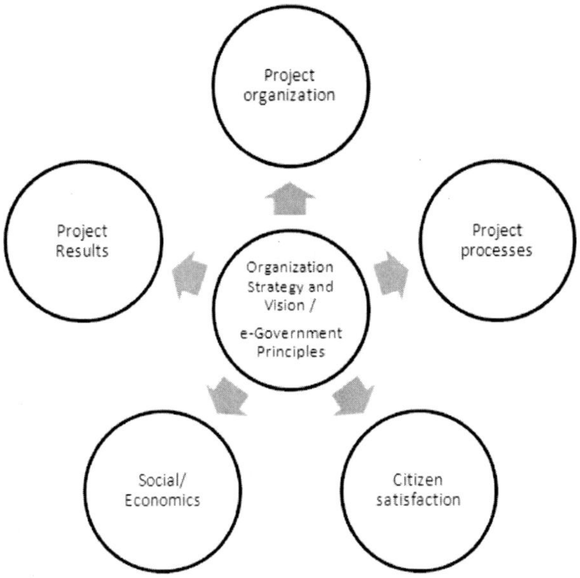

previous funding management; b) *staff's skills* and c) *organization's consistency* in delivering final products or services.

- *Project processes perspective* evaluates project processes concerning their alignment and their agility (interoperability) with other existing or ongoing e-government projects. Additionally, this perspective measures attributes concerning the conformation to existing strategic planning and to the *online availability* perspective from (Table 4), while it is inspired from the *business process perspective* from the balanced scoreboard. The indices defined for project process measurement (Table 6) evaluate a) *the process alignment* to software installation after project completion, and to strategic planning (number of services transformed and delivered online); and b) *process agility* regarding the interoperability with other projects.
- *Project results perspective* reflects deliverables' size, quality, complexity and their requirements concerning infrastructure resources and capacity. This dimension does not reflect directly to any of the indices described in (Table 3) and (Table 4), since most of its indices measure the social and economic effects of e-government projects, rather they analyze technically the results of e-government projects. However, this dimension is particularly useful in the programme design since it offers data and information on the effort, size and complexity of the planned projects, needed for achieving the objectives set. In (Table 7) the set of metrics that is proposed for this perspective is presented.
- *Social and economics perspective* considers the project's implications to its environment (Table 8). This dimension evaluates how the project affects social life and employment; it examines project's conformation to policies and strategy; and it evaluates how much the project supports the 'close' of the digital divide. Social and economics perspective deals as well partially as with citizen satisfaction from (Table 4), since it measures attributes concerning political

Table 5. Project organization metrics

Project organization metrics	
Direct cost measurement indices	
Initial estimated budget for the project	The budget declared during project planning
Final project cost	The project real cost
Costs for project preparation	Costs for research and planning
Costs for project management	Costs for the support of project management
Investment estimated "lifecycle"	Years that the investment is estimated to handle organization and citizen needs
Annual maintenance cost	Costs for technical support, update and supervision
Staff's skills measurement indices	
Training programs cost	Concerning e-skills for software use
Executives' maturity	Number of executives that participated in project management
Costs for personnel employment	Costs covering staff (internal or outsourcing) that need to administer installed software
Organization's consistency	
Project duration turnover	Project duration excess ratio compared to contractual duration
Organization Certified	Organization holds certificate for project management and for internal procedures
Organization maturity	Organization has invested on ICT projects and offers digital public services

and financial implications. The main difference is that *Social and economics* indices are *macro* indices, since they evaluate the progress of the society and economy in general (e.g. the contribution to quality of life, the contribution to democracy etc.), while citizen satisfaction indices focus on satisfaction achieved from using specific ICT services. Moreover, this perspective investigates alignment to e-government literature (like *openness* and *digital divide*).

- *Citizen satisfaction perspective* deals with the satisfaction of e-government stakeholders (citizens, enterprises, civil servants etc.). This perspective was inspired from *the citizen satisfaction* index from (Table 4) and the *customer perspective* of the balanced scoreboard. Both qualitative and quantitative criteria (Table 9) are combined to examine citizen satisfaction, such as the involvement of stakeholders during project design and management, quality surveys measuring the conformation of the project deliverables to citizen and others stakeholders' expectations etc. It also measures direct values such as deliverables' usage by the end-users, estimating deliverables' acceptance.

The proposed model offers a complete framework that can be used as a survey tool for measuring the success of e-government projects in achieving their targets and user satisfaction.

While benchmarking for e-government projects should be a staple in the government policy and priorities, it is important to remember that establishing useful and meaningful metrics is very much a comparative exercise. Therefore, the optimum set of metrics should depend on, not only the government's policies, technology levels, but as well on international practice.

The balanced scorecard approach defines dimensions of e-government projects need to be benchmarked and uses metrics defined in the

Table 6. Project processes metrics

Project processes metrics	
Process alignment	
Re-designed processes	Number of services that were re-designed to align to software needs
Process digitization	Processes that totally transformed to digital ones and delivered online
Hybrid Processes	Processes that are executed either electronically either in their traditional form
e-Service availability	Services delivered online as percentage to the total number of offering services
Electronic procedure ratio	Procedures executed via software deliverables compared to the total internal procedures
Processes with legal confirmation	Processes whose relative legal framework has been updated
Process agility	
Web services	Number of web services delivered within software projects
Interoperable services	Number of digital services interoperating with other organizations' software
Conformation with national strategy	XML schemas used to conform to national interoperability strategy (like e-GIF)

literature and in large organizations in order to define a complete framework of measurement. As such, the whole approach or parts of it can be used for practice the various facets of the product, process and project management process and service quality of e-government projects.

CONCLUSION

Our study presents recent existing evaluation frameworks and models for e-government progress, which show how various -yet large- organizations, measure Government performance on ICT investments and on delivering digital public services online. These data are useful for e-government audience in order to realise how strategic plans estimate progress evaluation, and on which axes of precedence strategic reviewing is based on. Our chapter focuses on using existing frameworks and models in order to implement an evaluation framework for e-government software projects. The presented method is also considered useful for e-government audience who would like to conduct individual evaluations. We consider e-government software as the most important aspect

Table 7. Project results indices

Project results indices	
Discrete subsystems	Number of subsystems that the software is analyzed in
Discrete modules	Number of software modules that the software is analyzed in (according to UML)
Internal interfaces	Number of internal interfaces between software modules (ADO, JavaBeans etc.)
External interfaces	Number of external interfaces for software interconnections and and UIs for multi-platform access
Service size	The number of services that the software offers
Process size	Data (in MB) that it produces per process execution
Transaction size	Data (in MB) that software sends and receives per service execution per second

Table 8. Social economics indices

Social economics indices	
Social implications	
Service usage	Number of service sessions (applications for services) executed by citizens and enterprises daily
Contribution to quality of life	Number of services offered that support quality of life (e.g. intelligent transport services)
Time savings ratio	Ratio of time decrease for citizen/enterprise per service execution
Contribution to competitiveness	Number of e-procurement, 'find a job' and other financial services offered by the installed software
Political implications	
Contribution to democracy	Number of new digital services concerning e-Democracy (decision making, e-voting etc.)
Contribution to social profiling	Data (records per month) delivered to social networks and other e-participation systems
Direct cost results	
Contribution to employment	Number of personnel that worked during software implementation
Operational cost savings	Paper cost savings, concerning ratio of electronically produced documents
Personnel decrease	Number of staff positions cancelled after software installation
Direct operational costs	Annual costs (for five years after deliverables installation) for administration, support and maintenance
Indirect cost results	
Personnel time savings	Ratio of time decrease per service execution for personnel activity (e.g. document creation, archiving etc.)
Return of Investment	Number of operational years needed for direct and indirect cost savings to cover funding

Table 9. Citizen satisfaction indices

Citizen satisfaction indices	
Direct end-user satisfaction	How well (scale 0-100) do end-users evaluate offered services?
Indirect end-user satisfaction	Ratio of end-users returned to the services rather than applying to traditional ones
Fully digitally execution	Number of services offered in fully digitally execution form, compared to total digital services
Semi-digitally execution	Number of services that request citizen visit to the agency, compared to total digital services
Public executives' satisfaction	How well (scale 0-100) do civil servants evaluate the installed software that they use?
Service reliability	Ratio of failed service executions against those that succeeded
Service complexity	Number of steps each service is analyzed in and citizen must follow during execution.
Service consistency	Ratio of Service execution time versus estimated execution time

to measure, since it is the final product of strategic planning and it structures the interfaces amongst e-government stakeholders. E-Government software project managers and strategic designers can apply the framework on the organization and on data concerning the project environment, achieving in both pre- and post- assessment of their projects and of their vision.

Well known evaluation methods -such as the SERVQUAL and the Balanced Scoreboard- were used to structure the framework, which includes indices able to measure unique software projects as parts of the organization's or central administration's vision. The resulted framework can become a useful tool for every organization that plans to move to e-government era, while it can deliver data to central benchmarking agencies, and to national and to supranational observatories. Our future objective is to apply the framework on small scale e-government projects in order to evaluate its ability to measure both projects' progress and their alignment to strategic vision and e-government principles.

REFERENCES

Accenture. (2005a, January). *Driving High Performance in Government: Maximizing the Value of Public-Sector Shared Services*. Retrieved April 29, 2009, from http://www.accenture.com

Accenture. (2005b, April). *Leadership in Customer Service: New Expectations, New Experiences. The Government Executive Series*. Retrieved April 29, 2009, from http://www.accenture.com

Anthopoulos, L., Siozos, P., Nanopoulos, A., & Tsoukalas, I. A. (2006). The Bottom-up Design of e-government. Development Methodology based on a Collaboration Environment. *e-Service Journal, 4*(3).

Anthopoulos, L., Siozos, P., & Tsoukalas, I. A. (2007). Applying Participatory Design and Collaboration in Digital Public Services for discovering and re-designing e-government services. *Government Information Quarterly, 24*(2), 353–376. doi:10.1016/j.giq.2006.07.018

Anthopoulos, L., & Tsoukalas, I. A. (2005). The implementation model of a Digital City. The case study of the first Digital City in Greece: e-Trikala. *Journal of E-Government, 2*(2).

Asubonteng, P., McCleary, K. J., & Swan, J. E. (1996). SERVQUAL revisited: a critical review of service quality. *Journal of Services Marketing, 10*(6), 62–81. doi:10.1108/08876049610148602

Barclay, C. (2008). Towards an integrated measurement of IS project performance: The project performance scorecard. *Information Systems Frontiers, 10*(3), 331–345. doi:10.1007/s10796-008-9083-6

Batini, C., Viscusi, G., & Cherubini, D. (2009). GovQual: A quality driven methodology for e-government project planning. *Government Information Quarterly, 26*(1), 106–117. doi:10.1016/j.giq.2008.03.002

Boonen, K., & Brand, H. (2008). *IT Governance CobiT 4.1 - A Management Guide* (3rd ed.). Amsterdam: Van Haren Publishing.

British Standards Institution. (2002). *BS 6079-1:2002 Project Management: Guide to project management*.

British Standards Institution. (2003). [*Quality management systems: Guidelines for quality management in projects.*]. *BS ISO, 10006*, 2003.

Cap Gemini Ernst & Young. (2005). *Online availability of public services. How is Europe progressing?* Retrieved April 29, 2009, from http://ec.europa.eu/information_society/eeurope/2005/doc/all_about/online_5th_measurement_fv4.pdf

Carnegie Mellon University. (2002). *Capability* Maturity *Model Integration: CMMI for Systems Engineering, Software Engineering, Integrated Product and Process Development, and Supplier Sourcing* (CMMI-SE/SW/IPPD/SS, V1.1). Carnegie Mellon University.

Council of the European Union. (2003). *Council Resolution on the implementation of the eEurope 2005 Action Plan*. Retrieved April 29, 2009, from http://ec.europa.eu/information_society/eeurope/2005/doc/all_about/benchmarking/resolution.doc

Dymond, K.M. (2005). A Guide to the CMMI: Interpreting the Capability Maturity Model Integration, Process Transition International Inc., 2005.

Esteves, J., & Joseph, R. C. (2008). A comprehensive framework for the assessment of e-government projects. *Government Information Quarterly*, *25*(1), 118–132. doi:10.1016/j.giq.2007.04.009

European Commission. (2002). *eEurope 2005: An information society for all*, European Commission - COM 263, 2002. Retrieved April 29, 2009, from http://europa.eu.int/eeurope

Fenton, N., & Pfleeger, S. L. (1997). *Software Metrics - A Rigorous Approach*. London: International Thomson Publishing.

Gant, J., & Gant, D. (2002). Web portal functionality and State Government E-service. In the *Proceedings of the 35th Hawaii international conference on system sciences (IEEE 2002)*.

German Federal Government. (2003). *BundOnline 2005. 2003 Implementation Plan*. Retrieved April 29, 2009, from http://www.en.bmi.bund.de

Greek Information Society Observatory. (2008). *Measuring e-Europe 2005 and i2010 indices*. Retrieved April 29, 2009, from http://www.observatory.gr/ files/meletes/eEuropei2010_05-07.pdf

Information Society DG. (2006). *i2010 Benchmarking Framework*. Retrieved April 29, 2009, from http://ec.europa.eu/information_society/eeurope/i2010/docs/ benchmarking/060220_i2010_benchmarking_framework_nov_2006.doc

International Project Management Association. (2009). *Project Excellence Model.* Retrieved April 29, 2009, from http://www.apm.org.uk/ProjectExcellence.asp

Kaplan, R. S., & Norton, D. P. (1999). *The Balanced Scorecard: Translating Strategy into Action*. Boston: Harvard Business Press.

Kaufmann, D., Kraay, A., & Mastruzzi, M. (2008, June 24). *Governance Matters VII: Aggregate and Individual Governance Indicators, 1996-2007*. World Bank Policy Research Working Paper No. 4654. Retrieved April 29, 2009, from http://ssrn.com/abstract=1148386

Kelly P., & Stalnaker M.L. (2002). Avoiding IT Project Disasters of Counsel. *ABI/INFORM Trade & Industry, 21*(7), 13-23.

Liu, A. N. N., & Walker, A. (1998). Evaluation of project outcomes. *Construction Management and Economics*, *16*(2), 209–219. doi:10.1080/014461998372493

Liu, J., Derzsi, Z., Raus, M., & Kipp, A. (2008). eGovernment Project Evaluation: An Integrated Framework. *Lecture Notes in Computer Science*, *5184*, 85–97. doi:10.1007/978-3-540-85204-9_8

National Technical University of Athens. (2008a). Implementation methodology for the study 'Improving ICT investment effectiveness in Public Administration.' *Greek Information Society Observatory*. Retrieved April 29, 2009, from http://www.observatory.gr/files/meletes/MVA_D0_gr.pdf

National Technical University of Athens. (2008b). Comparative evaluation of different stages of the ICT investment efficiency for the study Improving ICT investment effectiveness in Public Administration. *Greek Information Society Observatory*. Retrieved April 29, 2009, from http://www.observatory.gr/files/meletes/MVA_D1_gr.pdf

National Technical University of Athens. (2008c). Evaluation framework for the study 'Improving ICT investment effectiveness in Public Administration.' *Greek Information Society Observatory*. Retrieved April 29, 2009, from http://www.observatory.gr/files/meletes/MVA_D3_gr.pdf

Office of Government Commerce. The Stationary Office (2005). Managing Successful Projects with PRINCE2. London.

Pressman, R. (2009). *Software Engineering: A Practitioner's Approach* (7th ed.). New York: McGraw-Hill Higher Education.

Programme Management Maturity Model. (2009). *The Programme Management Web Site*. Retrieved April 29, 2009, from http://www.e-programme.com/

Project Management Institute Standard Committee (2004). *A guide to the Project Management Body of Knowledge*.

Shenhar, A. J., Levy, O., & Dvir, D. (1997). Mapping the dimensions of project success. *Project Management Journal, 28*(2), 5–13.

The Standish Group. (2001). Extreme Chaos. *The Standish Group*. Retrieved April 29, 2009, from http://www.standishgroup.com/sample_research

Treasury Board Secretariat. (2001, August 10). *Canada's Report on Portals*. Government of Canada.

UK Cabinet Office. (2000). e-government, a strategic framework for public services in the information age. *UK Cabinet Office*. Retrieved April 29, 2009, from http://archive.cabinetoffice.gov.uk/e-envoy/resources-pdfs/$file/Strategy.pdf

UK Cabinet Office. (2002). Office of the e-Envoy, e-government Interoperability Framework (e-GIF). Part two: Technical Policies and Specifications, Office of the e-Envoy. *UK Cabinet Office*. Retrieved April 29, 2009, from http://www.govtalk.gov.uk/ documents/e-GIF4Pt2_2002-04-25.pdf

United Nations. (2008). *UN E-Government Survey – From e-government to Connected Government*. Retrieved April 29, 2009, from http://unpan1.un.org/intradoc/ groups/public/documents/UN/UNPAN028607.pdf

US Federal Government. (2002). *E-Government Strategy: Simplified Delivery of Services to Citizens*. Office of Management and Budget, US Federal Government. Retrieved April 29, 2009, from http://www.firstgov.gov/Topics/ Includes/Reference/egov_strategy.pdf

Van Der Westhuizen, D., & Fitzgerald, E. P. (2005). Defining and measuring project success. In *the Proceedings of the European Conference on IS Management, Leadership and Governance,* 07-08 Jul 2005, Reading, United Kingdom.

Van Iwaarden, J., Van der Wiele, T., Ball, L., & Millen, R. (2003). Applying SERVQUAL to Web sites: an exploratory study. *International Journal of Quality & Reliability Management, 20*(8), 919–935. doi:10.1108/02656710310493634

Victor, G. J., Panikar, A., & Kanhere, V. K. (2007). E-government Projects–Importance of Post Completion Audits. In the *5th International Conference of e-government (ICEG, 2007)*. Retrieved April 26, 2009, from http://www.iceg.net/2007/books/1/20_308.pdf

Wang, Y.-S., & Liao, Y.-W. (2008). Assessing eGovernment systems success: A validation of the DeLone and McLean model of information systems success. *Government Information Quarterly*, *25*(4), 717–733. doi:10.1016/j.giq.2007.06.002

Wateridge, J. (1998). How can IT/IS projects be measured for success? *International Journal of Project Management*, *16*(1), 59–63. doi:10.1016/S0263-7863(97)00022-7

Zhen-Wei Qiang, C., Lanvin, B., & Minges, M. Swanson, E., Wellenius, B., Clarke, G., Halewood, N., Adamali, A., Coffey, J., & Safdar, Z. (2006). *Global trends and policies - 2006: information and communications for development.* Retrieved April 29, 2009, from http://www-wds.worldbank.org/external/default/WDSContentServer/WDSP/IB/2006/04/20/0000 12009_20060420105118/Rendered/PDF/359240PAPER0In101OFFICIAL0USE0ONLY1.pdf

KEY TERMS AND DEFINITIONS

E-Government: The implementation and delivery of digital public services to citizens and enterprises.

E-Governance: The transformation of the public sector into a more efficient form, able to execute simplified public services, to minimize operation costs and to respond with means closer to the private sector.

E-Government Principles: The implementation of modern public sector, whose characteristics are: a) openness (all citizens, even with disabilities or with no ICT skills) have access to modern public services and to public information of all kinds, b) transparency (corruption phenomena are avoided via digital transactions) and accountability (analysis of public expenditures and of their performance), c) security and privacy (transactions are secured and private information is protected), d) social inclusion and participation in decision making (public opinion is respected and requested by the political leadership), e) cost and time savings for public transactions are established, f) the implementation of and efficient and effective public administration, delivering goods and services to the citizens and to the enterprises in terms of the private sector.

Balanced Scorecard: The balanced scorecard is a strategic planning and management system that is used extensively in business and industry, government, and nonprofit organizations worldwide to align business activities to the vision and strategy of the organization, improve internal and external communications, and monitor organization performance against strategic goals. It was originated by Drs. Robert Kaplan (Harvard Business School) and David Norton as a performance measurement framework that added strategic non-financial performance measures to traditional financial metrics to give managers and executives a more 'balanced' view of organizational performance.

Chapter 6
Images of Citizenship:
A Content Analysis of Local Government Websites in the United States

Michael J. Jensen
University of California, Irvine, USA & Universitat Oberta de Catalunya, Spain

ABSTRACT

Local government websites are the primary place citizens interact with their local governments online. This research presents qualitative and quantitative content analyses of local government websites in the United States. It investigates these websites with respect to the participatory and consumer citizenship roles reflected and structured through their design. The websites are evaluated regarding their usability with respect to consumer and participatory interactions as well as the symbolic content framing users' interactions. While both participatory and consumer interactions were equally accessible in 2003, longitudinal analysis shows that governments are facilitating consumer interactions without a corresponding increase in participatory usability. Additionally, an evaluation of the symbolic content of the websites reveals that almost universally, they emphasize a consumer mode of interactions over a participatory mode of interactions. A detailed qualitative analysis shows that participatory aspects are subordinate to consumer dimensions and that political content is cast to discourage dissenting political interactions.

INTRODUCTION

As the Internet is becoming increasingly integrated in our everyday lives (Castells, 2009), the construction of local government websites has been a public policy for many municipalities (Drüke, 2005). This chapter is a study of how local government websites perform encourage certain modes of citizenship. As Robert Klotz notes, "cities without websites by 1999 were already being seen as behind the times" (p. 101). During the second term of the Clinton Administration, the National Partnership for Reinventing Government began evolving into electronic government (e-government) strategies with the goal of "putting people 'online, not in line'" (AccessAmerica: E-Gov., 2001). Alfred Tat-Kei Ho has found that these principles have filtered down to the local level, noting that his survey of munici-

DOI: 10.4018/978-1-61520-931-6.ch006

pal websites reveals the web designs emphasize "'one-stop shopping' and customer-oriented principles" (p. 434). Mary Maureen Brown and Shannon Schelin note that placing government services online "can potentially lead to advances in government responsiveness and accountability" by improving the "ability to promote visibility and transparency, productivity and efficiency, and horizontal integration" (p. 267). Websites achieve these goals through a hierarchical assemblage of images and text connected through hyperlinks. These link structures form the website architecture while the symbolic elements (text, images, and video) form the content which is ordered by the website architecture. The interrelationship of the website architecture, images, video, and text play an important role in how websites are able to achieve their public policy interests.

This chapter analyses local government websites with respect to their architectures and symbolic content using a sample of American municipalities. The chapter is divided into three sections. The first section considers the background literatures relating to controversies in government website construction from which we will build a framework for coding and analyzing local government websites. The second section presents the data collection and analysis of results in response to the issues raised by the current literature on website construction. This section utilizes a combination of qualitative and quantitative methods to catalogue and categorize websites. The third section presents conclusions and policy recommendations to improve website designs to facilitate participation and good governance goals.

BACKGROUND

Local government websites provide a rich surface to study the implementation of e-government implementation. They are both a tool of public policy and a policy output in their own right. Additionally, there are a number of audiences addressed by a government website. These may include businesses, other government bodies, organizations from civil society, and citizens. As public policy outputs, local government websites are theoretically important for two reasons. First, e-government portals provide the "cultural interface" between governments and members of a political system through their construction of an online scene of interaction between governments and users (Manovich, 2001). Websites can emphasize, marginalize, or omit certain interactions which can thereby define modes of online citizenship from the perspective of the government. Thus websites serve as an authoritative discourse to normalize citizen-government interactions (Edelman, 2001; Mehta, 1998). Second, in contrast to the kaleidoscope of images we receive from the fragmentary information flows communicated through media, direct interactions with government authorities and other networks, local government websites centralize a set of images and information in one place. Websites therefore project the online "face" of government (Chadwick, 2001). This chapter considers local government websites as a policy output in analyzing the images of citizenship communicated to users. It begins with a review of the approaches and findings of previous content analyses of government websites. It then suggests additional considerations for analyzing the spaces of government websites and the spaces within government websites.

Previous studies of local government websites tend to focus on cataloging functions (e.g. West, 2008; Ho, 2002) rather than the structuring of forms of citizen interaction. Generally, scholars have found, as of yet, little emphasis on the promotion of electronic democracy through e-government (Moon, 2002). Julliet Musso and her colleagues find that local government websites in California tend to prioritize consumer functions over political participation (Musso, Weare, & Hale, 2000). Studies of Scandinavian local government websites found similar results with generally easily accessible information retrieval but few mechanisms for input (Baldersheim & Øgård, 2008, pp. 131-132). As a result, it is not surprising that government websites are primarily used for the consumption of government services rather than participation (Jensen and Venkatesh, 2007). Finally, in contrast the stated goal of greater accountability and transparency in local government, there is evidence that e-government systems are surreptitiously collecting of vast amounts of information on citizens regarding their consumption of government services and other interactions (Taylor and Lips, 2008). However, user satisfaction with American Federal Government websites has been steadily increasing in line with advances in website navigability (Freed, 2009).

Murray Edelman famously noted the role symbols have in constructing and organizing political reality (1964, 1988). Governments regularly politicize and depoliticize issues in order to control the demands on the political system (Easton, 1965b, p. 117) and language is the medium in which politicization and depoliticization (Edelman, 1977, pp. 136-139). Websites play a significant role in these symbolic constructions of politics as the website defines a government's online presentation (Chadwick 2001) and prefigures its user as citizen.

The imbrication of images and text form "imagologies" which are a combination of text and images that communicate content to users (Taylor & Saarinen, 1994). Municipal websites translate the architecture of cities into the "electrotecture" of online environments such that, "the public square reappears on the private screen" (Taylor & Saarinen, 1994, Sec. 4, p. 9). The online representation of a city is not neutral. Given that websites are designed to advance public policy goals, they are designed to shape user interactions in particular ways. While local government websites are typically the product of a large number of actors (Brown and Schelin, 2005), we can take the end product of a website as a unified artifact presented to a user, even if it may contain "heterarchies," i.e. different structures of organization and contrasting goals (Adams, 2009, pp. 214-215).

Websites do their work through imagologies to position users as certain types of citizens. How a word or image depicts something always entails what Kenneth Burke calls a "terministic screen." If we take a given text or image as "a *reflection* of reality, by its very nature as a terminology it must be a *selection* of reality; and to this extent it must also function as a *deflection* of reality" (Burke, 1966, p. 45). Hence even otherwise "purely informational" imagologies have a persuasive function as they point our attention to certain elements and orientations by saying "not this, but that." That is text and images represent and they represent in a particular way (Leeuwen, 2001). Websites represent the place of localities online through the use of iconic images and text which also places the website user in relation to that representation (Adams, 2009, pp. 139-144). Therefore the irreducibly aesthetic nature of websites is not incidental, it is essential for achieving public policy objectives as they move website users to carry out certain functions.

Most local government websites are more than just a single page, the link structures organize the elements hierarchically and create spaces or communication topologies between users and website functions (Adams, 2009, pp. 82-83). Not all web pages have the same value as some are orphaned or updated less frequently (Phillips, 2009a). The link structure can impose orderand assess value on websites in three ways. First, it can prioritize certain functions by making some accessible by "clicking" through fewer links or prioritizing some features as a "quick link" on the homepage while leaving others harder to locate. Second, link structures connect objects relationally creating online spatial structures. Third, links can indicate directionally of information flows as information communicated to users or information sent from users to a website.

This chapter analyzes the images of citizenship on local government websites with respect attributes that orient users to consumer or participatory interactions. The idea of citizens as consumers did not begin with the emergence of e-government. It has had a long history in the United States, particularly since the New Deal (Cohen, 2001). These categories are not necessarily antagonistic as websites may have many attributes that support the consumption of services. Additionally, consumption practices may be in some cases considered a political act often called "political consumerism" (Bang, 2007; Stoll & Hoodge, 2004) and government websites employing consumer-oriented aspects may be described as part of a "politics of convenience" (Chadwick, 2003, pp. 451-452).

For this reason we need to be clear in what ways the politics of participation can be distinguished from the politics of consumption. We distinguish actions aimed at consumption and participation with reference to David Easton's political system by defining consumption and participation in terms of their relation to politics. Easton famously defined politics as "the authoritative allocation of values for a society" (Easton, 1953, pp. 129). Participatory actions, therefore, relate to taking part in or seeking to influence the authoritative allocation of values for a society. This includes not only the politics of interest recognition that constitute system inputs, but also participation in the implementation of policy outputs such as organizing a community center funded with pubic grant monies. Local government website may make this possible by providing information on officials, email contact information for officials, and information on policy matters and meetings. Consumer actions relate to the consumption of the values that have been allocated for a society and relate to addressing private rather than public needs. While consumption of government goods and services may create a system feedback or change the environment, which affects the system inputs, we can analytically separate system outputs from inputs (Easton, 1965a). Websites commonly include information on goods and services and some level of interactivity with respect to the consumption of goods or services. These conceptualizations of consumption and participation enable us to classify both participation on the input and output side of the political system as forms of participation and therefore do not exclude political consumerism from the category of political participation. Deciding on and designing services delivered would clearly be forms of participation while making use of services once they have been designed would be more properly a form of consumption.

The analysis presented in this chapter is driven by three research questions:

1. How accessible are the various consumer and participatory elements of these websites? Is the accessibility different for different kinds of cities?
2. Has the accessibility of consumer and participatory elements of these websites changed over time?
3. What is symbolically communicated to users of local government websites?

ANALYZING GOVERNMENT WEBSITES

Methods

These research questions are addressed using a content analysis of 24 local government websites from 12 geographically diverse metropolitan statistical areas (MSAs) across the United States.[1] These areas were selected according to two criteria. First, they are located in areas where there is a relatively high degree of broadband Internet access and use. Given that previous research shows those with broadband are heavier Internet users, these are areas where website local government websites would be in higher demand, *ceteris paribus* (Horrigan and Raine, 2002). Second, the governments were selected, to the extent possible, such that they included a center city as well as a suburb, or exurb so as to ensure variation in the types of governments selected as well as the level of urbanization and affluence in each MSA.

The websites were surveyed with respect to a wide range of functions, attributes, and images. These include the link structures of the websites to access certain functions, the presence or absence of types of images, the text on the front page of the website describing the city, appeals that direct our attention and towards participatory or consumer activities, and prioritization of images, and ideas directed at users. The data on website usability was collected in fall 2003 and spring 2006 in order to provide longitudinal data reflecting at least two fiscal cycles. This will allow us to chart changes in the websites they evolve which is a likely indication of priorities. The remainder of the website data was collected in spring 2006. Apart from the longitudinal analysis, all other analyses are based on the more recent data.

Website usability is significantly related to its navigability and content (Palmer, 2002; Vidrio Barón, 2009)Analyzing the formal structure of the website is a useful tool to ascertain the priority placed on certain functions and features of the website as well as the usability of these features. These categories are based in part on Gibson and Ward's (2000) categories for analyzing party websites. This includes the following website interaction measures: downloading forms, online transactions, email contact, information about authorities, and information about policy (p. 307). These particular features were included in the analysis because they appear on every website in the sample. These categories reflect a view of consumerism as service provision and participation not in terms of representation or deliberation but granular communications which favors a pragmatic rather than idealistic view of online participation (Chadwick, 2009). A second formal element of the website concerns the reading level of the council meeting minutes. This is a measure of the usability of the website to inform users of the business of the city measured by the complexity of a text measured by its average sentence length and the number of syllables per word. This measure is biased in that it underestimates the reading difficulties encountered with the jargonistic language used in bureaucratic and policy circles that are found in the minutes. These elements are minimal in that they do not survey features enabling the customization of government services which may signal a politicization of the consumption of government services. These features were selected since they represent the minimal elements found across the sample at both time points enabling longitudinal analyses.

While certain functions may be readily available on a website, the collage of images and text may not orient users to make use of them effectively. The use of such images is important because while we may not be able to judge the correct course of action in city politics or the proper role of the city as a political site and provider of services, we do recognize an appealing image when we see it (Lilleker, 2006). This goes beyond Gibson and Ward's "'glitz' factor" (2000. p. 308) as it refers to the ability of a website to draw in users, to direct their attention, and move them to engage with the site in specific ways. The website defines users in terms of specific types of relationships they may have and identities they may assume. Because we are not interested in interpretations of website features but only the presence or absence of certain items and features, multiple coders were not used.

Finally, this chapter integrates both forms of structural and symbolic analysis by analyzing in greater detail a paradigm case of the most participatory oriented website. The placement of images, text, animation, and the juxtaposition of objects are all devices by which the website can create meanings and position governments and users in relation to each other. These rhetorical tools are the different devices used to communicate ideas and capture their imaginations. The unit of analysis is the government website as a public policy output rather than the subjective assessments of users. The data analysis presented here does not tell us how users interpret government websites since such interpretations are subject to multiple feedback processes and assessments beyond the website itself (Katz and Lazarsfeld, 1955; Couldry, 2004). Instead, this is an analysis of the rhetorical structure of the website indicating how a government website orients users through its placement of symbols and structural organization.

Measures

Content and navigability are not completely separable as the elements that structure navigation are content and likewise the content can facilitate navigation as the "graphical design, layout, and actual content are prime components of making a page easier to use" (Palmer, 2002, p. 153). We separate navigability and content with respect to the website architecture and symbols that orient users. Navigability is operationalized in terms of the number of "clicks" required to reach a particular element. These include 3 consumer and 2 participatory functions. The three consumer items are: 1) obtaining information about government services, 2) downloading forms to apply for building permits, and 3) processing a transaction (specifically, paying a fine or a utility bill). The participatory elements include information on elected officials and locating the email address of the mayor or council members. All of these items were reachable within 4 "clicks." These values were then coded inversely (0 = 4, 1 = 3…). The participation usability analysis included a third element: the reading level of the city minutes.[2] This item was operationalized using a Flesch-Kincaid formula for readability.[3] The scale measures reading level in terms of grade levels ranging from 1-12. Given that the average American reads at an eighth grade level, this measure, these were recoded such that 8th grade or below = 4, 9th = 3, 10th = 2, 11th = 1, and 12th = 0.[4] Each individual item in the usability analysis ranges from 0-4. These items were aggregated into participation and a consumer scales ranging from 0-12. Higher numbers correspond with greater degrees of usability on the website for each scale.

In addition to the formal attributes of the website, a number of symbolic elements on the website were coded that impact the usability. These were coded with respect to evoking participatory or consumer images of the municipality. Participatory elements included the following items: whether there quick links for contacting government officials, text or images on the front page depicting the government as a site of political activity, instructions on how to participate in the political process, appeals to participate in the political process, and an image representing the city in terms of a political figure or image. These items help frame the government on the website as a political site where people can participate politically—they may even be encouraged to participate. The consumer elements included the following items: whether there were quick links regarding access to services, text or images depicting the city as a place for enjoyment, instructions on how to process a transaction with the government, appeals to make use of government services, and representation of the city in terms of a building or other bureaucratic element which creates distance from the user. Each item was coded as present or absent (1, 0).

Finally a paradigm case is considered examining the municipality with the highest score on the participatory index. This allows us to see how the text and visual symbols interact in context on the website—data which is not easily quantifiable. While the two previous forms of data provide an accounting of the items present or absent on a website or the accessibility of items, the in depth analysis of these two websites allows us to see how the images, text, and link structures work together in context to produce the context of the user interface with a local government online.

Table 1. Consumer and participatory usability index

	Minimum	Maximum	Mean	Std. Deviation
Consumer 2003	2	10	5.75	2.41
Consumer 2006	3	12	8.42	2.06
Participatory 2003	2	10.3	5.72	1.96
Participatory 2006	2	10	5.82	2.20

Results

We first report on consumer and participatory dimensions of website usability. These data indicate the facility of access for participatory and consumer functions of the websites. Before turning to an analysis of the participatory and consumer usability indexes, we briefly note some observations on the reading level of the council minutes. On average, the reading level of the minutes remained relatively unchanged at mid-way through the tenth grade level. This represents a reading level two and a half grades above the capacities of the average American adult (Smith, 1995; Bronson, 1993). Additionally, the minutes tend to omit any content of the political dialogue revealing the arguments for and against a policy and how proponents and opponents respond to each other. The minutes list the order of business, who spoke, and the outcome of votes rather than substantive content of the policy voted on and the positions taken by speakers at the meetings. Only seven of the 24 cities had any information on the policy positions taken by elected officials or speakers before the council.

These scores were aggregated into consumer and participatory indexes. The claim is not that these items empirically "hang" together, indeed they do not.[5] This indicates a significant degree of hybridity between accessibility of consumer and participatory attributes in the structure of the websites. That is, local government websites do not tend to be singularly consumer or participatory oriented in terms of accessibility. Nevertheless, the indexes are a way to describe the degree to which they exhibit attributes of both. These results are displayed in Table 1.

The indexes reveal that in 2003, on average, the consumer and participatory elements on the websites were roughly equally accessible. However, by 2006 this had changed with a notable increase in the accessibility of consumer functions while participatory accessibility remained relatively stagnant. Whether this change is statistically significant we will consider in Table 2.

The participation and consumer usability scales range from 0-12. These were summed for each city independently in 2003 and 2006. Table 2 presents these results along with the longitudinal change in scores along each dimension.

The results indicate that, on average, there has been a general trend towards increasing accessibility of consumer website functionality (+ 2.667) with a relatively small increase in the accessibility of participatory functions (+.092). The greatest change along either dimension is in Arlington, VA, which moved up eight points on the consumer usability scale. While 11of the 24 websites had decreasing accessibility for participatory items, only three decline in consumer usability. Six of the sites did not offer the ability to process transactions in 2003, all 24 now offer that feature. T-tests confirm that the change in the consumer scale is significant at the $p < .001$ level while the change in the participation scale is not significant. This evidence indicates policy changes decidedly favoring the facilitation of consumer interactions without a corresponding increase in the facilitation of participation.

We analyzed a variety of symbolic elements that the websites communicate to the user. These

Table 2. 2003 and 2006 website usability

	Participatory				Consumer	
Government	2003	2006	Change	2003	2006	Change
Arlington, VA	4	5	1	2	10	8
San Francisco, CA	5	6	1	5	12	7
Huntington Beach, CA	5	8.9	3.9	4	10	6
Minneapolis, MN	7.4	7.1	-0.3	5	11	6
Edison, NJ	10.3	8.4	-1.9	3	8	5
Portland, ME	3.3	6	2.7	4	9	5
Alexandria, VA	4	4	0	5	9	4
West Des Moines, IA	6.1	8	1.9	4	8	4
Austin, TX	5	5	0	4	7	3
Brunswick, ME	6.4	5.8	-0.6	6	9	3
Des Moines, IA	6.4	3.4	-3	7	10	3
Georgetown, TX	5	4	-1	5	8	3
Loveland, CO	9	4.4	-4.6	6	9	3
San Mateo, CA	4	4	0	8	11	3
Boston, MA	3.5	5	1.5	7	9	2
Cary, NC	2	3	1	4	6	2
Mission Viejo, CA	3.2	7.7	4.5	6	8	2
Newton, MA	4.5	10	5.5	10	11	1
St. Paul, MN	9	6	-3	5	6	1
Durham, NC	7	10	3	8	8	0
Yelm, WA	9.9	5.6	-4.3	8	8	0
Flemington, NJ	10	7	-3	5	3	-2
Olympia, WA	2.3	2	-0.3	8	6	-2
Ft. Collins, CO	5.1	3.3	-1.8	9	6	-3
Average	5.725	5.817	0.092	5.75	8.417	2.667***

***$p < .001$
t statistics: .143 participatory scale, 4.759 consumer scale.

items were coded as binaries (1,0) indicating the presence or absence of a feature. The extent to which these participatory and consumer features are co-present on these websites was analyzed using a multidimensional scaling (MDS) technique. The technique generates a spatial representation of the joint occurrence of each item such that spatial proximity indicates greater joint occurrence. The results are displayed in Figure 1.

The Rsq for the model is .99238, which indicates the model has a very close fit. These results indicate the data line up almost on a single dimension of participatory and consumer elements. The consumer cluster is particularly tight indicating that websites tend to feature almost all of the consumer items in common. Three of the five participatory items (characterization of the city as a political site, images of political officials on the front page, and appeals to participate in governance) are located fairly close together as well. However, in comparison to the tightness of the consumer items, there appears to be less

Figure 1. Consumer and participatory symbolic content

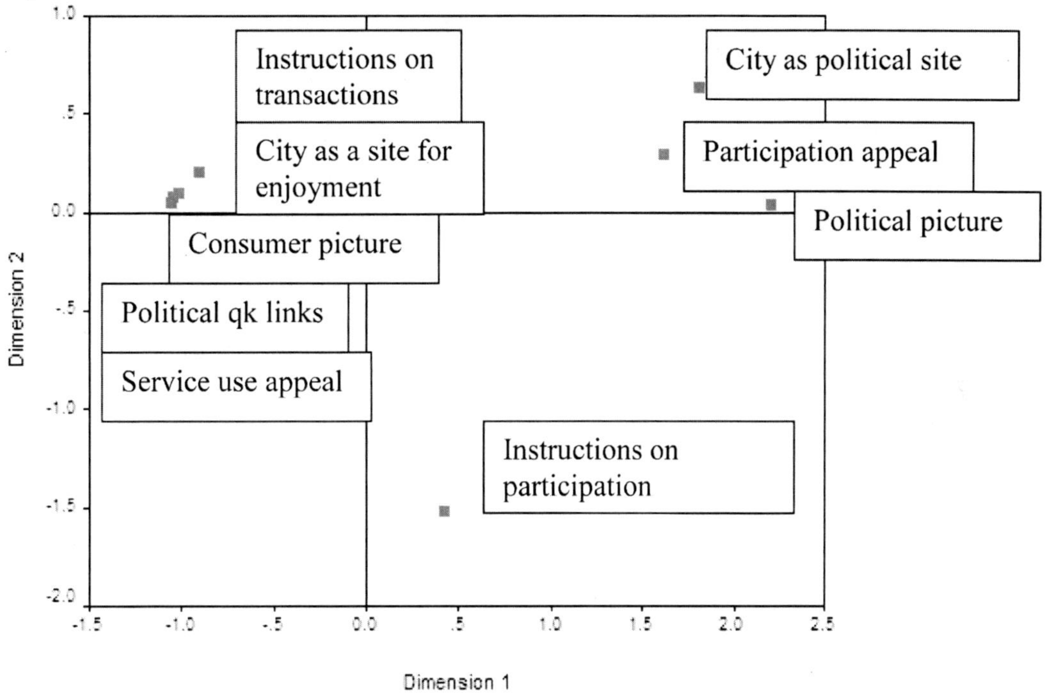

Stress: .05671
Rsq: .99238

of a coherent communication strategy revolving around participatory elements. There are two deviations from the consumer and participatory conceptualizations. One feature, "instructions on how to participate" is an outlier creating a second dimension, it is roughly equally distant from the other participatory items as it is from the consumer items. The second deviation is the appearance of "political quick links" amongst the tight cluster of consumer symbols. For almost every website, if there were quick links for information regarding and access to government services, there would also be quick links regarding information on political officials. In general, however, this result indicates that local government websites tend to have a considerable amount of symbolic coherence either in a consumer or participatory direction.

To identify which orientation tends to have a greater incidence on websites in terms of the variety of symbols displayed, we looked at the ratio of participatory to consumer (p/c) items on average across each of the 24 websites surveyed in 2006.[6] The higher the ratio, the greater the variety of participatory symbols on the website while lower ratios indicate a more consumer orientation. The possible values for p/c range between 0 and ∞. Given that there are an equal number of participatory and consumer elements surveyed for on the websites, a ratio of 1 indicates both are quantitatively equally present. These results are displayed in Table 3.

These results indicate that the websites strongly reflect a consumer-orientation. The average ratio of participatory to consumer symbols is .469. Flemmington, NJ is entirely bereft of participatory

Table 3. Ratio of participatory to consumer elements on municipal websites

Municipality	Ratio
Arlington, VA	1.25
San Francisco, CA	1.00
Cary, NC	0.80
Saint Paul, MN	0.75
Edison, NJ	0.67
Boston, MA	0.60
Yelm, WA	0.60
San Mateo, CA	0.60
Ft. Collins, CO	0.60
Des Moines, IA	0.50
Durham, NC	0.50
Olympia, WA	0.40
Portland, ME	0.40
Alexandria, VA	0.40
Huntington Beach, CA	0.40
Austin, TX	0.40
Georgetown, TX	0.40
West Des Moines, IA	0.20
Minneapolis, MN	0.20
Newton, MA	0.20
Loveland, CO	0.20
Brunswick, ME	0.20
Mission Viejo, CA	0.20
Flemington, NJ	0
Average	0.469444

symbols while Arlington, VA is the only government website with a greater degree of participatory than consumer symbols. This means that while websites may make participatory features relatively accessible (though not as accessible as consumer elements as we saw above), they tend not to enjoin visitors to use those functions nearly as much as they do consumer functions of the websites.

We examined the relationship between the type of government institution and the consumer and participatory functional and symbolic content analyses. Each local government was classified according to its governing structure: mayor-council, council-manager, and a mixed system. The one exception to this standard classification was Arlington, VA, which is an urban county. Since the county is governed by a five member council elected at large and there is an office that functions like a city manager, this was coded as a council-manager system. We analyzed the government structure with respect to the symbolic content and each of the website usability items. None of the relationships proved statistically significant except for the relationship between email accessibility and the type

Table 4. Relationship between government type and email accessibility

	Number of "Clicks" To Reach Officials' Email (Column %)			
Type	**1**	**2**	**3**	**4**
Mayor-Council	3 (60.0%)	4 (36.4%)	3 (42.9%)	0 (0%)
Mixed	1 (20%)	0 (0%)	0 (0%)	1 (100%)
Council-Manager	1 (20%)	7 (63.6%)	4 (57.1%)	0 (0%)
Total	5	11	7	1

$X^2 = 15.177$*
*$p < .05$

of government institution. These results are reported in Table 4.

This result indicates that the email addresses of elected officials in mayor ward systems of government are more accessible than in council-manager and mixed systems. This finding is consistent with what we would expect given mayor ward systems are more centered around ties between the electorate and individual politicians than council-manager systems which were developed as a hedge against a form of electoral politics predicated on personalism. This evidence shows a small connection between the electoral system and a municipality's online communication strategies.

We analyze the Arlington website in greater detail for two reasons: first, it was the only website with a higher participatory to consumer symbol ratio and it also showed the greatest rise in consumer item usability. The emphasis of the approach used here is on the images and tropes that frame the account of the local community and government to the website user. Together, these imagologies create the online cultural interface and structure the user's online experience.

The Arlington website is packed with a wide variety of links on the front page. In addition, there is a fairly comprehensive version of the website in Spanish to increase its accessibility to America's largest linguistic minority. The images presented are relatively small. The dark blue border frames the text and series of links available to website users. The link for information on the County Fair figures most prominently against the white background, its rich color photo making it a hotter media element relative to the blue framing and surrounding text. (McLuhan, 1955, pp. 161-162). The higher resolution of the photo in relation to the other content of the website facilitates the hold of a user's attention by reducing the amount of cognitive work required for attention and comprehension.

The symbolic content analysis gives us a quantitative analysis of the symbolic content, but it does not show us how these symbols direct our attention on the website. Despite the larger numerical presence of participatory items, the website directs a user's attention towards its consumer function. The website prioritizes consumer elements in four ways. First, the quick links that are associated with most of the subsites give a privileged the position of services over "topics, news, calendar, employment, and departments." The news link is a list of Arlington events rather than press releases relating to political matters. This website structure imposes an architecture centered around the service provision function of the website.

Second, there are services enumerated down the right side of the page that facilitate location of specific items. To be sure, the Arlington Council is one of the items accessible via these quick links. However, the same enumeration of participatory interactions is not carried out. There are no links to information on current policy issues, contacting officials, instructions on participating online or offline, etc. Third, the quick links listed down the left top of the site concern either information about living in Arlington or it provides general information about the County for the consideration of persons or businesses considering locating there. This information is practical for selling Arlington as a place to live and work and makes use of the website as a potentially effective marketing strategy to reach consumers (Phillips, 2009b) but a similar effort is not made to market Arlington's politics.

Fourth, the five items that are depicted in the largest font size with colored lettering tend to be consumer items in nature. These items change slightly every few days to reflect new events or issues as they emerge though the orientation of these items tends to be the same. These include the fair, which highlights leisure as an Arlington experience. This item is given the greatest prominence given its location at the top left of the page. The notification of the extension of the grace period for parking permits concerns the regulation of consumption—namely consuming parking as a scarce resource. Such regulation renders parking within a symbolic economy of consumption. Likewise, the application extension for real estate tax relief concerns the regulation of financial transaction with the local government.

Though not as central, there are a number of participatory elements on the site. First, in the top text box, there is a link soliciting public input on the master transportation plan. Second, attention is further drawn to this link by the placement of small montage of images (one of two links on the front page with a high resolution image). The link brings users to a page filled with a number of documents and reports that are written in non-technical language, which unlike many planning commission reports, makes these fairly accessible to the general public. However, this presentation tends to depoliticize transportation planning by detailing policy already decided on at an administrative level, rather than inviting a dialogue between possible alternative options for the transportation plan. This reduces its function as a source of information and facilitates their function as a source of legitimation. Depoliticization is reinforced through an additional statement on the website informing users that, despite its diversity, Arlington is a "community…where people unite to form a caring, learning, participating, sustainable community in which everyone is important." Fourth, there is a section on the front page under topics devoted to community and citizen participation. This section is mostly devoted to participation in community events rather than political participation and includes information on a bicycle race and Hurricane Katrina relief efforts. Finally, the Council is not present on the front page but repressed below. Despite the presence of the quick link to the Council, the political representatives are in no way represented on the front page of the website. This conveys a bureaucratic image of the Arlington County government by locating the elected officials in a recessed, compartmentalized manner.

DISCUSSION AND CONCLUSIONS

The findings presented here indicate that local government websites in the United States generally are consumer rather than participatory oriented. Political engagement is generally not reflected in the narratives of these localities revealed on their websites. To the extent politics is present, it is taken as either something distant and removed for "ordinary" members of the political community or it is presented as consensual in nature, thereby seeking to eliminate dissent in favor of conformity. This section summarizes the above findings and makes policy recommendations directed at improving both the participatory and consumer elements of the websites.

The preceding data analysis indicates that government websites predominantly direct users towards consumer interactions. Consumer activities are generally more accessible on the websites than participatory activities. While many items regarding access to services, processing transactions, or the regulation of consuming government goods are easily accessible from the front page and enumerated individually, most of the participatory functions are buried beneath the websites' front pages. Additionally, the political information that is available in the form of meeting minutes is written such that it is generally less accessible or useful than other information on the website. Further, between 2003 and 2006, we found that consumer interactions became more accessible to users while participatory activities did not. This likely reflects public policy priorities due to the fact that these participatory and consumer features require a revolution in software to produce, in contrast to some online deliberative forums. Additionally, software development is often driven by public policy. Government institutions seeking greater participation or deliberation have implemented such features (Wright and Street, 2007).

Second, there is a greater emphasis on consumer rather than participatory symbols on local government websites. There is a far greater occurrence of elements directing users to the consumption of government services rather than a political form of citizenship. Furthermore, we find greater joint occurrence of consumer symbols on websites than participatory symbols. This indicates that the consumer element is a more coherent image presented to users on government websites than participatory images of membership in the political system.

Finally, we find that the websites subordinate their political elements to consumer concerns. They do this by both prioritizing consumer concerns and by avoiding symbols evocative of political contestation. Consumer functions are facilitated with information, directing users in completing a transaction, these functions are normally easily accessible from the front page almost universally with quick links, and they tend to appear at the top or left side of the front page—locations which users in Western linguistic traditions are most readily drawn to when they first "read" a webpage. Participation on the other hand, receives a lower priority placement and there is less encouragement to participate. Information on policy matters is either nonexistent, particularly technical, or presents the conclusions of government reports rhetorically casting the matter as settled rather than a matter of political contestation. Finally, to the extent there are references to the city as a site for participation, participation is predicated on a politics of consensus (and this was the case on several of the websites)—a move that rhetorically empowers majority opinion against politically disruptive minorities. Political theorists William Connolly and Stanley Fish have demonstrated that this rhetoric of inclusion and other liberal platitudes often becomes a political device of exclusion used against those who challenge majority opinions using majority definitions of "caring" and "sustainable communities" to politically denigrate minority dissent (Fish, 1999; Connolly, 1995).

Regarding both access to services and facilitating participation, local governments might improve their websites using political marketing more effectively. Political marketing is often maligned as a cause of political alienation and a decline in participation as people become disenchanted with constant political marketing (Hay, 2007). However, it could also become a way to reengage members of the political system as governments and officials find better political communication strategies to connect with citizens regarding both political participation and access to government goods and services (Lilleker and Lees-Marshment, 2005).

The idea of the website as a government "portal" which provided "one-stop shopping" was a way to centralize access to governments online. Additionally, since many transactions between citizens and governments traverse administrative boundaries, portals provide a way for seamless interactions with government administration. However, the ease in finding functions may also be advanced through better searching and indexing mechanisms than placing everything on one site where certain functions may end up buried in clutter. Some governments have moved towards better indexing and even de-aggregating governmental portals as they have found users tend to use Google's search engine rather than government pages to find what they are looking for.

Second, websites can include links to additional groups representing different sides on a political issue along with information crafted by the bureaucracy written in a manner accessible to the public. This can give fiscal projections, environmental impact statements, and information outlining the axes in debates when such information is contested. Such input can be useful for political officials as they depend on information provided by individuals and other stakeholders in order to formulate a (Crozier, 2007). Officials can therefore use these inputs to make better informed decisions as well as legitimate decisions based on public consultation. At the same time it can make citizens demands and expectations more realistic by educating them on the difficult tradeoffs and competing interests at stake. Policymakers can directly contribute to this by blogging about particular issues before the council as a means to solicit feedback and educate the public. Additionally, online surveys can be used to provide feedback, updating the government on the level of the website's usefulness enabling governments to improve the sites over time. Such surveys and discussion forums were entirely absent on the websites analyzed at both time intervals. Cities can learn to use the same tools they use to market their cities to businesses to market policy input and discussion to citizens. In doing so, political marketing can become a tool to reengage citizens in local politics.

REFERENCES

Access America. *E-Gov*. (2001). Retrieved December 8, 2003 from http://govinfor.library.unt.edu/npr/initiati/it

Adams, P. C. (2009). *Geographies of media and communication*. Oxford, UK: Wiley-Blackwell.

Baldersheim, H., & Øgård, M. (2008). Innovatgion in e-government: Analysis of municipal web pages in Nordic countries. *Information Polity, 13*, 125–137.

Brown, M. M., & Schelin, S. (2005). American Local Governments: Confronting the E-government Challenge. In Drüke, H. (Ed.), *Local electronic government: A comparative study*. New York: Routledge.

Brownson, K. (1993). Patient Handouts? We're Wasting Our Time. *RN, 56*(7), 88.

Castells, M. (2006). The network society. In Castells, M., & Cardoso, G. (Eds.), *The network society: From knowledge to policy*. Washington, DC: Center for Transatlantic Relations.

Castells, M. (2009). *Communication power*. Oxford, UK: Oxford University Press.

Chadwick, A. (2001). The electronic face of government in the Internet age. *Information Communication and Society, 4*(3), 435–457.

Chadwick, A. (2009). Web 2.0: New challenges for the study of e-democracy in an era of informational exuberance. *I/S: A Journal of Law and Policy for the Information Society* *5*(1), 9-42.

Cohen, L. (2001). Citizens and consumers in the United States in the century of mass consumption. In Daunton, M., & Hilton, M. (Eds.), *The politics of consumption: Material culture and citizenship in Europe and America*. New York: Berg.

Connolly, W. E. (1995). *Ethos of Pluralization*. Minneapolis, MN: University of Minnesota Press.

Drüke, H. (2005). *Local Electronic Government: A Comparative Study*. New York: Routledge.

Easton, D. (1953). *The Political System: An inquiry into the state of political science*. New York: Alfred A. Knopf Publishers.

Easton, D. (1965a). *A Framework for Political Analysis*. Chicago: University of Chicago Press.

Easton, D. (1965b). *A systems analysis of political life*. Chicago: University of Chicago Press.

Edelman, M. (1964). *The symbolic uses of politics*. Chicago: University of Illinois Press.

Edelman, M. (1977). *Political language: Words that succeed and policies that fail*. New York: Academic Press.

Edelman, M. (1988). *Constructing the political spectacle*. Chicago: University of Chicago Press.

Edelman, M. (2001). *The politics of misinformation*. New York: Cambridge University Press. doi:10.1017/CBO9780511612640

Fish, S. (1999). Mutual respect as a device of exclusion. In Macedo, S. (Ed.), *Deliberative politics: Essays on Democracy and Disagreement* (pp. 88–102). New York: Oxford University Press.

Freed, L. (2009). *ACSI E-government Satisfaction Index*. Retrieved from http://fcg.nbc.gov/documents/ACSI_EGov_Report_Q4_2008.pdf

Gibson, R., & Ward, S. (2000). A proposed framework for studying the function and effectiveness of party and candidate websites. *Social Science Computer Review*, *18*(3), 301–319. doi:10.1177/089443930001800306

Ho, A. T. K. (2002). Reinventing local governments and the e-government initiative. *Public Administration Review*, *62*(4), 434–444. doi:10.1111/0033-3352.00197

Jensen, M. J., & Venkatesh, A. (2007). Government websites and political engagement: Facilitating citizen entry into the policy process. In B. Thönssen, et al. (Eds.), *Proceedings of TED conference on e-Government: Enhancing public administration back offices* (pp. 56-65). Linz, Austria: Trauner Verlag.

Lilleker, D. G. (2006). *Key concepts in political communication*. Thousand Oaks: Sage.

Lilleker, D. G., & Lees-Marshment, J. (2005). *Political marketing: A comparative perspective*. New York: Manchester University Press.

Manovich, L. (2001). *Language of the new media*. Cambridge, MA: MIT Press.

Margolis, M., & Resnick, D. (2000). *Politics as usual*. Thousand Oaks, CA: Sage Publications.

McLuhan, M. (1995). Media hot and cold. In McLuhan, E., & Zingrone, F. (Eds.), *The Essential McLuhan*. New York: Basic Books.

Mehta, M. D. (1998). Virtual control and disciplining on the Internet: Electronic governmentality in the new wired world. *The Information Society*, *14*, 107–116. doi:10.1080/019722498128917

Musso, J. A., Weare, C., & Hale, M. C. (2000). Designing web technologies for local governance reform: Good management or good democracy? *Political Communication*, *17*(1), 1–19. doi:10.1080/105846000198486

Needham, C. (2004). The citizen as a consumer: E-government in the United Kingdom and United States. In Gibson, R., Römmele, A., & Ward, S. (Eds.), *Electronic democracy: Mobilization, organization, and participation via new ICTs*. New York: Routledge.

Norris, D. F., & Moon, M. J. (2005). Advancing e-government at the grassroots: Tortoise or hare? *Public Administration Review*, *65*(1), 64–75. doi:10.1111/j.1540-6210.2005.00431.x

Phillips, D. (2009a). The value of online content. Posted to Leverwealth Blog on March 8, 2009. Retrieved April 21, 2009, from http://leverwealth.blogspot.com/2009/03/value-of-online-content.html

Phillips, D. (2009b). The real world of the Internet. Posted to Leverwealth Blog on March 19, 2009. Retrieved April 21, 2009, from http://leverwealth.blogspot.com/2009/03/real-world-of-internet.html

Smith, T. L. (1995). The resource center: Finding solutions for illiteracy. *HRFocus*, *72*(2), 7.

Taylor, J. A., & Lips, A. M. B. (2008). The citizen in the information polity. *Information Polity*, *13*, 139–152.

Taylor, M. C., & Saarinen, E. (1994). *Imagologies*. New York, NY: Routledge.

Vidrio Barón, S. B. (2009). Human-computer interaction: National culture and electronic government website usability. In Chabra, S., & Kumar, M. (Eds.), *Integrating e-business models for government solutions*. Hershey, PA: IGI Global.

Wright, S., & Street, J. (2007). Democracy, deliberation and design: The case of online discussion forums. *New Media & Society*, *9*(5), 849–869. doi:10.1177/1461444807081230

KEY TERMS AND DEFINITIONS

Communication Topologies: The structure of links and nodes between actors that tie them together in communication.

Frontpage: The first page of a website.

Heterarchy: Contrasting structures of organization contained within the same space.

Iconic Image: An image that has become generally identified with an object or event and therefore generally represents it for many. Iconic images normally also evoke an affective response.

Imagologies: The combination of image and text, text as image, and image as text, to communicate ideas.

Political Marketing: The use of marketing strategies within politics.

Semiotics: The study of how symbols create meaning.

Symbols: Typically thought of as words or other characters which communicate by drawing our attention to one aspect an object or event and thereby deflecting our attention from other aspects.

ENDNOTES

1. The full list of these websites can be found in Table 3.
2. The minutes selected were the most recent minutes from either the month of April or May 2006 and September or October 2003. Comparisons with other minutes from the surrounding weeks (not reported here) indicates that each government reports its minutes in a standardized format and that the reading level scores vary at most one grade level between weeks selected.
3. This method calculates the grade level according to the following formula: (.39 x ASL) + (11.8 x ASW) – 15.59 where ASL = average sentence length and ASW = average syllables per word. This figure is fairly crude since it measures individual words and sentences rather than the sentence in a context where it has meaning. Additionally, this measure presumes a native speaker of the language so nonnative speakers may encounter additional difficulties. Nevertheless it is a rough measure that at allows us to make rough as well as relative assessments of reading levels.

4 The values on reading may have decimals. In such cases they were then recoded within the scheme as a fraction of the scale points. For example, a reading level of 11.7 translates into a value of .3.

5 The results of a reliability analysis are not reported here.

6 The ratio was selected rather than an additive scale in order to capture which orientation tends to be the most prominent. A website may have a lot of both kinds of messages and symbols or very few of each. However, in both cases there is not a clear orientation for users on the website.

APPENDIX

Figure 2. Arlington, Virginia official website

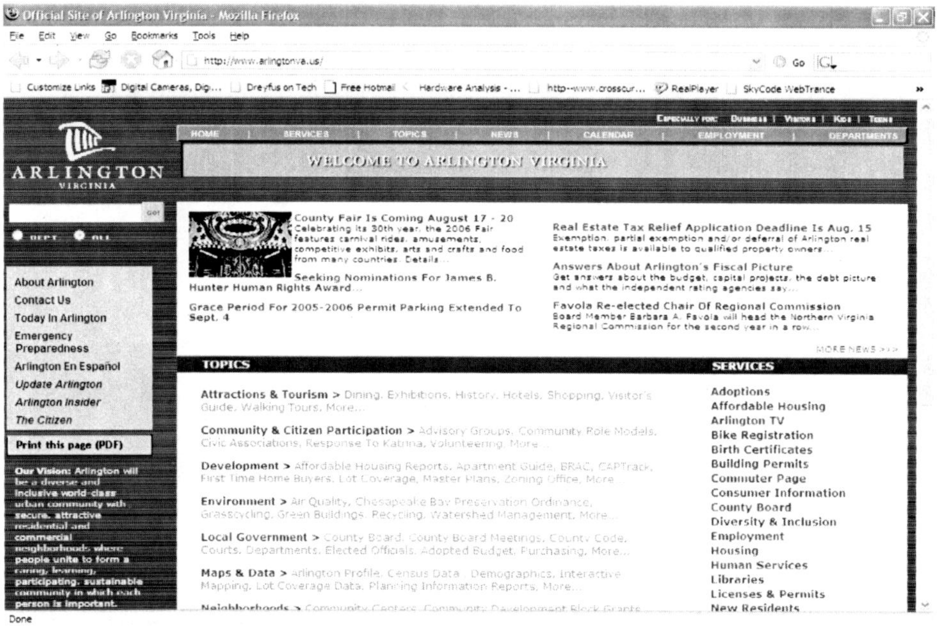

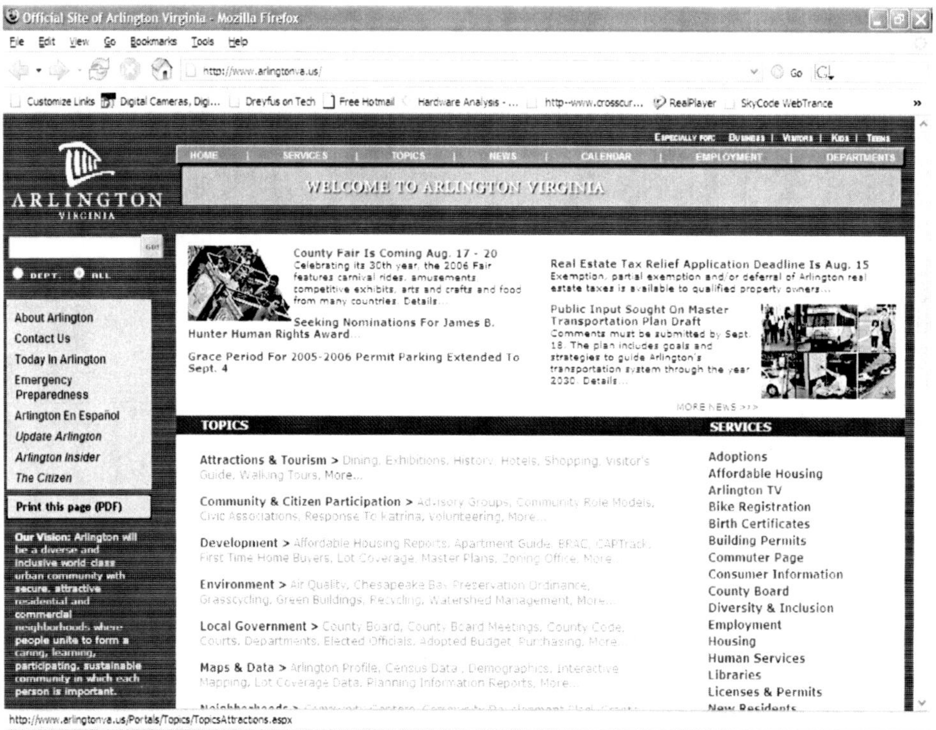

http://www.arlingtonva.us/ (Accessed: May 23, 2006)

Figure 3. Arlington, Virginia transportation plan

http://www.co.arlington.va.us/Departments/EnvironmentalServices/dot/planning/mplan/mtp/MTP_Draft.aspx (Accessed: May 23, 2006)

Chapter 7
Innovation in Democratic E-Governance:
Benefitting from Web 2.0 Applications in the Public Sector

Ari-Veikko Anttiroiko
University of Tampere, Finland

ABSTRACT

This chapter provides a brief introduction to Web 2.0 and its gradual adoption in public services and governance. Web 2.0 refers to the second generation of Web-based communities, networks and hosted services, which facilitates interaction between users. Since the invention of the concept of Web 2.0 version numbering has been attached to various activities and organizations, including government. Government 2.0 opens a horizon towards post-modern governance, in which government utilizes in its governance and stakeholder relations open and pluralist interactivity, community-centeredness and citizens' own content production and networking, following the logic of Web 2.0. The promise of Government 2.0 lies in the idea that the more direct citizen involvement there is in public affairs in Web 2.0 style, the more reason there is for people to take a constructive view of public policies, governance and organizations.

INTRODUCTION

Online communities, social networking and user-generated content production are bringing new elements to the development of electronic government. These new features are based on a new logic of the Web, referred to as Web 2.0. When applied to the public sphere, this idea has been labeled as Government 2.0. This is a new trend that challenges governments to assess their role in society and especially their relationship with citizens.

This article provides a brief introduction to Web 2.0 and its gradual adoption in public services and governance. Attention is directed to the concrete ways of utilizing Web 2.0 applications, on the one hand, and the identification of tensions and challenges associated with this new trend, on the other.

Methodologically this article is a descriptive and heuristically oriented discussion of a novel phenomenon, thus having basically an exploratory

DOI: 10.4018/978-1-61520-931-6.ch007

nature. Early forms of Web 2.0 applications in government are presented as exemplifications of how social networking and user-generated content production have been utilized by public organizations.

BACKGROUND

The core service of the Internet, the World Wide Web (WWW) or more briefly the Web, emerged in the 1990s essentially as the global publication and exchange network utilized by organizations. In the 2000s new forms of online communities, social networking and peer-to-peer content sharing started to change the logic of the use of this global network. These new forms became known as Web 2.0, a concept that was launched by consultants who aspired to map out the then new trends revolving around the Internet. The term appeared for the first time at the O'Reilly Media Web 2.0 Conference held in 2004. (O'Reilly, 2005.)

Web 2.0 refers to the second generation of Web-based communities, networks and hosted services, which facilitates interaction between users. It does not refer to technology as such – i.e. a new technological version of WWW – but rather to the way software developers and end-users use the Web. There are conceptions or approaches to Web 2.0 that emphasize the set of technologies that enable the new forms of interaction within the Web and those that associate Web 2.0 with the semantic Web (Breindl & Francq, 2008, p. 19). Our conception, however, draws on collaborative practices and visions of the Web, thus emphasizing the social dimension of the current trends in the development of the Web. This is the most fruitful approach when assessed from the government perspective.

An indication of the revolutionary nature of Web 2.0 is the nomination of "You" as the person of the Year 2006 by Time magazine, referring to ordinary people who form social networks and provide primary content for social networking and content sharing sites with a magnitude that reached new historic proportions (Grossman, 2006; Dutton, 2007). It was in 2003-2004, roughly ten years after the so-called Great Internet Explosion, when the numbers of subscribers to Web 2.0 applications started to grow exponentially. This shift has created pressure on government to follow the Web 2.0 trends more carefully and to start considering how to utilize the available Web 2.0 applications and particularly how to utilize the wisdom of crowds in the public service and governance processes, which are expected to increase the responsiveness of public organizations. (Anttiroiko, 2009).

There is a need to point out that the use of the concept of Web 2.0 has been criticized on various grounds. The research tradition on Web 2.0 has generally been fairly technology-oriented, even in such socially oriented areas as social network service (SNS) research, the bulk of which has focused on impression management and friendship performance, networks and network structure, online/offline connections, and privacy issues (Boyd & Ellison, 2007). This together with the novelty of the phenomenon explains why critical views are usually generated in blogs and other electronic media rather than in academic journals. Beside the generally held view of the fuzziness of the concept of Web 2.0, there is a lot of social and political criticism on it. For example, some sociologist bloggers and media critics have criticized it for being just another new feature of exploitative capitalism, sometimes labeled Web Capitalism 2.0. Some have also pointed to the underlying undemocratic features of Web 2.0 and the regressive nature of wisdom of crowds propagated by Web 2.0 enthusiasts. (See e.g. Carr 2005; Wilson 2008.) In addition, there have been reservations and concerns among experts, public managers and politicians about the risks of too deep involvement in the Web 2.0 trend in the public sector due to privacy and security risks and capacity problems of public administration (Sternstein, 2006). Even if Web 2.0 provides a lot of opportunities, it may also pose risks that we should be aware of in order to utilize its potential in a responsible and sustainable way.

Many recent trends in technological development have been attached to Web 2.0, from ubiquitous networks to radio frequency identification (RFID), location-based services (LBS) and open source software (OSS). The vagueness of this concept is increased by the fact that some have already started to speak of Web 3.0 due to the introduction of systemic intelligence into interactive Web and information systems (Viitaniemi, 2008; Strickland, 2009). In any case, Web 2.0 refers essentially to the new logic of the Web that revolves around users' networks and user-generated content and related hosted services. To sharpen the picture of the social dimension of this trend, let us next discuss social networking.

SOCIAL NETWORKS AT THE CORE OF WEB 2.0

There are various concepts that depict the social dimension of Web 2.0. One of the essential features of Web 2.0 is the new role of users, users' networks, and user-generated content. In this sense we may see social networking as an activity that is gradually changing the logic of the Web. In reality this process is based on generative interaction between innovative service providers and active end-users. Thus, corporate interests and activities play a crucial role in the Web 2.0 world and in the creation of added value from the critical mass associated with it.

The earlier form of social networking was usually discussed under the concept of online community, virtual community or some similar concepts. They belong to the older generation of Web-based community formations, the two basic forms being non-spatially built *virtual communities* (e.g. Rheingold, 1995) and spatially bound *community networks* (e.g. Schuler, 1996). Yet, in the late 1990s the new forms of social networking emerged gradually starting a new phase in this development, sometimes referred to as Community 2.0.

Social networks, social networking and social network service are fairly recently adopted terms. Social networking is about the building and functioning of online social networks for people who share an interest in creating connections and sharing content. These networks are facilitated by hosted services known as *social network services* (SNS), which can be broadly defined as "Internet- or mobile-device-based social spaces designed to facilitate communication, collaboration and content sharing across networks of contacts" (digizen.org, 2008). Most SNSs are primarily Web based and provide various ways for users to create their profile pages and to interact with each other. They allow relationship initiation and enable individuals to articulate and make visible their social networks. (Boyd & Ellison, 2007.)

The difference between online community or similar terms and social network is more or less arbitrary. The rule of thumb is that that 'community' implies a tighter social bond and inclusiveness than 'network'. The paradigmatic forms of 'community' and 'network' are actually quite different from each other, but they have apparently converged in the discourse on social dimension of Web 2.0. For example, does the large group of the subscribers of Bebo or Facebook constitute an online community or a social network? Is deviantART or WetCanvas a community or a network? Questions like these show that there will be no meaningful clear-cut demarcations between these concepts. If we approach this matter from a pragmatic point of view, we may say that paradigmatic forms of *social networks* are those that focus on human interaction for the purpose of gaining some instrumental benefits from gathering at a virtual meeting place or marketplace, usually associated with friendships, lifestyles and professional life, whereas *online communities* usually refer more dedicated groups of people who share an interest in some creative activity areas, such as art, culture, music, games or video, or in emotionally or ideologically oriented areas in religious or political life. As said, these boundaries are far from clear-cut and the use of these and similar concepts is currently rather vague. (Anttiroiko, 2009).

In addition to social networking the social dimension of Web 2.0 is associated with *content sharing*. These are, in fact, sometimes seen as two basic forms of SNS: profile-based SNS and content-based SNS. In most of the social network sites various kinds of content are published and similarly content-sharing sites include social networking functionalities, which indicates the convergence of social networking and content sharing services. For example, YouTube is based on video sharing, but it also includes selected social networking functionalities, such as user profiles as well as comment and messaging options. Similarly such social network services as Facebook, MySpace, Tagged, Friendster or Netlog provide various features that allow users to share verbal or media content. In their paradigmatic forms content sharing sites focus on sharing written content (diaries, opinions, stories, poems etc.) via blogs or some similar services or media content, be it photos, music, videos, games or webcam views, or as usual, some combination of these.

The technological side of this phenomenon is referred to by such concepts as Web technologies, social computing and social media. What is characteristic of all of them is that they utilize a range of Web technologies and related functionalities such as file-sharing, photo-sharing, video-sharing, music-sharing, blogging, vlogging (video blogging), instant messaging, voice chat, discussion groups, and so on. This field has become a world of services and platforms hosted by such players as Microsoft, Google and Yahoo (global portals for multi-modal social network services), MySpace and Facebook (social networking), Last.fm (personal music), YouTube (video sharing), Wikipedia (reference work), Second Life (virtual social networking), Flickr (photo sharing) and LinkedIn (professional networking), to name just a few well-known examples. (Anttiroiko, 2009.)

A Glance at the Evolution of Social Networking

The idea of social networking cannot be reduced to a web site, even if that is the most obvious manifestation of their emergence. Rather, they are a part of a generational habit related to how people want to interact with each other through social media. It is a phenomenon with literally millions of people networking online for business or pleasure. As most of the SNSs are primarily hosted Web-based services, they do not require the download of software to users' computers, which is another important feature of these sites with the exception of some messengers. webcam and virtual social networking services. (Alford, 2007.) Let us take a brief look at the development of hosted profile-based SNSs, which serves to highlight some key aspects of the emergence of this phenomenon.

The main features of social network Web sites are user profile, list of friends or contacts, private messaging and public comments feature (Boyd & Ellison, 2007). The first site to combine all these elements was SixDegrees, which was established in 1997 and due to its difficulties in becoming a sustainable business, was closed in 2000. In the last years of the 1990s a number of community tools began supporting various combinations of user profiles and publicly articulated friends in such sites as AsianAvenue, BlackPlanet and MiGente. Likewise, shortly after its launch in 1999, LiveJournal listed one-directional connections on its user pages. The Korean Cyworld, which was started in 1999, added social networking features in 2001. A new turn in SNS began when Ryze.com was launched in 2001 to help people leverage their business networks. This aspect became functional a little later, as shown by the success of LinkedIn. (Boyd & Ellison, 2007.) This history is illustrated in Figure 1.

Figure 1. Timeline of the launch and SNS-based re-launch dates of some major social network sites. (cf. Boyd & Ellison, 2007).

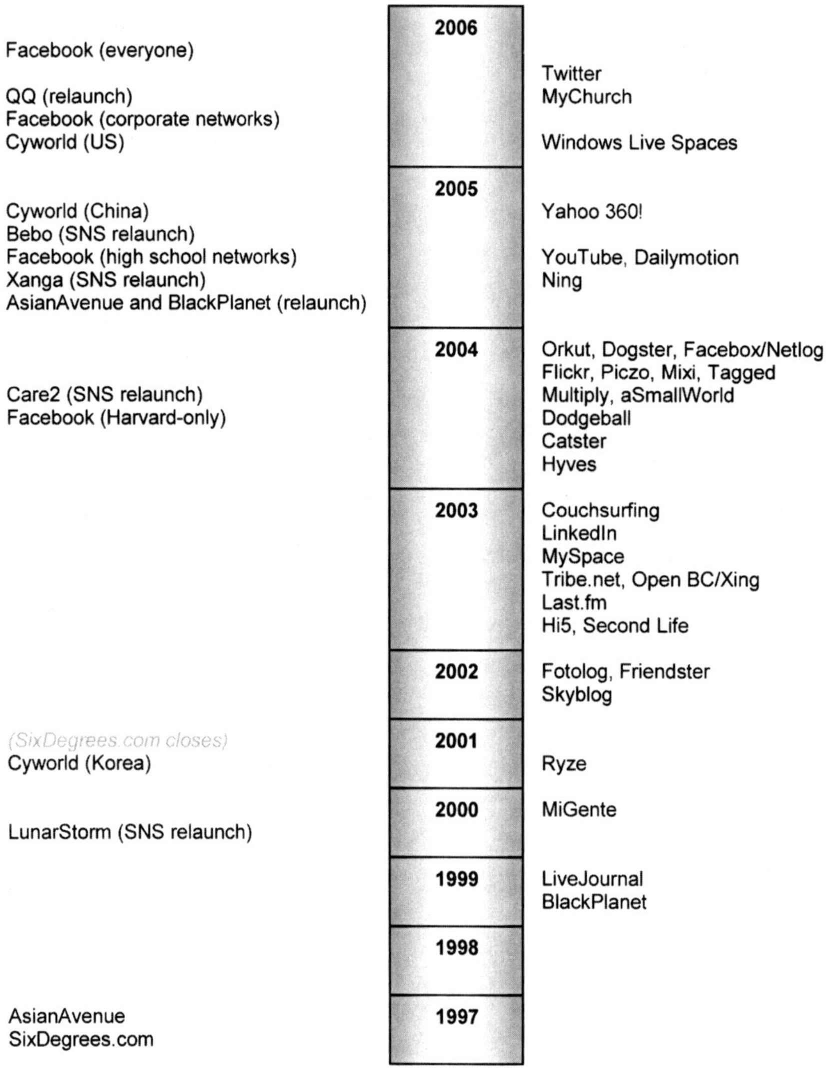

The development of SNSs was rather slow in the early 2000s, until some dramatic changes started to emerge after 2003. For example, in 2003-2004 such popular SNSs were created as MySpace, Facebook, hi5, Orkut, LinkedIn, Flickr, Piczo and Multiply. The fast development continued for several years. (Boyd & Ellison, 2007.) This is the time when social software analyst Clay Shirky (2003) coined the term YASNS ("Yet Another Social Networking Service"), which indicated the mushrooming of new social networking and content sharing sites. At that time many new SNSs took the form of profile-centric sites, imitating the early success of Friendster. Soon this field began to proliferate and diversify, spreading to such areas as professional network sites (LinkedIn, Visible Path and Xing), special interest networks (e.g. Dogster), local and regional SNSs (e.g. Fukuoka Local SNS known as VARRY), "passion-centric" communities (e.g.

Care2 or MyChurch) and peer-to-peer services (e.g. CouchSurfing). Furthermore, social media and user-generated content sharing grew and were integrated with genuine user profile-centric SNS development (e.g. Flickr, Last.fm, Slide.com and YouTube). (Boyd & Ellison, 2007.)

Web 2.0 Applications

As said, what is clearly the most obvious common denominator of different concepts related to the social aspect of Web 2.0 are applications or services, as they are more or less the same irrespective of the direction from which Web 2.0 or SNS is approached or conceptualized. The most widely discussed Web 2.0 applications and services to date are YouTube, Wikipedia, MySpace and Facebook. They are, however, only the tip of the iceberg of the multitude of applications that relate to this conceptual field.

On the basis of the features of Web 2.0 applications the most important Web 2.0-related functionalities are (Anttiroiko, 2009):

- *Social networking*: profile-based hosted services that allow people to create and maintain networks of friends and contacts based on general social interests (MySpace, Facebook, Bebo, Friendster, hi5, Tagged, Ning, Orkut, Netlog, PerfSpot, etc.)
- *Special interest networks (SINs)*: varieties of interest communities and networks in the Web (43 Things, Hobeze, Minti, WetCanvas, WAYN, MyTripz, Dogster, etc.), professional networks (LinkedIn, Xing, Visible Path, etc.), lifestyle and consumerist social networks (Stylehive, Zebo, ALL Consuming, etc.), activism and political movements (GoodTree, Care2, MySociety.org, etc.) and confessional communities (e.g. MyChurch).
- *Media communities and content-based SNSs*: producing, storing and sharing videos, webcam views, photos, music and other content materials (YouTube, Dailymotion, EarthCam, Flickr, Slide.com, imeem, Last.fm, Woophy, etc.)
- *Blogging*: sharing experiences and views using blogs and e-diaries (LiveJournal, Multiply, Blogger, WordPress, e-diary.uk.com, etc.)
- *Reference works*: collecting and sharing generic or thematic knowledge on a peer-to-peer basis in online forums (e.g. Wikipedia and other wiki applications).
- *Sharing opinions, reviews and news*: sharing experiential knowledge, opinions, evaluations and news releases on a peer-to-peer basis using opinion, review and rating sites (Epinions.com, PublicOpinion, etc.), news 2.0 sites (Fark, reddit, Gabbr, Wikio, etc.), alert features and RSS feeds (e.g. Sabifoo combines IM with RSS), social bookmarking (Delicious), short messaging (Twitter) and sharing knowledge and evaluations through user-centric market places and networks (eBay, book reviews in Amazon.com, user evaluations in travel web sites etc.).
- *Collective intelligence*: WWW sites or applications which combine content from different sources, synthesizes such content and utilizes new presentation tools in presenting them to the public, including such applications as mashups (e.g. Digg), map-based or location-based information presentation applications (e.g. EveryBlock, which presents crime statistics and data on Chicago, New York and San Francisco), knowledge networks and follow-up sites (e.g. Public Whip, which watches MPs voting patterns in the UK, or TheyWorkForYou.com, a site which follows the actions of British politicians) or facilitated consumer activism (e.g. MoneySavingExpert.com).
- *Communication services:* global multi-function portals with communication tools (MSN, Google, Yahoo, AOL etc.) and tools

Figure 2. Illustration of the Web 2.0 application field. (Cf. Anttiroiko, 2009).

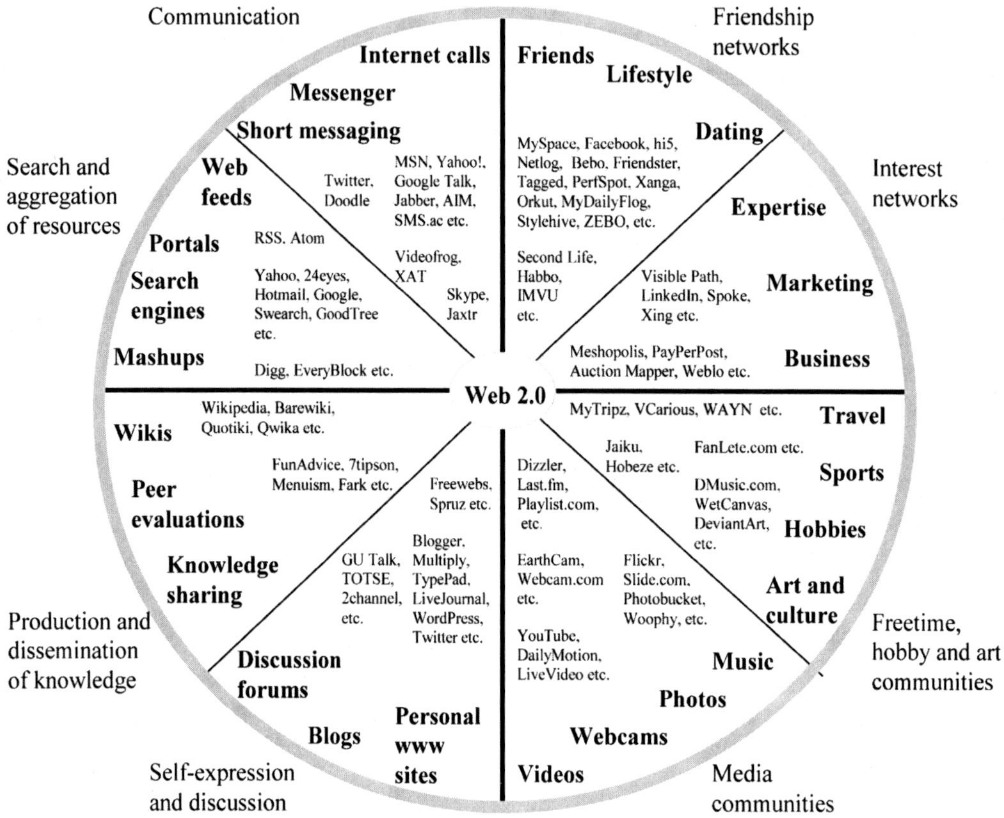

for real-time communication through instant messaging (IM), Voice over IP (VoIP), Internet Relay Chat (IRC) and other tools with a range of supporting SNS functionalities (MSN, Yahoo, Google, ICQ, AIM, Jabber, Skype etc.).

Figure 2 illustrates the field of Web 2.0 applications.

Most of the social networking applications so far offer one or more of the eight features or functionalities: (1) finding people, (2) building directories and social networks, (3) inviting people to join user's network, (4) managing access to user's network ("permissioning"), (5) connecting with people in user's network using various media, (6) managing relationships across media, (7) collaborating with people within user's network, and (8) content sharing with people in user's network combined with other learning, knowledge-finding and knowledge-sharing functionalities. (Pollard, 2006.) These features are a kind of first order networking and content sharing functionalities. In the second order functionalities these features are connected to a higher level of systemic intelligence, thus combining social networking and crowdsourcing with expert systems, location-based services, radio frequency identification and other advances in social informatics.

DIMENSIONS OF GOVERNMENT 2.0

Since the invention of the concept of Web 2.0 and related discussions about new value-adding logic of the Internet, version numbering has been at-

Table 1. Schematic typology of approaches to Web 2.0 for government

Type of e-government regime	Orientation towards Web 2.0 for government	Major reservations	Examples
Reform-oriented e-government	Web 2.0 seen fairly positively as a tool for building interactive public e-governance in the lead of government	Some reservations regarding community-based practices and UGC as they may challenge public authority and professional government services	Germany, France, USA
Managerial e-government	Web 2.0 seen positively as a tool for improving service processes and efficiency along NPM doctrine	Some reservations regarding contributions of online communities and citizens, as such an empowerment may challenge practices based on New Public Management	UK, New Zealand
Open e-government	Open and experimental approach to Web 2.0	Main concerns relate to conventional privacy, security and other risks	Sweden, Denmark
Authoritarian e-government	Negative or suspicious orientation towards the basic logic of Web 2.0	Web 2.0 contains too many areas that are beyond government control	China

tached to various activities and organizations, such as Enterprise 2.0, Media 2.0, News 2.0, Office 2.0, Education 2.0, University 2.0, Community 2.0 and Government 2.0. The overall message is that the work, communication, interaction and transaction logic is changing in all sectors of society and in all kinds of organizations. Public sector is not an exception, even if it has not been in the forefront of this trend. (Hintikka 2007, p. 43.)

The nature of the e-government regime determines how Web 2.0 is approached by governments. A general typology of e-government regimes is based on the nature of state intervention and governance style (interventionist or strong state vs. minimal state) as well as government's approach to information and network architecture (open vs. closed). On this basis Amoretti (2007) presents a four-fold typology of e-government regimes: reform-oriented e-government (or digital state paradigm), managerial e-government, open e-government, and authoritarian e-government. These paradigms determine government's willingness to utilize Web 2.0 tools and applications, as illustrated in Table 1.

At the moment it appears that open, managerial and reform-oriented e-governments are more or less active in introducing Web 2.0 functionalities into their e-government service palettes. Their approach to the utilization of this potential has a slight difference, as the managerial approach emphasizes commercial aspects of Web 2.0, such as consumer feedback and related knowledge processes, and reform-oriented approach places most efforts to internal use of Web 2.0 tools and information services, whereas open e-government approach tends to pay more attention to the democratic potential of Web 2.0. There is need to point out that this typology is only schematic, though, the idea being to show that there are different ways to look at and to utilize the potential of Web 2.0 in the public sector.

Key Functions of Government 2.0

Web 2.0 applications can be divided into two main application areas: (a) internal work and communication processes and (b) external governance and stakeholder relations. In the first area the principles of networking and sharing are applied to the internal organization and work processes of public sector organizations. One of the best-known examples of it is wikis used for storage place for work materials and records management as well as for collaborating and communicating with colleagues (Sternstein, 2006). There are also tools like Doodle for scheduling meetings (http://www.doodle.com/) and messengers for internal communication within an organization. The true

Figure 3. Supporting intersectoral collaboration and intelligence through Web 2.0

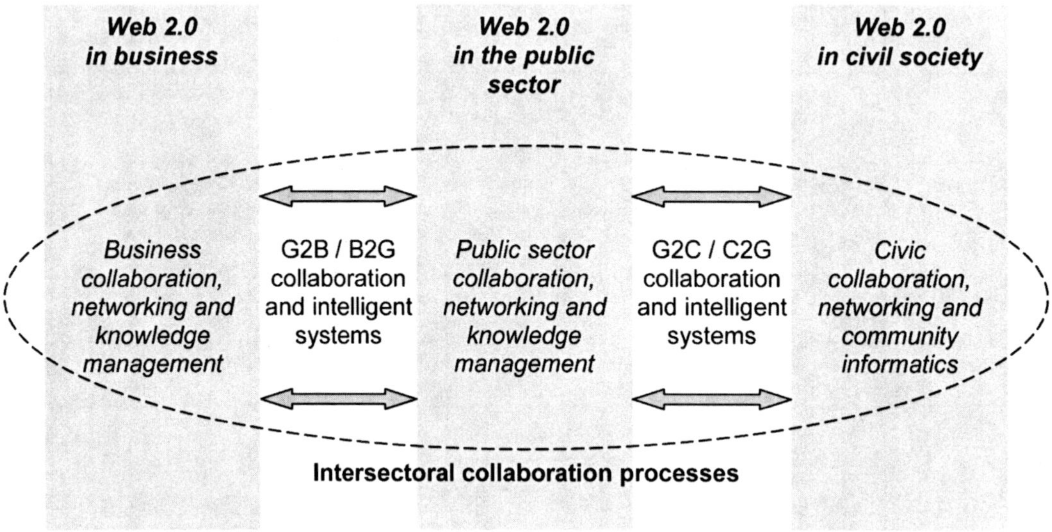

potential of Web 2.0 for government, however, lies in external relationship, service management and governance relations, which are our focus here.

At a very general level the added value of Government 2.0 is created by human collaboration and systemic intelligence. In this sense it is a sum of two fundamental aspects of e-government, which can be labeled as c-government and i-government. Web 2.0 for government is about c-government (c for 'collaborative') because communication, sharing and networking are the core features of Web 2.0 and can be applied to government activities in order to benefit from a broader knowledge base and interaction in service and governance processes (cf. Deloitte, 2008). The other side of this phenomenon is collective intelligence and smart community features, which include such services and tools as mashups, user reviews, RFID and LBS applications. The latter aspect of Government 2.0 can be called i-government (i for 'intelligent'). In the overall development of Web 2.0 for government the former is the more "socially" oriented side in terms of the nature of development efforts whereas the latter is often associated with more technically oriented systems, resembling traditional expert systems applied to collective problem solving that aggregate and process information and create intelligent solutions to collective problems.

These two aspects – internal vs. external applications and collaborative vs. intelligent systems – are combined in Figure 3 to illustrate the potentials of Web 2.0 for various organizational and intersectoral settings.

If we further elaborate this dichotomy and especially its collaborative aspect, we can end up with four fundamental categories of added value of Web technologies applied to users' networks and user-generated content: communication, content sharing, social networking and collective intelligence. These four interrelated areas indicate the ways how government can utilize Web 2.0, as illustrated in Table 2 below.

Inter-Sectoral Sharing in Focus

Government 2.0 is based on the idea of giving users a new role in public service and governance processes by utilizing their social networking and content sharing activities (cf. Osimo 2008). Content production, sharing and utilization processes

Table 2. Social functions of Web 2.0 and their implications for government

Applications / *Functions*	**Paradigmatic Web 2.0 application**	**Examples of Web 2.0 applications**	**Government 2.0 applications**
Communication	Messenger	MSN, Yahoo, AIM	Chat feature in government web site e.g. the State of Virginia
Short messaging and alerting services	Short messaging	RSS feeds, Twitter, Delicious	Government use of RSS feeds and Twitter
Content sharing in hosted services	Content sharing	YouTube, Slide.com, Flickr, Multiply	YouTube and blogs utilized by public organizations
Social networking	Creating and maintaining user profiles and social networks	Facebook, Tagged, Netlog, Friendster, Orkut	Public organizations' presence in Facebook and other social networking sites
Collective intelligence I: aggregated human intelligence	Sharing, aggregating and processing user-generated knowledge	Wikipedia, 7tipson	User-oriented sites such as Patient Opinion (UK) and TheyWorkForYou (UK)
Collective intelligence II: systemic intelligence	Generating and presenting knowledge using intelligent systems	Expert systems and RFID, LBS, GIS applications	Intelligent applications in community informatics (e.g. RFID applications of Seoul Metropolitan Government or crime maps of Metropolitan Police of London)

form a complex setting, which is simplified in Figure 4. The main point is that the collaborative aspect of Web 2.0 is not only about utilizing the content provided by individual service users or active citizens, but about generative production-sharing-utilization (PSU) relations in both intra-sectoral and inter-sectoral areas. Our focus is on inter-sectoral sharing, with citizen-to-government (C2G) and government-to-citizen (G2C) relationships at its core.

Figure 4. Simplified production-sharing-utilization (PSU) model

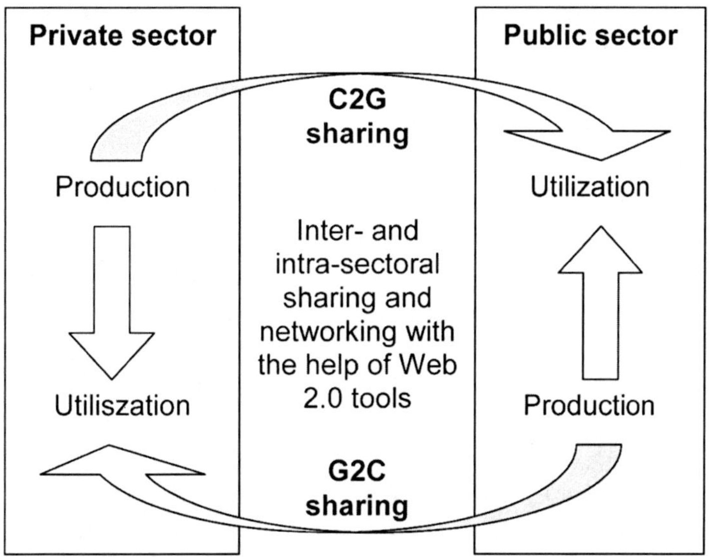

In practical terms, C2G sharing can be about service users' reviews of public services, which are utilized by public organizations to improve their services. Similarly, in governance processes users may generate content or disseminate information – e.g. making evaluations, writing blogs, drafting contributions to reference works and producing media content – that may have a role in shaping public policies or in improving the procedures or outcomes of public governance.

In G2C sharing governments may utilize Web 2.0 technologies in informing citizens and providing them with up-to-date information on what is happening in the public sector, of which good examples are RSS feeds, short messaging (e.g. Twitter) and social networking and content sharing sites. In the last case governments may utilize YouTube, Facebook and similar sites to disseminate information and services to a wide audience. Organization blogs serve the same purpose.

Development Stages of Government 2.0

The maturity of Government 2.0 is about the degree of sophistication in the utilization of Web 2.0 applications. Such a development can be systematized by using a conventional e-government development stage model, which describes a transition from a simple Web presence via interactive and transactional phases to a totally transformed system of government (see e.g. Al-Sebie, Irani, & Eldabi, 2005; Siau & Long, 2005). The steps from a lower level to higher levels of sophistication in the utilization of Web 2.0 in the public sector follow conventional logic of e-government maturity, starting from information provision and alerts and ending up with fully transformed citizen-centered e-government.

In a narrow sense Government 2.0 is increased use of tools like RSS feeds and organization blogs in government Web sites for the purpose of improving communication and information processes between government and citizens. More advanced utilization of the ideas and tools of Web 2.0 reflect a citizen-centric approach to the design and implementation of interaction and transaction processes, including the facilitation of the new forms of peer-to-peer support, new role given to user-generated content and the utilization of mashups and location-based services (LBSs). In the fully-fledged Government 2.0 system most suitable applications and features of Web 2.0 are used extensively and creatively together with intelligent systems, which transforms public organizations and their governance relations and service delivery. (Cf. Hintikka 2007, pp. 44-45; Venkatraman, 1994.) The development stage model of e-government applied to Web 2.0 applications is illustrated in Figure 5.

The development of Government 2.0 is not coherent and linear in the sense that all government activities develop with the same pace. Thus, the development of the key functions of government organizations – political, administrative, service and development functions – may develop asynchronously. For example, planning methods may be advanced in some public organization, but at the same time Web 2.0 may be applied to services only modestly in the very same organization. In general, most of the Web 2.0 applications currently applied by public organizations relate to provision of information, thus reflecting fairly low level of sophistication.

GOVERNMENT 2.0 APPLICATIONS

Even if the concept of Web 2.0 is a new one, similar applications have been used in the public sector for decades. Conventional electronic discussion forums are examples of early forms of e-democracy which reflect the idea behind Web 2.0. The same goes for feedback channels, user evaluations and similar participatory forums and Web services, which started to emerge around the mid-1990s. It was some years later in the

Figure 5. Evolution of the utilization of Web 2.0 in government

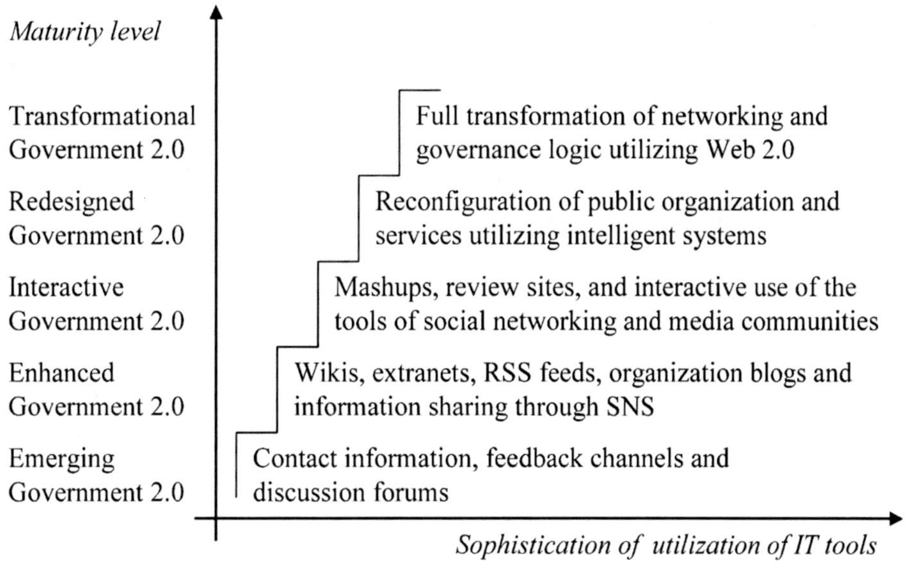

mid-2000s that the emerging logic of the Web gave some novel ideas of the future appearance of e-government. Web 2.0 emerged as an agenda which focused on new trends in Web technologies and especially concrete platforms, software solutions, and applications. The other side of the agenda was built on the social dimension of Web 2.0, reflecting the vision of active and constructive role of user networks and sharing in public governance and services processes.

The development of citizen-centered e-government has been fairly slow in all parts of the world, not least because of the capacity problems of public sector organizations. The other reason behind the sluggish development has been reluctance of key players in the public sector to take the decisive step from a representative system of government towards participatory and direct democracy. The first steps in this field have therefore been fairly conventional, mainly improving the G2C interaction by providing government information in Web 2.0 style.

The Nordic countries have inherent strengths in Government 2.0 due to their transparency and citizen-centric traditions, as exemplified by active development of Government 2.0 by Sweden. The Anglo-American countries also have special strengths due to their innovative NPM-oriented reforms. Another factor that has some relevance here is that in the USA there are a lot of Web 2.0 developers and people who are used to operating in the Web 2.0 environment. In the UK social networking is said to be the most popular phenomenon when compared with their European neighbors. Yet, in all cases, Government 2.0 is such a novel and challenging idea that it is not an integral part of the official governance policy of any government.

Web 2.0 Applications Gaining Popularity in the Public Sector

The most widespread Web 2.0 applications adopted by government agencies to date are basic communication and information sharing tools, such as RSS feeds, Twitter, Delicious and the like, which are useful for facilitating quick communication or short messaging and for keeping citizens informed of government activities.

The other common application area is the dissemination of government information through social networking and content sharing sites, such as YouTube, Facebook and Second Life. The training videos of the British Government in YouTube or the Second House of Sweden in Second Life are examples of this. The Commonwealth of Virginia's Web site is a good example of state-of-the-art Web site, which under the label "Stay Connected" provides links to RSS feeds, Twitter, Facebook, Podcasts and YouTube.

The third area of early adoption of Web 2.0 in government is to disseminate and utilize experiences of service users, such as in the case of Patient Opinion in the UK. This is a paradigmatic area of Web 2.0 applications for government. Yet, the number of such applications is still limited because there is no clear policy on how contributions from civil society can be effectively utilized in the provision of public services without compromising the quality and trust in public services. In any case, such applications, whether initiated by dedicated individuals, associations, professionals or companies, are making a difference in many fields. A good example of this trend is PatientsLikeMe (http://www.patientslikeme.com/), which is dedicated to making a difference in the lives of patients diagnosed with life-changing diseases. It is a platform for a global community of patients, doctors, and organizations that empowers individuals by providing them with access to the tools, information and experiences that they need to understand and to take control of their disease. Similar forums and platforms for service user empowerment and service-oriented collective intelligence are increasing and their potential in supporting the development of public services is enormous.

Lastly, the use of social network services, blogs and video-sharing sites in political debates, campaigns and elections has increased interaction in elections and also 'crowdsourcing' in political life.

Short Messaging

One of the most widely applied Web 2.0 applications in public organizations' Web sites is information services and short messaging in particular. An indication of this trend is that some Irish county councils and several other Irish, Northern Irish, and British government agencies have published press releases using the Nooked hosted online RSS publishing service. In the USA, too, there are many governments that already utilize some aspects of Web 2.0. At the state level a good example is the State of Virginia, which uses RSS feeds not only for alerts, but also as a monitoring service that keeps citizens informed of new resources and services added to the portal. Similarly the State of Georgia provides links to RSS feeds for various topics. (RSS in Government, 2008). Another example of information service is e-mail subscription to the services of the Federal Government of the USA, which provides e-mail notification when any user's favored USA.gov site is updated.

Some government agencies use Twitter, which is a real-time short messaging service that works over multiple networks and devices. In the use of government it provides access to government information. In Twitter the question "What are you doing?" is answered by a short message (less than 140 characters in length) and can be sent via mobile texting, instant messaging, or the Web. The idea is to make it easy for actors to stay connected.

Some governments, such as James City County, use Delicious to make bookmarking of interesting Web sites easier for users (http://delicious.com/jamescity). Delicious is a social bookmarking service that allows users to tag, save, manage and share Web pages from a centralized source. With the emphasis on the power of the community, Delicious improves how people discover, remember and share resources on the Internet.

Chat is not much used in government Web sites, but, for example, the US Federal Government provides a Web Chat option, which offers live personal assistance related to government services. Various departments of the State of Virginia also offer Live Chat.

Content Sharing

In many countries there has been discussion about public organizations' need to increase their visibility in Web 2.0 forums. The main purpose is to provide government information as widely as possible to citizens and user groups in popular forums and in a form that is attractive and easily understandable to users. For example, the results of food inspection, crime prevention and price comparisons or performance assessments of public institutions and utilities could be available in popular content sharing sites in the Web. They have enormous potential in helping to disseminate critical information on public policies and services.

The most widely used content sharing site to disseminate government information has so far been YouTube. An example of Web 2.0 style knowledge sharing is training video prepared in 2006 by the British Government, which was published in YouTube (http://www.youtube.com/watch?v=milFCLGiysI). In the same way Chief Gilbert C. Cruz of the Philippine National Police (PNP) started to use YouTube in 2007 to post anti-crime videos that discussed such topics as ATM scam, date rape, gang activities and anti-kidnapping techniques. (http://www.youtube.com/user/chiefgilbertcruz). They have not gained particularly impressive popularity, but videos like these may well form part of governments' information dissemination strategy, as many users can be reached more easily in YouTube than in the city halls.

Organization blogs are gradually becoming popular in the public sector. For example, the Federal Government in the USA provides information and tips on government issues in Gov Gab blog hosted by six bloggers (http://blog.usa.gov/roller/govgab/).

Government as a Social Networker

Government agencies are increasingly setting up their own sites in social networking services. Facebook gained exceptionally high popularity in the public sector compared with other similar services. Especially many US and UK local governments have subscribed to such services – to Facebook in particular – in order to disseminate information to those who actively use social media. Such sites are seen as a means to provide up-to-date information, news, job announcements and similar information in forums in which especially many younger users are active and in which they concentrate most of their social activities in the online world.

A special case of social networking took place at the beginning of 2007 when Sweden announced a plan to establish a virtual embassy to Second Life (SL). Virtual Embassy was opened in May in the same year. The virtual embassy building – named as the Second House of Sweden – is an almost accurate replica of the House of Sweden in Washington D.C. It is a forum that provides access to information on Sweden, but so far at least neither passports nor visas are available from this virtual forum. The most important function of this virtual embassy is to express the innovativeness and progressiveness of Sweden as an applier of technology. Related to this, it serves to promote a positive image of the country.

Lastly, there is a special form of social networking, local SNSs – sometimes referred to as community SNS, local area SNS, City 2.0 or the like – and wider regional SNSs, which are built around territorial communities of various sizes. Even if most of such services are run by private sector actors, there are also some that are hosted by local or regional authorities. For example, the Gorotto-Yacchiro SNS is a local SNS of Yatsushiro City in Japan, which has been up and running since 2003. Grotto-Yacchiro is a kind of local community site which was made an integral part of the Web site of Yatsushiro City. The site was considerably improved in October 2004 and again in 2005 by the addition of some SNS functionalities. Its development was inspired by Mixi, Japan's then largest social network site which was set up in early 2004. (Shoji, 2007; Toyama, 2007; Yoshida et al., 2008).

Gorotto-Yacchiro SNS was among the first of its kind in Japan, and gave an impetus to the development of community SNS especially with a view to using them for community building and citizen involvement in community development. Soon after the Gorotto-Yacchiro SNS had become a success in this field two experimental projects on local governmental SNS funded by the Ministry of Internal Affairs and Communications (MIC) were undertaken: Chiyoda ward in Tokyo Metropolitan area and the city of Nagaoka. Since then many other followed either with the support of the Ministry or on the basis of local initiatives. (Toyama, 2007). These and similar experiences in different parts of the world indicate that community networks can be integrated with local government Web sites and that local and regional governments are increasingly adding SNS functionalities to their Web sites with an aim at engaging citizens in community building and local development.

Crowdsourcing in Public Service

A paradigmatic example of Web 2.0 style applications adopted by public organizations is the utilization of 'the wisdom of crowds' in different phases of service provision. An example of such an application is Patient Opinion set up to improve the performance of the National Health Service (NHS), the national health service provider in the UK interested in improving its service by utilizing experiences and opinions of service users. In Patient Opinion patients and carers can find out what other people think of local hospitals, hospices and mental health services. People may also share stories of what happened to them or their family when they were ill. While using the system people may give suggestions on how to improve health services relying on their real-life experiences. The stories are sent to the managers of the relevant service providers for reference. The best anecdotes are featured in the Patient Opinion blog.

Patient Opinion has been set up as a not-for-profit social enterprise, i.e. a mediator independent of both the NHS and the Government, which is assumed to help in building trust among service users. It was founded by Paul Hodgkin, a family doctor who wanted to find a way to make the wisdom of patients available to the NHS. Its income is generated mainly by small annual subscription payments, which make the use of Patient Opinion easier and more efficient for hospitals and primary care trusts and many other organizations. (See Patient Opinion at http://www.patientopinion.org.uk/).

Politics 2.0

There are some signs of a tendency of Web 2.0 applications to increase pluralism in society and politics. For example, there are activist groups, such as mySociety.org (http://www.mysociety.org/), a project of UK Citizens Online Democracy, that together with media serve as the kind of watchdogs and channels of civic interests in the political system. TheyWorkForYou is mySociety's most visited site, providing citizens with a range of information on elected Members of Parliament (MPs) and unelected Peers in the UK (http://www.theyworkforyou.com/).

Other slowly emerging areas in which the Web 2.0 logic is gaining ground are urban planning, community informatics and local democracy, as reflected in the concept of City 2.0 or C2. One of its expressions originated in Santa Barbara, where citizens try to make the difference in local affairs by civic journalism and democratic discussions within C2 platform, which includes blogs, local headlines, photos and discussion forums (http://sb.city2.org/).

The early applications of Politics 2.0 or Democracy 2.0 revolve around blogs created to communicate on social and political issues. Blogging has become fairly common among political journalists and politicians. There is a phenomenon of 'influential bloggers', which shows that some bloggers may become extremely popular and have a significant impact on public discussions. The blogs of many journalists, columnists and commentators have gained popularity especially during elections. (Breindl & Francq, 2008). Indeed, blogs have become an integral part of elections and political campaigns, as exemplified by the French presidential elections of 2007 and the Australian federal elections of 2007 (Fraunholz & Unnithan, 2008). Moreover, it is common nowadays for leading politicians to have their own blogs, which are a convenient source for media constantly searching for news on political life. A good example of this trend is Finnish Prime Minister Matti Vanhanen and many other top politicians in Finland, who occasionally appear on national media due to their active blogging. Another example is the use of "mini hompy" (mini homepage), including communication tools and a blog feature, by Korean politicians. A well-known example is Park Geun-hye, a member of the National Assembly and a previous head of the conservative Grand National Party, who has kept a diary and communicated with the public through her Cyworld site (KoreAm, 2005).

Of content sharing sites especially video sharing has become widely utilized in campaigning, such as the use of Dailymotion in the French presidential elections of 2007 and the use of YouTube in various elections in the USA. Such videos include everything from conventional political campaigning to criticism and political satire. (Breindl & Francq, 2008; Fraunholz & Unnithan, 2008; Peña-López, 2008.) Content sharing sites and YouTube in particular are used increasingly as forums for debate on various political issues, representative examples being Senator Ted Kennedy's advocacy of net neutrality (http://www.youtube.com/watch?v=6UlCXXZTTh8), political discussions and breaking news by Bloomberg (http://www.youtube.com/user/Bloomberg), videos featuring dialogue and deliberation events, methods and conferences (http://www.youtube.com/user/sheierbacher), and the public speeches of politicians, such as Barack Obama's victory speech on November 4th 2008 at Grant Park, Chicago (http://www.youtube.com/watch?v=jSABjeD3ecc).

Wikis can be used to exchange views and to discuss political topics, especially as support for already existing communities. Similarly, social network service may find its expression in the form of political networking. Such a virtual SNS as Second Life was even utilized by all four major candidates in the French presidential elections in 2007. (Breindl & Francq, 2008; Fraunholz & Unnithan, 2008). In addition, social bookmarking services such as Delicious, may help citizens to access politically relevant information (Breindl & Francq, 2008). In all, networking and sharing are becoming an integral part of medialized politics and may have a potential to increase citizen involvement. The other side of the coin is the increased speed and personalization of politics, which may well pave the way to superficial democracy.

TENSIONS IN THE WEB 2.0 ENVIRONMENT

Applying Web 2.0 to government operations entails many risks and tensions. One of the shadowy prospects is the possibility of a chaotic relationship between government and citizens in the absence of clear leadership in the process. There are also privacy and security risks associated with dense online interaction and empowered Web users (Peña-López, 2008). It is also worth keeping in mind that besides helping citizens to express their opinions and increasing social inclusion Web 2.0 is also a realm of populism, manipulation, misinformation, and prejudice. This is a reason behind the reservations of the establishment and political elite regarding the development of crowdsourcing and other practices of Government 2.0.

Defining the role of government in the new networked environment is quite a challenge and requires a change in administrative and political culture. It is fairly easy to predict the emergence of Web 2.0 features in government Web sites. In the area of social network services their short-term contribution to public policy is to facilitate the exchange of information and to establish novel collaboration patterns across organizational boundaries (domain-b.com, 2008).

Yet, this trend should also do more to change the role of public administration in society and in the way public organizations work and interact with stakeholders. One critical question is whether civil servants should participate actively in discussions in civic forums and online communities, which are beyond public control. What would be the added value of such activity and, especially, what would be the alternative costs and transaction costs of such a policy? Without tensions such changes will not take place. Especially, a generally negative attitude towards public administration and politics increases sharp and sometimes simply inappropriate comments from the public. This, in turn, increases the psychological costs of such interaction to politicians and civil servants. (See Weiss, 2008).

A good example of tension around Government 2.0 is a social experiment made by the British Government to gain experiences of what people think of the distribution of government information via YouTube. When the training video prepared by the British Government was published in YouTube in August 2006, many users commented that public administration was pushing its tentacles to the realm of civil society. Youtubers presented such comments as "all governments suck." or "Government propaganda here. Ooook, Youtube is no longer safer place...". Such comments indicate broad freedom of speech, but they also indicate problems in public governance and in the stakeholder relations of public administration. (Anttiroiko, 2009). The promise of Government 2.0 lies in the idea that the more direct citizen involvement there is in public affairs in Web 2.0 style, the more reason there is for people to take a constructive view of public policies, governance and organizations.

FUTURE PROSPECTS

Web 2.0 may have either a modest or radical impact on the public sector. If the negative aspects of Web 2.0, the apathy of citizens and capacity problems of public machinery dominate the future development of e-government, there will be little added value from the idea of Government 2.0. In such a case Government 2.0 would mark an improvement especially in alerts and other information services. This is, however, both a most unlikely vision and also leaves most of the potentials of Web 2.0 underutilized.

The most radical views on the potential of Web 2.0 present a vision in which the scope of government activities together with the entire field of actors involved in public governance change. Gartner predicts that in the long-run the execution of many government processes in public finance, health care and education and other services will involve individuals who are neither employees nor contractors. This implies the utilization of networking, volunteering and sponsorships in public governance and service provision.

According to Andrea Di Maio, a distinguished analyst in Gartner Research, "the current global financial turmoil bolsters the case for government adoption of social networks as technology-budget cuts make tapping into societal resources, such as voluntary groups, philanthropists, associations and social network groups essential to complement weaker government action in some critical areas." (Domain-b.com, 2008.) If this takes place, many aspects of Web 2.0 must be reconsidered within the public policy framework. In addition, this development will most likely increase fragmentation and diversification in public service-related fields, which will require new ways of integrating Web 2.0 with public services and governance processes. This will be one of the key challenges to the Government 2.0 trend.

CONCLUSION

Government 2.0 opens a horizon towards postmodern governance, in which government utilizes in its governance and stakeholder relations open and pluralist interactivity, community-centeredness and citizens' own content production and networking, following the logic of Web 2.0.

If Government 1.0 is hierarchical, single channel and input-oriented, Government 2.0 is collaborative, multi-channel and outcome-driven (Deloitte, 2008). Government 2.0 is about determining the scope and nature of future government. It combines two basic elements: collaboration and intelligence, which intersect in crowdsourcing, a paradigmatic form of knowledge creation in Web 2.0 style. In this sense Government 2.0 is essentially about utilizing the experiences and knowledge of individual users and community members in public governance and services.

Utilization of user networks and user-generated content is a shift that has its problems from the point of view of collective action. Paradoxically, public organizations' presence in Web 2.0 forums may give rise to criticism among people. The other problem is how to guarantee that such principles as rule of law, equality and democracy are sufficiently taken into account in Web 2.0-related operations in which governments are involved. Thirdly, there are numerous privacy and security problems that are likely to increase due to Web 2.0 applications, especially in cases utilizing ubiquitous technologies.

REFERENCES

Al-Sebie, M., Irani, Z., & Eldabi, T. (2005). Issues relating to the transaction stage of the e-government system. *Electronic Government, 2*(4), 446–459. doi:10.1504/EG.2005.008334

Alford, B. (2007). *Social Networking and the Changing Face of Communication.* Retrieved May 1, 2009, from http://ezinearticles.com/?Social-Networking-And-The-Changing-Face-Of-Communication&id=843747

Amoretti, F. (2007). E-Government Regimes. In Anttiroiko, A.-V., & Mälkiä, M. (Eds.), *Encyclopedia of Digital Government* (*Vol. 2*, pp. 580–587). Hershey, PA: Idea Group Reference.

Anttiroiko, A.-V. (2009). Government 2.0: Towards interactive and enabling e-government. In A. Kaplan, A. Balci, C. C. Aktan, & C. Dalbay (Eds.), *Advances in eGovernment & eGovernance, Selected Proceedings of the First International Conference on eGovernment and eGovernance*, 12-13 March 2009, Ankara, Turkey (Vol. 1, pp. 51-65).

Boyd, D. M., & Ellison, N. B. (2007). Social network sites: Definition, history, and scholarship. *Journal of Computer-Mediated Communication, 13*(1), 11. Retrieved May 1, 2009, from http://jcmc.indiana.edu/vol13/issue1/boyd.ellison.html

Breindl, Y., & Francq, P. (2008). Can Web 2.0 applications save e-democracy? A study of how new internet applications may enhance citizen participation in the political process online. *International Journal of Electronic Democracy, 1*(1), 14–31. doi:10.1504/IJED.2008.021276

Carr, N. (2005, October 3). *The amorality of Web 2.0.* Posted to Rough Type, Nicholas Carr's blog. Retrieved June 19, 2009, from http://www.roughtype.com/archives/2005/10/the_amorality_o.php

Deloitte. (2008). *Change your world or the world will change you. The future of collaborative government and Web 2.0*. Retrieved May 1, 2009, from http://www.deloitte.com/dtt/cda/doc/content/ca_govt_web20_mar08_EN.pdfdigizen.org. (2008). *What are social networking services?* Retrieved November 29, 2008, from http://www.digizen.org/socialnetworking/what.aspx

Domain-b.com. (2008, October 23). *Citizen social networks may replace some government functions: Gartner*. Retrieved November 29, 2008, from http://www.domain-b.com/infotech/itnews/20081023_citizen_social_networks.html

Dutton, W. H. (2007). e-Democracy: Reconfiguring Participation in Governance and Public Policy. *Journal of Korean Association for Regional Information Society*, *10*(1), 11–26.

Fraunholz, B., & Unnithan, C. (2008). Anti apathy approaches in representative democracies: e-governance and web 2.0 – facilitating citizen involvement? *International Journal of Electronic Democracy*, *1*(1), 51–84. doi:10.1504/IJED.2008.021278

Grossman, L. (2006, December 13). Time's Person of the Year: You. *Time*. Retrieved May 1, 2009, from http://www.time.com/time/magazine/article/0,9171,1569514,00.html

Hintikka, K. A. (2007). Web 2.0 – johdatus Internetin uusiin liiketoimintamahdollisuuksiin. [Web 2.0 – Introduction to New Business Opportunities of the Internet]. TIEKE – Tietoyhteiskunnan kehittämiskeskus ry:n julkaisusarja 28. Helsinki.

KoreAm. (2005 August). Politics As E-Usual. The ubiquitous nature of the Internet is changing the face of South Korean politics. *KoreAm Journal*. Retrieved May 1, 2009, from http://www.koreamjournal.com/Magazine/index.php/kj/2005/august/korea_news

O'Reilly, T. (2005, September 30). *What Is Web 2.0. Design Patterns and Business Models for the Next Generation of Software*. Retrieved May 1, 2009, from http://www.oreillynet.com/pub/a/oreilly/tim/news/2005/09/30/what-is-web-20.html

Osimo, D. (2008). Web 2.0 in Government: Why and How? JRC Scientific and Technical reports, Seville, Spain. EUR 23358 EN – 2008. European Commission.

Peña-López, I. (2008). Towards e-Government 2.0: Review of the 4th Internet, Law and Politics congress – Political Track. In *IV Internet, Law and Politics Congress. Social Software and Web 2.0: Legal and Political Implications*. IDP. Revista de Internet, Derecho y Politica, 7. Retrieved March 20, 2009, from http://www.uoc.edu/idp/7/dt/eng/pena.pdf

Pollard, D. (2006, September 3). *Social Networking: Still Not Meeting its Critical Promise*. Retrieved November 29, 2008, from http://blogs.salon.com/0002007/categories/businessInnovation/2006/08/14.html#a1612

Rheingold, H. (1995). *The Virtual Community. Finding Connection in a Computerized World* (Surfing the Internet). London: Minerva. *RSS in Government*. (2008). Retrieved November 29, 2008, from http://www.rssgov.com/

Schuler, D. (1996). *New Community Networks. Wired for Change*. New York: ACM Press.

Shirky, C. (2003). *People on page: YASNS... Corante's Many-to-Many*. Retrieved July 21, 2007, from http://many.corante.com/archives/2003/05/12/people_on_page_yasns.php

Shoji, M. (2007). *Regional Social Networking Services (SNS) – The Current Situation and the Future Potential*. Center for Global Communications (GLOCOM), International University of Japan. February/March 2007. Retrieved May 1, 2009, from http://www.glocom.ac.jp/e/publications/Shoji_1.pdf

Siau, K., & Long, Y. (2005). Synthesizing e-government stage models - a meta-synthesis based on meta-ethnography approach. *Industrial Management & Data Systems, 105*(4), 443–458. doi:10.1108/02635570510592352

Sternstein, A. (2006, November 20). Web 2.0 for feds. *FederalComputerWeek*. Retrieved May 1, 2009, from http://www.fcw.com/print/12_42/news/96857-1.html

Strickland, J. (2009) *How Web 3.0 Will Work*. HowStuffWorks. Retrieved June 19, 2009, from http://computer.howstuffworks.com/web-30.htm

Toyama, S. (2007) *Local area SNS and community building in Japan*. Communities and Action: Prato CIRN Conference 2007. Retrieved May 1, 2009, from http://www.ccnr.net/prato2007/archive/toyama%20135.pdf

Venkatraman, V. (1994). IT-enabled business transformation: From automation to business scope redefinition. *Sloan Management Review, 35*(2), 73–87.

Viitaniemi, V.V. (2008). Olemme aivan uudenlaisen verkkomaailman kynnyksellä. [We are on the threshold of a novel networked world]. *Kauppalehti* 11.2.2008, Debatti, 12.

Weiss, T. R. (2008, June 17). Web 2.0 and City Hall: What's a local government to do? *Computerworld*. Retrieved May 1, 2009, from http://www.computerworld.com/action/article.do?command=viewArticleBasic&articleId=9099038

Wilson, C. (2008, February 22). The Wisdom of the Chaperones: Digg, Wikipedia, and the myth of Web 2.0 democracy. *Slate*. Retrieved June 19, 2009, from http://www.slate.com/id/2184487/

Yoshida, M., Shoji, M., Yamada, Y., & Minetaki, K. (2007). Analysis of Regional Social Networking Services: Community Participation and Regional Economic Revitalization in Japan. In M. Snaprud & A. Sawicka (Eds.), *T4P '07. Proceedings of the first T4P Conference*, 6 March 2008 (pp. 73-79). Retrieved May 1, 2009, from http://www.t4p.no/conference/conference/proceedings/T4P-proceedings-v5_1.pdf

KEY TERMS AND DEFINITIONS

Blog: (abbreviated from Web log) is a form of Web-based micropublishing, i.e. a Web site designed for personalized content creation and sharing, having typically a form of an online diary. It is a hosted Web service that enables personalized or organizational mass messaging – using text, photos, videos and other types of content – to disseminate diary-type stories on personal life and experiences, news and stories in the manner of civic journalism or continuous follow-ups or reports to internal or external stakeholders or to a wider unidentified audience. The whole formed by blogs is called the blogosphere. Examples of blogging services are TypePad, Blogger, Multiply, and WordPress.

Content sharing: is an activity in which users offer user-generated content or acquired media content to other users in open social networks or media communities.

Government 2.0: is the application of Web 2.0 to government activities. It is a subcategory of e-government.

Crowdsourcing: is the collaborative utilization of the creativity and potential of users in the development of software or Web-based applications or services.

Mashup: is a Web service that gathers thematically related content from various sources to provide an information service to users.

Online Community: refers to a group of people with a strong social bond who primarily interact via a computer network. It is a dedicated group of people who share an interest in some local community (often called community network) or some activity area, such as art, culture, music or videos (often called either virtual community or media community). Online community that utilizes Web 2.0 applications is sometimes called community 2.0.

RSS: (Really Simple Syndication) is a Web-feed format used to publish frequently updated content, such as news or blog entries. It is a service that helps users to stay informed on their favourite Web sites or organizations.

Social Media: is a new media that uses the "wisdom of crowds" to connect and share information and content in a collaborative manner. It is an online media where news, photos, videos, podcasts and other media content are made public and shared via dedicated Web sites. Sometimes a similar kind of activity area is referred to as social computing.

Social Network: refers to online social networks for people who share some interests and activities. Paradigmatic forms of social networks focus on human interaction for the purpose of gaining some instrumental benefits from gathering to some virtual meeting place or marketplace, usually associated with dating, friendships, lifestyles, hobbies, marketing, professional life or business.

Social Network Service: (SNS) can be broadly defined as Web-based service that facilitates civic networking. Such services provide electronic social spaces designed to facilitate communication, collaboration and content sharing across networks of contacts. The most famous SNSs include genuine social networking sites such as MySpace, Facebook, Tagged or Friendster and various kinds of special interest sites. Usually content-sharing sites and media communities, such as YouTube, are also included in this category due to their social networking features.

User Generated Content: (UGC), sometimes user created content (UCC), refers to various kinds of publicly available media content that are produced and shared by end-users, in such forms as video, blogging, podcasting, news, photography, and wikis.

Web 2.0: refers to the second generation of Web-based communities, networking and hosted services, which aim to facilitate creativity, sharing and interaction between users. In spite of the version number, it does not refer so much to Web technologies as to the way software developers and end-users use the Web.

Wiki: is a Web application that allows users to create and edit content in a collaborative manner, usually for the purpose of forming a user-generated systematic set of knowledge, such as work process descriptions, manuals or encyclopedias. A pioneer and currently the best-known example of this service is Wikipedia.

This work was previously published in International Journal of Electronic Government Research, edited by Vishanth Weerakkody, pp. 18-36, copyright 2010 by IGI Publishing (an imprint of IGI Global).

Chapter 8
Reducing the Administrative Burden by Online Information and Referral Services

Josep Lluis de la Rosa
Rensselaer Polytechnic Institute, USA

Mercè Rovira
University of Girona, Spain

Martin Beer
Sheffield Hallam University, UK

Miquel Montaner
Strategic Attention Management, Spain

Denisa Gibovic
Strategic Attention Management, Spain

ABSTRACT

Public Authorities have increasing difficulties in providing timely and accurate information in response to the wide variety of citizens' enquiries to which they are expected to respond. These often require the citizen to be redirected to elsewhere as the query refers to areas of responsibility of other Authorities. This often leads to frustration and wasted time for the citizen, who has to repeatedly explain their query, before obtaining a satisfactory answer. The Information and Referral Services (I&R) are created to help the citizen. This chapter demonstrates how online I&R can help to reduce the administrative burdens while improving the overall quality of service provided, increasing its availability to full 24/7, and significantly reducing the overall cost to the administration. It is shown the case of Community Answers, in Greenwich, Massachusetts, USA, where the online approach has helped to reduce by a third the required to man telephones while the number of calls increased by 25% between 2000 and 2008. That cased is compared with our own experiences with the Call Centre of the city of Terrassa, Catalonia, Europe, where the service with the on-line I&R has attended a third more questions in the years 2007 and 2008

DOI: 10.4018/978-1-61520-931-6.ch008

compared to 2006 without additional costs and similar satisfaction as a result of the adoption of the results of the iSAC6+ European project for the deployment of open source I&R on-line platforms.

INTRODUCTION

Information and Referral (I&R) services provide an important social function describing a unique process of assessment and information-giving that enables people to make informed choices regarding their particular needs and the services that might be helpful to them.

I&R specialists, who are typically public servants, combine skilful questioning and careful listening with sensitivity, support, and guidance to help callers "sort out" their situations and make reasoned and informed decisions. They will identify the agencies/services that are best able to meet the caller's needs and explain the potential outcomes of pursuing one option over another. It is a process that gives individuals a sense of control over their situation. After talking with an I&R specialist, individuals feel much better equipped to make what are often important life decisions.

Many I&R agencies collect data regarding the number and nature of the enquiries they receive, and the information that is used, as an aid to improving the service by identifying gaps in the information available. I&R staff record statistics frequently and forward the pertinent information to the appropriate agencies; we take advantage of this practice in this study.

There are thousands of I&R programs in operation across Canada, the United States, and Europe. In the USA many of these are comprehensive, community-based programs. Others are specialized programs catering to the needs of particular social groups, such as seniors, people with disabilities, children and youth, etc. I&R service providers include non-profit agencies, United Ways, libraries, hospitals, and employee assistance programs.

The most widely accepted definition of I&R is:

"the active process of linking a person with a need or problem with a service which will meet the need or solve the problem." (Croneberger and Luck, 1975)

For example, this type of service would provide detailed information, including the contact information, mailing address, and telephone number for organizations that are able to provide childhood immunizations. There are three basic requirements for an I&R service: creation of a resource file (which we are going to refer as the *database*, or the *I&R database*); distribution of the information; and updating of the file. I&R services were originally created to serve the disadvantaged members of underserved areas, but few have actually served this type of population exclusively.

I&R services are symptomatic of the complexity of the present mode for delivering human services by public administrations, and reflect a relatively conventional response to the problems created by such complexity. As quoted from (Kronus and Crowe, 1971):

"It is suggested that I&R services represent a conventional response because they grew out of the tangle of human services and have evolved essentially as partners and perpetuators of the present complexity of human services. [...] The fact remains that human services remain largely inaccessible to a great number of people who need them. The barriers, such as poverty, ignorance, and prejudice, which prevent the utilization of services, are not easily overcome. .... What appears to be needed is a revolution in the delivery of human services, or the development of an entirely new

approach to their delivery that lies completely outside the present structure."

This assertion, which dates from as early as 1971, is still valid in 2010, especially as the majority of US and EU administrations are planning to go entirely on-line in the coming years. In such a service environment, on-line I&R services will become indispensable. Despite many current citizens being considered digitally illiterate, their collective knowledge and that of society as a whole is very much greater than civil servants generally give credit for, and can be utilized in such a way as to answer many of the difficult questions directly (Howe, 2008). The revolution in service provision that we foresee is based on this, and is mediated by giving tools to citizens in terms of direct access to the I&R information, and letting them improve it.

Furthermore, the new trends of e-government suggest public services going online, in the sense suggested (Garson, 2006), referring e-government as the "*provision of governmental services by electronic means, usually over the Internet*". Garson assumes that e-government is a political curiosity that must be explored discursively with reference to big ideas about power, resources, control and bargaining. And this is our point: *let the information in the administration stored in its I&R databases be shared with the citizens*, who, as Howe claims, as a sort of insiders will contribute with their own experience, with information that will be highly valuable for other citizens, the ones who deserve such a service from their administration. And the benefits of sharing are immense, though the administration might feel some loose of control. For Garson it is clear that e-government will continue to evolve and embrace the crowdsourcing way of dealing with public information, and this is our point of view. Providing I&R services online is aimed at reducing the services' cost, while at the same time expanding their capabilities and effectiveness, as well as citizens satisfaction. These changes are discussed in this chapter. Moreover, this trend will of necessity increase rapidly as both the American and European governments, as already said, aim to go entirely on-line over the next few years.

Our research could be considered as a case of improving the back office of administrations. Back office functions are defined as those areas that support front line delivery of services. Back office definition (Gershon, 2004) includes finance, human resources, information technology, administrative support, legal services, facilities management, travel services, marketing and communication. In our case, the back office is the I&R database that is created from the information provided by the multiple departments that conform the administrations. One of the problems in the research of e-government research into detailed case studies on the one hand and highly abstract theoretical treatises on the other hand (West, 2005). There are a variety of case study publications that focus on particular agencies or jurisdictions. These are very useful, but hard to generalize to a larger universe of cases. At the other end of the spectrum are highly theoretical treatments of e-government that either glorify technology or study it at abstract levels. With either brand of theorizing, it is a challenge for practitioners and policymakers to figure out how to use this information to improve their performance.

Our goal in this chapter is also to bridge the worlds of theory and practice. E-government is a field in which practitioners and theorists need to address one another and share their respective insights. It is important to have clear conceptual frameworks for the analysis of e-government. It also is crucial that these frameworks rest on empirical analysis that actually shows what is happening and what problems need to be addressed.

Consistent with this objective, we look at *two* cases in the European Union (EU) and the United States of America (USA) from the point of view of how are their I&R being improved by going online, focusing on how do they share their I&R information with their citizens through internet.

Then we will find out whether computational linguistic resources strengthen the improvement or in cost or in satisfaction.

WHAT IS THE IMPACT OF I&R DATABASES GOING ON-LINE?

Using automatic answering machines introduces a barrier that prevents citizens from gaining direct interaction with real humans to meet their informational needs. The effect of this is to discourage of further phone calls. A similar effect will also occur when I&R services go on-line. We understand going *on-line* as providing individual citizens direct access to the I&R databases and FAQ (Frequently Asked Questions). The process of I&R services moving online could be accomplished in several ways:

a) Putting some I&R information on the web
b) Letting citizens make directory and other queries through the web using the I&R database
c) Attending to e-mails
d) Using natural language systems to help citizens make their queries directly to an I&R database.

In (a) updating the web with episodic events prevents phone calls. An automated system to assist in the transferring of the database to the web would be desirable. One further possibility is creating and providing a list of FAQs online.

In (b) the web interface has direct query access to the I&R database. This is very useful, especially for local authorities where agendas and city directory queries comprise nearly 80% of citizens' most common questions.

In (c) more sophisticated questions can be answered at times when the I&R service is less busy with incoming calls. This helps to reduce calls and optimizes the work of human agents, who are much better able to organize their workload.

In (d), more sophisticated questions can be answered on-line by making use of linguistic resources (namely with those Question Answering search engines of WebQA, Q-Go, and iSAC, among others). This is an improvement over (b) in terms of access to the I&R database and (a) in terms of the FAQ on the web.

These common approaches range from quite simple to highly complex. We now analyze their impact in two cases, one in America and the other one in Europe. The first Greenwich, Connecticut and the second, is Terrassa, Catalonia. These locations have two I&R services that share the same principle: to answer any question which has some connection to the city/town, regardless of whether it is about local government, other services provided by national or local services, life in the community, or the city in general. Both I&R services went online in recent years, and they have gathered a substantial quantity of data that can be used to understand their impact over the period that their online service has been running.

COMMUNITY ANSWERS: GREENWICH, CONNECTICUT

Greenwich is a town of over 60 thousand inhabitants in the outskirts of New York City. Its population is stagnant, with only 3.9% growth in the last 30 years. Greenwich's I&R service is very peculiar and quite different from the centralized 2-1-1 Connecticut call centre which is provided by the regional community representatives of the State of Connecticut. The Greenwich I&R service, which is known as *Community Answers (CA)*, is run independently from the Town Hall in Greenwich. Roughly 10% of its budget comes from the United Way of Connecticut, and the rest comes from local donors. However, *CA* is providing the service in the name of the whole town. Surprisingly, around 8% of its traffic arises from Town Hall civil servants asking questions about their own institution.

Figure 1. The I&R service in Greenwich, Connecticut accessible at http://www.greenwichlibrary.org/commanswers.htm

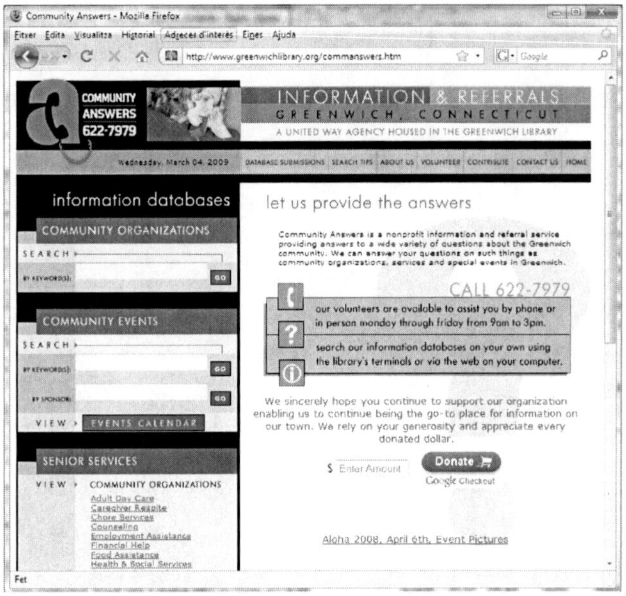

A common practice of American 2-1-1 services is to link volunteers with opportunities and donors with recipients who will benefit from the donation (Dan o'Shea et al., 2004). In most cases, this matching is handled directly by the call centre staff. In some instances, direct referrals are made to an ongoing, community-based volunteer broker. As the benefit estimates suggest, 2-1-1 services offer an enormous potential benefit to society. This is exactly the case of CA: it works with highly motivated volunteers at the phone desk.

CA also has an on-line I&R service (Figure 1).

Figure 2 displays the evolution of questions at CA. This organization had three phone shifts until 2005; shifts were reduced to two in 2006 after the successful addition of on-line information via the sharing the I&R database with citizens on the web. The on-line service, equipped with e-mails and the web, was inaugurated in July 2001. In 2004, a counter was installed on the website to determine how many consultations were performed directly via the web. These actions have provoked a yearly decrease in the number of phone calls.

The burden decreased by 33.3% (one of the former three shifts was discarded) between the years 1998 and 2008 after a 61.5% phone call reduction. In contrast, the number of questions answered grew by 99.8% (i.e., the service nearly doubled the number of answers it provided). The reduction of the number of shifts did not significantly reduce the costs (because CA is a volunteer based service), but it eased management responsibilities, and let the volunteers focus on more complicated, and thus more interesting, questions. Answering more challenging questions also provides a higher added value for citizens, as well as more interesting and rewarding for volunteers. It therefore has a double benefit. It is interesting that the number of questions doubled within the same population, and this statistic provides a rough idea of the service need in the town of Greenwich, as its population, though stagnant, is becoming increasingly digitally literate.

CA in Greenwich has three part-time staff devoted to the organization of the service, recruiting volunteers and donors, searching for

Figure 2. The expansion of service for Community Answers (Greenwich) while reducing phone calls, activity per capita

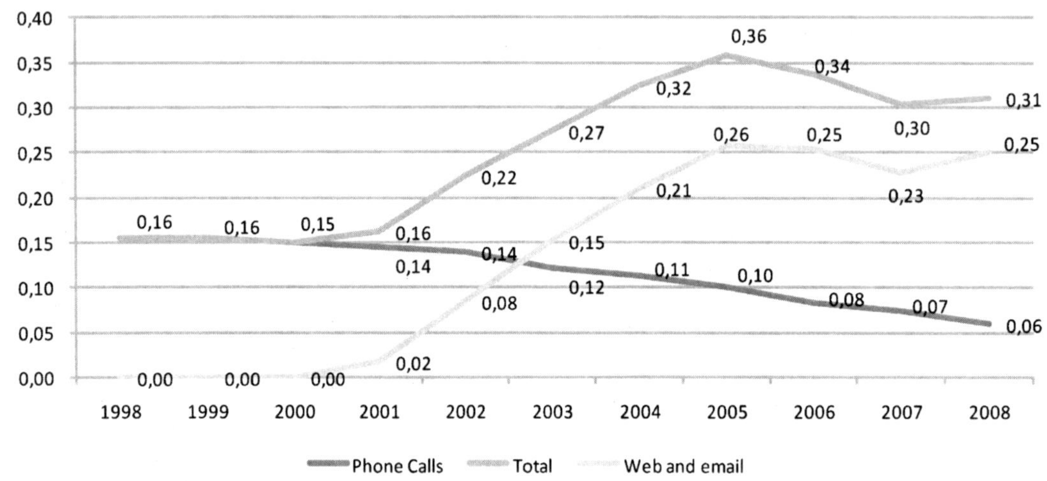

information updates, and tutoring and supervising the volunteers. As at many sites, significant staff effort is spent maintaining the completeness and accuracy of the resource database; these costs are embedded in non-call staff wages and other costs. It is interesting to compare the performance of CA vs. the 2-1-1 service of the State of Connecticut using data from (O'Shea et al, 2004) shown in Table 1. The CA deals with higher rates of calls per inhabitant (11.15% vs. 8.07% of the State of Connecticut) and is fully privately funded, very different from the state service that runs with 100% of governmental funds. It is very interesting to see that though CA is much smaller, its service is much more efficient in terms of the cost per call (US $5.43 per call compared to the state US $13.28) when the on-line and phone services are considered. In fact the CA costs per phone call have reduced nearly 3 times after putting their databases online. Many repetitive and simple calls are avoided by the presence of the on-line service, and the majority of the remaining calls require the human attention of volunteers who can more intensely engage the situation and needs of the caller or provide more complex and specialized services.

So, CA in Greenwich is a small I&R that is more efficient than his homologue at the state level, and part of his efficiency is because of putting his I&R database online apart from recruiting volunteers, citizens, that are entirely in charge of the phone service. CA regarding the state 2-1-1 is of different scale, different point of view, and better results.

SERVEI D'ATENCIÓ CIUTADANA: TERRASSA, CATALONIA

Terrassa is a city of over 207,000 inhabitants in the outskirts of the city of Barcelona. It has experienced a 21.8% growth in its population in the last 10 years. The city has a strong I&R phone and desk service funded by the City Hall that is accessible through a 0-1-0 number. Its model, similar to CA, is to provide citizens with answers to questions about the government and the city.

Between 1999 and 2002, the service counted only calls asking for general information about the city. It already had an on-line web service to answer straightforward informational queries,

Table 1. Comparison in 2004 of the 2-1-1 state of Connecticut I&R and the Community Answers (CA)

	2-1-1	CA phone	CA + on-line
Call volume	281,188	6,937	19,786
Population	3,483,372	62,236	62,236
Ratio Call/Pop	8.07%	11.15%	31.79%
Cost	$3,733,390	$107,418	$107,418
Ratio Cost/Call	$13.28	$15.48	$5.43
Model	Refer/Centralised	Volunteers	Volunteers/On-line
Staff	35	1.5	1.5
Ratio Staff/Call	1: 8,034	1: 4,625	1: 13,191
Funding	100% state	0% state & local	0% state & local

and the impact of this service was observable in the period between 1999 and 2003 with a slight reduction of the volume of phone calls (see Figure 4). In 2003 there was a campaign in the city to promote the I&R service while in 2004 the service was expanded to answer with not only city information but city applications and all administrative procedures, thereby causing an important increase in the volume of phone calls (more than 150%). Then, the consequent large increase in phone call volume and the growing population suggested that further on-line measures were required. The service received over 300,000 calls in 2006, at which point they initiated a full, on-line I&R service utilizing the open source platform for on-line I&R services known as iSAC[2].

The service's 0-1-0 phone call service steadily grew during this period. As shown in Figure 4 over period of 2006-2008, the number of phone calls to the Terrassa I&R service decreased by 17.2%. In contrast, the organization increased its service by answering more than 80,000 new questions per year at any time of any day. This figure represents an increase of the 23.4% in their question answering capacity. Consequently, the cost per question was reduced by 19%.

The online service thus helped to reverse the increasing trend in phone calls while expanding the service so that it was now available 24 hours a day, seven days a week. This I&R service was therefore *always* available while the phone based service was not.

REDUCING COSTS

We have seen two approaches that share the same principle of putting I&R databases on-line. Greenwich and Terrassa both demonstrate that the addition of an on-line service results in significant cost reduction accompanied by an increase in the volume of answered questions. To maintain this impact, it is essential that the I&R service is provided with a continuous stream of updated information. A new problem then arises in how this information is to be provided without increasing backup costs or requiring additional use of the I&R staff.

This problem is key for the adoption of the online I&R, but it is also very challenging and costly. The staff could work on this task full-time but there would still be plenty of missing, incorrect, or obsolete information. Another possibility is to take advantage of the knowledge of citizens or volunteers. This possibility is coherent with our theory of empowering citizens to have direct access to the I&R, not only for consultation but for contributions. To understand how to do this, we must first examine the state-of-the-art in FAQ technology. Then, we will determine how the

Figure 3. The on-line I&R service of Terrassa, with iSAC right in the middle of the screen, accessible at http://isac.terrassa.cat/isac, "Com us podem ajudar" (What can I help you, in Catalan)

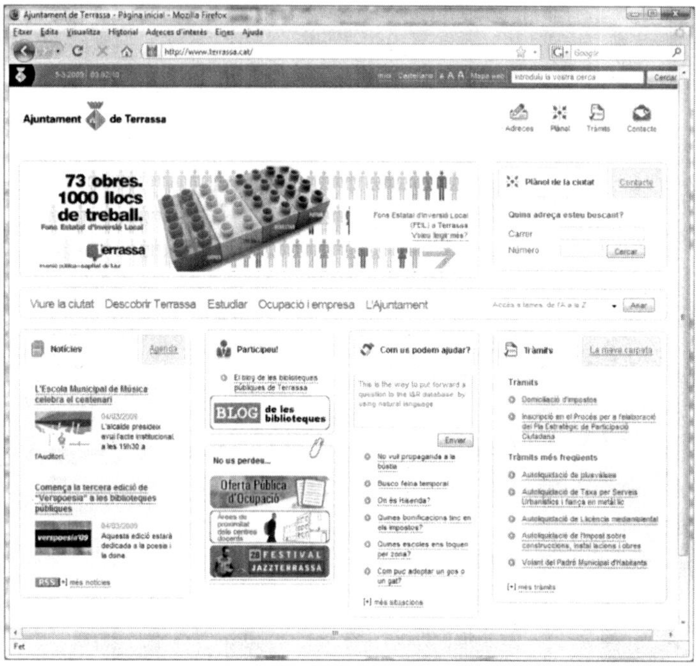

creation of FAQ lists can be assisted by citizen engagement.

A second issue that differentiates the two on-line I&R systems is that the I&R service of Terrassa had linguistic resources in its search engine. Since the on-line service deals with over 80% of the most frequently asked questions (i.e., those regarding the directory and agenda), the questions tend to be simple. They can therefore be expressed in terms of simple keywords and answered using search engines like Google. However, citizens appreciate that a natural language interface is friendlier and provides a higher degree of satisfaction than simple, keyword-based interfaces. A next section will measure the citizens' satisfaction, which though improved it has not yet been translated into, nor measured in terms of cost reduction.

THE UNDERGROUND TECHNOLOGY OF FAQ

A popular way of sharing inquiry-based, I&R information on the Internet involves listing FAQs and their answers on web pages or text documents. FAQ lists remain the most common way of providing answers to common questions online. Many internet-based organizations and corporations will first direct clients and citizens to a publicly available FAQ document before submitting questions to support personnel. This limits the number of redundant questions and reduces the resources spent on support personnel.

The history of so-called "question answering" goes back much farther than computerized systems. One of the most straightforward ways to learn is by asking someone who has intimate knowledge in the field a question. In the course of growing up, children often experience a period during which they frequently ask their parents questions about everything in their surroundings,

Figure 4. The I&R phone and online services in Terrassa, questions per capita

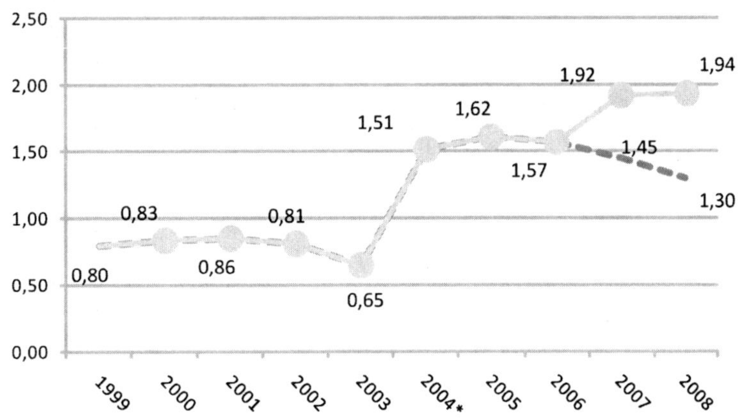

thus building up their knowledge about the world. In addition, there have been extensive studies on rewarding students (O'Brien, 2008) for their questions (Lietaer, 2006), an approach which may be of interest with regard to online Answer Communities.

The Bulletin Board Systems were the first forums to allow answers to questions to be shared across networked computers. These types of systems were hosted on computers connected through a phone network. Bulletin Board Systems (BBS) were popular in the 1970s and 1980s, especially in Europe. The servers hosting the bulletin boards used various methods and protocols to synchronize messages, such as FidoNet (Bush, 1995). The questions asked and knowledge exchanged in these early networks were mostly computer science related. A similar system named UseNet was developed as the Internet became more widely-adopted. UseNet was conceived in 1979 by Duke University graduate students Tom Truscott and Jim Ellis. Users can read and post public messages (called articles or posts, and collectively termed news) to one or more categories, known as newsgroups. Usenet resembles BBS in many respects. The key to Usenet's success was that news servers could be connected to the network very simply and exchange posts using the NNTP (Network News Transfer Protocol) (Kantor, 2004). This was initially achieved using the UUCP network of dialled connections, but this was later superseded by the developing Internet. The key was that when items were posted they would be propagated to all news servers in communication with it and eventually the item would appear on every news server that subscribed to that newsgroup. The number of articles, questions and answers grew exponentially, and today news servers are considered a major knowledge resource for almost any type of information. Various companies, such as Yahoo and Google, have realized that indexing this type of information can make this resource even more powerful. The information available in these archives consists mostly of users submitting questions, which other users, in turn, have answered. A keyword search can be used to quickly locate postings containing answers to common questions. However, locating answers for more specific questions using keyword searches usually requires some effort to analyse of the articles returned by the search. If quality results are to be achieved some practical knowledge is required in the choosing of appropriate keywords. Answers to unusual questions are much harder to find using this method, and the results do not guarantee a correct answer. Ideally, a user should be presented with a single answer, rather than a list of documents. The documents resulting from keyword searches may not even contain the answer, or they may contain false answers. Based on logs from popular search engines, approximately 15% of all queries posted are fully-formulated questions (Liljenback, 2007). The following are examples of typical questions users submit to search engines (Liljenback, 2007):

- What are the top-rated colleges in the USA?
- How many kilograms are 220 pounds?
- How do I lose weight?
- Where can I buy inexpensive but good quality headsets?

In a related work, (Radez et. al., 2002) concludes that when posting complete questions to search engines, correct answers are only returned three fourths of the time within the first 40 returned results. This shows that there is a great need to provide more precise answers instead of merely a list of links to documents that potentially hold the answer. However, the quality of the results for plain text questions is likely to degrade even further if question-answer (QA) systems do not become an integral part of regular search engine technology soon. The reason for this is that it is usually better to type in several well-thought-out keywords that correspond to the question context than an actual question. Plain text questions tend to generate poor results and are even discouraged by certain search engines.

That is why one popular way of sharing inquiry-based information on the Internet is by listing Frequently Asked Questions (FAQs) and their answers on Web pages or in text documents. FAQs originated as a text medium on ARPAnet mailing lists, and later became available on UseNet in the form of "*.answers"-moderated newsgroups. In addition to FAQs, another mechanism for answering questions exists online, namely Answer Communities. Web 2.0 approaches to Answer Communities have blossomed in the last 10 years, with companies like Yahoo Answers! and Answers.com encouraging individual users to participate in personal knowledge exchanges (or "answers"). In addition, knowledge management has become an important strategic initiative for some enterprises (Davenport et al., 2001). Organizations have implemented Internet-based applications and supported virtual communities to promote knowledge-sharing across internal organizational boundaries (Alavi and Leidner, 1999) (Davenport and Prusak, 1998). Knowledge management programs typically involve activities in different areas and are driven by different perspectives on knowledge. These range from human resource initiatives and organization design initiatives to information systems-focused efforts. A critical challenge plaguing these initiatives involves designing appropriate incentive mechanisms to foster the knowledge exploration and exploitation processes (Drucker, 2001). Market-based institutions offer promising mechanisms to evaluate knowledge and to design incentives to motivate and support valuable knowledge transfer (Malhotra, 2002).

As mentioned in the introduction, Internet-based exchanges have emerged that support the buying and selling of knowledge assets in the context of asking and answering questions. While web sites such as eBay have demonstrated the viability of the auction model for well-specified goods and services, it remains a question at this time whether similar mass markets can be created for intangibles that are difficult to specify and appraise prior to their exchange.

Personal knowledge exchanges are defined as market-based arrangements used to trade knowledge assets. Personal refers to the fact that the entities involved in the exchange are individuals, and reflects the often "personal" nature of knowledge. Industry reports use the label "P2P e-commerce information exchanges" to describe this kind of business, with revenues as high as billions of dollars per year ; these reports assert that the aggregation and identification of experts, the efficient categorization of knowledge databases and adequate pricing models are the critical factors for success in this industry (Datamonitor, 2000).

Also related, studies such as (Gosain, 2003) have tried to answer the following two questions:

(1) What are the key challenges in supporting the exchange of personal knowledge within web-based marketplaces?
(2) How can personal knowledge exchanges be designed to overcome these challenges?

Table 2 shows several approaches available at the time (Gosain, 2003) was published, which was prior to the existence of Yahoo or Google Answers. These approaches intend to address challenges such as how to build up a critical mass of questioners and answerers (that is, knowledge asset buyers and sellers, respectively), how to encapsulate that knowledge, how to ensure answer quality and build up trust, and how to establish a "price" with regard to the answering (that is, knowledge exchange) process.

Personal knowledge exchanges are a promising institutional development, and even the search engine site Google had launched an (unsuccessful) exchange to facilitate the discovery of hard-to-find knowledge. Google's knowledge exchange was interesting in that it was intended to complement Google's other knowledge sources, including its search engine that (already) mined knowledge available on the Web, its Usenet newsgroup forums that connected focused communities, and its Web directory that started with a collection of Web sites selected and ranked according to importance by volunteer editors. The design of Google's service reflected a model that included features used previously by ExpertCity and InfoRocket (see Gosain, 2003). In their approach, pre-screened experts provide an understanding of complex knowledge needs, are able to better situate the knowledge in the user context, and can convey tacit elements of knowledge that automated search engines cannot. Furthermore, the inclusion of experts allows for the creation of new knowledge through interaction between users and experts. While Google had a flow of visitors whom it could involve in building a critical mass of users and experts, it had to overcome initial trust and quality concerns. It tried to address these through a rigorous screening process and rating and feedback mechanisms. In their approach, the experts were free-agents, not enrolled in any particular organisation.

DRAWBACKS OF FAQ TECHNOLOGY

A FAQ document has several drawbacks in comparison to an interactive Question and Answer (QA) system. If the FAQ is too small, the questions are unlikely to cover sufficient breadth of the topic. A small size is positive in that it enables readers to quickly determine if their questions are covered. A large FAQ set, on the other hand, can be intimidating to read and is not always guaranteed to provide the correct answer. Sometimes, larger FAQ sets will be covered in several documents, each dealing with a more specific area or topic. This can provide some structural advantages, but makes it harder to search for specific keywords relating to a question, as the user may not be familiar with the hierarchy used to organize the FAQs. Another problem with a static FAQ set is that *there is no straightforward way for an I&R specialist to determine the types of questions citizens are actually asking*. This can be solved by providing some sort of feedback, such as email. However, the citizen typically looks for an immediate answer for their question and will search elsewhere before submitting any feedback. If feedback were to be provided, an administrator could theoretically refine the FAQs based on empirical knowledge as to the types of questions being asked most frequently.

Table 2. A comparison of approaches to challenges of Answer Communities cited from (Gosain, 2003)

	HotDispatch	ExpertCity	Soapbox	InfoRocket
Building a critical mass of buyers, sellers, and knowledge assets	Tie-in to developer communities such as Sun's Java community	Tie-in to technology—vendor customer support needs	Tie-in to Motley Fool's financial community	Mostly organic growth driven by breadth of areas covered
View of knowledge	Encapsulated in explicit exchanges of information, software code	Need to support exchange of tacit information through rich interaction	Encapsulated in documents supplemented by interactive exchanges for clarification and for monitoring reputation	User driven—could be professional advice, software code, etc.
Ensuring quality and building trust	Buyer and seller ratings Deep profiles about expertise	Ratings and pre-screening	Ratings, limited pre-screening, informal message board-based mechanisms Deep profiles on expertise and link to message board	Ratings, improve quality through re-use incentives Pre-bidding process
Price setting	Buyer-driven	Supplier-driven	Supplier-driven	Buyer-driven
Knowledge source	Synthesized from multiple solutions presented	Generated through interaction between subject and expert	Derived from explicit base and interactions around it	Explicit question and answer

One of the greatest drawbacks with static FAQ sets is that users are not given the option to ask free-form questions; rather, they are forced to rephrase the question in such a way that it matches the information available. Since citizens can be considered a type of insider, they may best understand and answer the questions of other citizens, then we expect to utilize citizens to answer each other. If storing the questions and answers, this will lead to complete FAQ sets that contain answers to virtually *any* question. A system that uses FAQ is combined with QA (question – answer) resources to conform a question answering machine shown in Figure 5.

The most important systems currently using the FAQ approach for I&R services are: WebQA[3], Q-Go[4], Artificial Solutions[5], IntelliResponse[6], and iSAC[7]. WebQA and IntelliResponse operate in America and the others in Europe. The main difference among these systems is that iSAC, installed in the city of Terrassa, addresses the main problems of FAQ lack of completeness. First, it crawls[8] inside the organization to search for information; then, it allows citizens to participate in the information exchange process, by providing with any information that helps citizens with their day to day problems and enables them to fully participate as members of their democratic community. It is information pertaining to the availability of local services such as health care, financial assistance, housing, transportation, education and childcare services; as well as information on recreation programs, clubs, community events, and information about all levels of government. This is what is called *community information* (Pettigrew, 1996).

The *Community Answers* of Connecticut also provides community information, though it does not have any self organized capability, so can be considered a directed community. We suggest that those communities which provide self-organizing capability to provide assistance to other members of the city/town, such as iSAC in Terrassa are much better in allowing citizens to freely interact. The question then becomes: how to empower citizens so that they generate the questions and answers that fill the FAQ?

Figure 5. Generalized question answering machine, as proposed by (Liljenback, 2007)

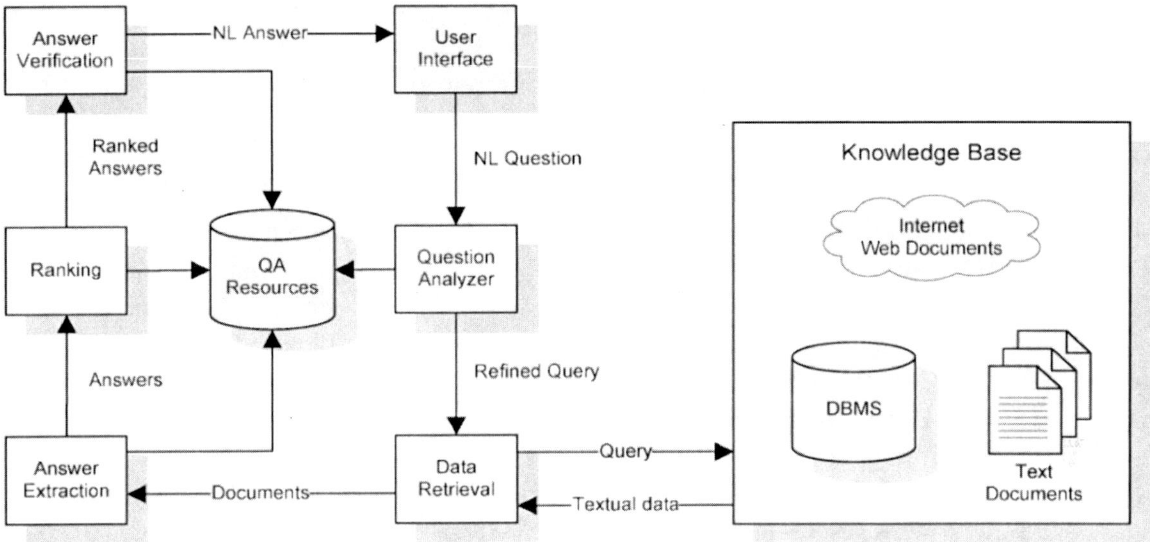

THE COMMUNITY SOLUTIONS FOR SOLVING THE DRAWBACKS OF FAQ TECHNOLOGY

Despite the successes of both iSAC and CommunityAnswers in delivering community information using the FAQ approach there are still considerable weaknesses that need to be addressed if the service is to be of maximum benefit to all citizens. (Sneiders, 1999) reports that FAQs have been traditionally presented as lists of answers which users have to scan to find the solution to their problem. This leads to a number of issues as it assumes that users all have similar issues that they wish to resolve, and that they can identify potential solutions easily when they are presented to them. In particular, users do not have the opportunity to ask any questions of their own. They are required to search among a long list of pre-canned questions until they find the one that comes closest to their problem, if one even exists at all. This is because the information provider does not know the actual questions that are currently being asked. They therefore answer the questions that they suppose that users might ask, or collect together answers to questions that have previously been answered, or a combination of the two. This leads to poorly organised lists with inadequate indexing, making it very hard for a user, who is unfamiliar with the language and concept used by the information provider.

When the list is too long or is disorganized, users normally adopt one of two strategies for working with it. They can either read all the questions in it or they can search for the question using a key word. This helps if the list is classified, but there are lists whose classification is ambiguous or the terms are unfamiliar and the users do not know where to look. This is a particular problem with the sorts of I&R systems we are considering as the information providers are typically Authority personnel whose knowledge and understanding is different from the normal citizen posing the question. The two systems discussed in this chapter deal with this issue in rather different ways. The provider might also provide assistance by constructing a list of FAQs within a FAQ. When users choose a question that comes close to their problem, they can find another list of possible questions. The problem with this approach is that the search can become too long if the users have followed an inappropriate branch and continue with the hope of eventually finding the correct answer.

One way in which these problems can be addressed is to allow users to propose their own questions to add to the FAQ. This allows the questions to be formulated and prioritised according to the needs of real users. It can however lead to excessive numbers of questions which may repeat information that is already available in a slightly different form. Careful editing is therefore required to maintain the integrity of the list and to prune outdated or repeated questions. This can be a time consuming process for the organisation that have to allocate significant resources for this task. A much greater degree of flexibility involving both formal and informal mechanisms is called for, many of which are often more horizontal than vertical in orientation. For this reason, government has been viewed by many as collaborative government (Allen et al., 2005). Unfortunately, today collaboration is viewed more as a cost than a virtue – even by many managers and elected officials who routinely espouse the benefits of collaborative activity (United Nations, 2008). Horizontal governance within the public sector must be collaborative to take hold: in the present system, running counter to tradition, creating such mechanisms and a corresponding culture takes time and energies that can paradoxically be seen as vices on the quick action and strong decision-making required to respond to new realities. Similarly, a more participative and consultative form of politics often contradicts how we most regularly frame leadership – as decisive and unwavering. While leadership is a key lens through which the conduct and interpretation of leadership must be understood, it is also a symptom of the larger organizational and managerial paradigm in good currency not only in government but in all sectors. Yet, it is government more than elsewhere that has continued to rely on the foundational pillars of Weberian bureaucracy that include hierarchy, clarity and specialized organization. In this largely vertical world, the interface between formal structures and informal culture creates a reflexive preference for top-down management and process control.

The notion of control is fundamental here to understanding the reframing that must occur. All organizations and institutions require some form of control, but the widening interest in new e-government systems is testament to the need to view control as less a means to shape every aspect of behaviour (i.e. process control) and more a basis for coordinated and shared actions orchestrated on the basis of outcomes and objectives. From the perspective of more horizontal but in reality networked e-government solutions that are the essence of service transformation and effective security strategies, the two fundamental questions that remain stubbornly unanswered include:

- How to motivate public managers to share data and, more generally, to work jointly for the public good; and
- How to understand and influence the range of barriers, from psychological and social to structural, political and technical, that mitigate across cross-agency initiatives (p. 33, Fountain, 2001); and
- How to encourage citizens to contribute with data

Our approach which can help with the problem of maintaining the currency of the information provided is to develop a social environment. These are highly dynamic; virtual span across a broad range of users, and allow rapidly changing collections of resources to be produced. In such environments, personalisation and adaptation are paramount to facilitating effective knowledge construction and information sharing and creating a trusting and motivating atmosphere for members of groups, teams and communities to share and work together seamlessly. By developing such a community, local government officials can work effectively with members of the community to draw together information that is useful to all, without excessive workload burdens. Information is updated rapidly as additional information is added, and outdated information is deprioritised. The problem is that with many government planners emphasizing a vision of electronic government that is technocratic and service-oriented rather than a tool for grass-roots empowerment, system-level transformation has been slow to develop (West, 2005). Regardless of the type of political system, many government officials are conservative when it comes to change. Rather than rushing to embrace new technology, major political and economic interests slow the pace of technical innovation until they can figure out how to make sure their own vested interests are well-protected. This keeps the danger from new technology as low as possible, and forces technology to accommodate existing power structures rather than the other way around. This is especially true when the government officials are concerned about the "quality" of their information when citizens are allowed to dig in and contribute to the I&R database. But as (Howe, 2008) suggests, citizens will outperform the experts in the administration, provided that they have the same privileged access to information, and because citizens will lead the change their administration need to follow and support.

The transformative potential of new technologies has recently been showcased and championed by (Tapscott and Williams, 2007) who invented the term "wikinomics", authors provide thorough accounts of companies and industries fundamentally reinventing themselves in order to adapt to a new era of openness and networking in terms of ideas, information and people. The resulting organizational forms and strategies on display bear little resemblance to the traditional corporate model that dominated much of the preceding century.

At the same time, however, the traditional corporation remains a predominant feature of the business and public landscape, much as hierarchy remains an important organizational reality in any large organization. Other business commentators thus underscore the importance of sustainability and long-term success in an era where all too often new ventures fail to live up to the hype and promise initially surrounding them. For such reasons, the success of Google[9] is the subject of increasing debate as to whether it personifies a new type of company predicated on dispersed innovation and limited control internally or instead whether more traditional forms of order and planning are required in order to ensure a sustainable and profitable expansion over the long term (United Nations, 2008).

The Internet itself is often a key part of the transformation puzzle, as technology enthusiasts champion online connectivity as a foundation for a fundamentally new society (Eggers, 2005). Other observers have been more cautious, pointing out that digital technologies more generally are incremental in reinforcing existing power structures in most societal, economic and political realms (Kraemer and King, 2003). The point is that the web 2.0 is here to change the government (Wyld, 2007) (Eggers, 2005) (Tapscott and Williams, 2007).

About supporting the citizen's leverage for a change in the public information provided by I&R, a recent study on developing communities, to be found in (Kim, 2000) points out that:

"Your community's purpose will evolve, but you need to start somewhere. Plant a stake in the ground and define your initial purpose as clearly as you can. To kick-start your thinking, see if you can identify an ongoing, unmet need that your members have in common and which your community is uniquely suited to address. Participating in this kind of project takes time and effort, and unless you fulfil a real need, your members won't be motivated to keep coming back. As you ponder this, you may find it useful to refer to Maslow's Hierarchy of Needs (see the following **Figure 6***), which can help you focus on the basics, while keeping up with the evolving needs*

Figure 6. The Maslow Hierarchy of Needs

of your members".

People rely on communities in all areas of their lives as we can see in Table 3. In this line, a study carried out in the AmI@work communities by the Computer Supported Collaborative Work (CSCW) research community [AmI@Work] in the Emerging Trends in Collaborative Technologies shows there is a number of Future Emerging Trends which are on the increase, such as based blogging, shared workspace and, last but not least, the wikis (on the increase by 53%). All these areas are of interest to I&R services, as they give a greater understanding of the ways that individuals interact online to solve their problems.

There is a solution in the model included in the research paper by (Moreno et al., 2006) stimulated to develop a virtual community for completing the FAQ in iSAC powered I&Rs. Its model was integrated into the iSAC platform with wikis to edit new answers from citizens, organised by means of knowledge contribution methods (Figure 7). This helps the completion of FAQ by citizens' participation (Moreno et al., 2009) while reducing its construction and maintenance costs. And citizens are satisfied by receiving answers that are better targeted by their own needs. Citizens (as well as experts) can be encouraged to engage in the QA synthesis process by empowering them with tools for answering questions. This makes sense, since first, citizens tend to be best at understanding the problems of other citizens. That is, they are insiders, and they understand the ways questions are posed. Second, they can share their personal experiences as citizens in their answers. This is applicable to questions ranging from very common curiosities to very rare, even personal questions regarding the public administration. As their participation cannot be taken for granted, rewarding mechanisms are explored (de la Rosa et al., 2009) to have theoretical guaranties of the FAQ completion (Moreno et al., 2009)

ABOUT CITIZENS SATISFACTION

In the previous sections we have seen how costs and burden can be reduced while, at the same time, expanding the I&R services. Two questions arose: how can the I&R database be maintained and updated at an affordable cost and keep the level of citizens' satisfaction high when using search engines for their questions. Let us focus on the second question, because it is not really valuable to reduce costs as long as the citizens are not satisfied with the new service. The satisfaction is the final measure of the I&R service, and the real aim at having sustainable on-line I&R services.

There are several measures of citizens satisfaction, namely first how many answers as qualified as "good" out of the total amount of questions put forward, second, how many questions are quali-

Table 3. Area of life and type of community

Area of Life	Type of Community
Family	Extended Family Play group PTA
Work	Workplace Professional Group
Play	Games Hobbies Sports Fan Club
Spirituality	Church or temple Meditation group Bible study group Support Group Drumming Circle
Politics	Political campaign Environmental group

fied as "good" compared to those are qualified as "bad", third, on-line marks from 0 to 10 of the service, and fourth, and indirect measure of the growth of how many people use the service.

Let us see the first measure, as compared fulfilment of on-line I&R vs. call centre and Google. The test consists of a set of questions to measure the satisfaction of citizens (good/bad answer) and compare it the performance (fulfilment) of the online service compared to the call centre (0-1-0 number) which answers at a first shot, when the call centre answers after requiring for further information (a 2nd question), the answers provided by a keyword oriented search engine (Google) digging inside the Terrassa City Hall databases and the general Google. For iSAC and Google search a valid (good) answer is considered if it can be found in the first 20 results page. The test was performed in May 2007 by several people asking to the call centre, to iSAC and to Google a same set of questions.

The output shown in Table 4 is that the online I&R with iSAC was able to match the same level of fulfilment of the call centre (64%) as long as the human agent asked for simple further clarifications and details about the questions put through by the citizens. Google with a 36% could barely reach the fulfilment of the call centre when the human agents asked no clarifications (as of 36%), and got worse when it included global information out of the city of Terrassa (27%, because a lot of "noise" comes in and it affected the ranking of the Google answers). The result was that the online I&R did a very good work, comparable to the human based call centre 0-1-0. The call centre only outperformed the on-line answers when they were allowed to ask further refinement questions, starting a conversation with the citizen. This is the pattern of very difficult questions, of very high added value, that remain for the call centre.

The analysis of the crisp feedback (good/bad) of the questions from January 1, 2008 to April 22, 2009 out of is 117,403 questions with consulted results (if no result is clicked then the question is considered "not answered"). The feedback was of 1.32% of the answered questions, 1,545 answers. The positive answers were 613, a 39.7%. Taking into account that the negative feedback of unsatisfied citizens is from 3 to 5 times higher the positive feedback of the satisfied citizens (Exposito et al. 2003) because the most of the satisfied citizens simply take the information and go without feedback, but unsatisfied citizens are much more willing and active at explaining their bad experience, then the statistics is corrected 3x1, that is the total number of satisfied citizens

Figure 7. Model of iSAC with WikiFAQ inside from (Moreno et al., 2006)

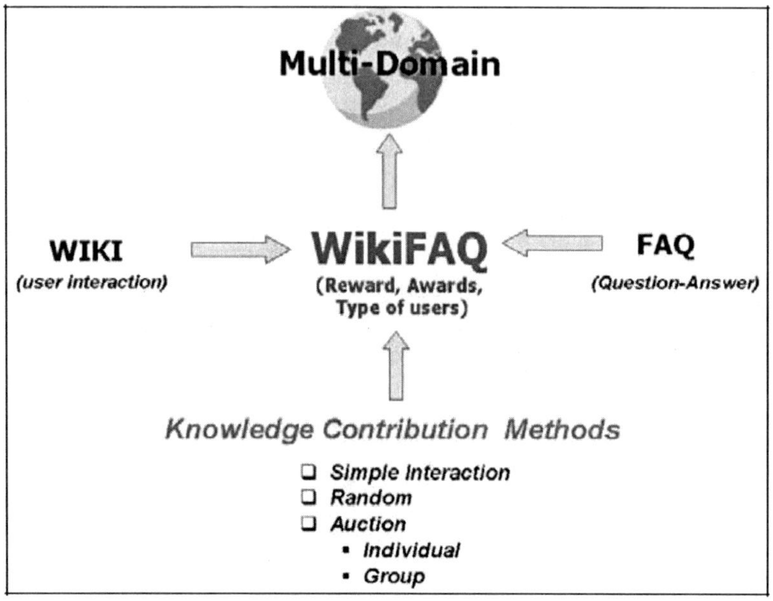

is multiplied by 3. Thus the proper reading of the test is that there are an estimated 66.4% of satisfied citizens.

The average satisfaction of people, measured in the 0 to 10 interval, was an average of 5.9 from May 2008 to April 2009 with a slightly growing satisfaction trend as shown in Figure 8. This result is given by 4,301 citizens who gave a numerical feedback, representing the 3.39% of the questions made in the period.

The number of questions of the online I&R service, rose from 70.914 in 2007 and 103,000 in 2008, that is a 45.25% of growth. This gives an indirect idea of the success of the service.

In conclusion, the satisfaction of the on-line I&R is comparable to the 0-1-0 call centre and sustainable through time. This sustains the core value proposition that the on-line I&R are able to answer the questions of citizens while reducing costs and burden of the public administration. However, there are aspects that have not being measured in this chapter as for example the usability and comfort of having 24/7 the I&R service. As an approximation, according to the iSAC statistics toolbox (see Figure 9) nearly 20% of questions are put forward out of the office time of the 0-1-0 call centre (from 8h to 20h), and in holidays. This is another symptom of the utility of such a service.

CONCLUSION AND FUTURE WORK

The transformative potential of new collaborative technologies can be used by administrations to fundamentally reinvent themselves in order to adapt to a new era of openness and networking in terms of ideas, information and people. The resulting organizational forms and strategies bear little resemblance to the traditional models that have dominated much of the past century. We have seen two cases of significant cost reduction accompanied by an increase in the volume of answered questions by sharing the I&R databases (as a sort of back office) with citizens, who have direct access to the information and can even contribute with further information.

The difference between the two on-line I&R systems discussed in this paper lies in the fact

Table 4. Comparison of iSAC (online I&R) vs. the call centre, and Google

	% fulfilment
Call center answers at one shot	36%
Call center aks for further information to answer	64%
iSAC answers at one shot	64%
Google Searches only inside the City Hall DataBase	36%
Google Searchers everywhere	27%

that the I&R service of Terrassa has linguistic capabilities built into its search engine. Since the on-line service deals with over 80% of the most frequently asked questions (i.e., those regarding the directory and agenda), the questions tend to be simple. They can therefore be expressed in terms of simple keywords and answered using search engines such as Google. However, citizens appreciate the natural language interface as being friendlier and providing a higher degree of satisfaction than simple, keyword-based interfaces. Unfortunately, it has not so far been possible to identify or measure an identifiable cost reduction resulting from this capability.

It should be noted that an I&R service has to have its information base updated very regularly when answering questions on-line, otherwise citizens would not use such a service. This creates a new problem in determining how the I&R database should be updated without increasing backup costs or requiring additional use of the I&R staff. This problem is key, but challenging and costly as well. The staff could work on this task full-time but there would still be plenty of missing, incorrect, or obsolete information. One possibility is to take advantage of the knowledge of citizens or volunteers. Then, we have determined how best to assist in the creation of FAQ lists through the use of citizens, creating tools that allow them to input information in a collaborative but managed way.

Both iSAC and Community Answers provide models where the community and officials work together effectively to provide timely and accurate answers that meet the citizen - enquirer's needs. Considerable human intellectual input is however still required for this to function effectively and

Table 5. Satisfactory answers of iSAC

From Jan 1, 2008 to April 22, 2009						
Satisfactory answers (Raw Data)				**Satisfactory answers (Correction 3x1)**		
Bad	932	60.3%		Bad	932	33.6%
Good	613	39.7%		Good	1839	**66.4%**
Total feedback	1545	100.0%		Total feedback	2771	100.0%
Number of users that has shown unsatisfaction compared to the total of questions						
Bad	932	0.8%				
#questions	117403	100.0%				

Figure 8. Satisfaction of users by getting their feedback in the scale of 0 to 10 (y-axis) at every two months (in the x-axis yy-mm)

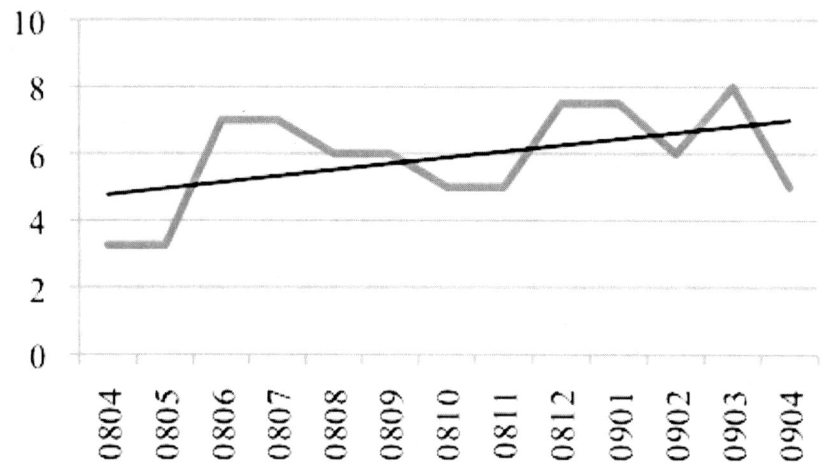

provide an accurate and authoritative set of answers to the complete range of potential queries. This level of service is inevitably expensive to provide, and it is necessary to explore further opportunities that can provide means of reducing this burden without compromising the level of service. This can best be done by automating some of the activities required using various artificial intelligence methods. For example, within the field of FAQ great effort has been made to develop information retrieval techniques. This research has explored different solution alternatives such as grammatical analysis, question-type evaluation (Jung et al., 2004), the use of WordNet and the Web (Hammond et al., 1995), noisy-channel transformations, semantic analysis and the inference model (Jijkoun and de Rijke, 2005). (Sneiders, 2002) examined problems with FAQ, focusing in particular on the answers provided, since these can be a source of user dissatisfaction. (Moldovan et al., 2003) explores the role of answer providers in FAQs, alluding that people behind them are experts in the field.

Another area that can be explored is the role of virtual assistants (Visseret al., 1999). These are intelligent pieces of software that act as intermediaries between the citizen requiring information and the various information sources that can provide the answers (Angioni et al., 2007). They attempt to provide an equivalent level of service to an I&R expert. The state of the art of virtual assistants includes private virtual assistants dedicated to customer service (Semeraro et al., 2008) and a virtual assistant dedicated to local government citizen information service (Baños et al., 2008). At present, there are some good public Citizens Attention Services in a number of countries which offer personalized attention in various forms, e.g. face to face, over the phone or internet. As a result, there has been more effective interaction between the citizens and the public administration. All virtual assistants share similar ways of capturing user questions and displaying answers that are when the question corresponds to an answer found in a static list of answers, it is presented to the customer. Alternatively, the customer is presented a set of answers that could be related to the question; or the virtual assistant may suggest other sources for locating the information, such as electronic mail, telephone assistance, or

Figure 9. Number of on-line questions per hour in a typical day

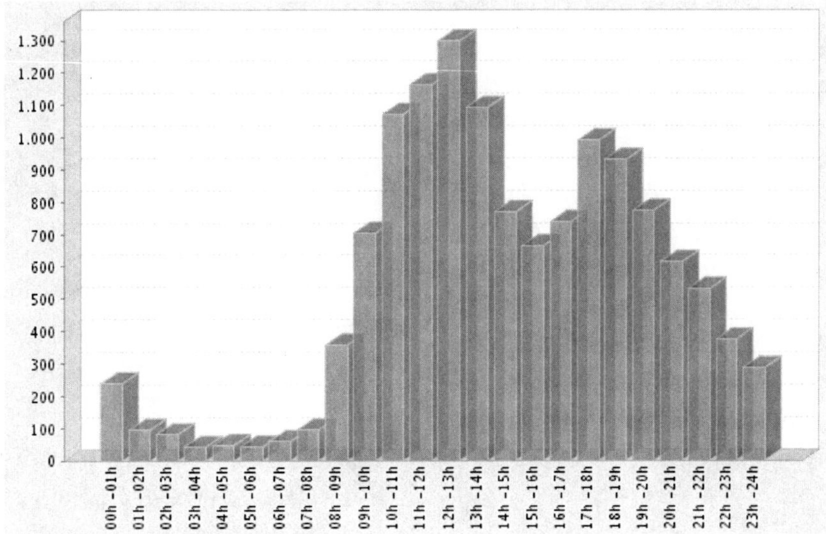

an address for face-to-face personalized service. The size and the maintenance of the static list of answers may vary, according to the local experts′ anticipation of possible questions.

Modern Citizen Information Systems need to fulfil a large number of criteria. Consequently, the development of these systems is a non-trivial process. In order to improve the citizen's experience, these systems often need to personalize the information based on the current user's needs and personal context (e.g., number of family members or their current employment state, their interests in dog's owner's communities/ hobbies, etc).

The technologies discussed in this chapter can be used effectively to improve the quality of Citizens Attention Services. This can be done by understanding citizens' demands through their natural language; it is based on the semantics of the communication process as a whole, and on structuring and semantic tagging of content to improve and simplify the retrieval process. Such systems need to take a citizen-centred approach to provide integrated views of information over heterogeneous data sources. Since these data sources are usually autonomous (i.e. maintained by different local, regional and national public administrations) and distributed, frequently overlapping and changing, citizen attention services have to work hard to extract useful knowledge; this is likely to prove to be a very challenging technology transfer issue.

Finally, in addition to blogs and wikis, there are other emerging trends which may also be important to I&R services. Such trends include service-oriented architecture, mash-ups, personalized web services, RSS, Twitter, and mobile government. We need to ask how these technologies can be leveraged in I&R services. We do not know yet, though from our point of view one thing is for sure: sharing the I&R information with the citizens empowers the I&R service, regardless of how this is achieved.

This and further discussions follow in the iSAC6+ epractice community, available at http://www.epractice.eu/community/isac6 where you are kindly invite to contribute.

ACKNOWLEDGMENT

This research was partially funded by the European Union project Num. 238887, a unique European citizens' attention service (iSAC6+) IST-PSP

VII European Frame Programme, Num. 216746 PReservation Organizations using Tools in AGent Environments (PROTAGE), FP7-2007- ICT Challenge 4: Digital libraries and content, as well as RDiSAC *Recerca en incentivació de la participació 2.0 i llenguatge natural per contexts per a la creació de serveis no presencials d'informació i atenció ciutadana SAC*, a grant from the ACC1O – Catalan Government, and the 2009 BE-1-00229 of the AGAUR, Generalitat de Catalunya. Special thanks to Boleslaw Szymanski from RPI, Chitra Shanbhogue from the town of Greenwich in Connecticut (USA) and Josep Monterde from the city of Terrassa in Catalonia (EU).

REFERENCES

Alavi, M., & Leidner, D. (1999). Knowledge management systems: issues, challenges, and benefits. *Communications of the Association for Information Systems, 1*, 1–28.

Allen, B. A., Paquet, G., Juillet, L., & Roy, J. (2005). E-Government as Collaborative Governance: Structural, Accountability and Cultural Reform. In Khosrow-Pour, M. (Ed.), *Practising e-Government: A Global Perspective* (pp. 1–15). Hershey, PA: Ideas Group Publishing.

Angioni, M., Demontis, R., Deriu, M., De Vita, E., Lai, C., Marcialis, I., et al. (2007). DART: the distributed agent-based retrieval toolkit. In D. Sharma, L. C. Jain, D. Tran, & W. Ma (Eds.), *Proceedings of the 2007 Annual Conference on international Conference on Computer Engineering and Applications* (Gold Coast, Queensland, Australia, January 17 - 19, 2007) (pp. 425-433). Stevens Point, WI: World Scientific and Engineering Academy and Society (WSEAS).

Baños, T. Y., Aquino, E., Sernas, F. D., López, Y. R., & Mendoza, R. C. (2007). EMI: a system to improve and promote the use of public transportation. In *CHI '07 Extended Abstracts on Human Factors in Computing Systems* (San Jose, CA, USA, April 28 - May 03, 2007) (2037-2042). New York: ACM. Retrieved from http://doi.acm.org/10.1145/1240866.1240946

Bush, R. A. (1995 September). *Basic FidoNet(r). technical standard.* Pacific Systems Group. Retrieved June 15, 2005, from http://www.ftsc.org/download/docs/fts-0001.016

Carrillo, C., de la Rosa, J. L., & Canals, A. (2007). Towards a Knowledge Economy. *International Journal of Community Currency Research, 11*, 84–97.

Croneberger, R. Jr, & Luck, C. (1975). Defining Information and Referral Service. *Library Journal, 100*(19), 1984–1987.

Datamonitor. (2000). *P2P eCommerce information exchanges*. Datamonitor Business Report. Retrieved from http://www.datamonitor.com/industries/research/?pid=DMTC0679&type=Report

Davenport, T. H., Harris, J. G., & Kohli, A. (2001). How do they know their customers so well? *MIT Sloan Management Review, 42*(2), 63–73.

Davenport, T. H., & Prusak, L. (1998). *Working Knowledge*. Boston, MA: Harvard Business School Press.

de la Rosa, J. L., Moreno, A., Rovira, M., Montaner, M., & Szymanski, B. (2009). Reward System for Completing Frequently Asked Questions. In *Proceedings of the AAAI 2009 Spring Symposium on Social Semantic Web: Where Web 2.0 meets Web 3.0, 2009.* Retrieved from http://tw.rpi.edu/portal/Reward_system_for_completing_frequently_asked_questionsDrucker, D. (2001). Knowledge mgm't revised – theory doesn't equal practice. *Internetweek, 1*(29), 60.

Eggers, W. (2005). *Government 2.0: Using Technology to Improve Education, Cut Red Tape, Reduce Gridlock and Enhance Democracy*. New York: Rowman and Littlefield Publishers.

Expósito, F., Mollet, R., Oliva, F., & Sanchez, J. A. (2003). *3A Un Sistema de Retención de Clientes: Análisis, Alarmas y Acciones One 2 One*. 27 Congreso Nacional de Estadística e Investigación Operativa, Lleida, April 8-11.

Fountain, J. E. (2001). *Building the Virtual State: Information Technology and Institutional Change*. Washington, DC: Brookings Institution Press.

Garson, G. D. (2006). *Public information technology and e-governance: Managing the virtual state*. Sudbury, MA: Jones & Bartlett Publishers.

Gershon, P. (2004). *Releasing Resources to the Front Line: Independent Review of Public Sector Efficiency*. London: HM Treasury. Retrieved from http://www.hm-treasury.gov.uk

Gosain, S. (2003). Issues in designing personal knowledge exchanges. *Information Technology & People*, *16*(3), 306. doi:10.1108/09593840310489403

Hammond, K., Burke, R., Martin, C., & Lytinen, S. (1995). FAQ finder: a case-based approach to knowledge navigation. In *Proceedings of the 11th* [Washington, DC: IEEE Computer Society.]. *The Conference on Artificial Intelligence Applications*, (February): 20–22.

Howe, J. (2008). *Crowdsourcing: Why the power of the crowd is driving the future of business*. Crown Business.

Jijkoun, V., & de Rijke, M. (2005). Retrieving answers from frequently asked questions pages on the web. In *Proceedings of the 14th ACM international Conference on information and Knowledge Management* (Bremen, Germany, October 31 - November 05, 2005) (pp. 76-83). New York: ACM. Retrieved from http://doi.acm.org/10.1145/1099554.1099571

Jung, S., Harris, K., Webster, J., & Herlocker, J. L. (2004). SERF: integrating human recommendations with search. In *Proceedings of the Thirteenth ACM international Conference on information and Knowledge Management* (Washington, D.C., USA, November 08 - 13, 2004) (pp. 571-580). New York: ACM. Retrieved from http://doi.acm.org/10.1145/1031171.1031277

Kantor, B., & Lapsley, P. (2004). *Network news transfer protocol, a proposed standard for the stream-based transmission of news*. Retrieved March 2004 from ftp://ftp.rfc-editor.org/in-notes/rfc977.txt

Kim, A. J. (2000). *Community Building on the Web: Secret Strategies for Successful Online Communities*. Englewood Cliffs, NJ: Peachpit Press.

Kraemer, K., & King, J. L. (2003). *Information Technology and Administrative Reform: Will the Time After e-Government Be Different?* Irvine, CA: Centre for Research on Information Technology and Organizations.

Kronus, C. L., & Crowe, L. (Eds.). (1971). Libraries and neighborhood information centers. Papers presented at an institute conducted by the University of Illinois Graduate School of Library Science, October 24-27, 1971. Urbana, IL: Graduate School of Library Science.

Lietaer, B. (2006). A Proposal for a Brazilian Education Complementary Currency. *International Journal of Community Currency Research*, *10*, 18–23.

Liljenback, M. E. (2007). *ContextQA: Experiments in Interactive Restricted-Domain Question Answering*. MSc. in CS Thesis, San Diego University.

Malhotra, Y. (2002). Enabling knowledge exchanges for e-business communities. *Information Strategy*, *18*(3), 26–31.

Moldovan, D., Paşca, M., Harabagiu, S., & Surdeanu, M. (2003). Performance issues and error analysis in an open-domain question answering system. *ACM Transactions on Information Systems*, *21*(2), 133–154. Retrieved from http://doi.acm.org/10.1145/763693.763694. doi:10.1145/763693.763694

Moreno, A., de la Rosa, J. L., & Carrillo, C. I. (2006). WIKIFAQ: Obtaining complete FAQs. *Frontiers in Artificial Intelligence and Applications – AI Research & Development, 146*, 283-290.

Moreno, A., de la Rosa, J. L., Szymanski, B. K., & Barcenas, J. M. (2009). *Reward System for Completing FAQs*. Frontiers in Artificial Intelligence and Applications – AI Research & Development.

O'Brien, R. (2008, June 27). *Paying City Students Is a Wise Investment*. New America Foundation, The Baltimore Sun. Retrieved from http://www.newamerica.net/publications/articles/2008/paying_city_students_wise_investment_7445

O'Shea, D., King, C. T., Greenfield, S., Shelton, E., Sullivan, L., & Taber, E. (2004). *National Benefit/Cost Analysis of Three Digit-Accessed Telephone Information and Referral Services*. Ray Marshall Centre for the Study of Human Resources, Lyndon B. Johnson School of Public Affairs, The University of Texas at Austin.

Pettigrew, K. (1996). Nurses' perceptions of their needs for community information. *Journal of Education for Library and Information Science*, *7*(4), 351–360.

Radev, D. R., Libner, K., & Fan, W. (2002). Getting answers to natural language queries on the web. *Journal of the American Society for Information Science and Technology*, *53*(5), 359–364. doi:10.1002/asi.10053

Sneiders, E. (2002). Automated question answering using question templates that cover the conceptual model of the database. In *Proceedings of the 6th International Conference on Applications of Natural Language to Information Systems-Revised Papers* (pp. 235–239).

Sombrero, G., Andersen, V., Andersen, H. H., de Gemmis, M., & Lops, P. (2008). User profiling and virtual agents: a case study on e-commerce services. *Univers. Access Inf. Soc., 7*(3), 179-194. Retrieved from http://dx.doi.org/10.1007/s10209-008-0116-1

Tapscott, D., & Williams, A. D. (2007). *Wikinomics – How Mass Collaboration Changes Everything*. New York: Portfolio.

United Nations. (2008). *United Nations e-government survey 2008: From e-government to connected governance. UN Publication ST/ESA/PAD/SER.E/112*. New York: United Nations.

Visser, P. R., Beer, M. D., Bench-Capon, T. J., Diaz, B. M., & Shave, M. J. (1999). Resolving Ontological Heterogeneity in the KRAFT Project. In T. J. Bench-Capon, G. Soda & A. M. Tjoa (Eds.), *Proceedings of the 10th international Conference on Database and Expert Systems Applications* (August 30 - September 03, 1999) (LNCS 1677, pp. 668-677). London: Springer-Verlag.

West, D. M. (2005). *Digital Government: Technology and Public Sector Performance*. Princeton, NJ: Princeton University Press.

Wyld, D. (2007). *The Blogging Revolution: Government in the Age of Web 2.0. IBM Endowment for The Business of Government.* Retrieved from http://www.businessofgovernment.org/pdfs/WyldReportBlog.pdf

ENDNOTES

1 iSAC6+ *a unique European citizens' attention service* is an European Project Num. 238887, IST-PSP VII European Frame Programme devoted to provide open source I&R platforms for on-line I&R

2 http://www.webqa.net

3 http://www.q-go.com

4 http://www.artificial-solutions.com

5 http://www.intelliresponse.com

6 http://www.isac.cat

7 Crawler is a software bot that autonomously follows connected paths such as webpage links.

8 See for example, Inside the Googleplex (Economist Magazine, 08/30/2007)

ANNEX 1

Table 6. A table of questions for the experiment shown in Table 4

Ciutadà anònim a Terrassa **Comparativa de canals d'accés**						
Question (Translated from Catalan to English)	**010 after a 2nd ques-tion**	**010**	**iSAC**	**Google Ter-rassa**	**Google Gen-eral**	**notes**
I want to study **an industirla textile pattern degree**	good	bad	good	bad	bad	el 010 no sap que a l'AG hi ha cursos, em dona les escoles
Is there any **public trans-portation to Terrassa from Barcelona**? I must com-munte daily from 8 to 9	good	bad	good	good	good	010- has de trucar a renfe, nosaltres no tenim horaris des d'iSAC hi és però és millorable, et fa nevegar molt... El millor és el web! Terrassa, com anar-hi! Fer FAQ!.
I'd like my **son learned painting**	bad	bad	good	good	0	el 010 em dona una escola
Is there any **ONG devoted to occidental Sahara?**	bad	bad	bad	bad	good	hi ha docs memòries anuals i el 010 em dóna tel de joventut Google gen hi ha 33.300 docs amb 0,09 segons...
Kindergarten plastic arts	good	bad	good	bad	bad	010 ni idea dels cursos... sols donen escoles...
Where is the **Terrassa's Public Tanatorium**	good	good	bad	good	bad	iSAC no entén la paraula. Afegit sinónim i ara ja va bé... web perfecte, 010 completa a petició meva, no a iniciativa pròpia
Where the **people is buried in Terrassa?**	good	good	good	good	bad	010 no proactiu, sols ha anat responent les meves preguntes...
Are there **summer camps** (activities) in the weekends for **teenagers?**	good	bad	bad	bad	bad	010 dona entitats que en fan, però no sap si ara n'hi ha
Are there **winter camps** for kids?	good	bad	bad	bad	bad	
I want to hear **the mayor;** when is he reading a **confer-ence** in Terrassa or nearby?	bad	good	good	bad	bad	010 refà la pregunta i me demana confirmació: contesta "dinar el 17/2/07, si vols més info., truca al partit o bé a l'alcaldia tel..."
I'm looking for a partner in Terrassa. Is there a place for dating widows?	bad	good	good	bad	good	Només el 010 és realment bo!!! -porquesolos.com-
Google, cercador AOC i iSAC, mirem si hi és la resposta en les primeres 20 informacions (primera pàgina)						
Als cerc Google, AOC i web Terr els treurem els patrons de comunicació del davant, el que busquem és saber què troben. Mireu les paraules clau en negreta						
Si el 010 comunica, i per variar, també es pot trucar al 937397000, és la centraleta, pero és el que dóna telefònica						
Si hi afegiu preguntes, per favor compartiu-les amb tothom						
en peplluis fa ses preguntes						
en deme						
na merce						
en miquel						

Section 2
Issues and Challenges

Chapter 9
Transparency and E-Government in Developing Countries:
The Case of Latin-American Municipalities

Maria del Carmen Caba Pérez
University of Almería, Spain

Manuel Pedro Rodríguez Bolívar
University of Granada, Spain

Antonio Manuel López Hernández
University of Granada, Spain

ABSTRACT

Information and Communication Technologies (ICTs) have become an important tool to be used in order to meet NPM objectives in public administrations, by enhancing information flows and active participation by citizens, constituting a valuable tool for building trust and enhancing government-citizen relations, by identifying, assessing and, thus, satisfying public needs. This chapter focuses on the Internet, one of the tools that is most widely used by the public, and on on-line access to government financial information (Borins, 2002). Concretely, this chapter examines and discusses the approach taken by local governments in developing countries to using the Web as a means of making government disclosures, thus combating corruption and enhancing accountability by means of information transparency. To achieve this aim, a series of aspects to provide an overview of the degree of on-line information and the accessibility of this information in Latin-American capital cities are analyzed. This way, this chapter discusses the e-government process and its implications on democracy, accountability and information transparency and describes the state of the art of e-government initiatives and legislation in the sample governments. The results obtained and the main conclusions of the research indicate that Latin-American capital cities are still not fully aware of the potential importance of the Internet in enabling the achievement of e-democracy initiatives. Indeed, the Internet is still not an important means by which sample governments disclose their local government information to the public.

DOI: 10.4018/978-1-61520-931-6.ch009

INTRODUCTION

In recent decades, governments all over the world have reformed their public administration in accordance with NPM tenets. Under this framework, most national governments have inexorably moved from a system of bureaucratic organization to a professionally managed one (Osborne & Gaebler, 1993), placing, among other major initiatives, greater emphasis on citizen satisfaction and more transparent information. In fact, it is now recognized that good governance in public administration depends upon transparent and publicly accountable institutions (MAC, 2004).

This process has led public administrations to search for tools which could be adopted from the business sphere, enabling them to provide greater transparency and involvement of citizens in the decision-making process (Bonson *et al.,* 2006). **Information and Communication Technologies (ICTs)** have become an important tool to be used in this process, which is particularly aimed at satisfying the citizen and at enhancing citizens' engagement in public policy-making (OECD, 2003a). Public administrations could adopt these new technologies in order to meet NPM objectives, thus meeting social demands efficiently and effectively (Welch & Hinnant, 2002).

In this context, the question of **e-government** has become one of today's most important issues on political agendas, and is a concept that is apparently in constant development (Jaeger, 2003). This trend is understood to be one of the forms of expression of the information society, as well as a central part of the process of modernizing public administrations (Borins, 2001; Chan & Chow, 2007). There is a firm belief that e-government, by enhancing information flows and active participation by citizens, constitutes a valuable tool for building trust – which is a fundamental value of ethics in public administration (Gilman & Lewis, 1996; Cooper & Yoder, 2002) – and enhancing government-citizen relations, by identifying, assessing and, thus, satisfying public needs (King & Stivers, 1998).

Tolbert and Mossberger (2006) indicate that e-government arises as a way of increasing citizens' trust in governments and of improving the evaluations made concerning political management. Its objective is focused on bringing public administration closer to citizens and restoring trust in governments (Cho & Choi, 2004; Shim & Eom, 2008; Kim *et al.*, 2009). As Siau and Long (2006) argue, digital government will provide governments with an effective and efficient channel to facilitate their internal administrations and improve their external services, thereby increasing transparency and generating a higher degree of trust.

In the light of the multiple possibilities of new technologies, this chapter focuses on the Internet, one of the tools that is most widely used by the public (Borins, 2002; Cuillier & Piotrowski, 2009), and on on-line access to government financial information. In fact, the most common form of e-government initiatives is a government-run web site or web portal (Joseph & Jeffers, 2009).

Nonetheless, although e-government applications are revolutionizing such areas as record keeping—particularly in the West—most nations still rely on offline channels to accommodate the majority of their daily governmental correspondence (Berhel, 2000; Bouras *et al.*, 2000; Jeffres, 2007). Indeed, the proportion of non-Internet population appears to be remaining fairly high, and so the oft-cited digital divide continues to be mean that e-government is not universal and that other channels must be kept open (Margetts, 2006b). Nonetheless, there is evidence to suggest that even non-users may benefit from e-government (Margetts, 2006b). Also, although most countries produce governmental information, such as financial information aimed at accountability, it has often been highlighted that citizens have difficulty in accessing it (Tayib *et al.,* 1999; OECD, 2003b), which, in practice, implies a lack of information transparency.

A key factor underlying the non-availability of online governmental information is the level of corruption in countries. Secrecy and lack of information create a breeding ground for corruption and abuses of power (World Bank, 2008). The development of e-government is one of the main changes that needs to be made. In fact, such a development could contribute to reducing corruption in government via greater transparency in information and public functions (Maor, 2004). Therefore, e-government projects focused on transparency and other anticorruption measures need to be implemented in these countries.

This chapter examines and discusses the approach taken by local governments in developing countries to using the Web as a means of making government disclosures, thus combating corruption and enhancing accountability by means of information transparency. Specifically, we focus on the capital cities of Latin-American countries to discover whether they are using the Internet to enhance citizens' access to public sector information, thus contributing to encouraging a benchmarking process –benchmarking process is the continuous process of measuring an entity's products, services, and practices against its toughest competitors (IFAC, 1993)-. To achieve this aim, a series of aspects are analyzed to provide an overview of the degree of on-line information and the accessibility of this information made available by these municipal Governments.

The chapter is organized as follows. The next section discusses the e-government process and its implications on democracy, accountability and information transparency. The third section describes the state of the art of e-government initiatives and legislation in Latin-American countries. We then describe the empirical research carried out, the results of which are presented in the fifth section of the chapter. Finally, we highlight the main conclusions of our research and discuss the potential implications.

BACKGROUND: TRANSPARENCY, E-GOVERNMENT, E-DEMOCRACY AND ACCOUNTABILITY

Nowadays, public administrations are required to be more efficient (Rocheleau & Liangfu, 2002), to provide more transparency to citizens (Piotrowski & Van Ryzin, 2007), to create an operative framework which facilitates competitiveness and to enhance greater information and participation in public life for all social agents (Fieldman & Khademian, 2007). In this regard, a receptive administration must be based on increasing citizens' involvement as clients, and on enhancing accessibility and transparency (Hughes, 1994).

Nonetheless, as there are different kinds of accountability, each kind of **transparency** needs to be assessed and understood in its own context (Wilson, 2006). Technological advances have clearly reduced the direct costs of transparency, as the incremental costs of making existing documentation available are often minimal (Margetts, 2006a). The reduction of logistical obstacles to transparency heightens the importance of determining which directions and varieties of transparency are appropriate for particular organizations and habitats. In addition, the beneficial nature of transparency is contingent upon the directions and varieties of transparency that occur and on the habitat with which they interact (Heald, 2006b). In this regard, in this chapter, information transparency is defined as the availability of online governmental information and access to this information. Therefore, according to this definition, transparency is characterized as transparency downwards and inwards, from the point of view of directions, and events transparency, transparency in real time and effective transparency, from the point of view of varieties, in the terminology used by Heald (2006a).

New technologies could improve government responsiveness and empower individual citizens (Ward, 1996), communicating government information to improve democratic governance (King,

2006) because citizens can only make effective decisions if they can evaluate information about government (Quinn, 2003; Jho, 2005). Furthermore, e-government can act as a conducting mechanism to accelerate the decentralization of public administration and, at the same time, improve the capacity of governments to supervise the main activities (Thorson, Chung & Ma, 2005), reducing both administrative costs and the time devoted to repetitive tasks by civil servants (Yen & Evans, 2005), offering greater transparency to public administration (Ya & Tat-Kei Ho, 2005; Wong & Welch, 2004), and expanding the access to services due to its availability twenty-four hours a day and seven days a week on the Internet (Scott, 2006; West, 2004).

Although there has been little systematic empirical analysis of the extent to which governmental use of technology provides the information and interactive capabilities that might meaningfully improve governance (Musso *et al.,* 2000), citizens appear to be generally satisfied with the electronic provision of information (transparency) (Welch *et al.,* 2005). In fact, although the three main reasons for citizens' visits to government websites are e-commerce, e-democracy and e-research (Clift, 2002), the single most important motivation for such website visits is to obtain information, in particular, regarding income tax (Borins, 2002).

Nonetheless, much of the research suggests that correlates with Internet use depend on motivation and the types of use (Van Dijk, Peters, and Ebbers, 2008). This is based on the proposed uses and gratification theory (Blumler and Katz, 1974), which suggests that people actively search out media messages to satisfy certain needs, rather than being passive receivers of information. Indeed, from a uses and gratification perspective, to foster civic engagement and political participation, public agencies should post information online that is particularly useful and relevant to people's lives and then proactively advertise it so people are alerted to it (Cuillier & Piotrowski, 2009).

In spite of these considerations, most websites lack the 'interactive quality crucial to other citizen-initiated contacts' (Thomas & Streib, 2003), which is especially relevant in those countries with a higher level of corruption. Indeed, as noted previously, the level of corruption of a country is also a key factor underlying the non-availability of online governmental information. Research has shown that those countries with low levels of corruption will be more transparent in the disclosure of information concerning the management of public funds and vice versa (Kim et al., 2009). Thus, in developing countries, where the level of corruption is higher (Transparency International, 2008) because scarcity is a major factor in perpetuating corruption (Caiden, 2003), e-government remains an alternative rather than a primary outlet for governmental communication (Lau et al., 2008). Accordingly, although most Latin-American countries have begun e-government initiatives in which notable emphasis is placed on improving state managerial and administrative processes and the quality of online services offered, the enhancement of methods for citizen interaction has taken a back seat (Betancourt, 2006).

By promoting transparency and accountability, freedom of information curbs abuses (World Bank, 2008). The right to access government records is essential in a democracy to foster citizen trust, deter corruption, and provide basic information for the public, companies and journalists (Altschull, 1990; Blasi, 1977; Cross, 1953; Florini, 2007; Foerstel, 1999; Meiklejohn, 1948). Nonetheless, transparency by itself is a very incomplete remedy for corruption, untrustworthiness, or poor performance in public and corporate life. It can achieve rather little unless the material disseminated is made accessible to and assessable by relevant audiences, and actually reaches those audiences (O'Neill, 2006).

On the other hand, numerous studies (King, 2006; La Porte *et al.,* 2002) have highlighted the importance of using new technologies to enhance e-democracy. This has become one of the main objectives underlying the information policies introduced in the national legislations that have addressed information technology and e-government performance requirements, together with the introduction of new technologies into the field of government.

In this regard, the development of e-government allows citizens to participate in democratic institutions and political processes (Justice *et al.*, 2006; Siau & Long, 2006), thereby perceiving governments as accessible, transparent, responsible, effective and participative (Tolbert & Mossberger, 2006). In this context, e-government could lead to an increase in citizens' trust and a perception of speed in the answers made by governments to their needs. All this leads to a stronger democracy (OECD, 2001b) and to the legitimacy of the state and its relationship with citizens and the rule of law, entering into the realm of e-democracy and e-governance (Brown, 2005).

This reform involves a new form of governance of society, entailing a new form of interaction between governments, citizens, the private sector and community organizations (Snellen, 2002). It also involves a new sharing of powers among the various internal and external players (Charih & Robert, 2004).

With respect to non-democratic governments, it is possible that e-government may result in their liberalization or democratization although, particularly in the short to medium term, they are likely to seek to utilize e-government initiatives to extend the control currently exercised over citizens and to perpetuate currently authoritarian regimes (Blakeley *et al.*, 2001). Nonetheless, in the long run, it is expected that e-government will promote the development of e-democracy in these countries (Blakeley *et al.*, 2001). Moreover, employing new technologies as tools of transformation can assist governments in fighting corruption and also in institutionalizing transparent public sector practices (Cho & Choi, 2004; Shim & Eom, 2008; Kim *et al.*, 2009). In this regard, global initiatives based on central and international values such as open democratic governance (Caiden, 2001 and 2003), a burgeoning consensus on integrity, responsibility, and transparency (Cooper & Yoder, 2002) and the inculcation of a culture of public accountability and transparency (Klitgaard, 1988) are crucial factors to tackle corruption and thus improve economic growth (Moilanen & Salminen, 2006).

In any case, e-democracy has arisen in the context of growing public concern about the openness and accountability of government and politicians (King, 2006). The governmental response to public demands for information and services is thus a contribution to openness, a measure of government accountability and a response to citizens' demands for information and services from government organizations (La Porte *et al.*, 2002) that often involve public policy (Thomas & Streib, 2005). Nonetheless, numerous studies have concluded that politics on the Internet remains simply politics as usual because easier access to information does not appear to lead to greater participation (Davis, 1999).

E-government could increase efficiency, transparency and **accountability** in the use of public resources (United Nations, 2003). In this context, the accountability of public entities would be enhanced, and information transparency is crucial to achieving this objective. Thus, the concept of transparency is of great significance in the contexts of accountability and democracy (Arellano-Gault, 2008) because it is an effective tool to ensure citizens' access to information (Haque, 2006). Indeed, in some countries such as the USA, good government groups have suggested their own proposals for increasing government accountability and transparency, many of these with a focus on providing more information online and on making agencies more responsive to public records requests (Cuillier & Piotrowski, 2009). This is consistent with the international trend toward increased use of e-government practices and the proactive release of information electronically and otherwise (Holzer & Kim, 2004; Moon, 2002; Piotrowski & Borry, 2009).

The citizens' access to information is an essential precondition for engagement, although the quantity of information disclosed is not necessarily equated with its quality (OECD, 2003b). The digitalization of government affairs increases transparency and efficiency and, therefore, seems to have a positive influence for the development of democratic institutions, increasing political participation and supporting democratic principles (Ferguson & Perse, 2000; Katz, Rice, & Aspden, 2001; Pierce & Lovrich, 2003; Shah, Kwak, & Holbert, 2001; White, 1997), which is an essential condition for the protection of human rights (Jho, 2005). Indeed, people who use the Internet for seeking news and information are more likely to exhibit greater support for democratic principles such as freedom of information because they see the practical value of open government records in understanding the political process and aiding their personal lives (Cuillier & Piotrowski, 2009). This process is of overriding importance in horizontal governments (Michels & Meijer, 2008).

Despite the above comments, the e-government process is not the same in all countries and it does not affect all citizens in the same way. E-government also entails risks to civilian society through the possible creation of a digital divide, further increasing the disadvantage of already disadvantaged citizens (James, 2008; Ryder, 2007; Dugdale *et al.,* 2005). Nonetheless, audience segmentation could make the digital divide less critical (Garnett, 1992; Margetts, 2006b).

In view of the foregoing comments and with respect to the e-democracy process, this chapter investigates the transparency of the information process within e-democracy and as a part of the NPM approach that has been implemented at a municipal level in developing countries. To this end, we carried out an empirical study of government disclosures on the Internet in the capital cities of various Latin-American countries.

PROMOTION BY GOVERNMENTS IN LATIN AMERICA OF INCREASED ACCESS TO PUBLIC INFORMATION

In recent years, Latin-American governments have taken various steps to foster the information society, developing programmes and initiatives to implement ICTs in diverse areas, including plans, specific actions, legislation and, at the very least, strategic documents; all of this shows that the issue is now firmly on the political agenda (United Nations, 2008).

The main initiatives that have been developed by these countries in the field of ICTs are aimed at enhancing the transparency of management, reducing current levels of corruption, improving the internal and external efficiency of public administration vis-à-vis the public, especially as concerns the provision of services, and promoting and expanding citizens' participation (Welp, 2008).

The countries in the region, to a greater or lesser extent, have passed **legislation** to ensure citizens' access to government information, especially via the use of ICT tools. In addition, organizations have been set up to guarantee and facilitate the provision of public information (see Table 1). As can be seen in Table 1, the area of application of most of the regulations established in these countries is that of the municipalities. The goal of this legislation is to regulate the right of access to public information as a prerequisite for public participation, thus enabling greater control over corruption, optimizing efficiency in government offices and enhancing awareness of public decisions.

Furthermore, numerous Latin-American governments have subscribed to the IMF's Special Data Dissemination Standard (IMF, 2007), while in the field of e-government, the Santo Domingo Declaration on Good Governance and Development in the Knowledge-Based Society was signed in 2006, at the General Assembly of the Organization of American States. In 2007,

Table 1. Agencies and legislation to promote access to public information

Country	Agency	Legislation	In force (year)	Area of Application
Argentina	Secretariat of the Cabinet Chief and Governmental Affairs, of the Office of the Cabinet Chief	Decree No. 252/2000 of 17/03/2000 (Official State Gazette 22/03/2000) National Programme for the Information Society.	2000	Offices and departments of the National Government
Bolivia	Agency for Development of the Information Society in Bolivia (ADSIB).	Supreme Decree No. 27329 of 31/01/2004 on transparency and access to governmental information.	2004	All the institutions of the executive, both centralized and decentralized.
Brazil	Executive Committee on Electronic Government (CEGE)	Act No. 9507 published on 2/11/1997, regulating the right to public information.	1997	Federal public administration.
Chile	Committee of Ministers for Digital Development	Act No. 20285 of 11/08/2008 on Transparency in the Public Sector and Access to Information in the National Administration	2008	Ministries, provincial authorities, local government agencies, regional governments and municipalities, among others.
Colombia	Intersectoral Commission for Information Policies and Management for Public Administration (COINFO)	Act 57 of 1985 (05/07/1985), on Transparency and Access to Government Information.	1985	Ministries, administrative departments, local government agencies, provincial authorities, city halls and municipal councils, among others.
Costa Rica	Technical Secretariat for Digital Government (STGD)	Act No. 7202 of 24/10/1990 on the National Record System.	1990	State-wide public sector organizations
Cuba	Ministry for Computing and Communications (MIC)	Decree-Act No. 199/1999 of 25/11/1999, establishing and regulating the System for the Security and Protection of Official Information.	1999	Public sector institutions and bodies
Ecuador	National Telecommunications Council (CONATEL).	Act No. 34 of 10/05/2004 Organic Act on Transparency and Access to Public Information	2004	Public sector bodies and departments
El Salvador	National Commission for the Information Society.	Legislative Decree No. 1038/2006 (DO 18/05/2006) Law on Governmental Ethics	2006	Public sector bodies and departments
Guatemala	Presidential Commission for the Reform, Modernization and Strengthening of the State and its Decentralized Agencies (COPRE).	General rules on access to public information regarding the Executive and its Agencies. Government Agreement 645-2005.	2005	State-wide public sector and decentralized bodies
Honduras	Presidential Commission for Modernization of the State (CPME). Governmental Committee on Infotechnology (CGI)	Law on Transparency and Access to Public Information No. 170-2006.	2006	All the organizations and bodies that constitute the three State powers (the Executive, the Legislative power and the Judiciary), and the municipalities, among others.
Mexico	Agency for E-Government and Information Technology Policy (UGEPTI) of the Secretariat for Public Administration.	National Law on Transparency and Access to Government Public Information, of 11/06/2002.	2002	The Federal Executive power, the Federal Public Administration, and the Federal Legislative power, among others.

Table 1. continued on following page

Table 1. continued

Country	Agency	Legislation	In force (year)	Area of Application
Nicaragua	National Integrity Committee	Access to Public Information Act No. 621 of 2007.	2007	The State powers (Legislative, Executive, Judicial and Electoral), with their subsidiary offices, and other organizations, whether associated or independent, the Municipal Governments and the Autonomous Regional Governments of the Atlantic Coast.
Panama	Secretariat of the President's Office for Government Innovation	Transparency Act No. 6-2002 (23/01/2002).	2002	All national agencies and offices, including those belonging to the Executive, Legislative and Judicial powers, the municipalities, local governments and district councils, among others.
Paraguay	Paraguay National Commission for the Information Society (CNSI)	Act No. 1028/1997 General Law on Technological Science	1997	
Peru	National Office for E-Government and Computing (ONGEI).	Act No. 27806 on Transparency and Access to public information, published on 02/08/2002	2002	The Executive Power, including Ministries and Decentralized Public Organizations; the Legislative Power; the Judicial Power; Regional and Local Governments.
Dominican Republic	National Commission for the Information and Knowledge Society (CNSIC).	Act No. 200/2004 of 28/07/2004. General Law on Free Access to Public Information.	2004	The departments of the central public administration and of municipal offices.
Uruguay	Agency for the Government Development of E-Management and the Information and Knowledge Society (AGESIC).	Act No. 18.381 published on 17/10/2008, concerning the regulation of the right to access to public information.	2008	State-wide and municipal public organizations.
Venezuela	National Centre for Information Technologies.	Organic Act for Public Administration (published in the Official State Gazette No. 37305 of 17/10/2001).	2001	Organizations and departments within the public administration (State-wide and municipal).

Source: the authors.

the Ibero-American Charter for Electronic Government was approved, in the framework of the Ninth Ibero-American Conference of Ministers for Public Administration and State Reform These international agreements recognize citizens' rights to easier access to public administrations, so that they may make use of the facility offered by electronic media to become aware of what these administrations are doing. Thus, government will be made more transparent and more controllable, contributing to the fight against corruption and generating confidence among the public, promoting inclusion and equality of opportunities so that all citizens, whatever their territorial or social situation, may access the benefits provided by the information society.

Legislation on the right of access to information, as well as being promoted by the public administrations themselves as a mechanism favouring responsibility and public participation, has been advanced as a result of the pressure exercised by international organizations, which have demanded greater transparency and accountability of countries in the region as a condition for access to international funding.

Table 2. Index of information transparency for the Latin-American capital cities

	Index of information transparency %	*Position*	Index of institutional and general information %	*Position*	Index of financial and management information %	*Position*
Ciudad de México (Mexico)	70.49	*1*	71.42	*2*	69.56	*1*
Santiago (Chile)	66.35	*2*	76.19	*1*	56.52	*3*
Santa Fe de Bogotá (Venezuela)	65.94	*3*	66.66	*3*	65.21	*2*
Buenos Aires (Argentina)	61.80	*4*	71.42	*2*	52.17	*4*
Quito (Ecuador)	56.21	*5*	42.85	*6*	69.56	*1*
Panamá (Panama)	52.48	*6*	57.14	*4*	47.82	*5*
Brasilia (Brazil)	45.54	*7*	47.61	*5*	43.47	*6*
San José (Costa Rica)	44.92	*8*	33.33	*8*	56.52	*3*
Lima (Peru)	44.92	*8*	33.33	*8*	56.52	*3*
Managua (Nicaragua)	33.85	*9*	28.57	*9*	39.13	*7*
Montevideo (Uruguay)	29.91	*10*	38.09	*7*	21.73	*8*
Guatemala (Guatemala)	25.56	*11*	38.09	*7*	13.04	*9*
Sucre (Bolivia)	18.84	*12*	33.33	*8*	4.34	*10*
Asunción (Paraguay)	18.84	*12*	33.33	*8*	4.34	*10*
San Salvador (El Salvador)	14.07	*13*	23.80	*10*	4.34	*10*

EMPIRICAL RESEARCH

Methodology of the Research

From a methodological point of view, we have drawn up a score table to capture the data we consider of outstanding importance in identifying on-line municipal transparency. To assess the degree of dissemination, this research study analyzes a series of aspects to provide the reader with an overview of the degree of on-line information and the accessibility of this information in these municipal Governments. Thus, based on Gandía and Archidona (2008), the design of the questionnaire has been divided into two sections: a) the *information disclosure* and b) certain basic elements of the presentation of and *navigation* within this information on the municipal website.

a) The first section of the study highlights the content of the information included on the website, and outlines the dissemination of two large areas of information analysis.
   a.1) The first area of information is focused on the need to disclose on the Web general and institutional information about the municipality and its government.

As remarked by Gandía and Archidona (2008), the web site content linked to aspects of the cul-

Table 3. Information on the websites of Latin-American capital cities

	%
A.1.INSTITUTIONAL AND GENERAL INFORMATION ON THE MUNICIPALITY (21 items)	
Information about the organization of the city council	
1. Functional structure chart	86.7
2. Government agencies and their functions	73.3
3. Political composition of elected officials and of government agencies	6.70
4. Dependent bodies (decentralized agencies, public or mixed municipal companies, etc.)	26.7
Information about the elected public officials of the city council	
5. Bibliographic data on the mayor and/or councillors or similar	66.7
6. Information on the salaries of the mayor and/or councillors or similar	33.3
7. Personal wealth of elected officials	67.0
Information about the adopted rules of the city council	
8. Texts of agreements adopted by government bodies	20.0
9. Non fiscal municipal rules and regulations	73.3
10. Fiscal regulations	73.3
General situation information	
11. Population statistics	60.0
12. Information on the surface area	33.3
13. Information on productive sectors (industry, agriculture, services, livestock farming, etc.)	40.0
14. Net family income (net family income and gross family income)	20.0
15. Information on service infrastructures (cultural, sporting, educational, healthcare, tourism, etc.)	20.0
16. Street maps and plans of the city	66.7
17. Environmental situation	46.7
18. News-provision services (notice board or municipal diary of activities)	86.7
19. Tourist information	66.7
20. Municipal publications (newspapers, gazettes, magazines, TV channels)	26.7
21. General town planning scheme	42.9
A.2. FINANCIAL AND MANAGEMENT INFORMATION (22 items)	
Budgetary information	
22. Budget approved	60.0
23. Budgetary amendments	26.7
24. Expenses executed	66.7
25. Income executed	66.7
26. Surplus or deficit	26.7
27. Budgetary indicators	53.3
Financial information	
28. Cash flows	26.7
29. Current debt	53.3
30. Variation in debt levels	53.3
31. Non-current assets or long term assets (Investments; Intangible assets; Tangible assets, etc.)	33.3

Table 3. continued on following page

Table 3. continued

32. Variation in non-current assets	33.3
33. Financial indicators	20.0
Non-financial information	
34. Indicators of effectiveness and efficiency	46.7
35. Human capital	26.7
Strategic management information	
36. Strategic Plan approved	73.3
37. Execution and monitoring of the Strategic Plan	6.7
Provision of services information	
38. Charter of services	0
39. Quality control systems established	0
40. Information on calls for tenders, contracting and public works	53.3
41. Resolution of tenders, contracts and public works	53.3
42. Information on procedures for the provision of non-fiscal services	73.3
43. Information on procedures for the provision of fiscal services	73.3

tural, social life and politics of the municipalities should be examined. Providing citizens, via the Web, with institutional information about the city council, that is its organization, political parties, the composition of the bodies of government, salaries, rules, etc., seems to be information that should really be made available as a matter of course so that a high degree of transparency may be achieved in all current laws on transparency and access to public information in Latin America (Table 3). Furthermore, items concerning this question have been taken into consideration in many papers in which municipal transparency has been analyzed (Transparency International, Spain, 2008; Transparencia por Colombia, 2007; Chile Transparente, 2008).

However, using the city's web site to transmit to citizens general information, including aspects such as population statistics, socio-cultural offerings and tourist information, could be considered non-fundamental to the goal of achieving greater information transparency for the municipal web site, as this kind of information could be located elsewhere. Nevertheless, as observed by Gandía and Archidona (2008), although such information is indeed merely 'decorative', and could be obtained via other web sites, a municipal web site should be as complete as possible, providing information enabling a broader vision of the municipality, so that it would not be necessary to resort to other sources to reach conclusions about the council's management of local affairs. Taking this into account, studies of Torrejon (2004) and of Gandía and Archidona (2008) have chosen to analyze, in addition, tourist and statistical information in their examination of the transparency of the municipal web site. Thus, in our view, the following information should be published on the Web (Table 3):

- *The website should disclose information about the organization of the city council:* The functional organization of the city council; a chart of its structure and chief officials; the government bodies and their functions; the political composition of the elected officers and of the local government bodies; and the organizations that are dependent on the municipality (municipal companies, decentralized agencies, etc.).

- *The website should disclose information about the elected municipal officials of the city council:* Elected public officials; who they are; biographical data; salaries received; data regarding their personal wealth situation.
- *The website should disclose information about the adopted rules of the city council:* Municipal rules and agreements; agreements adopted; current fiscal and non-fiscal rules.
- *The website should disclose general situation information about the city council:* So that the municipal population, average income, the infrastructure installed, etc. can be related to the funds administered by the municipal body. For this purpose, it would be useful to publish information on the following: the general situation of the city; statistics on population, surface area and available family income; information on productive sectors and of infrastructure available for the provision of services; environmental situation; street maps and town plans; tourist information; municipal news service; urban planning regulations and municipal publications.
    - a.2) The second area includes financial, budgetary and management information about the local government.

Prior studies indicate that citizens would be interested in accessing not only the traditional budgetary information provided by public sector entities, but also financial information. Likewise, they would appreciate the public administration offering them, in addition to financial information (Lin & Raman, 1998), other possibly relevant details that would inform them of how the taxes collected have been managed, i.e. *non financial information* (Tayib *et al.,* 1999).

Additionally, based on Transparency International, Spain (2008), Transparencia por Colombia (2007), Chile Transparente (2008), Gandía and Archidona (2008), this second area includes the on-line disclosure of strategic management information and information on services provided by the municipality.

This implies that we need to differentiate five groups within the information to be provided (Table 3):

- *Budgetary information*: In this section the budgetary information contained in the city council web sites is examined, including data on the budget approved and executed and additional information on the budget.
- *Financial information:* Data on the municipality's fixed and current assets and liabilities, the changes over time in its long term assets and details of its cash flow. These are all indispensable to knowledge of the economic situation of the city council, so that citizens may judge the use made of the funds administered by the municipal body.
- *Non-financial information:* management indicators of the services provided and policy on human resources.
- *Strategic management information:* strategic plans approved and their degree of execution.
- *Provision of services information:* The city should give high priority to facilitating information on the bureaucratic procedures of its fiscal and non-fiscal services. Moreover, it should inform of the quality systems established to control service provision; the commitments undertaken in service provision, reflected in a charter of services; information on calls for tenders, contracting and public works, as well as on the resolution of such calls.

b) The second section highlights the need to design a website that is easy to navigate and provides ready access to the information available. We have concentrated on analyzing some of the basic aspects to be borne in mind when designing a website and that could affect the availability of the municipal information (CYPRG, 2001; Fang, 2002; Holzer & Kim, 2003).

In particular, we have considered the presence of certain essential aspects that characterize the Web's structure:

- *The information on the site should be easily identifiable.* Elements should be included on the website to facilitate searching for municipal information. This would help users avoid confusion and prevent the dispersion of information.
- *The information should be easily located on the website.* As a tool to complement the existence, or to overcome the absence, of a specific section for municipal information, a site map structuring all the information offered by the municipal Governments would be appropriate. Moreover, the inclusion of a search mechanism is recommended.
- *Ease of transit through the information.* An adequate set of internal links –hyperlinks– should be provided within the information to enhance its utility and understandability.
- *The information provided should be user-friendly.* Firstly, users should have the option of storing the online information on their own PC, in a variety of electronic formats. Thus, the information should appear in "downloadable" formats, adaptable to their needs. Secondly, we evaluated whether the information can be adapted to users' needs (in -.xls- format), whether, although downloadable, the information cannot be manipulated (-.pdf or .doc-), or whether it simply appears as html text.
- *User interaction with the information.* The Web is the first ever two-directional mass medium. Therefore, we ascertain the existence or otherwise of an e-mail address other than that of the webmaster to be used for requesting general information; the existence or otherwise of a mailing list; and examine whether the municipal website provides contact information for those responsible for the data provided or for the services provided by the city council.
- *Personalization of the information supplied.* Whether there are any restrictions on access to certain services or information, or whether registration as a user is required to access information.
- *Using different languages to disclose the information.* Given that the Web opens the information up to a wider audience, the municipal information should be disclosed in languages other than the official language(s) of the country.
- *Responsibility for the information disclosed.* It is advisable to clearly distinguish on the website the existence of internal and external links to the city council, so that visitors to the site can know when they have left the site and entered that of another body.
- *Responsibility for the content disclosed on the website.* The municipal government should include in its website a declaration of intentions, stating that the information provided has been prepared and made available by the municipal agency specifically identified, and stating, where appropriate, any external source of information that may have been utilized.

In the content of this index of information transparency, we have taken into account the need for municipalities to transmit to society not only financial and management information, but also a more global vision, supplying information on both the institutional aspects of the municipal corporation and also on the general situation of the municipality. With this aim in mind, we have distinguished within the overall index of information transparency (*ITW*), two sub-indexes, a partial one on the municipal corporation and the general aspects of the municipality (IW_0) and an informative partial index on financial, strategic and service-provision management (IW_E). In total, 43 items of information were analyzed, grouped into the two sub-indexes described above; 21 of them corresponded to aspects of the municipal corporation and general aspects regarding the municipality, while 22 concerned the management of economic, strategic and service-provision aspects. Thus, the maximum number of items that could coincide in IW_0 is 21 and in IW_E it is 22.

Among the possible alternatives for scoring these items making up the index, we opted for a dichotomous classification, such that any given item (tw_i) was awarded a 1 if information in that respect was provided on the website, and a 0, otherwise. Given the absence of empirical studies that might justify awarding greater weight to one aspect of information transparency over another ($IW_{0;}$ IW_E), we decided to assign the same weight to both aspects. Accordingly, the index of information transparency on the Internet is calculated as follows:

$$ITW = IW_O + IW_E = \left(\frac{\sum_{i=1}^{21} tw_O}{21} + \frac{\sum_{i=1}^{22} tw_E}{22} \right) \times \frac{100}{2}$$

Where

tw_i = 1 if the item tw_i coincides with the information analyzed

= 0 if the item tw_i does not coincide with the information analyzed.

The percentage value is obtained by multiplying this by 100 and then dividing by two. In other words, ITW will achieve a 100% index of coincidence if the 43 items observed are published on the city's web site.

For the second section, we prepared an index of accessibility and navigability (INW) in a similar way to that employed for the ITW, although in this case a total of 14 items were analyzed. The value obtained can be transformed into a percentage by multiplying by 100.

$$INW = \left(\frac{\sum_{i=1}^{14} nw_n}{14} \right) \times 100$$

SAMPLE SELECTION

In this study, we focus on determining the degree of transparency provided on the websites of **Latin-American capital cities**, in order to evaluate the initiatives taken by Latin-American governments in the field of e-government. In order to achieve these aims, during the months of February and March 2009 we consulted the website of each Latin-American city and analyzed the information provided on the website. The following cities were included: Buenos Aires (Argentina); Sucre (Bolivia); Brasilia (Brazil); Bogotá (Colombia); San José (Costa Rica); Santiago (Chile); Havana (Cuba); Quito (Ecuador); San Salvador (El Salvador); Guatemala (Guatemala); Tegucigalpa (Honduras); México D.F. (Mexico); Managua (Nicaragua); Panama City (Panama); Asunción (Paraguay); Lima (Peru); Montevideo (Uruguay) and Caracas (Venezuela).

Firstly, we determined the presence on the Internet of an official website of the local governments under study. This was done by locating these websites using, on the one hand, general search engines and, on the other, pages listing the websites of local governments in Latin America. Through this process, we identified the websites of 17 of the 18 cities analyzed; it was not possible to locate one for the city council of Havana in browsers such as Google, Altavista or Lycos, or

Table 4. Index of navigability and accessibility for the Latin-American capital cities

	Index of navigability and accessibility %	***Position***
Santa Fe de Bogotá (Colombia)	76.92	*1*
Buenos Aires (Argentina)	69.23	2
Ciudad de México (Mexico)	69.23	2
Quito (Ecuador)	69.23	2
Managua (Nicaragua)	69.23	2
Santiago de Chile (Chile)	61.54	3
Brasilia (Brazil)	46.15	4
San José (Costa Rica)	46.15	4
Guatemala (Guatemala)	38.46	5
Montevideo (Uruguay)	38.46	5
Panamá (Panama)	30.77	6
Lima (Peru)	30.77	6
Sucre (Bolivia)	23.08	7
San Salvador (El Salvador)	7.69	8
Asunción (Paraguay)	7.69	8

on the websites of federations of Latin-American capital cities such as http://www.flacma.org.

Subsequently, during the data-acquisition process, problems arose with two of the websites. Regarding Tegucigalpa, the capital of Honduras, although a link was found, the website was still under construction. And on the website for the local government of Caracas (Venezuela), the link did not function, and remained non-operational during the entire data collection stage. Thus, our sample was eventually limited to 15 local governments.

ANALYSIS OF RESULTS

The index of information transparency for the sample of Latin-American local governments was found to have a value of 44.23% for the information supplied via Internet (see Table 2). The country with the highest value was Mexico, with over 70% of the items proposed, followed by Chile with 66.3%. On the other hand, the cities with the lowest value for this index were San Salvador, Sucre and Asunción, which failed to provide even 20% of the recommended items.

Analysis of the partial results obtained for this first block of information (the institutional information on the local government and general information about the city) showed that Santiago de Chile, followed by Buenos Aires and Mexico D.F are the local governments that incorporate most information on-line.

A more detailed analysis of Table 3 reveals that over 86% of the cities sampled offer on-line a graphic representation of the structure of their local government. However, very few local bodies provide information on their website about the political party to which their elected officers belong, or about that of the components of the municipal government's agencies.

With respect to the disclosure of information about the elected officers of the municipal government – items 5, 6 and 7 in Table 3 – the results show

Table 5. Navigability and accessibility of Latin-American websites

	%
NAVIGABILITY AND ACCESSIBILITY (14 items)	
The information on the site should be easily identifiable	
44. Existence of a specific section on the municipal website for access to each type of information	86,7
The information should be easily located on the website	
45. Map of the website	53,3
46. System for searching within the website	60,0
Ease of transit through the information.	
47. The website uses hyperlinks as a tool for investigating the information supplied	0
The information provided should be user-friendly.	
48. Possibility of downloading and printing the information supplied	93,3
49. Electronic formats enabling processing of the information supplied	26,7
57. The website of the public administration offers information in audio and/or visual format	66,7
User interaction with the information	
50. The municipal website presents an e-mail address other than that of the webmaster so that the public may request general information	66,7
51. The municipal website presents contact addresses for those responsible for the information supplied or for the services provided by the municipality	46,7
52. The municipal website allows the inclusion of a mailing list to provide updated information to those users who request it	20,0
Using different languages to disclose the information	
53. The information supplied by the local government is available in various languages	6,7
Responsibility for the information disclosed	
54. The website clearly distinguishes between internal and external links	33,3
Personalization of the information supplied	
55. Indications on the website of access restrictions to certain services or data	33,3
Responsibility for the content disclosed on the website	
56. The public body accepts responsibility for the content disclosed on the website	0

that over 65% of the websites analyzed reveal the political history of their elected officers. However, when it comes to providing information about salaries or personal wealth, information which could be used to prevent situations of corruption, we found that only five municipalities gave data on salaries and only one, information about the personal wealth of its elected officials. From the analysis of the disclosure on the municipal website of the rules and agreements adopted within the municipal government – items 8, 9 and 10 – we observed that over 70% disclosed both fiscal and non-fiscal regulations. However, regarding the content of the agreements adopted by the governing body, this proportion fell to 20%.

Together with this information on local government, we analyzed the inclusion on the websites of information about the city, via items 11-21 in Table 3. Examination of these aspects of the municipal websites revealed that the most frequently-occurring item was the provision of news about the city, this being included on 86% of the websites analyzed; thus, great importance appears to be attached to providing citizens with the latest news about the city and about the municipal agenda. Next in overall importance is tourist information, which is given by 66.7% of the Latin-American local governments analyzed. The items found to be of least apparent importance were data on net family incomes in the municipality and information on the city's infrastructure for the provision of services such as healthcare and tourist and sports facilities – such information was provided on only three city websites.

Although the Buenos Aires website presents most information of a general nature about the city, offering on-line data on 90% of the items recommended, it is in fact Santiago de Chile that pays most attention to institutional information on local government, covering 90% of the items, although it only makes available 63% of the recommended items regarding general information about the city.

With respect to the partial results obtained for the second section of the index on information transparency, those corresponding to financial and management information show that this is provided for only 40.2% of the items observed in our analysis.

México D.F and Quito are the two cities offering greatest financial and management information, by including on their websites 69.5% of the items listed in Table 3. As regards financial information, it is budgetary data, with figures for executed expenses and income, that is most commonly provided (in 67.7% of the cases), while financial indicators and data on human capital are least disclosed on municipal websites, being available on less than 27% of those sampled.

Regarding management information, over 73% of the local governments analyzed considered it appropriate to include information on the city's strategic plan and on the proceedings to be followed by citizens for the provision of both fiscal and non-fiscal services. However, it should be noted that none of these websites offered information on the commitments undertaken for the provision of services in the form of a charter of services, or on the quality-control systems established for this service provision.

Having analyzed the index of information transparency, let us now examine that of navigability and accessibility. As shown in Table 4, the websites achieving the highest rating on this index were Santa Fé de Bogotá, followed by Buenos Aires, Santiago de Chile, Quito, México D.F and Managua, with those for San Salvador and Asunción being the least accessible and most difficult to navigate.

Beginning our analysis of the various aspects observed to gauge the accessibility and navigability of the municipal websites, let us highlight the fact that most of those in our sample (86.7%) provided specific sections for the inclusion of each type of information, thus making apparent the type of information included, although these sections were not always located on the home page of the website. Regarding the ease of finding information, website search engines and maps – items 45 and 46 in Table 5 – were provided, but only on 60% of the pages sampled.

It seems to be generally accepted that one of the great advantages of using the hypertext (html) format is that it provides a system of hyperlinks, making it possible to gain easy access to different information sections contained on the website. However, in the content of the information analyzed, this characteristic was not taken advantage of by any of the local governments in our sample.

Analysis of the formats utilized in publishing information revealed that most of the websites (93%) used the pdf format – downloadable and printable – with only a much smaller proportion (26.7%) using Excel spreadsheets, a format that enables users to create their own reports.

The aspect related to interactivity between local governments and users of the information published on the Internet is analyzed in items 50, 51 and 52 in Table 5. We found that 66.7% of the websites analyzed provided an e-mail address other than that of the webmaster, although it was much less common (20% of the websites sampled) for users to be offered the possibility of receiving regular electronic information about given aspects of the municipality of interest.

Taking into account that the Internet makes it possible for any user anywhere in the world to access information that would otherwise be very difficult to obtain, we note that only a small number of the local governments sampled (6.7%) also provide information in other languages, as well as the country's own official one(s).

With respect to the personalization of the information supplied, it should be noted that 33.3% of the sample chose to include this tool as a security measure for personal information, and a means of discretionality and personalization for data consultations by users. Moreover, none of the websites analyzed clearly stated who was responsible for the information disclosed.

FUTURE DIRECTIONS AND CONCLUSION

In the move towards e-government in the public sector, the disclosure of government information is a highly significant factor in improving governance as part of the fulfilment of the requirement of public accountability in public administrations. Public administrations are required to be more efficient, to provide more transparency to citizens, to create an operative framework which facilitates competitiveness and to enhance greater information and participation in public life for all social agents.

Employing new technologies as tools of transformation can assist governments to fight corruption and also to institutionalize transparent public sector practices. It is a proven fact that secretism and the absence of information create a fertile breeding ground for corruption and the abuse of power. Diverse international organizations, such as Transparency International, have reported that developing countries present higher levels of corruption and offer scant information on the management of public funds, while countries with low levels of corruption are more transparent as regards the dissemination of information. The right of access to public information is thus essential within democracy so that confidence may be promoted among citizens and corruption prevented. The development of e-government could enhance transparency and accountability, thus contributing to increasing citizens' confidence and improving governments' capabilities of responding to their necessities. Nevertheless, in the case of governments that are non-democratic or present high levels of corruption, e-government initiatives could be used, in the short term, to extend control over the population and maintain such governments in power.

Anyway, most Latin-American countries have begun e-government initiatives which place notable emphasis on improving state managerial and administrative processes and the quality of online services offered. These initiatives have spurred new legislation aimed at enhancing information transparency, improving the rendering of public sector services, raising the internal and external efficiency of the public administration and promoting citizens' participation. Undoubtedly, these inclusions in Latin-American legislation on ICTs highlight the reality of the Internet as a tool facilitating this process through the disclosure of public information.

However, empirical research has revealed that Latin-American capital cities are still not fully aware of the potential importance of the Internet in enabling the achievement of e-democracy initiatives. The results obtained in studies of the question indicate that new technologies such as the Internet are still not an important means by which Latin-American capital cities disclose their local government information to the public.

Thus, the need to meet people's expectations as concerns public accountability means that Latin-American administrations must be made more aware of the importance of including information on their websites. Such an attitude requires capital city councils in Latin America to consider what information about governmental affairs should be made available, what parameters should be addressed and what should be done so that the website that is created may be readily accessible and straightforward to navigate. For this purpose, we must encourage a benchmarking process among local administrations in order to intensify the sharing of knowledge regarding best practices in this field.

In our study, the local government of Mexico City obtained the highest overall score in the field of information disclosure. On the other hand, excluding the local governments of Tegucigalpa and Havana, which do not have an official website, the local government of El Salvador City scored lowest on the general index. In any case, there is considerable heterogeneity among disclosure levels in our sample of local governments. The results indicate a dissimilar degree of commitment of these local governments to the implementation of the information society. Only 6 of the 15 local governments sampled exceeded 50% of the items analyzed. This means that although efforts in legislation have been made in Latin-American countries, the implementation of Internet as a tool for information transparency remains unsatisfactory. Thus, additional public policies in this way need to be adopted by the central government to achieve greater online information transparency; for example, by promoting an official website with a homogeneous structure and publishing a best practice code on the disclosure of local government information.

From the general and institutional point of view, empirical results indicate that the local governments of Santiago de Chile, followed by Buenos Aires and Mexico City are those that score highest in the ranking calculated in this study. In general, Latin-American capital cities are insufficiently aware of the need to disclose best practices in governance as a means of building trust among citizens.

From the standpoint of financial and management information disclosure, the local governments of Mexico City followed by Quito and Santa Fé de Bogotá are those that score highest in the ranking. Nonetheless many sample capital cities show a low level of disclosure for this type of information. This might imply high levels of corruption, as has been suggested in prior research. On the other hand, greater e-government might lead to the liberalization or democratization of such governments, helping to democratize the provision of information, by improving the transparency of public accountability.

As regards the aspects of navigability, design and information accessibility, in general terms, the local governments sampled leave much to be desired. Their official websites are not well designed for navigating and accessing the information and this impedes citizens' participation and interaction. Thus, our results indicate only an incipient development of ICTs, and thus the possibilities for online interaction remain limited.

As the methodology of this study has been applied to the practices implemented in Latin-American municipalities, studies in other countries and international comparisons of the practices and the determinants of public financial information would be useful to intensify the sharing of knowledge concerning best practice in this field, and to develop a comprehensive predictive model for information disclosure in the public sector using an electronic environment such as the Internet.

REFERENCES

Altschull, J. H. (1990). *From Milton to McLuhan: The ideas behind American journalism*. New York: Longman.

Arellano-Gault, D. (2008). An organizational analysis of transparency: transparency failures as an instrument for incorporating effective transparency policies into public organizations. *Open Government, 4*(1), 1–19.

Berhel, H. (2000). Digital Politics. The vote's. In The Web's potential in the political process is still lacking. *Communications of the ACM, 43*(11), 17–22.

Betancourt, V. (2006). *E-government: An opportunity for citizen participation in the era of digital development.* Retrieved April, 14, 2009, http://www.apc.org/en/news/all/world/e-government-opportunity-citizen-participation-era.

Blakeley, C. J., Matsuura, J. H., & Alliance Law Group LLC. (2001). *E-government: is e-democracy inevitable?* Paper presented at Innovations for an e-Society. Challenges for Technology Assessment, Berlin, Germany, Oct 17–19, 2001

Blasi, V. (1977). The checking value in First Amendment theory. *American Bar Foundation Research Journal. American Bar Foundation*, 521–550.

Blumler, J., & Katz, E. (1974). *The uses of mass communication.* Thousand Oaks, CA: Sage.

Bonsón, E., Escobar, T., & Flores, F. (2006). Online transparency of the banking sector. *Online Information Review, 30*(6), 714–730. doi:10.1108/14684520610716180

Borins, S. (2001). Public Management Innovation: Toward a Global Perspective. *American Review of Public Administration, 31*(1), 5–21. doi:10.1177/02750740122064802

Borins, S. (2002). On the frontiers of electronic governance: a report on the United States and Canada. *International Review of Administrative Science, 68*(2), 199–211. doi:10.1177/0020852302682003

Bouras, C., Kastaniotis, S., & Triantafillou, V. (2000). Citizen information services using Internet technologies. In ECIS 2000, European conference on information systems, Vienna, Austria (pp. 1123–1130).

Brown, D. (2005). Electronic government and public administration. *International Review of Administrative Sciences, 71*(2), 241–254. doi:10.1177/0020852305053883

Caiden, G. E. (2001). Dealing with Administrative Corruption. In Cooper, T. L. (Ed.), *Handbook of Administrative Ethics* (pp. 429–455). New York: Marcel Dekker.

Caiden, G. E. (2003). The burden on our backs, corruption in Latin America. En *VIII Congreso Internacional del CLAD sobre la Reforma del Estado y de la Administración Pública*, Panamá, 28-31 Oct. 2003.

Chan, H. S., & Chow, K. W. (2007). Public Management Policy and Practice in Western China: Metapolicy, Tacit Knowledge, and implications for Management Innovation Transfer. *American Review of Public Administration, 37*(4), 479–497. doi:10.1177/0275074006297552

Charih, M., & Robert, J. (2004). Government On-line in the federal government of Canada: the organizational issues. *International Review of Administrative Science, 70*(2), 373–384. doi:10.1177/0020852304044262

Chile Transparente. (2008). *Estándares de Transparencia Municipal, Convenio Asociación Chilena de Municipalidades.* Retrieved April, 14, 2009, http://www.munitel.cl/eventos/otros/chiletransparente/propuestatransparencia.pdf

Cho, Y. H., & Choi, B.-D. (2004). E-Government to Combat Corruption: The Case of Seoul Metropolitan Government. *International Journal of Public Administration, 27*(10), 719–735. doi:10.1081/PAD-200029114

Clift, S. (2002). *The Future of E-Democracy.* Democracy Online Newswire. Retrieved from http://www.e-democracy.org

Cooper, T. L., & Yoder, D. E. (2002). Public Management Ethics: Standards in a Transnational World. *Public Integrity*, *4*(4), 333–352.

Cross, H. (1953). *The people's right to know: Legal access to public records and proceedings*. Morningside Heights, NY: Columbia University Press.

Cuillier, D., & Piotrowski, S. J. (2009). Internet information-seeking and its relation to support for access to government records. *Government Information Quarterly*, *26*(3), 441–449. doi:10.1016/j.giq.2009.03.001

Cyberspace Policy Research Group (CYPRG). (2001). *Web attribute Evaluation System (WAES)*. Retrieved April 14, 2004, from http://www.cyprg.arizona.edu/waes.htm

Davis, R. (1999). *The web of politics: The Internet's impact on the American political system.* New York: Oxford University Press.

Dugdale, A., Daly, A., Papandrea, F., & Maley, M. (2005). Acessing e-government: challenges for citizens and organizations. *International Review of Administrative Science*, *71*(1), 109–118. doi:10.1177/0020852305051687

Fang, Z. (2002). E-Government in the Digital Era: Concept, Practice, and Development. *International Journal of The Computer. The Internet and Management*, *10*(2), 1–22.

Ferguson, D. A., & Perse, E. M. (2000). The World Wide Web as a functional alternative to television. *Journal of Broadcasting & Electronic Media*, *44*(2), 155–174. doi:10.1207/s15506878jobem4402_1

Fieldman, M. S., & Khademian, A. M. (2007). The Role of Public Management in Inclusion: Creating Communities of Participation. *Governance: An International Journal of Policy. Administration and Institution*, *20*(2), 305–324.

Florini, A. (2007). *The right to know: Transparency for an open world.* New York: Columbia University Press.

Foerstel, H. (1999). *Freedom of information and the right to know: The origins and applications of the Freedom of Information Act.* Westport, CT: Greenwood Press.

Fondo Monetario Internacional (FMI). (2007). *Washington: Informe Anual 2007, Por una economía mundial para todos*. Retrieved April, 14, 2009, http://www.internationalmonetary-fund.com/external/spanish/pubs/ft/ar/2007/pdf/AR07_ESL.pdf

Gandía, J. L., & Archidona, M. C. (2008). Determinants of website information by Spanish city councils. *Online Information Review*, *32*(1), 35–57. doi:10.1108/14684520810865976

Gilman, S. C., & Lewis, C. W. (1996). Public Service Ethics: A Global Dialogue. *Public Administration Review*, *56*(6), 517–524. doi:10.2307/977250

Haque, M. S. (2006). Modernising Government: The Way Forward – an analysis. *International Review of Administrative Sciences*, *72*(3), 319–325. doi:10.1177/0020852306068007

Heald, D. (2006a). Varieties of Transparency. In Hood, C., & Heald, D. (Eds.), *Transparency: The Key to Better Governance?* (pp. 25–43). Oxford, UK: Oxford University Press.

Heald, D. (2006b). Transparency as an Instrumental Value. In Hood, C., & Heald, D. (Eds.), *Transparency: The Key to Better Governance?* (pp. 59–73). Oxford, UK: Oxford University Press.

Holzer, M., & Kim, S.-T. (2004). *Digital governance in municipalities worldwide: An assessment of municipal web sites throughout the world.* National Center for Public Productivity.

Hood, C., & Heald, D. (Eds.). (2006). *Transparency: The Key to Better Governance?* Oxford, UK: Oxford University Press.

Hughes, O. (1994). *Public Management and Administration*. Londres: Macmillan Press Ltd.

International Federation of Accountants (IFAC). (1993). *Managing Quality Improvements*. New York: Author.

Jaeger, P. T. (2003). The endless wire: E-government as global phenomenon. *Government Information Quarterly*, *20*(4), 323–331. doi:10.1016/j.giq.2003.08.003

Jeffres, L. W. (2007). Media technology and civic life. In Lin, C., & Atkin, D. (Eds.), *Communication technology and social change*. Mahwah, NJ: LEA.

Jho, W. (2005). Challenges for e-governance: protests from civil society on the protection of privacy in e-government in Korea. *International Review of Administrative Science*, *71*(1), 151–166. doi:10.1177/0020852305051690

Joseph, R. C., & Jeffers, P. I. (2009). E-Government in the Caribbean Nations. *Journal of Global Information Technology Management*, *12*(1), 52–70.

Justice, J. B., Melitski, J., & Smith, D. L. (2006). E-Government as an instrument of fiscal accountability and responsiveness: Do the best practitioners employ the best practices? *American Review of Public Administration*, *36*(3), 301–322. doi:10.1177/0275074005283797

Katz, J. E., Rice, R. E., & Aspden, P. (2001). The internet, 1995–2000: Access, civic involvement, and social interaction. *The American Behavioral Scientist*, *45*(3), 405–419.

Kim, S., Kim, H. J., & Lee, H. (2009). An institutional analysis of an e-government system for anti-corruption: The case of OPEN. *Government Information Quarterly*, *26*(1), 42–50. doi:10.1016/j.giq.2008.09.002

King, C. S., & Stivers, C. (1998). *Government is us: Public administration in an anti-government era*. Thousand Oaks, CA: Sage.

King, J. (2006). Democracy in the Information Age. *Australian Journal of Public Administration*, *65*(2), 16–32. doi:10.1111/j.1467-8500.2006.00479.x

Klitgaard, R. (1988). *Controlling Corruption*. Berkeley, CA: University of California Press.

La Porte, T. M., Demchak, C. C., & De Jong, M. (2002). Democracy and bureaucracy in the age of the web. Empirical findings and theoretical speculations. *Administration & Society*, *34*(4), 411–446. doi:10.1177/0095399702034004004

Landsbergen, D. (2004). Screen level bureaucracy: Databases as public records. *Government Information Quarterly*, *21*(1), 24–50. doi:10.1016/j.giq.2003.12.009

Lau, T. Y., Aboulhoson, M., Lin, C., & Atkin, D. J. (2008). Adoption of e-government in three Latin American countries: Argentina, Brazil and Mexico. *Telecommunications Policy*, *32*(2), 88–100. doi:10.1016/j.telpol.2007.07.007

Lin, W., & Raman, W. (1998). The housing value-relevance of governmental accounting information. *Journal of Accounting and Public Policy*, *17*(2), 91–118. doi:10.1016/S0278-4254(98)10004-2

Management Advisory Committee. MAC. (2004). Connecting Government: Whole of Government Responses to Australian Priority Challenges. Canberra: Commonwealth of Australia.

Maor, M. (2004). Feeling the Heat? Anticorruption Mechanisms in Comparative Perspective. *Governance: An International Journal of Policy. Administration and Institutions*, *17*(1), 1–28.

Margetts, H. (2006a). Transparency and Digital Government. In Hood, C., & Heald, D. (Eds.), *Transparency: The Key to Better Governance?* (pp. 197–207). Oxford, UK: Oxford University Press.

Margetts, H. (2006b). E-Government in Britain—A Decade On. *Parliamentary Affairs*, *59*(2), 250–265. doi:10.1093/pa/gsl003

Meiklejohn, A. (1948). *Free speech and its relation to self-government*. New York: Harper.

Michels, A., & Meijer, A. (2008). Safeguarding Public Accountability in Horizontal Government. *Public Management Review*, *10*(2), 165–173. doi:10.1080/14719030801928490

Moilanen, T., & Salminen, A. (2006). *Comparative Study on the Public-service Ethics of the EU Member States. A report from the Human Resources Working Group, European Public Administration Network*. EUPAN.

Moon, M. J. (2002). The evolution of e-government among municipalities: Rhetoric or reality? *Public Administration Review*, *62*(4), 424–433. doi:10.1111/0033-3352.00196

Musso, J., Weare, C., & Hale, M. (2000). Designing Web Technologies for Local Governance Reform: Good Management or Good Democracy? *Political Communication*, *17*(1), 1–19. doi:10.1080/105846000198486

Naciones Unidas. (2008). *E-Government Survey 2008, From E-Government to Connected Governance*. Retrieved April, 14, 2009, from http://unpan1.un.org/intradoc/groups/public/documents/UN/UNPAN028607.pdf

O'Neill, O. (2006). Transparency and the Ethics of Communication. In Hood, C., & Heald, D. (Eds.), *Transparency: The Key to Better Governance?* (pp. 75–90). Oxford, UK: Oxford University Press.

Organization for Economic Co-operation and Development (OECD). (2001b). Citizens as partners. OECD handbook on information, consultation and public participation in policy-making. France: OECD publications.

Organization for Economic Co-operation and Development (OECD). (2003a). Engaging Citizens Online for Better Policy-making, *OECD Observer, Policy Brief*. Retrieved from http://www.oecd.org/publications/Pol_brief

Organization for Economic Co-operation and Development (OECD). (2003b). Promises and problems of e-democracy. Challenges of online citizens engagement. France: OECD publications.

Osborne, D., & Gaebler, T. (1993). Reinventing Government: How The Entrepreneurial Spirit Is Transforming The Public Sector. New York: Plume/penguin Books.

Pierce, J. C., & Lovrich, N. P. (2003). Internet technology transfer and social capital. *Comparative Technology Transfer and Society*, *1*(1), 49–71. doi:10.1353/ctt.2003.0008

Piotrowski, S. J., & Borry, E. L. (2009). Governmental transparency and websites: The case of New Jersey municipalities. In Reddick, C. G. (Ed.), *Strategies for local e-government adoption and implementation: Comparative studies*. Hershey, PA: IGI Global.

Piotrowski, S. J., & Van Ryzin, G. G. (2007). Citizen Attitudes Toward Transparency in Local Government. *American Review of Public Administration*, *37*(3), 306–323. doi:10.1177/0275074006296777

Quinn, A. C. (2003). Keeping the citizenry informed: Early congressional printing and 21st century information policy. *Government Information Quarterly*, *20*(3), 281–293. doi:10.1016/S0740-624X(03)00055-8

Rocheleau, B., & Wu, L. (2002). Public Versus Private Information Systems. Do they differ in important ways? A review and empirical test. *American Review of Public Administration*, *32*(4), 349–397. doi:10.1177/027507402237866

Scott, J. K. (2006). E the People: Do U.S. Municipal Government Web Sites Support Public Involvement? *Public Administration Review*, *66*(3), 341–353. doi:10.1111/j.1540-6210.2006.00593.x

Shah, D. V., Kwak, N., & Holbert, R. L. (2001). Connecting and disconnecting with civic life: Patterns of internet use and the production of social capital. *Political Communication*, *18*(2), 141–162. doi:10.1080/105846001750322952

Shim, D. C., & Eom, T. H. (2008). E-Government and Anti-Corruption: Empirical Analysis of International Data. *International Journal of Public Administration*, *31*(1), 298–316. doi:10.1080/01900690701590553

Siau, K., & Long, Y. (2006). Using social development lenses to understand E-government development. *Journal of Global Information Management*, *14*(1), 47–62.

Snellen, I. (2002). Electronic governance: implications for citizens, politicians and public servants. *International Review of Administrative Sciences*, *68*(2), 183–198. doi:10.1177/0020852302682002

Tayib, M., Coombs, H. G., & Ameen, J. R. M. (1999). Financial reporting by Malaysian local authorities. A study of the needs and requirements of the users of local authority financial accounts. *International Journal of Public Sector Management*, *12*(2), 103–120. doi:10.1108/09513559910263453

Thomas, J. C., & Streib, G. (2003). The new face of government: citizen-initiated contacts in the era of e-government. *Journal of Public Administration: Research and Theory*, *13*(1), 83–102. doi:10.1093/jpart/mug010

Thomas, J. C., & Streib, G. (2005). E-democracy, e-commerce and e-research. Examining the Electronic Ties between Citizens and Governments. *Administration & Society*, *37*(3), 259–280. doi:10.1177/0095399704273212

Thorson, S., Chung, J., & Ma, L. (2005). E-Government in China: Bringing economic development through administrative reform. *Government Information Quarterly*, *22*(1), 20–37. doi:10.1016/j.giq.2004.10.001

Tolbert, C. J., & Mossberger, K. (2006). The effects of E-government on trust and confidence in government. *Public Administration Review*, *66*(3), 354–369. doi:10.1111/j.1540-6210.2006.00594.x

Torrejón, A. M. (2004). *Ciudades Digitales Iberoamericanas. Análisis de las web de las principales capitales*. Available at: http://www.fundacionorange.es/areas/28_observatorio/pdfs/8_SPC.pdf

Transparencia por Colombia. (2007). *Índice de transparencia municipal – itm –2005 2006*. Retrieved April, 15, 2009, http://www.transparenciacolombia.org.co/Portals/0/descargas/itm/ITM_Esquema.pdf

Transparency International. (2008). *Global Corruption Report 2008. Corruption in the Water Sector*. Cambridge, United Kingdom: University Press.

Transparency International. Spain. (2008). *Metodología utilizada en el índice de transparencia de los ayuntamientos*. Retrieved April, 20, 2009, http://www.transparencia.org.es/INDICE%20TRANSPARENCIA%20AYUNTAMIENTOS/METODOLOGÍA%20UTLIZADA%20EN%20LA%20VALORACIÓN%20DEL%20ITA.pdf

United Nations. (2003). *World Public Sector Report 2003. E-Government at the Crossroads*. New York: United Nations.

Van Dijk, J. A. G. M., Peters, O., & Ebbers, W. (2008). Explaining the acceptance and use of government internet services: A multivariate analysis of 2006 survey data in the Netherlands. *Government Information Quarterly*, *25*(3), 379–399. doi:10.1016/j.giq.2007.09.006

Ward, M. (1996). The effect of the Internet on political institutions. *Industrial and Corporate Change*, *5*(4), 1127–1142.

Welch, E. W., & Hinnant, C. C. (2002). Internet Use, Transparency, and Interactivity Effects on Trust in Government. In *Proceedings of the 36th Hawaii International Conference on System Sciences–2003*, Hawaii, USA.

Welch, E. W., Hinnant, C. C., & Moon, M. J. (2005). Linking citizen satisfaction with e-government and trust in government. *Journal of Public Administration: Research and Theory*, *15*(1), 1–21.

Welp, Y. (2008). América Latina en la era del gobierno electrónico. Análisis de la introducción de nuevas tecnologías para la mejora de la democracia y el gobierno. *Revista CLAD Reforma y Democracia*, *41*, 42–57.

West, D. M. (2004). E-Government and the Transformation of Service Delivery and Citizen Attitudes. *Public Administration Review*, *64*(1), 15–27. doi:10.1111/j.1540-6210.2004.00343.x

White, C. S. (1997). Citizen participation and the internet: Prospects for civic deliberation in the Information Age. *Social Studies*, *88*(1), 23–28. doi:10.1080/00377999709603741

Wilson of Dinton, L. (2006). The Contribution of Scholarship to Good Government. *British Academy Review*, *9*(1), 44–47.

Wong, W., & Welch, E. (2004). Does E-Government promote accountability?A comparative analysis of Website openness and government accountability. *Governance: An International Journal of Policy. Administration and Institutions*, *17*(2), 275–297.

World Bank. (2008). Freedom of information. Briefing paper. 'freedom of information in Pakistan: drawing on international experience'. *World Bank Workshop,* June 19, 2008.

Ya Ni, A., & Tat-Kei Ho, A. (2005). Challenges in e-government development: Lessons from two information kiosk projects. *Government Information Quarterly*, *22*(1), 58–74. doi:10.1016/j.giq.2004.10.005

Yen, D. C., & Evans, D. (2005). E-Government: An Analysis for implementation: Framework for understanding cultural and social impact. *Government Information Quarterly*, *22*(3), 354–375. doi:10.1016/j.giq.2005.05.007

ADDITIONAL READING

Eschendefer, K. R., Beachboard, J. C., McClure, C. R., & Wyman, S. K. (1997). Assessing U.S. Federal Government Websites. *Government Information Quarterly*, *14*(2), 173–189. doi:10.1016/S0740-624X(97)90018-6

Governmental Accounting Standards Board (GASB). (1990). *Research Report: Service Efforts and Accomplishments Reporting: Its time has come*. Norwalk: GASB.

Hedlin, P. (1999). The internet as a vehicle for investor relations: The Swedish case. *European Accounting Review*, *8*(2), 373–382. doi:10.1080/096381899336104

Institute Of Chartered Accountants In England And Wales (ICAEW). (1998). *The 21st Century Annual Report*. Londres: ICAEW.

International Accounting Standards Committee. (1999). *Business Reporting on the Internet*. Discussion Paper, Noviembre 1999, IASC, London.

International City/County of Management Association (ICMA). (2002). *Electronic Government 2002*. Retrieved from http://www2.icma.org/upload/bc/attach/{613FEECD-7345-40DF-971E-00E2E327A5AF}egov2002web.pdf

Layne, K., & Lee, J. (2001). Developing fully functional E-government: A four stage model. *Government Information Quarterly*, *18*(2), 122–136. doi:10.1016/S0740-624X(01)00066-1

Spaul, B. (1997). *Corporate Dialogue in the Digital Age. The Institute of Chartered Accountants in England and Wales*. Londres: ICAEW.

KEY TERMS AND DEFINITIONS

Benchmarking Process: It is the continuous process of measuring an entity's products, services, and practices against its toughest competitors.

Developing Country: It is a term generally used to describe a nation with a low level of material well being.

E-Democracy: It represents the use of information and communication technologies and strategies by democratic actors within political and governance processes of local communities, nations and on the international stage.

E-Government: It is a term used to refer to the use of information and communication technology to provide and improve government services, transactions and interactions with citizens, businesses, and other arms of government.

Freedom of Information (FOI): It refers to the protection of the right to freedom of expression with regards to the Internet and information technology.

Information Transparency: It is defined as the availability of online governmental information and access to this information.

Political Corruption: It is the use of legislated powers by government officials for illegitimate private gain.

Chapter 10
Human Factors in Implementing E-Government in Developing Countries

Marvine Hamner
George Washington University, USA

Doaa Taha
Independent Consultant, USA

Salah Brahimi
Grey Matter International Ltd, USA

ABSTRACT

Even today only modest gains have been made since the implementation of E-Government. A veritable plethora of human factors affect the success, or failure, of technology initiatives like E-Government. These human factors include everything from simple resistance to change and peer pressure to more complex factors brought about by the value pluralism that exists in today's increasingly global society and its impact on technology acceptance. This chapter seeks to initiate a dialogue in which the broad range of issues and challenges for implementing E-Government can be discussed. It includes data and anecdotal information acquired from citizens, government managers, and experts in the field. This chapter also includes a discussion about reducing the risk associated with ICT initiatives such as E-Government by applying principles of systems engineering, usability engineering and human-computer interaction. Further, this article describes how risk reduction can be achieved by taking a phased approach to E-Government implementation.

INTRODUCTION

Thurow (1997) was right in his discussion about the loss of "classical comparative" advantage. "Brain power" industries and knowledge workers were (are) the "*neo* comparative" advantage of the future (Thurow, 1997). However, it is not clear that even Thurow could foresee all the ways the "*neo* comparative" advantages would appear. The benefits of E-Government for citizens, business and governments have been extolled for years (Jaeger, 2003). Claims have been made that E-Government will

DOI: 10.4018/978-1-61520-931-6.ch010

help government with everything from "radically shrinking communications and information costs, maximizing speed, broadening reach, and eradicating distance" (Norris, 2001, p 232) to increased efficiency of government agencies, enhanced service delivery to citizens and improved public management (Srivastava, 2007). In fact, Carnoy (2000) said that societies that are unwilling or unable to develop such public policies and supporting systems will suffer economically. Even so, many public initiatives, such as E-Government, are usually less than fully successful and some are outright failures.

There are many reasons E-Government initiatives do not succeed. Information and communication technology (ICT) initiatives themselves are inherently risky (Magda, 2009; Davis et al. 1989). But "human" factors appear to play the biggest role in the success, or failure, of E-Government initiatives. Issues and challenges with technology acceptance and usage abound. And, there is no single E-Government solution that countries wishing to launch an E-Government initiative can point to for guidance. In fact, local customization of E-Government plays a large role in its success. This is in part because of the broad, very diverse nature of countries and their citizens around the world. But it is also due to the different views, missions and requirements of the stakeholder groups E-Government typically seeks to integrate. Moreover, there will always be some resistance to change, some need for additional knowledge, skills and abilities, some concern about privacy and security.

BACKGROUND

This article considers human factors that affect the implementation of E-Government. Data and information was acquired from citizens, government managers and experts with regard to E-Government requirements and benefits. These data were compiled, analyzed and used to demonstrate how systems engineering can be applied to address human factors in implementing E-Government. A phased approach to E-Government implementation in which existing government processes and procedures can be maintained while implementing E-Government is discussed. And, using principles from usability engineering and human-computer interaction to design and develop a locally customized E-Government system is discussed. The background material below establishes a foundation so that these issues and challenges in human factors can be discussed, addressed, and, solutions and recommendations can be created.

Models of Acceptance and Behavior

In the real world many things affect whether an individual will use a technology as part of their personal or professional life. Often the factors that affect the individual's decision have little or nothing to do with technology. Resistance to change is often cited as a challenge to overcome in technology initiatives. But resistance to change can not explain why someone with every intention of using a technology does not actually use it. The sections below discuss additional factors that affect whether or not an individual uses technology.

The Technology Acceptance Model (TAM)

Since its beginning, information technology (IT) has diffused throughout the world. However, both the rate of IT diffusion and the rate of its acceptance have varied widely. Sometimes it is easy to understand this variation. Sometimes understanding has proved elusive. For example, lack of access to technology can be an effective barrier. However, even when sufficient infrastructure exists and service is readily available at affordable costs, technology is still under-utilized.

The technology acceptance model (TAM) is one of the models built to test variables that impact actual IT usage. The TAM (Davis, 1986)

Figure 1. The original technology acceptance model (Davis, 1986)

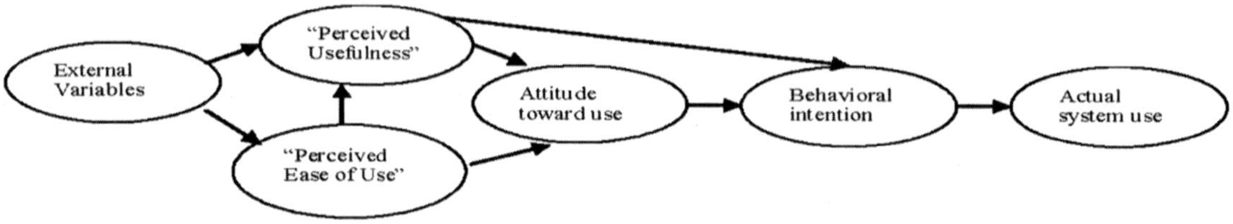

was based on the Theory of Reasoned Action (Fishbein, 1975) that predicted behavior is based on an individual's beliefs and society's norms. The original TAM is shown in Figure 1 below.

Since its inception the TAM has been expanded many times (Rouibah, 2008; Nasco, 2008; Qazi, 2006; Yang, 2004). One version of an expanded TAM is shown in Figure 2 below.

Data acquired during a research project focusing on public organizations in Pakistan discovered that real barriers to the actual use of IT start primarily in the area of "Perceived Personal Utility" (Qazi, 2006). Following the effect of these barriers highlighted a "disconnect" between an individual's "Behavioral Intention" and their "Actual System Use." This disconnect appears to be independent of "Systems Factors" and "Individual Factors". What is left is the effect of "Organizational Factors" such as social context. These factors impact an individual's perception of how they are viewed with regard to their use of technology; and, if the social context supports an individual's use of technology. This is true for both citizens and for employees and managers of government agencies.

The Value Pluralism Model

The original Value Pluralism Model derived by Tetlock et al (1996). Figure 3 was developed to explore an individual's decision-making process in view of their values. Similar to the TAM, the original Value Pluralism Model did not include "social context."

The Value Pluralism Model has also been revised and expanded many times. As an example, consider "peer pressure" in a social context. Peer pressure involves the interactions we have with our peers. It involves whether or not we will be held accountable for our own actions, and/or for our peers actions. We may believe technology will enhance our ability to do our job. We may have a good "attitude" with regard to using technology. In fact, we may fully "intend" to use

Figure 2. An expanded technology acceptance model

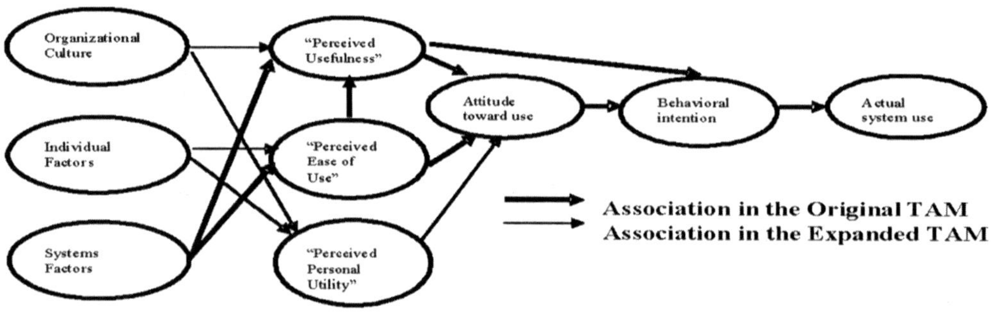

Figure 3. The original value pluralism model of ideological reasoning (Tetlock et al, 1996)

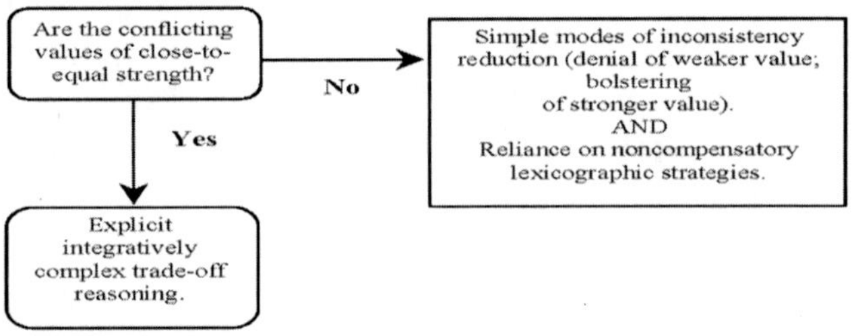

technology. However, if our peers decide not to use technology, then we probably will not use it either. The original reason technology was rejected is not particularly important. The revised value pluralism model (as shown in Figure 4) reflects an increasingly complex decision-making process (Tetlock et al, 1996).

Perceptions about Government and Technology

Government agencies must be perceived as "professional, transparent and efficient" (Grimsley, 2007), but not necessarily as perfect. Routine transactions must be performed, and when errors are discovered they should be corrected, in a "fair"

Figure 4. Schematic of the revised value pluralism model (Tetlock et al, 1996)

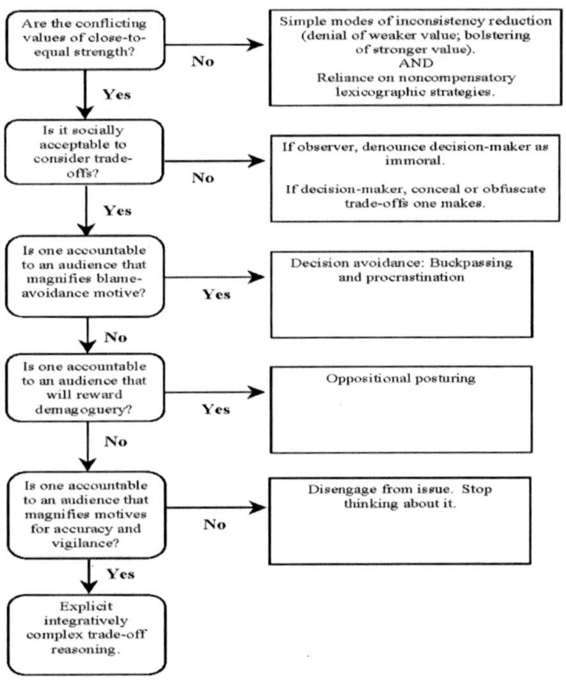

and expeditious manner. To achieve this, government agencies need to improve, or initiate, training programs for employees to increase both their IT skills and their people skills. Only after government agencies are perceived as professional and transparent will efforts to address a "lack of trust" by citizens be effective. A lack of trust creates a social context that is a much bigger challenge to overcome than any technological challenge for E-Government implementations.

In addition, technology initiatives are inherently risky (Magda, 2009; Davis et al, 1989). Heeks (2004) estimated that up to 35% of E-Government projects in developing countries were "total failures," and up to 50% more were "partial failures" while only 15% could be considered "successes". To ensure a successful implementation of technology organizations must consider the affect of the technology on its people. When a technology implementation fails it can create increased conflict, turnover and absenteeism; a decrease in morale; and, a variety of productivity challenges (Grady, 2005). Furthermore, past failures can impact current implementations (Jasperson & Zmud, 2005: Nelson & Cheney, 1987). When there have been failures in the past organizational memory may say, "It didn't work before so why should it work now?" Averett (2001) reported that the Gartner Group said;

In the planning phase of a strategic application project, up to 40 percent of the total cost should be allocated to people issues. Organizations that do not focus up-front on employee commitment, understanding and capabilities run the risk of spending too much time and money at the back end trying to resolve internal problems. (Averett, 2001)

Methods to alleviate the impact of technology include: leadership; end-user involvement; training and education; and, communication (Magda, 2009). Magda's (2009) research also found that the way an organization applies these methods (passively, reactively or proactively) is as important as the methods themselves. Proactively involving end-users throughout a technology implementation helped ensure success and reduced the time it took employees to fully utilize new technology by one-half (Magda, 2009). In addition, elements of designers' context, elements of users' context, and more importantly misperceived elements of users' social context get embedded in E-Government. In many cases, the situation gains "contextual collision" (Heeks, 2004). Such collisions lead to failures that have nothing to do with technology, access or connectivity. Situations like this are often encountered where E-Government projects are proposed as part of reform initiatives but where other issues in the social context, e.g. corruption or low administrative capacity, ultimately undermine the success of the project (Polidano, 1999).

A Phased Approach to E-Government

Many researchers have proposed a phased approach to implementing E-Government (Lau, 2008; Layne, 2001). A phased approach to E-Government might include a "Transactional Phase," an "Engagement Phase," and a "Participatory Phase," each with increasingly complex levels of interaction between citizens and government. Prior to the "Transactional Phase" governmental agencies may already have informational websites that describe their policies and procedures. These informational websites "broadcast" or "blast" information out of the government agency to citizens or businesses. To do this E-Government provides only the lowest level interface, typically a client-server interface. However, useful information for further E-Government implementation can still be obtained. Information about policies, procedures and transactions can be used to establish future requirements for E-Government, e.g. bandwidth requirements or establishing a bandwidth cap so that channels do not become overloaded. But, designing and developing an interface, or any kind

Figure 5. Notional schematic of the resource view for a system

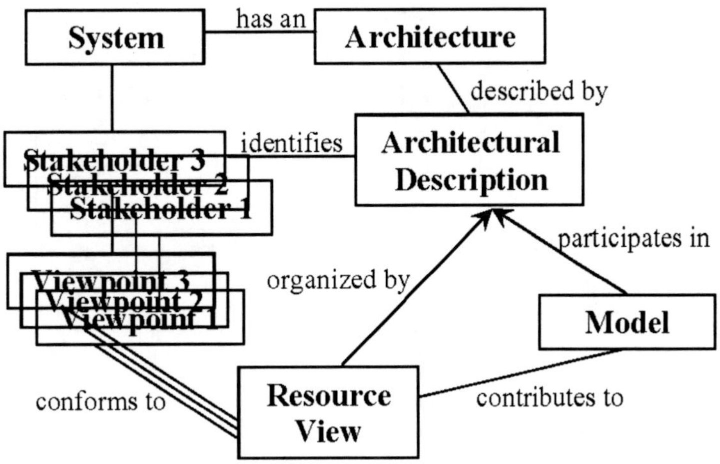

of ICT, based solely on technical specifications will probably not meet users' requirements and introduces risk to the initiative. Designing and developing ICT based on requirements that focus on service delivery to users inherently includes human factors and correspondingly reduce risk due to human factors.

Systems Engineering – E-Government

Systems engineering is interdisciplinary, a complex area of study that can be thought of as a "community of practice" focusing on the design, development and deployment of complex systems, or systems of systems (INCOSE, 2009). Within the systems engineering's community of practice several distinct methodologies exist, e.g. developing a block diagram, or a UML class diagram, or a common project model (CPM), or a "4+1" model (Maier, 2006; Ogren, 2000; Gacek, 1995). Creating a world view that encompasses each distinct view required to completely describe a system is another of these methods. This method is preferred when a comprehensive framework (architecture) is required to capture all the components in the system, including all its interactions and interfaces (Jonkers, 2004; Andrade, 2004). This method is particularly useful for "software" or "information" intensive systems within an enterprise such as those that fall under the standard IEEE-1471 (Hillard, 2000). Because of the enormous cost of failure building a comprehensive world-view model could be used as part of risk reduction for E-Government (Osvalds, 2001). A notional schematic of a "system of systems," Government-to-Citizen (G2C), Citizen-to-Government, Government-to-Business (G2B), etc. is shown in Figure 7. Distinct views, such as a "Resource View," conceptually fit within the corresponding architecture, as shown in Figure 5.

In Figure 5, each stakeholder group has its own "viewpoint" which conforms to (or within) a "view," which contributes to the model, and is organized by the overall architectural design. For example, in a resource view each stakeholder group will have its own viewpoint about the resources needed for E-Government. Each viewpoint will be different depending on the stakeholder. But each will contribute to the model that contains the specifics about resources, e.g. hardware, software, security, etc.

Within systems engineering the first step is to develop a complete set of requirements, i.e. a comprehensive set of requirements that takes into

Figure 6. Resident decision model for the use of e-government (Al-Qahtani, 2004)

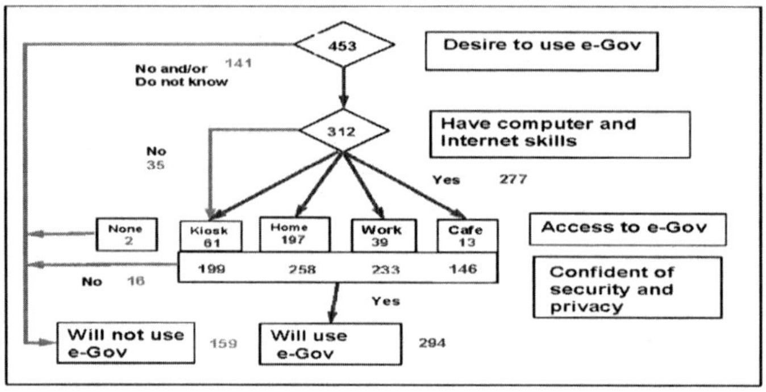

account all stakeholders (citizens, government, etc.), resources (infrastructure and technologies), systems and information, and processes (Leite, 1991). Then, breaking E-Government into four views; process, resource, information, and organization segregates the overall "world" into more manageable pieces. It also separates individual components in the architecture in a way that each component's interfaces and interactions can be studied. Each view can be thoroughly analyzed for local customization.

The synthesis of E-Government should continue to involve all stakeholders, at appropriate times. For example, stakeholder testing of E-Government's functionality, its hardware and software, is an integral part of this process and one way to ensure that E-Government is the usable interface desired. Synthesis and testing end with complete documentation. This documentation can then be used to extend E-Government's functionality in future phases, or simple to maintain and upgrade E-Government as required.

Usability Engineering – Human Computer Interaction Using a Computer Interface

Usability engineering, like systems engineering, has a number of principals that when applied in designing and developing E-Government will help ensure an interface that is useful, usable and sustainable. Usability engineering recognizes factors that include: details about users; details about the tasks performed; and, hardware resources and constraints, as well as social and cultural limitations. Usability engineering follows processes that involve:

- Understanding and documenting the context of the project.
- Understanding and documenting the problem to be solved
- Designing and documenting a solution in context.
- Implementing the solution.
- Testing and evaluating the solution.

These are not sequential steps to be followed in defining, designing and developing user interfaces but rather activities that may be repeated as required to achieve the desired result (Leventhal & Barnes, 2008). Within usability engineering the practice of participatory design includes end-users throughout the project and is congruent with mitigating the impact of technological change. In addition, usability engineering embraces customization of projects. Given the diversity of stakeholders, cultures, local infrastructure, and national strategies, customization will be a vital part of defining, designing and developing E-Government.

Table 1. Comparison of different classifications of developing countries

Country	Classification	per capita GDP (2008 US$)	HDI	per capita GDP Growth Rate
Mexico	NIC	12,235	0.842	3.2
China	NIC	3,315	0.781	13.2
Armenia	LMI	3,360	0.775	13.8

Country Classifications

Local customization of E-Government depends on the issues and challenges each country must address. Such customization requires that differences and similarities between countries be understood. The United Nations (UN), the World Bank, the International Monetary Fund (IMF), and others have all established different classifications for countries. According to the UN, a "least developed" country, or LDC, is a country with a per capita gross national income (GNI) less than $900 (US$) in 2006, in addition to hardships in other human factors. This is essentially the same classification as "low income" by the World Bank whose "income groups" also include: lower-middle income ($976-$3,855); upper-middle income ($3,856-$11,905); and, high-income ($11,906 or more) (World Bank, 2009a). Two additional classifications, newly industrialized country (NIC) and emerging market typically comprise the upper-middle income (UMI) countries. While NIC is a designation that began use over 40 years ago with the "new" industrialization of Asian countries (Fogel, 2009; Young, 1993), today this socioeconomic classification includes countries from around the world. NIC are countries still fall within the very broad classification of "developing" country but have significant advantages over an LDC and in many cases are growing rapidly, e.g. India and China. This article deals with two sets of countries. One set includes countries within the UMI countries including newly industrialized countries; the second set includes countries within the lower-middle income (LMI) classification. Newly industrialized countries include (but are not limited to): South Africa; Mexico; Brazil; China; India; Malaysia; Philippines; Thailand' and Turkey. Lower-middle income countries include (but are not limited to): Armenia; Bolivia; Ecuador; Georgia; Iraq, Pakistan, Sudan, Tunisia and so on.

Because many economic and human factors in these countries are very dynamic country classifications can change at any time and include some overlap as shown in Table 1.

The second set of countries this article includes, LMI countries, are countries that typically do not have as high an HDI and do not have as high a growth rate. They are at a much greater disadvantage than countries in the first set, but do not have the extreme disadvantages of the least developed countries. Table 2 includes a few of this second set of countries.

ISSUES AND CHALLENGES FOR E-GOVERNMENT

If human factors are the primary cause behind the success, or failure, of many technology initiatives then requirements should be developed accordingly. Unfortunately, this usually is not the case. There are many who do not believe that human factors are, or even can be, central to systems engineering; that systems engineering is only comprised of and interested in technology, i.e. components such as hardware and software. This is not true. Many facets of systems engineering deal explicitly with human factors, e.g. determin-

Table 2. Lower-Middle Income (LMI) developing countries with relatively lower per capita GDP combined with relatively lower per capita GDP growth

Country	per capita GDP (2008 US$)	HDI	per capita GDP growth rate (2007)	Population (2008 est.)	Literacy rate*
Bolivia	1,736	0.695	4.6	9,863,000	86.7
Georgia	2,561	0.763	12.4	4,714,816	98.6**
Guatemala	2,848	0.689	5.7	13,000,000	69.1
Morocco	2,748	0.646	2.7	31,352,000	52.3
Pakistan	1,044	0.562	6.0	172,900,000	49.9
Syria	2,756	0.724	6.6	19,405,000	80.8
Vietnam	1,040	0.718	8.5	86,116,559	90.3

Notes: *Literacy rates from UNESCO Institute for Statistics (estimates from censuses or surveys).
**Composite value for Central Asia.

ing and considering the needs of all stakeholders. Establishing requirements that include all stakeholders can greatly reduce the risks associated with technology initiatives. This article focuses primarily on two key stakeholders groups: citizens and managers of governmental organizations.

The Citizens' View

Research about E-Government in the early 2000's in developing countries often involved areas within which no such system existed, yet. This research often focused on the "supply side," i.e. technology requirements for the infrastructure required to implement E-Government (Reddick, 2004). Studies that did focus on the "demand side" often only considered what services citizens would like to have available such as the ability to pay taxes online. These studies did not consider whether or not citizens would accept or reject such systems. Nor did they explore what would be required, e.g. human capital, for such systems to be successful and sustainable. One study completed did use a people-centric approach to explore whether or not citizens would accept and use E-Government should it become available to them. This study took place in Saudi Arabia before any implementation of E-Government had begun and studied the processes of renewing driver's licenses and obtaining passports (Al-Qahtani, 2004).

Al-Qahtani (2004) distributed a total of 900 surveys of which 558 surveys were returned and 105 were invalidated due to missing or conflicting information. At the time of this study it often took days for a citizen to renew their driver's license. Since this was the process in place, this is what people did to obtain what they needed, i.e. completing this process was simply a reflection of people acting as required to satisfy personal needs. As such, it is a manifestation of personal utility not personal preference. At that time citizens reported the perceived benefits of E-Government included (Al-Qahtani, 2004):

- Reduction in over-the-counter costs associated with registration and submission of forms
- Reduction in errors and greater accuracy of data, as human error is reduced
- The ability to communicate directly and quickly with institutions
- Eliminating the need to appear in-person at government agencies
- Providing government services to citizens 24-hours-a-day, 7-days-a-week.
- Delivering government services from any place.

Figure 7. Schematic of e-government as the interface between government and citizens/business

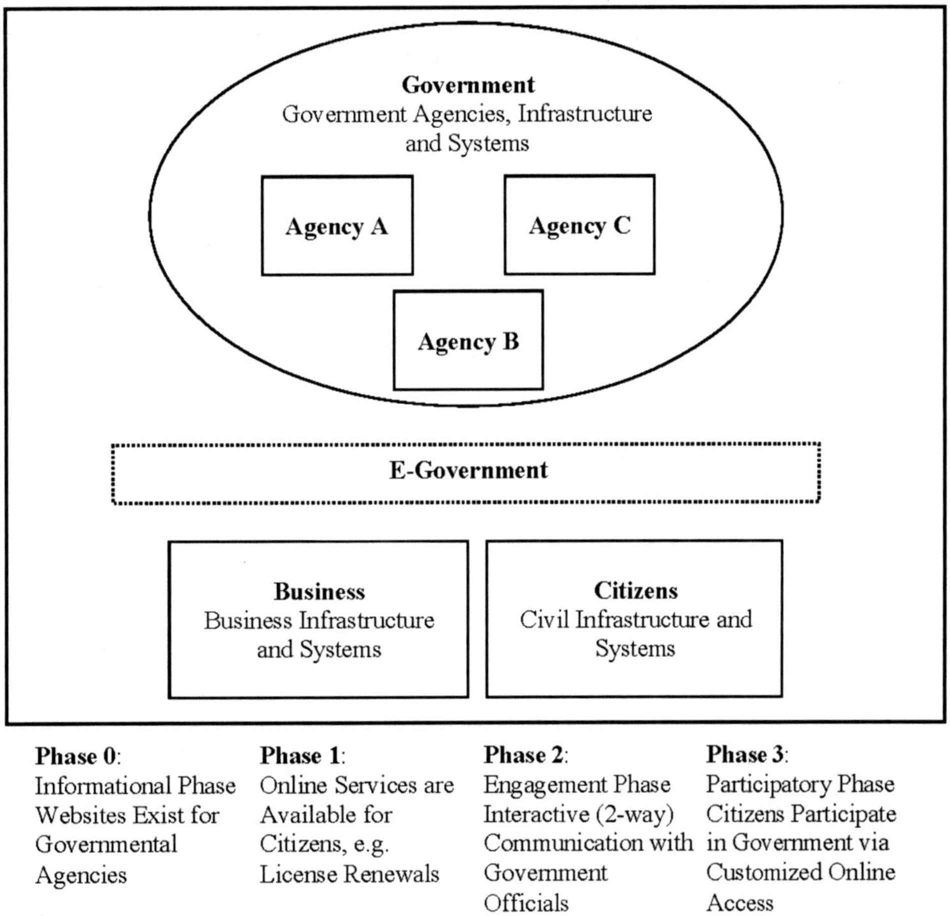

Note that this study was narrowly focused considering only specific transactions and, therefore, this list of perceived benefits is similarly narrow.

Figure 6 below shows the Resident Decision Model Al-Qahtani (2004) developed to illustrate citizens' use of E-Government. From data acquired during this study, 65% of the 453 respondents indicated that they would be willing to use E-Government. Various demographics were included in this study such as the effects of age, level of education, etc. In terms of technology acceptance and the TAM, citizens reported that they strongly coupled the "ease of use" of E-Government with its "usefulness." In general, these respondents indicated that they had sufficient skills and access that was sufficiently private and secure to use E-Government, if it were available. Although this conclusion was very positive, ancillary to this was the statement that "initial usage may be disappointing…" (Al-Qahtani, 2004). This was in part because the highest percentage of the Saudi population was still very young with limited connectivity. One conclusion was that as the population aged and access to the internet increased (estimated to triple over the three years following the research) increasing usage appeared to rest on educating and training Saudi youth about E-Government.

Since Al-Qahtani's (2004) study was completed, implementation of E-Government in Saudi Arabia has begun. In 2005 Al-Fakhri et al began to study the implementation of E-Government in Saudi Arabia and reported that research in three parts: "the types of E-Government initiatives that were being undertaken…; the awareness of Saudi governmental employees of (the) implementation of E-Government; (and) the problems and challenges that faced the Saudi government as it tried to implement E-Government…" (Al-Fakhri, 2008). In summary, this research found that most government employees had not been involved, connectivity was very limited, and employees did not have adequate knowledge about the E-Government implementation. Although Al-Fakhri's research evolved from a very different perspective, its conclusions are consistent with the prior research concerns that initial E-Government usage would be disappointing. In addition, the overall recommendation between the research projects remained the same. That is, education and training focused primarily on the youth coupled with increasing connectivity throughout society, over time. Both research projects concluded that would result in increased use of E-Government.

Benefits of E-Government for Citizens

The broader range of benefits to citizens has primarily been discussed in terms of what citizens "want." In this case, increasing personal utility will be something that provides a benefit to citizens perhaps in terms of greater ease of access or increased transactional efficiency. Since citizens in developing countries, particularly in LMI countries, pay little or no income or sales tax, reducing the cost of government does not directly benefit these citizens, e.g. increased personal utility through reduced taxes. However, a number of benefits to citizens, regardless of economic or political systems, do exist. Based on the review of current E-Government systems and E-Government literature, the list of benefits – what citizens want – includes:

- Access to information, e.g. government information, medical information, legal information, information on rural life such as agricultural information or information about state and national parks
- Income or residence certificates and land registration
- Birth, death or marriage certificates
- Sales certificates
- Driver's license renewal
- Access legal aid
- Access aid from non-governmental organizations (NGO's)
- Reporting broken infrastructure, e.g. roads, irrigation pumps, etc.
- Voter registration
- Voting on the Internet
- Filing taxes
- Other licenses (e.g. hunting and fishing) or official paperwork
- Passport services
- Access to "one-stop shopping," i.e. one portal for all government services

As evidenced by the first few items on this list, the key to benefiting citizens in LMI countries will be providing access to fundamental governmental services. Research in LMI countries has found that rather than focusing on national initiatives, focusing locally where large populations of the poor and marginalized interact with their government is crucial. This is supported by data from experts who indicate that easier access is important to citizens. In fact, the interaction involved in delivering local governmental services appears to have the added benefit of raising individuals' awareness of their rights and responsibilities as citizens (Zambrano, 2008). Incorporating this knowledge in the requirements for E-Government will help develop systems that are utilized faster and are more easily sustainable.

Table 3. Challenges to the deployment of e-government

Rank	Challenge
1	Developing the Required Infrastructure
2	Knowledge about Technology
3	Trust
4	Knowledge about E-Government
5	Knowledge about Government
6	Security

The Government Managers' View

To present the government managers' view a study was conducted including interviews and questionnaires with a group of experts involved with E-Government or similar ICT initiatives, primarily in UMI countries. The experts who participated were primarily located in the region comprised of the Middle East and North Africa (MENA). All the experts included in the study were highly qualified and their "expert opinion" well respected internationally. These experts represented good thematic and regional diversity and included representation from both larger and smaller countries, wealthier and relatively more developed countries as well as poorer and less developed countries. Many of the experts were nationals of one country but operated in others giving them a broader view than their sole own country's experience.

Interestingly, these experts are in concert with findings by previous research and discussions throughout the literature, e.g. what the benefits of E-Government are, what the requirements for E-Government are, and how E-Government can be successful, in developing countries. Furthermore, all of the perceived challenges (lack of infrastructure, need for development of human capital, and so on) posed to the experts were confirmed to be "real" challenges. One point of agreement among virtually all experts is that getting E-Government adopted internally at the institutional level is the initial litmus test for how serious a Government is in deploying E-Government. Hence, internal adoption of E-Government is a clear pre-cursor and indeed a pre-requisite to any wider dissemination of E-Government. In addition, a broad range of failures of E-Government were presented by the experts, albeit without any real understanding or discussion of the cause of the failure. This may indicate that (short-term) efforts with regard to deploying E-Government may have been attempted without planning for the multi-dimensional challenges (cultural, environmental, infrastructure, institutional, etc. challenges) which may be expected in developing countries. Alternatively, given that technology projects are "inherently risky," particularly in their early stages, such failures may simply be a reflection of the level of readiness of E-Government itself.

When asked more generally about challenges to the deployment of E-Government, experts said the biggest challenge will be infrastructure and the least challenge will be security. Table 3 below shows how experts ranked the challenges:

Other challenges experts cited include: people used to working in a paper-based system; conservatism of government; proliferation of computers; communication about the benefits of E-Government; and, knowing (believing) there is integrity in the (electronic) transaction.

The fact that experts found security to be the lowest challenge to the deployment of E-Government is of some concern. This is because privacy and security are critical areas for technology and are believed to be critical areas for

Table 4. Security and privacy challenges to government adoption of e-government

Rank	Challenge
1	Secure Government Technology
2	Security of Personal Records and Information
3	Security of Electronic Transactions
4	Potential for Unwanted Access to Government Databases
5	Privacy of Personal Records and Information
6	Security of Citizens' Technology

E-Government. To explore this paradox further, experts were asked to rank a number of security and privacy challenges. Experts indicate that the governments' technology (infrastructure, hardware, software, systems, etc.) is the single biggest security challenge for government adoption of E-Government. Table 4 below lists the ranks of all the security and privacy challenges experts were asked about.

Benefits of E-Government for Managers

The benefits of E-Government can be divided into two broad categories; benefits to government and benefits to the managers themselves. One example of the benefits to government is the potential for reallocating often scarce governmental resources to better enable achieving social and economic goals (Mok, 2002). In addition, there will also be unintended consequences which can be either positive or negative. Srivastava et al developed a research model to study the benefits to governments from the use of E-Government (Srivastava, 2007). Survey data acquired from experts further validates that model, indicating that enhancing service delivery to citizens would be the greatest benefit to government managers. This was followed closely by reducing costs. Other benefits described include: more transparency and precision by reducing the amount of human intervention in service delivery; and, enhancing the quality of government service to citizens.

Benefits to managers themselves can be viewed from the perspective of personal utility. From this point of view, government managers benefit as E-Government helps them solve problems in managing their agencies, helps them increase their agency's performance and accountability (through increased transparency), and correspondingly helps them increase their overall effectiveness as public managers (Gil-Garcia, 2007). For example, part of the development of E-Government involves codifying the "rules" used in governance. By codi-

Table 5. Managers' "essential" requirements for e-government

Rank	Requirement
1	Functionality
2	Accessibility
3	Security
4	Knowledge about E-Government
5	Knowledge about Technology
6	Technology Required

Table 6. Systems engineering views of e-government

Level 1	Level 2	Component	Interface	Interaction	Tasks
World View					
	Process View	Agency A	E-Government Portal	Website Development	Maintain and update webpages
		E-Government	E-Government Portal	Server for Agency A website client	Process and respond to client requests
					Maintain privacy and security, e.g. authentication process
		Citizens	E-Government Portal	Website Access	Access governmental information
		E-Government	Citizen Portal	Server for Citizen client	Process and respond to client requests
	Resource View	Agency A	Agency A ICT	Client-Server	Agency A's hardware and software
		E-Government	E-Government ICT	Server-Client	E-Government server hardware and software*
		Citizens	E-Government Portal	Client-Server	Citizens' hardware and software
	Information View	Agency A	Agency A Portal	Client	Post, maintain and archive website content
		E-Government	E-Government Portal	Server	Respond to Agency (client) requests to post website content
		Citizens	Citizen Portal	Client	Access governmental information on website
		E-Government	E-Government Portal	Server	Respond to Citizen (client) requests for website content
	Organization View	Agency A	Agency A	Governance	Develop website policies and processes
		E-Government	E-Government Portal	Server	Follow Agency policies and procedures
		Citizens	Citizen Portal	Access	Find information and learn about government policies and procedures

* E-Government resources (hardware and software) may be shared with other ICT initiatives, e.g. distance learning.

fying these rules managers establish the boundaries within which governmental agencies and their employees operate. Even if the "rules" had not been strictly followed in the past, the process of codifying those rules forces government managers, as stewards of the public's trust, to review, revise or eliminate if necessary, and enforce (in the future) those directives (rules) that run the government. This process introduces transparency in government and enables citizens' understanding of how and why specific actions are taken by the government. The process achieves this by enabling the evolution and standardization of organizational routines within government agencies that can then be explicitly understood, reviewed, and changed. Such changes could include modernization of record keeping such as the ability to build and maintain databases more easily.

SOLUTIONS AND RECOMMENDATIONS

E-Government is in reality a tool that could be used to solve some of the issues and challenges confronted by developing countries. For example, Figure 7 schematically illustrates a comprehensive "system" including E-Government as a "permeable" electronic interface between citizens, businesses, etc. and government. Consider the challenge of getting information about a government agency out to citizens in a very remote area. Table 6 below delineates various "views" of a world model for an E-Government portal (website) that provides (broadcasts) information, based on its depiction in Figure 7. These views show how this system (architecture) satisfies citizens' requirements for basic information about the government agency and additionally managers' requirements for more efficient dissemination of information about their agency.

However, the situation is generally more complex. Stakeholder groups in the system include all citizens, the government, government agencies, government employees, non-governmental organizations, technologists, businesses and contractors including those involved with ICT and infrastructure, E-Government researchers and practitioners, and more. A multiplicity of membership in stakeholder groups that invokes decision-making based on the tenets of value pluralism as discussed before. Applying a phased approach builds in time for stakeholders to make decisions; to develop, implement, review, and adjust as required E-Government concepts and supporting systems. It builds in time for making a thorough requirements' analysis for each phase. Data from citizens and experts has been compiled and analyzed to provide the more detailed discussion of citizens' and managers' requirements for E-Government below.

Citizens' Requirements for E-Government

Citizens' requirements for E-Government are crucial in designing a system that can be successfully implemented and is sustainable. Focusing on human aspects, the UN developed a weighted measure of human capital based on one third for the adult literacy rate and two thirds for gross enrollment in primary, secondary and tertiary programs of study. Alternatively, other researchers have considered a number of independent factors that affect citizens' requirements including level of education and social context. Regardless of how it is evaluated, the development of human capital is a fundamental part of the requirements for E-Government.

Prior research indicates that the diversity of human capital precludes the development of a single set of citizens' requirements for E-Government. For example, Kannabiran (2008) studied the Rural Access to Services through the Internet (RASI) initiative in India over several years and data was reported for 2004 and 2006. Demographic data included in this report indicate that roughly 66% of those included in the study were under the age of 25, roughly 60% were college graduates, and 85% held a "professional" job. Given these demographics, this study found that citizens' requirements included: location of kiosks (where E-Government access was provided); low fees; the variety of services offered; the amount of support available; and, the availability of other resources. These requirements are indicative of an UMI country.

However, this is not the typical demographics of citizens in LMI countries. For many citizens in LMI countries development of human capital must parallel or precede development of technology and associated infrastructure. Many initiatives have started in LMI countries, e.g. "ICT4E," ICT for education (Wagner, 2005). While these initiatives are intended to provide basic education, they also provide a foundation for building knowledge and skills required to use E-Government. Again, the success of E-Government is embedded in a broader context. In this way, citizens' requirements for E-Government are completely in accord with requirements for technology and infrastructure that support the development of human capital, bridge the digital divide and promote economic growth.

Despite the fact that computers have been available in schools in developing countries for over 20 years, despite the fact that literally billions of dollars have been spent on ICT for educational purposes in developing countries, despite 100's of projects, untold numbers of articles and presentations related to applying or using ICT for educational purposes in developing countries, very little knowledge exists about what impact, if any, that investment has had on developing "human capital" (Wagner, 2005). Steve Jobs famous comment that "Computers can't solve what is wrong with education" is still true. But equally true is that fact that computers can make an enormous impact on education anywhere. The United Nations Millennium Development Goal 2 which seeks to achieve universal primary education includes ICT an enabler (UN, 2003). Unfortunately, costs of programs like these may be much higher than estimated when initial investment in ICT includes associated investment in supporting infrastructure, recurring costs such as maintenance and training, and associated political costs of such high visibility projects. A broader discussion of these issues is ongoing including "bundling" multiple ICT initiatives to achieve national strategies (Heeks, 2001).

Managers' Requirements for E-Government

Managers' requirements for E-Government are as complex as Citizens' requirements. A preliminary look at managers' requirements, based on data acquired from experts, indicates that the biggest requirement will be functionality. Managers appear to be least concerned about technology requirements for E-Government. Table 5 below ranks mangers' requirements as conveyed by the experts.

These requirements are typical of those stated for E-Government and reflect a top-level view. In reality, like other types of technology projects, E-Government projects (initiatives) are inherently risky and the majority fail (Heeks, 2003). Causes for the failure of E-Government include a "design-reality gap" (Heeks, 2003). This gap represents the difference between where we are now (the current state) and where we intend to be (the desired state). For E-Government this gap represents the difference between government agencies now and the desired future state of these organizations. Ways of evaluating and closing the "design-reality gap" exist and include: hierarchical task and resource decompositions; applying the tenets of process improvement approaches such as capability maturity model integration (CMMI); and using systems engineering to develop a holistic "world view" based on "views" of processes, resources, information and organization. A complete set of managers' specific requirements must harmoniously and inclusively address not just the technical requirements of E-Government, but also the business, societal, cultural, educational, human and technological aspects of the systems interfacing with and supporting E-Government.

E-Government, the Technological Interface between Citizens and Government

It has been widely recognized that simply transferring E-Government and related systems from developed to developing countries is inappropriate. Correspondingly, applying the criteria used to evaluate the success or failure of E-Government in developed countries to developing countries is equally inappropriate. Implementation of E-Government in developing countries must include consideration of the different local, institutional and cultural contexts (Schuppan, 2009). Figure 7 below schematically depicts an E-Government "system," or architecture, as an electronic interface between government and citizens/business. The E-Government interface is a permeable architecture that allows both government and citizens (G2C or C2G), or government and businesses (G2B or B2G), to interact through it, as appropriate. Table 6 below delineates the views for an E-Government architecture representing a government website used to broadcast information to citizens. Using this type of government website, citizens have easier access to fundamental information about the government agency and its services. Government managers can begin to reap the intended gains in efficiency while allowing employees, as knowledge workers, to focus on more challenging aspects of processes and procedures. In taking a phased approach, this type of website provides other kinds of information and helps refine requirements. For example, citizens may find they need different hardware or software. In addition, it allows citizens to reflect on security issues without compromising their security or privacy at the outset. Government managers can review the effectiveness of processes and procedures in achieving goals of the associated policies. And, it allows an evaluation of government system hardware, software and security requirements that can be used to further evolve their E-Government system.

Supporting Systems

Moreno's (2007) articulates a vision of increased public service, increased public value as:

There is no doubt that with the adoption of new technology the public service will be able to increase its productivity and provide more and better services, doing more, more responsively. With new technology, public employment should not be diminished as a matter of course, but rather would require a new kind of professional official who has the capacity to learn, to innovate, and to manage information (Moreno, 2007).

This vision begets the question, "What is public value here, now and in the foreseeable future?" The answer will be different for every country. Once the answer is known, what (systems, hardware and software) will be necessary to provide public value; and, how (e.g. face-to-face or electronic) public value will be provided to citizens can be determined. Moore (2004) argues that at a top level public value comes from government managers' use of assets to provide services that the public is willing to pay for. In this way, what the public is willing to pay for represents those services that have "public value" (Moore, 2004). However, this broad view begins to fall apart as details about how to achieve this are discussed (Moore, 2004). Drucker (1992) said that,

Since the Middle Ages, no society has had as many centers o power as the one in which we now live... Who will take care of the Common (Public) Good? Who will define it? (Drucker, 1992).

That remains the core of the fundamental question. Social integration (Carnoy, 2000, pp 192) across stakeholder groups will play a central role in answering that question. UMI countries have the capabilities required to achieve that social integration among stakeholder groups within their country. LMI countries do not. Social integration for LMI countries will involve stakeholder groups within and outside their country boundaries, e.g. the UN, World Bank and others. This could introduce a level of conflict within some LMI countries that may render them unwilling or unable to engage in social integration. These countries will suffer economically (Carnoy, 2000). These issues are well beyond the scope of this article. Focusing on human factors in implementing E-Government, supporting systems to achieve Moreno's vision include updated/upgraded or entirely new systems for education and training.

Education and Training

As early as 1959 Peter Drucker coined the term "knowledge worker" and envisioned organizations of professionals who had (have) "highly specialized knowledge" that they autonomously applied (Drucker, 1959). Synonymous with Nonaka's (1998) concept of "Ba," in today's Information Society information and knowledge seem ubiquitous. Yet the digital divide continues to exist confirming that there are still challenges to be met. In fact, information may exacerbate differences in economic opportunities, even in developed countries (Bonaccorsi, 2002). While details of the technical, environmental and human challenges will vary between UMI and LMI countries, education and training will be critical in addressing these challenges.

For E-Government to be sustainable, education and training in LMI countries has to include both citizens and government employees. In UMI countries many citizens may have sufficient training to access and use E-Government through their use of E-Commerce. In these UMI countries education and training will likely focus on government employees. As E-Government evolves, a core requirement of education and training programs for government employees will be the development of competencies required to lead the strategic development of E-Government. Details of this strategic development in different countries will vary; but, since it focuses on public value, government managers and employees will need sufficient education and training to develop a deep understanding of theoretical and applied areas as outlined by Moreno (2007) including:

- information and the knowledge society,
- public management and electronic government,
- strategic management and digital government,
- technical and process applications of e-governance,
- the ethics of electronic governance,
- gender, equity, and e-government, and
- the knowledge management function in organizations.

SUMMARY AND CONCLUSION

Human factors issues and challenges for E-Government are numerous. Although citizens have repeatedly expressed their desire for E-Government, in fact they may never use it. If this happens it will more likely be because of the way citizens perceive their peers and how they want to be perceived by those peers than due to any technological issues. Any E-Government initiative must address the broken link between the intention to use technology and the fact that it is not really used. Understanding the decision making process with regard to technology acceptance and usage in terms of value pluralism will aide governments to establish programs or incentives promoting the use of E-Government by citizens. At the same time, governments can promote employees' use of E-Government by proactively including end users, and in fact representatives of all stakeholders, in its design, development and implementation. A phased approach builds in time to facilitate an inclusive decision making process. This process will be a vital part of establishing people-centric requirements, i.e. requirements that inherently include human factors.

Citizens and experts have agreed that with regard to citizens' adoption of E-Government and to governments' deployment of E-Government security ranks lowest of all challenges. However, when experts were queried about privacy and security challenges for governments' adoption of E-Government experts believe that the security of the governments' technology ranked highest and the security of citizens' technology ranked lowest. Consistent with other research findings, experts believe that developing the required infrastructure ranks highest of all challenges for deployment. Of all the challenges with regard to government employees' utilization of E-Government, the basic lack of knowledge about E-Government and the lack of trust by employees in completing government tasks online are the most significant. In fact, most experts believe that to be successful implementation of E-Government must begin in governmental agencies and then extended to citizens.

Facets of systems engineering, particularly determining the requirements of all stakeholders, will be critical to successful design, development and deployment of E-Government in developing countries. Local customization of E-Government will be an important part of E-Government. As requirements are established a business model can be developed that addresses issues relevant to sustainability. E-Government's sustainability will likely depend on its incorporation in the broader spectrum of a nation's strategy including distance learning, bridging the digital divide, etc. While the pattern among developed countries has been consistent between per capita GDP, fixed telephone penetration and Internet penetration, developing countries are breaking this pattern. Assuming appropriate caution about different definitions of literacy, developing countries that have high literacy rates also have greater acceptance of new technology. Future research in ICT should consider solutions that require less power to help enable sufficient localized power generation. However, this is not universal and many LMI countries have much lower literacy rates. In these cases the development of human capital will have to proceed before or at least in parallel with ICT initiatives for them to be successful.

REFERENCES

Al-Fakhri, M., Cropf, R., Higgs, G., & Kelly, P. (2008). E-Government in Saudi Arabia: Between Promise and Reality. *International Journal of Electronic Government Research, 4*(2), 59–82.

Al-Qahtani, F. (2005). *Use of e-government in developing countries: A people centric approach focusing on Saudi Arabia as an example*. D.Sc. dissertation, The George Washington University, District of Columbia, USA.

Andrade, J., Ares, J., Garcia, R., Pazos, J., Rodriguez, S., & Silva, A. (2004). A Methodological Framework for Viewpoint-Oriented Conceptual Modeling. *IEEE Transactions on Software Engineering, 30*(5), 282–294. doi:10.1109/TSE.2004.1

Averett, P. (2001). People: The human side of systems technology. *Journal for Quality and Participation, 24*(2), 34–37.

Bonaccorsi, A., & Rossi, C. (2002). *Measuring and modeling Internet diffusion*. Paper presented at DRUID's Summer Conference 2002, Copenhagen.

Carnoy, M. (2000). *Sustaining the New Economy: Work, Family, and Community in the Information Age*. Cambridge, MA, USA: Harvard University Press.

Davis, F. (1986). *A Technology Acceptance Model for Empirically Testing New End-User Information Systems: Theory and Results*. Ph.D. dissertation, Massachusetts Institute of Technology, Sloan School of Management, MA, USA.

Davis, F., Bagozzi, R., & Warshaw, P. (1989). User Acceptance of Computer Technology: A Comparison of Two Theoretical Models. *Management Science*, *35*(8), 982–1003. doi:10.1287/mnsc.35.8.982

Drucker, P. (1959). Long Range Planning: Challenge to Management Science. *Management Science*, *5*(3), 238–249. doi:10.1287/mnsc.5.3.238

Drucker, P. (1992). *The New Society of Organizations. Harvard Business Review Reprint 92503*. Cambridge, MA, USA: Harvard Business School Publishing.

Fishbein, M., & Ajzen, I. (1975). *Belief, Attitude, Intention and Behavior: An Introduction to Theory and Research*. Reading, MA: Addison-Wesley.

Fogel, R. W. (2009). *The Impact of the Asian Miracle on the Theory of Economic Growth*. NBER Working Paper No. 14967. Cambridge, MA, USA: National Bureau of Economic Research.

Gacek, C., Abd-Allah, A., Clark, B., & Boehm, B. (1995). *On the Definition of Software System Architecture* (Technical Report USC/CSE-95-TR-500). Los Angeles, CA, USA: University of Southern California, Center for Software Engineering.

Gil-Garcia, J., & Martinez-Moyano, I. (2007). Understanding the evolution of e-government: The influence of systems of rules on public sector dynamics. *Government Information Quarterly*, *24*, 266–290. doi:10.1016/j.giq.2006.04.005

Grady, V. (2005). *The impact of technological change on the overall effectiveness of an organization.* D.Sc. dissertation, The George Washington University, United States – District of Columbia.

Grimsley, M., & Meehan, A. (2007). e-Government information Systems: Evaluation-led design for public value and client trust. *European Journal of Information Systems*, *16*, 134–148. doi:10.1057/palgrave.ejis.3000674

Hamner, M. (2010). Potential Barriers to Implementing E-Government in Developing Countries. In Reddick, C. (Ed.), *Politics, Democracy and E-Government: Participation and Service Delivery*. Hershey, PA: IGI Global.

Heeks, R. (2001). *Understanding e-Governance for Development (Paper No. 11). Manchester M13 9QH*. UK: University of Manchester, Institute for Development Policy and Management.

Heeks, R. (2003). *Most eGovernment-for-Development Projects Fail: How Can Risks be Reduced? (Paper No. 14). Manchester M139GH*. UK: University of Manchester, Institute for Development Policy and Management.

Heeks, R. (2004) eGovernment as a Carrier of Context (Paper No. 15). Manchester M139GH, UK: University of Manchester, Institute for Development Policy and Management.

Hillard, R. (2000). *IEEE-Std-1471-2000 Recommended Practice for Architectural Description of Software-Intensive Systems*. Retrieved July 29, 2009 from http://www.incose.org/delvalley/Hilliard_11_14_00.pdf

INCOSE. (2009). Retrieved July 29, 2009, from http://www.incose.org/practice/whatissystemseng.aspx

Jaeger, P., & Thompson, K. (2003). E-government around the world: Lessons, challenges, and future directions. *Government Information Quarterly*, *20*, 389–394. doi:10.1016/j.giq.2003.08.001

Jasperson, J., Carter, P., & Zmud, R. (2005). A Comprehensive Conceptualization of Post-Adoptive Behaviors Associated with Information Technology Enabled Work Systems. *Management Information Systems Quarterly*, *29*(3), 525–557.

Jonkers, H., Lankhorst, M., van Buuren, R., Hoppenbrouwers, S., Bonsangue, M., & van der Torre, L. (2004). Concepts for Modeling Enterprise Architectures. *International Journal of Cooperative Information Systems*, *13*(3), 257–287. doi:10.1142/S0218843004000985

Kannabiran, G., Xavier, M., & Banumathi, T. (2008). E-Governance and ICT Enabled Rural Development in Developing Countries: Critical Lessons from RASI Project in India. *International Journal of Electronic Government Research*, *4*(3), 1–19.

Lau, T. Y., Aboulhoson, M., Lin, C., & Atkin, D. (2008). Adoption of e-government in three Latin American countries: Argentina, Brazil and Mexico. *Telecommunications Policy*, *32*, 88–100. doi:10.1016/j.telpol.2007.07.007

Layne, K., & Lee, J. (2001). Developing fully functional E-government: A four stage model. *Government Information Quarterly*, *18*, 122–136. doi:10.1016/S0740-624X(01)00066-1

Leite, J., & Freeman, P. (1991). Requirements Validation through Viewpoint Resolution. *IEEE Transactions on Software Engineering*, *17*(12), 1253–1269. doi:10.1109/32.106986

Leventhal, L., & Barnes, J. (2008). *Usability Engineering: Process, Products, and Examples*. Upper Saddle River, NJ: Pearson Prentice Hall.

Magda, B. (2009). *Increasing the efficacy of emergency departments through systems analysis of enterprise architecture: Mitigating the impact of technological change*. Ph.D. dissertation, The George Washington University, District of Columbia, USA.

Maier, M. W. (2006). System and Software Architecture Reconciliation. *Systems Engineering*, *9*(2), 146–159. doi:10.1002/sys.20050

Mok, K. (2002). Changing Government Role for Socio-economic Development in Hong Kong in the Twenty-first Century. *Policy Studies*, *23*(2), 107–124. doi:10.1080/0144287022000011468

Moore, M., & Khagram, S. (2004). *On Creating Public Value: What Business Might Learn from Government about Strategic Management* (Corporate Social Responsibility Initiative Working Paper No. 3). Cambridge, MA, USA: Harvard University.

Moreno, E. A. (2007). Competency-based Educational Models for Electronic Governance: Implications for Inclusion and Responsiveness in the Public Service. *Journal of Public Affairs Education*, *13*(1), 79–86.

Nasco, S., Kulviwat, S., Kumar, A., & Bruner, G. II. (2008). The CAT model: Extensions and moderators of dominance in technology acceptance. *Psychology and Marketing*, *25*(10), 987. doi:10.1002/mar.20249

Nelson, R., & Cheney, P. (1987). Training End Users: An Exploratory Study. *Management Information Systems Quarterly*, *11*(4), 547–559. doi:10.2307/248985

Nonaka, I., & Konno, N. (1998). The concept of ba: Building a foundation for knowledge creation. *California Management Review*, *40*(3), 40–54.

Norris, P. (2001). *Digital divide: Civic engagement, information poverty, and the Internet worldwide*. Cambridge, UK: Cambridge University Press.

Ogren, I. (2000). On Principles for Model-Based Systems Engineering. *Systems Engineering*, *3*(1), 38–49. doi:10.1002/(SICI)1520-6858(2000)3:1<38::AID-SYS3>3.0.CO;2-B

Osvalds, G. (2001). *Definition of Enterprise Architecture-centric Models for the Systems Engineer*. Paper presented at the Eleventh Annual International Symposium of the International Council on Systems Engineering (INCOSE), Melbourne, Victoria, Australia.

Polidano, C. (1999). *The New Public Management in Developing Countries* (Working Paper no. 13). Manchester M139GH, UK: University of Manchester, Institute for Development Policy and Management.

Qazi, R. (2006). *Expanding the technology acceptance model (TAM), a consideration of personal computer technology use in public organizations of a developing country in South Asia, Pakistan*. D.Sc. dissertation, The George Washington University, United States – District of Columbia.

Reddick, C. (2004). Empirical Models of E-Government Growth in Local Governments. *E-Service Journal*, *3*(2), 59–84. doi:10.2979/ESJ.2004.3.2.59

Rouibah, K. (2008). Social usage of instant messaging by individuals outside the workplace in Kuwait:A structural equation model. *Information Technology & People*, *21*(1), 34–68. doi:10.1108/09593840810860324

Schuppan, T. (2009). E-Government in developing countries: Experiences from sub-Saharan Africa. *Government Information Quarterly*, *26*, 118–127. doi:10.1016/j.giq.2008.01.006

Srivastava, S., & Teo, T. (2007). E-Government Payoffs: Evidence from Cross-Country Data. *Journal of Global Information Management*, *15*(4), 20–40.

Tetlock, P., Peterson, R., & Lerner, J. (1996). Revising the Value Pluralism Model: Incorporating Social Content and Context Postulates. In C. Seligman, J. Olson, & M. Zanna (Eds.), *The Psychology of Values: The Ontario Symposium Volume 8*. Mahwah, NJ: Lawrence Erlbaum Associates, Publishers.

Thurow, L. C. (1997). *The Future of Capitalism*. New York: Penguin Books USA.

UN. (2003). *Human Development Report 2003: Millennium Development Goals: A compact among nations to end human poverty. The United Nations Development Group*. New York: Oxford University Press.

UN. (2009). Retrieved on July 29, 2009 from http://www.un.org/esa/analysis/devplan/profile/criteria.html

Wagner, D., Day, R., James, T., Kozma, R., Miller, J., & Unwin, T. (2005). *Monitoring and Evaluation of ICT in Education Projects*. Washington, DC: The World Bank / The International Bank for Reconstruction and Development.

World Bank. (2009a). Retrieved on July 29, 2009 from http://web.worldbank.org/WBSITE/EXTERNAL/DATASTATISTICS/0,contentMDK:20420458~menuPK:64133156~pagePK:64133150~piPK:64133175~theSitePK:239419,00.html

World Bank. (2009b). Retrieved on July 29, 2009 from http://web.worldbank.org/WBSITE/EXTERNAL/DATASTATISTICS/0,contentMDK:20535285~menuPK:1192694~pagePK:64133150~piPK:64133175~theSitePK:239419,00.html

Yang, H., & Yoo, Y. (2004). It's all about attitude: revisiting the technology acceptance model. *Decision Support Systems*, *38*(1), 19–31. doi:10.1016/S0167-9236(03)00062-9

Young, A. (1993). *Lessons from the East Asian NICS: A Contrarian View*. NBER Working Paper No. 4482. Cambridge, MA, USA: National Bureau of Economic Research.

Zambrano, R. (2008). E-Governance and Development: Service Deliver to Empower the Poor. *International Journal of Electronic Government Research*, *4*(2), 1–13.

Chapter 11
E-Government, Security, and Cyber-Privacy:
Individual Rights versus Government Responsibility

Ross Wolf
University of Central Florida, USA

Ronnie Korosec
University of Central Florida, USA

ABSTRACT

E-government involves governments at all levels using advanced technology and communication tools to provide services, allow for transactions, and respond to citizen's needs and requests. This on-line version of government, which is designed to enhance efficiency and improve operations, relies heavily on a network of data structures that are currently in place. While much has been written about e-government, few studies exist that link the concepts of e-government and security with individual rights and government responsibility. Now more than ever, progressive changes in technology allow public and private sector entities to routinely collect, store, and disseminate large files of personal information about the citizens and clients they interact with. The power associated with the magnitude of this information requires great responsibility and accountability. This chapter is a beginning point to discuss how governments in the United States attempt to maintain secure fortresses of data, limit the dissemination of sensitive information to unauthorized parties, and ensure on line privacy for citizens.

INTRODUCTION

During the last decade, governments have increasingly embraced electronic technologies as a means to provide more efficient points of contact for citizens to access government information and services on line, as well as to collect necessary data and information about the citizens and communities they serve. While the expansion of electronic government services (or 'e-government') has resulted in various cost savings and service improvements for citizens and administrators, it has also created several challenges. Many citizens may appreciate the ease in accessing city council meeting minutes, reviewing police reports, analyzing property

DOI: 10.4018/978-1-61520-931-6.ch011

records, or applying for government jobs on line, but they may not realize that potentially sensitive information about them may be collected, stored, and accessed on line or through other media used in elaborate e-government networks. Although much of this information is readily available through the Freedom of Information Act (FOIA) and state open government laws, some citizens have argued that the scope of this information and the potential for it to fall into the hands of those who will use it for negative gains presents too great of a threat to their privacy.

While the US Constitution does not specifically mention individual rights to privacy, there are inherent references to it in the 3rd, 4th, and 5th Amendments. The forth amendment is perhaps most germane to this discussion, as it states (with emphasis added):

The right of the people to be secure in their persons, houses, papers, and effects, against unreasonable searches and seizures, shall not be violated, and no warrants shall issue, but upon probable cause, supported by oath or affirmation, and particularly describing the place to be searched, and the persons or things to be seized (The Constitution of the United States of America).

This has been interpreted broadly to mean that citizens have the right to keep sensitive information about themselves private, and also to limit the distribution of that information. The extent of, need for, and use of data by governments creates a quandary for them and their affected citizens. Government agencies collect personal information for a variety of reasons. However, as individual data becomes more and more readily available at the click of a mouse, citizens have raised concerns over the amount of data that is available to anyone with a computer, an internet connection, and an interest. Seen as one of the greatest accomplishments of the modern era, the internet is also responsible for most concerns about the privacy of personal information (Burgunder, 2007). Concerns over keeping on line information secure, or 'cyber-privacy' are not new. Americans have long been concerned with the government's collection of data, but the availability of information today through government-run or government-partnered websites has greatly amplified suspicion. Most governments rely on freedom of information or open government laws that insist that certain information be made public. There are few laws that shield information from public scrutiny.

As the internet has become the chosen means for municipal, local, and state governments to post information and allow for instant access, it has also simplified record searching, giving "individuals the opportunity to easily access enormous banks of information that once were available only to the most dedicated information sleuths" (Burgunder, 2007, p. 585). Real estate records, mortgage information, bankruptcy filings, home phone numbers and addresses, divorce records, and criminal charges are just some of the pieces of information available through government agencies. Before the internet, the fact that government agencies collected certain data and allowed public review of it upon request was of little concern to most citizens. In order for anyone to access data they would have to drive to a government building, locate the right person, often make a written request for information, and pay a copying charge for photocopies. Today, all an interested individual must do is find the correct agency website and enter the correct search parameters--no driving around, no confusing forms to fill out, no printing charges to pay. In essence, privacy as it once was known is dead. It has been replaced with a complex electronic web of seemingly infinite data, poised for infiltration from potential hackers, spyware, worms, viruses, data pirates, as well as nameless and faceless nosey neighbors.

How vulnerable is the information now available? Does personally identifiable data open individuals up to scammers, identity thieves, stalkers and other criminals? LoPucki (2003) commented that some of this individual data is compiled by

Departments of Motor Vehicles, universities, and other government entities, and has ironically been processed by federal prisoners while in prison. How safe is personal data if the government allows such open access to it?

The mission of this chapter is to build on the emerging dialog about how and where citizens are most concerned that their privacy and security may be breeched as a result of e-government. It will address how local governments are adopting new policies, protocols, and technologies in an attempt to provide a balance between protecting the privacy of citizens, ensuring the security of sensitive information, and maintaining effective service delivery systems that protect the public's best interests. Although this chapter is not empirical in nature, it still provides a valuable resource in building a framework for other (future) research to focus on key issues and concerns. In addition, it will suggest emerging issues that warrant additional consideration in order to enhance e-government without creating legal, ethical, or professional barriers to policy implementation.

BACKGROUND

The United States is one of the few countries in the world without comprehensive, general legislation that governs the collection, storage, or release of data on line, or recognizes privacy as a basic human right (Hiler and Belanger, 2001). Although legislation does exist to govern specific exchanges of data on line (such as those relating to the privacy of children or law enforcement officers), the type and scope of personal information that is assimilated can be staggering. Cross referencing data between online and off line data bases, often without the consent of the individual involved, is the single largest concern privacy advocates raise with on line interactions (Hiler and Belanger, 2001). Put simply, the potential for security breach involving sensitive personal information is a very real concern amongst most citizens. Clark (1994) identifies three different types of data which can be used to make positive identification of an individual. "Knowledge based" identifications are defined as information possessed by an individual that only that person would be expected to know, for example passwords, a mother's maiden name, or a social security number. "Token based" identifications are defined as the possession of some item, such as a driver's license, or passport. Lastly, identification that is based on some physical characteristic, such as DNA, fingerprint scans, facial scans, and personal descriptions would be considered "biometric" identifications. Any of these types of identification, however, has failed as a security device when a person other than the intended is able to identify themselves in the place of another, rightful, individual (LoPucki, 2003).

Identity Theft has been labeled as one of the "greatest threats to the U. S. economy...with losses expected to be in excess of $2.3 billion in the near future" (Allison, Schuck, & Lersch, 2005, p. 19). Allsion, et al. define identity theft as the unlawful use of another's personal information, including name, address, social security number, date of birth, and driver's license number, with criminal intent (see also: Ainscough, Brody & Trocchia, 2007; Anderson, 2006; Milne, Rohm, & Bahl, 2004). While there are low-tech ways to acquire this information (such as purse-snatching, or pick-pocketing), and high technology methods require some skills and expertise, even low-tech ways can lead to high-tech use of the data (Allison, Schuck, & Lersch, 2005; Bellah, 2001; Lee & Soberon-Ferrer, 1997). However, society functions on the verification of identities to do business. If you go to the doctor, you may be asked for your social security number or insurance card information. If you get in a traffic accident, and the police will ask you for your driver's license, vehicle registration information, and vehicle insurance card. If you can provide items in either of these scenarios that meet the scrutiny of the gatekeepers, your identity is accepted. But, could a person use someone else's insurance information to misidentify themselves to receive medical assistance? Could someone produce a false or stolen driver's license to a police officer at a crash scene? The answer to both of these questions is yes, and shows how these security devices may fail in certain situations.

While most states have enacted some type of legislation to define citizens' rights to privacy as they relate to electronic exchanges of data, not all of them are comprehensive in nature. Because data included in e-governance may be part of a business transaction that transcends state borders, most comprehensive privacy legislation has come from the Federal Government, and a preponderance of laws deal with one or more specific areas of electronic data. Fears over identity theft and personal invasion of privacy have fueled the movement toward increased legislation relating to both issues. Two recent and fairly well-known examples of federal attempts to control personal information stored or used electronically include HIPPA and FERPA. The Health Insurance Portability and Accountability Act (HIPAA) was originally enacted by Congress in 1996 as a vehicle to provide coverage for workers when they change or lose their jobs. Interestingly, this legislation has become more well-known for the privacy processes it has created, than anything else. Because of the type of data (personal medical information) and the potential for it to be abused or misplaced, the federal government included provisions in the legislation which established rigid requirements and protocols for the collection and storage of personal information from patients. (HIPAAcomply, 2009). FERPA, or the Family Education Rights and Privacy Act of 1974 also created new controls over, and expectations associated with students' grades, behaviors, school work, and other personally identifiable information. It includes regulations on how information can be posted, shared, and stored both on line and in person (Family Educational Rights and Privacy Act, 2009).

Other legislation is more generic in nature, but equally far reaching. Title 18, United States Code 1028, or the *Identity Theft and Assumption Deterrence Act of 1998,* made it an offense when anyone "knowingly transfers or uses, without lawful authority, a means of identification of another person with the intent to commit, or to aid or abet, any unlawful activity that constitutes a violation of Federal law, or that constitutes a felony under any applicable state or local law" (section 3(a)). Many states have closely followed the federal law, establishing that the victims of identity theft are not only those who suffer financial loss (such as banks and credit card companies), but those whose identities have been stolen to perpetuate unlawful activity (Burgunder, 2007).

Although many people are proponents of technology which makes things easier, less time-consuming, and more user-friendly, they are often just as concerned with too much reliance on data that can then be used to commit identity theft against them, or to infringe on their personal privacy. Simon (1992) argued that protections of privacy can be seen as a measure of how much citizens allow themselves to become "subjects of the ever-expanding technological empire" (pp. 1-2). In the early 1990s, Simon pondered how much the government should be allowed to ask personal questions about relationships and daily activities, and where and how this information is stored and used. Even earlier, Rule (1973) wrote of the ever-increasing concern with public controversy over the bureaucratic uses of personal information, fearing the realistic possibility of George Orwell's fictional story, *1984*. At about the same time, Westin and Baker (1972) addressed concerns over the right to privacy in the growing realm of computerized databanks. As we will discover later in this section, these questions and concerns have yet to be answered. While on one hand, we expect those we do business with to know who we are and details of our last transaction, we grow concerned when we find out the depth of information they keep (Rule, McAdam, Steams, and Uglow, 1980), and are even more disturbed when confronted with the potential for intrusion and collection of that data by unauthorized or ill-meaning individuals.

E-GOVERNMENT AND PRIVACY

Government data has gone beyond the information that we have provided on some bureaucratic form or legal description. New technologies have developed and are in use by governments around the world that automatically record information without human intervention. Most citizens are aware that when they use an electronic toll device that the toll agency records certain information, such as the time and date, lane of travel, and registered owner of the device; however, these toll booth equipment can also collect additional information, such as photographs of drivers, and the speed of the vehicle.

Police agencies have also recently begun collecting data through License Plate Recognition (LPR) devices, that utilize photographs of vehicles to automatically check information about the vehicle and registered owner. These LPR cameras can be fixed-mounted, or mounted on a police or government vehicle. License plates that are "seen" by the camera are checked against police data bases, and if something of interest is noted by the system, human operators are notified. In addition to capturing data about where a certain vehicle was located at a particular time, additional information, including possibly a photograph of occupants of the vehicle can be stored. Deployment of these devices in Europe is commonplace, London set up a "Ring of Steel" of these devices in the early 1990s to monitor the plates of every single vehicle entering the city (Wolf & Gordon, 2007). While the use of these devices is still new in the United States, similar uses are being considered, and citizen groups are keeping a watchful eye on the technology. Although the collection of this data may seem innocuous, a fear exists that images and data captured by the cameras violates personal privacy.

Related new technology allows for the downloading, or "cloning" of almost every single type of cell phone on the market in the world today. Marketed to police and military intelligence agencies, one device called "Cellebrite" can allow the operator to copy every single piece of data contained in an electronic phone, Blackberry®, Ipod®, MP3 player, or other storage device. The device is battery-operated and handheld and requires no computer for extraction, downloading information from the device's internal phonebook, text messages, pictures, videos, call logs, audio files, and deleted call histories (Portable, 2009). If an individual arrested by police has a cell phone on his person, case law may allow the police to copy this data for future intelligence.

Issues, Controversies, Problems

As noted earlier in this chapter, collecting, storing and using data on line is not a new phenomenon. What are more recent concerns, however, are differing perspectives of the security of this information, and implications associated with sensitive data falling into the wrong hands. The terms 'sensitive' and 'wrong' are the operative terms here. Each can be defined very broadly and very differently, given the situational context. In the event that personal information is accidentally or intentionally disseminated or accessed without the consent of the individual, complaints of invasion of privacy, unwarranted intrusion into personal lives, and breach of Constitutional rights escalate. The type of information that is currently being collected, stored, and used is staggering---and varies based on agency. Some of this information is common and is required for routine activities, such as applying for a marriage license or a home loan.

Consider, for example, the conventional practice of applying for a home loan. Since some loan funds are guaranteed by the US government, private mortgage companies often collect, store, and disseminate the following information about individuals to government agencies, private corporations and other stakeholders:

- name and any "aliases"—including maiden name and variations name;
- birth date, social security number, and gender;
- phone number(s), cell phone numbers, and email addresses;
- former addresses and length of time lived at each, as well as if owned or rented;
- educational background-- schools attended and addresses; degrees awarded and dates;
- outstanding debts (including credit card numbers, balances and bank names);
- listing of assets, such as cars, boats, other homes, savings accounts (again, including account numbers and bank names);
- marital status, name of spouse, name of dependents, their names, ages, and addresses;
- legal judgments;
- employment data, including current job title, salary, address, and length of time in that position, as well as previous jobs, titles, addresses and length of time in position;
- names of nearest family members, addresses, and phone numbers;
- insurance information; and
- retirement funds, stocks, bonds values, names and company information.

The collection of this information can certainly be important for government agencies, but is it really necessary? Certainly it is important for any business entity to verify the identity of those with which they have a relationship to curb fraudulent acts, and for government this can be especially important. Providing emergency relief funding to fictitious people, releasing arrestees who are wanted under a different name, or providing medical assistance to those who have not received care can all erode confidence in the ability of government to be effective stewards of the public purse. Internationally, many governments have considered the potential uses of a national government ID card to reduce inconsistencies in identification. The government of Dubai is the first to make such identification mandatory for all citizens. Instead of multiple identity cards such as driver's licenses, work permits, employee cards, and passports, the UAE Federal Government created a single national identity card in April 2006, mandating its use by citizens, nationals and others by 2009. The card contains smart features including biometrics and other features that will eventually eliminate the need to carry multiple cards (Get a National Identity Card, 2008). Where the identification of veiled women had been an issue, fingerprints are now compared against encoded records in the card to verify the identity of the holder without asking for the woman to uncover her face (Shaaban, 2009).

Collecting Personal Information

Governments have several ways that they use personal information through various e-government activities: to deliver services, to protect security, to enhance democracy, to work with businesses, and to work with other governments (Belanger and Hiller, 2000). The most prevalent reason that governments collect, analyze and use personal information and data is to be more effective in the way that they provide services to citizens. Services may include anything from requesting mail to be stopped via an interactive link to renting a pavilion in a public park. Another example of this may be citizen requests for assistance after a natural disaster. Citizens may make application to the Federal Emergency Management Agency for monetary assistance after a hurricane. The application is uploaded into a computer system, disseminated to adjusters in the area, verified electronically, and then assistance funding is provided. However, these databases can also serve as a method of checks and balances. The government keeps this information to insure that fraudulent acts have not occurred and that the same person is not receiving multiple payments. Obviously, these checks and balances are not fool-proof.

Governments also collect data to protect and provide homeland security, and for law enforcement. In 2002, the US Government established the Information Awareness Office (IAO) as a response to the 9/11 terrorist attacks (Defense Advanced Research Projects Agency, 2002) This mega-stealth organization was tasked with creating a macro systems approach to researching, developing, and integrating technologies to aggregate data virtually, and allow data mining of such information. (Defense Advanced Research Projects Agency, 2002). As a start up organization, IAO collected financial data on individuals from banks, educational institutions (elementary schools, high schools, colleges, trade school, and others), travel agencies (including data on vacations, business travel, and other travels), medical facilities (hospitals, doctors offices, pharmacies, and insurance agencies), veterinary clinics (relating to animals, doctors seen and medicines prescribed), housing data (location, tax value, purchased/rented, bankruptcy, liens), and transportation entities (cars, boats, planes, owned/leased) to identify and track potential terrorists and persons of interest in suspected terrorist activities. Although the agency was defunded in 2003 amidst public outcry over the extensively intrusive nature of this organization, other groups continue to collect data files on a less comprehensive level. A simple traffic stop can involve the collection and transfer of sensitive and personally identifiable information, including a personal photo, insurance data, and medical information, (such as driving restrictions due to physical limitations or health issues). Taking into account the additional questions that are asked, such as "Where were you going?," "Why?," "Who is in this car with you?," "How do you know each other?," "Where are you coming from?," "How long were you there?," "What were you doing there?," "What is in your car?," "Have you been drinking?," "What were you drinking?," "How many?," "When?," "Where?," and others, it quickly becomes clear that some in some instances, motorists may feel that the information being collected about them may potentially harm their public image, professional image, marriage, or other social stature.

Governments must have up-to-date information on citizens in order to be able to identify, communicate with, and serve them and insure democracy. A drivers license, birth certificate, social security card, draft card, or other personally identifiable document is used to help officially determine that the person in front of a government agency is really whom they say they are—and that they are eligible for the services and resources that all Americans enjoy. For example, swiping a driver's license or voter registration card at a polling place on Election Day allows governments to confirm the identity of an individual requesting to vote. Filing an on line claim as part of a class action suit with the Department of Justice is also part of this process, as is updating drivers license information on line.

Because much of what takes place in the US is affected by the private sector, governments have increasingly turned to on-line technology and resources to foster effective relationships. Lockheed Martin (a private company), for example, may respond to a RFP (request for proposal) from the National Aeronautical Space Alliance (NASA) to build the next generation of space shuttle orbiters. As part of the on-line application process, NASA may request names, resumes and qualifications from potential workers, workplace safety reports, information on the financial stability of the company, and other sensitive information. Working with other governments on line, governments at all levels also share information and collaborate on tasks.

Threats to Privacy and Security

The elements of virtual technology that make e-government successful are the parallel attributes that make it especially vulnerable for abuse. The low cost, expediency of data retrieval, user-friendliness and anonymous nature of cyber-based information technology may result in abuses of power. The extent of these exploitations may include accidentally/intentionally leaking sensitive data, cyber-stalking, government spying, invasion of personal privacy, and other unauthorized access to personal information.

Intentionally or accidentally leaking sensitive information can have long reaching effects on private citizens. Professional and social reputations can become tarnished, jobs can be terminated, friendships can become tainted and individual sense of self worth can be diminished----whether or not the information released is accurate or not. Once the information is out there, individuals have a hard time harnessing it or reversing the potential damage created by the breach.

Cyber-stalking is the use of the Internet, e-mail, or other electronic communication devices to harass or follow another person. Because the internet and email are fairly anonymous, the cyber-stalker is able to harass his/her victims with in pain view with complete coverage. As the US Attorney General indicated,

"Unbeknownst to the target, the perpetrator could be in another state, around the corner, or in the next cubicle at work. The perpetrator could be a former friend or lover, a total stranger met in a chat room, or simply a teenager playing a practical joke. The inability to identify the source of the harassment or threats could be particularly ominous to a cyber-stalking victim, and the veil of anonymity might encourage the perpetrator to continue these acts. In addition, some perpetrators, armed with the knowledge that their identity is unknown, might be more willing to pursue the victim at work or home, and the Internet can provide substantial information to this end. Numerous websites will provide personal information, including unlisted telephone numbers and detailed directions to a home or office. For a fee, other websites promise to provide social security numbers, financial data, and other personal information." (1999 Report on Cyber-stalking, 1999, Para. 19).

Aggressive government monitoring or "snooping" of citizens' electronic activities has become more pronounced since the Patriot Act was passed in 2001(Source: "Electronic Privacy Information Center, http://epic.org/privacy/terrorism/hr3162.html, retrieved on March 30, 2009). Every time a citizen logs into a website, places a cell phone call, swipes a credit card or reads an on line journal, a record of that action is created, and an electronic trail of the transaction is left behind. Massive and complex government "carnivore" programs endorsed and protected by the Patriot Act allow governments to legally hack into the private, on line lives of citizens and monitor their daily routines. Chat rooms, email, on line social networking or dating sites, blogs, and even reverse monitor cams on computers are used to methodically track the actions of citizens (Smith, 2001).

The scope and extent of the information collected about individuals can be staggering. To add an additional element to this equation, consider the issue of individuals who have common names, such as Jim Smith or Robert Jones. Information that is collected on these individuals may be mistakenly attributed to another person with the same name. This creates an even more complex breach of 'identify theft' for the individual who must then clear his or her own name.

System Failures/Gaps in Coordination

Rapid expansion of the use of computer applications in government and by private corporations doing government business has provided unprecedented opportunities for criminals. The new opportunities created by commerce in cyberspace have allowed individual offenders and criminal networks to outwit and avoid law enforcement agencies that have been unable to effectively respond (Broadhurst, 2006). "As never before and at little cost a single offender can inflict catastrophic loss or damage on individuals, companies, and governments from the other side of the world" (Broadhurst, 2006, p. 4). This has resulted in the need for reliable, effective, and efficient cooperation between law enforcement agencies and governments in the investigation and prosecution of cyber-crime, even though most policing agencies are still relatively powerless to discover or investigate these offenses within their jurisdictions. It may not always be clear where, and under whose jurisdiction, cyber-related crimes occur. A single offense may produce victims in many different cities, states, or countries. This results in cross-border conflicts of determining which jurisdiction should prosecute and how to deal with the logistical issues of witness or victim testimony, unnecessary duplication of law enforcement and prosecutorial efforts, civil and criminal offense standards, data collection and preservation practices, and other evidentiary factors (Broadhurst, 2006; Brungs & Jamieson, 2005; Hinduja, 2004; Hinduja, 2007).

These problems continue to gain complexity as criminals and criminal organizations recruit specialists trained by government and commercial companies to better gain access to information technology systems, and to entice government workers to provide access in exchange for payoffs. Criminals are also exploiting the lack of effective enforcement and jurisdictional issues by coordinating attacks from multiple jurisdictions (Broadhurst, 2006). Overlapping jurisdictions and a lack of coordinated agreements for prosecution only make this type of crime more profitable for criminals, while the information gleaned from these actions has a deep social and psychological impact on the individual victims.

Solutions and Recommendations

It is difficult to provide simple solutions and recommendations regarding these issues. For every possible solution, there are additional concerns and corollaries created. Regardless of security provided to databases, it is inevitable that unscrupulous individuals will go to extraordinary and imaginative lengths to attain personal information so that they can sell this information to others or engage in illegal transactions with this information themselves. As a beginning point for understanding and dealing with these issues, we suggest three main focal points for future research and consideration:

1. Targeted legislation that is coordinated and enforced. While it is imperative that state governments keep up with the times and provide legislation that criminalize new and innovative ways to breach data storage systems, it is also important that legislation is created that clearly defines what information is collected and retained by government entities, and why that information is important. One example of the need for this lies in integrated data sharing networks. Increasingly, government agencies have begun to use data systems that share information, rather than storing information in one secure location. Such programs, such as the Florida Integrated Network for Data Exchange and Retrieval (FINDER) allow previously impossible ways to find out information about individuals, transactions, and activities that cross jurisdictional boundaries. The system is designed to allow Florida's law-enforcement agencies to communicate important information "in a system designed to keep terrorists and criminals from using a lack of cross-jurisdiction communication to cover their tracks" (Greenemeier, 2005). Numerous operating systems such as FINDER have been developing throughout

the nation and the world, in an attempt to allow government agencies to better communicate with each other, and mine data that would previously sit uselessly in a single agency's computer memory. In the not-so-distant future, one division may have a need to know everyone who has come in contact with a particular individual, for example an individual who has been diagnosed with a disease but is unconscious. That agency may use one of these network software programs to find out everyone that the diseased individual has communicated with by phone, any contacts made with police agencies, use of ATM devices, where the person drove using his GPS device, and any transactions that person has made by credit card. While this is certainly a great way to attempt to head off the spread of disease, it is also a clear manifestation of the fear developed in the book *1984*. Legislation that mandates the use and scope of these types of networks is greatly needed. Governments and organizations must understand the extent of the power of these integrated networks, and must be aware that safeguarding them is not merely suggested, but mandated by law. A system of strict sanctions or penalties should be created to encourage organizations and governments to conform. A 'zero tolerance' policy should be created for those individuals who knowingly disseminate personal information for their own gain or pleasure.

2. Investment in security technology and public/private collaboration. It is also important that government agencies utilize the most up-to date security protocols for storage devices that hold personal information. While this may seem a simple solution, with the advent of multiple-data storage devices in networked systems, it becomes a nightmare. As more and more data is collected, and more and more people have access to shared system information, the data becomes more prone to infiltration or misuse. Those who have access to the data in these systems, such as law enforcement officers and other government administrators need to be trained and educated on the specific things they can and cannot do with the information obtained. Clearly established lines of conduct need to be communicated regarding government and private data, and misuse should not be tolerated. Encouraging extensive collaboration and research on cyber security should become a mainstay of federal educational funding or private grant efforts.
3. Enforcement and sanctions. Finally, there needs to be strict and severe punishment for the misuse of power and information tied to these systems. While infiltration and misuse of data records may not be immune to clever hackers, there is also a very real threat from those authorized to use the systems for legal means. Examples include finding and using information for blackmail, personal monetary gain, or stalking. While training and education of government employees and private contractors with access to systems plays an important role, there must also be sever sanctions for those who misuse the information. Currently, few cases are identified or publicized when individuals are associated with cyber crimes. Diligent tracking of these infractions and strict enforcement of expected norms, rules and laws will help break the semblance of anonymity that hackers and cyber criminals may currently enjoy.

CONCLUSION

This research is a beginning point in discussing the main issues relating to e-government, privacy, and security in the United States. As communities and regions continue to grow in size and complexity, there is a heightened expectation that governments will continue to respond to new needs and issues with greater efficiency. A large part of this movement in the last ten years has focused new applications of information technology and especially e-government. With the transition to more government functions and services being conducted on line has come a corresponding shift in the potential for misuse or abuse of data collected, managed and stored on line. Central to this discussion has been the concept of privacy—and especially cyber-privacy. Certainly individuals within society consider certain information about themselves to be privileged, but they may be surprised to find that this same information is maintained by numerous government and private entities, and may be more easily accessed than they would like. Governments at all levels hold a special level of responsibility to be vigilant in carefully monitoring the information that they collect, report on, and store. In addition, they must be respectful of privacy concerns, and careful in the factual, honest reporting of all information. Finally, and perhaps most importantly, governments must become more proactive in creating comprehensive legislation that protects individuals from the potential of unreasonable intrusions into their personal lives via the intentional or unintentional disclosure of personal information. As we continue to teeter between expanding technology and attempting to bridge the digital divide, governments must take the lead on creating new laws that more successfully protect the anomonity of private citizens, rather than providing cover to nameless and faceless cybercriminals. Future research should explore differing practices in e-government and security on a case by case basis in the United States and in international forums. In addition, we encourage other scholars to provide empirical evidence on the linkage between individual rights and government responsibility in e-government transactions.

REFERENCES

Ainscough, T. L., Brody, R. G., & Trocchia, P. J. (2007). Identity theft and consumers' reaction to preventative technological innovations. *Psychological Reports*, *101*, 250–258. doi:10.2466/PR0.101.5.250-258

Allison, S. F. H., Schuck, A. M., & Lersch, K. M. (2005). Exploring the crime of identity theft: Prevalence, clearance rates, and victim/offender characteristics. *Journal of Criminal Justice*, *33*, 19–29. doi:10.1016/j.jcrimjus.2004.10.007

Anderson, K. B. (2006). Who are the victims of identity theft? The effects of demographics. *Journal of Public Policy & Marketing*, *25*(2), 160–171. doi:10.1509/jppm.25.2.160

Bellah, J. (2001). Identity theft: Ruining credit and creating criminal records. *Law & Order*, *49*(10), 222–226.

Broadhurst, R. (2006). Developments in the global law enforcement of cyber-crime. *Policing: An International Journal of Police Strategies and Management*, *29*(2), 408–433.

Brungs, A., & Jamieson, R. (2005). Identification of legal issues for computer forensics. *Information Systems Management*, *22*(2), 57–66. doi:10.1201/1078/45099.22.2.20050301/87278.7

Burgunder, L. (2007). *Legal aspects of managing technology*. Mason, OH: Cengage Learning.

Censusof Governments Counts 16 million State and Local Employees. (2007). Retrieved April 20, 2009, from http://www.census.gov/Press-release/www/releases/archives/employment_occupations/012797.html

Clarke, R. (1994). Human identification in information systems: Management challenges and public policy issues. *Information Technology & People*, *7*(4), 6-37. Retrieved March 5, 2009 from http://www.rogerclarke.com/DV/HumanID.html

Family Educational Rights and Privacy Act (FERPA). (n.d.). Retrieved March 15, 2009 from http://www.ed.gov/policy/gen/guid/fpco/ferpa/index.html

Get a National Identity Card in the UAE. (2008, December 29). Retrieved April 10, 2009 from http://www.dubai.ae/en.portal

Greenemeier, L. (January 20, 2005). Florida Police Network Supports Post-9/11 Promises: Florida hopes to expand a data-sharing network aimed at spotting criminals or terrorists across jurisdictions. *Intelligent Enterprise*. Retrieved April 10, 2009 from http://www.intelligententerprise.com/showArticle.jhtml?articleID=57702947

Hiler, J. S., & Belanger, F. (2001). *Privacy Strategies for Electronic Government*. Retrieved February 10 from http://www.businessofgovernment.org/main/publications/grant_reports/details/index.asp?GID=6

Hinduja, S. (2004). Perceptions of local and state law enforcement concerning the role of computer crime investigative teams. *Policing: An International Journal of Police Strategies and Management*, *27*(3), 341–357. doi:10.1108/13639510410553103

Hinduja, S. (2007). Computer Crime Investigations in the United States: Leveraging Knowledge from the Past to Address the Future. *International Journal of Cyber Criminology*, *1*(1), 1–26.

HIPAAcomply - The Definitive Source for Information on HIPAA Security and Privacy Compliance. (n.d.). Retrieved April 5, 2009 from http://www.hipaacomply.com

Lee, J., & Soberon-Ferrer, H. (1997). Consumer vulnerability to fraud: Influencing factors. *The Journal of Consumer Affairs*, *31*(1), 70–89.

LoPucki, L. M. (2003). Human identification theory and the identity theft problem. *Texas Law Review*, *80*(89), 89–134.

Milne, G. R., Rohm, A. J., & Bahl, S. (2004). Consumers' protection of online privacy and identity. *The Journal of Consumer Affairs*, *38*(2), 217–231.

National ID Card Makes Transactions at Dubai Courts Faster. (2009). Khaleej Times. Retrieved April 10, 2009 from http://www.khaleejtimes.com/DisplayArticleNew.asp?section=theuae&xfile=data/theuae/2009/march/theuae_march73.xml

Portable, field proven forensic system for the quick extraction and analysis of cell phones, Smartphones and PDA devices. (2009). Retrieved April 10, 2009 from http://www.cellebrite.com/

Reporton Cyber-stalking: A New Challenge for Law Enforcement and Industry. (1999). Retrieved March 28, 2009, from http://www.usdoj.gov/criminal/cybercrime/cyberstaling.htm

Rule, J., McAdam, D., Stearns, L., & Uglow, D. (1980). *The politics of privacy: Planning for personal data systems as powerful technologies*. New York: Elsevier.

Rule, J. B. (1973). *Private lives and public surveillance*. London: Allen Lane Publishers.

Simon, D. (1992). *Big brother*. East Roseville, NSW: Simon & Schuster Australia.

Smith, C. (2001). *Invasion of your Privacy has Just Begun*. Retrieved March 15, 2009 from http://archive.newsmax.com/archives/articles/2001/3/5/220402.shtml

The Constitution of the United States of America. (n.d.). Retrieved March 20, 2009 from http://www.law.cornell.edu/constitution

Westin, A. F., & Baker, M. A. (1972). *Databanks in a free society*. New York: Quadrangle Books.

Wolf, R., & Gordon, A. (2007). License Plate Recognition (LPR) technology: Practical and legal issues for police implementation. *Law Enforcement Executive Forum*, *7*(7), 93–99.

ADDITIONAL READING

Aas, K. F., Gundhus, H. O., & Lomell, H. M. (2009). *Technologies of insecurity: The surveillance of everyday life*. Abingdon, UK: Routledge-Cavendish.

Arzt, C. (2005). Data protection versus Fourth Amendment privacy: A new approach towards police search and seizure. *Criminal Law Forum*, *16*(3-4), 183–230. doi:10.1007/s10609-005-4143-9

Belanger, F., & Hiller, J. (2006). A framework for e-government privacy implications. *Business Process Management Journal*, *12*(1), 48–60. doi:10.1108/14637150610643751

Chen, H., Brandt, L., Gregg, V., Traumailler, R., Dawes, S., & Hovy, E. (Eds.). (2007). *Digital Government: E-Government Research, Case Studies, and Implementation*. New York: Springer.

Curtin, G., Sommer, M., & Vis-Sommer, V. (2003). *The World of E-Government*. London: Routledge.

Garson, G. D. (2006). *Public Information Technology and E-Governance: Managing the Virtual State*. Boston, MA: Jones and Bartlett Publishers.

Graafland-Essers, I., & Ettedgui, E. (n.d.). *Benchmarking egovernment in Europe and the US.* Retrieved from http://www.rand.org/pubs/monograph_reports/MR1733/MR1733.pdf

Gritzalis, D., & Lopez, J. (2009). *Emerging Challenges for Security, Privacy and Trust* (24th ed.). New York: Springer.

Heeks, R. (2005). *Implementing and Managing eGovernment: An International Text*. New York: Sage.

Hempel, L., & Töpfer, E. (2009). The Surveillance Consensus: Reviewing the Politics of CCTV in Three European Countries. *European Journal of Criminology*, *6*(2), 157–177. doi:10.1177/1477370808100544

Homburg, V. (2008). *Information Systems in Public Administration: Understanding e-Government*. New York: Routledge.

LeBeuf, M. (2006). *E-policing in police services*. Ottawa, Canada: Research and Evaluation Branch, Community, Contract and Aboriginal Policing Services Directorate, Royal Canadian Mounted Police.

Lyon, D. (2007). Surveillance, security and social sorting: Emerging research priorities. *International Criminal Justice Review*, *17*(3), 161–170. doi:10.1177/1057567707306643

Mansell, R., & Collins, B. S. (2005). *Trust and crime in information societies*. Cheltenham, UK: Edward Elgar.

McGrath, J. E. (2004). *Loving big brother: Performance, privacy and surveillance space*. London: Routledge.

Murphy, M. C., & Wilds, M. R. (2001). X-rated X-ray invades privacy rights. *Criminal Justice Policy Review*, *12*(4), 333–343.

Nicholson, W. C. (2005). *Homeland security law and policy*. Springfield, IL: Charles C Thomas.

Pavlichev, A., & Garson, G. D. (2003). *Digital Government: Principles and Best Practices*. Hershey, PA: IGI Publishers.

Peterson, R. S. (2000). DNA databases: When fear goes too far. *The American Criminal Law Review*, *37*(3), 1219–1238.

Reynolds, K. M., Griset, P. K., & Scott, E. (2006). Law enforcement information sharing: A Florida case study. *American Journal of Criminal Justice*, *31*(10), 1–17. doi:10.1007/BF02885681

Simmons, R. (2007). Why 2007 is not like 1984: A broader perspective on technology's effect on privacy and Fourth Amendment jurisprudence. *The Journal of Criminal Law & Criminology*, *97*(2), 531–568.

Sullivan, B. (2004). *Your evil twin: Behind the identity theft epidemic*. Hoboken, NJ: John Wiley.

Wartell, J., & McEwen, J. T. (2001). *Privacy in the Information Age: A Guide for Sharing Crime Maps and Spatial Data*. Alexandria, VA: Institute for Law and Justice.

West, S. (2007). *Digital Government: Technology and Public Sector Performance*. Princeton, NJ: Princeton University Press.

Wood, D. M. (2009). The 'Surveillance Society': Questions of History, Place and Culture. *European Journal of Criminology*, *6*(2), 179–194. doi:10.1177/1477370808100545

KEY TERMS AND DEFINITIONS

Cyber-privacy: The condition of personally identifiable information being held securely in an electronic or on line basis, without the fear of unsanctioned intrusion from others.

Cyber-stalking: The use of electronic means, including the internet, GPS, and mobile devices, to harass, threaten, intimidate, bully, follow, observe, or contact another person without their permission.

E-Government: The use of electronic or on line information technology to provide government goods and services; governmental functions or processes provided in various formats including websites, downloadable government forms, and on-line chat systems with governmental representatives; may also include intra- and inter-governmental processes or communication that is conducted on-line or electronically.

Freedom of Information Act (FOIA): Legislation signed into law by President Lyndon B. Johnson on July 4, 1966 and amended several times. The law, applicable only to federal agencies, allows for the disclosure of certain information and documents controlled by the United States Government and defines agency records subject to disclosure, outlines mandatory disclosure procedures, and grants exemptions.

Identity Theft: The use of another's personal information with criminal intent to defraud, transfer, profit, or retain that information for future illegal use; or that aids or abets any unlawful activity that constitutes a violation of Federal, State, or local laws.

Information Technology: The study, design, development, support, and management of both computer hardware and software used to store, process, retrieve, protect, transmit, and manipulate information and data.

Information Privacy: The condition of personally identifiable information being held securely, without the fear of unsanctioned intrusion from others.

Chapter 12
Considering the Role of E-Government in Cybercrime Awareness and Prevention:
Toward a Theoretical Research Program for the 21st Century

J. Mitchell Miller
University of Texas at San Antonio, USA

George E. Higgins
University of Louisville, USA

Kristina M. Lopez
University of Texas at San Antonio, USA

ABSTRACT

Cybercrime has exponentially increased in recent years as an unavoidable byproduct of greater internet use, generally, and presents a wide range of criminal threats to large companies and individuals alike. While cyber offenses (e.g., cyberharassment, cyberstalking, identity theft, and intellectual property theft) and their address have been examined across diverse academic disciplines including criminology, electrical engineering, sociology, and computer science, minimal consideration has been given to the role of e-government in combating cybercrime – a somewhat ironic oversight given the computerized context of both. After reviewing the nature of cybercrime, this chapter considers e-government policies addressing cybercrime awareness, prevention, and victimization services. Discussion centers on the prospects for cybercrime theoretical research program development toward best practices public policy.

INTRODUCTION

Internet use is now normative daily practice in multiple life spheres at individual, group, institutional, and societal levels. The computerization of North America, Europe, and much of the rest of the world has vastly modified, and in many respects improved (e.g., speed and efficiency), the nature of interpersonal communication, information dissemination, and business transactions. Innovation

DOI: 10.4018/978-1-61520-931-6.ch012

rarely transpires, however, without unintended consequences. In the case of computerization, proliferated internet use has been coupled with new types of high tech computer crime threats that have redefined the nature of victimization and crime prevention.

Computer crime, conventionally referred to as cybercrime, regularly occurs in the virtual reality of cyberspace. Cybercrime typically involves illegal access to an information technology infrastructure and one or more of the following activities: illegal interception of data transfers, data disruption (e.g., intentional modification or deletion), electronic fraud, and/or forgery through identity theft (Higgins, 2009; Higgins, 2008; Douglas & Loader, 2000). These activities manifest in a variety of specific criminal offenses, both new types of crime inherent to virtual reality and traditional offenses facilitated by technology, that raise broad public policy issues and specific criminal justice system challenges.

The purpose of this chapter is to consider the role of e-government in addressing the growing and ever-evolving problem of cybercrime. After reviewing the extent and diversity of cybercrime, the government response, generally, and the role of e-government, primarily in American context, is observed. Discussion themes include an expanded e-government role necessary to meet current and future cyber-threats and advocacy for a research-based and best-practices public policy orientation. Accordingly, suggestions are provided for engaging a theoretical research program (TRP) facilitative of leveraging collective efficacy through virtual reality toward cybercrime reduction.

A BRIEF OVERVIEW OF CYBERCRIME

Cybercrime refers to a fairly broad range of criminal activities that can be generally dichotomized into acts that either attack individual central processing units or computer networks (e.g., malware and viruses) or utilize computer networks to engage crime (e.g., bulk email scams, identity theft, fraud, and cyberstalking). There are several aspects of deviant computer practices with criminal intent distinguishable by an offense-specific jargon that has permeated the popular culture. *Spam,* unsolicited and predatory bulk emailing that, although for genuine commercial purposes, violated numerous federal and international privacy, morality, and telecommunications acts (Wikipedia, 2009 E-mail spam legislation by country).*Zombies* are computers attached to and hijacked through the web that aggressively and resiliently randomly attack other machines. *Hackers* (i.e., cybercriminals) use internet connections to place a computer virus that regenerates without permission and compromises a computer's ability to function regularly.

The everyday use of the term *computer virus* has become a "catch-all" reference for malware generally, including worms, Trojan horses, adware, and spyware. Bulk email scams are widely known as *phishing*, an attempt to acquire personal financial information through communications disguised as being from a trustworthy or reputable source. These problems are spread across computers through emails, accessing internet sites, and through shared DVDs and floppy disks. Thus, problems are rarely contained to a single machine. Collections of compromised machines (the zombies) are called a *botnet* that, in turn, control multiple affected linked machines remotely by a *bot herder*, a head hacker.

The Bureau of Justice Assistance provides funding to the Internet Crime Complaint Center (IC3), previously named the Internet Fraud Complaint Center until 2003, which publishes regular reports reflecting the broad characteristics of internet crime. In 2008 alone, the center received and assessed 275,284 complaint submissions (BJA, 2008). As reflected in the IC3's "2008 Internet Crime Report", 72,940 of these complaints were referred to federal, state, or local law enforcement agencies, the vast majority of instances

Figure 1.

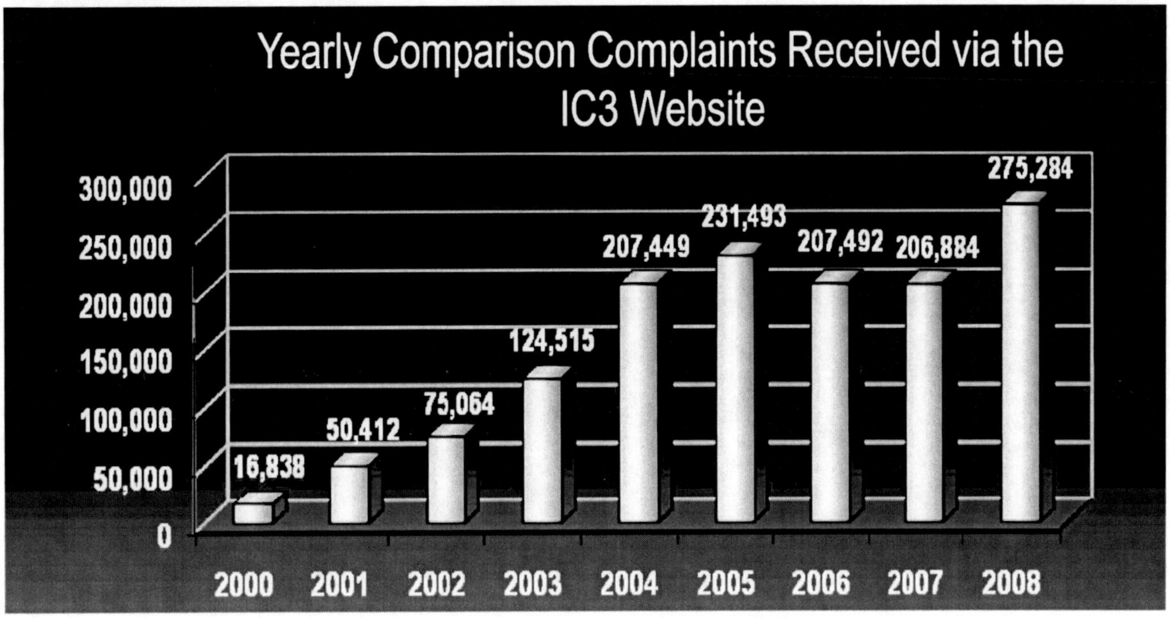

From January 1, 2008 – December 31, 2008, there were 275,284 complaints filed online with IC3. This is a 33.1% increase compared to 2007 when 206,884 complaints were received. Tracking of this data began in 2000, when there were 16,838 complaints. Since then, complaints doubled each year to 2004, when they hit 207,449. From 2004 through 2007 they remained around the same threshold. In 2008, there was again a spike of approximately 75,000 complaints that took it to the 275,284 total. Source: Internet Crime Complaint Center, 2008 Internet Crime Report

involving some type of attempted or executed fraud. While cybercrime, like any other criminal offense, fluctuates in both frequency and severity, IC3 data clearly suggests that cybercrime is a steadily worsening social problem. The number of reported events, for example, has grown from less than 20,000 in calendar year 2000 to over 275,000 in 2008 as described above (see Figure 1). This observed increased frequency of internet criminal activity has been coupled with a similar spike in property loss, from less than 18 million dollars in 2001 to over 264 million dollar loss in 2008 (see Figure 2).

As indicated in Figure 3 below, cybercriminals employ a variety of methods by which to snare potential victims. Emails and fraudulent webpages are by far the most frequent methods used to deceive people, but a range of conventional, low tech tactics are also utilized such as telephone and non-electronic communications that typically refer victims to the internet for money and data transfers.

Cybercrime victimization transpires in various forms as indicated in Figure 4 that can involve harassment or cyberstalking (i.e., threats and intimidation), but typically involves some kind of fraud. Most common is the non-delivery of items purchased from "fake" online stores. A similar scam involves online auctions wherein the seller receives funds from a winning bidder but never ships the auctioned item. Whereas reporting systems can identify and lead to the removal of altogether fraudulent websites, auction scams are usually embedded within legitimate sites, such as EBay, that simply have too many sellers to effectively regulate all. Fake charities and direct appeals from individuals appealing to the altruistic nature of others are also common.

Figure 2.

Dollar loss of referred complaints was at an all time high in 2008, $264.59 million, exceeding last year's record breaking dollar loss of $239.09 million. On average, men lost more money than women. Source: Internet Crime Complaint Center, 2008 Internet Crime Report.

Simple and elaborate stories of misfortune, sickness, and, especially, situations involving political insurgencies are bulk emailed through phishing and zombie networks in search of a bite from a recipient seeking to assist the alleged person in dire need of help. Some strategies simply seek donations while other, such as the well known Nigerian money transfer scheme, promise to share vast sums of monies with Americans willing to facilitate foreign funds into the country via their personal bank accounts (a crime itself). Of course, upon receiving account information, money is withdrawn rather than deposited.

THE GOVERNMENT ROLE IN ADDRESSING CYBERCRIME

Legislative Efforts

The government has attempted to manage and regulate cybercrime through implementing literally dozens of legal statutes that serve multiple related policy functions, including: 1) protect individual privacy, 2) provide access to government information, 3) protect government information and information services, 4) guarantee national critical infrastructure availability and reliability, and 5) establish formal definitions for investigatory and prosecutorial purposes (McQuade, 2006). Legislation has covered a wide range of cybercrimes, including privacy, identity theft, fraud, child pornography, and copyrighting, among others. An overview of major legislative efforts is provided below.

Figure 3.

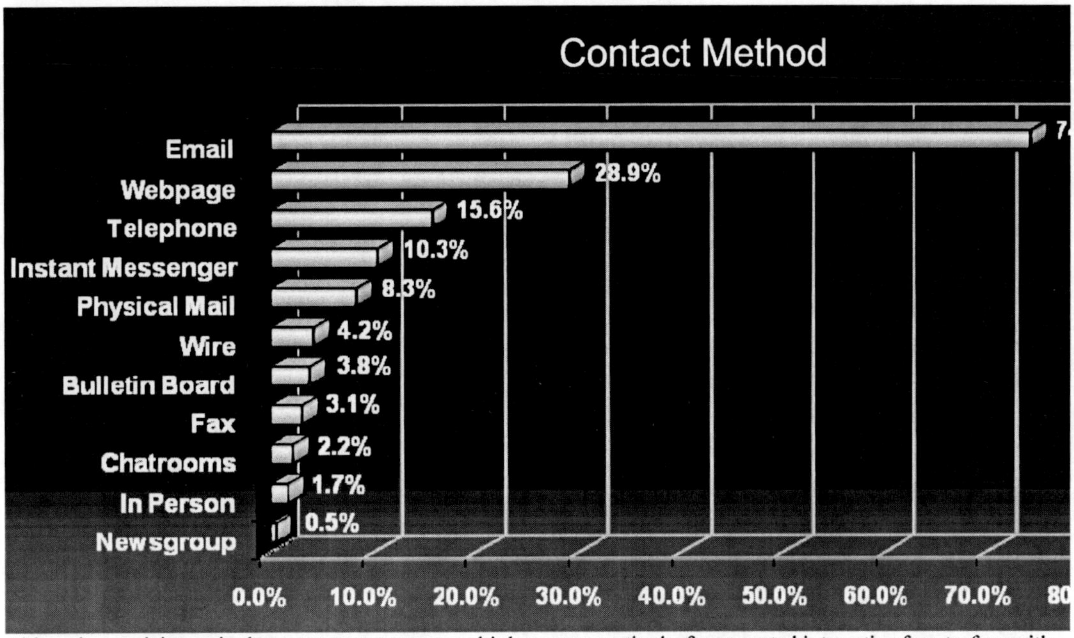

Although complainants in these cases may report multiple contact methods, few reported interacting face-to-face with the vast majority of perpetrators contact through e-mail (74.0%) or a webpage (28.9%). Others reportedly had phone contact (15.0%) with the perpetrator or corresponded through physical mail (8.3%). Interaction through chat rooms (2.2%) and in-person (1.7%) meetings were rarely reported. Source: Internet Crime Complaint Center, 2008 Internet Crime Report

Privacy, Identity Theft, & Fraud

Beginning with privacy concerns in relation to fraud and identity theft, the government has combated computer crime through statutes such as the first federal computer crime law known as the Access Device Fraud Act of 1984. This legislation prohibited the acts of creating, distributing, possessing, or using counterfeit-making equipment or devices (McQuade, 2006). This first law was later complemented by The Computer Fraud and Abuse Act that made it a federal felony to access unauthorized federal or financial institution computers that possess classified information or credit data (Reyes, O'Shea, Steele, Hansen, Jean, & Ralph, 2007). The final amendment to this statute led to the National Information Infrastructure Protection Act of 1996 in order to include all "protected computers" and specifically protect the confidentiality, integrity and availability of systems and information and incorporating stolen information that could be used to harm the United States or any foreign nation (Marcella & Greenfield, 2002,McQuade, 2006). Through the enactment of the 1996 Internet Fraud Watch, the National Fraud Information Center (NFIC) became an essential informant by offering consumers advice on protecting themselves from fraud schemes (Marshall, Robinson, & Kwak, 2005). Also among these early government attempts to regulate fraud in computer systems, the Gramm-Leach-Bliley Act (GLBA) was put into action to mandate financial institutions, establish appropriate safeguards to customer's data records, and protect their confidentiality (Reyes et al., 2007).

Other legislation has dealt with the relatively new phenomenon of "computer hackers". Unfortunately for the government and law enforcement, technology is consistently developing at a faster pace than they can familiarize themselves

Figure 4.

During 2008, non-delivered merchandise and/or payment was, by far, the most reported offense, comprising 32.9% of referred complaints. Internet auction fraud accounted for 25.5% of referred complaints. Credit/debit card fraud made up 9.0% of referred complaints. Confidence fraud, computer fraud, check fraud, and Nigerian letter fraud round out the top seven categories of complaints referred to law enforcement during the year.
Source: Internet Crime Complaint Center, 2008 Internet Crime Report

with in order to stay one step ahead of computer hackers. In order to regulate hackers, Congress enacted the Electronic Communications Privacy Act (ECPA), which regulated hacking, and the Stored Communications Act (SCA), which affected hacking activities by fortifying the privacy rights of computer users (such as their stored email and voicemail). The latter also authorized law enforcement engage surveillance and investigation of cybercrimes (Audal, Lu, & Roman, 2008).

To serve those victimized by fraud, the Identity Theft and Assumption Deterrence Act of 1998 was enacted to protect potential and actual victims of identity theft and illegalized the six following acts of knowingly; produce or transfer a false ID, possess five or more false IDs with intent to use them for a fraudulent purpose, use a false ID to defraud the United States, produce, transfer, or possess a device used for making false IDs or other documents with the intention of using it to create false identity documents, possess an ID that is or appears to be an identification document of the United States that is stolen or produced unlawfully and transfer or use, without lawful authority, a means of identification of another person with the intent to commit, or to aid or abet, any unlawful activity (McQuade, 2006). Ensuring the protection of individuals privacy and confidential information further, the Computer Security Act of 1987 and the Information Technology Management Reform Act of 1996 (ITMRA) were implemented to make sure every government system with case-sensitive information had a custom security plan with training and a chief information officer (CIO) within the federal government agencies to oversee that information systems were acquired and managed properly (McQuade, 2006). At a 1987 G-7 summit in Paris, the Financial Task Force (FATF) was established and become one of the most significant intergovernmental organizations dealing with money laundering at the time (Zombori, 2001). In the FATF 1999 report, one of the most respected money laundering documents was created known as The Forty Recommendations (Marshall et al., 2005). Specifically, in reference to Recommendation 13 of the report it stated, "Countries should pay special attention to money laundering threats inherent in the new or developing technologies that might favour anonymity, and take measures, if needed, to prevent their use in money laundering schemes" (FATF, 1999).

Educational systems have also been affected by the government's mandate for increasing security on information systems. Most importantly, the Family Educational Right to Privacy Act (FERPA) was implemented to protect the rights of students whose educational records are stored on large, potentially accessible servers. This Act increased the penalties for educational agencies and programs and promised the loss of federal funds if any policy or practice allowed the release of educational records (Reyes et al., 2007).

Online Child Pornography

Online child pornography is also a consistent concern addressed by federal and state legislatures which have enacted numerous statutes to address this criminal conduct. The Communications Decency Act of 1996 (CDA) prohibited the transferring of "indecent", "patently offensive", or "obscene" material to minors through the internet (Audal et al., 2008). Specifically, the CDA act set out to ban sexually explicit material from online sites that children would easily be able to find (McQuade, 2006). Also in 1996, President Clinton passed the Telecommunications Reform Act that was implemented to regulate the increasing issue of Internet pornography and terrorism (Finley, 2008). One of the most significant acts in 1996 was The Child Pornography Prevention Act (CPPA) which criminalized the production, distribution, and reception of computer generated, sexual images of children and this act attempted to outlaw any transmission of erotic photographs of adults created to resemble children (Audal et al., 2008).

With a combined effort from Congress, the Justice Department, and President Clinton, the Child Online Protection Act of 1998 (COPA) was enacted to prohibit anyone from knowingly using a commercial Web site to communicate pictures, writings, or recordings that were deemed obscene or harmful to minors (Finley, 2008). That same year, the Protection of Children from Sexual Predators Act (PCSPA) was created to include the provisions related to transmitting information or obscene materials electronically (Taylor, Caeti, Loper, Fritsch, & Liederbach, 2006). A more recent act passed by the Congress was the Prosecutorial Remedies and Other Tools to End the Exploitation of Children Today Act of 2003 ("Protect Act") that confronted the transmission of images of real children altered to appear as computer-generated pictures (Audal et al., 2008). In addition, in 2003, The Controlling the Assault of Non-Solicited Pornography and Marketing Act of 2003 ("CAN-SPAM") was implemented to set a stern boundary for email solicitations concerning deceptive subject lines, false or misleading titles, and fraudulent practices used in commercial emails and requires the Federal Trade Commission (FTC) to enforce its provisions (Audal et al., 2008, McQuade, 2006).

Electronic Copyright Theft

The increasing unlawful distribution of copyrighted material by computer has been addressed through copyright statutes such as the Criminal Copyright Infringement in the Copyright Act and the Digital Millennium Copyright Act (DMCA) (Audal, et al., 2008). These two acts address the illegal distribution of copyrighted material by computer use and any altering of digital copies of copyrighted work without the owner's authorization to gain access to their material. In 1997, the legislation put into act the No Electronic Theft (NET) Act in which prohibited any conspiracy to infringe software copyrights and in 2001 this statute was used to prosecute 17 defendants across the United States and Europe facing charges of infringing more than 5,000 computer software programs available through a hidden Internet site (Marcella & Greenfield, 2002). In 2002, the Technology, Education and Copyright Harmonization Act (TEACH Act) was enacted to require educational institutions to take "technological feasible" precautions and enforce information security in order to prevent unauthorized sharing of copyrighted information beyond the students particularly requiring the information for their studies (Reyes et al., 2007).

International Joint Efforts

Legislation's combat with cybercrime has even gone to global terms with uniform commitment internationally to address the issue. There are 39 countries that have signed the Council of Europe's Treaty on Cybercrime, including the United States, which mandates these countries to establish substantive laws against cybercrime, ensure their law enforcement officials possess necessary procedural authorities to investigate and prosecute cybercrime effectively, and provide international cooperation to other parties in combat against computer-related crime (Audal et al., 2008). Singapore, China, and Vietnam regulate their Internet activities by requiring users to register with authorities and by directly controlling Internet traffic entering their countries (Wall, 1997). The United States is also a party in the Subgroup on High-Tech Crime at G-8's Lyon Group that has developed a network allowing law enforcement authorities of member nations to contact one another for immediate assistance in investigations dealing with computer crime and protecting electronic evidence (Audal et al., 2008). The National Cyber Security Partnership (NCSP) was formed with the combination of the Business Software Alliance (BSA), the Information Technology Association of America (ITAA), TechNet, and the U.S. Chamber of Commerce in a voluntary partnership with academics, CEOs, federal government, and industry experts to protect America's information systems (McQuade, 2006).

Executive Efforts

In response to the growing threat of cybercrime the Executive branch of the government has developed a variety of computer crime units within law enforcement agencies to combat the problem. The FBI Cyber Division takes on one of the lead roles in investigations and preventions in all the various forms of cybercrime and partners with numerous other agencies in developing other programs such as the InfraGard and the National Center for Missing and Exploited Children (McQuade, 2006). The Cyber Division takes on jurisdiction of online child pornography through the known Innocent National Initiative (IINT) which achieved 5,840 convictions out of 17,691 cases between 1996 and 2006 (Audal et al., 2008).

With funding from the U.S. Department of Defense and the U.S. Department of Homeland Security the CERT Coordination Center was formed by the Software Engineering Institute (SEI) and the Defense Advanced Research Projects Agency (DARPA) in 1988 (McQuade, 2006). This center assists the FBI and other agencies that ask of its service in investigating information security problems and providing cybercrime investigation training. Also in assistance to the FBI, as well as other agencies, is the Computer Hacking and Intellectual Property (CHIP) program that is within the U.S. Attorney's offices and helps to network with high-tech communities and encourage referral of computer crime cases to law enforcement. The CHIP program is also significant for providing thorough training to law enforcement and businesses in prevention of cybercrime.

As an international effort, the InterGOV International Web Police works to serve and protect the citizens of the Internet community by gathering reliable information on Web crime (Marshall et al., 2005). Organizations such as the International Criminal Police Organization (Interpol) consists of dozens of units within member nations across continents including Europe, Asia, Africa, and the Americas to assist the criminal justice system in preventing international crime such as cybercrime. In 1995, a group consisting of about 1,300 volunteers in more than 14 countries came to be known as the CyberAngels and maintained a goal to educate those who are stalked and harassed on how to use their computer to research their stalker and change the hunter into the hunted (Karp, 2000). The SysAdmin, Audit, Network, Security Institute (SANS) was founded in 1989 and represents one of the largest and most trusted sources of information security training and certification worldwide as a cooperative research and education organization (McQuade, 2006).

Another collaborative endeavor implemented to fight cybercrime was the establishment of the Joint Anti-Piracy Initiative. This was accomplished through the combined effort of the Department of Justice, the Federal Bureau of Investigation, and the U.S. Customs service (Marcella & Greenfield, 2002). The goal of this law enforcement unit was to combat the increasing piracy and counterfeiting of intellectual property in the households as well as internationally.

As part of the Bush Administration multi-agency Strategy Targeting Organization Piracy (STOP), which included the Department of Commerce, Department of Homeland Security, and the Office of the United States Trade Representative, the Task Force on Intellectual Property was enacted to exemplify the priority to increase the combat on intellectual property crime (Audal et al., 2008). In order to conduct a variety of network monitoring and intrusion detection functions, the NFR Network Intrusion Detection (NID) was designed as a network monitoring device (Frederick, 2002). Within the U.S. Department of Homeland Security, a public-private partnership was formed called The United States Computer Emergency Readiness Team (US-CERT) to fight cybercrime and information security threats (McQuade, 2006). The U.S. Department of Justice has a similar unit known as the U.S. DoJ Computer Crime and Intellectual Property Section (CCIPS) that manages dozens of prosecutors and investigative staff and is responsible for prosecuting computer crimes, lobbying for strengthened penalties, and promoting for expansion of federal computer crime statutes coverage.

E-GOVERNMENT IN THE WORKS: A THEORETICAL RESEARCH PROGRAM FOR THE 21ST CENTURY

Cybercrime is a 21st century growing criminal attraction that the government and law enforcement agencies are still attempting to understand what works best to manage and deter it all together. In a 1999 Annual Report to Congress by the U. S. Department of Justice's Office it was expressed that electronic crime presents new obstacles to effective law enforcements efforts at all levels (U.S. Department of Justice, 2000b). In an alternate attempt to prevent and manage cybercrime, e-government is playing a role in creating online sources, policies and practices specifically to cybercrime awareness, prevention and victimization services. The e-government combat with cybercrime is rapidly developing, for example; National White Collar Crime Center, Working to Halt Online Abuse (WHO@), Internet Crime Complaint Center, American Intellectual Property Law Association (AIPLA), American Law Institute, Information Systems Audit and Control Association, International Information Systems, Security Certification Consortium, National Colloquium for Information Security Education,

National Cyber Security Alliance, and NetSmarz Workshop to name numerous of these developed online sources currently in action (McQuade, 2006). The following sections will address the e-government role in combating cybercrime and define the purpose and goals of the e-government sources in reference to cybercrime awareness, prevention and victimization services.

Before considering specific elements and research issues in need of address comprising an e-government theoretical research program, we review the characteristics of theoretical research programs, generally. A theoretical research program is an anatomic "set of related theories" (Wagner, 1984: 90) engaged (i.e., empirically tested and examined) by science. The theoretical research program's orienting strategy controls the types of issues and strategies employed by researchers. For example, e-government is concerned with crime prevention while simultaneously attempting to maintain privacy and civil liberties, particularly First Amendment rights. Are these issues congruent or is utilitarian choice required in order to move forward, both politically and social for scientific declaration of being best-practices based? Clearly, this delicate balance disadvantages lawmakers and criminal justice efforts to beat cybercrime through limiting policy and strategy options.

A theoretical research program is composed of core and auxiliary formal theory sets, both of which may be falsifiable (Berger and Zelditch, 1993). Program growth transpires either through composition of the sets or in the organization, clarity, or refinement of elements already in the set. A theoretical research program also leads to theory growth in five possible ways: elaboration, variation, proliferation, integration, and competition. Elaboration occurs when a new theory assumes a structure similar to an old theory but is "more comprehensive, more precise, more rigorous, or has greater empirical support. Variation occurs when a new theory is a slight modification of a prior theory, typically conflicting over a small part of a domain. Proliferation occurs when a new theory adopts a structure similar to an old theory but the predictions apply to different explanatory domains. Integration occurs when a new theory consolidates two other theories and subsumes many (though typically not all) of the predictions of the old theories. Finally, competition occurs when a new theory attempts to displace another by establishing its comparative inadequacy. Each aspect of theoretical growth has useful properties, but, of the five, competition has proven the least useful: Competing social scientific theories have rarely been resolved by direct comparison, and social and behavioral scientists alike cling to inadequate theories even under relatively clear demonstrations of inadequacy. These unfortunate reality means that popular perspectives are apt to be accepted without sufficient empirical confirmation and major or driving conceptual elements recycled and extended to additional topics. If faulty, the potential for greater harm through misinformation dissemination will result. As the government continues to offer a greater variety and number of services online, regular online transaction procedures may be coupled with risk of criminal victimization as security levels vary within and across computer systems.

Routine activities theory, a prominent criminological perspective that has received considerable empirical support (see Miller, Schreck & Tewksbury, 2008 for overview), provides a good example in the case of e-government and cybercrime. In short, the theory posits that crime is a function of three elements coming together in time and place: a motivated offender, a suitable criminal target, and a lack of (effective) guardianship. The theory seems applicable enough to internet crime as there certainly are enough hackers and other cybercriminals throughout society as indicated by the increasing volume of complaints to satisfy the first required element of a motivated offender pool. The theft of financial information and intellectual property in electronic form, child pornography, cyberstalking, and human and drug trafficking all involve criminal targeting in the context of cyberspace. The guardianship element, however, is less directly applicable as the theory was originally conceptualized around the notion of physical rather than virtual space and thus presents challenges to researchers and practioners alike. Presumably, the success of the former enhances the viability of the latter. While security races to keep pace with hackers in an ever escalating technology frenzy to block and access systems, the physical realities comprising social ecological conditioning of criminal opportunities and individuals' daily routines that present vulnerabilities in physical locales are rendered largely irrelevant in many cybercrime contexts.

Therefore, unless rigorous theory and testing processes are logically embedded in cyberworld realities, a theoretical research program can easily further complicate and confuse a general theoretical perspective or philosophy. The best-practices for situational crime prevention, for example, are still germane in principle to internet security but clearly assume different forms. The very fact that calls are made for a theoretical research program in a given area often indicates either pure or applied theoretical stagnation but in the case of e-government addressing cybercrime, the newness of the phenomenon presents the more fundamental challenge of developing a seminal knowledge base on the characteristics of offenders and culprits across situational and environmental contexts.

In short, while cybercrime research has typologized cybercriminals, provided sociolegal analysis of cybercrime legislation, and explored characteristics associated with risk of victimization, micro-level theories specific to cybercrime have not been crafted. Similarly, minimal attempts have been made to apply conventional criminological theories to the topic of internet crime, with very few exceptions (Holt & Bossler, 2009). More theory without sound empirical support has been abundant in the case of some policy efforts like the restorative justice movement and begs evaluative scrutiny of restorative programs toward the focused goal of establishing accountability. The opposite problem exists with e-government, however, namely the lack of an offense specific theoretical framework. Beyond simple quasi-experimental, before-after outcome assessments of whether various e-government initiatives work and to what extent, mixed-methodological research models are needed to determine the saliency of specific concepts, it is largely unknown which, if any, existing crime explanations inform our understanding of cybercrime. If cybercrime solutions are to be effective, a fundamental understanding of the nature of the offense, the offender pool, victimization, and the dispersion of virtual crime events is requisite.

Engaging a theoretical research program for e-government cybercrime prevention will force choices - the emphasis of some priorities and thus programs over others, the naturally result from the infusion of science. There will be winners and losers as some programs will be found effective and others will not. Funding implications and political choices will likely result. Assuming empirical confirmation, it is probable that policymakers and the general public will favor crime prevention approaches that offer broad social benefit over victim service activities. Major issues to be considered include: 1) the government versus the private sector role in combating cybercrime, particularly public access to free or subsidized security technology 2) the accessibility and utilization of awareness and prevention information, 3) cybercrime reporting systems, and 4) victimization assistance.

REFERENCES

Audal, J., Quincy, L., & Roman, P. (2008). Computer Crimes. *The American Criminal Law Review*, *45*, 233–264.

Berger, J., & Zelditch, M. Jr., (Eds.). (1993). *Theoretical research programs: Studies in the growth of theory*. Stanford, CA: Stanford UP.

Douglas, T., & Loader, B. D. (2000). *Cybercrime: Law Enforcement, security and surveillance in the information age*. New York: Routledge, Taylor & Francis Group.

Financial Action Task Force. (FATF). (1999). *Financial action task force on money laundering: The forty recommendations*. Paris: Organization for Economic Co-operation and Development. Retrieved April 19, 2009 from www.oecd.org/searchResult/0,2665,en_2649_201185_1_1_1_1_1,00.html

Finley, L. L. (2008). *Hawking Hits on the Information Highway: The Challenge of Online Drug Sales for Law Enforcement*. New York: Peter Lang.

Frederick, K. (2002). NFR Security. In Casey, E. (Ed.), *Handbook of Computer Crime Investigation Forensic Tools and Technology* (pp. 93–113). San Diego: Academic Press.

Higgins, G. E. (2008). 5-10 Cybercrime. In J. M. Miller (Ed.), The 21st Century Criminology: A reference handbook. Thousand Oaks, CA: Sage.

Higgins, G. E. (2009). *Cybercrime: An introduction to an emerging phenomenon*. New York, NY: McGraw-Hill Companies.

Holt, T. J., & Bossler, A. M. (2009). Examining the Applicability of Lifestyle-Routine Activities Theory for Cybercrime Victimization. *Deviant Behavior, 30*, 1. doi:10.1080/01639620701876577

Karp, H. (2000, April). Angels online: Special report. *The Reader's Digest*, 74–80.

Marcella, A. J., & Greenfield, R. S. (2002). *Cyber Forensics: A Field Manual for Collecting, Examining, and Preserving Evidence of Computer Crimes*. Boca Raton, FL: Auerbach Publications. doi:10.1201/9781420000115

Marshall, C. E., Robinson, T. H., & Kwak, D. (2005). Computer Crime in a Brave New World. In Reichel, P. (Ed.), *Handbook of Transnational Crime & Justice* (pp. 114–138). Thousand Oaks, CA: Sage Publications, Inc.

McQuade, S. C. (2006). *Understanding and Managing Cybercrime*. Boston: Pearson Education, Inc.

Miller, J. M., Schreck, C. J., & Tewksbury, R. (2008). *Criminological Theory: A Brief Introduction* (2nd ed.). Boston: Allyn & Bacon.

Reyes, A., O'Shea, K., Steele, J., Hansen, J. R., Jean, B. R., & Ralph, T. (2007). *Cyber Crime Investigations: Bridging the Gaps Between Security Professionals, Law Enforcement, and Prosecutors*. Rockland, MA: Syngress Publishing, Inc.

Taylor, R., Caeti, T., Loper, D., Fritsch, E., & Liederbach, J. (2006). *Digital crime and digital terrorism*. Upper Saddle River, NJ: Prentice Hall.

U.S. Department of Justice. (2000b). *Office of Justice Programs annual report to Congress Fiscal Year 1999*. Washington, DC: U.S. Department of Justice.

U.S. Department of Justice (Fraud Section-Criminal Division). (2000a). *Internet fraud*. Retrieved April 19, 2009, from http://www.internet-fraud.usdoj.gov

Wagner, D. G. (1984). *The Growth of Sociological Theories*. Beverly Hills, CA: Sage.

Wall, D. (1997). Policing the virtual community: The Internet, cyberspace and cybercrime. In Francis, P., Davies, P., & Jupp, V. (Eds.), *Policing futures: The police, law enforcement and the twenty-first century* (pp. 208–236). New York: St. Martin's.

Wikipedia. (2009). *Email spam legislation by country*. Retrieved April 19, 2009, from http://www.wikipedia.org

Zombori, G. (2001). e + finance + crime: A report on cyber-crime and money laundering (Working document). Toronto: York University, Osgood Hall Law School, Nathanson Centre for the Study of Organized Crime and Corruption.

Chapter 13
Citizen Centric or Government Centric?
Perceptions of Risk in New Identity Management Systems

Ruth Halperin
London School of Economics, UK

James Backhouse
London School of Economics, UK

ABSTRACT

This chapter explores citizens' perceptions of information risks inherent in the move towards eGovernment that deploy identity management systems (IdMS). The new plans for electronic identity management in the UK sparked a furious public debate but the related perceptions of citizens have not yet been systematically explored. The findings presented in this chapter were developed using grounded theory methods of open-coding content analysis and depict how a sizeable group of UK citizens regard the risks. Five areas of perceived risk emerged and they testify to the diversity of issues and concerns preoccupying citizens: technology failure, public authority competence, public authority integrity, lack of control over personal data, and, the overpowering state. Further, the authors present findings that express how citizens might ultimately act in the light of their perceptions. Drawing on social risk theory and current political developments, the authors discuss these emerging perceptions and suggest that citizen-centricity and joined-up systems - central to the transformational government agenda - stand in considerable jeopardy and require the government's attention and a suitable response.

INTRODUCTION

As the move towards eGovernment gathers pace in UK and other countries around the world, the impact of the digitalisation of many citizen-state interactions is beginning to challenge accepted wisdom on what digital citizenship consists of, what its risks are, and how they might be managed in the new digital era. The aim of this chapter is to explore the information risks perceived by citizens, identity risks in particular, that are seen to emerge from eGovernment vision and its underlying systems. We define information risk here as the harm

DOI: 10.4018/978-1-61520-931-6.ch013

that may arise from the loss of confidentiality, integrity or availability of information under public custodianship.

An important characteristic of eGovernment applications is its dependence on technologies for managing identity. eGovernment, and its current UK variant, tGovernment (transformational government) is predicated on the collection, storage and use of personal information on citizens. For tGovernment to succeed, 'means must be provided for citizens and businesses to engage electronically with government via secure networks that maximize user confidence and respect data protection requirements. A system of authentication of electronic documents must also be planned and developed' (Saxby, 2006: 1). Hence, tGovernment projects must deploy electronic identity management systems (IdMS) in some form or another.

Major plans for digital identity management were tabled by the UK government as part of the Identity Cards Act, 2006, including a new central database – a National Identity Register (NIR). Personal information identifying every UK citizen is to be stored on the NIR, which will allow data sharing between governmental agencies and authorized organizations (Crossman, 2007). Data sharing[1], which underpins the joined-up government concept (Six et. al., 2005), is one of three themes in the UK tGovernment strategy (Transformational Government, 2006). Citizen-centricity is another such theme, and the two are closely linked:

We must be relentlessly customer-focused. Many people want a single point of contact for a range of services. The public are not interested in whether their needs are met by department X or agency Y, they just want a good, joined-up service where X and Y talk to each other and share the information the public have provided. We should strive to meet this demand'.

Sir Gus O'Donnell, Cabinet Secretary (Transformational Government, 2006: 14)

The notion of citizen-centricity or customer-focused services, central to the eGovernment agenda, is epitomised in systems such as CRM (consumer relationship management) (Bose, 2002) extensively adopted from the private sector into the UK public sector (Lips, 2007). CRM relies on identity technologies, profiling systems in particular, and their claimed benefits mirror many of the objectives of the new tGovernment programme (King and Cotterill, 2007: 339). Likewise, the national identity card is supposed to achieve a broad set of benefits for the individual citizen: 'protect your identity from theft; protect vulnerable people from those who have lied to gain positions of trust; speed up many everyday transactions; make it easier for you to travel in Europe; make the internet easier to use; make it easier to replace lost and stolen documents'.[2]

However, despite the citizen-centric rhetoric and the proposed benefits, the implementation of new IdMS also brings with it new risks. We argue that understanding how the risks arising from new IdMS deployed in eGovernment are perceived and addressed may be critical to citizen acceptance of eGovernment. Large-scale systems have proved to be failures when end-users practise resistance during implementation (Bauer, 1997). A UK research programme, "Ensuring privacy and consent in identity management infrastructures"[3], currently under way, lent support to this view that without consent, acceptance will be difficult to obtain. An identity system for the UK should be based on public trust and user demand rather than on enforcement of criminal and civil penalties. The winning of public trust could be realized, in part, through the creation of a more flexible citizen-centred model[45]. Therefore, citizen perceptions, their fears and expectations, have important implications for any future attempts at implementing eGovernment systems deploying IdMS, as they may well result in resistance to use, misuse, or non-use.

In this brief introduction we have presented the rationale underlying the research reported in this chapter, and highlighted the need for studying how citizens perceive identity-related risks. The next section introduces the underlying question: what information risks are perceived in the move to 'citizen-centric' eGovernment which deploys IdMS? In this introductory discussion we draw on the literature criticising the prevailing notion of 'citizen as consumer', central to the eGovernment strategy, and point to information risks introduced for the citizen. We then report on an empirical study that explored the perceptions of UK citizens on information risk in the context of IdMS. Deploying a citizen-centric approach, we argue, warrants consideration and analysis of the risks as the citizen perceives them: what is their nature and scope, and can they be mitigated? The methodology used to uncover citizen perceptions is then introduced. We explain why we have chosen a qualitative, interpretivist approach to guide this study, describe how we collected the data and used a grounded research method for analysis. We then present the empirically grounded findings that emerged from the analysis, uncovering a diverse set of risk perceptions. There follows a discussion reasoning that the present goal of citizen-centric and joined-up tGovernment stands in jeopardy unless governments respond appropriately to the risks perceived by citizens.

BACKGROUND

E-Government, the Citizen as Consumer and Emerging Information Risks

eGovernment has been strongly associated with what is called a citizen-centric approach in government reform efforts and should lead to a situation in which citizens have an improved, central position in their service relationship with their government. eGovernment takes into account the desires and needs of citizens and aligns the new digitally based public service system more closely to their perspectives and aspirations (Lips, 2007). The strategy has been modified by tGovernment proposals, in which a more radical citizen-centric agenda is set by central government (King and Cottrerill, 2007: 351).

The notion of citizen-centric eGovernment is intimately linked to an underlying and persistent metaphor: the citizen-as-consumer:

... in this new view of citizen as customer [.. .], the Internet represents more than just a new channel for service delivery. On its deepest level, the Internet is a catalyst that challenges age-old assumptions about how governments operate [.. .] In fact, in just a few short years, the Internet has started to shift the organizing logic of government from a product or process-centric approach to a customer-centric model (Deloitte Research, 2001).

The new public management movement (NPM) (Ferlie et al., 1996; Barzelay, 2001), recasts citizens as customers (Mosse and Whitley, 2008) and forms part of the wider transformation that envisages public administration as a firm operating in a market (Ciborra, 2005). However, concerns have emerged about the appropriateness of the 'customer' concept in the context of public services (Gray, 2005; Bevir and Rhodes, 2003; Warner and Hefetz, 2002). The replacement of the term 'citizen' by that of 'consumer' and the idea that government agencies should be 'customer-focused': that public managers should view their clients as consumers and serve them using management concepts drawn from effective private sector service firms – demand closer scrutiny (Fontain, 2001: 56).

In the following section, we critically review the citizen-as-consumer notion advanced by governments both in Europe and beyond. Paradoxically, it seems the citizen-centric approach in its market-like interpretation might actually be weakening the position of the citizen and creating new risks. While we are mainly concerned with the implications of public sector IdMS for the citizen, we address the current trends in the broader context of eGovernment in which IdMS play a central role; identity management is the life-blood of eGovernment. eGovernment projects are by definition information-intensive, involving large-scale sharing of personal data and requiring the identification and authentication of individual citizens as they interact with the state. (Lips, 2007: 38). Characterizing the next generation of eGovernment, Lips (2007) concludes that digitalized personal identification and authentication systems, that is, IdMS, become an essential pre-condition for successful eGovernment. Whereas previously a separate profile for the same citizen was needed by each department say for the patient, the driver, and the taxpayer, with the introduction of new IdMS it becomes much easier to create and manage an integrated identity profile on the citizen. Combining new types of personal data moreover affords new forms of eGovernment provision (Lips, 2007: 42).

But where does this leave the citizen? In an environment where the government is the only provider of a range of crucial services, a critical issue for the citizen-consumer concerns choice; the notion of customer entails a number of market mechanisms that cannot be transferred to a public administration monopoly. In a competitive market the customer has choice (Ciborra, 2005), but unlike the real consumer who is able to choose trusted service providers and terminate the relationship with them if, for example, trust has been violated, the citizen-consumer is deprived of both options and will find it difficult, if not impossible, to disengage with government agencies. Citizens have no real exit option. Lack of choice, as we discuss later, also raises an information risk management issue.

If tGovernment reflects the private sector experience, adopting CRM-like systems will mean services will become less standardized. Governments will resort to stereotyping through large-scale use of profiling, increasingly serving those clients who are easiest to serve. Ciborra (2005: 267-268) contends that this will generate a new form of *discrimination* based not on price, but on access and relative ease of interaction, both predicated on the information held on the citizen. With little control over what personal information is held by the state, its accuracy and how it is processed, the ordinary citizen is in a difficult position6. Inaccuracies in personal information might result in profiling outcomes whose result is to blacklist citizens or exclude them from a given category leading to, say, loss of benefit or service.

With its plans for public sector IdMS, the NIS and the introduction of identity cards, the UK government is bent on transforming service provision. The NIS proposals gave rise to a fierce public debate in the UK with privacy concerns being aired by civil rights movements (Crossman, 2007) and with serious doubts arising on the costs, legality and security of the scheme. Despite this however, there is almost complete lack of evidence on eID services perceptions (Wainer and Miltgen, 2009)8. Little heed has been taken hitherto of the perspective of the UK citizens, although a recent public event did highlight its importance: 9

If they [citizens] did not have confidence in a scheme, take up would be slow, motivations of some to undermine it strong, and the net result would be an ineffective scheme. Hence, research to uncover the precise nature of citizen fears with an aim of developing at the very least a communication programme or hopefully a dialogue with citizens should be a high priority.

A perceptible gap in research exists, therefore, which deserves attention and consideration, and the next section describes the methodology used to explore perceptions of UK citizens of information risks in relation to new public sector IdMS.

METHODOLOGY

The methodology adopted in this study draws from grounded theory (Glaser and Strauss, 1967; Martin and Turner, 1986) as it offers a research method that seeks to develop accounts that are grounded in data. This generative approach seemed particularly useful here, given that no systematic research on this topic has been published to date. In particular, we adopted the analytical technique of open coding (Strauss and Corbin, 1990) as explained further below. This method provides for an exploratory and context-based research into the phenomenon at hand.

The inductive and contextual characteristics of the methodology suggested by grounded theory fit with the interpretive orientation of this research. The focus here is on developing a context-based description, with an aim of generating an account of UK citizens' risk perceptions regarding public sector IdMS.

Data Collection

The data for this study was collected using a web survey method. The survey was designed in two parts, one consisting of a closed questionnaire (Backhouse and Halperin, 2009)10 and a second part, aimed at obtaining qualitative data, consisting of an open-ended question that invited respondents to comment freely on the subject of electronic identity in the public sector, government context. This technique generated a wealth of data – statements made by respondents in the form of free text. The overall number of qualitative responses from UK citizens was N=377.

Statements varied in terms of length and their level of elaboration, for example, one respondent stated: *'1984'* whereas another explained in more detail:

It's an absolute necessity to pare the amount of centrally stored electronic data to the absolute minimum. Especially cross-comparison of different data bases must be permitted by law, just as access to this data by companies/business. Additionally, it must not be possible to read out electronic data stored on regular ID cards by radio frequency or any other contactless method, because every encoding, encryption or access protection will be cracked, which is just a question of time. Business/companies, banks and insurances have economical interests to get access to this data, so that access must be permitted by law.

Whilst the dataset obtained for this study provided a rich and revealing source about citizens' perceptions, some limitations associated with the chosen method of data collection are nevertheless evident because web surveys are self-selected samples. We could have opted for in-depth interviews but this method has its own drawbacks. Interviews would not have provided large, diverse and anonymous responses derived through the web survey. Another issue with a web survey is the potential response bias. It may be argued that those with strong opinions on IdMS were most eager to respond. Given these considerations, our findings cannot be said to represent the UK population in general as no controlled sampling was applied. However, this does not undermine the validity of the data nor lessen the importance of the findings that emerged from the analysis. Validity in qualitative research stems not from a statistical basis, but from the plausibility and cogency of the logical reasoning used in describing the results from the cases, and in drawing conclusion from them (Agerfalk, 2004). The study was not designed to provide statistical generalisability (Yin, 1984), however, it may properly lay claim to analytical generalisability, in particular, to the common type of generalising from data to descriptions (Lee and Baskerville, 2003).

Data Analysis

Making sense of the large body of unstructured text required the creation of a grounded analysis framework. Content analysis of the text gradually led to the creation of a framework of underlying reasoning or beliefs that characterised the range of responses and attitudes. This technique uses a form of content analysis where the data are read and categorized into concepts that are suggested by the data themselves rather than imposed from outside (Agar, 1980). This method of open coding (Strauss and Corbin, 1990) relies on an analytical technique of identifying possible categories and their properties and dimensions. As the data are examined, concepts are organized by recurring themes. These themes become prime candidates for a set of stable and common categories, which link a number of associated concepts. This is known as axial coding (Strauss and Corbin, 1990) and relies on a synthetic technique of making connections between sub-categories to construct a more comprehensive scheme. The goal is to determine a set of categories and concepts that covered as much of the data as possible (Orlikowski, 1993). This iterative examination yielded a set of broad categories and associated concepts that describe the range of risk perceptions held by UK citizens. In the findings section we introduce the refined categories by turn, illustrating each one with the data from which it emerged.

FINDINGS

We present the findings from the study arranged in terms of the key risks that were perceived by the respondents. Five main areas of risk emerged from the grounded analysis: technology failure, public authority competence, public authority integrity, lack of control over personal data, and the overpowering state. The section closes with the findings related to expressions of how citizen might ultimately act in the light of their perceptions.

Technology Failure

On the question of systems and technology, mainly concerning dependability of the technology, there were diametrically opposed views. While some respondents were adamant that biometric based ID cards offered unbreachable security:

Biometric based ID cards are secure as only you can provide the live match with biometric stored on the card, therefore the information help is useless without the individual present...

Others, on the contrary, had a low regard for the reliability of technology currently in the identity management systems area. The feeling persisted that the claims being made for the effectiveness of biometric based ID technology would have to be confirmed by lengthy testing in live contexts that were less critical:

Currently, the error rates for biometrics are too high to allow practical application in high-volume fast throughput application areas.

I do not believe such a (safe) technology exists, nor that it can be proven to exist without many years of use in a less critical mission application.

Still others decided to sit on the fence and to side neither with the former nor the latter, instead remaining ambivalent about the dependability of the systems and technology in this specialized domain –

Electronic ID provides many benefits and are (probably) technically realizable but doubts remain about the integrity of the IT system...

Although technology was seen to be more dependable than in the past there were fears about the robustness of identity management systems in particular. Centralised databases, biometrics and wireless technology, vulnerable open standards that interoperability requires together with the lack of platform independence – all were mentioned as examples of reasons why citizens should fear the large-scale deployment of interoperable electronic IDs:

the idea of a centralized ID databases is foolish in the extreme. It will be a honeypot for criminals, and lead to less security rather than more. Identity in the digital world is important, but centralized systems are not the way to provide. Federated, distributed systems are much safer, and work just as well.

such a system does not need to be centralized (as the British Government is currently suggesting to do). My main issue is with the "One Big Database" which will accumulate on every person in the UK, which is not being talked about - issues such as terrorism and benefits fraud are used to divert discussion away from this issue instead.

Public Authority Incompetence

Citizens saw a risk in the *competence* of the state and its departments in securing and managing personal data. It is important to recall that the data were gathered before the 2007 spate of breaches of security in several UK government departments, referred to below. Often reference was made to previous unsuccessful government IT projects and the outlook of many was pessimistic:

Trusting a bunch of civil servants to safeguard personal information, or to interpret it correctly is stupid beyond belief.

In some cases there remains still a reservoir of goodwill towards the authorities but nevertheless this was overshadowed by a disbelief in their ability to deliver.

I don't take the people at the authorities for incapable but if you see how little they know about IT-security I don't believe that they will be able to protect my data sufficiently.

I believe the authorities will attempt to be honest and secure but ultimately will be unsuccessful in maintaining the confidentiality of my data.

I feel the authorities will fail to deliver a secure, working system. It will be a monumental waste.

In these responses there is conveyed also the notion of the second order risk that the significant sums being expended would prove to be a waste of money for the taxpayer who is ultimately underwriting these projects; another related facet of the incompetence charge lies in the perceived inability of the government to manage large-scale IT projects properly:

...we also already have all the evidence we need to know that massive governmental IT projects are massive disasters, since every single one in the past twenty years has been

My concern is the ability of Government organisations to effectively implement, maintain and operate this system based on many displays of total ineptitude in delivering large IT transformational change programmes in the past. The fact that I cannot think of a single example of a successful Government programme of this kind is deeply concerning...

A further second order consequence of this competence risk is the linked risk of identity fraud, often referred to as identity theft: with access to this kind of personal data, criminals could set up new accounts or access existing accounts, and steal funds.

I'd love to believe that the ID authorities will be technically competent and ID fraud will become a thing of the past. But I just can't, and the potential problems here are very serious.

Important risks are not only located with technology, as we see below, but also with the institutional failures of state in managing the human aspects of information risk and security:

I am not against ID cards in principle, but have grave doubts about the competence of those running the system. Human error is probably a bigger risk then IT.

Public Authority Integrity

Alongside concerns about the competence of public authorities a further question was raised about integrity and trustworthiness. One view that emerged was of a government set on giving UK citizens' personal information to third parties without informed consent, and which furthermore could not be relied upon to maintain its commitments.

...our Government will hand over our data to the CIA or any other organisation they care to without telling us.

[the] government do not have the slightest regard to any promises or guarantees of secrecy or data security they may have made.

I am very concerned about the misuse of ID information especially considering links between government and industry.

Of course such links could be very beneficial in that they might reduce the number of times citizens are asked to fill out forms requesting the same data. Citizens seem to appreciate the potential benefits of a more joined-up government with better access to personal information thorough IdMS which, *if implemented correctly could make general travel and access to public services more convenient.* Unfortunately citizens also perceive a downside in which the information risks are heightened once the value and usefulness of that information are enhanced.

Another issue is that of Goverments gradually expanding the scope of their powers to share personal data "in the public interest", but without seeking informed consent.

Requiring informed consent is an essential step in minimizing perceived risks to privacy and identity.

A risk is perceived that data sharing between government departments and between government departments and private industry might take place without the citizen's informed knowledge or consent.

Lack of Citizen Control Over Personal Data

As well as the risk perceptions in relation to public authorities' integrity and competence, there emerged clear concerns regarding the citizen's inability to control personal data.

As a citizen I have virtually no say in what the government does: or a quick and easy way to control it...I don't want them managing my own data.

Much of the risk will be beyond the ability of the individual to manage, with the data being held in government databases and under the control of public sector information risk and security managers.

While I have no great problems with the idea of a proof of identity (e.g. Passport), the ID schemes proposed will shift the balance of control of identity from the Citizen to the State

...even the large private companies are pretty poor at managing personal data. However, as a consumer/employee I have a lot more influence over that company.

This last response touches on the diminished redress that digital citizens have when compared with digital consumers. Perhaps both government and private sector present real inadequacies, but a private company must be more responsive to pressure. Looking at the balance between benefits and risks implicit in the large-scale deployment of interoperable electronic IDs, different citizens find different trade-offs, but for many this calculation is a constant consideration.

The Overpowering State

A recurring theme saw the ID card as the harbinger of a totalitarian state.

ID cards are the biggest threat to personal liberty that Europeans are facing since 1930-40s fascism.

The idea of a general ID Card for all citizens is very wrong and a manipulative way of certain people in power seizing the rights of its citizens. It is a modern form of dictatorship

The states and the EU seem to consider their citizens as "enemies", that have to be surveilled, controlled, harassed and restricted in their rights.

The main thrust of these responses is that civic freedom from unfettered surveillance is at risk. Even more apocalyptic was: *What happens, if tomorrow another Hitler is rising? And if he then has access to all these data?* - raising the spectre of an end to the democratic political system. The risk perceived in both these notions is a political one, but for the latter, the mere accumulation of all this personal data into one logical place itself constitutes an unacceptable ratcheting up of risk to citizens.

Recalcitrant Citizens

What emerges beyond just the perceptions of the risks associated with the deployment of IdMS is the expression of citizens' commitment to follow up with actions. Again the strength of some of the language is remarkable. The language smacks of resorting to civil disobedience in order to resist the UK government scheme. Several wrote of their willingness to go to jail rather than submit to the government's blandishments:

I would rather go to prison than give my personal details to an ID database register.

I would rather go to prison than participate in the UK ID card scheme even though I am a Labour Party supporter in general, pay my taxes, and have never been in trouble for the law for so much as a parking fine.

the data transferred by airlines to the USA has altered my plans travel to North America because of the invasive nature of the information given to them. I will therefore never be prepared to register for an ID card, whatever the penalty.

In addition, the use of powerful verbs such as "fight" and "resist" gave the impression that citizens would be prepared go to some lengths in their opposition:

I will fight vigorously to oppose their introduction here.

If put into use, I would be inclined to move to another continent. I will resist it at every turn

I will fight to preserve my liberty against this disgraceful fascist onslaught

People I talk to are going to sabotage or resist this nonsense.

Even more extreme were these two responses. Of course such expressions of sentiment are relatively easy to pronounce but what action ensues remains to be seen.

I would sooner renounce my citizenship than submit to the British government's evil scheme

I will never, never, NEVER have my fingerprints, retina scans or DNA profile taken from me and put on a Government Database. I would rather die than have that happen..

DISCUSSION

Irani et al (2008) state that eGovernment must be evaluated in terms of its benefits, costs and risks, and focusing on the last of these we review our findings against some notions of the risk society and of modernization found in the work of Beck 1994, Giddens 1990 and Hanseth and Ciborra (2007). For these researchers, the control revolution (Beniger (1986) has exploded into the risk society, leading to increasing unpredictability and, ironically, less control because of the unanticipated effects of new systems; 'the expansion and heightening of the intention of control ultimately ends up producing the opposite' (Beck et al. 1994:9, in Hanseth and Ciborra, 2007).

The increased sharing of data among departments and agencies will be a certain outcome of eGovernment, and the term *joined-up systems* conjures up closely-coupled systems in which the output of one system becomes the input of another. Personal health care data captured on a citizen will ultimately be made available to other systems, perhaps taxation or housing benefit, or perhaps as we see below, law enforcement. As the systems are tightly coupled, any change in a personal record will be quickly reflected throughout all the systems that are 'joined-up'. But this will also mean that the side-effects, including errors (or failures) in capturing data, in managing and communicating data, and in technology, will be replicated in very short order through the whole ensemble. As Beck states, 'the side-effect, not instrumental rationality, is becoming the motor of social change'(1994: 175). Greater integration of systems could paradoxically, instead of increasing control, lead to less control and more risk. The November 2007 loss in the post of 2 CDs holding 25m personal records of UK citizens by HMRC, the UK tax authority, was just one in a lengthening list of unmitigated disasters for UK citizens' security and privacy. A side-effect was the risk that the leaked identity data might (still) increase incidents of identity fraud with known dire consequences; the UK Cabinet Office estimated that for 2008 identity fraud costs amounted to 1.2 billion GBP 11. But it could have been much worse. With integrated, joined-up systems a similar scale breach might have cascaded the risks throughout all the attached systems in other government departments.

Joined-up systems are intended to provide better knowledge to the state about citizens and their needs, and thereby reduce health and social risks in the process. Giddens (1990: 28) questions the idea that better knowledge reduces risks on four grounds, including differential power and the impact of unintended consequences. He sees power differences ensuring that the better knowledge is put to the use of those with more power rather than in an even-handed fashion. With only minimal citizen control and if the perceptions of the risk of integrity prove to be true, public authorities may decide to disclose citizens' personal information to more agencies than envisaged at the outset, and hence considerably increase the risk of breach of confidentiality, not to mention identity fraud. So, having reviewed the benefits and the risks as presented, the citizen might consent to sharing personal data with a given set of agencies and possibly other states, only to find later that this list is being continually and unilaterally lengthened. A straw in this wind was the revelation in February 2008, by a UK minister12, that the police would have access to the new 60 million patient record database being developed for the National Health Service (Brennan, 2007) in cases where there is an "overriding public interest". No definition was given for this term.

Our respondents see risks in technology, administrative competence and integrity, in lack of control over personal data and in an overpowering state. As joined-up systems endow the state with unlimited access to knowledge about an individual, there is undoubtedly a yawning gulf in power between the citizen and the state. After the police, might other actors be lining up for the same access, for example, social security and private sector bodies, such as employing organisations and insurance companies, with concomitant detrimental outcomes for the citizen? The more the access, the more users involved, the greater the information risks. However the realization of exceptional power eventually will filter through to ordinary citizens. In the absence of a consensus about these new powers, the conduct of administration could be politicised to a far greater degree than seen hitherto, as ordinary citizens become deeply suspicious of the power reposing in joined-up systems and the motives of public administrators. Indeed the very idea chills the blood of a future much less democratic state inheriting deeply intrusive and powerful public IdMS. Our findings show that some citizens claim they would resort to sabotage and resistance. However the power is not all one-sided, and there could emerge a weapon useful to aggrieved citizenry. Joined-up systems will constantly require major input from the data subjects themselves: changes of address, job, names, titles, status etc., therefore submitting false values for personal information into one system will quickly result in inaccurate data operating in all the others.

Unintended consequences are often bedfellows of technological change. No matter how much knowledge the state has about the likely impacts of new public IdMS on the normal conduct of social and business affairs, it will never be able to predict all the consequences that might emerge from the introduction of its new systems. How quickly will the banks and other commercial institutions adopt the same IdMS and standards as tGovernment, and with what outcomes? It is already impossible in the UK to open a new bank account without a passport, so the consequences of alignment with national IdMS will be to isolate further those on the other side of the digital divide, and 'refuseniks' will find life very hard going. How will they react? Will they cease resisting, or merely find new ways to strike back? Unless the state finds a way of convincing opponents of the benefits, the potential for conflict is considerable.

How can the citizen respond to the growing information and especially identity risks associated with eGovernment deploying IdMS? In risk management procedure, once the priority of risks has been decided, appropriate assurance, security and countermeasures should be set in place. But what form might these risk-countervailing actions take? In theory, risks can be avoided, mitigated, transferred or accepted. Perhaps the digital citizen can avoid eGovernment systems, but only for as long as the paper-based alternatives survive, and there will often be an extra cost. Mitigating risks refers to the setting of controls and limits - on money values or periods of time for example - in order to constrain risk, and it is unlikely that eGovernment will allow such manipulations. Limiting the risk might for example mean refusing consent for data sharing, possibly resulting in the loss of certain services or priorities. Transferring risk to third parties, such as taking out insurance, is equally problematic since in eGovernment personal information is not managed by the citizen but by the state.

Managing risks requires the ability to mitigate, transfer, avoid or accept the risks involved. These options however require the person managing the risk to have some choice in the course of actions open to them. The problem for the digital citizen is exactly this lack of choice. Unless significant alternatives are to be offered, the citizen will simply have to accept that as the digital state continues to develop their personal data remain in the custody of the state with the added risks that this brings.

With web-based eGovernment systems requiring access from home, the ability of the citizen to secure their own computers or mobile devices will also become a critical part of managing eGovernment information risk. Currently home information security is a very weak link in the overall information risk management picture, needing especial attention at a professional and policy level. If, as Anderson (2003) claims, information security is '*a well-informed sense of assurance that information risks and controls are in balance*', then we must conclude that citizens do not currently possess this sense, and feel powerless to protect themselves in the face of these looming scenarios.

CONCLUSION

The new IdMS underpinning eGovernemnt and the transformational government vision present new risks to citizens. New services deploying CRM-like applications, and the implementation of joined-up systems that increase data sharing, were seen to jeopardise both the security and privacy of citizen and ultimately to bring about a detrimental shift in the balance of power between state and citizens. The objective of transforming citizens from 'passive recipients of standardised services to active partners in customised service design and delivery' (King and Cotterill 2007:336) will require more data sharing. However, the nature of identity management in eGovernment might bring considerably more uncertainty and risk into the delivery of public administration than is currently being recognised. Our empirical study found that a considerable number of UK citizens are deeply nervous of how electronic identity management might usher in a degree of risk never before encountered. Technology failure, public authority competence and integrity, lack of control over personal data, and, the overpowering state are the key areas of concerns identified. The UK government, and perhaps others intending to move in a similar direction, might well reflect on the implications of those perceptions if it is to avoid failure of a critical public sector programme.

DIRECTIONS FOR FURTHER RESEARCH

One important issue highlighted in this chapter concerns the ever-increasing risk to the citizen brought about by new IdMS, while the current practices and divisions of responsibilities and accountability fall short of adequately securing the citizen. Currently, it seems, 'citizen centricity' dominates the discourse while government centricity underpins practice. Redress for victims of IdMS must be addressed and resolved for risks to be managed and this suggests reappraisal of responsibilities between eGovernment and digital citizens – perhaps towards a social digital contract, setting out rights and responsibilities, duties and liabilities. This is one avenue we propose in further developing and expanding this research.

Additional developments of this work also include refinements to the analytical framework. This chapter focused on data from UK only but a comparative analysis is called for, exploring perception of citizens in other countries that are moving towards similar trends in eGovernment identity management.

Further theoretical development to the research involves proposing and employing a theory of interpretation and in so doing shifting the focus of the analysis from grounded theory to theory driven. This, we propose, should provide further insight into the pressing contemporary issues associated with eID-related risks and increase understanding of citizens' perceptions of it.

REFERENCES

Agar, M. H. (1980). *The Professional Stranger: An informal introduction to ethnography*. New York: Academic Press.

Ågerfalk, P. J. (2004). *Grounding through Operationalization: Constructing Tangible Theory in IS Research.* Paper presented at the European Conference on Information Systems, Turku, Finland.

Anderson, J. M. (2003). Why We Need a New Definition of Information Security. *Computers & Security*, *22*(4), 303–313. doi:10.1016/S0167-4048(03)00407-3

Backhouse, J., & Halperin, R. (2009). Approaching Interoperability for Identity Management Systems. In Rannenberg, K. (Ed.), *Identity in the Information Society: Challenges and Opportunities*. New York: Springer.

Barzelay, M. (2001). *The New Public Management*. Berkley, CA: University of California Press.

Bauer, M. (Ed.). (1997). *Resistance to New Technology: Nuclear Power, Information Technology And Biotechnology*. Cambridge, UK: Cambridge University Press.

Beck, U. (1992). *Risk Society – Towards a New Modernity*. London: Sage.

Beck, U. Giddens. A., & Lash, S. (1994). Reflexive Modernity. Cambridge, UK: Polity Press.

Beniger, J. (1986). *The Control Revolution: Technological and Economic Origins of the Information Society*. Cambridge, MA: Harvard University Press.

Bevir, M., & Rhodes, R. A. W. (2003). Searching for civil society: changing patterns of governance in Britain. *Public Administration*, *81*(1), 41–62. doi:10.1111/1467-9299.00336

Bose, R. (2002). Customer Relationship Management: key components for IT success. *Industrial Management & Data Systems*, *102*(2), 89–97. doi:10.1108/02635570210419636

Brennan, S. (2007). The Biggest Computer Programme in the World Ever! How's it going? *Journal of Information Technology*, *22*, 202–211. doi:10.1057/palgrave.jit.2000104

Ciborra, C. (2005). Interpreting e-government and Development: efficiency, transparency or governance at a distance? *Information Technology & People*, *18*(3), 260–279. doi:10.1108/09593840510615879

Crossman, G. (2007). The ID Problem. In Birch, D. (Ed.), *Digital Identity Management* (pp. 175–183). Hampshire, UK: Gower.

Deloitte Research. (2001). *E-government's Next Generation: Transforming the Government Enterprise Through Customer Service*. New York: Deloitte Consulting.

Ferlie, E., Pettigrew, A., Ashburner, L., & Fitzgerald, L. (1996). *The New Public Management in Action*. Oxford, UK: Oxford University Press.

Fountain, J. E. (2001). Paradoxes of Public Sector Service. *Governance: An International Journal of Policy and Administration*, *14*(1), 55–73.

Giddens, A. (1990). *The Consequences of Modernity*. Cambridge, UK: Polity Press.

Glaser, B. G., & Strauss, A. L. (1967). *The Discovery of Grounded Theory: Strategies for Qualitative Research*. New York: Aldine.

Gray, A. (2005, November 7). Q&A: Professor Andrew Gray, editor of Public Money and Management. *eGov Monitor*. Retrieved August 10, 2008, from http://egovmonitor.com/node/3403

Hanseth, O., & Ciborra, C. (2007). *Risk, Complexity and ICT*. Cheltenham, UK: Edward Elgar.

Irani, Z., Elliman, T., & Jackson, T. (2007). Electronic Transformation of Government in the U.K.: a research agenda. *European Journal of Information Systems*, *16*, 327–335. doi:10.1057/palgrave.ejis.3000698

Irani, Z., Love, P. E. D., & Jones, S. (2008). Learning lessons from evaluating eGovernment: Reflective case experiences that support transformational government. *The Journal of Strategic Information Systems*, *17*, 155–164. doi:10.1016/j.jsis.2007.12.005

King, S., & Cotterill, S. (2007). Transformational Government? The role of information technology in delivering citizen-centric local public services. *Local Government Studies*, *33*(3), 333–354. doi:10.1080/03003930701289430

Lee, A. S., & Baskerville, R. L. (2003). Generalizing Generalizibility in Information Systems Research. *Information Systems Research*, *14*(3), 221–243. doi:10.1287/isre.14.3.221.16560

Lips, A. M. B. (2007). E-Government Under Construction: Challenging Traditional Conceptions of Citizenship. In Nixon, P., & Koutrakou, V. (Eds.), *E-Government in Europe Rebooting the State* (pp. 33–47). London: Routledge.

Martin, P. Y., & Turner, B. A. (1986). Grounded Theory and Organizational Research. *The Journal of Applied Behavioral Science*, *22*(2), 141–157. doi:10.1177/002188638602200207

Mosse, B., & Whitley, E. A. (2008). (forthcoming). Critically Classifying: UK E-Government Website Benchmarking and the Recasting of the Citizen as Customer. *Information Systems Journal*.

Orlikowski, W. (1990). CASE tools are organizational change: Investigating Incremental and Radical Changes in Systems Development. *Management Information Systems Quarterly*, *17*(3), 309–340. doi:10.2307/249774

Saxby, S. (2006). eGovernment is dead: Long live transformation. *Computer Law & Security Report*, *22*, 1–2. doi:10.1016/j.clsr.2005.12.002

Six, P., Raab, C., & Bellamy, C. (2005). Joined-up Government and Privacy in the UK part I: Managing tensions between data protection and social policy. *Public Administration*, *83*(1), 111–133. doi:10.1111/j.0033-3298.2005.00440.x

Strauss, A., & Corbin, J. (1990). *Basics of Qualitative Research: Grounded Theory, Procedures, and Techniques*. Newbury Park, CA: Sage.

Transformational Government Enabled by Technology Annual Report. (2006). *HM Government*. Retrieved August 10, 2008, from http://www.cio.gov.uk/documents/annual_report2006/trans_gov2006.pdf

Van Loon, J. (2002). *Risk and Technological Culture: Towards A Sociology Of Virulence*. London: Routledge. doi:10.4324/9780203466384

Warner, M., & Hefetz, A. (2002). Applying Market Solutions to Public Services: an assessment of efficiency, equity and voice. *Urban Affairs Review*, *38*(1), 70–89. doi:10.1177/107808702401097808

Yin, R. K. (1984). *Case Study Research: Design and Methods*. Thousand Oaks, CA: Sage.

ADDITIONAL READING

Bennet, C. J., & Raab, C. D. (2006). *The Governance of Privacy*. Cambridge, MA: MIT Press.

Birch, D. (Ed.). (2007). *Digital Identity Management*. Hampshire, UK: Gower.

Dunleavy, P., Margetts, H., Bastow, S., & Tinkler, J. (2006). *Digital Era Governance*. Oxford: Oxford University Press.

Gutwirth, S., Poullet, Y., De Hert, P., de Terwangne, C., & Nouwt, S. (Eds.). (2009). *Reinventing Data Protection?*Berlin: Springer. doi:10.1007/978-1-4020-9498-9

Hildebrandt, M., & Gurtwith, S. (Eds.). (2008). *Profiling the European Citizen*. Berlin: Springer. doi:10.1007/978-1-4020-6914-7

Kerr, I., Steeves, V., & Lucock, C. (Eds.). (2009). *Lessons from the Identity Trail: Anonymity, Privacy and Identity in a Networked Society*. New York: Oxford University Press.

Lace, S. (Ed.). (2005). *The Glass Consumer*. Bristol, UK: The Policy Press.

Lupton, D. (1999). *Risk*. London: Routledge.

Lusoli1, W., Maghiros, I., & Bacigalupo, M. (2009). eID policy in a turbulent environment: is there a need for a new regulatory framework? *Identity in the Information Society Journal*. Retrieved from http://www.springerlink.com/content/bw4r060035250522/fulltext.html

Lyon, D. (Ed.). (2005). *Surveillance as Social Sorting: Privacy, Risk and Digital Discrimination*. London: Routledge.

Royal Academy of Engineering. (2007). *Dilemmas of Privacy and Surveillance: Challenges of Technological Change*. London: RAE.

Silverman, D. (1993). *Interpreting qualitative data: methods for analysing talk, text and interaction*. London: Sage.

Taylor, J. Lips, M., & Organ, J. (2009). Identification practices in government: citizen surveillance and the quest for public service improvement. *Identity in the Information Society Journal*. Retrieved from http://www.springerlink.com/content/2pl2731712732452/fulltext.html

Wodak, R., & Chilton, P. (Eds.). (2005). *A new agenda in (critical) discourse analysis: theory, methodology, and interdisciplinary*. Philadelphia: John Benjamins Publishing Company.

ENDNOTES

1 http://www.dca.gov.uk/foi/sharing/information-sharing.pdf

2 http://www.ips.gov.uk/identity/benefits-individual-british.asp

3 http://www.epsrc.ac.uk/CallsForProposals/Archive/EPAC.htm

4 http://identityproject.lse.ac.uk/identityreport.pdf

5 http://www.digitalchallenge.gov.uk/links-and-resources/research/study-on-organisational-change-for-citizen-centric-egovernment

6 Article 29 Working Party on Data Protection issued a Working Document on E-Government (WP73) that called for more control by the citizen over the processing of their personal data, but whether and how this will be implemented by Member States remains to be seen.

[7] http://identityproject.lse.ac.uk/identityreport.pdf

[8] http://ftp.jrc.es/EURdoc/JRC50089.pdf

[9] http://www.kablenet.com/KE.nsf/EventsSummaryView/0CFE397AFD0FF888802572E50050D62B?OpenDocument

[10] Results can be found at http://www.fidis.net/fileadmin/fidis/deliverables/fidis-wp4-del4.4.survey.pdf

[11] http://www.cifas.org.uk/default.asp?edit_id=561-56

[12] http://www.computerweekly.com/blogs/tony_collins/2008/02/police-will-be-allowed-searche.html#more

Chapter 14
Citizens and Service Channels:
Channel Choice and Channel Management Implications

Willem Pieterson
University of Twente, The Netherlands

ABSTRACT

The arrival of the electronic channels in the 1990s has had a huge impact on governmental service delivery. The new channels have led to many new opportunities to improve public service delivery, not only in terms of citizen satisfaction, but also in terms of cost reduction for governmental agencies. However, until now these promises of e-government have not been met. Surely, the usage of the electronic channels has skyrocketed in recent years and some organizations do witness cost reductions, but in general the usage of the traditional channels remains high and the costs of introducing and maintaining the electronic channels have merely been additional costs. These observations call for a deeper understanding of the behavior of citizens. Why do citizens choose the channels they use to obtain services? Furthermore, how should knowledge about these behaviors be used to improve governmental multi-channel service strategies and marketing activities? In this chapter the authors will analyze citizens' channel behavior. They will discuss channel usage and explore the channel choices of citizens. Further, the authors will discuss how these findings may help in improving channel strategies and marketing and thus help in improving citizen satisfaction and reduce cost of governmental service delivery.

INTRODUCTION

Citizens and governmental agencies interact through various channels. For example, a governmental agency may send me a letter telling me to pay my taxes and I may phone the tax agency to ask them why. A governmental agency has full control over the information it sends out, in terms of the channels they deploy to do so. However, in most situations, citizens are free to choose heir channels if they need governmental services. Yet, governmental agencies try to influence the behavior of their citizens. Service delivery is expensive and, given budgetary constraints, governments need to optimize their

DOI: 10.4018/978-1-61520-931-6.ch014

service policies and service channel management. In order to do so, governments need to understand why citizens use the channels they choose for their contacts with governmental agencies.

Further, a number of important developments have altered the service channel landscape fundamentally in the past decades. The first development is the change in governmental agencies themselves: the shift from bureaucracy to customer centeredness. Nowadays, governmental agencies pay loads of attention to public services and the improvement of the services (Bekkers, van Duivenboden, & Lips, 2005). However, this is no common situation. Before thinking about services became popular, governmental agencies were merely occupied with the implementation of policies and maintenance of the law (Bekkers, et al., 2005). Where governmental agencies until the 1970's could be characterized as Weberian bureaucracies (see below), influences such as the New Public Management (NPM) caused governmental agencies to start thinking about services and paying attention to the demand of citizens. For a long time, governmental agencies thought in terms of supply, rather than demand (van Dijk & van Deursen, 2006). Changes in management approach caused organizations to think more in terms of the needs of their citizens, rather than merely the supply of services. This development caused governmental agencies to develop specific (multi)channel strategies and determine largely how services and channels are perceived by the public sector.

A second development is the impact of ICT in governmental agencies. ICT did not only impact organizational aspects of the public sector, such as new ways of information handling and new work tools that affected how service provision is organized, but, more important, ICT has given us new service channels, such as the World Wide Web, e-mail and more recently chat and SMS. The arrival of these new channels has led to more thought about the different characteristics of service channels and the ways in which channels are positioned in an ideal service channel mix.

It appears that the service channel landscape has changed enormously in the past decades. But what insights have the developments led to? And have the developments actually improved service delivery? The purpose of this chapter is to give an overview of the relevant developments in public service delivery and to determine whether those developments have affected a) service channel strategies and b) actual citizens' behavior. Hereby we draw insights from various relevant domains on service delivery and service channels, such as the e-Government literature, marketing and information science (Pieterson & van Dijk, 2007).

First, we discuss the background of the topic. The current status quo is largely determined by developments such as the arrival of the NPM and the birth of new (electronic) service channels in the 1990's. Next, we discuss citizens' channel behavior and channel management strategies. Based on the analysis of the current situation, we present some suggestions for future research and we finish the chapter with a number of concluding remarks.

BACKGROUND

Usually, governmental organizations are seen as "bureaucratic" organizations. This Weberian type of organization focuses on such aspects as departmentalization, specialization, standardization and routinization of the production process (Simon, 1976). Consequence of this focus is that "cost-efficiency" is a central goal of bureaucratic governmental organizations (Tat-Kei Ho, 2002). This primary focus on internal processes and procedures led to a low service orientation in the public sector until the 1970's. As a consequence, within the public sector, there was little attention for the relationship with its environment; why ask citizens about their needs if you are able to assess those needs yourself?

This perception changed slightly in the 1970's, when the traditional Weberian bureaucracy became increasingly criticized. Main points of critique on the Weberian bureaucracy are that it is a rigid organization type characterized by proceduralism and the incapability to treat customers as humans who have preferences and feelings (Bozeman, 2000). At the same time, external influences also put pressures on governmental agencies, there were economic and fiscal pressures, due to budget deficits. In addition, citizens and businesses increasingly demanded good services, resulting from service delivery developments in the private sector. Hence, a shift started towards a customer orientation in the public sector, as Albeda and Van Bijlert (2001) argue. This resulted in various new management doctrines, from which the most influential was the New Public Management (NPM). It has impacted the functioning of the public sector in general in most Western countries and most notably the service orientation in the public sector. Even today, many policy programs are rooted in the NPM principles. The influence of NPM on government's channel perceptions and channel strategies are therefore noteworthy.

The focus of NPM is on the relationship between governments and their citizens. Citizens were no longer seen as subjects of the state, but had to be treated as clients (Hood & Peters, 2004). In NPM, the emphasis of the way governments influence their citizens shifted from reinforcement of the law towards service provision. A more service oriented approach would not only improve the relationship between citizens and governments, but should also lead to higher levels of compliance to the law. During the second half of the 1990's, most Western countries based their service policies on the ideas of NPM (Duivenboden & Lips, 2001). One of the consequences of the NPM is that it strongly emphasizes the needs of the citizen. But to be able to satisfy the need of the citizen, one has to know what the citizen wants. Fountain (2001) argues that governmental agencies often simply assume what the needs of the citizen are. On reason for this is that it is rather difficult to assess the preferences of citizens. Intrapersonal tradeoffs among preferences make it difficult to understand what citizens want, because there are so many ways in which people make those tradeoffs (Sen, 1982). This might explain why the level of knowledge within governmental agencies about the behavior of citizens is rather low (Pieterson, 2008).

Nevertheless, the focus on the citizen as customer has enhanced the attention for service delivery and hence the attention for service channels and the behavior of citizen. Governmental programs aimed at improving public service delivery, such as the Dutch "Overheidsloket 2000" (OL2000) were strongly based upon the ideas of NPM. In this project, the national government worked for several years on a project to provide all citizen services using a one-stop shop approach (Programmabureau Overheidsloket 2000, 2000). In this and various similar programs in other countries explicit statements were made about service channels and the behavior of citizens. Further, although it started as a project to improve services through the creation of a physical one-stop shop, it gradually shifted to a more ICT oriented project ending in a transition to a one-stop shop on the Internet. It nevertheless makes clear how the NPM has impacted the thought about services and services channels and the needs of the citizen as a 'customer' of public organizations.

There is, however, an important drawback in the view of the citizen as a customer. A citizen is more than just a customer of (public) services. Citizens have different roles in their contacts with governmental agencies and therefore administrators should primarily see citizens *as* citizens (King & Stivers, 1998). Citizens can have contact with governmental agencies in various ways. As a citizen I have rights, for example, I may receive healthcare or education, but I also have duties. If I don't comply by the rules I may have to pay a fine or go to jail. Further, I can vote or participate in policy making processes. I can also contact governmental agencies when I have questions or problems. The different relations citizens have with governmental agencies determine how contacts within these relations look like; a prisoner is treated different than a *customer*. A common (see for example Bekkers, 1998; Ringeling, 2001; van Duivenboden, 2002) distinction between the different roles of citizens is the division in citizens as 1) *voter*, 2) *subjects of the state,* 3) *citoyen*, 4) *customers* of public services. It is likely that the roles put different requirements on the interaction process between citizen and government. Therefore, it is likely that, if the citizen is aware of his role, this influences his channel choices. This also leads to the notion that this awareness is an important factor in the channel choice process of citizens. Within the public administration context, this awareness is closely related to the concept of bureaucratic competence. This concept means that citizens know what their rights and duties are, further, that they know how they have to realize these rights and duties and finally that they master the needed pattern of behavior to effectuate the rights and duties (Daemen & Thomassen, 1989). In terms of channel choice, it is likely that bureaucratic competences are displayed through a) a recognition of the characteristics of the problem (knowing what the right or duty is), b) knowledge of the available channels (knowing how to realize the right or duty) and c) choosing the proper channel (the needed pattern of behavior).

On behalf of the governmental agency, it is important to offer the right channels for the right roles. If a service delivery process requires co-production, channels should be offered that allow for this co-production. If an organization decides to just offer those channels that are cost-efficient (such as the electronic service channels), the risk arises that the loss of effectiveness in the process overshadows the (financial) efficiency gains. Scheepers and Kommers (1994) argue that the *McDonald's effect* may occur when cost-efficiency is chosen above a proper alignment to the roles of citizens and governments; smooth and efficiently satisfying superficial short term needs may lead to a neglect of the complex, fundamental and long-term needs (p. 327).

However, this does not imply that governmental agencies should develop a holistic approach towards the citizen in which all roles are addressed simultaneously. In most cases a citizen can be addressed in a specific role and can e.g. be addressed as a citizen. It does imply however, that governmental processes should be citizens centric and that services and resources are tailored to the service and resource needs of all roles (Bertot & Jaeger, 2008). This implies that governmental agencies should have an understanding of the needs and behaviors of their citizens in all different roles (Bertot & Jaeger, 2006; Evans & Yen, 2006).

The Rise of ICT and the Emergence of New Channels

A second historical development that impacted public service delivery has been the rise of ICT. In the Netherlands, the government has always been one of the pioneers in the use of ICT (Donk & Meyer, 1994). The role of ICT has been described in various policy plans since then, whereby the focus slowly shifted from ICT as a tool for the design and functioning of the public sector in the back-office to the possibilities of ICT to improve public service delivery in the front-office. In most western countries similar developments took place. Arguably this shift is due to the influence of NPM on public management practices. NPM advocates have been eager in the adoption of ICT to realize their ambitions. One of the first governmental NPM programs specifically on ICT in this context was the US' National Performance Review. This program was among the first to acknowledge the potential of ICT the better serve citizens and reduce the costs of ICT.

When ICT became more and more influential in government organizational strategies, the term e-Government, derived from e-Commerce became in fashion to describe aspects of the implementation of ICT in public administration. Although e-Government is the most fashionable term, the term "digital government" has (mostly in the US) been used as well since the 1990s. The rise the e-Government movement led to enormous enthusiasm about the possibilities of ICT to improve public service delivery. It is apparent that e-Government seems to be narrowed down to just the delivery of services. The other roles of citizens seem to be neglected and the possibilities of ICT to improve the (internal) processes seemed to be neglected at the end of the past millennium. There was, however, a sheer sense of optimism about ICT, not in the least inspired by the commercial sector, and the new electronic service channels.

Optimism About the New Channels

When new technologies are introduced there is always some kind of arousal, especially amongst those enthusiastic about it. ICTs are, of course, no exception. A general example of the enthusiasm is provided by Tom Stonier revealing a utopian view of the impact of ICT on society:

"In late industrial society, we stopped worrying about food. In late communicative society, we will stop worrying about material resources. And just as the industrial economy eliminated slavery, famine and pestilence, so will post-industrial economy eliminate authoritarianism, war and strife. For the first time in history, the rate at which we solve problems will exceed the rate at which they appear. This will leave us to get on with the real business of the next century. To take care of each other. To fathom what it means to be human. To explore human intelligence. To move out into space. (Stonier, 1983, p. 214)

This view on ICT in general is not that much different than the optimism about ICT and especially the new service channels to improve public service delivery and reduce the costs of government. An example is the following quote of Symonds:

"Within the next five years the Internet will transform not only the way in which most public services are delivered, but also the fundamental relationship between government and citizen. After e-commerce and e-business, the next Internet revolution will be e-government" (Symonds, 2000, p. s3).

Fountain was also optimistic about ICT and their potential to transform bureaucracies, as she argues that ICT has the potential "to substantially redistribute power, functional responsibilities, and control within and across federal agencies and between the public and private sectors" (Fountain, 1999, p. 150). Not only scholars have formulated optimistic statements about ICT, practitioners in the field of public administration have expressed their optimism as well. Stephen Goldsmith, at the time an advisor of President George W. Bush argued that "electronic government will not only break down boundaries and reduce transaction costs between citizens and their governments, but between levels of government as well" (cited in West, 2005, p. 4).

Based on a number of associated characteristics, the Internet was believed to be an ideal medium to realize those aims. In most cases, the Internet was seen as the channel with unlimited possibilities, rendering the traditional service channels. Potential advantages for citizens of electronic government are summarized by Michael Cross (Guardian Online 16.07.98): Round the clock government, one-stop shops (tell the government only once instead of form filling for different departments), electronic benefits (no more queuing and information-sharing across departments reducing fraud) and open and cheaper government (better public access to information encouraging efficiency and democracy).

However, not everyone was this optimistic about how the new media would replace the old traditional media. Some scholars have been more cautious towards this thesis. Hall (1998) already argued before the end of the past millennium that the diffusion of ICT could lead to stimuli for personal contact. An increase in ICT use and the need for understanding would e.g. call for courses, and a person seeing a video clip online might want to see the artist in real life. The ambiguities arising from ICT use need to be addressed via other (traditional) means of communication. Various authors argue that the new means of communication are strongly linked to the old means, or as Mitchell puts it: "bits meet the body" (Mitchell, 1995), thereby stressing the idea that ICTs are not replacing old means, but providing strong linkages to them (Baym, 1998; Jones, 1998). Wellman (1997) thereby argues that many of our online relations are embedded in the offline relations, many people use computers at work or at schools and develop online relations next to the existing relations with friends, colleagues and family.

It has been argued that the strategies followed by governmental agencies, to just 'electronify' existing traditional services will not result in much organizational benefit. Pavlichev and Garson (2006) argue that the productivity potential of ICT initiatives will not be achieved as long as governmental agencies merely automate their existing process. Reason for this might be that governments mostly transpose existing procedures to the electronic environment. It has been argued that, despite the different characteristics and possibilities of ICT as opposed to the traditional means, the bureaucratic "maze" has simply been duplicated on the web (R. Davis, 1999). This means that the bureaucratic ways of working are also reflected online. This tendency is also observable in a more general sense. Margolis and Resnick (2000), for example argue that the Internet in many instances is a reflection and reinforcement of the behavioral patterns in the real world.

Nevertheless, the general tendency at the end of the past millennium is that of positivism towards the electronic service channels. Although the crash of the Internet bubble led to most businesses revise their channel strategies, most governmental agencies remain focused on the electronic channels (Pieterson & van Dijk, 2006) This is a surprising development, given the fact that the Internet hardly resulted in a more cost efficient government. A survey by Moon (2002) among municipalities showed that, even in municipalities with online transaction services, there were hardly any cost-savings in service delivery. Next, chief administrators on the municipalities indicated that their e-government initiatives increased, rather than decreased their staff demands. More important, however, is that the developments in channel usage by citizens has not been so favorable towards the Internet in recent years. In the following section we will briefly discuss what the developments have been in channel usage in recent years and what factors determine the channel choices of citizens.

CITIZENS' CHANNEL BEHAVIOR

What is channel choice, and how does it relate to channel use? Building on the work of media theorists, we can decompose the general concept of channel behavior in a number of steps. Trevino, Webster and Stein (2000) define the concept of 'Media behavior' as the product of general use and specific choice. Here, general use refers to an individual's broad pattern of medium use over time. Trevino, Webster and Stein (2000) further define choice as follows:

"Choice is an individual's specific decision to use a medium in a particular communication incident."

Use and choice can also be seen as 'using the communication medium for a certain task (use)' and 'the picking of a medium' (choice). We want to extend this interpretation with an extra step of 'channel evaluation' in which the citizen evaluates his or her channel choice. The experience acquired influences both channel perceptions (Carlson & Zmud, 1994, 1999) and future channel choices

(Pieterson & Van Dijk, 2007). Channel behavior in real life is far more complex, because, for example, citizens can use multiple channels simultaneously. Furthermore, information seeking usually consists of more stages. However, it seems obvious that for channel management use and choice are the most relevant steps in channel behavior. Below, we will shortly discuss these.

Channel Usage

As mentioned before, governmental agencies had high hopes of the possibilities of the Internet to improve service levels and the expectations were that citizens would turn to these channels *en masse*. However, it seems that this promise has not been realized yet. Millard (2006) showed that within the EU the face-to-face channel is still the most important channel. In various separate countries were studies have been conducted on channel usage (such as Canada, the US and the Netherlands (for an overview see Pieterson, 2008)) the traditional service channels (telephone and face-to-face) were still the most popular. When analyzing developments in use, in most countries the use of the Internet increases. The number of visits on websites has grown at a tremendous pace since the arrival of the electronic channels. However, except from a decline in the use of the written channel (Berner

Fachhochschule and Unisys, 2005), the use of the traditional service channels did not decrease until now. This implies that the total number of contacts with most governments has increased in recent years.

From the fact that the total number of interactions in most countries, and with most organizations only increases, we can hypothesize that people use more and more channels in their interactions. This hypothesis seems to be confirmed in various studies. Pieterson and Ebbers (2007) did a survey among Dutch citizens and found that citizens in practice are multi-channelers: on average, they have contact with governmental organizations via three different channels. But citizens do not only use an increasing number of channels in general, they use more than one channel within the same service-delivery process. American research found that 22% of all Americans had used multiple channels during their last service encounter with a governmental organization (Horrigan, 2004). Further, the Citizen First study from Canada found that citizens used an average of 1.9 channels to obtain the last used service (Erin Research, 2003). One half used a single channel, while the other half used two or more channels.

So people use more channels in general (the Internet appears to be an 'extra' channel), but also use more channels in one service delivery process. This leads to the question what factors determine citizens' channel choices.

Channel Choice

Very little research has been conducted on why citizens' choose their channels for the interactions with governmental agencies. Reddick (2005b) has examined interactions from citizens with governments. However, he focuses solely on the use of the Internet. Pieterson and Ebbers (Pieterson & Ebbers, 2008) found that different groups of citizens choose different channels and that task characteristics affect channel choices. The impact of these factors has been confirmed in other studies (2005a) (2003). Reddick (2005a) added trust and satisfaction as possible channel choice determinants and Schellong and Mans (2004) found that the use situation in terms of *time* and the *emotional form* of the respondent are possible determinants. Other disciplines have also studied how and why people select service channels or communication media. For example, Media Richness Theory (MRT) (Daft & Lengel, 1986) has been the focal point of both theoretical and practical research on (communication) channel choices. Additional theories such as the Social Influence Model and Channel Expansion

Theory have also been used to study channel or media choice.

If we try to assess which factors are mentioned most in the different studies, we can group the possible channel choice determinants into four groups (see also Pieterson and Van Dijk, 2007). The first group consists of *task characteristics*, such as complexity (see for example Belkin, Brooks, & Oddy, 1982; Byström & Järverlin, 1995) and ambiguity (Choo, 1998; Daft & Lengel, 1986). The second group consists of *channel characteristics*, such as personalization (Daft & Lengel, 1986), interactivity (Alba, et al., 1997) and ease of use (F. D. Davis, 1989). The third group consists of *personal characteristics*, such as the demographic characteristics (Reddick, 2005a; Schellong & Mans, 2004). The final group consists of *situational characteristics*, such as time (Schellong & Mans, 2004) and distance (Kwast, Martha, & Wolken, 1998).

Most recently, Pieterson (2009) presented a theory of channel choice, based on earlier work (Pieterson & van Dijk, 2007). In this theory he argues that people may follow two decision strategies in their channel choices. One strategy is based on reasoning in order to achieve a match between tasks and channels (task-channel elaboration). Within this strategy, people may do fairly comprehensive reasoning to reach an optimal solution, or they may adopt a strategy that entails little cognitive effort that leads to decisions with low accuracy. The second strategy (habits) involves no conscious reasoning and is based on unconscious habitual action, guided by experiences. Pieterson argues that what decision strategy is followed is influenced by the four groups of factors presented above. In a quantitative study among 2461 Dutch citizens, Pieterson tests the main premises of this theory. One of the main findings in his study is that people are guided by habitual decision making in their primary choice and that this shifts to elaboration in their second choice. Habitual decision making is guided by situational and emotional constraints. The results demonstrate that, primarily, people want the fastest answer, they choose the channels that are associated with 'ease of use' and speed their decision process is guided by their habits and by the experiences they have in the decision making process. Furthermore, if people don't succeed in their first attempt they engage in a second channel choice processes. The results demonstrate that this process is guided by a rational elaboration on the fit between task and channel. Now situational and emotional factors as well as habits do not play a role anymore.

If we conclude that citizens use all available service channels alongside each other, for different purposes and different situations, how does this relate to channel management strategies of governmental agencies?

CHANNEL MANAGEMENT STRATEGIES

Currently, many governmental organizations follow different strategies in the management of their service channels. Some public agencies still stick to the model in which the Internet is the preferred channel for public service delivery. For example, for service delivery, the Internet is the primary service channel for both the Canadian and UK Inland Revenue Agencies. The Dutch Tax and Customs administration also follows this strategy but goes even further; it has made the electronic delivery for business taxes mandatory. Hereby, e-Government services are implemented, specifically to reduce the number of channels. The focus of these countries or organizations is to replace one channel with another. Hence, this strategy can be seen as a 'replacement channel strategy'.

Other governmental agencies follow different strategies. The central governments of Canada and Australia for example want to integrate all channels in one service delivery concept. Under the label 'Multi-channeling' various initiatives are deployed for this integration of channels, but

Table 1. Channel management strategies (Pieterson & van Dijk, 2006)

Nr	Name	Explanation
1	Parallel positioning	Channels are positioned next to each other. Citizens are free to choose their channels and services are available through each channel.
2	Replacement positioning	Channels can replace each other. Assumption is that channels can be superior or inferior to each other. Customers would prefer to use the best channel and therefore one channel would replace another.
3	Supplemental positioning	Channels have supplemental values; each channel has its own characteristics that make it suitable for certain types of services. Therefore, governments should offer services via the best suited channels.
4	Integrated positioning	All channels are integrated in the entire service delivery process. This means that all services are offered via all channels, but that strengths and weaknesses of channels are used in their design. Citizens are guided to the 'best' channels and channels seamlessly refer to each other.

what exactly is multi-channeling and what types of channel strategies can be distinguished?

We can distinguish between four different service channel strategies (Pieterson & van Dijk, 2006). Table 1 shortly summarizes these strategies.

In time these strategies are linked to different (historical) phases in channel positioning, as will be discussed below. Both supplemental and integrated positioning can be seen as multi-channel management strategies. Kotler (2000) defines multi-channeling as the use, by one single firm, of two or more marketing channels to reach one or more customer segments. In the public service context, Pieterson and Van Dijk (2006) define multi-channeling as:

The use of multiple service channels within one public service delivery process or the use of different channels for different service delivery processes, whereby the different channels relate to each other.

This definition emphasizes the fact that channels have different characteristics which makes them useful for purposes with different requirements. Multi-channeling is not about using multiple channels, alongside each other, but is about multiple channels that relate to each other and to the service requirements. However, as mentioned above, different channel management strategies exist and different organizations follow different channel management strategies.

Parallel Positioning

The traditional way of dealing with service channels is that of parallel positioning. Before the advent of the Internet, this was the basic strategy that most governmental agencies followed. The strategy rests on the idea that all different channels are used alongside each other; each question could be answered via each channel. For example, some twenty years ago I could contact most government agencies by phone, letter or in person and get a reply to my question via each of the channels.

Replacement Positioning

The second strategy arrived after the advent of the Internet. The Internet gave us a number of new channels, e-mail and especially websites that were conceived as superior to the other channels. Hence it was conceived that channels were able to replace each other. The replacement of the written tax form for entrepreneurs by the obligatory electronic form in the Netherlands is a striking example of this strategy.

The crash of the Internet hype and the enduring popularity of the traditional channels have led to rethought of the replacement strategy.

Figure 1. Parallel channel positioning

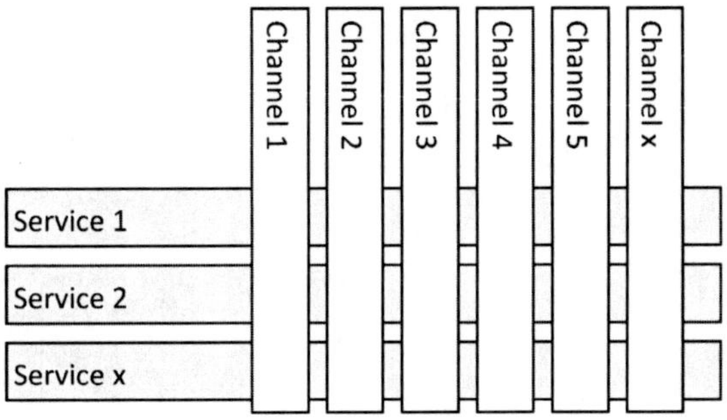

Supplemental Positioning

There is however a, theoretical, more important reason why replacement positioning might not be the ideal channel management strategy. From a communication point of view; channels have different characteristics that turn them suited for different types of (communication) tasks. One of the most prominent (media) communication theories; Media Richness Theory (Daft & Lengel, 1986), for example, argues that media differ in richness and that rich media are needed to solve ambiguous problems. Van Dijk (2005). Reviewed numerous media theories and argues that the electronic channels are *fast*, have a high *geographical reach*, have a *high storage capacity*, and are *accurate* and *selective.* The electronic channels, however, also score low on their *social reach*, degree of *interactivity*, their *stimulus richness*, *complexity* and *privacy protection.*

This knowledge would call for simple and fast services to be dealt with via the electronic channels and the complex and ambiguous services via the traditional channels. Hence, channels supplement each other and services should be offered via the best channel for that particular task.

This strategy has gained importance in the private sector were for example transferring money is done electronically with banks, but mortgages are mostly sold in person. Such policies attempt to implement a multi-channel approach that has originated in the business sector and in marketing (examples from the private sector are Kumar & Venkatesan, 2005; Neslin, et al., 2006). This strategy potentially has two benefits (Pieterson & van Dijk, 2006). Service delivery would be for efficient if not all services need to be offered through all channels. Second, citizens are better served if service delivery is tailored to their needs.

Figure 2. Replacement channel positioning

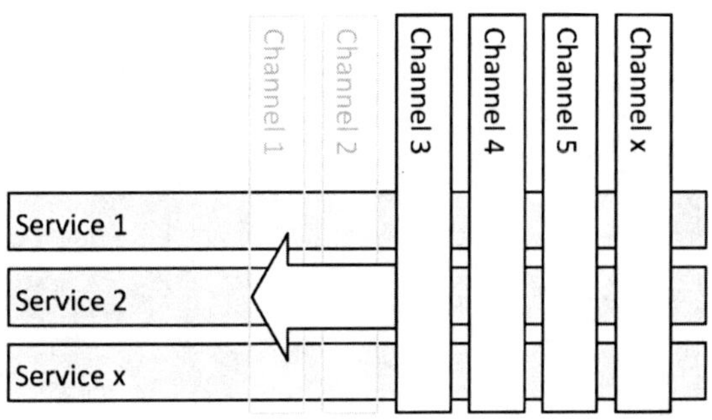

Figure 3. Supplemental channel positioning

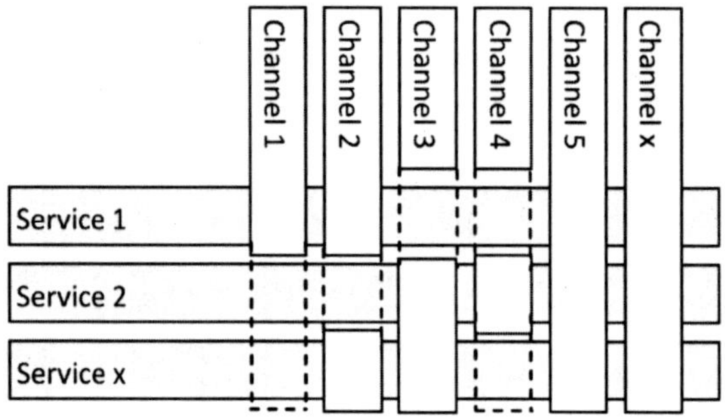

However, this strategy also has a number of drawbacks. First, there are some differences between the public and private sector that turn the applicability of this strategy difficult (Ebbers, Pieterson, & Noordman, 2008), governments have the duty to deliver services to their citizens. A governmental agency, for example, cannot exclude citizens who do not posses a computer from services that are delivered solely via the Internet. A second reason why this strategy is hard to realize is that it assumes that citizens are rationally able to match a certain channel with a certain service. As the channel choice section made clear, citizens often do not behave rationally, but choose their channels habitually. This might easily lead to citizens picking channels via which services are not offered, rendering service delivery less efficient.

Integrated Positioning

A better strategy might be the integrated strategy (Pieterson & van Dijk, 2006). This strategy combines elements of the supplemental strategy and the parallel strategy (Ebbers, et al., 2008), The basic idea behind this strategy is that, principally, all services are offered via all channels, but that in the design of the channels its strengths and weaknesses are taken into account. Channel integration – as perceived by the customer – implies a strong level of compatibility and a seamless interaction across the channels (Teerling, 2007). Or as Payne and Frow (2005) indicate; the structure and flow of activity in the various channels should be integrated in such a manner that they consistently deliver the value proposition in the eyes of the customer.

Figure 4. Integrated channel positioning

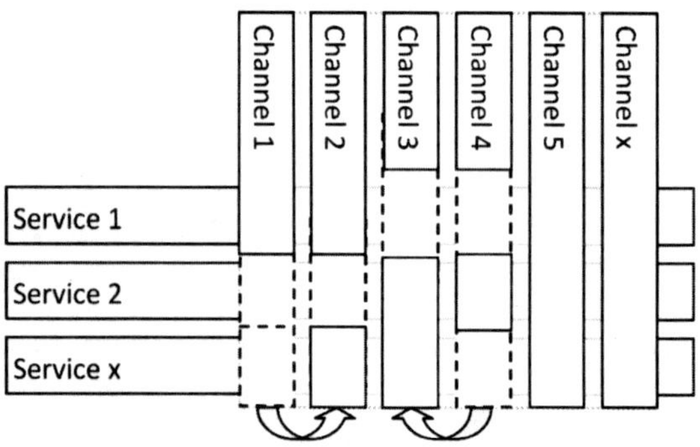

Table 2. Examples of linkages between channel choice determinants, task suitability and channel referral

Channel	Chosen why?	Suited for what tasks?	Suited for what situations?	Refers to other channels
Website	- easy to use - high contact speed	- Simple & standard tasks - much information (background)	- To reduce low levels of uncertainty - When emotions play a minor role	- The telephone when ambiguity is high - The front desk when complexity and ambiguity are high - The telephone when closure is needed
Telephone	- high contact speed - High immediacy of feedback - Gives closure	- Ambiguous tasks	- To reduce high levels of uncertainty - When emotions play a major role When people are in a rush	- The website when ambiguity is reduced - The front desk when complexity and ambiguity are still high
Front desk	- Out of habit - Gives closure - Is personal - offers high levels of service	- Ambiguous tasks and (highly) complex tasks	- To reduce high levels of uncertainty - When matters are of high importance - When emotions play a major role	- The website when ambiguity is reduced
E-mail	- easy to use - Gives closure	- Simple & standard tasks - much information (backgrounds)	- To reduce medium levels of uncertainty	- The telephone when ambiguity is high - The website when (simple) information is needed. - The front desk when complexity and ambiguity are high

Layne and Lee propose a model of e-Government development, in which integration takes a central position. Their model distinguishes between horizontal and vertical integration. Horizontal integration means that at the same level systems are integrated across different functions. An example of horizontal integration is conditional access techniques (user names and passwords used in every service), such as the Dutch DigiD system that allows for a single logon for many governmental services. Vertical integration entails a real one stop shop for citizens; portals such as the US' usa.gov are heading in that direction. However, the integrated channel strategy focuses on integration across channels and in this it takes a broader perspective of the Layne and Lee model.

To give an example of the integration across channels; the front desk is better in reducing ambiguity than a website, so ambiguous services should be mostly dealt with in person. However, since all services should be offered via all channels, information regarding ambiguous tasks should also be posted on a website, but ambiguous services might be put deeper in the site. The front pages of the website should then be used to deliver relatively simple and standard services. Given the fact that citizens do not autonomously choose the best channel given the task, another key element of this strategy is that within the strategy the citizens are directed to the proper channels. Citizens calling a helpdesk out of habit should be guided to the advantages of another channel if the required service could be better served via this channel. Or as Pieterson suggests "[w]hy not send such citizens an e-mail or SMS linking to the desired information after their ambiguity is reduced and they have closure about the correctness of the information?" (p. 251).

Using this strategy, governmental agencies should not aim at reducing the number of contacts via a channel or replace one channel with another, but they should make the contacts via the expensive channels as efficient as possible. "The aim should not be the reduction of the number of calls but shortening the calls' duration" (Pieterson, 2009, p. 251). Pieterson (2009) gives suggestions for what purposes the channels are best suited. In the following table some suggestions are given for the connection between certain services (tasks) and service channels.

Although this integration strategy has important (potential) benefits in improving the quality and efficiency of public service delivery it requires a lot of effort to become reality. Most importantly, governmental agencies need to gather loads of information about their citizens' behaviors. Knowledge that, in most cases, is not present yet. Further, it requires that the data provided through the different channels are the same in all channels and that the content of the information is synchronous across the available channels. Those conditions are not often met in public agencies and it requires many changes in both front and back offices to become reality. Further, it requires coordination between the different channels. Often, channels are managed separately by different organizational units and communication and cultural aspects are seen as important obstacles in realizing proper alignment between the organizational units and hence the channels (Pieterson, 2008).

The strategy of integrating channels is interesting and some examples of organizations that integrate channels exist. A first example is the Service Canada model that offers citizens multi-jurisdictional access to customer oriented services and one-stop multi-channel access (Flumian, Coe, & Kernaghan, 2007). Another example is the 311 call center from New York City in which different telephone channel of various organizations are integrated. However, no examples are known that integrate multiple channels and provide linkages between different channels.

In some, the integrated strategy may have important benefits in terms of increasing customer satisfaction and reducing costs. Goals that are often seen as hard to combine (Bertot & Jaeger, 2008). However, at present it is largely a theoretical and hypothetical model; we lack the understanding to realize such a perspective at present. Nevertheless, the idea that channels have different characteristics that should be used for different tasks has be acknowledged widely, both in theories, such as media richness theory (Daft & Lengel, 1986) and policy plans of governmental agencies (Australian Government, 2006). Hence it seems an important future direction for channel management.

FUTURE RESEARCH DIRECTIONS

After the Internet hype, it has become clear that public service delivery works best when adjusted to the needs and behaviors of citizens (van Deursen & Pieterson, 2006). Service delivery should be based on the demand, rather than the supply of services (van Deursen, van Dijk, & Ebbers, 2006). However, in order to turn from supply to demand, we need more knowledge about the actual needs, desires and behaviors of citizens. Further, we need to develop new theories and models that translate the behavioral determinants of citizens in generalizable channel management guidelines. Finally, we lack understanding of some of the behavioral determinants of citizens, such as the role of emotions in citizen-government interactions. Future research should explore these directions.

CONCLUSION

In this chapter, it has been argued that governmental service delivery has changed through the years. After the 1970's the orientation of governmental service delivery shifted to an external 'customer' orientation. Especially the NPM and the arrival of the new service channels in the 1980's and 1990's have impacted current practices, such as the shift from the 'supply' to the 'demand' of public services. Although the customer orientation has succeeded in some cases, empirical research has shown that, in practice, governmental agencies still remain bureaucratic (Parker & Bradley, 2004).

Given the bureaucratic rationality of governmental agencies, these agencies have a tendency to view citizens as rational beings who weigh the characteristics of channels and tasks before choosing channels. Based on this rational thought, it was predicted by some during the dot-com hype that the electronic channels would replace the traditional service channels. However, this did not happen. Our discussion of citizens' channel behavior shows that the traditional service channels remain popular. In many cases throughout the world, the traditional service channels remain the most important means of interaction for citizens with their governments. Developments in use show that only the written channel has become less important in recent years. The electronic channels have proven to be additional channels rather than replacements.

In this chapter we argued that channels should not be seen as replacements. Channels have different characteristics that turn them suited for different types of services. If one would rationally match channels with services a supplemental service channel strategy would be an ideal strategy. However, citizens do not always rationally choose the best channel for the task: rather, they act out of habits and emotions. If citizens choose channels where they cannot get the service they need, then service delivery is less efficient and effective in terms of citizen satisfaction and costs than in situations were they do receive the desired service.

The most important conclusion is that an integrated strategy in which channels are seamlessly connected might be the best future channel management strategy. This strategy exploits the strengths of the different service channels and it anticipates on the unpredictable behavior of citizens. Finally, it has the potential to enhance the cost-effectiveness of public service delivery. A goal that is in the interest of both citizens and governmental agencies.

REFERENCES

Alba, J., Lynch, J., Weitz, B., Janiszewski, C., Lutz, R., & Wood, S. (1997). Interactive Home Shopping: Consumer, Retailer and Manufacturer Incentives to Participate in Electronic Marketplaces. *Journal of Marketing*, *61*, 38–53. doi:10.2307/1251788

Albeda, H., & van Bijlert, J. (2001). Oude klanten verwachten inspanningen, nieuwe klanten verwachten resultaten. In van Duivenboden, H., & Lips, M. (Eds.), *Klantgericht werken in de Publieke Sector*. Utrecht: Lemma.

Australian Government. (2006). *Delivering Australian Government Services: Managing Multiple Channels*. Canberra: Commonwealth of Australia.

Baym, N. K. (1998). The Emergence of On-Line Community. In Jones, S. G. (Ed.), *Cybersociety 2.0. Revisiting Computer-Mediated Communication and Community*. London: Sage.

Bekkers, V. (1998). *Grenzeloze overheid. Over informatisering en grensveranderingen in openbaar bestuur*. Alphen aan den Rijn: Samson.

Bekkers, V., van Duivenboden, H., & Lips, M. (2005). ICT en Publieke dienstverlening. In Lips, M., Bekkers, V., & Zuurmond, A. (Eds.), *ICT en Openbaar Bestuur*. Utrecht: Lemma.

Belkin, N. J., Brooks, H. M., & Oddy, R. N. (1982). As for information retrieval. *The Journal of Documentation*, *38*(2), 61–71. doi:10.1108/eb026722

Bertot, J. C., & Jaeger, P. T. (2006). User-centered e-government: Challenges and benefits for government Web sites. *Government Information Quarterly*, *23*(2), 163–168. doi:10.1016/j.giq.2006.02.001

Bertot, J. C., & Jaeger, P. T. (2008). The E-Government paradox: Better customer service doesn't necessarily cost less. *Government Information Quarterly*, *25*(2), 149–154. doi:10.1016/j.giq.2007.10.002

Bozeman, B. (2000). *Bureaucracy and Red Tape*. Upper Saddle River, NJ: Prentice Hall.

Byström, K., & Järverlin, K. (1995). Task Complexity Affects Information Seeking and Use. *Information Processing & Management*, *31*(2), 191–213. doi:10.1016/0306-4573(94)00041-Z

Carlson, J. R., & Zmud, R. W. (1994). Channel Expansion Theory: A dynamic view of media and information richness perceptions. In *Academy of Management Best Papers Proceedings 1994* (pp. 280-284).

Carlson, J. R., & Zmud, R. W. (1999). Channel Expansion theory and the Experimental Nature of Media Richness Perceptions. *Academy of Management Journal*, *42*(2), 153–170. doi:10.2307/257090

Choo, C. W. (1998). *The Knowing Organization: How Organizations Use Information to construct Meaning, Create Knowledge, and Make Decisions*. New York: Oxford University Press.

Daemen, H. H. F. M., & Thomassen, J. J. A. (1989). Afstand tussen burgers en overheid. In Hoogerwerf, A. (Ed.), *Overheidsbeleid. Alphen aan den Rijn, Nederland: Samson*.

Daft, R. L., & Lengel, R. H. (1986). Organizational Information Requirements, Media Richness and Structural Design. *Management Science*, *32*(5), 554–571. doi:10.1287/mnsc.32.5.554

Davis, F. D. (1989). Perceived Usefulness, Perceived Ease of Use, and User Acceptance of Information Technology. *Management Information Systems Quarterly*, *13*(3), 318. doi:10.2307/249008

Davis, R. (1999). *The Web of Politics: The Internet's Impact on the American Political System*. New York: Oxford University Press.

Donk, W. d., & Meyer, O. (1994). Beleid voor informatisering. In Zuurmond, A. (Ed.), *Inofmatisering in het openbaar bestuur. 's Gravenhage, Nederland: VUGA*.

Duivenboden, H. P. M. v., & Lips, A. M. B. (2001). Klantgericht werken in de publieke sector: introductie. In H. P. M. v. Duivenboden & A. M. B. Lips (Eds.), Klantgericht werken in de publieke sector. Utrecht, Nederland: Lemma.

Ebbers, W., Pieterson, W., & Noordman, H. (2008). Electronic government: Rethinking channel management strategies. *Government Information Quarterly*, *25*(2), 181–201. doi:10.1016/j.giq.2006.11.003

Erin Research. (2003). *Citizens First 3*. The Institue for Citizen Centred Service.

Evans, D., & Yen, D. C. (2006). E-Government: Evolving relationship of citizens and government, domestic, and international development. *Government Information Quarterly*, *23*(2), 207–235. doi:10.1016/j.giq.2005.11.004

Flumian, M., Coe, A., & Kernaghan, K. (2007). Transforming Service to Canadians: The Service Canada Model. *International Review of Administrative Sciences*, *73*(4), 557–568. doi:10.1177/0020852307083458

Fountain, J. E. (1999). The virtual state: Toward a Theory of Federal Bureaucracy in the 21 st Century. In Kamarck, E., & Nye, J. Jr., (Eds.), *Democracy.com? Governance in a Networked World*. Hollis, NH: Hollis Publishing.

Fountain, J. E. (2001). Paradoxes of Public Customer Service. *Governance: An International Journal of Policy and Administration, 14*(1), 55–73.

Hall, P. (1998). *Cities in Civilization. Culture Innovation, and Urban Order*. London: Weinfeld & Nicholson.

Hood, C., & Peters, G. (2004). The Middle AGeing of New Public Management. *Journal of Public Administration: Research and Theory, 14*, 267–282. doi:10.1093/jopart/muh019

Horrigan, J. B. (2004). *How Americans Get in Touch With Government*. Washington, DC: Pew Internet & American Life Project.

Jones, S. G. (1998). *Cybersociety 2.0. Revisiting Computer-Mediated Communication and Community*. London: Sage.

King, C., & Stivers, C. (1998). *Government Is Us: Public Administration in an Anti-government era*. Thousand Oaks, CA: Sage Publications.

Kotler, P. (2000). *Marketing Management; The Millennium Edition*. Upper Saddle River, NJ: Prentice Hall.

Kumar, V., & Venkatesan, R. (2005). Who are Multichannel Shoppers and How do They Perform? Correlates of Multichannel Shopping Behavior. *Journal of Interactive Marketing, 19*(Spring), 44–61. doi:10.1002/dir.20034

Kwast, M. L., Martha, S., & Wolken, J. D. (1998). Market Definition and The Analysis of Antitrust in Banking. *Antitrust Bulletin, 42*(4), 973–995.

Margolis, M., & Resnick, D. (2000). *Politics as usual: The cyberspace revolution*. Thousand Oaks, CA: Sage Publications.

Mitchell, W. J. (1995). *City of Bits. Space, Place, and the Infobahn*. Cambridge, MA: MIT Press.

Moon, M. J. (2002). The evolution of e-government among municipalities: Rhetoric or reality? *Public Administration Review, 62*(4), 424–433. doi:10.1111/0033-3352.00196

Neslin, S. A., Grewal, D., Leghorn, R., Shankar, V., Teerling, M., & Thomas, J. S. (2006). Challenges and Opportunities in Multichannel Customer Management. *Journal of Service Research, 9*(2), 1–18. doi:10.1177/1094670506293559

Parker, R., & Bradley, L. (2004). Bureaucracy or Post-Bureaucracy? Public Sector Organisations in a Changing Context. *The Asia Pacific Journal of Public Administration, 26*(2), 197–225.

Pavlichev, A., & Garson, G. D. (2006). Five great ideas in Public Information Technology Literature. In Rabin, J., Hildreth, W. B., & Miller, G. J. (Eds.), *Handbook of Public Administration*. Boca Raton, FL: CRC/Taylor & Francis.

Payne, A., & Frow, P. (2005). A Strategic Framework for Customer Relationship Management. *Journal of Marketing, 69*(oktober), 167-176.

Pieterson, W. (2008). Kanaal Strategie [Channel Strategy]. Enschede, Nederland: Telematica Instituut.

Pieterson, W. (2009). Channel Choice; Citizens' Channel Behavior and Public Service Channel Strategy. Enschede, Nederland: University of Twente.

Pieterson, W., & Ebbers, W. (2008). The Use of Service Channels by Citizens in the Netherlands; implications for multi-channel management. *International Review of Administrative Sciences, 74*(1). doi:10.1177/0020852307085736

Pieterson, W., & van Dijk, J. (2006). *Governmental Service Channel Positioning*. Paper presented at the Fifth International EGOV Conference 2006, Krakow, Poland.

Pieterson, W., & van Dijk, J. (2007). *Channel Choice Determinants; An exploration of the factors that determine the choice of a service channel in citizen initiated contacts*. Paper presented at the Proceedings of the 8th annual international conference on Digital government research: bridging disciplines & domains.

Programmabureau Overheidsloket 2000. (2000). *Een loket op het Internet*. Den Haag: Programmabureau Overheidsloket 2000.

Reddick, C. G. (2005a). Citizen-Initiated Contacts with Government Comparing Phones and Websites. *Journal of E-Government, 2*(1), 27–53. doi:10.1300/J399v02n01_03

Reddick, C. G. (2005b). Citizen Interaction with E-government: From the Streets to Servers. *Government Information Quarterly, 22*, 38–57. doi:10.1016/j.giq.2004.10.003

Ringeling, A. (2001). Rare klanten hoor, die klanten van de overheid. In H. P. M. van Duivenboden & A. M. B. Lips (Eds.), Klantgericht werken in de publieke sector. Utrecht, Nederland: Lemma.

Scheepers, A., & Kommers, C. (1994). De overheid als dienstverlenende instelling. In Zuurmond, A., Frissen, P. H. A., Huigen, J., Snellen, I. T. M., & Tops, P. W. (Eds.), *Informatisering in het openbaar bestuur. Den Haag, Nederland: Vuga.*

Schellong, A., & Mans, D. (2004). *Citizens preferences towards one-stop government*. Paper presented at the The 2004 annual national conference on Digital Government research.

Sen, A. (1982). *Choice, Welfare, and Measurement*. Oxford, UK: Basil Blackwell.

Simon, H. (1976). *Administrative Behavior*. New York: Free Press.

Stonier, T. (1983). *The Wealth of Information. A profile of the post-industrial economy*. London: Methuen.

Symonds, M. (2000). The nex revolution: a survey of government and the Internet. *The Economist,* (355), 1-34.

Tat-Kei Ho, A. (2002). Reinventing Local Governments and the E-Government Initiative. *Public Administration Review, 62*(4), 434–443. doi:10.1111/0033-3352.00197

Teerling, M. L. (2007). *Determining the Cross-Channel Effects of Informational Web Sites (doctoral dissertation Rijksuniversiteit Groningen)*. Ridderkerk, Nederland: Labyrinth Publications.

Thomas, J. C., & Streib, G. (2003). The new face of government: Citizen-initiated contacts in the era of E-government. *Journal of Public Administration: Research and Theory, 13*(1), 83. doi:10.1093/jpart/mug010

Trevino, L. K., Webster, J., & Stein, E. W. (2000). Making Connections: Complementary Influences on Communication Media Choices, Attitudes, and Use. *Organization Science, 11*(2), 163–182. doi:10.1287/orsc.11.2.163.12510

van Deursen, A., & Pieterson, W. (2006). *The Internet as a service channel in the Public Sector.* Paper presented at the ICA Conference, Dresden, Germany.

van Deursen, A., van Dijk, J. A. G. M., & Ebbers, W. (2006). Why E-government Usage Lags Behind: Explaining the Gap between Potential and Actual Usage of Electronic Public Services in the Netherlands. *Lecture Notes in Computer Science, 4084*, 269–280. doi:10.1007/11823100_24

van Dijk, J., & van Deursen, A. (2006). Van Aanbod naar Vraag, Tijd voor een Perspectiefwisseling. Enschede, Nederland: Universiteit Twente.

van Dijk, J. A. G. M. (2005). The Network Society, Social Aspects of New Media (2nd ed.). London: Thousand Oaks.

van Duivenboden, H. P. M. (2002). Responsive E-Government Services: Citizen participation in public administration. The impact of Citizen oriented public services on government and citizen. Utrecht, Nederland: Cap Gemini Ernst & Young.

Wellman, B. (1997). An electronic group is virtually a social network. In Kiesler, S. (Ed.), *Cultures of the Internet*. Mahwah: Lawrence Erlbaum.

West, D. M. (2005). *Digital Government. Technology and Public Sector Performance*. Princeton, NJ: Princeton University Press.

Wirth, W. (1986). Public Administration and Publics. In Kaufman, F. X., Majone, G., & Ostrom, V. (Eds.), *Guidance, Control, and Evaluation in the Public Sector*. Berlin: Walter de Gruyter.

ADDITIONAL READING

Ebbers, W., Pieterson, W., & Noordman, H. (2008). Electronic government: Rethinking channel management strategies. *Government Information Quarterly*, *25*(2), 181–201. doi:10.1016/j.giq.2006.11.003

Pieterson, W. (2009). Channel Choice; Citizens' Channel Behavior and Public Service Channel Strategy. Enschede, Nederland: University of Twente.

Reddick, C. G. (2005a). Citizen-Initiated Contacts with Government Comparing Phones and Websites. *Journal of E-Government*, *2*(1), 27–53. doi:10.1300/J399v02n01_03

Reddick, C. G. (2005b). Citizen Interaction with E-government: From the Streets to Servers. *Government Information Quarterly*, *22*, 38–57. doi:10.1016/j.giq.2004.10.003

Thomas, J. C., & Streib, G. (2003). The new face of government: Citizen-initiated contacts in the era of E-government. *Journal of Public Administration: Research and Theory*, *13*(1), 83. doi:10.1093/jpart/mug010

van Dijk, J. A. G. M. (2005). *The Network Society, Social Aspects of New Media* (2nd ed.). Thousand Oaks, CA: Sage.

This work was previously published in International Journal of Electronic Government Research, edited by Vishanth Weerakkody, pp. 37-53, copyright 2010 by IGI Publishing (an imprint of IGI Global).

Chapter 15
Comparing Citizens' Use of E-Government to Alternative Service Channels

Christopher G. Reddick
The University of Texas at San Antonio, USA

ABSTRACT

This chapter examines the role that e-government has over citizens' lives when they initiate contact with their government. It also compares the influence that other contact channels have on citizens' contacts with government. A public opinion survey is analyzed to determine what factors explain the different methods of contacting government, namely through the phone, e-government, visiting a government office, or a combination of approaches. There also is an analysis of the preferred choice of contacting government, examining different types of information or assistance that citizens' can get from government. The results of this study indicate that e-government is just one of many possible service channels that citizens' use, with the phone being the most commonly used. Citizens that use e-government, compared to other contact channels, are more likely to have high expectations of its impact on their search. When citizens need government information they are more likely to prefer the Internet; however, when citizens have a problem they are more likely to prefer the phone. The overall importance of the survey results indicate that e-government is just one contact channel for citizens, and resources should also be devoted towards other contact channels given their importance as well to citizens.

INTRODUCTION AND BACKGROUND

Citizen engagement is thought to be the key to the success of e-government and its development. E-government can only achieve true transformation through citizen engagement (Jones, Hackney, and Irani, 2007). Research indicates that citizens who use the Internet to contact government express higher levels of satisfaction with their contact experience (Cohen, 2006). A satisfactory contact experience by citizens improves their feelings of trust and support for government and its leaders thereby enhancing democracy (Cohen, 2006).

DOI: 10.4018/978-1-61520-931-6.ch015

There is a growing body of literature that examines channel choice and e-government use (Reddick, 2005a; Pieterson, 2009). Research is starting to focus on non Internet forms of e-government such as CRM or customer relationship management systems (Schellong, 2008). There is a growing body of research that examines citizen-initiated contacts with government, and the approaches that governments use to handle these contacts (Reddick, 2005a; Ong and Wang, 2009).

Compared to the Internet, telephones in many developed and developing countries are a more popular means of accessing information from government. In addition, research shows that a combination of contact channels works best to increase e-government service adoption (Singh and Sahu, 2008). Citizens prefer to use a combination of contact channels; therefore, government should address this by providing multiple contact points (Chen, Huang, and Hsiao, 2006; Ebbers, Pieterson, and Noordman, 2008). This article presents an analysis of the most popular contact channels currently used and preferred by citizens to get information and assistance from their government.

On the supply side of e-government, there is a fairly extensive literature that indentifies the importance of e-government to public sector organizations (Coursey and Norris, 2008). However, on the demand side we know less about how and why citizens initiate contact with their government via the Internet (Thomas and Streib, 2003; Thomas and Streib, 2005; Reddick, 2005b). The purpose of this article is to examine citizens and their contacts with e-government through different service channels, a relatively understudied area of research.

The next section of this article examines the existing literature on citizens' contacts with government through e-government and factors that are predicted to explain their choice of contact channel. This section is followed by a presentation of a public opinion survey that examines what citizens look for when they go online, the service channels they use to initiate contact with government, and the preferred method of gathering government information. Towards the end of this article, there is a statistical analysis examining factors that explain actual and preferred contact methods. The conclusion section summarizes the most important findings of this research and provides future research opportunities.

LITERATURE ON E-GOVERNMENT AND CITIZENS

The e-government literature that examines citizens and their contact with government can be grouped into two important themes: issues and constraints and socio-economic and demographic factors. These two themes should have an impact on citizen adoption of e-government compared to other contact channels such as the phone. This section examines the literature on each of these themes with reference to its impact on citizens' use of e-government to initiate contacts with their government.

Issues and Constraints

There are several issues and constraints mentioned in the e-government literature that should affect the choice of contact channel citizens' choose to use. One measure is the level of satisfaction that the individual has with the ways things are going in their community (Cohen, 2006). Citizens that are satisfied with the ways things are going in their community, are more likely to use e-government to contact government.

A second measure of issues and constraints that individuals face is their success at finding the information that they want on the Internet (Carter and Belanger, 2005; Streib and Navarro, 2006). According to this research, individuals that are more successful at finding information online would most likely turn to this source. Individuals that have more challenges at finding the information, they may turn to other contact channels. There is research that examines the preferred method of contacting government and its relationship to satisfaction and success (Reddick, 2005a).

A third measure of issues and constraints that individuals face is privacy of personal indefinable information (PII). Individuals that are more concerned about privacy are less likely to want to go online to get information and assistance from government (Carter and Belanger, 2005). Someone in this state of mind would most likely use an alternative contact channel, such as visiting a government office, where there may be the perception of greater security of PII.

Another measure is if someone expects to get information or services from a government website, this should translate into the individual having a greater likelihood of going online. Therefore, expectations of success should drive choice of contact channels. Research shows that increased expectation of finding government information online influences citizens' use of the Internet (Thomas and Streib, 2005). There is much research that examines e-government technology and its adoption in governments, but there is less research that examines actual user satisfaction with e-government (Verdegem and Verleye, 2009).

There is research that examines the level of trust by citizens and its impact on the use of e-government, which is another predictor of choice of service channel. One aspect of citizen interaction with e-government is the notion that it will have an impact on citizen trust in government (West, 2004; West, 2005). Research shows that e-government will not create more trust in government, but it will enhance trust in those already trusting government (Parent, Vandebeek, and Gemino, 2005).

Another issue and constraint with regards to using e-government compared to other contact channels is if the individual feels overloaded with all of the information that they receive. The prediction is that citizens' that feel overloaded with information are not as likely to go online using e-government. These individuals believe that their ability to find the right information is impaired because they feel overwhelmed with the information they receive.

A final predictor of e-government use compared to other contact channels is control citizens' feel over how technology has influenced their lives. The prediction here is that citizens that feel computers and information technology give them more control over their lives, are more likely to use e-government compared to other contact channels.

Socio-Economic and Demographic

Along with the issues and constraints on individuals when they initiate contact with government, there are several socio-economic and demographic factors that should influence whether someone will use e-government compared to other contact channels. There is existing research that examines socioeconomic factors and their impact on e-government use, with a focus on e-government enhancing trust in government (Welch, Hinnant, Moon, 2004; Tolbert and Mossberger, 2006).

Research shows that there is a digital divide in terms of access and skills (Dugdale, Daly, Papandrea, and Maley, 2005). The digital divide refer to the difference between the information have and have-nots, which is the gap between computer literate and the computer illiterate. Lack of access to the internet by certain demographic groups is the most common form of digital divide; this is related to age, income, education, and ethnicity. There also is the skills digital divide, which is based on experience with using the Internet (Belanger and Carter, 2009).

In the digital divide, individuals that have lower access to the Internet are not as likely to use e-government compared to alternative contact channels. For instance, African-Americans, Latinos, lower income individuals, and dial up Internet users are less likely to access the Internet because of the digital divide. This should translate into these groups using other contact channels to get information or assistance from government either by the phone of visiting a government office.

Another demographic factor that should influence channel choice is gender. According to existing research, e-government content and service use is closely related to gender (Akman, Yazici, Mishra, and Arifoglu, 2005). Individuals that are younger between the ages of 18-29 should be more likely to use the Internet and e-government. In addition, individuals that are college educated should be more likely to use e-government. Citizens that work for government might have a different attitude of government, and what is can offer, and may be more likely to use e-government (Moon and Welch, 2005). There may also be differences between individuals that live in urban settings, compared to rural and suburban areas of the country. There is research that supports a rural-urban digital divide in Canada, with the odds of using the Internet in an urban area being much greater than a rural area (Noce and McKeown, 2008). These social and demographic factors are what are commonly found in the literature to explain citizen use of e-government and are used to explain service channel choice in this article.

METHODS

This article used data collected from a survey produced for the Pew Internet & American Life Project. The telephone survey consisted of random selection of individuals throughout the United States. Telephone interviews were conducted by Princeton Survey Research Associates International between June 27 and September 4, 2007, among a sample of 2,796 adults 18 years of age and older. The final response rate for the survey was 27%. The methods used in this article to analyze the survey results were simple descriptive statistics and frequencies of responses. There was also logistic regression done because this study does a comparison of individuals that used the phone compared to other communication channels. The following section indentifies the sources of information that citizens' search for when they need information of help in a situation. This provides the context of the impact of the Internet on citizens' lives.

SOURCES OF INFORMATION AND ASSISTANCE

Table 1 presents the sources of information or assistance that citizens commonly use. This information gives the impression of the role that the Internet and government play in the lives of individuals when searching for information. The most common source is to ask a professional advisor such as a doctor, lawyer, or financial expert (55.7%). The Internet was the second most commonly used source for citizens to get information or assistance (47.1%). Asking family or friends was the third most commonly used source, according to 41% of respondents. Contacting a government office or agency was done by 33.2% of respondents. Libraries were used as a source for information and help according to only 13.5% of respondents.

Overall the results in Table 1 indicate that the go to source for information and help for citizens is the Internet (Estabrook, Witt, and Rainie, 2007); it was the second most commonly used source among the ones indentified. The Internet is so important, that almost half of the population used this source when they needed information. Government was the fifth most commonly used source of information for citizens, demonstrating the important role that it plays in U.S. society.

CITIZEN-INITIATED CONTACTS WITH GOVERNMENT

Table 2 examines how citizens contact a government office or agency. This question looks

Table 1. When citizens need information or assistance in a situation they get help from the following sources

	Yes, I used this source %	*No, I did not use that source %*	*Don't know refused %*
Ask professional advisors, such as doctors, lawyers or financial experts	55.7	43.7	0.6
Use the internet	47.1	52.4	0.5
Ask friends and family members	41.0	58.5	0.5
Use newspapers, magazines, and books	37.4	62.2	0.4
Contact a government office or agency	33.2	66.5	0.3
Use television and radio	19.3	80.3	0.4
Go to a public library	13.5	86.1	0.3
Use another source not mentioned already	10.8	87.8	1.5
Go to a local place where you can use a computer for free	9.4	90.2	0.3

Notes: Total response is 2796

specifically at the responses in Table 1 from individuals that contacted a government office or agency. Recall that contacting a government office or agency was the fifth most commonly used information or assistant source. The most common method was to call the government office or agency on the phone, according to 39.2% of respondents. Doing a combination of methods was the second most commonly used approach (27.4%). Visiting a government office or agency was done by 18.1% of respondents. While visiting a government office or agency website was only completed by 8.0% of respondents. Emailing a government office or agency was completed by 2.8% of respondents. Therefore, if you just look at the role of e-government in citizens' contacts, only including those that contacted government by website or email, this represents a mere 10.8% of respondents.

Overall, the results presented in Table 2 show that e-government was not a very common method for getting information or assistance compared to the other service channels. A similar finding for low e-government use, compared to other service channels, was found in another study that examines different service channels in the Netherlands

Table 2. How citizens contact a government office or agency to find information and help in their situation

	Frequency	*Percent*
Call on the phone	269	39.2
Do a combination of the above	188	27.4
Visit a office or agency in person	124	18.1
Visit a government website	55	8.0
Other	22	3.2
Send email	19	2.8
Write a letter	9	1.3

Notes: Total response is 686

Table 3. If citizens ever needed to contact government would they prefer to use the phone, Internet, or some other way

	Over the Phone %	*On the Internet %*	*Some other way %*
A personal tax issue	57.0	11.7	28.0
Getting a license or permit for your car	12.8	22.6	59.1
Exploring government benefits for yourself or someone else	30.5	33.9	30.1
Doing research for school or work	12.5	52.3	21.1
The kinds of programs different agencies offer	26.1	41.8	24.1
Community issues such as education, crime, and traffic	30.4	24.5	38.2

Notes: Total response is 2796

(Pieterson and Ebbers, 2008). In fact, the most common approach was to call the government office or agency on the phone. Therefore, placing too many resources on Internet development may be problematic for government because of its low usage among citizens compared to other contact channels such as the phone. The focus for government would be better served devoting resources to the phone system, or making sure that multiple service channels are available for citizens to contact their government (Horrigan, 2004).

PREFERRED CHANNEL CHOICE

Table 3 provides an interesting picture of the preferred contact channels that citizens would use if they had to solve a problem or look for information. For instance, when a citizen has a personal tax issue they prefer to use the phone to contact a government office or agency (57.0%). There were 28% of respondents who would prefer to use some other method such as a combination of approaches to solve a personal tax issue. Doing research for school or work, the preferred method to contact government was the Internet, according to 52.3% of respondents. Exploring the kinds of programs that different agencies offer the preferred method is over the Internet (41.8%). The results in Table 3 indicate that for more problem-solving issues the preferred method is over the phone, while conducting information gathering or searchers the preferred method is over the Internet.

Overall, the results in Table 3 show that citizens do prefer to have choice and e-government will not solve all of the issues they need addressed. From this table, it appears that the Internet is the channel that helps citizens the most with general information, but when there is a problem citizens' will most likely turn to the phone or some other contact channel. The following section examines more closely the issues and constraints and socio-economic and demographic predictor variables that are used to predict choice of actual and preferred contact methods.

PREDICTOR VARIABLES

Table 4 provides information on the various predictor variables used in this research. These variables, as previously mentioned, take into account both the issues and constraints and socio-economic and demographics of citizens and their contact with various service channels. The results in this table show that 65.8% of respondents were satisfied with the ways things were going in their community. There were 43.7% of respondents that were very successful at finding the information they wanted. Privacy was a factor in choosing a contact

Table 4. Predictor variables of factors that explain choice of contact channel

Predictor Variables	*Frequency*	*Percent*
Issues and Constraints		
Satisfied with the way things are going in their community	1839	65.8
Very successful at finding the information you wanted	1223	43.7
Privacy was a factor in choosing the information source	399	14.3
Expect to get information or services from the government agency's website	1748	62.5
Just about always and most of the time trust Washington to do the right thing	350	12.5
Feel overloaded with all the information they receive	427	15.3
Computers and technology give people more control over their lives	603	21.6
Socio-Economic and Demographic		
Male	1065	38.1
African American	430	15.4
Latinos	227	8.1
18-29 age range	269	9.6
2006 Household income before taxes greater than $40,000	1094	39.1
College Educated	812	29.0
Urban	965	34.5
Low Access or infrequently use the Internet and have dial up access	1579	56.5
Employed federal, state, or local government	252	9.0

Notes: N=2796

channel, according to 14.3% of respondents. A majority of citizens expect to get the information or services that they want from the government website (62.5%). Only 12.5% just about always and most of the time trust Washington, D.C. to do the right thing. Only 15.3% of citizens feel overloaded with the information they received from any source. In addition, only 21.6% of respondents believed that computers gave them more control over their lives.

The typical demographic makeup of those surveyed showed that males composed 38.1% of the sample, African Americans composed 15.4% of the sample, and Latinos were 8.1% of the sample. Less than 10% of those surveyed were young between 18-29 years of age. There was 39.1% of the respondents that had an average household income in 2006 of $40,000 or greater. There were 29% of respondents that were college educated. Only 34.5% of respondents lived in an urban setting. There was a majority of respondents that have low access to the Internet, meaning that they have a dial up connection to the internet and/or limited Internet access. Finally, there were only 9% of respondents that worked for federal, state, or local government. These sixteen predictor variables demonstrated issues and constraints and socio-economic and demographic characteristics that are predicted to influence choice of service channel for both actual and preferred contacts with government.

LOGISTIC REGRESSION RESULTS OF ACTUAL CONTACTS

The following section uses these predictor variables to determine if they have an influence on the choice of citizen contact with their government for information or service requests.

Table 5 uses the subsample of citizens that have contacted government for information or service requests. This regression is composed of 686 respondents out of the total sample size of 2796. Since it is a much smaller sample, caution should be used when reviewing the results. The regressions were run for the various contact channels outlined in Table 2. The possible choices that we did regressions for were calling on the phone, visiting a government office, e-government, and a combination of methods. For the e-government logistic regression, we combined the response of visiting a government website with emailing a government office or agency. The purpose of this question is to determine the impact that these sixteen factors have on choice of channel for contacting government.

The results in Table 5 revealed that the only predictors were urban and employed in government, had an influence on whether someone contacted government by phone. With logistic regression the Odds Ratios (OR) can be used to determine the likelihood of a predictor variable explaining the dependent variable. If someone lived in an urban setting they were almost one and a half times (OR=1.41) more likely to use the phone to contact their government. If the individual was employed for the federal, state, or local government they were less likely to use the phone (OR=0.58) to contact government.

For visiting a government office, individuals with over $40,000 household income in 2006 were less likely to visit a government office for information or help with a situation (OR=0.58). An individual with a college education was less likely to visit a government office for information or help with a situation (OR=0.41). These results show that access to resources and education indicates that visiting a government office is not as likely.

Factors that explained the use of e-government show that when individuals expect to get information or services from a government agency's website they were two times more likely to use e-government (OR=2.10). E-government users were almost three times more likely to be young, between the age of 18 and 29 years (OR=2.78). E-government users were also over one and a half times more likely to have a college education (OR=1.60). The results show that e-government users are confident that they will find something useful on government websites; they tend to be younger and well educated.

Of the four modes, the most robust regression was from individuals that used a combination of methods to contact their government for information or help with a situation. Males were slightly more likely to use a combination of methods (OR=1.34). African Americans were less likely to use a combination of methods (OR=0.56). Individuals that were college educated were more likely to be use a combination of methods (OR=1.65). Those individuals that worked for government were over one and a half times more likely to use a combination of methods (OR=1.55).

Overall, the results in Table 5 indicated that e-government users were different from those that use the phone to contact government. E-government users tended to be younger and college educated, they had higher expectations that government would deliver the information they wanted through their websites. Individuals that used the most common service channel, the phone, were more likely to live in an urban setting, but less likely to be employed by the federal government. What was most interesting is that the combination of contact methods had the greatest predictive power, compared with the other service channel choices, predicting four of the 16 independent variables.

LOGISTIC REGRESSION RESULTS OF PREFERRED CONTACTS

Table 6 provides information on the issues and constraints and socio-economic and demographic factors that are thought to explain the preference

Table 5. Logistic regression examining the different methods of contacting government

Predictor Variables	*Beta*	*Prob. Sign.*	*Odds Ratio*	*Beta*	*Prob. Sign.*	*Odds Ratio*	*Beta*	*Prob. Sign.*	*Odds Ratio*	*Beta*	*Prob. Sign.*	*Odds Ratio*
Issues and Constraints												
Satisfied with the way things are going in their community	-0.03	0.86	0.97	-0.18	0.41	0.84	-0.05	0.81	0.96	0.35	0.22	1.42
Very successful at finding the information you wanted	0.16	0.34	1.18	-0.29	0.17	0.75	0.05	0.79	1.05	0.28	0.32	1.32
Privacy was a factor in choosing the information source	-0.28	0.17	0.76	0.23	0.35	1.26	-0.01	0.96	0.99	0.06	0.84	1.06
Expect to get information or services from the government agency's website	0.00	0.99	1.00	-0.18	0.43	0.83	0.09	0.66	1.10	0.74**	0.04	2.10
Just about always and most of the time trust Washington to do the right thing	-0.09	0.74	0.91	0.00	0.99	1.00	0.34	0.30	1.41	0.19	0.68	1.21
Feel overloaded with all the information they receive	0.07	0.78	1.08	0.30	0.35	1.34	0.07	0.83	1.07	-0.80	0.16	0.45
Computers and technology give people more control over their lives	0.21	0.38	1.23	0.04	0.88	1.05	-0.27	0.36	0.77	0.05	0.92	1.05
Socio-Economic and Demographic												
Male	-0.17	0.30	0.84	0.05	0.82	1.05	0.30*	0.10	1.34	-0.27	0.31	0.76
African American	0.30	0.19	1.35	0.35	0.21	1.42	-0.58**	0.04	0.56	-0.69	0.15	0.50
Latinos	-0.02	0.96	0.98	0.28	0.46	1.32	-0.28	0.41	0.75	0.19	0.66	1.21
18-29 age range	0.01	0.98	1.01	-0.23	0.53	0.79	-0.25	0.46	0.78	1.02***	0.01	2.78
2006 Household income before taxes greater than $40,000	0.20	0.28	1.22	-0.54**	0.03	0.58	0.15	0.47	1.16	0.17	0.56	1.18
College Educated	-0.14	0.43	0.87	-0.89***	0.00	0.41	0.50***	0.01	1.65	0.47*	0.09	1.60
Urban	0.35**	0.04	1.41	-0.22	0.33	0.80	-0.03	0.89	0.97	-0.43	0.13	0.65
Low Access or infrequently use the Internet and have dial up access	0.29	0.22	1.33	-0.24	0.43	0.79	-0.38	0.17	0.69	0.00	0.99	1.00
Employed federal, state, or local government	-0.54**	0.04	0.58	-0.07	0.85	0.94	0.44*	0.09	1.55	0.26	0.46	1.29
Constant	-0.73***	0.01	0.48	-0.63*	0.07	0.53	-1.20***	0.00	0.30	-3.23***	0.00	0.04

Notes: ***Significant at the 0.01; ** significant at the 0.05; * significant at the 0.10 levels. N=686

of citizens contacting government for information or assistance. Odds Ratios (OR) are only reported in order to conserve space in this table. Unlike the previous logistic regressions, that examined the actual use of the different service channels, the regression results for citizen preference in Table 6 explained many of the predictor variables. These logistic regressions results examined six common issues: personal tax issue, getting a license or permit for a car, exploring government benefits for yourself or someone else, doing research for school or work, the kinds of programs that different government agencies offer, and community issues such a education, crime, and traffic.

When examining the six issues, there were four predictors that consistently explained the preference for the Internet being used for information and help. The odds ratios indicated that citizens that expect to get information or service requests from a government agency were more likely to use the Internet for various problems they needed help with. Essentially, citizens that had high expectations of what the government provided online gave them confidence that they will be able to get things done when visiting a government website. For instance, individuals that believed they could get information on a government website were almost four times more likely to want to explore government benefits online for themselves or someone else.

The second predictor that explained the six issues citizens' dealt with when initiating contact with government was IT and its control over individual lives. Individuals that believed computers and technology gave them more control over their lives were around two times more likely to prefer to go online and visit a government website for information or assistance. For example, individuals who believed that computers gave them more control were over two times more likely to want to visit government websites for community issues such as education, crime, and traffic.

The third predictor of the six issues that citizens commonly get information or assistant from showed that household income was an important factor. If the individual's 2006 household income before taxes was greater than $40,000, they were more likely to prefer contacting the government for these six issues. For example, higher income individuals were almost two times more likely to prefer to go online to get a license or permit for their car.

A fourth predictor of using the Internet for going online to solve an issue or problem was the level of Internet access. The logistic regressions showed that individuals that infrequently used the Internet and/or had a dial up connection were less likely to go online for these six issues. This is not surprising, but it confirms much of the literature on the digital divide.

Some interesting results surface when comparing citizens' preferences for contacting government using the phone or Internet. First, individuals that expect to get information from a government website are less likely to use the phone to explore government benefits, are less likely to use the phone to do research for school, and are less likely to use the phone to examine different programs that government offers. Individuals are more likely to do all three tasks if they use the Internet. Essentially, individuals that are more comfortable with government websites tend to gravitate towards this contact channel to do research rather than use the phone.

A second finding when comparing preferences for phone and Internet for the six issues was that if someone feels overloaded with information they will use the phone to do research for school, and they are less likely to use the Internet for this purpose. Third, individuals that have a college education are less likely to do research for school over the phone, less likely to learn about programs over the phone, they are more likely to use the Internet for these purposes. Finally, individuals that have low access to the Internet are more likely to prefer the phone for research and learn about community issues.

DISCUSSION

The following section provides a discussion of the most important results of the regression analysis presented in this article. For individuals

Table 6. Logistic regressions odds ratios of preferred method of contacting government

	Personal Tax Issue		*Getting a license or permit for a car*		*Exploring government benefits for yourself of some else*		*Doing Research for school or work*		*The kinds of programs different government agencies offer*		*Community Issues such as education, crime, and traffic*	
Predictor Variables	*Phone*	*Internet*	*Phone*	*Internet*	*Phone*	*Internet*	*Phone*	*Internet*	*Phone*	*Internet*	*Phone*	*Internet*
Issues and Constraints												
Satisfied with the way things are going in their community	1.21**	1.43**	0.97	0.91	1.00	1.27**	1.10	1.06	1.20*	1.07	1.15	1.20
Very successful at finding the information you wanted	1.06	1.15	1.03	1.02	1.05	1.21**	0.86	1.38***	0.91	1.33***	0.90	1.13
Privacy was a factor in choosing the information source	0.82*	1.07	0.96	0.82	1.09	0.86	1.21	1.05	1.05	1.03	0.90	1.23
Expect to get information or services from the government agency's website	1.17*	1.86***	1.04	2.18***	0.73***	3.94***	0.72***	3.11***	0.77***	3.77***	0.97	2.57***
Just about always and most of the time trust Washington to do the right thing	1.10	1.36	1.20	1.16	1.06	0.82	1.34*	0.75**	1.09	1.15	0.87	1.26
Feel overloaded with all the information they receive	1.00	0.58*	1.14	0.95	1.08	0.87	1.38**	0.58***	1.15	0.66***	1.12	0.88
Computers and technology give people more control over their lives	1.06	2.34***	1.11	2.10***	1.17	1.92***	1.03	1.91***	1.22*	1.82***	1.26**	2.41***
Socio-Economic and Demographic												
Male	0.83**	1.19	1.00	1.22*	0.85*	1.18	1.17	0.88	1.11	0.97	1.01	1.01
African American	0.64***	0.87	1.06	0.65***	0.93	0.60***	1.13	0.96	0.80*	0.76**	0.76**	0.78*
Latinos	0.74**	1.33	0.92	1.11	0.82	0.95	1.21	1.19	0.90	1.03	1.04	1.00
18-29 age range	0.98	1.47**	1.28	1.19	1.04	1.40**	0.63*	2.79***	0.76	1.62***	0.81	1.88***
2006 Household income before taxes greater than $40,000	1.43***	1.37**	0.70***	1.83***	0.93	1.90***	0.87	1.82***	0.80**	1.80***	0.99	1.48***
College Educated	0.94	1.13	0.89	1.89***	1.04	1.16	0.57***	1.41***	0.77**	1.45***	0.96	1.12
Urban	1.05	0.99	1.08	1.14	1.05	0.97	0.98	0.95	0.98	1.10	0.99	1.02

Table 6. continued on following page.

Table 6. continued

	Personal Tax Issue		*Getting a license or permit for a car*		*Exploring government benefits for yourself of some else*		*Doing Research for school or work*		*The kinds of programs different government agencies offer*		*Community Issues such as education, crime, and traffic*	
Low Access or infrequently use the Internet and have dial up access	0.98	0.22***	1.08	0.18***	1.53***	0.24***	2.13***	0.20***	1.45***	0.21***	1.33**	0.16***
Employed federal, state, or local government	1.06	1.09	1.18	1.38**	0.83	1.31*	0.64	2.20***	0.70**	1.47**	0.87	0.98
Constant	1.08	0.07***	0.14***	0.17***	0.42***	0.20***	0.10***	0.74**	0.35***	0.33***	0.38***	0.19***

Notes: ***Significant at the 0.01; ** significant at the 0.05; * significant at the 0.10 levels; N=2796; odds ratios are just reported to conserve space.

that contacted government through e-government, these individuals were more likely to expect to get information or services from a government website, they tended to be younger and college educated. While citizens that use the phone to contact government are more likely to live in an urban area and are less likely to be employed by government. While using a combination of methods the results indicate that citizens are more likely to be male, college educated, and employed by government, but were less likely to be African American. The results on the contacts with government through different service channels showed that the socio-economic and demographic factors partially explained all four contact channels. For the category of issues and constraints, only the expectation of getting information or services from a government agency's website was a driver of e-government use. Therefore, when citizens expected e-government, they were more likely to use this method of contact.

This article also examined the preferred methods of contacting government through either the phone or Internet; examining the six issues. When examining the preference for the Internet for getting information or help, the results showed that when citizens expect to get information or services from a government website they are more likely to use the Internet; individuals that believe computers give them more control over their lives are more likely to use the Internet. There also was the impact of the digital divide on those that preferred to use the Internet to contact government; individuals that have low access to the Internet and lower household income were more likely to use the phone than the Internet. When comparing phones to the internet, individuals conducting more research-oriented activities such as exploring government benefits are more likely to use the Internet than phone if they expect to find information on government websites. The college educated individual is less likely to use the phone for research purposes. Citizens making greater than $40,000 per year are more likely to use the Internet to do research than use the phone. The results show that the task at hand had an influence on service channel used. This research showed differences in Internet and phone preference was dependent upon if it was a research task, where the internet was preferred choice controlling for other factors.

CONCLUSION AND RECOMMENDATIONS

This article examined citizens and their use of e-government to contact government. The purpose of this research was to examine citizens and their contacts with e-government through different service channels. The results of this study indicated that the Internet was the second most commonly used source of information and assistance for citizens; with almost half of respondents using this source. The phone was the most common service channel that citizens use to initiate contact with their government. E-government was almost the last service channel that citizens used. Other popular methods of contact was visiting the government office or agency or doing a combination of methods. The results of this study indicate that governments should be aware of three things about e-government: (1) it is only one possible service channel for citizens among many others; (2) the phone is still the most popular service channel; (3) governments should invest resources in a multiple service channels in order to adequately serve their citizens.

Another major finding of this research is that service channel use is dependent upon task at hand for the citizen. For more information gathering tasks the preferred service channel was the Internet. While for more personal issues, such as tax problems, the preferred method was to contact government over the phone. Therefore, governments should better understand demand for their service channels in order to understand how much development should be placed on each channel.

The results of this study showed that e-government use was driven by the expectation of citizens of what the government agency or department offers online. If there was a greater expectation of e-government there was more demand by citizens for e-government. Government should spend more resources promoting what they currently offer online; this would improve the perceived expectations of what is available and improve demand.

A final result shows that for information gathering the preferred method of contact government was over the Internet. For more interaction the preferred method is to call the government agency over the phone. This supports much of the qualitative literature indicating that for more complicated problems individuals turn to the Internet to initiate contact with their government. A recommendation for government would be to make sure that information placed online be regularly updated and accurate.

There are some notable limitations to this study that should be mention and future research recommendations are provided. One limitation is that the survey data used in this study was taken from a preexisting survey; therefore, some of the factors that we use are rather crude compared to more precise measures if we designed the survey ourselves. The second limitation is that this study explored service channel use and preference in one country, which can be problematic since the results would provide much different findings for developed countries like the U.S. compared to developing countries. Therefore, future research should provide a more custom built survey on citizen-initiated contacts comparing two or more countries exploring the similarities and differences in choice of contact. This research was one of the first to explore the impact of why citizens prefer one contact channel over another and the factors that lead to their choice. However, there is more research that needs to be done on this understudied area of citizens and e-government.

REFERENCES

Akman, I., Yazici, A., Mishra, A., & Arifoglu, A. (2005). E-Government: A Global View and an Empirical Evaluation of some Attributes of Citizens. *Government Information Quarterly*, *22*(2), 239–257. doi:10.1016/j.giq.2004.12.001

Belanger, F., & Carter, L. (2009). The Impact of the Digital Divide on E-Government Use. *Communications of the ACM*, *52*(4), 132–135. doi:10.1145/1498765.1498801

Carter, L., & Belanger, F. (2005). The Utilization of E-government Services: Citizen Trust, Innovation and Acceptance Factors. *Information Systems Journal, 15*(1), 5–25. doi:10.1111/j.1365-2575.2005.00183.x

Chen, D.-Y., Huang, T.-Y., & Hsiao, N. (2006). Reinventing Government through On-Line Citizen Involvement in the Developing World: A Case Study of Taipei City Major's E-Mail Box in Taiwan. *Public Administration and Development, 26*(5), 409–423. doi:10.1002/pad.415

Cohen, J. E. (2006). Citizen Satisfaction with Contacting Government on the Internet. *Information Policy, 11*(1), 51–65.

Coursey, D., & Norris, D. F. (2008). Models of E-Government: Are They Correct? An Empirical Assessment. *Public Administration Review, 68*(3), 523–536. doi:10.1111/j.1540-6210.2008.00888.x

Dugdale, A., Daly, A., Papandrea, F., & Maley, M. (2005). Accessing E-Government: Challenges for Citizens and Organizations. *International Review of Administrative Sciences, 71*(1), 109–118. doi:10.1177/0020852305051687

Ebbers, W., Pieterson, W., & Noordman, H. N. (2008). Electronic Government: Rethinking Channel Management Strategies. *Government Information Quarterly, 25*(2), 181–201. doi:10.1016/j.giq.2006.11.003

Estabrook, L., Witt, E., & Rainie, L. (2007). *Information Searches that Solve Problems*. Retrieved July 31, 2009 from http://www.pewinternet.org/Reports/2007/Information-Searches-That-Solve-Problems.aspx

Horrigan., J.B. (2004). *How Americans get in Touch with Government*. Retrieved July 31, 2009, from http://www.pewinternet.org/Reports/2004/How-Americans-Get-in-Touch-With-Government.aspx

Jones, S., Hackney, R., & Irani, Z. (2007). Towards E-government Transformation: Conceptualising "Citizen Engage". *Transforming Government: People. Process and Policy, 1*(2), 145–152.

Moon, M. J., & Welch, E. W. (2005). Same Bed, Different Dreams? A Comparative Analysis of Citizen and Bureaucratic Perspectives on E-Government. *Review of Public Personnel Administration, 25*(3), 243–264. doi:10.1177/0734371X05275508

Noce, A. A., & McKeown, L. (2008). A New Benchmark for Internet Use: A Logistic Modeling of Factors Influencing Internet use in Canada, 2005. *Government Information Quarterly, 25*(3), 462–476. doi:10.1016/j.giq.2007.04.006

Ong, C.-S., & Wang, S.-W. (2009). Managing Citizen-Initiated Email Contacts. *Government Information Quarterly, 26*(3), 498–504. doi:10.1016/j.giq.2008.07.005

Parent, M., Vandebeek, C. A., & Gemino, A. C. (2005). Building Citizen Trust through E-Government. *Government Information Quarterly, 22*(4), 720–736. doi:10.1016/j.giq.2005.10.001

Pieterson, W. (2009). *Channel Choice: Citizens' Channel Behavior and Public Service Channel Strategy*. Netherlands: Thesis, University of Twente.

Pieterson, W., & Ebbers, W. (2008). The Use of Service Channels by Citizens in the Netherlands: Implications for Multi-Channel Management. *International Review of Administrative Sciences, 74*(1), 95–110. doi:10.1177/0020852307085736

Reddick, C. G. (2005a). Citizen-Initiated Contacts with Government: Comparing Phones and Websites. *Journal of E-Government, 2*(1), 27–51. doi:10.1300/J399v02n01_03

Reddick, C. G. (2005b). Citizen Interaction with E-Government: From the Streets to Servers? *Government Information Quarterly, 22*(1), 38–57. doi:10.1016/j.giq.2004.10.003

Schellong, A. (2008). *Citizen Relationship Management: A Study of CRM in Government*. Berlin: Peter Lang Publishing Group.

Singh, A., & Sahu, R. (2008). Integrating Internet, Telephones, and Call Centers for Delivering Better Quality E-Governance to all Citizens. *Government Information Quarterly*, *25*(3), 477–490. doi:10.1016/j.giq.2007.01.001

Streib, G., & Navarro, I. (2006). Citizen Demand for Interactive E-Government: The Case of Georgia Consumer Services. *American Review of Public Administration*, *36*(3), 288–300. doi:10.1177/0275074005283371

Thomas, J. C., & Streib, G. (2003). The New Face of Government: Citizen-Initiated Contacts in the Era of E-Government. *Journal of Public Administration: Research and Theory*, *13*(1), 83–102. doi:10.1093/jpart/mug010

Thomas, J. C., & Streib, G. (2005). E-Democracy, E-Commerce, and E-Research: Examining the Electronic Ties between Citizens and Governments. *Administration & Society*, *37*(3), 259–280. doi:10.1177/0095399704273212

Tolbert, C. J., & Mossberger, K. (2006). The Effects of E-Government on Trust and Confidence in Government. *Public Administration Review*, *66*(3), 354–369. doi:10.1111/j.1540-6210.2006.00594.x

Verdegem, P., & Verleye, G. (2009). User-Centered E-Government in Practice: A Comprehensive Model for Measuring User Satisfaction. *Government Information Quarterly*, *26*(3), 487–497. doi:10.1016/j.giq.2009.03.005

Welch, E. W., Hinnant, C. C., & Moon, M. J. (2005). Linking Citizen Satisfaction with E-Government and Trust in Government. *Journal of Public Administration: Research and Theory*, *15*(3), 371–391. doi:10.1093/jopart/mui021

West, D. M. (2004). E-Government and the Transformation of Service Delivery and Citizen Attitudes. *Public Administration Review*, *64*(1), 15–27. doi:10.1111/j.1540-6210.2004.00343.x

West, D. M. (2005). *Digital Government: Technology and Public Sector Performance*. Princeton, NJ: Princeton University Press.

This work was previously published in International Journal of Electronic Government Research, edited by Vishanth Weerakkody, pp. 54-67, copyright 2010 by IGI Publishing (an imprint of IGI Global).

Chapter 16
Social Tagging to Search and Recommend Government Information

Janice Warner
Georgian Court University, USA

Soon Ae Chun
College of Staten Island - City University of New York, USA

ABSTRACT

The amount of data, documents and services provided by the US government and all its agencies is overwhelming for citizens as well as employees of government agencies that need to collaborate. The US federal government offers several portals and associated search engines. In addition, to aid in inter-agency coordination, there are some platforms deployed to exchange information and share resources. This chapter investigates how social tagging technology can support citizen information and service requirements by facilitating discovery of needed information, services and knowledge. The authors also show how governmental agencies and departments can use the technologies to better service citizens through integration of their capabilities and knowledge. The proposed service could have a big impact in helping citizens with a relatively small incremental cost to implement because the "work" done is by the users in a distributed fashion. The impact derives from improving the accessibility and sharing of information resources.

INTRODUCTION

In order for citizens (and other constituents hereafter referred to together as citizens) to make fully informed decisions about the factors that may impact their lives and their communities, access to information is essential. They want to find government services, property and financial information, educational choices, social benefits, business opportunities, health information, statistical summary information, public affairs, professional career information and many others in order to make informed decisions. In addition, citizens want to participate in the governments' policy and decision making processes. Open government gives citizens the right to access government information. The US Freedom of Information Act (FOIA) legislates that government information is accessible to all

DOI: 10.4018/978-1-61520-931-6.ch016

citizens. Open government entails government transparency, accountability, public trust and shared governance, allowing more accessible citizen participation in the democratic processes. The Internet and the Web support open government under the digital government initiatives. Federal, state and local governments have pushed their information on the Web, and have begun to provide services from the Web.

The amount of data, documents and services provided by the US government and all its agencies is overwhelming for citizens. It is a challenge for citizens to be able to find the right information without sifting through many potential web pages, attached documents, and services. Employees of government agencies face a similar challenge when they need to collaborate in an attempt to provide seamless integrated services for both the public and for backend government business processes.

The US federal government offers several portals that provide access to a host of information and services. The main portal is "usa.gov" but there are many other portals specific to groups of people or areas of interest. These portals characterize various types of information and offer search capabilities. The usasearch.gov search engine, which supports the usa.gov portal, provides a more structured search environment than a general search engine provides since it does use knowledge about the contents of the websites it supports. Like most search engines, it is based on keyword search which can be limited to certain website address (i.e. urls). However, despite its attempts to focus results, searches still generate large numbers of documents and resources through which end users must sift.

Besides direct searching, citizen's access to services that cross government boundaries requires inter-agency collaboration and process coordination which would be supported by efficient search for data and web services among government agencies. To aid in inter-agency coordination, there are some platforms deployed. For example, a platform called CORE.gov, which is built on the federal enterprise architecture, is a central repository for various "components" such as software, processes, case studies and best practices. The difficulty is that all components need to be approved and the shared information needs to be transferred to the repository. Any agency offering to post a component also has the responsibility of updating it. These limitations impact what individuals share and post because the process is so burdensome.

This chapter investigates how IT tools support citizen information and service requirements. Our analysis is in two parts. First we examine the websites, information and services available directly to citizens in the USA. Then we examine the collaborative capabilities offered to government agency members in order to foster cooperation. In both cases, we use the US federal government websites and policies in order to illustrate what is possible as well as what is lacking.

Many of these websites do incorporate Web 2.0 technologies. In our background section, we review current capabilities in the areas of portals, search, and interactivity and assess their strengths and weaknesses. We then propose advances that can be made and the advantages they might bring. In particular, we look at semantic community tagging to facilitate finding of information, services and people. We also consider integration of relevant web services through mashups. Our goal is to show how governmental agencies and departments can use Web 2.0 technologies to better service citizen needs through integration of their capabilities and knowledge.

BACKGROUND

Most governments provide portals to help citizens find information. The information is categorized and special search engines are established as might be found in a corporate web site. Internal portals provide governmental employees the ability to collaborate and share information. In this section, existing capabilities as implemented by the US federal government are explored and limitations are highlighted. To help illustrate, we consider a search on "foreclosures", an issue of major importance in 2009 in the United States.

GOVERNMENT WEB PORTAL AND SEARCH ENGINE TECHNOLOGIES

The US Government's official Web portal (usa.gov) is an example of a portal where information is categorized. Similar portals are provided by the government or by citizen groups in other countries (e.g. http://www.citizensinformation.ie/categories for Ireland). The Web portal provides a directory service where content is categorized. Users typically navigate down to more and more specific categories until they find the content in which they have an interest. This facilitates discovery of the information through organization of the content. However, because the categories are established by the portal providers, it may not be completely in line with how the particular users would organize the resources.

Government search engines (e.g., usasearch.gov) provide a more structured search environment than a general search engine since their search domain is within the government website. Typically, a government search engine makes use of knowledge about the contents of the websites it supports. A government search engine is typically based on keyword search with advanced search features allowing a user to specify government domains of interest. The advanced search function at usasearch.gov allows a user to select file type and language and organizes the results in ways that are relevant for someone who has a need to access government services and information.

To illustrate, consider a search using usasearch.gov on "foreclosures" which provided over 58,000 results. A similar Google search on the WWW provided over 8 million results although that can be limited under the Google US Government Search Engine to around 82,000. However, in the usasearch.gov search, the top 109 were shown and these were categorized by subtopic as well as agency and source. The search engine relies on standard metadata in response to Office of Management and Budget mandates for all federal agencies to organize and categorize government information and make it searchable across agencies in order to improve public access and dissemination (Johnson, 2004; Johnson, 2005). At a minimum, federal websites are mandated to include metadata for the title, description, content creator (i.e., name of the organization), date created, date reviewed and language. These six suggested metadata elements are based on internationally recognized Dublin Core standards (DCMI, 2008). Metadata can be used to filter resources that match a keyword search.

Similarly, the citizen services from different governments can be searched using usasearch.gov. The keyword-based search will bring the available services from different governments, such as permit services or compliance check services, online business registration filing services, tax filing services, social welfare services, motor vehicle services, and many more. The search can be restricted to a specific state or to a specific language or a specific website.

US GOVERNMENT COLLABORATION PLATFORM

For federal inter-agency and intra-agency as well as inter governmental (federal, state, and local) collaboration, a platform called CORE.gov has been initiated to promote standardization and reuse of agency business functions and IT services. This collaborative environment advocated a development of service-oriented components that can be reused by sharing them through a central repository organized for various interest groups.

A community of users, including program managers, enterprise and data architects, and other government stakeholders, develop software components that provide interoperability across agencies, share the design of business processes, develop policies and protocols for interagency use, and discuss other strategies for collaboration and sharing resources, using community wikis. All components need to be approved and the shared information needs to be transferred to the repository. Any agency offering to post a component also has the responsibility of updating it. There are host of information services such as federal employment information system, contractor performance information retrieval system, payment service, billing service, products and services directory service to retrieve company contact and available products and services provided by the company, acquisition related vendor/trading partner information retrieval system, federal business opportunity system, authentication service component, and many more.

In order to make the sharing and collaboration work, we need to consider not only the fact that the end users need to be able to search the components easily, but also the fact that the author/publishers of the resources or components not be burdened when sharing them. Thus our research focuses on helping people to find material without burdening the authors/managers of the resources. What we propose is that search be augmented with an annotation system. This system would not only allow authors and managers to indicate that resources exist but would allow anyone else who has found and used the resources to generate metadata on the resource including content description, use and usefulness. Through this annotation system, a user searching for information resources will be able to assess relevance not only based on keyword matching but also based on the annotation of anyone who used the resource. If many people have found the resource to be useful, the searcher might also find it useful. In addition, if some of the annotators are considered to be experts, a searcher could take advantage of their expertise to find those resources that they found more useful. Finally, if the searcher knows which annotators have searched for resources based on similar context to their own, the searcher might look first at the resources found most useful to those annotators. Thus we are proposing a multi-faceted approach to resource discovery where the searcher could use the input of annotators to narrow down the list of potentially relevant resources.

Results presented by portal categorization and search engines do not incorporate end user input. Users of these web sites are considered to be information consumers and the government agencies are considered to be information or service providers. Standard metadata is provided and managed by the information providers without input from the end users including private citizens, business representatives or employees of government agencies. Any personalization of search results is based on log-in information and user specified profiles. To date, there has been limited use of web site usage data or direct user input, such as comments or ratings, to provide further personalized recommendation of information potentially interesting to the citizens given a particular context. However, on some commercial websites such as amazon.com, users are provided with recommended products and services based on the behavior or direct input of other users. Users can also see comments that others have left on any given product. This indirect interaction among end users is not seen on government sites. By supporting it, governments would not only help their citizens locate what they need, but they might be able to gain insight into the issues with which citizens are currently concerned, lending support to policy decisions.

WEB 2.0 TECHNOLOGIES FOR GOVERNMENT INFORMATION SEARCH, COLLABORATION AND SERVICE INTEGRATION

The US government has made a conscious effort to incorporate Web 2.0 technology into federal websites. A comprehensive matrix can be retrieved on the Web from the GSA site (Godwin 2008). There is a wiki (http://colab.cim3.net/cgi-bin/wiki.pl/) hosted by the GSA Intergovernmental Solutions which includes brainstorming results. There are blogs with the goal of putting a human face on government. These blogs usually describe current general issues such as increases in postal prices. Some agencies, such as the EPA and NASA, have also initiated Facebook groups to facilitate collaboration. Links also appear on multiple sites to allow users to bookmark the pages. While mashup potential was identified, the only mashups implemented to date put map services on sites to support provision of directions to physical locations. Additionally, informal groups have been developed including a social network call govloop.org which connects interested government employees and contractors.

In addition to these social networks that facilitate collaboration by bringing interested parties together, government resources such as documents, services and web resources should be easily searched and shared. For this purpose, we propose social tags, i.e. the collective tags created by the citizens and government officials. These tags should be organized in terms of their semantics and pragmatics to be useful for organizing and searching the government information. We discuss the social tagging, the challenges and opportunities, and a social tagging system architecture.

SOCIAL TAGGING

Tagging is an increasingly popular mechanism for adding personal categorization to information resources of all types that are available on the Web. It is an aid to organizing results of an unstructured search. When tagging is done by the individual, their personal conception or use of the resource is highlighted. If made available to others, people with similar questions or needs would benefit. If done in a distributed fashion, personal tags could be aggregated across a community to allow for a common understanding. Making tags available for community usage aids in search, acting as a filter that narrows the range of potential resources that might be of interest to the searcher. Thus, social tags are community based shared tags created by individuals. When aggregated together, tags reveal patterns indicating consensus or general "agreements" created in distributed and asynchronous fashion without any prior plan.

Several examples of social tagging systems are in existence and very popular. Del.icio.us was one of the first to allow users to share bookmarks (or tags) of sites. ZigTag has taken steps to consider search and tagging history to discern what a user is actually looking for. CiteULike, another example, allows users to tag actual documents or articles, not just websites. These resources might be in repositories or in personal collections and can be uploaded for sharing if the user has permission to do so. ZigTag and CiteULike allow users to create interest groups, thus carving out communities or people that share interests and tags.

When tags are designed and made available for a community to use, a type of ontology is built. Such a naturally grown ontology has been referred to as a folksonomy (Kroski, 2005). Thus, tags and their meanings can more efficiently be built through a community which includes the author or manager of the resources as well as any one who has used them. Such a dynamic process not only promotes quick labeling and categorization of the resources but also linkages between resources and people who use them.

Semantic tagging can help make searching more relevant to a user by categorizing resources using expertise of others. It promotes discovery of new and dynamic content because it does not depend upon a web crawler to find the content. Instead, other users who are members of a distributed community post or advertise the resource metadata via semantic tags. Finally, if the use for a particular resource evolves, the types of tags that may be associated with the resource will also evolve, adapting to the current usage.

On the other hand, such an open process of categorizing resources presents some difficulties. First, if a large population creates tags which have little commonality, their benefit is not apparent. We've named this the tag space issue. For many tagging services, tagging clouds are used to organize tags. These clouds indicate all tag values and highlight those that are most popular. If the clouds are also presented when a user is tagging an item, consensus can develop. Halpin et al. (Halpin, 2007) found empirically that tag distributions tend to stabilize into power law distributions. They found that given sufficient active users over time, a stable set of tags develop indicating consensus around the categorization of the resources. Mass collaboration on tag values can be achieved by having users pick from existing tags unless their chosen concept is not reflected in those existing tag values. In that case, they can add to the tag cloud. Such interactive choosing of labels or tags not only builds consensus but makes tagging less labor intensive, thus helping in another issue, the tag administration issue which will be discussed later in this section.

Tag space can also be minimized by using syntactical methods such as extracting stem words. The words tag, tags, tagging, and tagged should be linked as one label "tag*". Similarly, synonyms should be linked. Since all words have at least subtle differences in meaning, they should not be eliminated but linked for user perusal. If a synonym is more popular and just as useful a label, a user might choose the more popular word, thus limiting the tag space. An additional enhancement might be to provide generalization of the tag concept as well as more specific versions (specializations) of the tag concept. These would be read from an ontology, such as WordNet. Again, the generalization or specialization might be a better tag for the resource either from a semantic perspective or because of the popularity of the tag. Semantic comparisons of tag values allow users to also find related items.

Another issue associated with tagging systems that limits collaboration is the tag reference issue. When users are given free reign to create tags, they may choose tags that have no semantic meaning to anyone else. For example, many users tag documents with the label "toread". Clearly, this label is not useful to a collaborative community unless it is taken in context. Is it also labeled with a keyword? Is the tagger active in a particular field of interest to the searcher? If there is some semantic information outside of the "toread" tag, it might be used as an indicator of a newer resource to consider. Therefore, a collaborative system would want to move such a label outside of the semantic tag arena as use it as a secondary tag or an attribute tag.

Similarly, there are other types of metadata that should be considered in conjunction with semantic tags that give indications of content. Adjectives describing use, how well something is written, time frame covered, location considered, etc. might help a searcher narrow down their search. In a particular community, community specific information could also be useful. For example, if the resource is a result of a certain project, details and the project might be included as secondary labels. In general, to deal with the tag reference issue, primary tags should be keyword or concept tags with all other tags being secondary, attribute based tags that can act as filters.

Finally, collaborative tagging systems should address the tag administration issue, the issue that if tagging takes too much effort, it will not be done. Based on a quantitative study, Suchanek et al (Suchanek, 2008) found that tag suggestion is an important feature. They found that up to one third of tag applications were induced by suggestion. However, an important counterbalance must be to have good suggestions, otherwise the tags applied in haste will be useless because they also found that tag selection inhibits creation of new tags. Many existing systems provide tag suggestion. For example, del.icio.us suggests the tags that have been most popular so far, reducing participation effort and limiting tag space.

A SOCIAL ANNOTATION SYSTEM ARCHITECTURE FOR GOVERNMENTAL RESOURCES

Social tagging can be used to support citizen search as well as e-government collaboration for indirect citizen support. To address the tag space issue, the system should be based on existing natural language taxonomies and ontologies such as WordNet. A formal ontology in support of the Federal Enterprise Architecture is being developed (Allenmang, 2005). While the formality is important to relieve ambiguity in many applications, for the annotation application we envision, natural language will promote quicker development and acceptance. Connectivity between natural language concepts and the Federal Enterprise Architecture ontology can be added later.

To alleviate the tag reference issue, the system separates tag semantics (concept associated with the contents of the resource) from tag pragmatics (context attributes such as who, when, where and why associated with the resource). To alleviate tag administration and promote use, resource users are automatically asked to tag resources and are presented with a structured set of potential conceptual tags.

The overall architecture is shown in Figure 1. The government data and resources are distributed in each government site as they normally would in repositories. Users visit the tag service site or visit a government site and use a web service interface to the tagging environment. Users obtain log-in ids which give them access to the tagging environment. Depending upon their role – private citizen, governmental employee, contractor, etc., their view of tags as well as resources may be different but the underlying tagging system will be the same. The proposed service would be implemented in software and supported by databases that house only tags and hyperlinks to the tagged resources.

The social tagging system architecture would have several modular software components. Two would be concerned with subscription and authentication and are typical components of any web service. The others are specific to the tagging capabilities we are advocating. To implement, software would have to be developed or modified and databases to store the tags would have to be deployed. The service and component deployment could be performed incrementally as users sign up for the service and begin to use it.

In order to sign up, the system should support a subscription service. Collaborating government agencies and other partner organizations (e.g. NGO's, data service organizations or citizen groups), or private citizens can subscribe to the tagging service, using the subscription service. Access to individual tags and or resources will depend upon the affiliation of the requesting person. Having a subscription service would allow for general use of the system while allowing for various levels of access.

The Subscription Service would support an Authentication and Access Control Service. The scope of a subscribers' access will depend upon the subscription associated with their login identifier. Thus the public will only have access to tags associated with public resources. Governmental employees or employees of partner organizations

Figure 1. Government collaboration network functional architecture

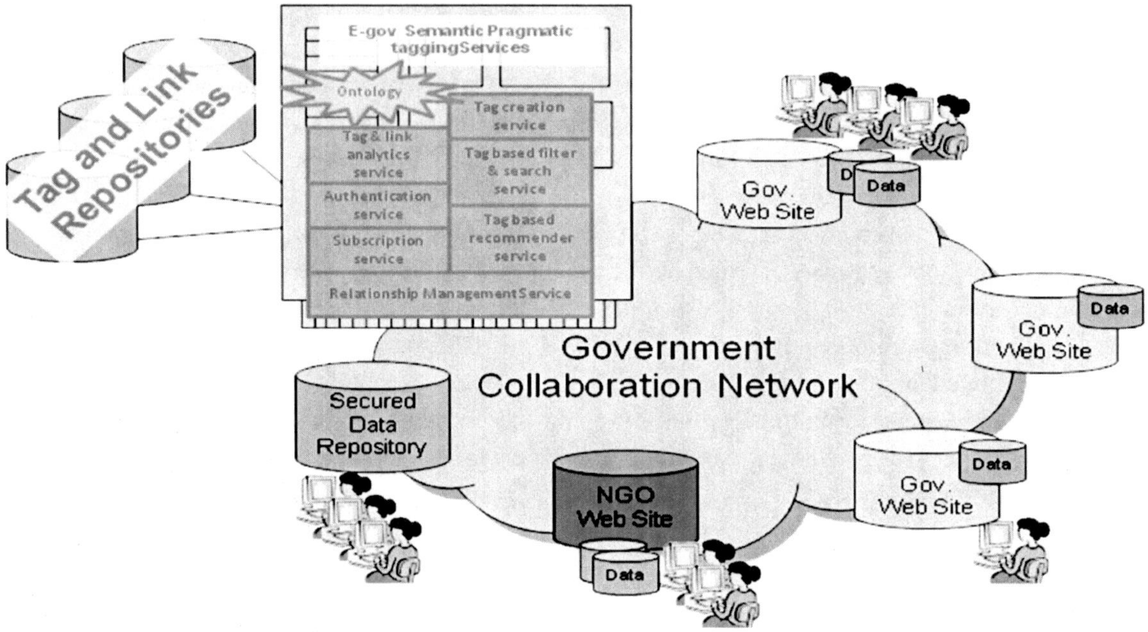

will gain wider access to tags. Note that although the goal would be to authenticate once, individuals might need to authenticate themselves with a digital repository service once a resource is located that appears to meet their needs. This depends upon the policies set at that repository.

Once subscribed and authenticated, use will be supported via the tagging application. When users want to identify a useful resource, they will use the Tag Creation Service, All authenticated users will be able to create tags for government resources. This service provides them with a natural language ontology or taxonomy that may guide them in selecting proper semantic tags that reflects the content of the resource. It also captures the pragmatic tags, including spatio-temporal tags, personal tags (i.e. tags that may be meaningful for a particular user), and security tags that specify who may be authorized to access the resources. Tagged resources are not put into a central repository. Instead, tagged resources remain in their original networked location. Tags and links to tagged resources are kept in the tagging service repository.

The key service provided by the system is the Tag-based Filter and Search Service. This service provides tag structures (concept clouds and relations) based on the frequency of tags used to describe the resources. The tags are used to locate the resources, and links are used to access the resources. Users that have access to repositories in which the resources are held would use normal means to access them once hyperlinked to the spot. Those who do not have access will be provided meta-information (e.g. semantic and pragmatic tags) about the resource. The search process is detailed in the following section. This service is used not only by tagging system subscribers but also by governmental search engines.

To support the Tag-based Filter and Search Service, a Tag and Link Analytics Service could be implemented. Tags used to describe resources of different agencies can be analyzed, using statistical and other data mining and analytics methods. The analytics service includes the learning and classification that can be used to

Figure 2. Structure tag cloud for combined concept "subprime" and "mortgage"

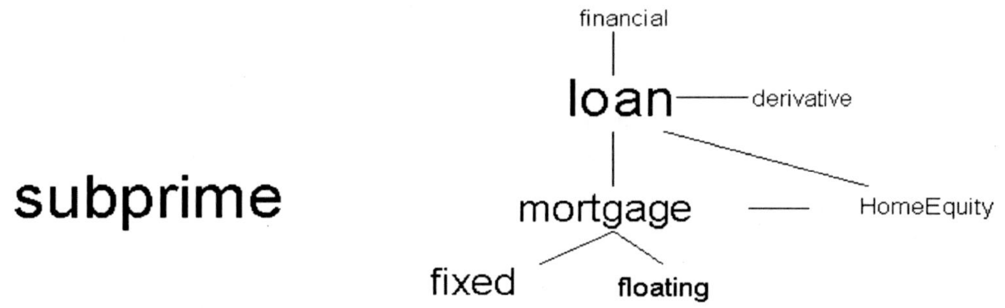

automate the tagging of the resources, or resource recommendations in search.

The Tag and Analytics Service also supports a Tag-based Recommender Service. Multi-faceted recommendation of resources can be provided using semantic and pragmatic tags. Facets include concept, author, and other resources tagged by groups of interest to the searcher.

Finally a Relationship Management Service allows the collaborating agencies to find other government agencies that are related to the participating agencies, either through resource sharing in other projects or through "friend links" of the agency established in past collaborations. The resources of one agency or one project may be available through the common agency, although this access may be limited as needed based on the subscription service.

Citizens need not subscribe to the tagging service to gain benefits. The search engines supported on governmental portal should link into the tagging system via a tagging web service. Thus, when a user of a search engine like usasearch.gov searches on a keyword, the search engine would not only present results based on their search algorithm but would also present results based on tagging. If the searcher chooses to peruse the tagged resources, they would automatically be asked to register for the tagging service and then be allowed to tag.

Another interesting integration opportunity concerns integration with other tagging systems. As part of the registration process, users might indicate their preferred tagging system. When accessing government resources, if their preferred system is another tagging system, the governmental tagging system would piggyback on that system and capture any annotation made. Of course any tagging system might use the governmental tagging system as a web service and include tag matches from it.

Although our tagging system is similar to existing systems in the public domain, we focus on solutions to the tag space, tag reference and tag administration issue. To illustrate, we will present the Tag-based Filter and Search and the Tag Creation services in more detail. For search, the user is asked to provide a concept on which to search. The system will respond with a structured cloud of tags related to that concept. For example, in line with the financial crisis we presented earlier in the paper, suppose a user searched on the tags "subprime" and "mortgage". He or she would be presented with a structured tag cloud that would look like that illustrated in Figure 2.

From the cloud, the user can than confirm use of the original tag or move through the cloud until the appropriate concept is found. Note that in combined tags either tag can be made more general or more specific without changing the other one.

When a user enters a tag concept for search, the user will also be asked if there are other attributes of interest such as author, resource type, date or time. These attributes will be used as filters, limiting the returned resources as requested so that the most relevant objects are presented for review.

Under the tag creation service, users need to indicate that they want to create a tag. However, we make it simple in several ways. First, all subscribers have access to a pop-up window that can be installed are part of their web browser to tag items at will. Second, any user who retrieves an item from a governmental source will be presented with the offer to register for the tag creation service (if they are not already a subscriber) or with a structured tag cloud of tags already applied to the retrieved resource. The user can select a tag concept from that structured cloud or add a concept. At the same time, they can add attributes in various categories including level of usefulness and quality. Third, any subscriber who retrieves a governmental resource and chooses to tag through a preferred tagging service, could automatically have the tag included within the governmental tagging system as well. No separate process is needed.

Our proposed annotation system is a knowledge management system which has the indirect beneficial result of allowing searchers also to find other subscribers who have similar interests or expertise in the area of interest. When users search via tags, they can also find other users who have tagged items that they find interesting. Browsing the libraries of these like-minded taggers is another mechanism for finding relevant resources. Support of social tagging will not only make the searchers more productive but will allow new resources to be discovered much more quickly. By examining tags, experts and their domain knowledge become automatically apparent. Those authors whose resources are tagged and those taggers whose tags are referenced by others can be sources of expertise in the areas indicated by the tag concepts.

SOCIAL TAGGING FOR DISCOVERING GOVERNMENT WEB SERVICES

Web services are becoming more widely used in e-government initiatives because they are cost effective as compared to paper based systems and offer convenience. State residents can register their cars, apply for social services such as food stamps, and obtain a wealth of information. In addition, public records are available on-line including court records, bankruptcies, real estate records, births and deaths. Likewise, web services of other such as mapping applications are integrated into governmental sites.

Government agencies can go even further by making their on-line applications and public data accessible from other web services. Thus if a user is accessing a web site of a non-governmental agency, that agency might integrate governmental services through the web service interface. This benefits the individual seeking services by allowing them to discover all possible services while visiting a single site. It also benefits the governmental agency by making its capabilities know and also by potentially off-loading customer contact to the non-governmental agency. The same would be true between agencies. By allowing one agency to take the lead while using the services of others, the services provided to citizens will be more integrated and less customer contact and coordination would be needed.

To allow the discovery of these Web services, the standard oriented approach has been to use a directory called UDDI. However, one can adopt the social tagging system for Web services and find appropriate services and compose them for integrated services, based on the social tags recommended by other users. This addition would be incremental to the proposed system because our social tagging system saves tags and hyperlinks, not actual resources. Thus instead of tagging a web page or a document, a user would tag the url for the web service. For such tags, the most important attribute associated with the tag would be "resource type". Thus users looking just for services would filter on that attribute to find web services associated with the concept tag. Alternatively, services can be filtered out if users are looking for information resources and not services.

FUTURE RESEARCH DIRECTIONS

We focused our work to date on using social networking to help find "traditional" web resources and services. As social networks are implemented in the government sector and grow, more and more resources created from direct user input will become available. While many of these artifacts will benefit others in narrowing their search, they also exacerbate the growing information resource problem because they increase the overall amount of information available. Thus future research should consider how all of the end-user annotation and input can best be managed. This work should include development of automated organization and categorization, aggregation, and summarization capabilities.

There are many members of the government community exploring uses of Web 2.0 technology. Many different services are being prototyped. Additional research is needed to evaluate all the potential applications and how best they can be delivered to end users. The solutions should not be more overwhelming then current information discovery.

Social tagging is already being implemented. Many users may already be familiar with it. A social tagging system for government should integrate with these existing systems. Thus there is a need to standardize the interfaces between tagging systems. The more people tag, the better the tags will be and the more easily systems will be able to gleam the semantic meaning of the tags. Care must be taken, however, to ensure that tags that have semantic conceptual meaning are separated from those that are associated with other attributes of the resource. Tags themselves, therefore, need labels and these labels need to be defined if they can be universally used. Therefore, not only do we propose that a system be put in place strictly for government usage, but it be made more widely available through interfaces to other similar annotation systems and search services.

CONCLUSION

Sophisticated knowledge management services will benefit citizens greatly by giving them easier access to information and expertise. Indirectly, they will also benefit because governmental organizations will have the tools to collaborate and to find information and human resources. To date, focus has been on providing information portal and collaboration spaces. We have proposed adding resource annotation using social tagging service.

Social Tagging has advantages over traditional search engines because it makes use of the knowledge and expertise of human taggers. If tags are defined in a distributed fashion, many beneficial outcomes are possible:

- New and dynamic as well as hidden resources will more easily be brought to light.
- Information about how resources relate will be generated.
- Navigation between resources in a search will be facilitated through semantic relationships.

Tagging is becoming popular particularly in research communities. However, to our knowledge, no specific work has been done to apply social tagging to government resources. Instead, well structured and defined categorizations have been developed and do help narrow down searches within federal government portals. Our work to date has been exploratory. We have examined what exists and how it is used. We move now into developing a tagging service specific for the government domain as a proof of concept.

Outside of tagging, we note that agencies in the US have explored other web services to aid in their support of citizens. Examples include the use of wikis, blogs and discussion boards. Both at the state and municipal level, agencies have also developed on-line applications so that users can perform mundane tasks such as car registration without appearing at a governmental office. Following that path, we propose not only that more agencies allow users to perform tasks on line but that these very applications be offered with open application interfaces so that several services could be integrated into one. For example, if a person moves to Cleveland, OH, they should be able to update their driver's license, register to vote, and update and records associated with themselves through one application derived from a set of web services offered by the various agencies. Social tagging could facilitate this integration by allowing other people who moved to tag the resources they needed to establish themselves in their new home thus helping those that come later. These tags might have been generated as bookmarks for their own use as they went through the process but with no additional effort they could be made available for the wider community. Tagging brings personal benefits that through sharing can be multiplied to benefit all.

REFERENCES

Ager, T., Johnson, C., & Kiernan, J. (2006). *Policy-Based Management and Sharing of Sensitive Information Among Government Agencies* (pp. 1–9). MILCOM.

Allenmang, D., Hodgson, R., & Polikoff, I. (2005). *FEA Reference Model Ontology (FEA RMO)*. GSA Osera Deliverable V1.2, February 2005.

Cook, M. (2000). *What Citizens Want from E-Government*. Albany: Center for Technology in Government.

Covington, M. J., & Sandhu, R. (2006). A usage-based authorization framework for collaborative computing systems. In *Proceedings of the Eleventh ACM Symposium on Access Control Models and Technologies* (Lake Tahoe, California, USA, June 07 - 09, 2006) (pp. 180-189). New York: ACM.

DCMI Usage Board. (2008). *DCMI Metadata Terms*. Retrieved from http://dublincore.org/documents/dcmi-terms/

Ding, L., Finin, T., Joshi, A., & Pan, R. (2005). *Search on the Semantic Web*. IEEE Computer.

Dix, A., Levialdi, S., & Malizia, A. (2006). *Semantic halo for collaboration tagging systems* [Online]. Retrieved from http://www.sis.pitt.edu/~paws/SNCBAT06/program.html

Dong, X., Halevy, A. Y., Madhavan, J., Nemes, E., & Zhang, J. (2004). Similarity Search for Web Services. *VLDB 2004*

Godwin, B. (2008). *USA.gov and Web Best Practices, GSA Office of Citizen Services. Matrix of Web 2.0 Technology and Government.* Retrieved July 18, 2008, from http://www.usa.gov/webcontent/documents/Web_Technology_Matrix.pdf

Golder, S. A., & Huberman, B. A. (2006). Usage patterns of collaborative tagging systems. *Journal of Information Science*, *32*(2), 198–208. doi:10.1177/0165551506062337

Halpin, H., Robu, V., & Shepherd, H. (2007). The complex dynamics of collaborative tagging. In *Proceedings of the 16th international Conference on World Wide Web* (Banff, Alberta, Canada, May 08 - 12, 2007) (pp. 211-220). New York: ACM.

Handschuh, S., Volz, R., & Staab, S. (2003, September/October). Annotation for the Deep Web. *IEEE Intelligent Systems*.

Johnson, C. (2004, December 17). *Policies for Federal Agency Public Websites*. Memorandum M05-04 for the Heads of Executive Departments and Agencies.

Johnson, C. (2005, December 16). *Policies for Improving Public Access to and Dissemination of Government Information and Using the Federal Enterprise Architecture Data Reference Model*. Memorandum M06-02 for the Heads of Executive Departments and Agencies.

Kroski, E. (2005). The Hive Mind: Folksonomies and userbased tagging. *Infotangle*. Retrieved December 11, 2008, from http://infotangle.blogsome.com/2005/12/07/the-hive-mind-folksonomies-and-user-based-tagging/

Liu, D., Hua, X., Yang, L., Wang, M., & Zhang, H. (2009). Tag ranking. In *Proceedings of the 18th international Conference on World Wide Web* (Madrid, Spain, April 20 - 24, 2009) (pp. 351-360). New York: ACM.

Lu, Y., He, H., Zhao, H., Meng, W., & Yu, C. (2007). *Annotating Structured Data of the Deep Web* (pp. 376–385). ICDE.

Suchanek, F. M., Vojnovic, M., & Gunawardena, D. (2008). Social tags: meaning and suggestions. In *Proceeding of the 17th ACM Conference on information and Knowledge Mining* (Napa Valley, California, USA, October 26 - 30, 2008) (pp. 223-232). New York: ACM.

VandenBos, G., Knapp, S., & Doe, J. (2001). Role of reference elements in the selection of resources by psychology undergraduates. [from http://jbr.org/articles.html]. *Journal of Bibliographic Research*, *5*, 117–123. Retrieved October 13, 2001.

Verma, K., & Sheth, A. (2007). Semantically Annotating a Web Service. *IEEE Internet Computing*, *11*(2), 83–85. doi:10.1109/MIC.2007.48

Wang, J., & Lochovsky, F. H. (2003). Data Extraction and Label Assignment for Web Databases. *WWW Conference, 2003*.

Wetzker, R., Alpcan, T., Bauckhage, C., Umbrath, W., & Albayrak, S. (2007). An unsupervised hierarchical approach to document categorization. In *Proceedings of the IEEE/WIC/ACM international Conference on Web intelligence* (November 02 - 05, 2007) (pp. 482-486). Washington, DC: IEEE Computer Society.

Wu, L., Yang, L., Yu, N., & Hua, X. (2009). Learning to tag. In *Proceedings of the 18th international Conference on World Wide Web* (Madrid, Spain, April 20 - 24, 2009) (pp. 361-370). New York: ACM.

Xu, Z., Fu, Y., Mao, J., & Su, D. (2006). Towards the Semantic Web: Collaborative Tag Suggestions. *Workshop on Collaborative Web Tagging, WWW2006*.

KEY TERMS AND DEFINITIONS

Folksonomy: A taxonomy or ordered classification of labels built via a collaborative process.

Mashup: A Web application that uses open application program interfaces (APIs) to combine data or functionality from one or more sources into a single integrated application.

Ontology: A formal representation of conceptual knowledge within a domain, that consists of a set of concepts and the relationships between concepts. It is a model of a domain, providing a shared vocabulary, such as the type of objects and/or concepts that exist, and their properties and relations. The ontology is used for reasoning and inferences to deduce further knowledge by computer software, as humans would do.

Open Government: Government processes designed to facilitate citizen participation through transparency, accountability, public trust and shared governance.

Semantic Annotation: Labeling of web pages, attachments, or services with words that have meaning and can be used by other people and or computer applications to aid in search.

Social Bookmarking: Bookmarking is the keeping of electronic pointers to web pages of interest. When these electronic bookmarks set by individuals are shared, it is called social bookmarking.

Social Tagging: Descriptive keywords created by the users, often in social network sites to annotate the Web contents or rich social media contents such as images or videos as in Flickr. The social tags function as metadata that can be used for search and access the shared Web contents.

Tag cloud: A visual presentation of user-generated tags or the word content of a Web site that describe the content of web sites. The tag or word size carries the weight of the word, i.e. the frequency of the words that may represent the importance or relevance of the tag to the site.

Web Portal: A Web portal is a website where diverse enterprise information is provided as a single entry point with a consistent look and feel. An example of a web portal is Yahoo!, AOL, MSN and iGoogle. A Government Web portal provide a list of web links to direct access to government information such as agency and department web sites, citizen-related information, business-related information, and other public records and documents.

Web 2.0: The second generation of Web design that promotes interactivity and services rather than static web pages.

Section 3
Case Studies

Chapter 17
Engaging Citizens on the Internet:
An Assessment of Local Governments in Ohio

Mark K. Cassell
Kent State University, USA

John Hoornbeek
Kent State University, USA

ABSTRACT

Some literature on E-government has envisioned that the internet would foster a linear progression toward new, productive, and more democratic relationships between governments and citizens (Layne and Lee, 2001). Recent literature has questioned the pace at which these relationships are developing (Coursey and Norris, 2008). This chapter presents empirical results relating to citizen-government relations on the internet that are based on an assessment of the worldwide web presence of 428 local governments in northeast Ohio. Northeast Ohio provides a useful picture of E-government-citizen relationships because it includes a range of local government forms (counties, townships, etc.), urban and rural populations, and Midwestern influences that many consider "typical" of American states. The website reviews conducted assess citizen-government engagement in a variety of areas. The measures used include simple engagements such as the ability to sign up for email updates and the presence of event calendars to more involved interactions such as blogs, e-pay services, and open records requests. Using these measures, we assess citizen-government engagement among local governments in our sample. Follow up interviews with local governments that rate high on these measures are used to further ascertain the extent of engagement and the benefits they yield for government-citizen relationships and service delivery. This information, in turn, provides lessons relating to citizen-local government relationships that may be useful to other government entities. Analyses to ascertain why some local governments seek greater internet engagement with citizens than others are also be conducted.

DOI: 10.4018/978-1-61520-931-6.ch017

INTRODUCTION

Citizen engagement is at the core of how we understand democracy. Citizen engagement is often messy and frustrating. However, a central promise of democracy is that engaging citizens brings broader interests into the decision-making process, diffuses power, and inhibits corruption by concentrated power elites. And while governments have long wrestled with the question of how best to engage citizens, advances in technology over the past two decades are forcing governments at all levels to rethink how they should engage with citizens. As Reddick (2004) put it, "The Internet is one communication tool that has the potential to radically change the face of government in the 21st century" (38). In response to the charge by Reddick and others that technology is changing the way governments engage citizens, the goal of this chapter is two-fold: first, to contribute to an understanding of how local governments in the United States are using the internet to engage citizens; and second, to test several hypotheses to explain the conditions under which governments pursue different models of citizen engagement.

The chapter draws on an analysis of 428 local governments in northeast Ohio. Northeast Ohio, which includes 13 counties with a total population of 4 million citizens, offers a useful case study for assessing web-based citizen engagement efforts. There are a lot of local governments in northeast Ohio (Ohio ranks sixth in the number of local governments in the country, and northeast Ohio is well represented among these local governments), so analyzing citizen engagement efforts in this area is likely to provide a rich sample of alternative approaches. The region also includes the four major forms of general purpose local governments in the United States: counties, cities, villages, and townships). In addition, the region's mix of urban and rural areas, its socio-economic variation, and its racial diversity make it a useful prism through which to view web based citizen engagement practices.

This study differs from existing literature on e-government in two-ways. First, it looks at government websites in terms of how web applications (which we also refer to as website "attributes") reflect particular goals or understandings of citizen engagement. Much of the existing literature examines governmental websites through the lens of technological capacity. Scholars often make the case that governments' use of the internet evolves over time along a continuum of technological sophistication – from simple posting of information on a website to more advanced Web 2.0 application like on-line forums or social networking sites. This study builds on the work of Kakabadse *et al.* (2003) in conceptualizing web applications not in terms of their technological sophistication but how specific website attributes promote different types of citizen engagement. Specifically, three distinct models of engagement are examined which Kakabadse and his colleagues term "electronic bureaucracy," "information management," and "populist." By focusing on these three models, the study offers an alternative perspective to the "stages" approach that characterizes much of the e-government literature.

A second way in which our study differs from existing work is that our analysis extends to local governments that have traditionally been left out of the research because they were too small or the information was too difficult to collect. Our study includes 13 counties, 102 cities, 201 townships, and 112 villages. In Ohio, townships are the most common form of general purpose local government: they are unincorporated areas which develop general purpose government capacities and are governed by boards of trustees. Incorporated areas with more than 5,000 residents are cities, and those with less than 5,000 residents are considered villages. By including all local governments in our study we provide a more comprehensive picture of how local governments are using (or not using) technology to engage citizens. We also seek to assess what factors determine the type of engagement local governments seek to promote with their websites.

To examine the relationship between citizens and local governments, the chapter is divided into several parts. In section II, we briefly discuss the literature on how government websites are conceptualized. This section also outlines the models of citizen engagement developed as an alternative to traditional accounts. In section III, we present a descriptive summary of the results of our analysis of local government websites in northeast Ohio. The analysis presents information on the types of website attributes governments are using most often, from which we infer the types of citizen engagement governments seek to promote through their websites. In the following section, four theoretical models are presented and tested. Our interview findings are also summarized in this section. And finally, we conclude with a brief summary of our overall findings and some lessons regarding what we have learned from this study.

CITIZEN ENGAGEMENT AND THE WEB

The means by which governments engage citizens through the internet has grown exponentially over time creating a small growth industry among academics and consultants in the development of typologies that seek to make sense of the exploding number of *website* applications (Ho 2002; Moon 2002; Layne and Lee 2001; Cousey and Norris 2008). This section discusses the conventional ways of conceptualizing websites and then offers an alternative approach which is then examined in later sections of the chapter.

Conventional Wisdom

The most common approaches in the literature conceptualize government websites in terms of a series of evolutionary stages. The stages begin with an informational presence such as a posting of on-line brochures or general information, followed by two-way interaction where citizens can download material and send emails to public officials. The next stage becomes a seamless integration across government services. And in the final stage, governments use technology to promote greater citizen participation and democracy. Eventually, as policy makers and citizens come to realize the advantages of e-government, the technology becomes so pervasive and powerful that it culminates into a "virtual government:" an automated, citizen-centric operation capable of delivering government services to citizens, businesses, and other government agencies 24 hours a day, seven days a week (Fountain 2001; Siefert and Petersen, 2002; The Gartner Group 2000; Baum and Di Maio 2000).

Two factors distinguish the stages approach. First, it conceptualizes government websites in terms of their technological complexity rather than according to what the intent of government officials or web designers might be. Websites are grouped into different stages based on the websites' level of technological sophistication. Little attention is given to the possibility that governments might seek to promote distinct forms of citizen engagement with their websites that may or may not require higher levels of technology complexity. Second, the stages approach assumes that adoption occurs in a linear and step-wise fashion (Layne and Lee 2001; Baum and Di Maio 2000; Ronaghan 2001; Hiller and Belanger 2001; Moon 2002; and Wescott 2001). Once on the e-government train, local, state and national governments steadily move forward along a technological continuum. Moreover, as governments understand the value of new website attributes, they will share knowledge with other governments and over time all governments will move down the track toward Web 2.0 and beyond. In short, e-government research on the development of government information technology uses a stages approach and assumes that, despite some bumps in the road, administrative evolution (where the most efficient processes win out) eventually drives governments to adopt the latest and best technology.

While the stages approach has become a way of conceptualizing government websites, Coursey and Norris (2008) and others (Akesson *et al.* 2008; Walker 2001) point out that, after a dozen years of data, the conventional story lacks empirical support. Despite the benefits touted by information technology consultants and scholars, governments in the United States appear to have either gotten off the e-government train or at the very least appear stalled. This should not be that surprising because Silvia Bolgherini (2007) notes that since 2001, two-thirds of e-government programs "fail in full or in part, thus involving relevant expenses, both direct and indirect"(264). In the developing world, the failure rate is 85 percent. Drawing on ICMA survey data for 2000, 2002, and 2004, Coursey and Norris (2008) find that few governments have moved beyond an informational web presence.[1] Brown (2007), using the same ICMA data, offers a more positive spin arguing that although local governments have achieved only minor benefits this reflects a "maturation model", a process that is more incremental and slower than previously anticipated.

Coursey and Norris (2008) also note that there is little empirical evidence to support the hypothesis that e-government transforms or changes local governments in the way the conventional narrative predicts. There is little evidence that e-government reduces costs. And there is even some evidence that e-government has reinforced the political and administrative structures of traditional government (Coursey and Killingsworth 2001). Pina *et al.* (2007) also find that e-government at the local level has done little to increase transparency or accountability. Finally, in contrast to conventional wisdom, e-government has not developed in a linear or step-wise fashion. Local governments appear to have adopted an informational presence very quickly and then stalled and failed to move toward a more transactional approach. Brown (2007) reaches a similar conclusion: that between 2000 and 2004 the "average change differences on a variable-by-variable basis indicate relatively small to flat growth in terms of e-government services and benefits" (p. 189). If the conventional story is incorrect, where does that leave us?

Citizen Engagement Models

Kakabadse *et. al.*(2003) offer an alternative theoretical perspective from which to view citizen engagement on the web. While acknowledging that the technological capacity of a government is important, we build on their work to suggest that technological capacity makes sense only in the context of how a government views the purpose(s) of their websites. Kakabadse and his colleagues develop a typology organized around different models of citizen engagement. The models reflect not technological capacity but distinct forms of citizen engagement that are promoted through the Web. Models corresponding to three forms of citizen engagement are proposed: "electronic bureaucracy," "information management," and "populist."

The electronic bureaucracy model refers to the delivery of government services. Web applications designed to "allow for easier, quicker, and cheaper transactions with government on behalf of businesses and citizens, and to *reduce*, over time, the size of the public sector" (*Ibid.* 47). Under this model, governments use the Web to replace street-level bureaucracy with system-level bureaucracies (Reddick 2004, 39). The electronic bureaucracy model emphasizes web applications that allow one to circumvent real life bureaucratic transactions. These include website attributes that allow one to pay taxes and fees on line, file for building permits, or register for recreational activities.

Information management is another model, distinct from electronic bureaucracy, in which the goal is to increase communication between government and citizens (we also refer to it as the mass communication or communication model). The model includes one- and two-way forms of communication but also suggests viewing the government's website as a means of marketing the governmental jurisdiction and communicating with prospective citizens and businesses who might be considering locating to the area. Policies that fall within the information management model include: placing computers in public places; posting decision-makers' contact information on line; posting public information such as speeches, meeting minutes, or notices on-line; and offering "text-only" applications that allow those physically challenged to also communicate.

Finally, the populist model seeks to promote democratic engagement among citizens through forums, blogs, social-networking sites, and other types of electronic town-hall meetings (London 1994). Electronic voting, electronic polling, and on-line discussions between candidates and citizens also fit within this perspective of citizen engagement. What distinguishes website attributes in the populist model is that while they disseminate facts and information, the applications seek to involve citizens in a dialogue with each other around public issues (Kakabadse et al. 2003).

In short, a theoretical perspective that is based on differing citizen engagement models attempts to incorporate the intentions of public officials into an understanding of website development. In particular, it assumes that public officials and web designers seek to promote particular types of citizen engagement. The model thus acknowledges the possibility that a government may prefer to remain at stage one or two of their website development simply because it fits with their understanding of citizen engagement.

This kind of perspective thus views government choices regarding web based citizen engagement strategies as a policymaking process that is affected by political influences which, in turn, produce particular kinds of web based policy outputs. In the sections that follow, we examine Kakabadse *et. al.'s (2003)* models of citizen engagement empirically. We also draw on theories of sub-national policy variation to identify and test differing explanations for choices of web based citizen engagement strategies made by local governments in northeast Ohio.

Data and Methodology

The data underlying this research were compiled through searches of local government websites in northeast Ohio during a six-month period, from October 2008 through March 2009. The area consists of 13 counties, which comprise majority of northeast Ohio. To compile the data, we enlisted the professional help of a government information technology specialist in northeast Ohio who is knowledgeable regarding both the management of local government websites and e-government practices among northeast Ohio local governments[2].

Using an annual report published regularly by the Ohio Secretary of State's office (Brunner, 2006-2007), we identified a total of 428 general purpose governments: 13 counties, 102 cities, 112 villages, and 201 townships, and we were able to compile complete data on all but two villages in a data set for analysis[3]. This annual report, along with numerous internet web queries and links from northeast Ohio county websites, enabled us to identify and locate web addresses for local government jurisdictions in our sample[4]. This effort yielded the identification of a total of 285 local government jurisdictions with worldwide websites.

We evaluated websites to assess how they are used to engage citizens. Thirty-three evaluative criteria were used to code attributes that reflect citizen engagement.[5] Each criteria was coded as "1" if the attribute existed and "0" if did not exist. Drawing on the work of Kakabadse *et al.* (2003) the web attributes were organized into three groups that correspond to three types of models: 1) electronic bureaucracy; 2) information management; 3) and populist model. The group identification of each attribute was based on Kakabdse *et al's* description of each model. In some cases, we placed an attribute into more than one category. For example, a blog is a form of communication between citizens and government. However, blogs also allow citizens to discuss and interact with each other, which reflects a populist model. Out of 33 attributes: 23 are coded as information management; 15 are coded as electronic bureaucracy; and three attributes are coded as populist.

Several steps were taken to increase the validity of the coding. First, our information technology specialist developed a coding guidebook and trained website coders on how to use it. Each website was coded separately by two individuals, and the results of these coding processes were then compared to identify discrepancies. In cases of discrepancies a third reviewer was used. And finally, these resolved discrepancies were then spot-checked using a fourth review conducted by our information technology specialist to identify any idiosyncratic or systematic sources of error on the part of the third coder. The coding designations which resulted after this final review are those which we present in this chapter. Website data were then supplemented with socio-economic and demographic data from the US Census Bureau for each government jurisdiction in the dataset.

The statistical software package, STATA 9.0 was used to conduct descriptive and analytical analyses of the data. These quantitative analyses were supplemented with qualitative information. Four separate interviews were conducted with Information Management (IT) professionals employed by local governments that scored high on indices of citizen engagement. Two interviews were conducted with chief technology officers in two counties, one interview was conducted with a city manager in medium size city located in a relatively sparsely populated area, and a fourth interview was conducted with the Web and Communications Editor of a medium size city located in an urban area. Although the interviewees are employed across a range of local governments, our intent here was not to be representative. Instead, the goal of the interviews was to understand how governments that are particularly innovative in their use of web technology view the purpose of their websites; and to identify what strategies these governments found helpful to conduct government business and enable citizen input for local governance processes. The interviews were conducted using a semi-structured instrument, and they served as a helpful descriptive supplement to our quantitative analysis of local government websites.

CITIZEN ENGAGEMENT THROUGH THE INTERNET IN NORTHEAST OHIO

How do local governments in northeast Ohio use the Web to engage citizens and the public? To address this question, we first look at all local governments in the region. Next, we break down the analysis according to our three models of citizen engagement and by government type. Our findings in these areas are presented in Tables 1 and 2, and in Figure 1 below.

All Local Governments

In our analysis of websites we found all 102 cities and 13 counties in northeast Ohio have websites. Among smaller governments, Web presence is more uneven. Just under half of townships (49 percent) and nearly two-thirds of villages (63 percent) in our study have government websites. Overall, two-thirds of the local governments in our sample had websites. These findings are in line with the e-government literature that finds smaller governments are less likely to use the Web than larger governments. At the same time, we find smaller local governments with less than 5000 residents are making significant in-roads in their use of the web. The finding is particularly striking given their lack of resources.

Table 1. Website presence among northeast Ohio local governments, by local government type

Local Government Type	Total Number	With Website	Without Website	Percentage with Website
County	13	13	0	100%
City	102	102	0	100%
Village	112	71	41	63%
Township	201	99	102	49%
All NE Ohio Local Governments	428	285	143	67%

Source: Authors' analysis of local government websites in northeast Ohio.

As Table 2 below suggests, there is a significant range of website attributes used by local governments to engage citizens. The most common forms of citizen engagement include the placement of phone directories on line (56 percent), posting of government contact email addresses (51 percent), calendar/event listings (48 percent), posting of minutes and agendas (47 percent), and downloading forms (47 percent). A sizeable number of governments also post job listings on line (22 percent), enable record searches (12 percent), and allow the payment of taxes online (13 percent). These findings are consistent with previous work on e-government.

Table 2. Local government website attribute distribution

Model	Website Attributes	% of Counties with Website Attribute	% of Cities with Website Attribute	% of Villages with Website Attribute	% of Townships with Website Attribute	% of NE Ohio Local Governments with Website Attribute
Electronic Bureaucracy Website Attributes	Downloadable Forms	100	91.18	41.07	24.38	46.96
	Employment Opportunities	*84.62*	*60.78*	*10.71*	*3.98*	*21.73*
	Contact Us Forms	*23.08*	*34.31*	*20.54*	*9.45*	*18.69*
	Citizen Complaints	*30.77*	*34.31*	*17.86*	*10.45*	*18.69*
	Search Engine	*53.85*	*44.12*	*10.71*	*6.97*	*18.22*
	Online Taxes	46.15	42.16	5.36	1	13.32
	Public Records Searches	92.31	25.49	8.93	2.49	12.38
	Contract Opportunities	*76.92*	*23.53*	*3.57*	*3.48*	*10.51*
	Pay Utility Bills	15.38	17.65	5.36	1	6.54
	Public Records Forms	15.38	15.69	0	2.49	5.37
	Pay Parking/Court Fines	15.38	14.71	0.89	0	4.21
	Building Permits Online	7.69	5.88	3.57	0.5	2.83
	Licenses Online	30.77	5.88	0.89	0	2.57
	Public Records Requests	23.08	5.88	0.89	0.5	2.57
	Online Form Submittal	0	2.94	0.89	1	1.4

Table 2. continued on following page

Table 2. continued

Information Management Website Attributes	Phone Directory	100	93.14	49.11	38.81	56.31
	Email Contact Addresses	*84.62*	*83.33*	*48.21*	*34.83*	*51.4*
	Calendar	53.85	86.27	42.86	30.85	47.9
	Online Meeting Minutes	84.62	82.35	37.5	32.84	47.43
	Special Links - Visitors, etc.	84.62	58.82	21.43	10.95	27.34
	Employment Opportunities	*84.62*	*60.78*	*10.71*	*3.98*	*21.73*
	Contact Us Forms	*23.08*	*34.31*	*20.54*	*9.45*	*18.69*
	Citizen Complaints	*30.77*	*34.31*	*17.86*	*10.45*	*18.69*
	Search Engine	*53.85*	*44.12*	*10.71*	*6.97*	*18.22*
	Citizen Feedback Request	*38.46*	*28.43*	*8.04*	*6.97*	*13.32*
	Audio Files	30.77	41.18	3.57	1.99	12.62
	Email Updates	38.46	25.49	11.61	2.99	11.68
	Privacy Statements	30.77	28.43	4.46	4.98	11.21
	Date of Last Update	30.77	13.73	4.46	10.95	10.51
	Contract Opportunities	*76.92*	*23.53*	*3.57*	*3.48*	*10.51*
	Emergency Notification	30.77	18.63	8.04	4.48	9.58
	Road Closure Alerts	53.85	18.63	0	5.47	8.64
	RSS Feeds	23.08	7.84	4.46	0	3.74
	Blog(s)	*7.69*	*6.86*	*0*	*1*	*2.34*
	Text Only	0	0	3.57	0	1.17
	Podcast(s)	7.69	0.98	0	1	0.93
	Language Translator	15.38	1.96	0	0	0.9
	Live Video Streaming	0	1.96	0	0	0.47
Populist Website Attributes	*Email Contact Addresses*	*84.62*	*83.33*	*48.21*	*34.83*	*51.4*
	Citizen Feedback Request	*38.46*	*28.43*	*8.04*	*6.97*	*13.32*
	Blog(s)	*7.69*	*6.86*	*0*	*1*	*2.34*

*Italicized elements characterize more than one model. Source: Authors' analyses of NE Ohio websites.

Models of Citizen Engagement

Figure 1 below illustrates that governments commonly use websites as means of promoting communication between citizens and government. Counties have on average nine website attributes that fit the information management model, cities have seven, and villages and townships have three and two such attributes, respectively. Moreover, among those villages and townships that have websites, the number of Web applications that fit within a information management model increases to five and four, respectively.

We also find evidence that local governments are following an electronic bureaucracy model through their website. Counties and cities have, on average, six and four applications on their website that fit within an electronic bureaucracy model. Smaller governments are far less likely to follow an electronic bureaucracy model: townships have on average less than one application; and villages have just over one application. Again, among townships and vil-

Figure 1. Web application by government and model type

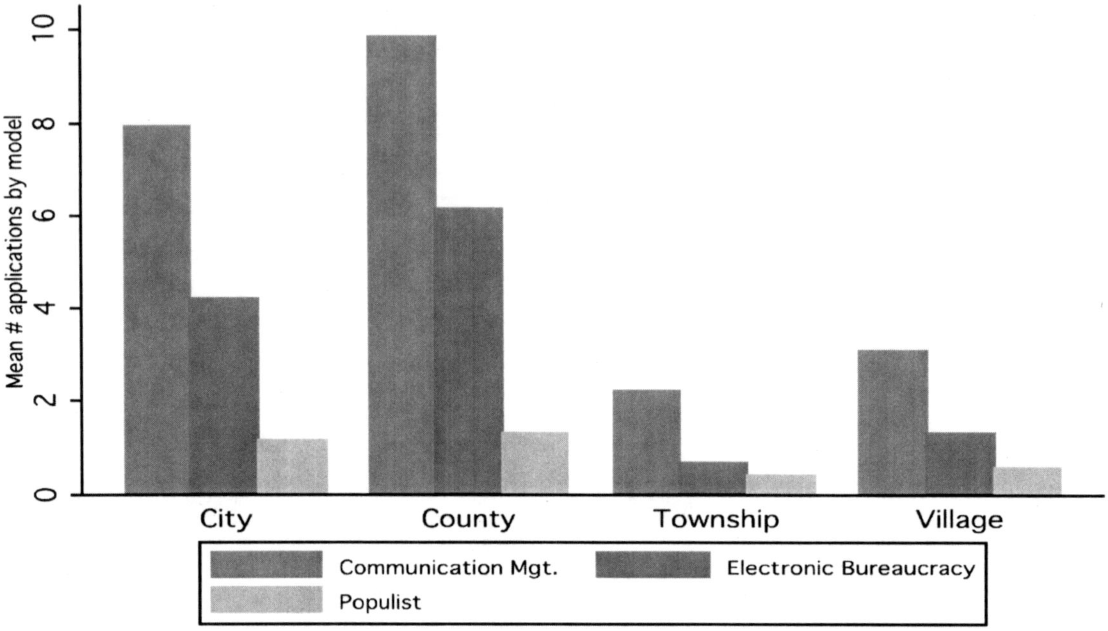

lages that have website, the usage of (electronic bureaucracy) website attributes increases as the mean number of applications grows to one and two, respectively.

Finally, we find minimal evidence that local governments are promoting a populist model through their website. Cities and counties in northeast Ohio have adopted on average one application that fits within a populist model. In most cases these are applications that solicit citizen feedback. In a very small number of cases, local governments use blogs as way to encourage participation and debate among citizens. However, there appears to be little evidence that local governments are pursuing a populist model in an intensive or widespread way.

Table 3. Dependent variable information (unstandardized)

Dependent Variables	N	Minimum Value	Maximum Value	Mean Value
Information Management	428	0	20	4.05
Electronic Bureaucracy	428	0	15	1.8
Populist	428	0	3	.67
All Attributes	428	0	25	5.035047

Source: Authors' analysis of local government websites in northeast Ohio

WHY DO SOME GOVERNMENTS MAKE GREATER USE OF THE INTERNET THAN OTHERS?

We now draw on the work of Kakabadse, *et. al.* and the theoretical literature on sub-national policy variation to construct models which enable us to test the influence of policy relevant variables on web based citizen engagement strategies. We first describe our measures of citizen engagement – our dependent variables, and we construct these variables based on the work of Kakabadse *et. al.* We then draw on theories of sub-national policymaking and recent adaptations of them in the e-government literature to identify appropriate independent variables to test in our models. And finally, we present the results of our analyses, and offer insights from our discussions with local government information management professionals.

Dependent Variables

To determine what factors influence the type of citizen engagement promoted through a government website, we constructed an engagement index for each of our theoretical models of engagement. For each website attribute associated with each of our models, a "yes" response received a point. Therefore the maximum obtainable score for information management is 23, the maximum for electronic bureaucracy is a 15, and the maximum for populist is a three. The maximum for all website attributes is 33 (Note: some website attributes are located in more than one model).

The results indicate that information management is the dominant model used by local governments in developing their websites. The mean score for information management is 4.05. Therefore, on average just over four information management website attributes existed on local government websites. Electronic bureaucracy is also important, although less so than information management. We find that website attributes drawn from the electronic bureaucracy model averaged 1.8. And we find that the populist model of citizen engagement is promoted only minimally among local governments, as the average number of attributes identified that are consistent with that model is .67. These results are summarized in Table 3 below.

After developing indexes for our models of engagement we wanted to increase the comparability across models. We therefore standardized each of the scores on a 100 point scale where 0 is the least amount of applications and 100 is the most amount of applications possible for each model. This is a linear transformation on our dependent variables that has no affect on the estimates except to make them interpretable in a percentage metric. For example, a mass communication score of 60 means the government had 60% of the applications possible to observe for the citizen engagement model. A score of 40 on the electronic bureaucracy index means the government had 40 percent of the applications possible to observe for the electronic bureaucracy model. This allows us to compare across models that have different numbers of website attributes possible.

It is important to stress at this point that without a systematic survey of website managers and government officials it is impossible to be certain of the intent behind the development of websites. During the course of this study we conducted several interviews. However, the findings presented here are preliminary and infer a type of model of civic engagement based upon the types of attributes found on the governments' websites.

Independent Variables

Drawing on theories of sub-national policy variation and recent e-government literature, we now identify and then proceed to test hypotheses regarding factors that influence various forms of web based citizen engagement. These hypotheses can be grouped into three broad categories: government capacity, socio-economic, and population density.

Table 4. Predicting local government citizen engagement efforts, by type of effort

	Electronic Bureaucracy Model		Mass Communication Model		Populist Model		All Attributes Model	
Independent Variable	Coefficient (Robust SE)	T-stat (Prob)	Coefficient (Robust SE)	T-stat (Prob)	Coefficient (Robust SE)	T-stat (Prob)	Coefficient (Robust SE)	T-stat (Prob)
Village	2.48*	1.93	1.08	0.65	1.48	0.54	1.36	.99
	(1.29)	(0.055)	(1.66)	(0.517)	(2.76)	(0.59)	(1.38)	(.324)
City	18.42***	8.27	16.84***	7.73	16.24***	4.28	16.46***	8.99
	(2.23)	(0.00)	(2.17)	(0.00)	(3.79)	(0.00)	(1.83)	(0.00)
County	31.45***	8.30	26.05***	7.15	20.92***	2.77	26.64***	9.36
	(3.78)	(0.00)	(3.64)	(0.00)	(7.55)	(0.006)	(2.85)	(0.00)
Education	0.4523***	4.74	0.6387***	5.79	0.739***	3.93	0.544***	6.14
	(.095)	(0.00)	(0.1103)	(0.00)	(.188)	(0.00)	(.088)	(0.00)
Population Density	0.9567	1.75	1.66***	2.51	1.55	1.33	1.40**	2.56
	(0.62)	(0.125)	(0.66)	(0.012)	(1.16)	(0.184)	(.545)	(0.011)
% White Population	-0.08	-1.52	-.0871*	-1.70	-.145	-1.39	-.064	-1.46
	(0.052)	(0.129)	(0.0511)	(0.09)	(.103)	(0.164)	(.0438)	(0.146)
Per Capita Income	-0.0001054**	-2.05	-0.0000872	-1.34	-0.0000986	-.94	-0.0000736	-1.36
	(0.00005)	(0.041)	(0.000065)	(0.182)	(0.0001)	(0.346)	(0.000541)	(0.174)
Constant	9.288*	1.79	12.57**	2.45	21.89**	2.15	9.197**	2.10
	(5.196)	(0.075)	(5.12)	(0.015)	(10.16)	(0.032)	(4.37)	(0.036)
Model Level Results	Prob. > F = 0.00*** R-squared = 0.5386 N=426		Prob. > F = 0.00*** R-squared = 0.4929 N=426		Prob. > F = 0.00*** R-squared = 0.2575 N=426		Prob. > F = 0.00*** R-squared =0.5557 N=426	
Interpretive Information	Significance: * < .10; ** < .05; *** < .01 Dependent Variable = Standardized measure of the proportion of attributes present on local government websites as a percentage of the total number of attributes in each conceptual category (E-bureaucracy, Mass Comm., Populist, All). It is defined by the following formula: $(X_1 / n^{category}) * 100$, where x_1 is the number of attributes in a particular category for a local government website and n is the number of attributes in that category. This is a standardized variable.							

Source: Authors' analysis

Government capacity hypotheses – For many years, scholars analyzing sub-national policy variation have asserted that policy development depends on government capacity (Bowman & Kearney, 1988). This broad hypothesis has also been applied by scholars of e-government. Larger governments, with greater capacity and greater demands on their bureaucracy, are likely to have more applications on their website than smaller governments (Norris and Moon 2005). This means we would expect county governments to have more applications across the three models of citizen engagement than cities, villages, and townships, respectively. And we would expect cities to have more applications across the three citizen engagement models than villages and townships. And finally, we would expect villages to have more applications on their websites than townships because, as incorporated areas, villages are responsible for more public services than townships. In our model we include dummy variables for county, city, and village, leaving township as the reference variable.

Socio-economic hypotheses – For many years, students of sub-national policy variation have also asserted that racial (Hero, 1998), educational (Gray, 1996), and economic (Dye, 1967) characteristics of a community influence policy development, and these variables have also been applied by scholars to the study of e-government (Reddick 2005, Tolbert and McNeal 2003). A digital divide that exists along racial lines means that communities of color are less likely to see governments rely on the Web as means of citizen engagement. Wealthier communities and those with higher levels of education, by contrast, should be more likely to rely on the internet and to expect government to adopt new technological innovations through which to communicate.

We measure the influence of race in our model by including the percentage of the population that is white. Our indicator for education is the percentage of the population that has graduated from college with a Bachelor of Arts (BA), Bachelor of Science (BS), or equivalent degree. And, our measure of economic status is the per capita income in the community.

Population density hypothesis – Basic economic theory suggests that highly populated areas create economies of scale for governments in the development of their websites, independent of the government type. We thus expect a more extensive development of government websites in more densely populated areas. We measure density by dividing total population into the land area of the community.

Model Results

To improve our understanding of local government choices regarding web-based citizen engagement strategies, we tested our hypotheses across all three models of citizen engagement and with an overall count of the number of website attributes. We used ordinary least squares regression to conduct the analysis because our dependent variables are continuous and our data are from individual government websites not panel data over time. Each of our models is statistically significant. The results are presented in *Table 4.*

Electronic bureaucracy model. Our model for electronic bureaucracy explains nearly 54 percent of the variance (R-square is .54) and suggests that government capacity and education matter.

Coefficients for village, city and county are statistically significant and positively related to the dependent variable. The coefficients also increase substantially with the size of the government. A county government increases our dependent variable by 31.45 percentage points, city government by 18.42, and village by 2.5. The findings also point to a gap between villages and cities, and suggest that the decisions about pursuing electronic bureaucracy forms of engagement are in part traceable to government capacity.

Education also predicts electronic bureaucracy forms of citizen engagement. Our measure of education is statistically significant and positive. The coefficient of .45 means that a 10 percent increase in the number of BAs in the community leads to 4.5 percent increase in our electronic bureaucracy index.

And finally, we expected governments in wealthier jurisdictions to make greater use of the Web to promote electronic bureaucracy forms of citizen engagement. However, we find that per capita income does not influence e-bureaucracy forms of engagement as we expected. Rather, it is inversely related to our index of electronic bureaucracy, after controlling for government capacity, education, race, and population density.

Communication management. Our model of communication management form of citizen engagement explains nearly fifty percent of the variance (R-square is .49) and suggests that government size, education and population density matter.

Coefficients for county and city are statistically significant and positive. A county government increases our communication index by 26 percentage points and a city government increases our index nearly 17 percentage points. Village is not statistically significant. Our socio-economic variables indicate that the number of college graduates in the community lead to a greater number of communication management attributes, even after controlling for the type of government and population density. At the same time, per capita income is not statistically significant. Finally, population density is a useful predictor of a communication management form of engagement. The 1.66 coefficient means that an increase of 1000 residents per square mile leads to a 1.6 percent increase the communication attributes. Race is statistically significant (at the .10 probability level), but its influence does not operate in the direction that we had expected. Here, surprisingly, we find that increases in the percentage of the population that is white tends to result in reductions in the mass communication engagement index.

An interesting finding is that the coefficients for government size are smaller than with our electronic bureaucracy index. This suggests that government size may play less of a role in predicting website attributes in the communication form of citizen engagement than in the electronic bureaucracy form. At the same time, coefficients for education and population density are larger in the communication management model than in the electronic bureaucracy model, which suggests that education and population density have a larger impact in promoting communication than electronic bureaucracy services through the web.

Populist. Our populist model explains the least amount of variation across our models (R-square is .26) and suggests that only government size and education are good predictors of the degree to which governments seek to promote citizen participation and dialogue through their website.

Coefficients for city and county are statistically significant and positive. The coefficient for county is 20.9 and for city it is 16.2, suggesting again that the larger the governmental unit the more populist attributes will be found on the governmental website. Village was not statistically significant.

Of our socio-economic variables, only education is statistically significant and positive. The coefficient for education is .74 which means that a one percent increase in the number of college graduates in the community leads to a .74 percent increase in level of populist citizen engagement. An interesting finding is that education appears to have a greater impact on a populist use of government website than other models. The coefficient for education in the populist model is 64 percent higher than in the electronic bureaucracy model of engagement.

Discussions with Local Government Information Management Professionals

We conducted four interviews with information management professionals from communities in our sample. Several significant points emerged from these discussions.

First, while those whom we interviewed emphasized both the dissemination of information to large audiences and the use of the internet to enable more efficient and effective bureaucratic services, none of the four focused extensively on fostering citizen-to-citizen engagement as the primary purpose for their current website engagement efforts. Where populist conceptions of citizen engagement were raised, they tended to be discussed in terms of being potentially valuable directions for future development, rather than descriptions of current purposes or activities.

Second, while populist conceptions of website purposes were not prevalent, several of those interviewed emphasized the important role of their worldwide web sites in enhancing democratic governance. By and large, their comments in this area focused on information provision, and the growing role of their websites in educating citizens about issues in their communities and in enabling more effective input from citizens to their governments. Several pointed to increases in email traffic to local officials and to improvements in the quality of input because of information available to citizens on the web. Several of those interviewed also pointed out that systems for tracking responses to citizens with email inquiries had been established to help ensure government responses to citizen inquiries.

It is useful to note in this context, however, that concerns about the value of open ended citizen-to-citizen uses of websites were also highlighted. At least one of the officials interviewed, for example, expressed concern about the potential abuse of blogs by small numbers of individuals who may seek to impersonate public officials and/or make comments that are inappropriate for community consumption, thus enabling a degradation of the quality of democratic dialogue. Consequently, while most of those interviewed suggested that the web could inform citizens and enable improvements in democratic processes, at least some of them also suggested that it could not – and perhaps should not seek to -- replace person to person contacts in local government settings.

A third and final insight offered by some of those interviewed focused on the politics underlying website engagements. As information management professionals, some viewed their role as primarily a technical one, and they at least implicitly suggested that true efforts to foster democratic engagement are appropriately directed by elected officials. Others suggested that their primary role was to disseminate information and provide efficient services, and that some local politicians had not yet expressed strong interest in using the web for purposes of democratic engagement. In this rendering, local government websites are recognized as valuable tools for democratic input, but also as tools which may be used to funnel that input in ways that are both efficient and relatively easy for governments to handle – particularly given growing resource constraints among local governments in Ohio during the time in which this research was being conducted.

SUMMARY OF FINDINGS AND LESSONS LEARNED

Several findings and lessons emerge from the results described above, and they relate to both the state of current local government efforts to engage citizens on the web and to the factors that appear to influence web-based citizen engagement efforts.

First, the results of our website surveys are consistent with previous suggestions that the development of e-government capacities is not inevitable. Among the 428 local governments in our sample, only a handful of them appear to be heavily engaged in using a wide range of website elements to engage citizens. Most of them have a reasonably modest web presence, as the average number of website attributes identified was approximately 5 – less than one-sixth of the potential universe of website attributes we identified for investigation. In addition, one-third of the local governments we investigated still do not appear to have any worldwide web site presence at all. The worldwide web is now well over ten years of age, and this study re-enforces the conclusion that we are still some distance from realizing the full potential that some observers have envisioned for the conduct of governance and citizen engagement.

Second, local governments undertake different kinds web based citizen engagement efforts. However, while we found evidence of citizen engagement efforts focused on both information management and the delivery of e-bureaucracy services, we found little evidence of populist interventions – less than 3% of the websites in our sample included a blog, for example. In addition, we did not identify any standard, or "cookie-cutter", set of website attributes. No single website attribute was used by more than 60% of governments assessed, and only 2 website attributes were used by more than 50% of the local governments we investigated. Web-based telephone directories and email contact address lists were the only two attributes that were present on websites for more than one-half of the local governments in our sample. While our effort in this chapter to distinguish e-government citizen engagement strategies according Kakabadse *et. al.'s* (2003) three major types provides initial insights regarding this variation, more extensive efforts to verify the results presented here and to differentiate web based citizen engagement efforts (both theoretically and empirically) are appropriate if we are to understand fully why local governments choose the strategies they do.

Third, our analyses confirm once again that government capacities do matter, but they also suggest that the extent to which they matter depends at on the kinds of citizen engagement strategies that local governments emphasize. Not surprisingly, larger governments (counties and cities) with greater capabilities tend to have a more extensive website presence than smaller governments with less developed capacities. This is the case across measures of all three of the models of website engagement that are assessed, although these capacity based factors appear to be most important in explaining the development of e-bureaucracy related website attributes. Thus, it appears that the capacities of local governments affect not only the extent of citizen engagement effort, but also the types of efforts that are undertaken.

Fourth, of the socioeconomic variables we assessed, education appears to have the strongest and clearest impacts on citizen engagement efforts. The education level of the community is a strong and statistically significant predictor of citizen engagement according to all three of the models of it that we investigated. However, our standardized analyses also suggest that education is particularly important in predicting citizen engagement strategies that are consistent with populist and information management website engagement strategies. This, in turn, suggests that highly educated communities may be quicker to develop website based tools that are designed to foster democratic governance processes than less educated communities. By contrast, our measures of race and economic capacity yield relatively weak results which are not consistent with our initial hypotheses.

Fifth, while our analyses suggest that government capacities and education are important determinants of web-based citizen engagement efforts, they also suggest that the policy dynamics underlying varying forms of engagement may differ from one another. Government capacities appear to contribute more to E-bureaucracy efforts than to information provision and populist engagement efforts.[6] On the other hand, education appears to be a particularly strong determinant of populist and information management forms of citizen engagement – both of which are more democratically oriented forms of engagement than E-bureaucracy. In addition, while population density does not appear to have a significant influence on all forms of engagement, it does appear to be significantly related to information management efforts. By contrast, neither diversity nor wealth appears to provide theoretically and empirically defensible explanations for any of the three major forms of web-based citizen engagement. While we view all of these findings as suggestive rather than conclusive, we do believe that they provide a foundation for further research and inquiry into the policy dynamics underlying varying forms of web-based citizen engagement.

And finally, even though some of our analyses call the extent of local government progress in fostering citizen engagement through e-government into question, they also confirm its fundamental value as a potential tool of democratic governance. Efforts to provide basic information to engage citizens in governance are clearly one of the most common uses of the local government websites we investigated, and these kinds of website attributes -- phone directories, email contact addresses, calendars, and meeting minutes – were also some of the most common elements of the websites across all sizes and types of local governments. If an educated populace is a central key to democracy as our forefathers suggested, this is a good sign. Our discussions with website professionals associated with some of the more developed local government worldwide web sites we investigated also emphasized the importance of information provision to their work, and they seemed to view it – along with simplifying the business of government – as a central purpose of their work. At the same time, however, they were also clear in their view that democratic engagement is fundamentally a political process and that their website related activities are not immune from these kinds of influences.

CONCLUSION

While the research presented here confirms many of the conclusions reached in previously published literature, it also suggests that the e-government literature has not yet accounted fully for a fundamental characteristic of democratic governance – the politics underlying local government administration. Local governments are using their websites to accomplish their purposes, and the extent to which they are doing so appears to depend on their capabilities, the education levels of their citizens, and the density of their populations. At the same time, however, it is also clear that the growth in e-government engagement is neither uniform nor inexorable. Many local governments are not advancing their efforts as quickly as some observers have suggested would occur, and many smaller governments are not moving forward in this area at all. While the research underlying this chapter must be viewed as preliminary, it does provide a foundation for future research that takes account of the differing purposes of government and the ways in which political and policy dynamics may affect e-government now and in the future.

ACKNOWLEDGMENT

The authors would like to express their appreciation to Great Lakes Innovations for providing funding support to Kent State University's Center for Public Administration and Public Policy to conduct the research underlying this chapter. We would also like to express our appreciation to the following individuals for their leadership and important contributions to this research effort: Mr. Brian Kelley, Ms. Melissa Koeka, Ms. Yunnan Li, Mr. Kent Sowards, Mr. Matthew Flemming, Ms. Sayantani Satpathi, Mr. Sam Janson, Ms. Ashley Lerch, Ms. Kerry Macomber, and Dr. Ryan Claaussen. We would also like to thank the four northeastern Ohio public officials who were willing to share their insights about citizen engagement activities associated with their local government websites.

REFERENCES

Accenture. (2005). *eGovernment Leadership: High Performance, Maximum Value*. Report published by the consulting firm Accenture.

Akesson, M., Skalen, P., & Edvardsson, B. (2008). E-government and Service Orientation: gaps between theory and practice. *International Journal of Public Sector Management*, *21*(1), 74–92. doi:10.1108/09513550810846122

Baum, C. H., & Di Maio, A. (2000). *Gartner's Four Phases of E-Government Model*. Retrieved July 25, 2008, from http://www.gartner.com

Bolgherini, S. (2007). The Technology Trap and the Role of Political and Cultural Variables: A Critical Analysis of the E-Government Policies. *Review of Policy Research*, *24*(3), 259–275. doi:10.1111/j.1541-1338.2007.00280.x

Bowman, A., & Kearney, R. C. (1988). Dimensions of State Government Capability. *The Western Political Quarterly*, *41*(2), 341–362. doi:10.2307/448542

Brown, M. M. (2007). Governments Understanding E-Government Benefits: An Examination of Leading-Edge Local. *American Review of Public Administration*, *37*(2), 178–197. doi:10.1177/0275074006291635

Brunner, J. (Ohio Secretary of State). (n.d.). *The Ohio Municipal, Township, and School Board Roster 2006-2007.* Columbus, OH: Ohio Secretary of State's Office.

Coursey, D., & Killingsworth, J. (2001). Managing Web Services: Lessons from Florida. In David Garson, G. (Ed.), *Handbook of Public Information Systems* (2nd ed., pp. 331–345). New York: Marcel Dekker/CRC.

Coursey, D., & Norris, D. F. (2008). Models of E-government: Are They Correct? An Empirical Assessment. *Public Administration Review*, (May/June): 523–536. doi:10.1111/j.1540-6210.2008.00888.x

Dye, T. (1967). *Politics, Economics, and Public Policy Outcomes in the American States*. Chicago: Rand McNally.

Fountain, J. (2001). *Building the Virtual State: Information Technology and Institutional Change*. Washington, DC: Brookings Institution Press.

Gray, V. (1996). The Socioeconomic and Political Context of States. In *Politics in the American States: A Comparative Analysis* (6th ed.). Washington, DC: Congressional Quarterly Press.

Hero, R. (1998). *Faces of Inequality: Social Diversity in American Politics*. Oxford, UK: Oxford University Press.

Hiller, J. S., & Bélanger, F. (2001). *Privacy Strategies for Electronic Government*. Washington, DC: IBM Center for the Business of Government. Retrieved January 28, 2008, from http://www.businessofgovernment.org/pdfs/ HillerReport.pdf

Ho, A. T.-K. (2002). Reinventing Local Governments and the E-government Initiative. *Public Administration Review*, *62*(4), 434–444. doi:10.1111/0033-3352.00197

Holzer, M., Manoharan, A., Shick, R., & Stowers, G. (2008). *U.S. Municipalities: E-Governance Report. The E-Governance Institute National Center for Public Performance School of Public Affairs and Administration Rutgers, the State University of New Jersey*. Campus at Newark.

Kakabadse, A., Kakabadse, N. K., & Kouzmin, A. (2003). Reinventing the Democratic Governance Project through Information Technology? A Growing Agenda for Debate. *Public Administration Review*, *63*(1), 44–60. doi:10.1111/1540-6210.00263

Layne, K., & Lee, J. (2001). Developing Fully Functional E-government: A Four Stage Model. *Government Information Quarterly*, *18*, 122–136. doi:10.1016/S0740-624X(01)00066-1

London, S. (1994). *Electronic Democracy: A Literature Survey. Paper prepared for the Kettering Foundation*. CA: Santa Barbara.

Moon, M. J. (2002). The evolution of E-government among municipalities: Rhetoric or reality? *Public Administration Review*, *62*(4), 424–433. doi:10.1111/0033-3352.00196

Moon, M. J., & Norris, D. F. (2005). Does managerial orientation matter? The adoption of reinventing government and e-government at the municipal level. *Information Systems Journal*, *15*(1), 43–60. doi:10.1111/j.1365-2575.2005.00185.x

Pina, V., Torres, L., & Royo, S. (2007). Are ICTs Improving Transparency and Accountability in the EU Regional and Local Governments? An empirical study. *Public Administration, 85*(2), 449–472. doi:10.1111/j.1467-9299.2007.00654.x

Reddick, C. G. (2004). A two-stage model of e-government growth: Theories and empirical evidence for US cities. *Government Information Quarterly, 21*, 51–64. doi:10.1016/j.giq.2003.11.004

Reddick, C. G. (2005). Citizen interaction with e-government: From the streets to servers? *Government Information Quarterly, 22*, 38–57. doi:10.1016/j.giq.2004.10.003

Ronaghan, S. A. (2001). *Benchmarking E-Government: A Global Perspective.* New York: United Nations Division for Public Economics and Public Administration and American Society for Public Administration. Retrieved May 11, 2009, from http://www.itpolicy.gov.il/topics_egov/docs/benchmarking.pdf

Seifert, J. W., & Petersen, R. E. (2002). The promise of all things E? Expectations and challenges of emergent electronic government. *Perspectives on Global Development and Technology, 1*(2), 193–212. doi:10.1163/156915002100419808

The Gartner Group. (2000). *Key Issues in E-Government Strategy and Management. Research Notes, Key Issues*. Stamford, CT: The Gartner Group.

Tolbert, C., & McNeal, R. (2003). Unraveling the effects of the Internet on political participation. *Political Research Quarterly, 56*(2), 175–185.

Wescott, C. (2001). E-Government in the Asia-Pacific Region. *Asian Journal of Political Science, 9*(2), 1–24. doi:10.1080/02185370108434189

ENDNOTES

1. Vicente Pina and his colleagues (2007) also find that local governments in the European Community have not moved beyond an informational presence. The note that "most ICT initiatives still view people from a passive perspective" (465)
2. The individual we enlisted serves as the Information Technology Manager for a northeast Ohio County. He is recognized as an e-government leader in the state of Ohio and has been in his current position for more than 15 years.
3. Throughout the remainder of the chapter, the reader will observe noted sample sizes of 428 or 426, depending on whether the data we were able to compile for these two villages was sufficient to support the analyses shown.
4. This search took place in three stages. First, graduate students affiliated with Kent State University's Center for Public Administration and Public Policy were assigned local governments and searched for their worldwide websites using the tools noted in the text. Next, our information technology specialist reviewed the websites identified to ensure that they actually represented the websites of the jurisdictions in our sample. And finally, this same specialist conducted an independent search to identify any sites that might have been missed.
5. The evaluate criteria used in our study builds on the work of Marc Holzer and his colleagues (2008).

6 It is appropriate to recognize, however, that the capacities of counties and cities are likely to lead them to have more extensive bureaucracies than villages and townships, so it is possible that higher levels of E-bureaucratic forms of web-based citizen engagement may be related not only to greater capacities, but also to a greater need to make bureaucracy efficient.

This work was previously published in International Journal of Electronic Government Research, edited by Vishanth Weerakkody, pp. 68-85, copyright 2010 by IGI Publishing (an imprint of IGI Global).

Chapter 18
Assessing e-Government Services:
The Case of e-Filing of Personal Income Tax in Malaysia

Maniam Kaliannan
Universiti Teknologi MARA, Malaysia

Murali Raman
Multimedia University, Malaysia

Magiswary Dorasamy
Multimedia University, Malaysia

ABSTRACT

Introduction of Electronic Government (e-Government) is seen as a tool to improve government service delivery to external and internal clients for the benefit of the government and the citizens and businesses that it serves. E-Government holds tremendous promise for improvements in the public service delivery as well to overcome many of the persistent public service problems. Successful delivery of online services has rapidly become an important measure of effective public sector management. The e-Government initiative in Malaysia was launched with the aim to improve the efficiency and effectiveness of government service delivery to its stakeholders, namely, citizens and businesses. The vision of e-Government is a vision for people in government, business and citizenry working together for the benefit of Malaysia and all of its citizens. The dual objectives of e-Government are to reinvent the government of Malaysia in terms of service delivery through the use of information technology and to catalyze the successful development of the Multimedia Super Corridor with IT as one of the leading sectors of the economy. One of the services that was launched as part of e-Government Flagship is on line tax filling or known as e-Filing by the Inland Revenue Board. Via this system, the taxpayers are able to complete an electronic application form and the necessary payment details within few keystrokes and hence complete their revenue declaration within minutes. The purpose of e-Filing service is to encourage every taxpayer to submit their income tax return through an online system, thus reducing the manual paper-based submission method. This system has received good response from the taxpayers. However, there is still a sizeable number who have yet to adopt e-Filing. An empirical assessment of

DOI: 10.4018/978-1-61520-931-6.ch018

adoption of **e-Filing** *system involving 200 tax payers was carried out. The study aims to assess the extent of* **e-filling** *acceptance among the tax payers who have filed their tax forms online. Beyond this, the chapter also analyses the factors that contribute towards adoption of such system in Malaysia. The findings revealed that taxpayers have positive attitude in using the* **e-Filing** *system as they perceive that tax submission method via internet is more convenient than submission by post or by hand and that perceived readiness towards using this technology is paramount to their belief for using* **e-Filing** *system.*

INTRODUCTION

Tax filing whether it is done manually or via digital means is an important phenomenon for most income earners and business entities. Governments worldwide are moving towards utilizing the power of information, communication and technology (ICT) by embarking into the new dimension which is electronic filing (henceforth referred as e-Filing). In order to improve taxpayer service, governments are leveraging ICT in many ways to tap the potential cost saving and efficiency in providing online services to the citizens. Malaysia too is in this bandwagon. However, low system acceptance by the end-users is one of the major hurdles to the proliferation of e-government projects (Sahu & Gupta, 2007).

This paper discusses the relationship between four major factors that are affecting the behavioural intention of tax e-Filing systems users in Malaysia in adopting this method in contrary to the manual submission method. Using three of the important theories on assessing users' behaviour against ICT system usage, Technology Acceptance Model (TAM), Technology Readiness Index (TRI) and Diffusion of Innovation (DOI), this study analysed and discussed the relationship of perceived ease of use, perceived usefulness, perceived readiness and complexity in using e-Filing system in Malaysia.

The academic nature of this paper stresses on how (ICT), manifesting itself in the form of e-Filing system, can enhance e-government efforts in providing fast and efficient service to its citizens. The paper is written based on our involvement with prior work that pertains to the use of e-government services. Understanding how and why people accept or reject an information system has proven to be one of the most challenging issues in information system research (Delone & McLean, 1992). Having invested huge amount of capital in ICT for better info-structure and infrastructure, governments will benefit from this nature of study to assess the intention to use and factors affecting the usage of such systems.

FOCUS OF THE STUDY

In Malaysia, the government's Multimedia Super Corridor (MSC) project has been instrumental in providing necessary platform for change or transformation. As one of the seven MSC flagships, E-government will contribute to the nation's rapid development. E-Filing in this context, is expected to be widely used by the Malaysian citizens. However, despite all the efforts aimed at developing better and efficient tax filing system, the e-Filing system remained unnoticed by many citizens and still seriously underused in spite of their availability (Wang, 2002). There is very little research done on this area due to infancy of e-Filing in Malaysia. This is due to insufficient evidence to date pertaining e-Filing system associated to Malaysian tax settings (Lai, Sheikh Obid, & Meera, 2005). In fact, there was lack of ability to obtain certain information relevance on these studies in Malaysia. In addition, there is still ambiguity on whether Malaysian tax practitioners are prepared to embrace the e-Filing system (Lai at al., 2005). Lai at al. (2005) examined the level of technology readiness and intention to use among Malaysian tax practitioners. This research reveals what and how Malaysians are in relation with the e-Filing systems adoption.

This study makes an attempt to examine the determinants of behavioural intention to the use of e-Filing systems in the case of tax submission in Malaysia. The significance of this study is two-fold. First, this study provides vital information for government to identify factors influencing taxpayers towards e-Filing systems adoption. Malaysian government will be able to use the result of this study as a guide to plan its strategies to improve the usage level of e-Filing systems. Since usage of e-Filing systems is at present completely voluntary, the challenge that Malaysian government has to face is to encourage the tax payers to use online submission instead of manual submission by highlighting the benefits of such systems and by making them realize the simplicity of the on-line process. Second, this study has significantly integrated three theories to describe a new technology acceptance, e-Filing systems in the case of tax return submission among individual tax payers in Malaysia.

LITERATURE REVIEW - E-GOVERNMENT DEFINED

E-Government refers to the automation of government-to-government and government-to-citizen interactions (Dan, 2000). Collaborative software and other tools are expected to help make transactions with government agencies much faster and more efficient. E-Government is a way for governments to use the new technologies to provide people with more convenient access to government information and services to participate in our democratic institutions and processes (State Service Commission (SSC), 2006). Information technology (IT) initiatives in government services known as electronic government, or e-government, are changing the way the government works and interacts with citizens, businessmen, its employees, and other governments (Sahu & Gupta, 2007). The purpose of e-government is to bring people together and for that to happen, the government must plan e-government in such a way that conventional means to access to government are maintained for those people who need them; community access to the Internet is available for those people who, for any reason, cannot access it from their homes; educational and public information programmes are used to help citizens in using the new technologies; review and strengthen where necessary, all legislation designed to protect people's privacy and provide safeguard around the sharing of people's personal information among government agencies.

Over the past decade, governments, worldwide, have invested heavily in E-government services. The scale of this investment can be gauged from the various benchmarking reports on e-government (Connolloy & Bannistern, 2008). Having invested in this technology, governments are naturally interested in both the level and the nature of the use of online services made by citizens and business and they have employed a variety of instruments to try to measure this, from crude hit rate counts to citizen surveys.

The use of Information and Communications Technology (ICT) in general, has also changed government service delivery process, business models and people's expectations of the quality and efficiency of information sharing and service delivery. Successful implementation of various e-Government initiatives worldwide (e.g. e-Seva and e-Bhoomi initiative in India, e-Citizen initiative in Singapore and e-firstgov.com in the USA) are being touted as the next wave of creating innovative supply chain management processes in the context of the civil/public sector worldwide (Maniam, 2007).

E-FILLING - GLOBAL SCENARIO

E-Filing as an important application that automates tax related processes in an attempt to improve efficiency in assessing and collecting tax information (Fu et. al.2006). The e-Filing service improves tax-filing service while at the same time reducing costs to both taxpayers and tax collecting agencies and emphasizes the effective and efficient use of IT and networks to achieve paperless culture (Fu et. al. 2004). Benefits of e-Filing systems are five fold:

i. On time submission

The e-Filing system encourages taxpayers to submit their returns on time, although most of the submissions are done at the eleventh hour. Unlike the manual submission, e-Filing system improves the convenience and flexibility besides providing ubiquity for users.

ii. Streamline procedures

The moment data or figures are entered in the system, it is sent to the central database or server. Thereafter, the process of revision or refund can be carried out efficiently and again the bottom line is speed.

iii. Provision of evidence

When someone makes an e-Filing, the users will be receiving verification which provides significant evidence that the IRB has received the return.

iv. Reduction in error rate in the tax returns processing.

According to the finding, over 18% of tax returns prepared on paper have numerous errors, which mostly arise from miscalculations (Hwang, 2000). It is proven that only 1% of taxes prepared electronically have errors (Hwang, 2000). In tax years 1996 and 1997, the US tax statistical records demonstrated that the preliminary error rate in e-Filing tax returns is about 1% to 3% compared to approximately 16% to 20% for paper filing returns (Wongtrakool, 1998). Other experience showed that the error rate for electronically filed income tax returns was less than 1% versus 20% for paper returns (Fletcher, 2002).

However, in the case of UK, Barnes & Vidgen (2007), in their survey on the users' perception of online self-assessed tax return of UK's Inland Revenue, found that the system interactors indicated lower quality of the site. Key problems affecting the perceptions of the interactive users are the usability of the self-assessment facility and difficulty communicating with the organisation (Barnes & Vidgen, 2007). Nevertheless, the latest information from the Inland Revenue shows that there has been a major increase in take up in the year ended April 5, 2003, when 329,420 users accessed the system to submit their tax return (Barnes & Vidgen, 2007).

Singapore is an excellent example on e-Filing implementation. The Inland Revenue Authority of Singapore (IRAS) launched in 1992 to remove the bureaucratic red tape by restructuring the taxation system (Lim, Wee & Pan, 2007). The desirability of the e-Filing system was reflected in a 2001 survey where 94.1% of individual taxpayers, 89.6% of corporate taxpayers, and 94.6% of goods and services taxpayers expressed high levels of satisfaction with the refurnished tax services (Lim et al., 2007). Out of the 1,510,020 individual income tax returns issued for year 2007, close to 93 per cent of the year 2007 returns were received by the filing due date last year. This is a 1 per cent point improvement from 92 per cent for year 2006 (Lim et al, 2007). By 31 March 2007, 1,462,017 returns were submitted, representing 96.8 per cent of the total returns issued (Lim et al., 2007). The high compliance rate could be attributable to the ease of e-Filing through myTax Portal, the new "No-Filing Service", and timely reminders to taxpayers to file on time through publicity in newspapers and outdoor advertisements. As at the close of the e-Filing deadline of 18 April 2008, 87 per cent taxpayers e-filed their taxes, or close to nine out of ten. This is a remarkable increase of 7 per cent points as compared with the 80 per cent who e-Filed last year (IRAS Annual Report, 2007/08).

Taiwan is another well-known case in the e-Filing plan with its online tax filing system and tax tracking system. The online tax filing and payment system (OTFPS) allows Taiwan taxpayers to submit tax returns using online ID and electronic transaction authentication mechanisms. The OTFPS provides various reports on income tax withholding (exemption) data, online filing and payment of general income tax, online filing and payment of business income tax, online payment of business tax, and online payment of taxes owed following a tax audit (Hung, 2006). Tax e-Filing was launched and available nationwide in 1998 with the usage of 18,000 to over 2.1 million representing 43.5 per cent of total taxpayers in 2003 (Fu et al., 2006).

E-FILING IN MALAYSIA

Following the Malaysian government policy of becoming a technologically enabled government through its Vision 2020, the Inland Revenue Board of Malaysia (IRB) has introduced e-Filing in 2006. The IRB is a collecting agency under the Ministry of Finance. It acts as the Malaysian Government agent in administering, assessing, collecting and enforcing payment of a range of taxes. These include income tax, petroleum income tax and real property gains tax. It was formed in 1957, known as Inland Revenue Department. In 1996, it becomes a statutory body in accordance with the Inland Revenue Board of Malaysia Act 1995 to give more autonomy especially in financial and personnel management and to improve the quality and effectiveness of tax administration.

Initially, this application was introduced to corporate taxpayers in 2003 and later it was expanded to individual taxpayers in 2004. The Inland Revenue Board (IRB), the agency in charge for tax filing took this challenge to reshuffle the tax filing process by utilising ICT to embrace an electronic income tax filing systems (Malaysian Institute of Accountants (MIA), 2000). The intention of launching the e-government in Malaysia is to pilot the country into the information age and to further guarantee the materialisation of knowledge society.

Recently, the Inland Revenue Board (IRB) has surpassed its target on electronic submission of e-Filing returns forms. At the end of March 2007 there were 70,000 people who sent in return forms through e-Filing system compared to the previous year results which is only 4,500 people used until end of March 2006 (Hamid, 2007). On April 30, 2007, nearing the deadline of tax return form submission, a total of 569,990 taxpayers have sent in their return forms through e-Filing system (Hamid, 2007). CEO of IRB, Hasmah Abdullah, the nation top taxwoman had initially targeted 360,000 people to use e-Filing in year 2007 which is double of the previous year's actual online tax returns, 180,000. (Hamid, 2007). There was a 60 percent rise to 1.2 million users in year 2008 as compared to about 800,000 in year 2007 ("IRB confident of collecting," 2008).

Based on senior officials from IRB, the 180,000 taxpayers have utilized the e-Filing systems in the last years can considered as a "good rate" (Hamid, 2007). The result reveals that about seven per cent of total taxpayers had utilised e-Filing systems when newly introduced in Malaysia. In comparison with United Kingdom (UK), when the system was newly introduced, UK could only achieve one percent usage rate among taxpayers. Surprisingly, Malaysia has fetched far higher usage rate compared in the UK (Hamid, 2007). The Deputy Finance Minister, Datuk Dr. Awang Adek Hussin anticipated about 80 per cent of taxpayers to use e-Filing system in the next five years (Hamid, 2007).

The Board has around 10,000 employees working over 40 branch offices nationwide. With the introduction of e-Filing in year 2006, the Board has successfully collected direct taxes amounting to RM 65 billion and the amount has increased to RM 74.669 billion in 2007 as the response to the e-Filing system for 2007 has been overwhelming (The Star, September 4, 2008). According to M.Krishnamoorthy (2008), a total of 874,814 taxpayers e-filed their tax return in 2007, compared with 186,343 in 2006. An interview with IRB chief executive officer Datuk Hasmah Abdullah reported that, in 2008, the number of income tax returned received through e-Filing has increased by 369% (Hariati, 2008).

In the effort to boost the e-Filing usage, the IRB officials made numerous visits to companies and government departments nationwide to brief and enlightened the private and public sector employees on how to use e-Filing. In addition, handouts on how to utilize the e-Filing system were distributed in the shopping malls and public places. Interestingly, the IRB has added a new feature to the e-Filing system known as "e-bayaran" or e-payment. The e-bayaran allows the taxpayers to pay tax online through Internet banking for the account holders of the banks which are members of Financial Process Exchange (FPX). This includes CIMB Bank, Public Bank, Hong Leong, Maybank2U and Bank Islam.

The current development of e-Filing system in Malaysia enables the taxpayers to submit their tax return forms online conveniently and hence expedite the tax refunds if any. The e-Filing system provides easy, accurate, safe and fast processing compared to manual tax return form submission. Another significant benefit for Malaysians is that the system imposes no risk of lost of mails and produce high accuracy rate as the e-Filing computes the tax for taxpayers.

Research conducted by Jasmine & Zurina (2008) revealed that majority of respondents in their study on e-filling in Malaysia preferred e-Filing because of ease of use (46.9%) and convenience (28.1%). Only 25% of the respondent chooses e-Filing because of the promise on tax return within one month. Majority of the respondents indicated positive perception towards e-Filing. This is a positive sign of a positive acceptance of the system amongst the Malaysians.

RELATED THEORIES

This study has attempted to analyse the behavioral intention of tax e-Filing users' perception by integrating constructs from Davis **(1989)** Technology Acceptance Model (TAM),Rogers (1995)Diffusion of Innovations Theory (DOI) andParasuraman (2000)Technology Readiness Index (TRI).

TAM was introduced by Davis (1989) is an adaptation of the Theory of Reasoned Action (TRA) specifically tailored for modeling user acceptance of IS. TAM was developed to explain and predict computer usage behavior. The goal of TAM is "to provide an explanation of the determinants of computer acceptance that is general, capable of explaining user behavior across a broad range of end-user computing technologies and user populations, while at the same time being both parsimonious and theoretically justified" (Davis et al.. 1989; p 985). It states that beliefs influence attitudes; which lead to intentions and to behaviors. TAM proposes two specific belief constructs, that is, perceived usefulness (the extent to which a technological innovation is expected to improve the potential adopter's performance) and perceived ease of use (the degree to which the potential adopter expects a technological innovation to be free of effort in use) as critical antecedents to an individual's technology adoption process (Davis, 1989; Davis et al., 1989). Both perceived usefulness and perceived ease of use are specific perceptions and are anchored to specific beliefs users hold about the system. In sum, it was found that TAM could successfully predict IS acceptance behavior under different technologies and different situations. In addition, it was found that TAM was a much simpler; easier to use and more powerful model of the determinant of user acceptance of computer technology than other models. In the recent years, TAM is been used extensively in the study of e-Government (Warkentin et al, 2002; Carter & Belanger, 2003, 2004, 2005). Findings of TAM suggest that IT acceptance is determined by person's perceived usefulness (PU), the user's "subjective probability that using a specific application system will increase this or her job performance" (Davis, 1989) and perceived ease of use (PEOU), "the degree to which the user expects the target system to be free of effort". Fu et al., (2004, 2006) pointed out that TAM is useful in evaluating application in organisational context. It may not reflect the variety of user task environment beyond organisational dimension.

The process of diffusion is defined as the acceptance of an idea or practice, over time, by individuals, groups or other adopting units, linked to specific channels of communication, to a social structure, and to a given system of values, or culture. Rogers described "diffusion" as the process by which an innovation (new - idea, object or practice) is communicated through certain channels over time amongst the members of a social system. Diffusion of innovation consists of four elements, namely: the innovation, communication channels, time, and the social system (Rogers 2003). An innovation is an idea, practice, or a phenomenon perceived to be novel by an individual or a community. Therefore, E-Government services can be considered to be an innovation as they are perceived to be novel by citizen, and are delivered via the Internet (communication channel) to citizens, a community of potential adopters. DOI theory sees innovations as being communicated through certain channels over time and within a particular social system (Rogers, 1995). Individuals are seen as possessing different degrees of willingness to adopt innovations (Rogers, 1995). The rate of adoption of innovations is impacted by five factors: relative advantage, compatibility, trialability, observability, and complexity (Rogers, 1995). This study only uses the complexity of technology construct due to the fact that it can be studied together with the perceived ease of use factor under the TAM's model. The complexity is generally negatively correlated with rate of adoption (Rogers, 1995), i.e., higher rate of adoption normally due to ease of use and vice-versa if the system is complex to use.

Through TRI, the technology-readiness construct refers to people's propensity to embrace and use new technologies for accomplishing goals in home life and at work (Parasuraman, 2000). Technology readiness can be defined as "people's propensity to embrace and use new technologies for accomplishing goals in home life and at work". Technological readiness is a good predictor of technology-related behavior. Four main dimensions of TRI were:

- Optimism: A positive view of technology and a belief that it offers people increased control, flexibility, and efficiency in life
- Innovativeness: A tendency to be a technology pioneer and thought leader
- Discomfort: A perceived lack of control over technology and a feeling of being overwhelmed by it
- Insecurity: Distrust of technology and skepticism about the ability to work properly

Of these dimensions:

- optimism and innovativeness are drivers of technological readiness
- discomfort and insecurity are inhibitors of technological readiness

This study had devised items from these components to represent the construct perceived readiness which reflect the readiness of user towards usage of new technology. Parasuraman (2008) ascertains that the extant literature pertaining to adoption of new technologies and people-technology interactions strongly suggests that consumers simultaneously harbor favorable and unfavorable views about technology-based products and services. The two components optimism and innovativeness are the drivers of technology readiness, whereas discomfort and insecurity are inhibitors. The perceived readiness is wider than

TR (Chang et, al. 2007). The PR is kind of belief that is an individual's self-confidence in his/her ability to perform a behavior (Bandura, 1977).

There are many theories exist related to evaluating technology behavioural intentions such as Theory of Planned Behaviour (TPB), Theory of Reasoned Action (TRA), Unified Theory of Acceptance and Use of Technology (UTAUT) and Delone and McLean IS Model (D&M IS). TPD concludes that attitude toward behavior, subjective norm, perceived behavioral control are the main constructs that influence the behaviour intention of users of technology. TRA posits that individual behavior is driven by behavioral intentions where behavioural intentions are a function of an individual's attitude toward the behaviour and subjective norms surrounding the performance of the behavior. UTAUT holds that four key constructs (performance expectancy, effort expectancy, social influence, and facilitating conditions) are direct determinants of usage intention and behaviour (Venkatesh et, al. 2003). D&M IS model holds that a system can be evaluated in terms of information, system, and service quality; these characteristics affect the subsequent use or intention to use and user satisfaction. As a result of using the system, certain benefits will be achieved. The net benefits will (positively or negatively) influence user satisfaction and the further use of the information system (Delone & McLean 2002, 2003). [edit]

RESEARCH MODEL AND HYPOTHESES DEVELOPMENT

In view of the discussions earlier, we have adopted three important theories to examine the behavioural intention (BI) which was to lead us to the acceptance of e-Filing systems in Malaysia. The first theory is TAM (Davis, 1989), which includes perceived usefulness (PU) and perceived ease of use (PEOU). The second theory is PRI (Parasuraman, 2000) which is the base for perceived readiness (PR) in this study. Finally, DOI (Rogers, 1995) were used by selecting only one of its construct which is complexity (C). On the other hand, BI is widely discussed by Taylor and Todd (1995). Thus, the following hypotheses are proposed.

H_1: Perceived Usefulness has a significant correlation with Behavioural Intention.

H_2: Perceived Ease of Use has a significant correlation with Behavioural Intention.

H_3: Perceived Readiness has a significant correlation with Behavioural Intention.

H_4: Complexity has significant a correlation with Behavioural Intention.

Figure 1 illustrates a research model for e-Filing services acceptance, as constructed based on TAM. The details of the above hypotheses and their supporting studies are summarized in Table 1.

METHODS AND MEASURES

A self-administered questionnaire-based survey was conducted in Klang Valley. Klang Valley is an area in Malaysia comprising Kuala Lumpur (the capital city of Malaysia) and its suburbs, and adjoining cities and towns in the state of Selangor. It is the heartland of Malaysia's industry and commerce with the population of 5.2 million in 2006. The unit of analysis is individual taxpayers. A total of 200 taxpayers' responses were collected using a non-probability convenient sampling method and it was a cross-sectional study.

The development of the constructs and the measures used to measure them were consistent with the literature. The measurements for independent variables; perceived ease of use and perceived usefulness were adapted from Davis (1989), whereas, input items measuring perceived readiness (with wording changes from technology readiness) were adapted from Para-

Figure 1. The research model

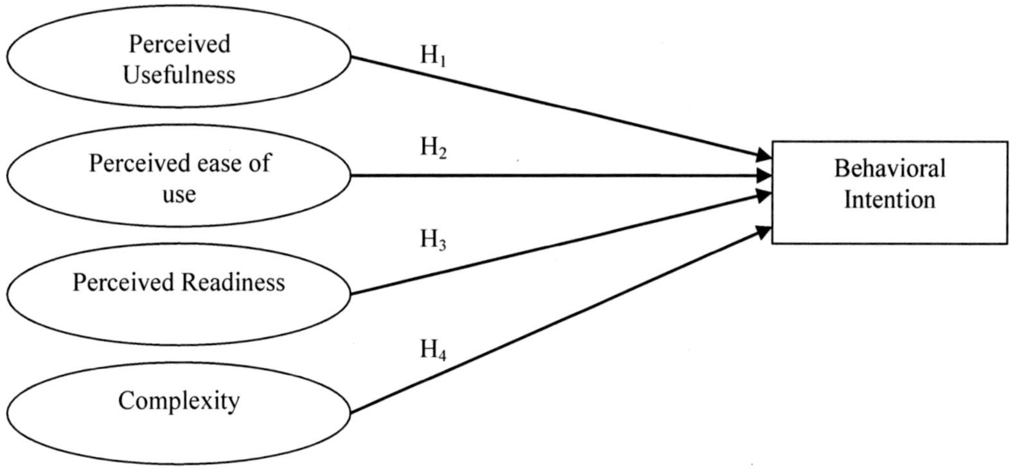

suraman (2000), and input items for complexity of technology were adapted from Rogers (1995). Measurements for behavioural intention were derived from Davis (1989). The details of the measures for each constructs are given in the Appendix 1.

The constructs were measured using a seven-point Likert-scaling with anchors ranging from "strongly disagree" to "strongly agree". The analyses encompassed descriptive statistics, reliability test, correlations and regression.

RESULTS AND DISCUSSIONS

This section presents some of the main findings from the survey which includes demographic profile of the respondents, reliability analysis and other measurements to test hypothesis.

DEMOGRAPHIC PROFILE

As given in Table 2 below, in terms of gender, male accounted for 56 per cent and female accounted for 44 per cent. The age groups; below 20, 21-30, 31-40, 41-50 and above 50 were 0.5 per cent, 39.5 per cent, 29 per cent, 17 per cent and 14 per cent respectively. Meanwhile, 40 per cent (80) of the respondents were still single, 59.5 per cent (119) were married and only 1 respondent (0.5 per cent) was divorced. In terms of education, 2 per cent and 43 per cent of the respondents were from primary school secondary school, 39 per cent

Table 1. Summary of research hypotheses- need to put it in a paragraph form, not clear

	Hypotheses	Supporting studies
H_1	Perceived Usefulness	Davis (1989); Taylor and Todd (1995)
H_2	Perceived ease of use	Davis (1989); Taylor and Todd (1995)
H_3	Perceived Readiness	Parasuraman, (2000); Chang, (2007); Bandura (1982); Zeithaml et al., (2002); Compeau and Higgins, (1995)
H_4	Complexity	Rogers (1995)

Table 2. Demographic profile

Profile	Frequency	Percentage (%)
Gender	112	56.0
Male	88	44.0
Female	200	100.0
Total		
Age	1	0.5
<20	79	39.5
21-30	58	29.0
31-40	34	17.0
41-50	28	14.0
>50	200	100.0
Total		
Marital	80	40.0
Single	119	59.5
Married	1	0.5
Divorced	200	100.0
Total		
Education	4	2.0
Primary school	86	43.0
Secondary school	72	36.0
Bachelors degree	38	19.0
Masters and above	200	100.0
Total		
Income (per year)	129	64.0
RM50,000 or below	47	22.5
RM50,001- RM100,000	8	4.0
> RM100,000	16	8.0
Systems Missing	200	100.0
Total		

and 19 per cent were with bachelors and masters (or above) degrees. Where income groups are concerned, 64 per cent of the respondents were earning up to RM50, 000, 22.5 per cent were earning between RM50,000 and RM100,000 and only 4 per cent were earning above RM100,000 in a year, however, 16 cases were considered as systems missing.

STATISTICAL ANALYSIS

Some important statistical techniques were adopted; reliability test, correlation and regression analyses. The reliability test (Table 3) is essentially important to evaluate the successfulness of the constructs considered in the study. The correlation results (Table 4) reveal the relationships among the variables considered in the study and

Table 3. Reliability tests

Variables	Cronbach's Alpha	No of items	No of cases
Behavioural Intention (BI)	0.882	4	200
Perceived Usefulness (PU)	0.903	4	200
Perceived Ease of Use (PEOU)	0.915	4	200
Perceived Readiness (PR)	0.877	4	200
Complexity (C)	0.929	4	200

Table 4. Mean, standard deviation and bivariate correlation results

	Mean	Std D	1	2	3	4	5
1.Behavioural Intention (BI)	5.09	1.36	1				
2.Perceived Usefulness (PU)	5.39	1.18	.0704**	1			
3.Perceived Ease of Use (PEOU)	4.83	1.27	.660**	.621**	1		
4.Perceived Readiness (PR)	4.64	1.32	.659**	.543**	.793**	1	
5.Complexity (C)	4.67	1.37	.457**	.380**	.487**	.510**	1

* $p < 0.05$, ** $p < 0.01$

the regression analysis explains the effect of the factors affecting the behavioural intention with regard to e-Filing operations.

The regression model is obtained using the OLS (ordinary least squares) estimators but since, all the variables were strongly correlated, we even conducted a diagnostic test on the multi-collinearity effect, and it was verified that the VIFs (Variance-inflating factors) for all the four independent variables (PU = 1.66, PEOU = 3.15, PR = 2.87 and C = 1.40) were within the acceptable range. Thus, the model shown below is free from multi-collinearity effect.

Table 3 shows that the Cronbach's Alpha value for behavior intention is *0.882*, perceived usefulness is *0.903*, perceived ease of use is *0.915.*, perceived readiness is *0.877*, and the value of complexity is *0.929*. All of the constructs obtain Cronbach's Alpha value is exceeding recommended value of 0.70. Therefore, this signifies the measures used to measure the constructs are relevant and these constructs can later be used for other types of analyses (correlations and regressions).

The mean, standard deviations and correlation are coefficients shown in Table 4 above. As for correlation analysis, behavioural intention is positively and significantly correlated with all other variables at 0.01, but however, the strongest correlation is found with perceived ease of use, ($r = 0.660$, $p < 0.01$). Though, even all independent variables are significantly correlated, however, highest correlation coefficient exists between perceived ease of use and perceived readiness ($r = 0.793$, $p < 0.01$).

Table 5 shows the regression model on the behavioural intention. It seemed that Perceived

Table 5. Regression results for predicting behavioural intention (BI)

	Behavioural Intention (BI) **Beta Adj R^2 F**
Constant	-0.003 60.6% 77.68*** (-0.010)
Perceived Usefulness (PU)	0.508*** (7.728)
Perceived Ease of Use (PEOU)	0.137 (1.613)
Perceived Readiness (PR)	0.277*** (3.581)
Complexity (C)	0.088* (1.685)

* $p < 0.1$, ** $p < 0.05$, *** $p < 0.01$
t-statistics are given in parentheses.

Usefulness (PU) and Perceived Readiness (PR) significantly affected behavioural intention at 0.01, meanwhile complexity was also found to correlate with behavioural intention but at 0.1. Thus, we came to know that perceived ease of did not have any impact on behavioural intention though it appeared to be significantly correlated with behavioural intention in the earlier discussion. Thus, hypothesis 1 and 3 are supported at 0.05, and hypothesis 2 and 4 are statistically not supported. Meanwhile, the model is significant at 0.01 (F-test = 2.456) and it seems 60.4 per cent of the variation in the dependent variable (behavioural intention) is explained by the model.

Overall, the findings revealed that in order to attract more users to use e-Filing systems, it is not enough to develop a useful system. Developing a useful system is hence about getting the technology ready for the public use. The real task is to attract more users to use the e-Filing system which touches the behavioural part of the users. This study indicates that the paramount reasons that correlate with the intention to use of the e-Filing systems are that perceived usefulness where the use of this system will be beneficial for users and perceived readiness reflects that users feel that they are somehow ready and have knowledge to use the e-Filing systems. Based on these findings, government of Malaysia can use these two factors, the PU and PR to formulate activities, strategies, campaign and policies to encourage the usage level of tax e-Filing systems. As suggested by TAM, TRI and DOI, these factors could improve positive psychological inclination towards embracing new technologies and belief that it be fruitful if being used whether it is for their personal or work use. Wang (2002) recommends government authorities to employ training and promotion approaches to develop people's beliefs of usefulness, ease of use and credibility, which in turn influence their behavioural intentional to adopt e-Filing system.

DISCUSSIONS & RECOMMENDATIONS

The advent of technological revolution has ushered in an era of convenience for the Malaysian tax payer. The tech savvy individuals having requisite knowledge of the provisions of Income tax can file their tax returns directly with the Income tax department through digitally signed returns online. The research reveals that generally the Malaysians agree on the benefits that can be derived from the online tax filling. However, there are many issues and challenges that need to be addressed by the implementing agencies in order to get more tax payers go online to file their income tax.

The design of an online tax filing system must address a number of specific challenges that do not usually apply in other online government service applications. Two that are paramount are a high level of security and the ability to handle large peaks in traffic and processing. Taxation is, by its nature, a complicated subject and most businesses as well as many self employed individuals and even PAYE employees use intermediaries, such as accountants, to complete and file their tax returns. An online system must inevitably reflect these complexities. At the same time, any such system has to be sufficiently clear and simple to use that an ordinary tax payer, who might not have a high degree of computer literacy, can complete and file their taxes without undue difficulty.

On the other hand, the implementation of the e-Filing system must be consistent with the other online government services. The relevant authorities should take necessary steps to reduce the problems faced by the online tax payers in the past few years of its implementation in order to satisfy their needs. Moreover, government should embark into heavy promotional activities to educate the public on the ease of use of the e-Filing system. The government should organize road shows throughout the country and educate the public on the importance and simplicity of the system. Both the individuals who submit their personal income tax and business owners should be the target group for this purpose. One of the initiatives would be the establishment of computer kiosks during January to May each year for the public to file their tax returns online with the assistance of the income tax officers.

The findings of this study impacts both research and practice. Research on e-Filing in Malaysia is still at an infant stage given that the system was only introduced few years ago. The model used in the study suggests that the constructs PU and PR are vital in addressing e-fling adoption issues in Malaysia. These constructs and model therein increases our understanding of e-Filing utilization and adoption in the context of Malaysia. This model can be used as a basis for future work. In terms of practice, this study can be used by the relevant government authorities to incorporate PU and PR issues in the context of larger scale systems implementation within the broad-based e-Government initiative in Malaysia. Specifically, the Inland Revenue department in Malaysia (Lembaga Hasil Dalam Negeri) should be aware that greater acceptance of e-Filing systems is influenced by citizens' perception about technology vis-à-vis is usefulness, and use. In addition the department must also conceptualize how e-Filing can be rolled out to rural areas in Malaysia where access to and awareness of technology and e-Filing is limited. In addition, vendors appointed by the government in improving the e-Filing system should ensure that all future enhancements to the system in terms of its functionality and use, is kept relatively simple (Schaupp et al. 2008) to ensure that citizens can readily accept and use the system (Bandura 1977, Barnes, and Vidgen, R. 2007).

LIMITATIONS & FUTURE DIRECTIONS

Several limitations must be addressed here. Firstly, the number of respondents is insufficient. This study only collected 200 questionnaires and in a specific location which is Klang Valley. This may not be sufficient to generalize the result to the overall behavioural intention of Malaysian tax payers. Nevertheless, this is a preliminary study which is aimed to role out the coverage to every e-Filing tax payers in the future studies with the cooperation of IRB. Secondly, the researchers understand that different working groups may have different perception. Thus, this study may not be generalized for all groups of workers and have different levels of involvement in ICT related services. Future research should segment the respondents into different working groups and different ICT knowledge level to extract more accurate scenario of e-Filing intentions and usages. Thirdly, application of DOI theory should not be limited to only one component rather should include all the important components under this theory.

CONCLUSION

TAM, TRI and DOI are the central models tested in this research and have been successfully integrated to predict and to understand the critical factors influencing the taxpayers' perception to accept or neglect the e-Filing systems. The critical factors included perceived usefulness, perceived ease of use, perceived readiness, and complexity were examined and statistically tested in regards to identification of the causal relationships with behavioural intention, divulged that the behavioural intention to use the e-Filing systems could be explained by perceived usefulness and perceived readiness. The Constructs PU and PR have produced important implications for the Malaysian government in successfully attracting the individual tax payers to effectively make use of the e-Filing systems. In conclusion, applying TAM, TRI and DOI to the e-Filing system studies could lead to an understanding of public acceptance to the system and shed some light on research of the G2C e-Government system in the future.

REFERENCES

Agarwal, R., & Prasad, J. (1999). Are individual differences germane to the acceptance of new information technologies? *Journal of Decision Science, 30*(2), 361–391. doi:10.1111/j.1540-5915.1999.tb01614.x

Bandura, A. (1977). Self-efficacy: Toward a unifying theory of behavioral change. *Japanese Psychological Review, 84*(2), 191–215. doi:10.1037/0033-295X.84.2.191

Barnes, S. J., & Vidgen, R. (2007). Evaluating the web site of the UK Inland Revenue. *International Journal of Electronic Government Research, edit3*(1), 19-37.

Carter, L., & Belanger, F. (2003). *The Influence of Perceived Characteristics of Innovating on e-Government Adoption.* Paper presented at the First International E-Services Workshop, September, 2003.

Carter, L., & Belanger, F. (2004). Citizen Adoption of E-Government Initiatives. In *The Proceedings of the 37th Hawaiian International Conference on Systems Sciences (HICSS 04').*

Carter, L., & Belanger, F. (2005). The Utilization of e-=Government Services: Citizen Trust, Innovation and Acceptance Factors. *Information Systems Journal, 15*, 15–25. doi:10.1111/j.1365-2575.2005.00183.x

Chang, M. Y., Ching, W. C., & Chao, K. H. (2007). *The impact of perceived readiness to citizen's acceptance of e-government services.* Unpublished master's thesis: National Kaohsiung First University of Science and Technology, Yenchao, Kaohsiung, Taiwan, Republic of China.

Compeau, D. R., & Higgins, C. A. (1995). Computer self-efficacy: Development of a measure and initial test. *Management Information Systems Quarterly, 19*(2), 89–211. doi:10.2307/249688

Connolloy, R., & Bannister, F. (2008). eTax & Service Quality: The Case of the Revenue Online Service. In Proceedings of World Academy of Science, Engineering and Technology (Vol. 28).

Dan, V. (2000, Aug 28). *Electronic government.* Retrieved on August 28, 2000, from http://www.computerworld.com/managementtopics/ebusiness/story/0,10801,48989,00.html

Davis, F. D. (1989). Perceived usefulness, perceived ease of use, and user acceptance of information technology. *Management Information Systems Quarterly, 13*(3), 319–339. doi:10.2307/249008

Delone, W. H., & McLean, E. R. (1992). Information systems success: The quest for the dependent variable. *Information Systems Research, 3*(1), 60–95. doi:10.1287/isre.3.1.60

Delone, W. H., & McLean, E. R. (2002). Information systems success revisited. In *Proceedings of the 35th Hawaii International Conference on System Sciences* (HICSS 02) (pp. 238-249).

Delone, W. H., & McLean, E. R. (2003). The DeLone and McLean Model of information systems success: A ten-year update. *Journal of Management Information Systems, 19*(4), 9–30.

Fletcher, P. D. (2002). *E-file: Electronic tax administration in the United States.* Projet CEFRIO TNouve aux Mode`les de Collaborationr, re'alise′ par Center for Technology in Government, Janvier 2002 1. Retrieved on June, 2004, from http://www.cefrio.qc.ca/./projets/Documents/NMC_ETA.pdf

Fu, J. R., Chao, W. P., & Farn, C. K. (2004). Determinants of taxpayers' adoption of electronic filing methods in Taiwan: An exploratory study. *Information & Management, 30*, 658–683.

Fu, J. R., Farn, C. K., & Chao, W. P. (2006). Acceptance of electronic tax filing: A study of taxpayer intentions. *Information & Management*, *43*, 109–126. doi:10.1016/j.im.2005.04.001

Hamid, H. (2007, May 10). New IRB chief on mission to improve tax compliance. *New Straits Times*. Retrieved September 26, 2008, from http://www.camtech.com.my/news_21.htm

Hung, S. Y., Chang, C. M., & Yu, T. J. (2006). Determinants of the user acceptance of the e-Government services: The case of online tax filing and payment system. *Government Information Quarterly*, *23*, 97–122. doi:10.1016/j.giq.2005.11.005

Hwang, C. S. (2000). A comparative study of tax-filing methods: Manual, Internet, and two-dimensional bar code. *Journal of Government Information*, *27*(2), 113–127. doi:10.1016/S1352-0237(00)00129-5

IRAS. (2007). *Annual report 2007/08*. Singapore.

IRB confident of collecting more than RM77 bln for assessment year 2007. (2008, September 3). *Bernama.com*. Retrieved September 26, 2008, from http://www.bernama.com/bernama/v5/newsbusiness.php?id=356860

Jasmine, A., & Zurina, M. N. (2008). *An Application of TAM Model: Public Perception on E-Filling*. Paper presented at the e-Asia Conference, November 2008, KLCC, Malaysia.

Lai, M. L., Sheikh Obid, S. N., & Meera, A. K. (2005). Tax practitioners and electronic filing system: An empirical analysis. *Electronic Journal of Tax Research*, *9*(1), 93-107. Retrieved 20, September 2008, from http://www.austlii.edu.au/au/journals/eJTR/2004/5.html

Lim, E. T. K., Wee, C. T., & Pan, S. L. (2007). E-Government implementation: Balancing collaboration and control in stakeholder management. *International Journal of Electronic Government Research*, *3*(2), 1–28.

Maniam, K. (2007). *Technology Innovations in Government Supply Chain Management Processes: A Case Study of e-Perolehan Initiative in Malaysia*. Paper presented at the 4th Asialics International Conference, Kuala Lumpur, Malaysia.

MIA. (2000). *Income Tax (Amendment Bill 2000)*. Malaysian Institute of Accountants (MIA), Circular No.20, November.

Parasuraman, A. (2000). Technology readiness index (tri): A multiple item scale to measure readiness to embrace new technologies. *Journal of Service Research*, *2*(4), 307–320. doi:10.1177/109467050024001

Rogers, E. (2003). *Diffusion of Innovation, Free press*. New York: Simon and Schuster.

Rogers, E. M. (1995). *Diffusion of Innovations* (4th ed.). New York: Free Press.

Sahu, G. P., & Gupta, M. P. (2007). User's acceptance of e-government: A study of Indian Central Excise. *International Journal of Electronic Government Research*, *3*(3), 1–21.

Schaupp, L. C., & Carter, L. (2008) The impact of trust, risk and optimism bias on E-file adoption. *Information Systems Frontiers*. Retrieved from http://www.springerlink.com/content/e5516xp043116327/?p=a9291f0187884793951d5ae39cad254c&pi=6

State Services Commission. (2006). *E-government: A vision for New Zealanders*. New Zealand. Retrieved on September 20, 2008, from http://www.e.govt.nz/about-egovt/vision.html

Taylor, S., & Todd, P. (1995). Assessing IT usage: The role of prior experience. *Management Information Systems Quarterly*, *19*(4), 561–571. doi:10.2307/249633

Venkatesh, V., Morris, M. G., & David, G. B. (2003). User acceptance of information technology: toward a unified view. *Journal of MIS Quarterly*, *27*(3), 425–478.

Wang, Y. S. (2002). The adoption of electronic tax filing system: an empirical study. *Government Information Quarterly*, *20*, 333–352. doi:10.1016/j.giq.2003.08.005

Wongtrakool, B. M. (1998). *Does paperless mean painless? Electronic tax return filing in the new millennium.* Retrieved September 25, 2008, from http://www.cyber.law.harvard.edu/is98/final_papers

Zeithaml, V. A. (2002). Service excellence in electronic channels. *Managing Service Quality Journal*, *12*(3), 135–139. doi:10.1108/09604520210429187

KEY TERMS AND DEFINITIONS

E-Government: use of ICT to improve the internal management of the government administration to offer more efficient and effective public services.

Ninth Malaysian Plan (2006-2010): Malaysian government's five year development plan which covers all aspects of socio-economic growth of the country.

E-Services: providing public the regular services such as payment of taxes and summons online

E-Filling: One of the e-Government Flagship initiative launched under the care of the Inland Revenue Board of Malaysia (IRB).

Related Theories- this study has attempted to analyse the behavioral intention of tax e-Filing users' perception by integrating constructs from Davis (1989)

Technology Acceptance Model (TAM): Rogers (1995) Diffusion of Innovations Theory (DOI) and Parasuraman (2000) Technology Readiness Index (TRI).

APPENDIX 1

Table 6.

Behavioral intention	Perceived Usefulness	Perceived ease of use	Perceived readiness	Complexity
I intend to use Internet facility for my income tax submission.	Using electronic tax filing systems enables me to finish income tax computation quickly.	Learning to use electronic tax filing systems would be easy for me.	I have basic knowledge and opportunities to use an electronic tax filing systems.	Electronic tax filing is difficult to learn compared to manual tax computation methods.
Tax submission method via internet is more convenient than submission by post or by hand	Using electronic tax filing systems can improve income tax computation more accurately. (calculation is computed by the system itself)	I find that electronic tax filing systems is easy to use.	There is no barrier for me to utilize electronic tax filing.	Electronic tax filing is difficult to utilize compared to manual tax computations methods.
I would like to recommend electronic tax filing systems to my relatives and friends	Using electronic tax filing systems can enhance income tax computation efficiency. E.g. save time and cost.	It is easy for me to input and modify data when I use electronic tax filing systems	I have access to the information and instructions that I need for using the electronic tax filing systems.	Electronic tax filing systems is difficult to set up compared to manual tax computations methods.
I will use other E-government service provide by government. E.g. check and pay traffic summons.	Using electronic tax filing systems makes the income tax computation easier.	The instructions provisions for utilizing an electronic tax filing systems are clear and understandable	I would be able to use electronic tax filing systems in irrespective of time and location.	Electronic tax filing takes a lot of efforts to learn.

Chapter 19
Factors Influencing Intention to Use e-Government Services Among Citizens in Malaysia

Ooh Kim Lean
Universiti Sains Malaysia, Malaysia

Suhaiza Zailani
Universiti Sains Malaysia, Malaysia

T. Ramayah
Universiti Sains Malaysia, Malaysia

Yudi Fernando
Universiti Sains Malaysia, Malaysia

ABSTRACT

With the liberalization and globalization, Internet has been used as a medium of transaction in almost all aspects of human living. This study is investigating the factors that influencing the intention to use e-government service among Malaysians. This study integrates constructs from the models of Technology Acceptance Model (TAM), Diffusion of Innovation (DOI) which been moderated by culture factor and trust model with five dimensions. Structured questionnaire was used to collect data from 195 respondents. The result of the analysis showed that trust, perceived usefulness, perceived ease of use, compatibility, perceived relative advantage and perceived image respectively has a direct positive significant relationship towards intention to use e-government service and perceived complexity has a significant negative relationship towards intention to use e-government service. While perceived strength of online privacy protection and perceived strength of data integrity have a positive impact on a citizen's trust to use e-government service. However, the uncertainty avoidance (moderating factor) used in the study has no significant effect on the relationship between the innovation factors (compatibility, complexity, relative advantage and image) and intention to use e-government service. Finally in comparing the explanatory power of the entire intention based model (TAM, DOI and Trust) with the studied model, it has been found that the DOI model has a better explanatory power.

DOI: 10.4018/978-1-61520-931-6.ch019

INTRODUCTION

As one of the strategies to achieve Vision 2020, Multimedia Super Corridor (MSC) has been introduced to accelerate Malaysia's entry into Information Age (Muhamad Rais & Nazariah, 2003). The services provided through the website are the Government's proactive way to help enhance the public delivery system. Electronic Government (e-Government) was initiated in Malaysia on 24 February 2004. The Vision of e-Government is to transform administrative process and service delivery through the use of IT and multimedia. E-Government is an initiative aimed at reinventing how the Government works and to improve the quality of interactions with citizens and businesses through improved connectivity, better access, furnishes high quality services and better processes and systems.

The Malaysian government has launched a website to collate all the services provided under one roof or portal rather than having separate website for respective services provided (http://www.msc.com.my/msc/flagships.asp). Under the e-government flagship, 7 pilot projects of E-Government Flagship Application are identified as Generic Office Environment (GOE), Electronic Procurement (EP), Human Resource Management Information System (HRMIS), Project Monitoring System (PMS), Electronic Services Delivery (E-Services), Electronic Labor Exchange (ELX), and E-Syariah (MDC,2004). The myGovernment Portal (www.gov.my) could be described as one-stop source of Malaysian government information and services for the citizens. The digital government plays an important role to provide public service a fast, easy and with integrity information at a click. For instance, E-Syariah portal plans to allow teleconferencing and mediation via the internet to upgrading the service level and will be able to bring down the current number of backlog cases at the Syariah court (The Star, 19 Apr 2007). Through the portal, public will be able to file suit or affidavits online, get mention date for a hearing and follow up on the status of their cases without having to step foot into the hallowed halls. Under the application of Electronic Labor Exchange (ELX) designed exclusively to Malaysians only, it provides free online services to help match potential employers with jobseekers. The website lists down 395 online services of ministries, departments and agencies and 3,300 Government forms can be downloaded for free.

The Malaysian Administrative Modernization and Management Planning Unit (MAMPU) is promoting the use of e-Government among the public. Among the online services provided under the website include zakat, loan and quit rent payments, application to update mailing address with the Employees Provident Fund, application to the Museum Department to extend the archaeological search license and to apply for foreign workers with the Immigration Department. There are also "Quick Links" direct to the Government machinery, directory, tenders, job vacancies, public complaints and even to get information on the weather. Information pertaining to taxation, health, education, legal and family such as pregnancy, adoption and even marriage issues, are just a click of the mouse away (The Star, 27 March 2007).

From a technological perspective, e-Government is the use of information and telecommunication (ICT) and multimedia technologies to improve the access to and delivery of government's services to benefit all citizens individually, businesses or organizations. E-Government is the application of ICT and multimedia technologies to transform the efficiency, effectiveness, transparency and accountability of informational and transactional exchanges between the government and the citizens. Generally, e-Government portal will be the one-stop gateway to administrative and commercial services.

With the e-Government portal, the citizens would undoubtedly benefit by able to access the various government's services at any time and any place conveniently. However, relatively little has been known about the adoption of e-Government among public citizens so far. If many citizens are not keen to adopting and using e-Government services, those large investments from governments could be simply wasted. Motivated by this important issue, this research intends to explore the key factors influencing the intension to use e-Government among the public citizens.

E-Government in Malaysia

As one of the strategies to achieve Vision 2020, Multimedia Super Corridor (MSC) has been introduced to accelerate Malaysia's entry into Information Age. The services provided through the website are the Government's proactive way to help enhance the public delivery system. Electronic Government (e-Government) was initiated in Malaysia on 24 February 2004. The Vision of e-Government is to transform administrative process and service delivery through the use of IT and multimedia. The Malaysian government has launched a website to collate all the services provided from one roof or portal rather than having separate website for respective services provided (http://www.msc.com.my/msc/flagships.asp). Under the e-government flagship, seven pilot projects of E-Government Flagship Application are identified as Generic Office Environment (GOE), Electronic Procurement (EP), Human Resource Management Information System (HRMIS), Project Monitoring System (PMS), Electronic Services Delivery (E-Services), Electronic Labor Exchange (ELX), and E-Syariah (MDC, 2004).

The myGovernment Portal (www.gov.my) could be described as one-stop source of Malaysian government information and services for the citizen and non-citizen. The illustration of portal is described in Figure 1. The digital government plays an important role to provide public service a fast, easy and with integrity information at a click. For instance, E-Syariah portal plans to allow teleconferencing and mediation via the Internet to upgrading the service level and will be able to bring down the current number of backlog cases at the Syariah court (The Star, 19 Apr 2007). Through the portal, public will be able to file suit or affidavits online, get mention date for a hearing and follow up on the status of their cases without having to step foot into the hallowed halls. Under the application of Electronic Labor Exchange (ELX) designed exclusively to Malaysians only, it provides free online services to help match potential employers with jobseekers. The website lists down 395 online services of ministries, departments and agencies and 3,300 Government forms can be downloaded for free.

Government E-Payment Adoption Ranking

The Economist Intelligence Unit conducted the Government E-Payment Adoption Ranking (GEAR), measures the extent to which 43 countries provide key government payment services on electronic platforms (Ranking result shown in Figure 2). The 31 indicators in this study were built into a dynamic scoring model (Indicators shown in Figure 3). Based on the research, Canada is the world's leading nation for government e-payments (with the highest score of 92.4 out of 100), edging the UK in second (92.1), Germany and the United States in third (90.1). The ranking followed by Sweden (89.6), Australia (88.0) and South Korea (86.8) round out the top seven. These countries' government combines well-developed information and communications infrastructures, technologically and financially sophisticated populations, and governments committed to electronic payments and to integrating the economy.

In Asian countries, Hong Kong was ranked in 9th (86.4), Singapore in 10th (85.6) and Taiwan in 11th (84.5). The governments of these countries have encouraged online services and electronic payments in recent years as part of their successful economic-development strategies. The report revealed that Malaysia was ranked in 24th (49.1),

Figure 1. Shows the mygovernment portal. This is a one-stop source of Malaysian government information and services for the citizen and non-citizen.

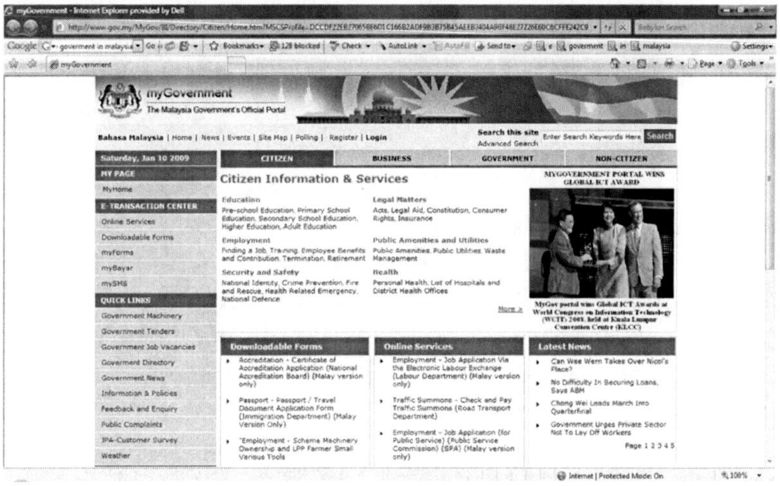

Figure 2. Ranks and scores in the government e-payment adoption ranking (GEAR)

Rank	Countries 1-22	Score	Rank	Countries 23-43	Score
1	Canada	92.4	23	Philippines	51.2
2	United Kingdom	92.1	**24**	**Malaysia**	**49.1**
3 tie	Germany	90.1	25	Mexico	48.2
3 tie	United States	90.1	26	Russia	45.5
5	Sweden	89.6	27	Poland	45.3
6	Australia	88.0	28	Argentina	44.7
7	Korea, Rep. of	86.8	29	Thailand	42.0
8	France	86.6	30	Kazakhstan	40.8
9	Hong Kong	86.3	31	United Arab Emirates	39.1
10	Singapore	85.6	32	Pakistan	38.4
11	Taiwan	84.5	33	India	34.6
12	Netherlands	81.6	34	Colombia	31.2
13	Spain	76.4	35	Morocco	28.3
14	Ireland	75.0	36	Costa Rica	28.2
15	Italy	74.2	37	Iran	23.8
16	Hungary	73.4	38	Saudi Arabia	20.9
17	Japan	66.4	39	Egypt	19.0
18	Turkey	61.6	40	Venezuela	18.7
19	China	61.1	41	Ukraine	14.6
20	Czech Republic	58.8	42	Nigeria	13.6
21	South Africa	53.8	43	Indonesia	12.8
22	Brazil	52.8			

Source: The Economist Intelligence United Limited, Oct 2007

showed that Malaysians are still low in utilizing e-services provided by government.

Based on the Government E-Payment Adoption Ranking (GEAR), Malaysia was ranked in 24th out of 43 countries in the world. This report indicated that more study need to be done to analyze factors influencing the intention to use e-government services among citizens in Malaysia. In addition, the government authorities also have to study their strategies in encouraging more citizens to use e-government services in future. This study is intention to use e-Government among citizens in Malaysia. This study can help the policy maker to know the information on factors that influence and affect citizens' intention to use e-Government services in Malaysia. Hence, it would value add in establishing better understanding and more practical security and control policies that would strengthen the government portal or websites that citizen concern the most. This would also help the government to identify which critical area that needs to be enhanced. Ultimately, the most critical outcome that we would expect out of this study is to increase the confidence of citizens to use e-Government in future.

The chapter is divided into five major sections. First, we give and highlight the problem with e-Government adoption, describe research objectives and methodology. Then, taxonomy of theories and models in technology acceptance are discussed. We analyze the adoptions of e-Government by testing the entire hypothesis. Finally, we draw some conclusions from the suggested approach and indicate future directions for further e-Government-related research.

LITERATURE REVIEW AND THEORETICAL FOUNDATION

Technology Acceptance Model (TAM) by Davis et al. (1989) and Diffusion of Innovation (DOI) by Rogers (1995) were deployed as fundamental framework in this study with the extension of trust element. To enhance the model, the culture factor of uncertainty avoidance has been placed in to see the moderating effect between each of the innovation factors and intention to use e-government services. The trust element was used in term of interpersonal trust in this study. TAM model focuses on perceived benefit. According to Horst and Kuttschreuter (2006), introducing a new technology may involve both benefits and risks to the end users and the individual may want to weigh the risks and benefits before deciding to use the technology. Electronic government services will not be an exception to this general rule too. Perceived risk can be defined as a combination of uncertainty and seriousness of outcome involved (Featherman & Pavlou, 2002). Individual users will base on their own perception on risk and benefits and not on the actual risk and benefits. The magnitude of the perceived risk is inversely related to perceived benefits. The more perception of risk will reduce the perceived benefits of the technology (Gefen et al., 2002).

The Development of Hypotheses

Generally, across discipline there is agreement that trust only exists in an uncertain and risky environment. Mayer et al. (1995) as cited in Sonja and Ewald (2003) explained that trust would not be needed if actions could be undertaken with complete certainty and no risk. One important reason for the importance of trust in e-government service is the fact that in a virtual environment the degree of uncertainty of online transactions is higher than in traditional setting. The decision to engage in e-government transaction requires users' trust in the state government agency providing the service and users' trust in the technology through which electronic transactions are executed via the internet (Lee & Turban, 2001). Higher degree of trustworthiness will lead to higher intention to use e-government services.

There are few basis online requirements of electronic commerce that should be fulfilled, in

Figure 3. The 31 indicators in the government e-payments adoption ranking

Indicator name	Indicator type
Consumer-to-government (C2G)	
1. Income tax payments	Score
2. Social security contributions	Score
3. Obtaining and paying for a new or replacement ID card or driver's license	Score
4. Automotive costs: Toll roads, bridges, zones, fines, tickets etc	Score
Government-to-consumer (G2C)	
1. Income tax refunds	Score
2. Social security benefits	Score
3. Unemployment, workers' comp and welfare benefits	Score
4. Government health benefits	Score
Business-to-government (B2G)	
1. Income tax payments	Score
2. Sales/VAT tax payments	Score
3. Social security and other contributions	Score
4. Company registration and payment of fees	Score
Government-to-business (G2B)	
1. Income tax refunds	Score
2. Sales/VAT tax refunds	Score
3. Payments for goods and services	Score
4. Disbursements of loans (such as SBA in the US)	Score
Infrastructure	
1. Number of ATMs per 10,000 people	Statistic
2. Number of POS terminals per 10,000 people	Statistic
3. Diffusion of broadband	Score
4. Diffusion of narrowband/dial-up	Score
5. Public-access terminals per capita	Score
6. Mobile phone usage per capita	Score
7. Level of development of stored value cards/phones	Score
8. Level of development of 3G and other technologies	Score
Educational, economic and political context	
1. Literacy levels	Statistic
2. Educational levels	Statistic
3. Internet/technology savvies	Score
4. Percentage of population using banks/other financial institutions	Score
5. Percentage of businesses using banks/other financial institutions	Score
6. Government commitment to electronic payments	Score
7. Government commitment to integrating the informal economy	Score

Source: The Economist Intelligence United Limited, Oct 2007

order to attract more citizens' willing to use the web site for transactions. They are authentication, integrity, confidentiality, non-repudiation, and privacy. Authentication allows a certain operation to be carried out only after identification, or if there are guarantees of the identity of the party one is dealing with (e.g. a web site). Non-repudiation refers to procedures that prevent an individual or organization from denying that they had carried out a certain operation. According to Bomil & Ingoo (2003), Non-repudiation means that neither of the trading parties should be able to deny having participated in a transaction after the fact. Pauline (1998) defined non-repudiation as a mechanism to ensure that if a party to some transaction or communication later denies that it has ever happened, some mechanism is in place to facilitate dispute resolution. Confidentiality involves the data being seen by authorized individuals. According to Pauline (1998), confidentiality has been defined as the act of warranting that data are only revealed to parties who have a legitimate need to know it or have access to it. Perception of Privacy Protection is defined as an individual's ability to control the terms by which his personal information is acquired and used (Westin, 1967; Galanxhi-Janaqi and Fui-Hoon Nah, 2004). When online services is concerned, privacy affects aspects such as the obtaining, distribution or the non-authorized use of personal information (Wang et al, 1998). According to Bomil & Ingoo (2003), privacy protection ensures that personal information about customers collected from their electronic transactions is protecting from disclosure without permission. Perception of Data Integrity of an information system refers to the impossibility of the transmitted or stored data being modified by third parties without permission. According to Bomil & Ingoo (2003), data integrity means that data in transmission are not created, intercepted, modified, or deleted illicitly.

In addition, web trust principles (business practices disclosure, transactions integrity, and information protection) were used to provide guidance for practitioners to use in testing and evaluating web sites (Pauline,1998). Bomil and Ingoo (2003) found that the impacts of perceived strength of non-repudiation, privacy protection, and data integrity on trust were significant. However, their research's results shown that there were no significant relationships between trust and perceived strength of authentication and confidentiality. Therefore, the following hypotheses were proposed:

H1: Perceived strength of authentication has a positive impact on a citizen's trust toward intention to use e-government services
H2: Perceived strength of non-repudiation has a positive impact on a citizen's trust toward intention to use e-government services
H3: Perceived strength of confidentiality has a positive impact on a citizen's trust toward intention to use e-government services
H4: Perceived strength of privacy protection has a positive impact on a citizen's trust toward intention to use e-government services
H5: Perceived strength of data integrity has a positive impact on a citizen's trust toward intention to use e-government services

Trust is the belief that the other party will behave as expected in a socially responsible manner and in doing so; it will fulfill the trusting party's expectation (Gefen 2000, Lewis and Weigert 1985, Luhmann 1979, Mayer et al. 1995). Trusting beliefs will relate positively to trusting intentions because a consumer with high trusting beliefs perceives the Internet vendor to have attributes that enable the consumer to hold a secure willingness to depend on vendor (McKnight et al., 2002). Trust should be preferred alternative, facilitating citizen choice to take advantage of the ability to file taxes online. Indeed, trust also a crucial enabler in online services (such as e-commerce), where consumers are exposed to far lesser degrees of dependence and risk, affecting

Figure 4. Research model

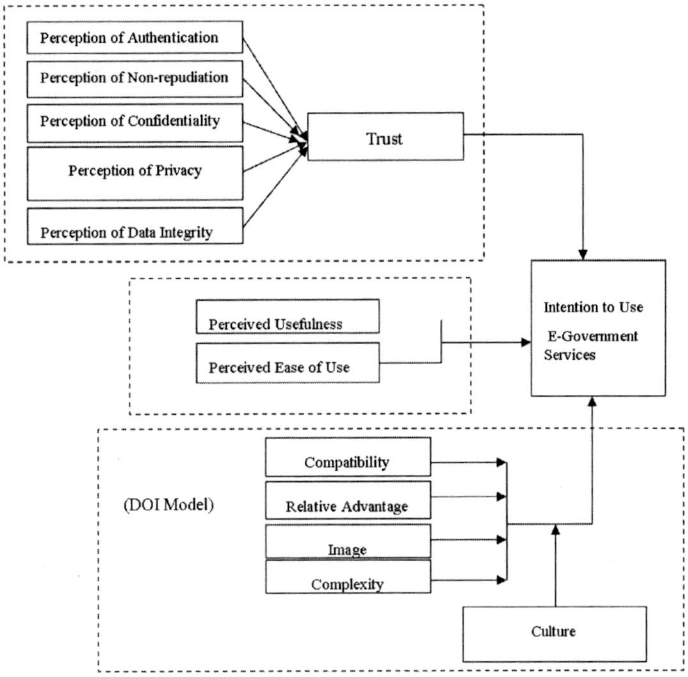

purchase intention, inquiry intentions and sharing personal information(Gefen 2000, Jarvenpaa and Tractinsky 1999, Pavlou 2001). Since trust is an important element of e-government, hypothesis as below was proposed:

H6: Higher levels of trust will be positively related to higher levels of intention to use e-government services

According to Davis (1989) Technology Acceptance Model (TAM) is widely used to study user acceptance of information technology. It suggests that perceived usefulness (PU) and perceived ease of use (PEOU) of IT are major determinants of its usage. PU was defined as the degree of which a person believes that using a particular system would enhance his or her job performance and PEOU was defined as the degree which a person believes that using a particular system would be free of effort. Carter and Belanger (2005) used TAM to evaluate e-government previously. Based on TAM, perceived usefulness (PU) and perceived ease of use (PEOU) influence an individual's behavioral intention to use a system. TAM is intended to be capable of explaining user behavior across a range of end-user computing technologies while being parsimonious and theoretical justified. Therefore, TAM is proposed to be integrated for this study of user acceptance of e-government website because it constitutes a class of IT projects.

H7: Higher levels of Perceived Usefulness will be positively related to higher levels of intention to use e-government services

H8: Higher levels of Perceived Ease of Use will be positively related to higher levels of intention to use e-government services

Another model frequently used to explain user adoption of new technologies is Rogers' (1995) DOI theory. Diffusion refers to "the process by which an innovation is communicated through certain channels over time among the members of a social society (Rogers, 1995)". Rogers (1995) defines compatibility as the degree to which an innovation is seen to be compatible with values, experiences, beliefs, and needs of adopters, relative advantage is defined as the degree to which an innovation is seen as being superior to its predecessor, image refers to one's perceptions of innovation as a status of symbol and complexity is the degree to which an innovation is seen by the potential adopter as being relatively difficult to use and understand. The e-government adoption model includes the four constructs from the DOI stream, namely compatibility, relative advantage, image and complexity. The following hypotheses were proposed:

H9: Higher levels of perceived compatibility will be positively related to higher levels of intention to use e-government services
H10: Higher levels of perceived relative advantage will be positively related to higher levels of intention to use e-government services
H11: Higher levels of perceived image will be positively related to higher levels of intention to use e-government services
H12: Higher levels of perceived complexity will be negatively related to higher levels of intention to use e-government services

The cultural difference, uncertainty avoidance is examined in the proposed e-government adoption model as a key moderator. Uncertainty avoidance represents the extent to which a society's members wish to avoid uncertain and ambiguous situations (Hofstede, 1980, 2001). Cultures high on uncertainty avoidance prefer structured situations (Singh, 1990) and view human behavior as predictable (Kale and McIntyre, 1991). Cultures low on uncertainty avoidance are relatively comfortable with situation lacking in structure and see human behavior as unpredictable (Gundykunst, 1997). Thus, low uncertainty avoidance cultures would have members who tend to take for granted the existence of facilitating conditions for online transactions. Hence, the following hypotheses were proposed:

H13: The relationship between perceived compatibility and intention to use e-government services is weaker among Malaysians characterized by high uncertainty avoidance.
H14: The relationship between perceived relative advantage and intention to use e-government services is weaker among Malaysians characterized by high uncertainty avoidance.
H15: The relationship between perceived image and intention to use e-government services is weaker among Malaysians characterized by high uncertainty avoidance.
H16: The relationship between perceived complexity and intention to use e-government services is weaker among Malaysians characterized by high uncertainty avoidance.

METHODOLOGY

Population, Sample Size and Sample Technique

The population of this research is Malaysia citizen who work in northern region of Malaysia. Specifically, the population of this study is individual across any industries and hierarhy in the organization with or without experience of using e-governmnet service. Sampling is a process of selecting a sufficient number of elements from the population. By selecting the right sample, it would be possible to generalize the characteristics of the elements to the population elements (Sekaran, 2003). The non-probability convenience sampling design was undertaken because it was a viable alternative and due to constraint of time, cost and manpower in conducting the present study. Based on Hair et al. (1998), the acceptable ratio would be ten-to-one ratio of independent variables. Thus, the minimum number of respondents should be 130 respondents. A total of 195 pieces of questionnaire papers are given out to the community randomly. However those questionnaires that not fill in properly and completely have been taken out. Hence, the actual sample used for the study are 150 respondents.

Questionnaire Design

The questionnaire consists of questions to identify possible factors that may effect the acceptance of e-Government. The questions consist of (6) sections and (5) sections from it are related to the construct / theoretical framework of the study. Section B consists of (23) items measuring five types of antecedents of trust, 6 items of trust; Section C consists of (9) items for TAM model; Section D consists of (5) items for uncertainty avoidance (moderator); Section E consists of 16 items for DOI models and Section F consists of (5) items for dependent variable. The mentioned total 64 items were taken from previous study, which were developed by Bomil and Ignoo (2003) and Carter & Belanger (2005). All the items were modified for this study according to the domain of the study. There were also another (10) questions placed in section A in the questionnaire to collect respondents' profile, such as age, gender, race, highest academic qualification, total years of working experience, occupation, total years of Internet usage, awareness on e-government website, experience of using e-government and total years of e-government usage. The measurement scale that has been deployed in the questionnaire is a five points Likert type scale, which ranges from (1) strongly disagree to (5) strongly agree. All instruments were adapted from various literatures and were modified for the adaptation to the e-Government context.

ANALYSIS AND RESULTS

A total of 195 questionnaires were distributed to Internet users personally and via email by using convenience-sampling technique. Out of the 195 the questionnaires distributed to colleagues, course mates, friends and neighbors, 172 questionnaires were received, however, only 150 questionnaires were usable for the purpose of this study. Hence, the response rate was 77%. From gender perspective, there is no big difference in term of number of male and female responding to the survey. Majority of the respondents were between 30 to 39 years old, which was 46% of the total respondents. In terms of racial distribution of the respondents, 54.7% of the respondents were Chinese, followed by 30% Malay, 14.7% Indian and other races representation of 0.70%. Majority of the respondents were well educated, which total 47.3% of the respondents were university graduates and 17.3% were post-graduate. More than 50% of the respondents originated from middle and upper corporate levels, the distribution were 30% for managers and 20.7% for senior executives. Majority of the respondents have been working more than 5 years, which contributed 61.3% to the total respondents. Nearly 30% of the total respondents had less than five years of working experiences but more than a year of working experiences.

Technology Usage

Among the respondents, there were two big group of users had total years of Internet usage 1 to 5 years and between six to ten years respectively, and they were nearly equally distributed by 38.00% and 40.00% respectively. 18.70% of the total respondents had more than 10 years of Internet usage, and respondents whom had less than one year of Internet usage only contributed 3.30% of the total respondents.

Goodness of Measures

To assess the goodness of measures, a within factor, factor analysis was carried out whereas to assess reliability we used the inter-item consistency measure of Cronbach's Alpha. The results are shown in Figures 6-9. All items exhibited sufficiently strong factor loadings and reliability values confirming the validity and reliability of the measures used in this study.

Hypotheses Testing

Basically, there were three different tests have been used to validate all the hypotheses, namely simple regression, multiple regression and hierarchical regression.

Trust and its Antecedents

Trust was entered as dependent variable, and perceived strength of online authentication, perceived strength of non-repudiation, perceived strength of confidentiality, perceived strength of privacy protection and perceived strength of data integrity were entered as independent variables. The regression output is presented in Figure 10. The three independent variables together explained 67% of the variance in trust, which was highly significant as indicated by the F-value. An examination of the t-values indicated that only perceived strength of privacy protection was significantly related to trust (Beta = 0.231, $p < 0.01$) and perceived strength of data integrity was significantly related to trust (Beta = 0.534, $p<0.01$). The other three were not significant as such H4 and H5 were supported whereas H1, H2 and H3 were not supported.

Trust and Intention to Use E-Government Services

The first simple regression was carried out to examine the relationship between independent variables (trust and intention to use e-government website). The independent variable explained 21% of the variance in intention to use e-government services, which was highly significant as indicated by the F-value. An examination of the t-values indicated that trust was significantly related to intention to use e-government services, and the relationship type was positive at Beta = .46, $p < 0.01$ giving support for H6.

Perceived Ease of Use and Usefulness and Intention to Use E-Government Services

The second simple regression was carried out to examine the relationship between independent variables (perceived usefulness and intention to use e-government website). The independent variable explained 47.3% of the variance in intention to use e-government services, which was highly significant as indicated by the F-value. An examination of the t-values indicated that perceived usefulness (Beta = 0.218, $p<0.01$) and perceived ease of use (Beta = 0.523, $p<0.01$) was significantly related to intention to use e-government services giving support for H7 and H8 of this study.

Diffusion of Innovation (DOI) Variables and Intention to Use E-Government Services

This hierarchical regression test was carried out to evaluate the relationship between three independent variables from Diffusion of Innovation model namely complexity, relative advantage, image and complexity which were moderated by uncertainty avoidance toward intention to use e-government services. The results are presented in Figure 13.

The result indicated that the three independent variables namely compatibility (Beta = 0.224, $p<0.01$), relative advantage (Beta = 0.253, $p<0.01$) and image (Beta = 0.381, $p<0.01$) were positively related to intention to use e-government services while complexity (Beta = 0.214, $p<0.01$) was negatively related to intention to use. This finding gives support for H9, H10, H11 and H12 of the study.

The third model where the interaction terms between uncertainty avoidance (moderator) with the four independent variables were entered showed that the change was not significant as such we can conclude that there was no moderation effect. Thus H13, H14, H15 and H16 are not supported.

DISCUSSION

Next the findings will be discussed from the antecedents to trust, followed by trust, perceived ease of use and usefulness, and the DOI variables and concluded by the moderating effect.

Antecedents of Trust

In the present study, four antecedents variables to trust was investigated, only Perceived Strength of Online Privacy and Perceived Strength of Data Integrity were proven to have a significant positive relationship with trust. In other words, when citizens perceived strength of online Privacy and Data Integrity to be high, the level of trust would also increase. Hence, we can conclude that this result supports the earlier finding by Kelly and Erickson (2004, 2005) where new technologies' growing capacity for information processing, plus its complexity, have made privacy an increasingly important issue. Udo (2001), also points out that the protection of privacy is the greatest concern of internet purchasers.

This may suggest that the citizens are very sensitive to prevent e-government from denying that they had carried out a certain operation or transaction, the accuracy of the transactions that has been committed and honesty of the e-government in virtual space. The citizens would feel less risky if these factors were greatly emphasized throughout the whole e-services or transaction cycle. In addition, most of the citizens that use online services are aware of the threats that might occur when their personal information was leaked out to third parties for any type of purposes. They may think that the impacts of this type of violation are extremely great as it has indirect negative impacts to the personal financial losses. As a result, greater privacy protection would increase citizens' belief and confidence in adoption of e-government.

In addition, perceived strength of authentication was found to have no significant relationship with trust. This is again consistent with the result from Bomil and Ignoo (2003). This finding may imply that this factor was not a hindrance for citizens using e-government service. As long as there is some authentication mechanism in place, they would assume that the other parties have no way to access to their information and to be granted the transactions.

Trust

In this study, trust is an assessment of customers on the trustworthiness of government from online perspective. Moreover, due to the physical setting of the actual e-government was normally remotely from the users, and the users may not fully understand the actual implementation of the e-services provided by government. Therefore, the assessment of trustworthiness was based on perception of each of the individual, whom has performed e-government transactions over the Internet.

Last but not least, government can enact institutional guarantees, improve their social characteristics and make the public knowledgeable about e-government services and encourage citizen to use the e-services through social campaigns. This may increase the level of trust among the citizens to interact with e-government services. Hence, the greater level of positive feeling in customers to inquire and perform transaction via e-government website.

Figure 5. Respondents' technology usage and e-government website usage

Usage / Awareness	Frequency	Percentage	
Total years of Internet usage	< 1 year	5	3.30
	1 - 5 years	57	38.00
	6 - 10 years	60	40.00
	> 10 years	28	18.70
Awareness of E-Government website	Yes	104	69.30
	No	46	30.70
Used the E-Government before	Yes	80	53.30
	No	70	46.70
	Total	150	100
Total years of using E-Government website	< 1 year	90	60.00
	1 - 2 years	43	28.70
	3 - 4 years	8	5.30
	> 4 years	9	6.00
	Total	150	100

Perceived Usefulness and Perceived Ease of Use

Perceived usefulness direct positive relationship towards intention is also in line with the TAM studies conducted by Davis et. al (1989), Mathieson (1991), Taylor and Todd (1995), Venkatesh and Davis (2000), Chau and Hu (2001), Ramayah and Suki (2005), Ramayah and Ignatius (2005), Ramayah and Jantan (2003), Ramayah et al. (2005), May (2005) and Guriting and Ndubisi (2006). Citizen's intentions to use e-government services such as electronic tax-filing will increase if they perceive the e-service to be useful. Tax submission is an activity that majority citizens should participate after exceed certain salary levels. The finding suggested that it is important for the agency to incorporate usefulness and valuable functions into the e-filing system. Taxpayers possibly would accept to use the e-filing if the usefulness of e-filing is consistent and convenience than the existing manual form filing method.

The implementation of online government services may not work equally well for every state in Malaysia and every levels of citizens. However, it could be start in communities that have strong sense of community, or advisable to seek individuals who are more open to adoption first which include high power distance segments, technology savvy users or risk takers. Then each success story could be shared among others by "word of mouth" communication.

Diffusion of Innovation Variables (Compatibility, Complexity, Relative Advantage and Image)

Based on the analysis, all the four variables, compatibility, complexity, perceived relative advantage and perceived image were significant

Figure 6.

Perception of Non-repudiation	0.87	66.19		3.53	0.662
The myGovernment portal (www.gov.my) will not deny having participated in a transaction after processing it			.726	3.55	.700
The myGovernment portal (www.gov.my) will not deny having sent me a message			.768	3.48	.809
The myGovernment portal (www.gov.my) will not deny having received a transaction from me			.843	3.46	.800
The myGovernment portal (www.gov.my) will provide me with some evidence to protect against its denial of having sent a message			.877	3.61	.858
The myGovernment portal (www.gov.my) will provide me with some evidence to protect against its denial of having received a transaction from me.			.845	3.56	.894
Perception of Confidentiality	0.85	69.88		3.83	0.710
All the communication with myGovernment portal are strictly to the site and me			.760	3.69	.725
I am convinced that myGovernment portal respects the confidentiality of the transactions received from me.			.850	3.79	.973
MyGovernment portal uses some security controls for the confidentiality of the transactions.			.863	4.05	.763
MyGovernment portal checks all communications between the site and me for the protection from wiretapping or eves dropping			.866	3.81	.953
Perception of Privacy Protection	0.82	59.08		3.58	0.661
MyGovernment portal will not use my personal information for any purpose unless I authorize it to do so.			.824	3.65	.935
MyGovernment portal would never sell my personal information in their computer databases to other companies.			.769	3.65	.743
MyGovernment portal would devote time and effort to preventing unauthorized access to my personal information.			.722	3.54	.738
Databases that contains my personal information would be protected from unauthorized access.			.771	3.69	.948
MyGovernment portal will really remove my personal information when I request it to do so.			.754	3.37	.924

in explaining intention to use of e-government. Compatibility, perceived relative advantage and perceived image have direct positive relationship with intention to use; whereas perceived complexity has negative relationship toward intention to use e-government.

The negative relationship between perceived complexity and intention to use e-government can be explained as the more unfriendliness or inaccessibility of e-services provided by the government, the lower of intention to use e-government service. Citizens' willingness to use e-government service will be affected if the online system was perceived to be too complicated and difficult to understand and take too much time in entering the data or input.

The positive relationship between perceived relative advantage and intention to use e-government mainly because they perceived the online system would enhance their efficiency in gathering information and interact with government. The relative benefits perceived by the citizens is by using the e-government portal, they would eliminate the need to visit the service provider personally. In short, it may include greater convenience and accessibility, reduced waiting time and faster response.

The positive relationship between perceived image and intention to use e-government can be explained that the users who have concern over their personal image have higher intention to use e-government service. An individual may believe that the online system is useful because the system will enhance their image and social status. Hence, to preserve a positive image within a social group, individuals often respond to social influences such as to be internet savvy.

Figure 7. Factor and reliability analysis results

	Cronbach Alpha	Variance Explained (%)	Factor Loadings	Mean	Standard Deviation
Perceived Usefulness	0.78	60.95		3.84	0.590
The E-government would enable me to complete transactions with E-government more quickly.			0.782	4.07	0.766
I think the E-government would provide a valuable service for me.			0.737	3.70	0.849
The E-government would enhance my effectiveness in searching for and using E-government services.			0.701	3.75	0.685
I would find the E-government useful.			0.890	3.84	0.733
Perceived Ease of Use	0.75	56.96		3.59	0.554
Learning to interact with the E-government would be easy for me.			0.688	3.65	0.634
I believe interacting with the E-government would be clear and understandable process.			0.768	3.59	0.696
I would find the E-government to be flexible to interact with.			0.831	3.35	0.852
It would be easy for me to become skillful at using the E-government.			0.724	3.75	0.744
Perception of Authentication	0.80	62.49		3.66	0.527
The transactions I send would be transmitted to my online website			.807	3.66	.674
The messages I receive would be transmitted from my online website.			.802	3.75	.604
The myGovernment portal (www.gov.my) ascertains my identity before sending any messages to me.			.822	3.55	.719
The myGovernment portal (www.gov.my) ascertains my identity before processing the transaction received from me.			.727	3.64	.671

Uncertainty Avoidance (Moderating Effect)

Unexpectedly, the finding revealed no moderating influence for uncertainty avoidance with respect to the connection between DOI's factors and intention to use e-government service. This could perhaps be explained by the age group of the respondents in this study was majority (78%) below 40 years old. Age disparity could offer a potential understanding for the lack of cultural effect on this relationship.

Implication of the Study

Government should seriously look into every opportunity that would create more trust in e-government services among citizens, as it would directly translated to higher volume of transactions over the Internet. The increased volume of e-government transactions would bring much benefit to government in several perspectives, such as operational excellence, cost and time saving; hence increasing the effectiveness, efficiency and quality of public services. According to European Commission (2006), policy maker may oblige government agencies to conduct Privacy Impact Assessments (PIAs) for new electronic information systems and information collections that involve the use of personally identifiable information. Moreover, government agencies should also ensure appropriate privacy practices are implemented and the public is well informed of their nature.

At the end of this study, several key conclusions had been made and they are very important for government to extend their knowledge based on citizens needs. Understanding adoption factors would able to lead the policy maker and government to formulate and execute better strategies in their e-government portal and website.

Figure 8.

Perception of Data Integrity	0.87	66.47		3.49	0.681
MyGovernment portal would check the information communicated with me for accuracy.			.726	3.32	.789
MyGovernment portal would take steps to make sure that the information in transit is accurate.			.810	3.71	.754
MyGovernment portal would take step to make sure that the information in transit is not deleted.			.791	3.53	.766
My Government portal would devote time and effort to verify the accuracy of the information in transit.			.872	3.43	.908
MyGovernment portal would devote time and effort to verify that the information in transit is not deleted.			.869	3.47	.946
Trust	0.84	62.65		3.40	0.547
E-government services is trustworthy.			.872	3.50	.721
I trust in the benefits of the decisions of e-government services.			.709	3.63	.727
E-Government services would keep its promises and commitments			.812	3.55	.807
E-Government services would keep customers' best interests in mind			.844	3.65	.845
I trust myGovernment portal.			.704	3.50	.976
Compatibility	0.75	66.90		3.91	0.632
I think using the web would fit well the way that I like to gather information from the E-government.			.827	4.09	.819
I think using the web would fit well with the way that I like to interact with the E-government.			.827	3.87	.805
Using the web to interact with the E-government would fit into my lifestyle.			.800	3.76	.692
Relative Advantage	0.75	68.51			
Using the web would enhance my efficiency in gathering information from the E-government.			.871	4.00	.705
Using the web would enhance my efficiency in interacting with E-government.			.879	3.97	.755
Using the web would make it easier to interact with E-government			.724	3.63	.938

The trust model was validated applicable in local environment of the study. They have become valid fundamental model to predict the intention to use e-government services. To re-cap, the trust factor was also triggered by the antecedents namely perceived of privacy and perceived of non-repudiation. In short, it is very important to formulate and implement correct strategy to increase the positive level of citizens' trust among Malaysia citizens toward using e-government services.

Government should seriously look into every opportunity that would create more trust in e-government services among citizens, as it would directly translated to higher volume of transactions over the Internet. The increased volume of e-government transactions would bring much benefit to government in several perspectives, such as operational excellence, cost and time saving; hence increasing the effectiveness, efficiency and quality of public services.

An attractive e-government portal or website starts with good contents. There are many ways in which government agencies can increase perceived usefulness. One is through their website: the information in the website has to be accurate, timely, informative, updated and relevant to citizens' needs. A good site not only contains sufficient information but also designed to be user friendly for all level of users. The website should have a search and help features to enable users to quickly and effortlessly find relevant information, provide for two way communications between users and the site; and also respond quickly to users' search and browsing needs. State government should also elicit and analyze citizens' feedback about their

Figure 9.

Image	0.66	59.98		3.35	0.626
People who use the web to gather information from the E-government have a high profile.			.688	3.42	.780
People who use E-government services on the web have a high profile.			.856	3.38	.766
People who use the web to gather information from the E-government have more prestige than those who do not.			.770	3.24	.887
Complextiy	0.89	75.08		2.99	0.803
Using the E-government services would take too much time from my normal duties.			.853	3.09	.976
Working with the online system would be so complicated; it would be difficult to understand what is going on.			.890	2.88	.969
Using the E-government would involve too much time doing mechanical operations (Eg: Data input)			.866	3.10	.865
It would take too long to learn how to use the E-government service to make it worth the effort.			.857	2.88	.897
Uncertainty Avoidance				4.09	0.432
It is important to have instructions spelled out in detail so that I always know what I'm expected to do			0.711	4.00	.676
It is important to closely follow instructions and procedures.			0.644	4.00	.624
Rules and regulations are important because they inform me of what is expected of me			0.608	4.17	.484
Standardized work procedures are helpful			0.770	4.11	.640
Instructions for operations are important			0.800	4.15	.612
Use Intentions	0.66	50.94		3.91	0.480
I would use the web for gathering information from E-government.			.753	3.97	.601
I would use E-government services provided over the web.			.781	3.99	.675
Interacting with the E-government over the web is something that I would do.			.527	3.67	.755
I would use the web to inquire about E-government services.			.763	4.03	.685

*One item each from the Trust, perceived usefulness, compatibility, relative advantage, image and usage were dropped due to low loadings.

site. These valuable feedbacks will enable government to redesign sites to present information and services in a way that is easy for citizens to utilize, enhance their efficiency in gathering information as well as interacting with e-government.

Government authorities can decrease perceived complexity by making the adoption of online services as seamless and as natural as possible. E-service should resemble traditional government services to encourage citizen acceptance. For instance, for online tax filing, the agency should present a form that resembles the more familiar paper-based tax form.

The adoption of e-government services processes is a critical component in the creation of an efficient and responsive New Public Management (Warkentin, Gefen, Pavlou and Rose, 2002). Due to the nature of government services over Internet was in virtual form, rather than the physical interaction in physical premises, the government portal or website should incorporate some online capabilities to ensure the users that each and every transactions committed over Internet is valid and undeniable. The capabilities could be transaction id generated for every transactions committed as prove and reference of transactions.

For perceived relative advantage to use e-government service, e-government website should always provide log or history of the transactions that had been committed, so that citizens could save and retrieve it anytime from their computer or print them out for tracking or filing.

To increase perceptions of trustworthiness, government agencies can reassure citizens of the

Figure 10. Regression results on antecedents of trust to trust

Variables	Std. Beta	t-value
Perceived Strength of Authentication	0.014	0.246
Perceived Strength of Online Non-repudiation	-0.006	-0.090
Perceived Strength of Confidentiality	0.129	1.650
Perceived Strength of Privacy Protection	0.231	2.903**
Perceived Strength of Data Integrity	0.534	5.721**
R Square	0.67	
Adjusted R Square	0.66	
F Value	58.495	

Note: **p<0.01, *p<0.05

Figure 11. Regression results of trust and intention to use

Variables	Std. Beta	t-value
Trust	0.46**	6.243**
R Square	0.21	
Adjusted R Square	0.20	
F Value	38.977	

Note:**p<0.01, *p<0.05

reliability of e-services by including easily visible privacy statement on their sites. If citizens have positive experience with e-government services, they will be more likely to use the service again and probably share this positive experience with others, thereby encouraging adoption of e-government service. However, negative experiences such as erroneous information or technical error will bring reverse effect to discourage adoption by the citizen.

Limitations and Suggestions for Future Research

In this study, only a small size of sample has been collected. The total number of usable sample in this study was 150 out of 195 questionnaires that had been distributed. Majority of the respondents were between 30 to 39 years old, which was nearly half of the total respondents. More than 60% of the total respondents were university graduates and post-graduates. Furthermore, majority of the respondents (78%) were at executive position and above. These constraints might lead to difficulties to generalize the findings of this study to all level of citizens in Malaysia. Another fact is that, this study is only confined to the Northern region especially Penang state. Hence, the sample of this study may not be a true representation of the behavioral intention of the entire Malaysia population towards using e-government service. Another limitation of this study is that we did not look at the different type of e-services (fully executable online and informative only) which may also may also have an impact on people's intention to use it. Future study is suggested to expand the scope of research to whole Malaysia, in order to better understand the role of trust, perceived usefulness,

Figure 12. Regression results of perceived ease of use and usefulness on intention to use

Variables	Std. Beta	t-value
Perceived Usefulness	0.218	2.693**
Perceived Ease of Use	0.523	6.467**
R Square	0.473	
Adjusted R Square	0.466	
F Value	65.543	

Note: **p<0.01, *p<0.05

Figure 13. Hierarchical regression results

Variable	Model 1	Model 2	Model 3
	Std. Beta	Std. Beta	Std. Beta
Model Variables			
Compatibility	0.224*	0.223**	-0.452
Relative Advantage	0.253**	0.262**	-0.762
Image	0.381**	0.367**	-0.421
Complexity	-0.214**	-0.213**	-0.479
Moderator			
Culture		-0.069	-1.592**
Interaction Terms			
Compatibility * Culture			0.739
Relative Advantage * Culture			1.243
Image * Culture			0.864
Complexity * Culture			0.302
R Square	0.473	0.478	0.513
Adjusted R Square	0.459	0.460	0.482
R Square Change	0.473	0.005	0.035
F Change	32.346**	1.259	2.534

Note: **p<0.01, *p<0.05

diffusion of innovation and uncertainty avoidance (culture effect) in e-government adoption in Malaysia as a whole.

CONCLUSION

This study could provide some valuable references to Malaysia government, and also hope that they could get some benefits out of this study by putting these three models namely trust model, TAM model (perceived usefulness) and Diffusion of Innovation (DOI) model into practices. Also, take into consideration the interaction effects of other cultural dimensions, providing a deeper and richer understanding of e-government in the global setting by conducting studies in multiple countries with different cultural variation across Hofstede's dimensions.

REFERENCES

Ajzen, I. (1991). The Theory of Planned Behaviour. *Organizational Behavior and Human Decision Processes*, *50*, 179–211. doi:10.1016/0749-5978(91)90020-T

Ajzen, I. (2002). Perceived Behavioral Control, Self-Efficacy, Locus of Control and the Theory of Planned Behavior. *Journal of Applied Social Psychology*, *32*, 1–20. doi:10.1111/j.1559-1816.2002.tb00236.x

Ajzen, I., & Fishbein, M. (2005). The influence of attitudes on behavior. In Albarracín, D., Johnson, B. T., & Zanna, M. P. (Eds.), *The handbook of attitudes* (pp. 173–221). Mahwah, NJ: Erlbaum.

Bandura, A. (1986). *Social Foundations of Thought and Action: A social Cognitive Theory*. Englewood Cliffs, NJ: Prentice Hall.

Bandura, A. (1991). Social cognitive theory of self-regulation. *Organizational Behavior and Human Decision Processes*, *50*, 248–287. doi:10.1016/0749-5978(91)90022-L

Belanger, F., Hiller, J., & Smith, W. (2002). Trustworthiness in electronic commerce: The role of privacy, security, and site attributes. *The Journal of Strategic Information Systems*, *11*, 245–270. doi:10.1016/S0963-8687(02)00018-5

Bomil, S., & Ingoo, H. (2003). The impact of customer trust and perception of security control on the acceptance of electronic commerce. *International Journal of Electronic Commerce*, *7*(3), 135–161.

Breaking Barriers to eGovernment: Solution for eGovernment. (n.d.). EGovernment Unit, DG, Information Society, European Commission. Retrieved from http://www.egovbarriers.org

Carrigan, R., Milton, R., & Morrow, D. (2005). *More Efficient E-Government Services for Citizens*. Computer World Honors Case Study.

Carter, L., & Belanger, F. (2004). The influence of perceived characteristics of innovating on e-government adoption. *Electronic. Journal of E-Government*, *2*(1).

Carter, L., & Belanger, F. (2005). The utilization of e-government services: citizen trust, innovation and acceptance factors. *Information Systems Journal*, *15*(1), 5–25. doi:10.1111/j.1365-2575.2005.00183.x

Chai, L., & Pavlou, P. A. (2002). Customer relationship management.com. In *Proceedings of the 2002 Americans Conference in Information System*, Dallas, Texas (pp. 9-11).

Chai, L., & Pavlou, P. A. (2004). From ancient to modern: a cross cultural investigation of electronic commerce adoption in Greece and the United States. *The Journal of Enterprise Information Management*, *17*(6), 416–423. doi:10.1108/17410390410566706

Chau, P. Y. K., & Hu, P. J. H. (2001). Information technology acceptance by individual professionals: A model comparison approach. *Decision Sciences*, *32*(4), 699–719. doi:10.1111/j.1540-5915.2001.tb00978.x

Chen, K., Yen, D. C., & Huang, A. H. (2004). Media Selection To Meet Communication Context: Comparing E-Mail and Instant Messaging in an Undergraduate Population. *Communications of the Association for Information Systems*, *14*, 387–405.

Cohen, S., & Eimicke, W. (2002). The use of the Internet in government service delivery. In Abramson, M. A., & Means, G. E. (Eds.), *E-Government 2001* (pp. 9–43). Lanham, MD: Rowman & Littlefield Publishing, Inc.

Davidsson, B., & Patel, R. (2003). Forskningsmetodikens grunder. Lund, Sverige: Studentlitteratur.

Davis, F. D. (1989). Perceived usefulness, perceived ease of use, and user acceptance of information technology. *Management Information Systems Quarterly*, (September): 318–340.

Davis, F. D., Bagozzi, R. P., & Warshaw, P. R. (1989). User Acceptance of Computer Technology: A Comparison of Two Theoretical Models. *Management Science*, *35*(8), 982–1002. doi:10.1287/mnsc.35.8.982

Douglas, M. (2002 May). A tight net against terror. *Government Technology*, 46-48.

Ebrahim, Z., Irani, Z., & Al Shawi, S. (2004). Factors influencing the adoption of e-government in public sector. *European & Mediterranean Conference on Information System*, 25-27 July 2004.

Egidius, H. (1986). Positivism-fenomenologihermeneutik. Lund, Sverige: Studentlitteratur.

Evangelidis, A. Akomode. J., Taleb-Bendiab, A., & Taylor, M. (2002). Risk assessment & success factors for e-government in a UK Establishment. In R. Traunmueller & K. Kenk (Eds.), EGOV 2002 (LNCS 2456, pp. 395-402).

Evanschitzky, H., & Wunderlich, M. (2006). An Examination of Moderator Effects in the Four-Stage Model. *Journal of Service Research*, *8*, 330–345. doi:10.1177/1094670506286325

Featherman, M. S., & Pavlou, P. A. (2002). Predicting E-services adoption: A perceived risk facets perspective. In *Proceedings of the eighth Americas conference on information*, Dallas.

Felix, B. T., & Paul, S. (2004). Online consumer trust: a multiple-dimensional model. *Journal of Electronic Commerce in Organizations*, 40.

Fishbein, M., & Ajzen, I. (1975). *Belief, attitude, intention and behaviour: An introduction to theory and research*. Reading, MA: Addison-Wesley.

Fukuyama, F. (1995). *Trust: The Social Virtues and the Creation of Prosperity*. New York: The Free Press.

GAO (General Accounting Office), & McClure, D. (2001). *Electronic government challenges must be addressed with effective leadership and management*. Retrieved from http://feapmo.gov/links.asp

Gefen, D. (2000). E-Commerce: the role of familiarity and trust. *Omega: The International Journal of Management Science*, *28*, 725–737. doi:10.1016/S0305-0483(00)00021-9

Gefen, D., Pavlou, P. A., Rise, G. M., & Warkentin, M. (2002). E-government adoption. In *Proceedings of the eighth Americas conference on information system*, Boston, MA.

Gefen, D., & Straub, D. W. (1997, December). Gender Differences in the Perception and Use of E-mail: An Extension to the Technology Acceptance Model. *Management Information Systems Quarterly*, 389–400. doi:10.2307/249720

Gefen, D., & Straub, D. W. (2000). Managing user trust in B2C e-services. *E-Services Quarterly, 1*(1).

Gundykunst, W. (1997). *Communicating with strangers: An Approach to Intercultural Communication*. New York: Random House.

Guriting, P., & Ndubisi, N. O. (2006). Borneo online banking: evaluating customer perceptions and behavioural intention. *Management Research News*, *29*(1/2), 6–15. doi:10.1108/01409170610645402

Hair, J. F., Anderson, R. E., Tatham, R. L., & Black, B. C. (1998). *Multivariate data analysis* (5th ed.). Englewood Cliffs, NJ: Prentice-Hall International.

Hair, J. F., Anderson, R. E., Tatham, R. L., & Black, W. C. (2006). *Multivariate Data Analysis* (6th ed.). Upper Saddle River, NJ: Prentice-Hall.

Harris, B. (2002, August). E-government makes global progress. *Government Technology*, 22-28.

Hoffman, D. L., Novak, T. P., & Peralta, M. (1999). Building consumer trust online. *Communications of the ACM, 42*(4), 80–85. doi:10.1145/299157.299175

Hofstede, G. (1980). *Culture's Consequences*. Beverly Hills, CA: Sage.

Hofstede, G. (1991). *Cultures and Organizatios: Softwareof the Mind*. London: McGraw-Hill.

Hofstede, G. (2001). *Culture's Consequences* (2nd ed.). Thousand Oaks, CA: Sage.

Horst, M., Kuttschreuter, M., & Gutteling, J. M. (2006). Perceived usefulness, personal experiences, risk perception and trust as determinants of adoption of e-government services in The Netherlands. *Computers in Human Behavior*, *23*, 1838–1852. doi:10.1016/j.chb.2005.11.003

Huang, W., Ambra, J. D., & Bhalla, V. (2002). An empirical investigation of the Adoption of e-government in Australian Citizens: Some unexpected research Findings. *Journal ofComputer Information Systems*, *43*(1), 15–22.

Hung, S. Y., Chang, C. M., & Yu, T. J. (2005). *Determinants of user Acceptance of the e-Government services: The case of online tax filing and payment system*. Elsevier Inc.

Igbaria, M., Livari, J., & Maragahh, H. (1995). Why do individual use computer technology. A finish case study. *Information & Management*, *29*, 227–238. doi:10.1016/0378-7206(95)00031-0

Jarvenpaa, S., Tractinsky, N., Saarinen, L., & Vitale, M. (1999). Consumer trust in an Internet store: a cross-cultural validation. *Journal of Computer-Mediated Communication*, *5*(2). Retrieved from http//www.ascusc.org/jcmc/vol5/issue2/jarvenpaa.html.

Jorgensen, D., & Cable, S. (2002). Facing the challenges of e-government: a case study of the city of Corpus Christi, Texas. *SAM – Advanced Management Journal, 67*(3), 15-21.

Kale, S. H., & Mclntyre, R. P. (1991). Distribution channel relationships in diverse cultures. *International Marketing Review*, *8*(3), 31–45. doi:10.1108/02651339110004069

Kelly, E. P., & Erickson, E. G. (2005). RFID tags: commercial applications v. privacy rights. *Industrial Management & Data Systems*, *105*(6), 703–713. doi:10.1108/02635570510606950

Kelly, E. P., & Erickson, G. S. (2004). Legal and privacy issues surrounding customer databases and e-merchant bankruptcies: reflection on Toysmart.com. *Industrial Management & Data Systems*, *104*(3), 209–217. doi:10.1108/02635570410525762

Kovacic, Z. (2005). The impact of national culture on worldwide e-government Readiness. *Journal of Informing Science*, *8*, 143–158.

Lee, J. K., Braynov, S., & Rao, H. R. (2005). Effects of a Public Emergency on Citizens Usage Intention toward E-Government: A Study in the Context of War in Iraq. In *Proceedings of the Eleventh Americas Conference on Information System,* Omaha, NE, USA.

Lee, M. K. O., & Turban, E. (2001). A trust model for internet shopping. *International Journal of Electronic Commerce*, *6*(1), 75–91.

Lekvall, P., & Wahlbin, C. (2001). Information for Marknadsforingsbeslut. Goteborg: IHM forlag.

Leoi L. S. (2007, April 19). Bold Plan For Syariah Portal. *The StarSpecial Paper*, 2

Leong, L. (2003). *Theoretical Models in IS Research and the Technology Acceptance Model (TAM)*. Hershey, PA: Idea Group Inc.

Leslie, S. (2007). Government E-Payments Adoption Ranking. *The Economist Intelligence Unit Limited*, 3-11

Loei, L. S., & Hong, Y. P. (2007, April 19). Public Service: Digital Government. *Newpaper StarSpecial.*

Malaysia, M. S. C. *The MSC Malaysia Flagship Applications.* (n.d.). Retrieved from http://www.msc.com.my/msc/flagships.asp

Malhotra, Y., & Galletta, D. F. (1999). Extending the Technology Acceptance Model to account for Social Influence: Theoretical bases and empirical validation. In *Proceedings of the 32nd Hawaii International Conference on System Science*.

Mathieson, K. (1991). Predicting user intention: Comparing the technology acceptance model with the theory of planned behavior. *Information Systems Research, 2*(3), 173–191. doi:10.1287/isre.2.3.173

Mayer, R. C., Davis, J. H., & Schoorman, F. D. (1995). An integrative model of organizational trust. *Academy of Management Review, 20*(3), 709–734. doi:10.2307/258792

McKnight, D. H., & Chevancy, N. L. (2002). *What trust means in e-commerce customer relationships: An interdisciplinary conceptual typology*. Internet. J. Electronic Commerce.

Moore, G. C., & Benbasat, I. (1991). Development of an instrument to measure the perceptions of adopting an information technology innovation. *Information Systems Research, 2*(3), 192–222. doi:10.1287/isre.2.3.192

Pauline, R. (1998). The important of trust in electronic commerce. *Internet Research: Electronic Networking Applications and Policy, 8*(4), 313–321. doi:10.1108/10662249810231050

Pavlou, P. A. (2001). Integrating trust in electronic commerce with the technology acceptance model – model development and validation. In *Proceedings of the 2001 Americas Conference in Information Systems*, Boston, MA, 2-5 August.

Pavlou, P. A. (2003). Consumer acceptance of electronic commerce- integrating trust and risk with the technology acceptance model. *International Journal of Electronic Commerce, 7*(3), 69–103.

Phang, C. W., Li, Y., Sutanto, J., & Kankanhalli, A. (2005). Senior Citizens' Adoption of E-Government: In Quest of the Antecedents of Perceived Usefulness. In *Proceedings of the 38th Hawaii International Conference on System Science* (pp.1-8).

Plouffe, C. R., Hulland, J. S., & Vanderbosch, M. (2002). Research report: Richness versus Parsimony in Modeling Technology Adoption Decisions–Understanding Merchant Adoption of a Smart Card-based Payment System. *Information Systems Research, 13*(2), 208–222.

Public, A. in Waiting. (2007, July 31). *The Star Paper*. Retrieved February 20, 2008 from http://archives.thestar.com.my

Ramayah, T., & Ignatius, J. (2005). Impact of perceived usefulness, perceived ease of use and perceived enjoyment on intention to shop online. [IJSM]. *ICFAI Journal of Management, 3*(3), 36–51.

Ramayah, T., & Jantan, M. (2003). Attitude And Intention To Use Web-Based Supply Chain Management (SCM) Among SME'S: Moderating Effect Of Self Efficacy. In *The Third International Conference on Electronic Commerce Engineering* (ICeCE2003), Hangzhou, China.

Ramayah, T., Jantan, M., Mohd Noor, M. N., & Koay, P. L. (2003). Receptiveness of Internet Banking by Malaysia Consumers: The Case of Penang. *Asian Academic of Management Journal, 8*(2), 1–29.

Ramayah, T., Siron, R., Dahlan, N., & Mohamad, O. (2002). Technology Usage Among Owners/Managers of SME's: The Role of Demographic and Motivational Variables. *The Proceedings of The 6th Annual Asian-Pacific Forum for Small Business on Small and Medium Enterprises Linkages,* Networking and Clustering, Kuala Lumpur: Malaysia.

Riemenschneider, C. K., Hardgrave, B. C., & Davis, F. D. (2002). Explaining Software Developer Acceptance of Methodologies: A comparison of Five Theoretical Models. *IEEE Transactions on Software Engineering, 28*(12), 1135–1145. doi:10.1109/TSE.2002.1158287

Rogers, E. M. (1995). *Diffusion of innovations* (4th ed.). New York: The Free Press.

Rogers, E. M. (2003). *Diffusion of Innovation* (5th ed.). New York: Free Press.

Rose, M. (2004). Democrating information and communication by implementing e-government in Indonesian regional government. *The International Information & Library Review, 36,* 219–226. doi:10.1016/j.iilr.2003.11.002

Rotter, J. (1967). A new scale for the measurement of interpersonal trust. *Journal of Personality, 35,* 651–665. doi:10.1111/j.1467-6494.1967.tb01454.x

Rousseau, D., Sitkin, S., Burt, R., & Comerer, C. (1998). Not so different after all: A Cross-discipline view of Trust. *Academy of Management Review, 23*(3), 393–404.

Sekaran, U. (2003). *Research methods for business. A skill-building approach* (4th ed.). New York: John Wiley and Sons, Inc.

Siau, K., & Long, Y. (2005). Synthesizing e-government stage models – a meta Synthesis based on meta-ethnography approach. *Journal of Industrial Management & Data Systems, 105*(4), 443–458. doi:10.1108/02635570510592352

Singh, J. (1990). Managerial culture and work related values in India. *Organization Studies, 11,* 75–101. doi:10.1177/017084069001100106

Slyke, C. V., Belanger, F., & Comunale, C. L. (2004). Factors influencing the adoption of web-based shopping: The impact of trust. *The Data Base for Advances in Information Systems, 35*(2), 32–49.

Sohaimi, M. S. (2003). *The Multimedia Super Corridor (MSC) and E-government Initiatives in Malaysia. School of Global Information and Telecommunication Studies (GITS).* Waseda University.

Sonja, G. K., & Ewald, A. K. (2003). Empirical research in on-line trust: a review and critical assessment. *International Journal of Human-Computer Studies.*

Steyaert, J. C. (2004). Measuring the performance of electronic government services. *Journal of International Management, 41,* 369–375.

Taylor, S., & Todd, P. (1995). Assessing IT Usage: The role of Prior Expereince. *Management Information Systems Quarterly, 19*(4), 560–570. doi:10.2307/249633

Tee, L. D. (2007, March 27). Digital Government Portal. *The Star Paper,* 24

Toregas, C. (2001). The politics of e-gov: The upcoming struggle for redefining civic engagement. *National Civic Review, 90*(3), 235–240. doi:10.1002/ncr.90304

Udo, G. (2001). Privacy and security concerns as major barriers for e-commerce: a survey study. *Information Management & Computer Security, 9*(4), 165–174. doi:10.1108/EUM0000000005808

Vassilakis, C., Laskaridis, G., Lepouras, G., Rouvas, S., & Georgiadis, P. (2003). A framework for managing the lifecycle of transactional e-government services. *Journal of Telematics and Informatics*, *20*, 315–329. doi:10.1016/S0736-5853(03)00011-X

Venkatesh, V., & Davis, F. D. (2000). A Theoretical Extension of the Technology Acceptance Model (Four Longitudinal Field Studies). *Management Science*, *46*(2), 186–204. doi:10.1287/mnsc.46.2.186.11926

Venkatesh, V., & Morris, M. G. (2000). Why Don't Men Ever Stop To Ask For Direction? Gender, Social Influence, and Their Role in Technology Acceptance and Usage Behaviour. *Management Information Systems Quarterly*, *24*(1), 115–139. doi:10.2307/3250981

Venkatesh, V., Morris, M. G., Davis, G. B., & Davis, F. D. (2003). User Acceptance of Infroamtion Technology: Toward A Unified View. *Management Information Systems Quarterly*, *27*(3), 425–478.

Walker, R. H., & Johnson, L. W. (2006). Why consumers use and do not use technology-enabled services. *Journal of Services Marketing*, *20*(2), 125–135. doi:10.1108/08876040610657057

Wan, A. H. (2000). Opportunities to enhance a commercial web site. *Information & Management*, *38*(1), 15–21. doi:10.1016/S0378-7206(00)00048-3

Wang, Y. S., Wang, Y. M., Lin, H. H., & Tang, T. I. (2003). Determinants of user acceptance of Internet banking: An empirical study. *International Journal of Service Industry Management*, *14*(5), 501–519. doi:10.1108/09564230310500192

Warkentin, M., Gefen, D., Pavlou, P. A., & Rose, G. M. (2002). Encouraging citizen adoption of e-government by building trust. *Electronic Markets*, *12*(3), 157–162. Retrieved from http://www.electronicmarkets.org. doi:10.1080/101967802320245929

William, G. Z. (2003). *Business Research Method* (7th ed.). Oklahoma City, OK: South-Western.

Wimmer, M. A. (2003). E-Government services in future. Short abstract for the JANUS workshop, Brussels.

Wu, I., & Chen, J. L. (2005). An Extension of Trust and TAM model with TPB in the initial adoption of on-line tax: An empirical study. *International Journal of Human-Computer Studies*, *62*(6), 784–808. doi:10.1016/j.ijhcs.2005.03.003

Yoo, B., Naveen, D., & Lenartowicz, T. (2004, August). The Effects of Marketing Education and Individual Cultural Values on Marketing Ethics of Students. *Journal of Marketing Education*, *24*, 92–103.

Zucker, L. G. (1986). Production of trust: institutional sources of economic structure, 1840-1920. *Research in Organizational Behavior*, *8*, 53–111.

Chapter 20
Assessing China's E-Government and Its Impact on Government and Citizen Relationship

Xia Li Lollar
University of Wisconsin-Whitewater, USA

ABSTRACT

The goal of this chapter is to examine the e-government development in China and its political impact on the communist countries' transition to democracy by transforming relations between the government and citizens. It is widely accepted that e-government can help to encourage government transparency, expand the information flow, promote work efficiency and increase citizens' political participation. This may be true in open democracies, yet there is little scholarly support for this conventional wisdom applied in authoritarian societies. This chapter will test hypotheses that e-government can improve the quality of government by enhancing citizens' accessibility to information and service, increasing citizens' political participation and promoting citizen outreach of the Chinese government. The chapter will indicate that e-government is transforming relations between citizens and the Chinese government and show how it is playing an essential role in China's incremental process of democratization.

INTRODUCTION

It has been a decade since the Chinese government launched China's Government Online Project in 1999. Today, 96.1% of national government agencies, 100% of provincial and metropolitan governments and 99.1% of local governing bodies have websites (Yang, 2009). The websites perform broad government functions including e-information, e-service, e-openness/transparency and e-citizen outreach/responsiveness.

It is widely accepted that e-government can help to expand the information flow, promote work efficiency, encourage government transparency and increase citizens' participation in the political process (Western 2000, Watson and Mundy 2001, Lenihan 2002, Yang 2003, Holliday and Yep 2005). This may be true in western democracies, yet there is little scholarly support for this conventional wisdom applied in authoritarian societies. Indeed,

DOI: 10.4018/978-1-61520-931-6.ch020

e-government in last 10 years has offered many opportunities for Chinese citizens to engage in political activities, such as accessing government documents, participating in online public opinion surveys, chatting with public officials online and sending e-mails to governors and mayors. However, questions must be raised about how effective e-government can be as an engine for political transformation. This chapter will test the hypotheses that e-government can improve the quality of government by enhancing citizens' accessibility of public information and service, increasing citizens' political participation and promoting citizen outreach of the Chinese government.

This study will be based on a comprehensive analysis of 31 provincial and metropolitan websites. The websites will be evaluated for the presence of four major e-government features: e-information, e-services, e-transparency, e-citizen outreach and responsiveness. The chapter will look at what kinds of features are available online, such as information posted and services provided to the public. It will also examine the government transparency and citizen outreach efforts by the Chinese provincial and metropolitan governments. For instance, what e-mails citizens sent to their governors and mayors and how public officials responded to citizens' requests and complaints. Finally, the chapter will indicate how e-government is transforming relations between citizens and the Chinese government and how it is playing an essential role in China's incremental process of democratization.

LITERATURE REVIEW

Scholars have been debating the role of e-government in e-democracy since the new technology was developed. Tracy Western (2000) delightfully points out "the world is rapidly going digital. This new communications technology will not just affect democracy, it will transform it. Because democracy is an interactive form of government, the revolution in interactive communications will inevitably have its greatest effect on the most important 'interactive institution'-the government itself" (p.218). Watson and Mundy (2001) identify e-government and e-politics as elements of e-democracy. They argue that democracy requires an informed citizenry and that e-government informs citizens about their public officials and how to obtain access to them. E-government allows an unimpeded flow of information between citizens and government officials. Lenihan (2002) states that e-government is a move from a more closed to a more open system. He notes that e-government is likely to produce a wide range of new ways to connect government officials with organizations and individuals usually outside their organizational boundaries. This is changing the way information enters and flows around the political system and introducing influences into decision making.

Holliday and Yep (2005) support the idea that the conventional wisdom does apply in authoritarian societies like China. They argue that the current Chinese leaders, President Hu Jintao and Premier Wen Jiabao, are strongly interested in working the crowd. "In this government environment, e-government can be turned into a useful tool for forging closer links between the government and the people. In spite of its subversive potential, e-government is very much a preferred option for encouraging greater participation" (p. 248)

With a neoinstitutional perspective to address the evolution and implementation of e-government in China, Yang (2003) notes that democratization in authoritarian countries like China may be a long-term incremental process, and "e-government will definitely play a significant role" (p.439)

However, some e-government researchers do not fully agree with the conventional expectations regarding the role of e-government in e-democracy in authoritarian states such as China. In its truest sense, Seifert and Chung (2009) argue, e-government is not about democracy. By launching e-government, China is trying to bring greater transparency and efficiency to its citizens, while at the same time the central government has improved its ability to monitor the interactions between public officials and citizens and also brought local governments under greater control of the central government. Zhang (2005) believes "China's e-government strategy reflects the state of an authoritarian system which is seeking a basis for legitimacy. Its present priority in building e-government lies not in promoting participation and democracy, but rather in enhancing its own governmental functionality and professionalism" (p.62).

In her comparative study of e-government and democracy in the North and South, Netchaeva (2002) believes that e-government proves to be a useful tool for administrations, politicians, big businesses and non-governmental organizations, but does not serve ordinary people in the same degree. E-government can make public officials more accountable to people but it can also let the politicians advertise themselves more effectively and provide unreliable or patently false information. Wong and Welch (2004) also expressed a similar argument in their study of e-government development in 14 countries including China. They state that government can stipulate what they want people to know. There is a danger that the new government-and-citizen interface created by e-government may simply be used as an additional channel for more political propaganda and control rather than real accountability enhancement.

It is clear that e-government development in non-democratic countries like China has been accompanied by a debate on its political impact on democracy in an authoritarian state. The seriousness of the debate is reflected by Yang's 2003 article:

It must be noted that comparative analysis should be performed in a careful manner not subject to cultural and political prejudices. Fountain (2001), for example, had some problematic observations: "In authoritarian regimes, the Internet threatens domination by the state over information and communication but at the same time, paradoxically, serves as an instrument of consummate state surveillance and control over society" (p.3); and "the central government of the People's Republic of China (PRC) enacts networked computing as an instrument of social control and surveillance. Technologies used for jamming, blocking, and filtering information dominate" (p.33). The assertion that technologies are used in authoritarian countries such as China primarily for control and surveillance is problematic and simplistic, indicating a dualist view of democratization and related epistemological prejudices. ... Regimes different from Western liberal democracy are viewed as necessarily undemocratic, and whatever they do is also undemocratic. This assumption neglects that no regime is perfectly democratic and every regime is practicing democracy. (Yang, 2003, p.439)

In this chapter, I will review the current development of e-government in China and add more insights to the debate.

METHODOLOGY

A number of organizations, academic and non-academic, have developed frameworks to assess e-government development in different countries. Some noticeable ones are the United Nations, Brown University of the United States, Beijing University of China, IBM, etc (Hu, Xiao, Pang & Xie, 2005). Brown University has conducted e-government assessments since 2001 in the United States and around the world. Beijing University has focused on the research of Chinese e-government development since 2003. Both universities are well known and advanced in leading e-government assessments. Brown University's model examines four major features of e-government: online information, service delivery, democratic responsiveness and public opinion about government (West, 2001). Beijing University's framework has 10 indexes which also include online information, online administrative work, interactions and connections of governments and citizens (Hu, Xiao, Pang & Xie, 2005). These features embrace the whole range of e-government activities such as providing services and engaging citizens.

This study more or less follows the Brown University and Beijing University's measurements to assess the current e-government development in China. The study is based on a comprehensive analysis of 31 provincial and metropolitan websites. A list of web-addresses of the Chinese governments can be found at www.govonline.cn. The websites are developed and managed by the executive branch of Chinese provincial/metropolitan governments.

Websites are assessed for the presence of four different features:

- E-information: for information, I look at the availability of government documents, government laws and regulations, news and current events (international, national and local), links to major public agencies/departments websites, live broadcasting of important news and events.
- E-services: for services, I assess four features: service guidelines, fully executable service, emergency management and "One Hundred Service Online Project" launched by the central government in 2008. The goal of the project is to encourage each province and metropolis to provide at least 100 services online for the public. Emergency management is the service handling emergencies such as natural disasters and traffic accidents. A fully executable service is the entire transaction can be completed online such as filling taxes and applying business licenses and loans. Service guideline informs people how to get things done and examples include instructions on getting marriage/divorce certificates, passports, citizen ID cards and downloading the required forms.
- E-transparency and openness: to examine the degree of transparency and openness of each government website, I look at features such as information on bidding for public projects, government purchasing, employment opportunities for civil service, price of goods and services and areas where citizens can pour out their grievance and expose public officials' crimes and bad behaviors.
- E-citizen outreach and responsiveness: websites are evaluated on their capability of connecting government officials with ordinary citizens. The major feature of citizen outreach/responsiveness is the Governor's/Mayor's Mail box. The questions we ask are, for instance, what e-mails citizens sent to their governors and mayors and how their e-mails are handled by government officials. Other features include online live discussions with citizens, discussion forums and public opinion surveys and feedback. Features also include public officials' biographical information, contact information of the main office of each government.

Resources of assessing the current e-government development in China come also from Chinese government documents, news media reports and public opinion surveys conducted by Chinese academics.

FINDINGS AND DISCUSSIONS

E-Information

One of the important benefits of e-government is to facilitate greater access to government information. The information includes government documents, government laws/regulations, public announcements, news/current events, links to other agencies, links to medium, local attractions and live broadcasting. Table 1 shows information provided by Chinese provincial and metropolitan websites.

Of the 31 government sites reviewed, 100% of the sites provide government documents, public announcements, news/current events and links to other agencies. Ninety seven percent of the sites have information of local attractions with pictures or videos and 68% incorporate audio/video clips or live broadcasting into their sites. These features rarely existed a few years ago. Surprisingly, slightly over one half of the sites do not have direct links to medium on the front page.

Reviewing e-information of Chinese provincial and metropolitan websites, two realities caught my attention. First, the sites carry mostly local news, little national and barely any international events. For instance, among 12 news events reported at the Shanghai site front page on March 6, 2009, 9 were local events and 3 were about national leaders' activities. It shows that the news coverage of provincial/metropolitan sites is very local –centered and emphasizes local affairs and developments. Second, information offered is more economic in nature and less political driven. For example, all of the news events on the Shaanxi site on March 6, 2009 were economic events, such as development of Xian subway construction and the number of people covered by the government insurance program. The only significant political report was the March 14 Incident posted by Tibet site. The site had 15 stories on March19, 2009 about violent ethnic protest in Tibet. Stories addressed China's firm position that Tibet is part of Chinese territory and criticized the Dalai Lama's anti-China speeches and activities.

E-Service

As West (2003) points out, online service delivery benefits both government and its citizens. Online services can lower the cost of service delivery and make services more widely accessible to the general public. As more and more services are put online, e-government will revolutionize the relationship between government and citizens.

In assessing e-service of Chinese government sites, we include four categories which are One Hundred E-Service Project, emergency management, executable service and service guideline. Among the sites examined, 100% of the sites provide guidelines for various services such as getting permission to have a second child and how to apply for retirement benefits. Sixty-one percent of the sites provide some kind of executable services such as making appointments online, online banking and paying taxes. According to the Chinese government online report, Guangdong is the first province in China to pass a law that makes secret codes, passwords and fingerprints as legitimate as a written signature, thereby formalizing electronic transactions. Another advanced site is Shanghai which adopted a foreign exchange e-payment settlement system so it can provide automatic fund transfer service online.

Twenty six government sites give people direction on how to deal with emergencies. Tibet, known by its severe weather and harsh road conditions, is advanced at providing emergency services including drills and case analyses. One Hundred Service Project is launched by the State Council in 2008 to call each province and metropolis to provide 100 services online. Sixty-five percent of governments have responded to the call and created this service category. Some services are interactive and some are simply instructions. Not surprisingly, most of the governments without this feature are from remote regions away from Beijing. Both the One Hundred Service Project and the emergency management are new features launched recently. It shows that Chinese government has been expanding its e-services to the public.

E-Transparency and Openness

E-government can make the political and economic decision-making process more open and transparent. As Watson and Mundy (2001) point out, ordinary citizens can drill into the process and discover how a particular piece of legislation is being made and carried out. To examine the degree of transparency and openness, I look at five features: government contract bidding information, government purchasing, public employment information, officially approved price of public

Table 1. Information provided by Chinese provincial/metropolitan websites

Province/ Metropolis	**Government documents**	**Government laws/ regulations**	**Public announce-ments**	**News/ current events**	**Links to other agencies**	**Links to medium**	**Local attractions**	**Live broad-casting Audio/video clips**
Beijing	yes	yes	yes	yes	yes	yes	yes	yes
Shanghai	yes	yes	yes	yes	yes		yes	yes
Tianjin	yes	yes	yes	yes	yes		yes	yes
Chongqing	yes	yes	yes	yes	yes	yes	yes	
Anhui	yes	yes	yes	yes	yes		yes	yes
Fujian	yes	yes	yes	yes	yes		yes	yes
Guangdong	yes	yes	yes	yes	yes		yes	yes
Guangxi	yes	yes	yes	yes	yes		yes	
Gansu	yes	yes	yes	yes	yes	yes	yes	yes
Guizhou	yes	yes	yes	yes	yes	yes	yes	
Hainan	yes	yes	yes	yes	yes	yes	yes	yes
Henan	yes	yes	yes	yes	yes	yes	yes	yes
Hebei	yes	yes	yes	yes	yes	yes	yes	yes
Heilongjiang	yes	yes	yes	yes	yes		yes	yes
Hunan	yes	yes	yes	yes	yes		yes	yes
Hubei	yes		yes	yes	yes	yes	yes	
Jiangsu	yes	yes	yes	yes	yes	yes	yes	yes
Liaoning	yes	yes	yes	yes	yes	yes	yes	yes
Jiangxi	yes	yes	yes	yes	yes		yes	
Jilin	yes	yes	yes	yes	yes		yes	yes
Neimeng	yes	yes	yes	yes	yes		yes	yes
Ningxia	yes		yes	yes	yes		yes	yes
Shandong	yes	yes	yes	yes	yes		yes	
Shanxi	yes	yes	yes	yes	yes	yes	yes	yes
Shannxi	yes	yes	yes	yes	yes	yes		yes
Sichuan	yes	yes	yes	yes	yes	yes	yes	yes
Tibet	yes	yes	yes	yes	yes		yes	
Qinghai	yes	yes	yes	yes	yes	yes	yes	yes
Xinjiang	yes	yes	yes	yes	yes	yes	yes	
Yunnan	yes	yes	yes	yes	yes	yes	yes	
Zhejiang	yes	yes	yes	yes	yes	yes	yes	
Total (%)	100	94	100	100	100	55	97	68

Table 2. Service provided by Chinese provincial/metropolitan websites

Province/ Metropolis	One Hundred Service Project	Emergency management	Executable service	Service guideline
Beijing	yes		yes	yes
Shanghai	yes	yes	yes	yes
Tianjin	yes	yes	yes	yes
Chongqing	yes	yes	yes	yes
Anhui	yes	yes	yes	yes
Fujian	yes		yes	yes
Guangdong	yes	yes	yes	yes
Guangxi		yes	yes	yes
Gansu		yes		yes
Guizhou	yes			yes
Hainan	yes			yes
Henan		yes		yes
Hebei	yes	yes	yes	yes
Heilongjiang		yes		yes
Hunan		yes	yes	yes
Hubei	yes	yes		yes
Jiangsu	yes	yes		yes
Liaoning		yes	yes	yes
Jiangxi	yes	yes	yes	yes
Jilin	yes	yes		yes
Neimeng		yes	yes	yes
Ningxia		yes		yes
Shandong			yes	yes
Shanxi	yes	yes	yes	yes
Shannxi	yes	yes	yes	yes
Sichuan	yes	yes	yes	yes
Tibet		yes		yes
Qinghai	yes	yes		yes
Xinjiang		yes	yes	yes
Yunnan	yes	yes	yes	yes
Zhejiang	yes	yes		yes
Total (%)	65	84	61	100

goods and services and an accusation box that citizens can pour out their grievances and expose public officials' crimes and bad behaviors. Table 3 shows the results.

Among all the sites measured, 81 percent of the government websites provide information on contract bidding, 87% have information on government purchasing, 71% have information on civil service position openings and 65% post the officially approved price of public goods and services such as school tuition and prescription drugs. Tianjin is one of the leaders with the most detailed and transparent information on bidding and purchasing. For instance, on March 9 and March 10 2009, 6 public projects were listed for bidding and 10 products for purchasing. Examples include bidding for public building remodeling, software development and purchasing government

Table 3. Transparency/openness of Chinese provincial/metropolitan websites

Province/ Metropolis	Bidding information	Government purchasing	Employment information	Price information	Accusation Box
Beijing	yes	yes			yes
Shanghai	yes	yes	yes	yes	yes
Tianjin	yes	yes		yes	yes
Chongqing	yes	yes	yes		yes
Anhui	yes			yes	yes
Fujian	yes		yes	yes	yes
Guangdong	yes	yes	yes	yes	yes
Guangxi		yes	yes		yes
Gansu	yes	yes	yes		yes
Guizhou	yes	yes	yes	yes	yes
Hainan	yes	yes	yes	yes	yes
Henan	yes	yes		yes	yes
Hebei	yes	yes	yes	yes	yes
Heilongjiang			yes	yes	yes
Hunan	yes	yes	yes	yes	yes
Hubei		yes	yes		yes
Jiangsu	yes	yes	yes	yes	yes
Liaoning	yes	yes	yes	yes	yes
Jiangxi	yes	yes	yes	yes	yes
Jilin	yes			yes	yes
Neimeng		yes			yes
Ningxia	yes	yes		yes	yes
Shandong		yes		yes	yes
Shanxi	yes	yes	yes		yes
Shannxi	yes	yes	yes	yes	yes
Sichuan		yes	yes		yes
Tibet	yes	yes	yes	yes	yes
Qinghai	yes	yes		yes	yes
Xinjiang	yes	yes	yes		yes
Yunnan	yes	yes	yes		yes
Zhejiang	yes	yes	yes		yes
Total (%)	81	87	71	65	100

vehicles and furniture. On the same days, the site also posted the bidding and purchasing results of eleven projects such as a new civil center at Wuqing District and new equipment for Tianjin Medical College. Shaanxi leads the list with the most price information on 20 indexes of goods and services such as water, electricity, prescription drugs, and school books and tuition. Guizhou is advanced in terms of public employment information. The site breaks down the civil service to different categories such as government employee, police officer, public school teacher and pharmacist. It then provides detailed information on how to register and take the examination.

Openness and transparency of government can serve as a powerful weapon for fighting corruption, which is one of the most significant challenges facing the Chinese government today. All of the sites have an Accusation Box where citizens can report corrupt public officials anonymously and pour out their own experiences with officials who abused their power and public trust. Some sites expose violations of rules and punishment of corruptions based on public accusations. On 9 December 2008, the Chongqing site exposed 23 online "black pharmacies" which sold fake drugs. It showed their web addresses, name of products, what illnesses the drugs are suppose to cure and who produces/provides the drugs. Another example of government transparency is Sichuan. To inform the public that appropriations and donations for earthquake victims have been used properly, Sichuan site posts the detailed information on how the funds were distributed.

Strong indicators for e-transparency and openness should include political decisions, decision making processes and policy results. To accomplish this, it is necessary to measure not just what is available in the "front" office, virtual reality on website, but how decisions have been made in the "back" office as well. This issue should be addressed in the future studies.

E-Citizen Outreach and Responsiveness

Having an advanced stage of e-government means it could become more than an information board but a space for political participation. Table 4 shows websites with interactive features to bring ordinary people closer to their governments. Key features examined include Governor/Mayor's Mail Box, officials' responses and citizens' comments, online live discussions with citizens, discussion forums and public opinion surveys and feedback.

The most significant interactive e-government function is the Governor/Mayor's Mail Box. The mail box posts the picture and biographical information of the governor or mayor and a brief introduction on how to use it. Citizens can send e-mails of their concerns directly to the mayor of their city or the governor of their province. Some sites list mail boxes of lieutenant governors as well. "In order to attract people to get involved in online consultations and discussions, government must respond to people and actively demonstrate that there is a relationship between the citizen's engagement and policy outcome" (Waller, Livesey & Edin, 2001, p. 5). Seventy-seven percent of governors and mayors posted their response letters online. Some inform the public of the number of e-mail letters received and how they had been handled. For example, Governor's Box of Hunan received 4,326 letters between October and December 2008. Of them, 1,171 were about personal issues and 167 were suggestions on government regulations and measures. Ninety-three percent of the e-mails had been processed and 12 were under the consideration (*Hunan.gov.cn*, February 4, 2009). Another example is the governor of Heilongjiang. In one of the letters he received, a parent of young school child reported an illegal gambling machine installed in a neighborhood restaurant where it attracted many local kids to gamble. His son stole 7,000 yuan one time from home and lost it all in two hours. After fruitless

Table 4. Citizen outreach and responsiveness of Chinese government websites

Province/ Metropolis	**Governor's/ Mayor's biographical information**	**Governor's/ Mayor's Mail Box**	**Governor's Mayor's response**	**Citizens' comment**	**Live online chat with citizens**	**Online Public opinion Survey**	**Government Hotline/ contact information**
Beijing	yes	yes	yes	yes	yes	yes	yes
Shanghai	yes	yes	yes	yes	yes	yes	yes
Tianjin	yes	yes	yes		yes	yes	yes
Chongqing	yes	yes	yes	yes	yes	yes	yes
Anhui	yes	yes			yes	yes	yes
Fujian	yes	yes	yes	yes	yes	yes	yes
Guangdong	yes	yes	yes	yes	yes	yes	yes
Guangxi						yes	yes
Gansu	yes	yes	yes	yes	yes	yes	yes
Guizhou	yes	yes	yes	yes		yes	yes
Hainan	yes	yes	yes	yes	yes	yes	yes
Henan	yes				yes	yes	yes
Hebei	yes	yes			yes	yes	yes
Heilongjiang	yes	yes	yes	yes	yes	yes	yes
Hunan		yes	yes		yes	yes	yes
Hubei		yes	yes	yes	yes	yes	yes
Jiangsu	yes	yes	yes	yes	yes	yes	yes
Liaoning	yes	yes					yes
Jiangxi	yes	yes	yes	yes	yes	yes	yes
Jilin	yes	yes	yes	yes	yes	yes	yes
Neimeng	yes	yes			yes	yes	yes
Ningxia	yes	yes	yes		yes	yes	yes
Shandong	yes	yes	yes	yes	yes	yes	yes
Shanxi	yes	yes	yes	yes	yes	yes	yes
Shannxi	yes	yes	yes	yes	yes	yes	yes
Sichuan	yes	yes	yes	yes	yes	yes	yes
Tibet	yes	yes	yes	yes	yes	yes	yes
Qinghai	yes	yes	yes	yes	yes	yes	yes
Xinjiang	yes	yes	yes		yes	yes	yes
Yunnan	yes	yes		yes	yes	yes	yes
Zhejiang	yes	yes	yes	yes	yes	yes	yes
Total (%)	90	94	77	68	90	97	100

effort fighting with the owner of the restaurant, the parent sent an e-mail to the governor. Soon after police wrecked the place, destroyed 23 gambling machines and arrested one restaurant staff and two gamblers (*Hij.gov.cn,* September, 2008).

In addition to mail boxes, Governors of Jilin and Jiangxi also post their cell phone numbers online. Jilin site has a diagram showing how the calls were received, processed and responded. On 12 March 2009, there were 300 phone records of contents and feedbacks posted on the site of Jilin government. Jiangxi has cell phone numbers of both the governor and lieutenant governor. It also gives regular bulletins to inform the public how the phone calls were handled and issues resolved. Sixty-five percent of the government sites post citizens' comments on how government officials have handled their cases. Most comments are "thank you notes" to governors and mayors. For instance, all 10 comments one day at Guizhou site were about citizens appreciations to the governor for solving their problems. In the same day, 9 out of 10 comments posted at Jiangxi site were "appreciation letters" to the governor and other leaders of the province.

Another feature to bring citizens and governments closer is online public opinion survey. Hainan and Henan sites post the entire questionnaires and results. For instance, in one survey, the Hainan website asked the following question: "What do you think the current employment situation is under the global financial crisis caused by the United States sub-prime mortgage scandal?" Ninety percent of respondents said it was very difficult to find jobs and 42% witnessed layoffs of their work units. The Henan site asked for public opinion on their goals of visiting government website. Respondents could check more than one choice. Fifty one percent were for contacting public officials, 42% for getting information on public policies, and 40% for using e-services.

In addition, 90% of the government websites offer live online chat with citizens and reporters. Through such features, citizens and public officials can talk and respond to each others' comments online. Hu Jintao, the General Secretary of CCP, chatted directly with citizens online at people.com.cn in June 2008 and the Primer Minister Wen Jiabao "met" people at Xinhua network in February, 2009.

In July 2008, People's Daily Online launched a new feature called "Message Board to Local Leaders." Over one thousand of party secretaries, governors and mayors have message boards. People can freely leave messages to their selected officials and these massages and officials' responses are exposed to citizens nationwide. For instance, Lu Hao, the Party Secretary of Gansu, responded to 114 messages in 45 days between September 1 and October 15, 2009.

Compared with a few years ago, Chinese e-government shows more effort to reach out to citizens and respond to their needs. Online chat between citizens and public officials was not available several years ago, for example, yet today it becomes a common tool to connect the officials and citizens.

IMPACT OF E-GOVERNMENY ON TRANSFORMING RELATIONSHIP BETWEEN THE GOVERNMENT AND CITIZENS

We highlight four important issues to illustrate the impact of e-government on transforming relations between the government and citizens. The issues are e-information, e-service, e-openness and transparency, e-citizen outreach and responsiveness.

One of the e-government's main uses is for seeking information. The Chinese government has traditionally practiced a system of information and censure, as Saich (2004) points out, with an intricate grading process for who at what level are allowed to see which kinds of information. For instance, certain government documents could only be available to officials at a certain level, and some newspapers were solely for members of the communist party. The Internet has changed all that and provided users equal access to information. However, news and current events are local centered and economic driven. Chinese provincial and metropolitan sites do not often carry national and international news and political events.

Another issue reviewed is online service provided by government websites. Prior to the arrival of the Internet, government services were solely delivered face-to-face or on paper. Ordinary citizens complained that government buildings were too hard to get in to; public officials were too rude to talk to; and government regulations were too complicated to follow. Today, as more and more government services are put online, e-government is changing the way that government interacts with citizens. Without the internet, it took a whole day to fill in forms in different agencies for mortgage loans in Beijing, yet with online service it takes only about 10 minutes. Compared with 2003, most sites today have lunched One Hundred Service Project and provided emergency management service. Nevertheless, most services online are guidelines in nature and not interactive. Many people are even not aware of e-services provided by government websites and therefore never use them.

The third issue discusses how e-government can encourage transparency and build trust in government. Saich (2004) has noted that the Chinese system of intense bureaucratic control over distribution, the increasing arbitrary control over personal life, and the concentration of power in individual hands, undermined social cohesion and trust in officials and laid the basis for the corrupt behavior by officials that dogs the system to this day. In pre-Internet days, the public had neither access to information on job openings in government branches nor to the procurement of government goods and services and bidding for government contracts. Citizens who wanted to track applications to jobs or public services would have to come to city halls and speak to officials who were in charge of applications. Also if citizens wanted to report corrupt officials they would have to make appointments with local accusation offices or might wait for months or even years to get their appointments scheduled. Today, because of e-government, ordinary people can track public works online and report corrupt public officials anonymously and instantaneously.

The last issue surveyed is citizen outreach and responsiveness. This initiative is designed to facilitate citizen interaction with government. Under the authoritarian rule, Chinese officials are selected not elected. They do not have to be responsible to the public and reach out to citizens. Government buildings are still guarded by armed soldiers and governors and mayors scarcely have any face-to-face contact with citizens. E-government has built a bridge between public officials and ordinary people. Some public officials opened office hours online to "meet" people. Citizens can chat with officials online on topics they are interested in. Citizens can also e-mail their governors or mayors on issues concerning them and expect responses from the contacted officials. However, as Lau, Fung and Ji (2005) point out providing online interactions can be advantageous to the authorities. While it can enable citizens to voice their grievances, the government could also use the collected information to generate support as well. Postings of the positive comments citizens made sound more like political advertisements on government work.

A new phenomenon in Chinese politics today is to use Internet as a weapon against government corruption. There are numerous examples of how citizens have used the internet to bring corrupt officials to justice. One demonstrates:

Zhou Jiugeng, a director of the Real Estate Management Bureau of Jiangjing District, Nanjing, Jiangsu, a nicely rich province, has lost his job because of a photograph shown on the web. Two weeks ago, Zhou was photographed at a meeting he was attending and the happy snap was posted on the Internet. Also showing was a 150 yuan pack of smokes on his table. How, many internet users wondered, could Zhou afford such expensive cigarettes on his normal salary? Not long after, another internet user spotted a photo of Zhou, this time wearing a Vacheron Constantin watch, valued at over 100,000 yuan, and the fat was in the fire. Great pressure was exerted over the net, and the local government was forced to investigate and then remove him from his position for his extravagant use of public funds (Ma, December 29, 2008).

However, the impact of such internet-based anti-corruption effort is questionable. One Chinese newspaper questions "it took millions of internet users a year to bring about the downfall of a few low-ranking officials. Once the enthusiasm of internet users wears off, who will take over the anti-corruption campaign" (Lin, 2008, p. 2)? It also questions the performance of government disciplinary agencies whose mission is to carry out investigation and punishment of corruptions of public officials. "Even after the Internet had already turned Zhou into a household name, disciplinary officials still refused to look into the case, saying they had not received any official complains about Zhou" (Lin, 2008, p. 2.).

CONCLUSION

This chapter provides an overview of provincial/metropolitan websites in China. It explores the key features of government websites in terms of online information, e-service, government transparency/openness and citizen outreach/responsiveness. Overall, e-government has played a massive role in providing public information and improving transparency and citizen outreach while playing a less significant role in delivering efficient services and including citizens in the decision making process.

Chadwick (2005) identifies two kinds of e-democracy. One is consultative and another is deliberate (in Ainsworth, Hardy & Harley, 2005). Consultative democracy focuses on vertical communication between government and citizens in process of information sharing. Deliberative democracy, on the other hand, includes citizens in the decision making process. In the case of consultative e-democracy, different participants of e-government produce opinions and concerns that are sent "upwards," in a largely vertical and one-way process, to government officials who then decide to factor them into their decision making or not (Ainsworth, Hardy & Harley, 2005). The challenging questions are: what are the selection criteria of the officials and how do they decide to factor them into the policy making process? To answer these questions, researchers need to interview public officials to discover how a particular piece of policy is being made and implemented. Compared with 2003, Chinese government websites have made significant effort to reach out citizens and listen to their opinions, but in terms of promoting e-democracy, they adopt the "e-consultation" approach (Lenihan, 2002, p.34).

A country's e-governance is coherent with its national policy and political ideology. "China can be regarded as a political control tight and an economic control free nation. This has strong implications for the development of its e-government"(Lao, Fung & Ji, 2005, p. 26). Thus Chinese provincial and metropolitan government websites emphasize more economic issues and less political debates. Political debates could threaten political stability and then weaken the economic growth. Currently, features of Chinese e-government serve the goal of enhancing economic development, maintaining political stability and building a harmonious society.

Still, it is significant to remember that Chinese Internet population has the fastest growth rate in the world. China now has 210 million Internet users which are slightly lower than the 215 million in the Unites States and ranks the second in the world. China also has 400 million mobile phone subscribers and 50.4 million of them have used their mobile phones to access Internet. Furthermore, China has 1.5 million websites today and 35,000 of the websites have gov.cn domain names (CNNIC, 2008). These factors will continue to influence China's e-government development and transfer the relationship between the government and citizens.

FUTURE RESEARCH DIRECTIONS

E-government development in China and its role in China's transition to democracy has become a significant research topic in Internet studies. Future research should examine websites of all three-level governments, local, provincial and national, and compare their online features. The comparison will help us understand the primary role each level of e-governments plays and answer questions such as are they being driven by the desire to promote democracy or enhance communist ideology? Future studies should also conduct an extensive review of contents of governor/mayor mailboxes. Do they consist primarily of positive portrayals of public officials or serve as means of reaching out to ordinary citizens? Furthermore, future studies should find out not only what is being provided by the e-government but how decisions are being made and carried out as well. Finally, e-government researchers in the United States should explore collaborative research opportunities with Chinese academics to exchange research ideas or work on research projects associated with e-government development in China.

REFERENCES

Ainsworth, S., Hardy, C., & Harley, B. (2005, August). Online consultation: e-democracy and e-resistance in the case of the development gateway. *Management Communication Quarterly*, *19*(1), 120–145. doi:10.1177/0893318905276562

Ban Yue Forum. (2009, February 10). *Behind the high numbers of government sites.* Retrieved March 19, 2009, from www.henan.gov.cn/zwgk/system/2009/02/10/010118335/shtml

China Internet Network Information Center. (2008 January). *Statistical survey report on the internet development in China.* Beijing: CINIC.

China Youth Daily. (2008, December). *Survey: 85.6% visited government web sites, 61.3% were not satisfactory.* Retrieved March 19, 2009, from http://www.henan.gov.cn/zwgk/system/2008/12/16/010110657.shtml

Hij.gov.cn. (2008 September). *Governor's mail box.* Retrieved March 10, 2009, from http://www.hlj.gov.cn/szxx/hfxd/200811/t20081114_143012.htm

Holliday, I., & Yep, R. (2005). E-government in China. *Public Administration and Development*, *25*, 239–249. doi:10.1002/pad.361

Hu, Y., Xiao, J., Pang, J., & Xie, K. (2005, August 15-17). *A Research on the Appraisal Framework of E-Government Project Success.* Paper presented at ICEC Conference, Xian, China.

Hunan.gov.cn. (2009, February 4). *Report on governor's mail box in the fourth quarter, 2008.* Retrieved March 19, 2009, from http://www.hunan.gov.cn/hdjl/szxx/qkfk/200902/t20090204_151543.htm

Lau, T., Fung, A., & Ji, M. (2005). E-government in China: keeping up with the Joneses? *Journal of E-Government*, *2*(4), 15–38. doi:10.1300/J399v02n04_03

Lenihan, D. (2002, April). *Realigning Governance: From E-Government to E-Democracy.* Paper presented at the E-Government Working Group of OECD, Paris, France.

Lin, Y. (2008, December). Exposing corruption on the Internet: illusory victories? *The China Blog.* Retrieved March 31, 2009, from http://china.blogs.time.com/2008/12/31/exposing-corruption-on-the-internet-illusory-victor…

Ma, W. L. (2008, December). Human flesh search-China-style anti-corruption. *ChinaStakes*. Retrieved March 31, 2009, from http://www.chinastakes.com/WatchFullArticle.aspx?articleid=937

Netchaeva, I. (2002). E-government and e-democracy. *Gazette: The International Journal for Communication Studies*, *64*(5), 467–477. doi:10.1177/17480485020640050601

Saich, T. (2004). *Government and Politics of China*. New York: Palgrave Macmillan.

Seifert, J., & Chung, J. (2009). Using E-government to reinforce government citizen relationships: comparing government reform in the United States and China. *Social Science Computer Review*, *27*(1), 3–23. doi:10.1177/0894439308316404

Waller, P., Livesey, P., & Edin, K. (2001). E-government in the service of democracy. *ICA Information, 74*(5).

Watson, R., & Mundy, B. (2001). A strategic perspective of electronic democracy. *Communications of the ACM*, 44.

West, D. (2001). E-government and the transformation of service delivery and citizen attitudes. *Public Administration Review*, *64*(1), 15–27. doi:10.1111/j.1540-6210.2004.00343.x

West, D. (2003). *State and federal e-government in the United States*. Retrieved March 2, 2004, from http://www.InsidePolitics.org/DwestPubs.html

Westen, T. (2000). E-democracy: ready or not, here it comes. *National Civic Review*, *89*(3), 217–227. doi:10.1002/ncr.89304

Wong, W., & Welch, E. (2004). Does e-government promote accountability? an analysis of website openness and government accountability. *Governance: An International Journal of Policy*, *17*(2), 290.

Yang, K. F. (2003). Neoinstitutionalism and e-government: beyond Jane Fountain. *Social Science Computer Review*, *21*(4), 432–442. doi:10.1177/0894439303256508

Yang, X. S. (2009, January). Direction of 2009 e-government development. *Saidi Net.* Retrieved March 19, 2009, from http://www.henan.gov.cn/zwgk/system/2009/01/16/010115118.shtml

Zhang, J. H. (2005). Good governance through e-governance? Assessing China's e-government strategy. *Journal of E-Government*, *2*(4), 39–71. doi:10.1300/J399v02n04_04

ADDITIONAL READING

Chadwick, A. (2003). Bring e-democracy back in: Why it matters for future research on e-governance. *Social Science Computer Review*, *21*, 443–455. doi:10.1177/0894439303256372

Davison, R. M., Wagner, C., & Ma, L. (2005). From government to e-government: A transition model. *Information Technology & People*, *18*(3), 280–299. doi:10.1108/09593840510615888

Flew, T. (2005, July). *From e-government to online deliberative democracy*. Paper presented at Oxford Internet Institute summer Doctoral Program, Beijing, China.

Garson, G. D. (2006). *Public Information Technology and E-Governance*. Sudbury, MA: Jones and Bartlett Publishers.

Hartford, K. (2005). Dear mayor: Online communications with local governments in Hangzhou and Nanjing. *China Information*, *19*(2), 217–260. doi:10.1177/0920203X05054682

Holliday, I. (2002). Building e-government in East and Southeast Asia: Regional rhetoric and national in action. *Public Administration and Development*, *22*(4), 323–335. doi:10.1002/pad.239

Kluver, R. (2005). The architecture of control: A Chinese strategy for e-governance. *Journal of Public Policy*, *25*(1), 75–97. doi:10.1017/S0143814X05000218

Kluver, R. (2005). US and Chinese policy expectations of the internet. *China Inforamtion*, *19*(2), 299–324. doi:10.1177/0920203X05054685

Kluver, R., & Yang, C. (2005). The internet in China: A meta-review of research. *The Information Society*, *21*, 301–308. doi:10.1080/01972240591007616

Lagerkvist, J. (2005). The rise of online public opinion in the People's Republic of China. China. *International Journal (Toronto, Ont.)*, *3*(1), 119–130.

Ma, L. J., Chung, J., & Thorson, S. (2004). E-government in China: Bring economic development through administrative reform. *Government Information Quarterly*, *22*, 20–37. doi:10.1016/j.giq.2004.10.001

McHenry, W., & Borisov, A. (2006). E-government and democracy in Russia. *Communications of the Association for Information Systems*, *17*, 1064–1123.

McNally, C. A. (2005). Global capitalism vs. Leninist controls: "Information" and e-government in the People's Republic of China. *Journal of E-Government*, *2*(4), 3–14. doi:10.1300/J399v02n04_02

Mulvenon, J. C., & Chase, M. S. (2005). Breaching the great firewall: External challenges to China's internet controls. *Journal of E-Government*, *2*(4), 73–84.

Shi, Y. Q. (2007). The accessibility of Chinese local government web sites: An exploratory study. *Government Information Quarterly*, *24*, 377–403. doi:10.1016/j.giq.2006.05.004

Song, G. (2005, July). *Transcending e-government: A case of mobile government in Beijing.* Paper presented at the First European Conference on Mobile Government, Sussex.

Tsui, L. (2005). The sociopolitical internet in China. *China Information*, *19*(2), 181–188. doi:10.1177/0920203X05054680

United Nations. (2008). *United Nations E-government Survey 2008*. New York: United Nations.

Xie, B., & Jaeger, P. T. (2008). Older adults and political participation on the internet: a cross-cultural comparison of the USA and China. *Journal of Cross-Cultural Gerontology*, *23*, 1–15. doi:10.1007/s10823-007-9050-6

Xiong, J. (2006). Current status and needs of Chinese e-government users. *The Electronic Library*, *24*(6), 747–762. doi:10.1108/02640470610714198

Yang, D. L. (2001). The great net of China. *Harvard International Review*, *22*(4), 64–69.

Yang, G. B. (2003). The co-evolution of the internet and civil society in China. *Asian Survey*, *43*(3), 405–422. doi:10.1525/as.2003.43.3.405

Yao, W. X. (2005). Interoperability: An indispensable propellant of e-China. *International Journal of Services and Standards*, *1*(4), 446–452. doi:10.1504/IJSS.2005.007471

Zhang, J. H. (2002). Will the government "serve the people"? The development of Chinese e-government. *New Media & Society*, *4*(2), 163–184. doi:10.1177/14614440222226325

Zhou, X. (2006). E-government in China: A content analysis of national and provincial web sites. *Journal of Computer-Mediated Communication*, *9*(4), 1–16.

Chapter 21
Exploring Citizens' Visions of 2020 E-Government in Taiwan:
Results from a 2008 Scenario Workshop

Lung-Teng Hu
Taiwan e-Governance Research Center & Shih Hsin University, Taiwan

Don-Yun Chen
Taiwan e-Governance Research Center & National Chengchi University, Taiwan

Kuan-Chiu Tseng
Taiwan e-Governance Research Center & Tamkang University, Taiwan

ABSTRACT

"Why do citizens not use government e-services when they are provided?" This is a question always bothering academics and practitioners of e-government. This chapter will argue that, although e-government initiatives usually are advocated as "consumer- or citizen-centered" reform efforts, the initial plans to implement them are, at best, paternalistic. The authors further argue that citizens should play a critical role in initiating e-government and make those initiatives more citizen-centric. This chapter presents the case of the "2020 E-governance Scenario Workshop," which was held in the fall 2008 in Taiwan, to provide evidence for our argument. By discussing the results of the workshop, this chapter will not only describe the visions and action plans derived from the workshop participants' perspective but will also show that a problem of professional asymmetry still exists in e-government planning. Further, the authors ask how elected officials can be convinced to adopt citizens' visions and plans, as their reluctance presents an obstacle that should be overcome. Despite these challenges, the authors wish to emphasize that e-government planning is in need of a paradigm shift from a technocrat-driven to a citizen-centric model.

DOI: 10.4018/978-1-61520-931-6.ch021

INTRODUCTION

Reinventing the public sector through e-government initiatives has become a worldwide movement, and, in the past decade, information technology (IT) applications providing productive services have been widely recognized as governmental innovations. Administrative reform through e-government initiatives has become one of the core strategies to promote consumer-centered reforms as well. However, the promises of e-government, such as the transformation of how the government does business, the reduction of both transaction costs and government expense, the reinstallation of social capital and restoration of trust through e-participation and e-democracy, and the formation of e-citizenship have been questioned and criticized (Garson, 2004). Among these criticisms rests the practical but fundamental question bothering academics and practitioners of e-government, a question about follow consumer-centered logic: why do citizens not use these e-services? Brewer and others (2006) argue that offering e-government initiatives does not merely serve to improve instrumental efficiency. Indeed, public managers should serve to protect public interests, maintain governmental legitimacy, and uphold democratic values. E-government should be leveraged as the public manager's new instrument for fulfilling these missions, rather than solely for short-term efficiency. Thus, e-government is another channel through which the government can deliver its services and information and interact with the public. To this end, public managers need to seriously consider the legitimacy of e-government initiatives, because any flaw in those initiatives' legitimacy may undermine citizens' adoption of the services. Thus, this chapter argues that this practical problem results partially from a lack of input or requests from the citizens' perspective during the initial stages of most e-government projects, such as the planning process.[1] Although e-government initiatives usually are advocated as consumer- or citizen-centered reform efforts, their initiating decisions are, at best, paternalistic.

As highlighted by the editor C. Reddick, the purpose of this book is to show that most existing literature focuses on what e-government currently offers, but much less is dedicated to evaluating the effectiveness of e-government, especially the impact of e-government and how it has changed citizens' contact with the government. There is an emerging need to look back at e-government from the perspective of the public. Since the legitimacy of instituting e-government initiatives has never been recognized as a question before, the authors attempt to argue that the public should take a critical role in initiating e-government and making such initiatives more citizen-centric. By presenting as a case study the "2020 E-governance Scenario Workshop" held in the fall of 2008 in Taiwan, this chapter demonstrates the importance of citizens' perspective in e-government, as well as showing empirical evidence that citizens can play significant roles at the very early stages of policy deliberation. Moreover, this chapter presents a picture regarding the next-generation of e-government in Taiwan.

In the following sections, we first look at the literature surrounding the debates concerning e-government development. Additionally, we wish to emphasize that participatory governance must be introduced into e-government initiative development to serve as the foundation upon which the legitimacy of e-government initiatives can be built. The chapter then continues with a short historic review of Taiwan's development of e-government initiatives in the past decades, followed by the results of a scenario workshop held in late 2008 to consider the 2020 e-governance initiative in Taiwan. The next section discusses the implications of using a participatory approach in planning e-government development and the picture of future e-governance in Taiwan. Finally, we conclude the chapter with some remarks and suggestions.

BACKGROUND

Worldwide governments at all levels are using technology to enhance citizens', businesses', and agency partners' access to government information, as well as delivery of that information and related services to the public (Heeks, 2001). This phenomenon is being fostered particularly by the shift in paradigm since the 1980s of the New Public Management, characterized by a slogan of "work better, cost less." In this regard, public service delivery through electronic approaches has been recognized as the best instrument for matching these aspirations. Not surprisingly, e-government has been proposed as a way to increase service delivery efficiency, service quality, information transparency, citizen participation in public affairs and decision making, and even citizens' trust in government (Heeks, 2001; Tolbert & Mossberger, 2006). It seems optimistic to suggest that placing information and services online will solve all government problems currently existing. Doubts are raised by scholars on various grounds, such as the problem of the digital divide (Norris, 2001; Compaine, 2001), the possibility of overloaded administrative systems (Neu, Anderson, & Bikson, 1999), and the insufficiency of using "infrastructure readiness" as an indicator of online democratic development (Rodan, 1998; Yang, 2003).

Even with an increasing number of e-government initiatives diffusing worldwide, the possibility of citizen participation in the planning process remains relatively unexplored. The following subsections will discuss the consequences of not engaging citizens in the planning process as potential users, as well as the underlying philosophy of the currently prevalent phenomenon.

Low Usage of E-Government Services: Why?

The imaginary ideal—(if we) build it, they will come—is always intuitively expected by most e-government initiatives. As e-government portals and services have become widespread and adopted across many countries, most governments still confront the challenge of low usage. According to Accenture's survey, the number of Internet users who have rarely or never visited a government web site is 41% in Canada and 48% in the U.S. (Accenture, 2004). Yet Canada and the U.S. are not alone. The level of usage of e-government services in the U.K. is quite low as well (Olphert & Damodaran, 2007). A similar situation is unfolding in Europe. According to Curwell et al. (2005), even though the connectivity of the Internet has dramatically increased in the EU, usage of government e-services is largely lagging behind. The United Nations also indicates that the problem of modest and uneven usage of government online services needs to be overcome (UN, 2008). It is significantly evident that fancy e-government initiatives do not guarantee a high usage of these services—not even web sites. In the meantime, a major scholarly effort has been dedicated to e-democracy (Mahrer & Krimmer, 2005; Scott, 2006; Torres, Pina, & Acerete, 2006) and e-participation (Sæbø, Rose, & Flak, 2008)—which are major sub-fields of e-government-related studies—as the ease, efficiency, and accessibility of information and communication technologies (ICTs) hold the potential to fulfill democratic scholars' aspirations of direct democracy. However, results revealed by e-democracy studies are still frustrating (Torres, Pina, & Acerete, 2006). It stands to reason that there might be a myth in e-government debates.

Using e-government services is not something that people necessarily choose to do, because citizens may not be aware of the presence of e-services (Curwell et al., 2005), even though e-government adoption and practice have rapidly increased (Ho, 2002; Moon, 2002; Norris & Moon, 2005). If citizens cannot fully recognize the benefits of e-government initiatives, then the usage rates of government e-services will logically fall far below expectations, regardless of the level of investment (Olphert & Damodaran, 2007). To address this practical dilemma, scholars state that there is a need to consider the provision of e-government from the perspective of demand, as the supply-side viewpoint has failed (Burroughs, 2009; Reddick, 2005; Sæbø, Rose & Flak, 2008; Thomas & Streib, 2003). The EU, for instance, in order to build up a "knowledge-based information society" by 2010 and achieve sustainable development by 2030, undertook the eEurope Action Plan, beginning with trying to understand citizens' preferences, explore their perception of future needs, and then aim to stimulate their usage of on-line services (Curwell et al., 2005). The emergence of a demand-side perspective in e-government design is not only an economic notion, but it also supports the argument that citizens' adoption of e-government initiatives depends upon whether the process of planning and decision-making is legitimate or not.

In contrast with the advocates of direct and deliberative democracy (those who recommend completely embracing the Internet as the new means of embodying their ideals), a more pessimistic view is that the features of ICTs may serve to undermine the public sphere and political interaction, which essentially underpin authentic public deliberation. The underlying thinking of demand-side planning echoes the emerging concept of so-called "participatory governance," which means that government and public administrators no longer dominate policy-making (Fung and Wright, 2001). Under the influence of participatory governance, the style of interaction between government and citizens has changed. Meanwhile, citizens' attitudes toward government have changed as well. Citizens have become more aware of their right to participate in the decision-making process; as a result, whether the public recognizes a policy is legitimate and acceptable or not certainly depends upon whether they are involved in the policy-making process. In this regard, there is evidence to suggest that the inflated expectations of the effect of e-government could result from a lack of input from citizens during the initial stages of most e-government projects. Thus, planners optimistically anticipate that citizens will want to visit the government's web sites once they are built. However, if the public does not even know of or notice government web sites, and if they never joined in the design process, why would they come to use the information and services available on the web sites voluntarily? Thus, this chapter attempts to fill this gap in the field and contributes a model for properly regarding the process of as well as the participants in building e-government visions.

Who Should Drive the Planning Behind E-Government Initiatives?

Despite the rich literature concerning the availability, accessibility, usability, technical applications, and usage of e-services, the underlying intentions of e-government remain unexplored (Jaeger, 2005). E-government is not simply a platform for new technological applications; it should be a strategy for making services more efficient and effective as well as more responsive to citizens' demands and concerns. Much of the existing literature regarding e-government initiatives assumes a supply-side perspective; discussions from a demand-side perspective are relatively rare (Reddick, 2005). As a result, what a government's websites are offering may be relatively well-understood; in contrast, what citizens need from e-government remains unknown. Yet the underlying concern here is over who should stand at the center to drive the planning of e-government development: bureaucrats, experts, or the public?

The formulation and planning of technological development seems conventionally to be the turf of experts. Probably due to e-government's information technology characteristics, a prevalent suggestion is that the development of e-government needs strong leadership (Weerakkody, Jones, & Olsen, 2007). In addition, the design of ICT systems or platforms has been criticized as traditionally carried out in isolation from users (Finn & Detlor, 2002). As a result, it seems that e-government is a top-down subject in society. A project exploring e-government strategies in Turkey using a strengths, weaknesses, opportunities, and threats (SWOT) analysis, along with an analytic hierarchy process (AHP) technique, is one of the manifest instances of expert-oriented e-government planning (Kahraman, Demirel, & Demirel, 2007).

A critical reflection on the dominant, technocratically oriented model, is, however, emerging. The traditional technocratic model for technological policies is confronting the strong challenge of democratization in technological decision making (Abelson et al., 2007; Bäckstrand, 2003; Bates et al., 2005; Cambrosio & Limoges, 1991; Holemans, 1999; Kloman, 1974; Pidgeon & Rogers-Hayden, 2007; Rask, 2003; Ross, 2007; Weinel, 2007). The importance and role of participatory decision-making in technological policies has been emphasized in advanced countries in biotech and medical technologies (Pidgeon & Rogers-Hayden, 2007; Rask, 2003; Weinel, 2007). The emergence of the democratization of technological policy grows out of the longstanding distrust of the public in bureaucrats, scientists, and even technological industries' decision-making process and capacity for risk management (Rask, 2003). According to Ross (2007), the democratization of technological policy has to empower ordinary people to participate in the deliberation of science and technology. Granting power to scientists to make decisions may result in the ignorance of discrepancies between various citizens and stakeholders' perceptions. To remedy the insufficient democratization of decision-making, as Pidgeon & Rogers-Hayden (2007) hold, citizen participation and engagement in technology-oriented policies should be started as early as possible; further, public administrators need to find a proper balance between public values and technological governance (Ross, 2007). Specifically, technological policies should not be decided by a small group of experts; instead, it should be co-decided by various policy stakeholders through informed public debate (Pidgeon & Rogers-Hayden, 2007: 193). In this regard, participating in the deliberation of technological policy is obviously not a privilege; instead, it is a right, especially for all policy stakeholders. Accordingly, a technological issue like e-government is surely not excluded from this principle.

The central issue that should be addressed, therefore, is that a supply-side approach to e-government development that depends solely on expert advice is unable to deal with the unwelcome result of low usage of e-services. Ironically, it is rarely questioned who should stand at the center of e-service designs, especially in the context of e-government. Empirical evidence suggests that knowing that government Internet services are available is one of the significant factors influencing citizens' acceptance and use of e-government services (Sæbø, Rose, & Flak, 2008). Even though no clearly citizen-driven demand for e-government services has been found, Curwell et al. (2005) still claim that a more inclusive, more democratic, bottom-up e-government strategy can be developed out of a citizen-to-citizen and citizen-to-planner dialogue. Scholars argue that most current academic and practical concerns in e-government are focused narrowly on ICTs' applications; however, "paradoxically, although an explicit objective of e-government is the enhancement of democracy, the design approach adopted in most cases has not been a democratic one" (Olphert & Damodaran, 2007, p. 500). Unquestionably, involving citizens/users in the design process is a critical means to uncover the public's collective preferences in e-government services, systems, and applications (Chen et al., 2006). In an era of participatory governance, the possibility of a participatory approach to policy analysis (deLeon, 1992; Dryzek, 1989; Korac-Kakabadse & Korac-Kakabadse, 2001) and "authentic" public participation in e-government initiative-building are worth exploring (King, Feltey, & Susel, 1998).

Since the emergence of a demand-side perspective, there is yet a small body of literature concerned with citizen engagement in shaping e-government services and initiatives (Olphert & Damodaran, 2007). Thus, the major concern of this chapter is neither e-democracy itself nor participation through government websites; instead, this is a chapter about the democratic planning of e-government, including a model and process for instituting such planning. The authors ask: is the basic mission of e-government to provide citizens and potential users more information as well as easier access to more efficient services? If e-government's users cannot be the designers, then who should be? If e-government users' desires cannot be matched or satisfied, then whose should be? The emphasis that the authors attempt to raise is that of "applying information technologies to realize deliberative democracy" and "applying democratic deliberation to strengthen the legitimacy of e-government initiatives" as two differentiated but equally important matters. However, the former has been over-accentuated while the latter has been neglected in the literature.

The Need for a Citizen-Centric E-Governance Planning Model

Future studies in the e-government field have become an emerging topic. Among the associated studies, scenario building techniques are depicted as a useful method. For example, Cairns et al. (2004) explored the future development of e-government through scenario planning. Janssen et al. (2007a) constructed the future development of e-government in 2020 using a scenario-building technique. The scenario-building process was based upon regional workshops held in EU member countries. As a result, eight scenarios that e-government applications may confront in 2020 were derived from 29 regional scenarios. Janssen et al. (2007b) conducted scenario-building workshops in Europe and the United States, which concluded with fifteen scenarios for future e-government. In addition, Dawes (2008) has recently suggested that relevance, confidence, interoperability, and innovation will be critical factors influencing the future vision of e-government.

The findings of these studies might be appealing, since possible scenarios that future e-government is going to confront and the future issues that public managers have to address in advance are outlined. However, it is worth noting that the people who were involved in the process and production of these scenarios deserve much more careful attention. In the Northshire case, addressed in Cairns and others' (2004) study, scenarios were constructed by elected Northshire Council members and officials, as well as by partners in public and nonprofit organizations, facilitated by experts in scenario planning. As for the others, the participants involved in Janssen and colleagues' (2007b) scenario-building workshops were academics, consultants, government officials, software providers, and private sector members. Obviously, citizens were still absent in these e-government scenario-building cases. However, do the examples cited here represent the prevalent model driving e-government projects in the field? Is this model sufficient for participatory governance as outlined above? Do we have another alternative?

It has been pointed out by scholars that the crucial problem with current e-government practices is their technocentric approach, which only minimally involves the public (Olphert & Damodaran, 2007); it has been further suggested that e-governance strategy must go beyond technical goals and issues (Ulrich & Chacko, 2005). According to Moon & Welch (2005), citizens and bureaucrats have different perspectives, attitudes, and concerns regarding e-government strategy and adoption. While scholars emphasize the potential impact of e-government on the democratization of policy planning or political issues through online dialogue and deliberation (Jaeger, 2005), the authors of this chapter would further argue that even though e-government absolutely has the potential and responsibility to promote and realize democracy via digital channels, the model selected to construct these digital channels deserves more attention. In our viewpoint, e-government should not only encourage societal dialogue and participation as an instrument of democratization (Jaeger, 2005), but further, the process of e-government development as such should be democratized and participatory as well.

Taking the socio-technical systems perspective, Mumford (1983; 1991) has convincingly emphasized the necessity of a user-participatory approach in new systems design. Mumford (1983) not only advocates the participatory design model, but also points out that potential users of the system should be involved in the initial stages. Olphert & Damodaran (2007), echoing Mumford's theory, claim that engagement with the stakeholders in e-government services during the design process may provide developers with understanding of different stakeholders' needs, aspirations, levels of experience, problems, priorities, and values; as a result, mutual respect and understanding, social inclusion, and enhanced democracy can be achieved. Apparently, information policies and strategies stand as a road map guiding a nation's direction for information technology development (Ulrich & Chacko, 2005). Yet who should decide the direction of the development of the road map?

It has become a new consensus in the field that e-government strategies should be citizen-centric (Ulrich & Chacko, 2005). As Olphert & Damodaran (2007: 496) state, "Engagement was most effective when citizens were engaged throughout and from the earliest stages of development, and when they were motivated and empowered to participate in relevant decision making." Even though difficulties in discovering users' desires, their lack of awareness of available technological solutions, and their lack of time and resources have been uncovered as hurdles to involving citizens in the e-government development process (Finn & Detlor, 2002), it is believed that there is no chance of achieving a high adoption of e-government services, increased social inclusion, and an enhanced democracy as expected without engagement with the public (Olphert & Damodaran, 2007). Thus, involving the public in the process of shaping e-government initiatives is an unavoidable issue confronting e-government decision-makers in the era of public management reforms.

Yet how do we engage citizens in e-government development effectively? In particular, we need to deal with and overcome the professional asymmetry between experts and ordinary people as they participate in e-government discussion together. Researchers claim that the formulation of e-governance strategy must include as components: visions, consensus, and plans for implementation (Ulrich & Chacko, 2005). Moreover, an effective civic participation model for e-government development must be derived from a meaningful project where cooperative actions are undertaken in which citizens are fairly and diversely represented and participate meaningfully in the process (Finn & Detlor, 2002). Additionally, engagement with ordinary people in e-government designs essentially requires building the capacities of those citizens who want to be involved in the development of e-services (Olphert & Damodaran, 2007). To fit all these requirements, we examine a deliberative democracy model—the scenario workshop—through which citizens can not only achieve a consensus in visions of the future of e-government and create action plans based upon these visions through a fair and meaningful process, but can also exchange their plans and goals informed by basic knowledge. Therefore, this chapter provides an illustrative case and aims to prove, by demonstrating the concrete results derived from a scenario workshop in Taiwan, that ordinary people are as capable as experts of developing their views regarding future e-government.

THE CASE OF TAIWAN'S 2020 E-GOVERNANCE SCENARIO WORKSHOP

In this section, first we introduce the brief history of the development of e-governance in Taiwan. Then, the operation and process of the Taiwan 2020 E-Governance Scenario Workshop will be described. In the next section, visions and action plans derived from the workshop will be presented and discussed.

A Brief History of the Emergence of E-Governance in Taiwan

From 1980 to 1990, several departments and committees at the level of central government initiated e-government plans pertaining to the creation of administrative information systems across certain policy fields. And, all of the e-government efforts enhance the goal of long-term national development and administrative efficiency and effectiveness by computerizing inter-government processes for the most part and promoting the information industry through work contracts.

At this time, contributions towards the organization of e-government were made by "the Information Development Office (IDO), Executive Yuan", which was established in February, 1982. Many achievements in e-government today are based upon the earlier contributions of the IDO, in particular to the management information systems (MIS) needed for the computerization of services and the automation of office duties needed to modernize official document processing. However, due to the rapid advance of information, technology, and communication and to the global reform of public management, the government authority in Taiwan was forced to reorganize the IDO in August, 1994.

Put differently, in order to respond positively to western countries of advanced IT who were engaged in various ICT projects, such as "The Project of National Information Infrastructure (NII)" proposed by the American government in 1993, government authorities in Taiwan decided to establish the National Information Infrastructure Steering Committee (NII), Executive Yuan, to be in charge of the infrastructure for information and communication, in order to keep pace with the changing world. Since then, resources and budget for e-government were largely allocated for the construction of infrastructure and to provide preliminary government website services.

While the NII Committee certainly made great efforts in steering the creation of the national IT infrastructure, this organization eventually was formally replaced by the so-called "National Information and Communication Initiative Committee (NICI), Executive Yuan" on April 4, 2001. The overall missions of NICI include not only the government sector but also the business and industrial sectors. Moreover, these missions include both hard engineering and soft engineering.[2] Regarding the NICI's substantial contributions, after 2001, certain influential e-government projects, such as Challenge 2008, the e-Taiwan Program, the Mobil Taiwan Program, and the Ubiquitous Taiwan Program, were initiated by the NICI. Unlike earlier investment in ICT, these programs operate essentially across sectors. In some respect, it can be seen that these programs represent gradual steps to widen and deepen the scope of information applications in Taiwan, with the intention of achieving the goal of a ubiquitous networked society as soon as possible.

The organizational arrangement of NICI is such that members are mainly from government agencies, enterprises, and research institutions. This makes a bit of difference in comparison to earlier stages, since more and more stakeholders began to be invited to participate in the decision-making process. Nevertheless, one of the senior public managers has admitted that, in past years, mid-level public bureaucrats have been responsible for drafting e-government initiatives, and experts from the public and private sectors have provided recommendations to government

Table 1. The evolution of e-government in Taiwan

	'80-'90	'90-'97	'98-'00	'01-'04	'03-'07	'08-'12
initiative name	administrative information system	Computerization of services	Web/ e-government program	e-government project	e-Taiwan program	U-Taiwan program
initiator	IDO		NII	NICI		
representation	officials, scholars			officials, scholars, businessmen		
vision	efficiency	administrative effectiveness and service delivery				public value
deliberation	median			Extended		

Source: The authors

authorities. Ordinary people, as expected, have been completely excluded from participating in the decision-making process. In the language of public policy, the agenda-setting power is proportionately dominated by public authorities rather than by ordinary citizens, and clearly this leaves room for improvement in the way of policy democratization.

What can we learn from the story of e-government in Taiwan? We think that the history of e-government initiatives in Taiwan might be summarized as follows (see Table 1). First, members of those steering committees are solely public officials and scholars in the early stages but gradually open to stakeholders from business sectors in the later stages. Unfortunately, the power of agenda-setting is by and large dominated by the so-called "societal elite," although many kinds of stakeholders have started to join the steering committees. Second, in the near future, the ideas for initiating e-governance projects apparently will not be limited to the instrumental values of administrative efficiency and service quality; rather, those involved will begin to appreciate the possibility of fostering the higher values of social equity and justice through innovative applications of ICT.

Further, students with a training background in public policy can see that the decision-making style for e-government projects is moving gradually from being a centralized authority to becoming a decentralized authority, especially when multiple stakeholders are willing to participate in and capable of enjoying deliberation with an open mindset and communicative skills. Nevertheless, as mentioned, a clear fact is that these stakeholders still do not consist of ordinary people or nonprofit organizations (NPOs). From the viewpoint of participatory governance and consumer-oriented ideals, to enlarge the base of policy legitimacy and societal acceptance of e-government initiatives, it seems that the best way is to authentically invite them to participate in the initial decision-making circle, and, through an elaborate and sophisticated procedural arrangement, a great contribution might be made.

Process of the Scenario Workshop

This chapter utilizes the "scenario workshop" as a way to practice the ideal notion of deliberative democracy. This kind of method originated in Denmark and was developed by the Danish Board of Technology in the early 1990s with the aim of overcoming the challenges of improving the ecological sustainability of urban life (Goven and Langer, 2005). In order to explore a well-supported vision of the future of e-government and simultaneously to encourage various actor groups to collaborate in formulating and implementing action plans, we created this experimental platform for empirical data collection and analysis.

To accomplish this goal, the authors attempted to invite representatives with different backgrounds to attend the meeting. The authors stimulated them to submit ideas boldly and exchange arguments freely with each other. We expected that consensus could be fostered via the well-designed process of social learning. However, stakeholders with multiple perspectives will not achieve consensus smoothly and automatically unless we consciously design a reasonable methodology. To clarify the whole process, four crucial dimensions are necessarily illuminated in the first place. They are:

(1) Organizations: Two organizations played key roles in the operation of the scenario workshop: the "research team" and the "consulting committee". The former was responsible for planning and implementing the scenario workshop, and the latter was to provide professional judgments and assistance. According to the objectives of the scenario workshop, the members of the consulting committee had concrete backgrounds in either e-government or deliberative democracy.

(2) Issues: This refers to "agenda setting" or "problem definition". After reviewing the literature, four main issues were proposed for deliberation, including "Convenient Life and Virtual World", "Information and Communication Safety and Technology Development", "Boundary-spanning and Integrated Service", and "We are the Government and Ubiquitous Democracy". Apparently, these issues are directly linked to current theories of e-governance, and many have to do with every citizen's life, which is worthy of inquiry.

(3) Scenario: This designates an account or synopsis of a projected course of actions, events, or situations. Participants may or may not have been familiar with the related issues outlined above, and thus the pros and cons of the arguments in relation to specific issues had to be explicated in a friendly and simple way for most participants to read and to criticize more easily.

(4) Participants: Four categories of clients were identified, and they were representatives from government authorities, enterprise, nonprofit organizations, and ordinary citizens. The quota of participants in each of the first three groups was ten, but the last one was 15. Accordingly, in total, 45 participants were recruited[3]. To balance the power of representatives from different sectors, factors that might affect claims or concerns, such as geographic locality, industrial classification, and even level of position (i.e., managers and non-managers), were seriously considered.

We will now introduce the substantial procedure. The scenario workshop was a two-day meeting, held on September 27th and October 18th in the school of management at Shih-Hsin University in Taipei, Taiwan. The whole procedure can be divided into two main parts; each of them was concerned with how to build participants' common vision and how to propose action plans.

The vision-building strategy was composed of five detailed steps. Specifically, they are: (1) Formulating an initial vision of the role of the group. (2) Comparing the discrepancies between the initial vision and the scenario provided. (3) Formulating each of the groups' ideals (after comparing the discrepancies above, each of the groups had to formulate its concluding vision). (4) Delivering their respective visions to all audiences (the point here is to clarify which visions are more desirable and feasible and to find out the plausible convergences and discrepancies among them). (5) Formulating the common vision (the common vision, which undergoes myriad deliberations, is the crucial output of the first-day meeting, and participants could use it to produce further action plans later).

The action plan itself was also derived from several steps, which are as follows: (1) Participants

Table 2. Coding numbers of interviewees

Panels	Coding numbers
Government panel	G1~G7
Business panel	B1~B8
NPO panel	N1~N9
Citizen panel	C1~C15
Total	39

Source: The authors.

are divided again. After the common vision is constructed, all participants have to be classified again into four groups without considering their original backgrounds. (2) Participants select the initial five action plans from each of the groups and then market these action plans to all audiences to win their support. (3) The final five action plans are decided upon and prioritized, and then further discussion takes place regarding respective challenges when these action plans are actually put into practice in the future.

As mentioned, since one of our research interests lies in figuring out the best configurations for allowing ordinary people to voice their ideas, we are naturally curious as to whether there is something special in their ideas and plans acquired through brainstorming. Also, we took this opportunity to assess the effectiveness of the scenario workshop. That is, we tried to grasp what participants thought of this activity and what they had learned during the process of deliberation. To solve the puzzle, a total of 39 participants were interviewed after the scenario workshop (see Table 2). By and large, our protocol surrounded the key aspects for assessing the scenario workshop. But for those representatives from the public sector, we especially designed an extra protocol focusing on their attitude toward citizen participation. Since public officials have played a dominant and decisive role in policy decision-making, we suppose that their attitudes will certainly be influenced by this kind of activity. This is the main reason why we would like to raise more questions for them.

Results of the Scenario Workshop

This section presents the results of the 2020 E-Governance Scenario Workshop in Taiwan. The scenario workshop agenda centered on three major issues: I. What are the services that citizens are most eager for e-governance to provide? II. In 2020, how could government balance the conflict between information openness and personal privacy while promoting e-governance? III. What extent do you expect that the development of political democracy in Taiwan will achieve based upon the progress of e-governance in 2020? For each issue, participants in the scenario workshop were asked to propose three visions, and, in turn, participants had to formulate three action plans for achieving each vision. The issues, visions, and action plans discussed and produced in the e-governance scenario workshop were as follows.

The first issue discussed in the workshop was: "What are the services that citizens are most eager for e-governance to provide?" Three visions were proposed, and three action plans were devised for each of the visions. They are as follows:

- **Vision I-I:** Strengthening the current hard and soft infrastructures, as well as minimizing the digital divide in Taiwan.

Action Plans I-I

1. Regulating Internet services' management and quality, and addressing through

legislation such issues as those resulting from telecommunication market leaders' domination. Cutting the price of Internet access to an affordable level for the general public, and further, offering subsidies for residents in remote districts. Promoting information education by collaborating with industries and NPOs.
2. Establishing business information-sharing systems and partially integrating them with governmental systems.
3. Establishing governmental promotion unit by contract, privatization, or public tender and formulating standards for mobile devices and information exchange.

The digital divide is still the principal challenge confronting governments worldwide, including Taiwan's. Therefore, the first vision proposed by the participants is the reduction of the digital divide in Taiwan. In this vision, cutting the price of Internet access and managing the telecommunication market were concerns of the participants. Further, participants also asked government to enhance information accessibility, citizens' information literacy, and information education through collaboration among government, businesses, and non-profit organizations.

- **Vision I-II:** Providing integrated e-services across boundaries and sectors, as well as without time and place limitations; further, these e-services should be able to be processed and completed in real time.

Action Plans I-II

1. Instituting a high-level information authority, such as a ministry of information or bureau of information, with independent budget and personnel, to which the formulation and implementation of national information policies shall be responsible, and with which the cooperation of local authorities are required.
2. By building up hard and soft mobile devices, citizens can: (1) process applications and other business with governments via TV and remote, or cell phone, instead of computers; (2) equip businesses with mobile devices in village offices or convenience stores.
3. Making it possible that people can deal with any government-related business in any public agency. The government has to get rid of departments and units constituting barriers to the integration of information systems and provide convenient services (e.g., information integration for household registration, land administration, the National Health Insurance Bureau, the Internal Revenue Service) through legislations or administrative orders.

"Real time" and "integration" will certainly become the core values of the next generation of e-government. According to the participants, the future government will be an ambient government. In the future, people may not perceive the existence of government, but the government will be nonetheless ubiquitous. People will be able to deal with governmental businesses anytime and anywhere via mobile devices. More importantly, on-demand-style e-services will not satisfy the public anymore; in contrast, citizens surely will ask the government to process and respond to their business in a real time. To this end, the back-office of government agencies should be integrated across boundaries and sectors. In this regard, legislation and institutional reforms must be undertaken to achieve vertical and horizontal agency integration.

- **Vision I-III:** Public information should be openly shared; further, public service information (e.g., disaster, security, transport, and other related information) could be collected in real time, reported by individuals immediately, and relayed to the person who needs information from the government instantly.

Action plans I-III

1. Offering disaster, security, transport, elderly safety, and other related information from the government through various media; in addition, the information should be released, delivered, and returned immediately.
2. Establishing competitive and monitoring mechanisms for public service information and adopting the rule that the user pays.
3. Setting up local service centers commissioned by the government to provide instant public information.

In this vision, participants are asking for openly shared public information. Further, citizens need the public information to be offered immediately to the person who needs it. Moreover, the collection and delivery of public information should be monitored.

The second issue discussed in the workshop was: "In 2020, how could government balance the conflict between information openness and personal privacy in promoting e-governance?" There were three visions proposed and three action plans devised for each of the visions, except vision II-III. These outcomes were as follows:

- **Vision II-I:** Establishing comprehensive and forward-looking legislation regarding personal information security and protection by which responsibilities of government, business, and individuals are regularized.

Action Plans II-I

1. Speeding up the progress of legislation regarding personal information protection; in addition, establishing a promoting unit to define personal information through public dialogue. Additionally, setting up a monitoring agency to oversee the use of personal confidential information (if such information is used in unlawful conduct, offenders should be subject to heavy penalties).
2. Legislation must be the primary condition. In addition, building dedicated units not only to enhance public education and the promotion of information security, but also to strengthen law enforcement for combating Internet crimes.
3. To preserve fair trade in the market, government must fulfill oversight responsibility to investigate and disclose the information of manufacturers which abuse personal information.

Personal information security is always the primary concern of the public. Responsibility for information protection not only by the government but also by businesses and individuals should be regularized by legislation. Most violations, theft, and misuse of personal information derive from businesses and individuals; however, neither of them is included in present regulations. Therefore, participants are looking for a remedy for this problem. Legislation, monitoring, and public education are the major strategies to address personal information security problems, participants say.

- **Vision II-II:** Empowering individuals with the right of decision over personal information openness: as personal information is being accessed or used in any media, individuals should be notified and should even have the right to decide whether to allow its use.

Action Plans II-II

1. Individuals shall be empowered by the right to decide whether to offer personal information, including biological characteristics, to government archives or for further open use. However, if the information is associated with public policies (e.g., comprehensive income tax, housing tax, land tax, or medical information), the government reserves the right to query and integrate it but is not allowed to release it.
2. Personal information should be classified at different levels of importance, which should be identified as standards by legislation or business agreements. As personal information is being accessed or used, the individual should be notified immediately and be able to decide whether to allow its use.
3. Personal information should be verified digitally at different levels, such as general information, personal information, policy-associated information, and personal property information.

Due to the rampant theft of personal information, citizens are requesting the right to choose whether to offer their personal information or not when someone is accessing and using it. To this end, participants propose that personal information should be classified at different levels of importance, and the classification should be identified by legislation.

- **Vision II-III:** The security of personal information management and storage should be verified by the latest technologies, using DNA, pupil profile, and/or fingerprinting as the verification code. Further, personal information should be secured and classified based upon the levels of information importance.

Action Plans II-III

1. Personal information should be encrypted by the government. The government should establish a flawless data verification code system, a faultless data classification system, and an ad hoc security management system with a specific person in charge.
2. The government should establish a universal personal identification database in which personal fingerprints and DNA information should be collected by the household registration authority. The government then should develop a non-repudiation mechanism, such as Perfect ID or certificate of natural person, and set up the classification system.

Following the previous vision, participants propose that personal information should be secured by a flawless system according to the highest standards and latest technologies. According to the participants, management of personal information must incorporate a classification system in which personal information can only be accessed by non-repudiation mechanisms and verification codes such as Perfect ID. Further, the use of various verification codes should be combined differently according to the different levels of information importance.

The third issue discussed in the workshop is: "To what extent do you expect the development of political democracy in Taiwan will proceed based upon the progress of e-governance in 2020?" Three visions are proposed and three action plans devised for each of the visions. The outcomes are as follows:

- **Vision III-I:** Open all information in the government's decision-making processes through an e-governance platform. In addition, promote the direct participation of citizens in parliament through digital information and reporting systems. Moreover, monitor the government's integrity and operational effectiveness; for example, monitor public construction during preliminary, middle, and concluding stages.

Action Plans III-I

1. Providing non-edited audio-visual materials of legislators' meetings and public hearings through channels, MOD, and/or digital databases and empowering citizens to search and monitor the government in real time or afterward, without the limitation of time and space.
2. Integrating with cell-phones and video systems, empowering citizens to participate in congress meetings, in which citizens can join in the legislative process: to be able to vote, inspect, query, and express opinions in real time, as well as get officials' responses immediately.
3. Legislatively establishing foundations whose representatives include political appointees, public officials, academics, NPOs, and private organizations, and setting up classified databases containing every record of policy implementation, use of funds, and implementation of political views. Further, openly recruiting a project manager, who comes from society but is familiar with the operation of government as well, to offer efficient, perfect, and convenient services for various demands.

For furthering political democracy development in Taiwan, the participants are looking forward to a state with "transparent government", "direct democracy", and "direct monitoring" that represents the progress of e-governance in 2020. In 2020, the public hopes to participate in making decisions in the executive, legislature, and even judicial branches. Citizens may be empowered to join in the discussion of legislation, voting, and, policy-making and to get responses from legislators and officials instantly, with the assistance of information communication technologies.

- **Vision III-II:** Through established internet platforms, every individual could become a civil reporter initiating, participating in, and summarizing discussions on issues. Provided by the Internet, information could make deliberation of public policies possible. Also, these activities will activate and deepen the dynamic participation of citizens in public affairs.

Action Plans III-II

1. Establishing an e-petition system to collect citizens' opinions for both the executive and legislative branches. Several conditions should be fulfilled. First, the initiation of issues should be controlled by NPOs, NGOs, or ordinary citizens. Second, for a new petition to be considered, there would have to be a minimum number of comments attached (for example, over 5000). Third, the responsibility for summarizing opinions should be given to a neutral NPO or NGO.
2. Formally empowering citizen reporters to induce public officials to respond to or even implement collected opinion from the Internet.
3. Establishing legal status to empower mechanisms related to direct democracy and to delegate discretionary power to civil servants to take into consideration all the opinion collected from the Internet.

Participants proposed a realization of the idea of direct democracy through the leveraging the advantages of ICTs. The participants asked for direct participation and informed deliberation in public affairs. It was also proposed that empowering citizens to become civil reporters would activate participatory energy at the grassroots level. Further, legal status and responsibility should be established and delegated to citizens, neutral NPOs, and NGOs in order to exercise direct democracy.

- **Vision III-III:** Utilizing ICTs to realize direct democracy, including i-voting, e-rulemaking, e-recall, e-referendums, e-initiation, e-approvals, and so on.

Action Plans III-III

1. Concerning the issue of i-voting, the implementation should be incremental. The goal is to use i-voting to secure the voting rights of overseas students, overseas working populations, and trans-regional voters in Taiwan. The location could be an ATM or 7-11. This action plan should be connected with action plan number one in vision I-II.
2. Business and government sectors should collaborate to establish a direct democracy Internet platform, and the expense should be covered by the government budget. Businesses could provide computers, PDAs or other necessary hardware for ICTs. The purpose of this collaboration is to realize i-voting, e-petitioning, and all other direct democracy activities.
3. Information revealed in the budgetary process between executive and legislative branches should be readable and understandable to the citizens. Then these processes should be approved or monitored by citizens on the Internet.

The participants are looking forward to realizing direct democracy, removing the representatives from the political system, and exercising comprehensive civil rights by utilizing information technologies. The participants expect that the civil rights of i-voting, e-recall, e-initiative, e-referendum, e-rulemaking, and e-approvals can be realized and exercised by electronic channels. But the progress should be incremental rather than radical. The plan should first be attempted with overseas students, overseas employees, and trans-regional voting in Taiwan; then it should be implemented from the local to the central level incrementally. Additionally, the budget and final account reports revealed by the executive and legislative branches should be readable and understandable to the public without professional terminologies and jargons, in order to protect citizens' exercise of civil rights.

In sum, the scenario workshop reveals that citizens expect that the future e-government should be characterized by: (1) real-time information and service provision, (2) back-office systems integrated across boundaries and sectors, (3) open and shared government information, (4) ubiquitous government, (5) transparent and accountable government, (6) empowered decision-making rights so that citizens can choose whether to disclose personal information, (7) a highly-secured personal information management system, (8) enhanced e-citizenship, (9) direct monitoring of government operation, and (10) direct participation and direct democracy. The visions and action plans presented above imply that ordinary people may be capable of discussing and envisioning the future of e-government with officials, business persons, and experts. While some ideas in these visions have emerged recently, the participants considered seriously the mechanisms for implementing and bringing these visions into practice. Next, the implications of the visions and action plans, as well as the practice of scenario workshops for vision building, will be discussed.

Table 3. Willingness to utilize channels to engage governments

	Applying for Services	Collecting Information	Expressing Opinion	Voting
Telephone/Fax	22%	25%	25%	1%
In Person	**40%**	20%	12%	**80%**
Internet (users only)	21% (31%)	**41% (60%)**	**32%** (48%)	17% (25%)
Letters	5%	2%	6%	0%
Third Person	6%	5%	13%	0%
No-response	5%	7%	12%	2%

Source: Chiang et al. (2004).

REFLECTIONS AND DISCUSSIONS

In this section, we will combine all we collected and found to respond to the argument raised in the very beginning of this chapter: that citizens should take a critical role in initiating e-government and in making the initiatives more citizen-centric in order to establish the projects' legitimacy. Based on the review of Taiwan's e-government planning history, first, we can definitely say that it has been an "elitist" process since the 1980s. The vision of promoting "citizen participation" has entered into e-government initiatives as late as 2007. Bureaucrats and experts led the process of e-government vision-building, and there was almost no direct participation from the potential users. Although there are more and more business representatives joining in the process in recent decades, ordinary citizens—even members from NPOs—are never invited into the process. As a result, the e-service initiatives provided by government could not fit in with the public's demands and preferences. According to a national survey done in Taiwan by Chiang and others (2004), we can see in Table 3 that ordinary citizens prefer to apply to government services in person rather than online. However, placing services online has been the focus of e-government initiatives in past decades. Rather than using e-services, citizens would like to use the Internet to collect information from and express opinions in government websites. That is, people prefer that the initiatives of e-government focus on "let me know" and "listen to me" rather than "serve me well" in their online function. Also, an earlier national survey in the US partially confirmed the preference of users in Taiwan (see Larsen & Rainie, 2002). Thus, there is a gap between what people need and what government provides in terms of e-government initiatives. Eventually, the gap between demands and provisions of e-service may diminish citizens' interest in searching and using e-government initiatives.

As the 2003 UN e-government report (2003: 66-67) states, the low usage of e-government services is a governance issue related to the lack of early involvement from potential users. In this regard, the 2020 E-Governance Scenario Workshop was an experiment with the purpose of involving ordinary citizens in the beginning stages of e-government planning and, further, of providing a platform for citizens to voice their ideas about e-government development. A further concern may be what citizens' visions will look like or whether such a citizen-oriented scenario workshop engaging technological issues would yield meaningful output. Let us evaluate them in a systematic way. Following the 2003 UN e-government report, we can see in Table 4 that the visions collected from the Scenario Workshop are distributed in all three major dimensions of e-government (e-readiness, e-service, and e-democracy). Several areas of issues can be discussed here.

Table 4. Visions collected from the scenario workshop in UN's e-government categories

		Issue I			Issue II			Issue III		
		I-I	I-II	I-III	II-I	II-II	II-III	III-I	III-II	III-III
e-readiness		▲	▲		▲		▲			
e-service			▲	▲		▲				
e-democracy	e-information		▲	▲	▲	▲		▲	▲	
	e-consultation			▲		▲		▲	▲	
	e-decision-making							▲	▲	
	e-voting									▲

Source: The authors.

First, there are four visions related to the infrastructure of e-government. They are: (1) building equality into the setting of e-government or alleviating the problem of the digital divide (I-I), (2) having basic equipment for building ubiquitous services such as wireless Internet (I-II), (3) brokering seamless legislation on e-government related issues such as e-government information acts (II-I), and (4) installing secure protection of personal privacy in e-government programs (II-III). Second, we can see that the vision of future e-service must have the features of being informative, boundary-spanning, and in real time. Third, the proposed directions for technological development for future e-government are: (1) developing ubiquitous e-service portals where all services are in real time (I-II; II-II); (2) designing a personal "perfect ID" system to alleviate ID problems on the internet; (3) constructing a personalized service business model to enhance personal choice (I-III and II-II), and (4) constructing an online monitoring system to hold representative institutions and administrative procedures accountable to citizenry (III-II). Based upon the analysis here, the results reached by the scenario workshop significantly demonstrate the quality of citizen-oriented deliberation, even for a technological issue like e-governance, since the workshop definitely grasps the global tendency of e-government development.

In general, through the collective efforts in the scenario workshop, the participants' visions on e-governance in 2020 Taiwan were found to look like the following:

1. The initiatives should be preoccupied with Internet human rights and provide personalized and real-time service;
2. In the process of promoting initiatives, the government should establish adequate legislation as the background for a secure and personalized information sharing system;
3. In order to deepen democracy, the initiative should assist people in effectively holding their representatives accountable at all times and offer equal chances to participate in the decision-making process in order to realize citizen's rights online.

Finally, and in addition to the concrete results from the scenario workshop, we are concerned about the capability of citizens in deliberating e-government issues. That is, is it possible for ordinary people to participate in the vision-building process of e-government initiatives as an instance of democratic decision making? We use interview information from after the scenario workshop to respond to this concern. First, we are interested in whether the process of forming visions or action plans is dominated by the experts in the group. One NPO participant said that:

No, they (visions and action plans) are not minority opinions. Although I might not agree with certain opinions, I am willing to listen. Some might not talk in the process, but all we talked about is listed on the board, right? As I said, people listening to these arguments without replying back might mean they are consenting with what other people are saying... (N3)

However, a few participants express their negative feelings about how some really dominated the process.

Some might be of no opinion or they did not know how to think throughout the meeting. They talk very little. So I am not sure those (visions and action plans) are consensus opinions, because these people were only passive followers. (C13)

One of the participants from the government expresses the same pessimistic opinion about the real meaning of citizen participation in the workshop. He said that:

Some are really capable of participating, such as those from the NPO and businesses. However, comparatively speaking, a citizen is less capable of attending a meeting like this. The participants from the government are able to lead the people. They were trying to influence others' opinions. My personal opinion is that this is not good for the independence of the meeting... (G6)

The message is mixed in the interview data. It can be said that the workshop is a formal way to include ordinary people to participate in government policy formation. However, the problem of "professional asymmetry" is still a critical obstacle to effective and meaningful participation. Although the workshop was designed to conquer that obstacle by offering participants a readable handbook and various lectures, the problem was only partially alleviated rather than solved.

Further, the authors wonder whether participants think the results of the workshop will be realized by the government. This concern is related to the curiosity as to whether the government will consider the results of the workshop seriously or not. Participants from different groups express their opinion as follows:

I think if the government moves in the direction revealed in the workshop—I mean that even if there are only three or five action plans collected here among the twenty-some action plans being realized by the government in 2020, I think that it will be worthwhile to have had this workshop. (B5)

I think that it is very important to bring citizens back these days. However, you should inform your supervisor and persuade those with power to agree that citizen participation is important and an acceptable idea of governing. (G1)

Probably, some of the opinions can be realized, but the problem is that government is not willing to change. Maybe change is risky, or usually they only need to tell you that they are professional bureaucrats. There is nothing you can do. (N6)

From these opinions, we can see that participants have reservations concerning the realization of visions or action plans collected in the workshop. By summarizing all the opinions expressed in the interviews, we can recognize the following four obstacles: (1) participants from the government expressed reservations about the feasibility of certain action plans; (2) some expressed their concern that because government is not fully transparent, citizens have no way of monitoring whether these action plans will be implemented; (3) some believe the government's usual image of being willing only to "take into consideration" rather than being mandated to follow these action plans; (4) many participants think that government officials only have election-oriented rather than public policy democratization mentalities. In this regard, there are still hurdles to be overcome in terms of realizing the visions and action plans indicated in the citizen-oriented E-Governance Scenario Workshop. However, the hurdles revealed above exist precisely in the government.

CONCLUSION

This chapter is concerned that current vision building practices of e-government initiatives are insufficient and lack a participatory planning approach for citizens or users. As a result, citizens who are the potential users of e-government services have little intention of using e-services because they are not involved in the planning process, not informed about e-services' existence and benefits, and further, do not recognize any relevance of the e-services for themselves. Consequentially, e-government services are rarely used. The fundamental solution for reversing this unwanted phenomenon, as demonstrated in this chapter, is a participatory vision-building model of e-government initiatives in which citizens are not only engaged at the beginning stages of the e-government planning process but can also participate in a fair, informed, and meaningful deliberation on the issues. Indeed, there is a need for a paradigm shift in e-government vision building from being a technocrat-driven to becoming a citizen-centric model.

Furthermore, the authors demonstrate an illustrative case with the 2020 E-Governance Scenario Workshop held in Taiwan. The model, operationalization, and process of the scenario workshop are presented to illustrate its feasibility in the real world. The visions and action plans reached at the scenario workshop reveal the capacity of ordinary people, serving as participants, to deal with technological issues such as e-government initiatives, and evidence of how citizens can play a critical role in initiating e-government is offered.

The technocentric approach to vision-building and planning of e-government initiatives, in which technocracy and experts dominate the process and decision making, should be replaced by a democratic participatory approach. In this participatory model, citizens would stand at the center of issues and concerns and participate in the initial stages of e-government development. Citizens' visions, desires, and plans, rather than bureaucrats' or experts', should be incorporated at the beginning of e-government initiative planning. Based upon the experience of the e-governance scenario workshop held in Taiwan, as well as on the analyses above, we are somewhat hopeful that the aspiration of moving toward a citizen-centric participatory vision building approach can be achieved, although there remain obstacles. It is surely heartening that the civic-oriented inclination of the participants was enhanced after they participated in the deliberative workshop. However, the problem of professional asymmetry between ordinary people and experts should first be overcome. Further, elected officials' support and perception of the visions and action plans constructed by citizens are the decisive factor which may eventually influence whether the visions and plans can be fulfilled or not. The problems mentioned here are still the challenges confronting e-government academics and practitioners.

ACKNOWLEDGMENT

The authors would like to acknowledge the Taiwan e-Governance Research Center (TEG) supervised by the Research, Development and Evaluation Committee (RDEC) of the Executive Yuan in Taiwanese central government for sponsoring the project of the 2020 Taiwan E-Governance Scenario Workshop. The project number is 09640D002503.

REFERENCES

Abelson, J., Giacomini, M., Lehoux, P., & Gauvin, F.-P. (2007). Bringing the Public into Health Technology Assessment and Coverage Policy Decisions: From Principles to Practice. *Health Policy (Amsterdam)*, *82*, 37–50. doi:10.1016/j.healthpol.2006.07.009

Accenture. (2004). *2004 eGovernment report: High performance, maximum value.* Retrieved on January 14, 2006, from http://www.accenture.com/NR/rdonlyres/D7206199-C3D4-4CB4-A7D8-846C94287890/0/gove_egov_value.pdf

Bäckstrand, K. (2003). Civic science for sustainability: Reframing the role of experts, policy-makers and citizens in environmental governance. *Global Environmental Politics*, *3*(4), 24–41. doi:10.1162/152638003322757916

Bates, B. R., Lynch, J. A., Bevan, J. L., & Condit, C. M. (2005). Warranted Concerns, Warranted Outlooks: A Focus Group Study of Public Understandings of Genetic Research. *Social Science & Medicine*, *60*, 331–344. doi:10.1016/j.socscimed.2004.05.012

Brewer, G. A., Neubauer, B. J., & Geiselhart, K. (2006). Designing and implementing e-government systems: Critical implications for public administration and democracy. *Administration & Society*, *38*(4), 472–499. doi:10.1177/0095399706290638

Burroughs, J. M. (2009). What users want: Assessing government information preferences to drive information services. *Government Information Quarterly*, *26*, 203–218. doi:10.1016/j.giq.2008.06.003

Cairns, G., Wright, G., Bradfield, R., van der Heijden, K., & Burt, G. (2004). Exploring e-government futures through the application of scenario planning. *Technological Forecasting and Social Change*, *71*, 217–238. doi:10.1016/S0040-1625(02)00371-2

Cambrosio, A., & Limoges, C. (1991). Controversies as Governing Process in Technology Assessment. *Technology Analysis and Strategic Management*, *3*(4), 377–396. doi:10.1080/09537329108524067

Chen, D.-Y., Huang, T.-Y., & Hsiao, N. (2006). Reinventing government through on-line citizen involvement in the developing world: A case study of Taipei City Mayor's e-mail box in Taiwan. *Public Administration and Development*, *26*(5), 409–423. doi:10.1002/pad.415

Chiang, M.-H., Chen, D.-y., Huang, T.-y., Hsiao, N., & Chuanh, K.-J. (2004). *An exploratory study of utilizing ICTs to promote citizen participation in Taiwan. A Project Sponsored by the Institute for Information Industries*. Taipei, Taiwan: III.

Compaine, B. (Ed.). (2001). *The digital divide: Facing a crisis or creating a myth.* Cambridge, MA: MIT Press.

Curwell, S., Deakin, M., Cooper, I., Paskaleva-Shapira, K., Ravetz, J., & Babicki, D. (2005). Citizens' expectations of information cities: Implications for urban planning and design. *Building Research and Information*, *33*(1), 55–66. doi:10.1080/0961321042000329422

Dawes, S. S. (2008). *An exploratory framework for future e-government research investments*. Paper presented at the 41st Hawaii International Conference on System Sciences, Hawaii.

deLeon, P. (1992). The Democratization of the Policy Sciences. *Public Administration Review*, *52*(2), 125–129. doi:10.2307/976465

Dryzek, J. S. (1989). Policy Sciences of Democracy. *Polity*, *22*(1), 97–118. doi:10.2307/3234848

Finn, K., & Detlor, B. (2002). Youth and electronic government: Towards a model of civic participation. *Quarterly Journal of Electronic Commerce*, *3*(3), 191–209.

Fung, A., & Wright, E. O. (2001). Deepening democracy: Innovations in empowered participatory governance. *Politics & Society*, *29*, 5–41. doi:10.1177/0032329201029001002

Garson, G. D. (2004). The promise of digital government. In Pavlichev, A., & Garson, G. D. (Eds.), *Digital government: Principles and best practices* (pp. 2–15). Hershey, PA: Idea Group Press.

Goven, J., & Langer, E. R. (2005). *Invitation to design the future: Christchurch scenario workshops on biosolids management*. Retrieved May 6, 2009, from http://www.ccc.govt.nz/wastewater/treatmentplant/InvitationToDesignTheFuture.pdf.

Heeks, R. (2001). Building e-governance for development: A framework for national and donor action. i-Government working paper series (paper no. 12). Institute for Development Policy and Management, University of Manchester.

Ho, A. (2002). Reinventing local governments and the e-government initiative. *Public Administration Review*, *62*, 434–444. doi:10.1111/0033-3352.00197

Holemans, D. (1999). The Democratic Separation of Technology and Ethics—The Case of the Flemish Regulation of Genetic Engineering. *Democracy and Nature*, *5*(3), 511–522.

Jaeger, P. T. (2005). Deliberative democracy and the conceptual foundations of electronic government. *Government Information Quarterly*, *22*(4), 702–719. doi:10.1016/j.giq.2006.01.012

Janssen, M., van der Duin, P., Wagenaar, R. W., Bicking, M., & Wimmer, M. A. (2007a). Scenario building for e-government in 2020. In *Proceedings of the 8th Annual International Digital Government Research Conference*.

Janssen, M., van der Duin, P., Wagenaar, R. W., Bicking, M., Wimmer, M. A., Dawes, S., & Petrauskas, R. (2007b). *Scenario building for e-government in 2020: Consolidating the results from regional workshops*. Paper presented at the 40th Hawaii International Conference on System Sciences, Hawaii.

Kahraman, C., Demirel, N. Ç., & Demirel, T. (2007). Prioritization of e-government strategies using a SWOT-AHP analysis: The case of Turkey. *European Journal of Information Systems*, *16*(3), 284–298. doi:10.1057/palgrave.ejis.3000679

King, C. S., Feltey, K. M., & Susel, B. O. (1998). The question of participation: Toward authentic public participation in public administration. *Public Administration Review*, *58*(4), 317–326. doi:10.2307/977561

Kloman, E. H. (1974). Public Participation in Technology Assessment. *Public Administration Review*, *34*(1), 52–61. doi:10.2307/974401

Korac-Kakabadse, A., & Korac-Kakabadse, N. (2001). Information technology's impact on the quality of democracy: Reinventing the 'democratic vessel. In Heeks, R. (Ed.), *Reinventing government in the information age* (pp. 211–228). London: Routledge.

Larsen, E., & Rainie, L. (2002). *The rise of the e-citizen: How people use government agencies' web sites*. Washington, DC: Pew Internet & American Life Project. Retrieved from http://www.pewinternet.org/Reports/2002/The-Rise-of-the-ECitizen-How-People-Use-Government-Agencies-Web-Sites.aspx

Mahrer, H., & Krimmer, R. (2005). Towards the enhancement of e-democracy: Identifying the notion of the middleman paradox. *Information Systems Journal*, *15*, 27–42. doi:10.1111/j.1365-2575.2005.00184.x

Moon, M. J. (2002). The evolution of e-Government among municipalities: Rhetoric or reality? *Public Administration Review*, *62*(4), 424–433. doi:10.1111/0033-3352.00196

Moon, M. J., & Welch, E. W. (2005). Same bed, different dreams? A comparative analysis of citizen and bureaucrat perspectives on e-government. *Review of Public Personnel Administration*, *25*(3), 243–264. doi:10.1177/0734371X05275508

Mumford, E. (1983). *Designing human systems for new technology: The ETHICS method*. Manchester, UK: Manchester Business School.

Mumford, E. (1991). Participation in system design: What can it offer? In Shackel, B., & Richardson, S. (Eds.), *Human factors for informatics usability* (pp. 267–290). Cambridge, UK: Cambridge University Press.

Neu, C., Anderson, R., & Bikson, T. (1999). *Sending your government a message*. Santa Monica, CA: RAND Science and Technology.

Norris, D. F., & Moon, M. J. (2005). Advancing e-government at the grassroots: Tortoise or hare? *Public Administration Review*, *65*(1), 64–75. doi:10.1111/j.1540-6210.2005.00431.x

Norris, P. (2001). *Digital divide? Civic engagement, information poverty, and the Internet worldwide*. Cambridge, UK: Cambridge University Press.

Olphert, W., & Damodaran, L. (2007). Citizen participation and engagement in the design of e-government services: The missing link in effective ICT design and delivery. *Journal of the Association for Information Systems*, *8*(9), 491–507.

Pidgeon, N., & Rogers-Hayden, T. (2007). Opening up Nanotechnology Dialogue with the Publics: Risk Communication or Upstream Engagement? *Health Risk & Society*, *9*(2), 191–210. doi:10.1080/13698570701306906

Rask, M. (2003). The Problem of Citizens' Participation in Finnish Biotechnology Policy. *Science & Public Policy*, *30*(6), 441–454. doi:10.3152/147154303781780236

Reddick, C. G. (2005). Citizen interaction with e-Government: From the streets to servers? *Government Information Quarterly*, *22*, 38–57. doi:10.1016/j.giq.2004.10.003

Rodan, G. (1998). The internet and political control in Singapore. *Political Science Quarterly*, *113*(1), 63–89. doi:10.2307/2657651

Ross, K. (2007). Providing Thoughtful Feedback: Public Participation in the Regulation of Australia's First Genetically Modified Food Crop. *Science & Public Policy*, *34*(3), 213–225. doi:10.3152/030234207X211500

Sæbø, Ø., Rose, J., & Flak, L. S. (2008). The shape of e-participation: Characterizing an emerging research area. *Government Information Quarterly*, *25*, 400–428. doi:10.1016/j.giq.2007.04.007

Scott, J. K. (2006). E the people: Do U.S. municipal government web sites support public involvement? *Public Administration Review*, *66*(3), 341–353. doi:10.1111/j.1540-6210.2006.00593.x

Thomas, J. C., & Streib, G. (2003). The new face of government: Citizen-initiated contacts in the era of e-government. *Journal of Public Administration: Research and Theory*, *13*(1), 83–102. doi:10.1093/jpart/mug010

Tolbert, C. J., & Mossberger, K. (2006). The effects of e-government on trust and confidence in government. *Public Administration Review*, *66*(30), 354–369. doi:10.1111/j.1540-6210.2006.00594.x

Torres, L., Pina, V., & Acerete, B. (2006). E-governance developments in European Union cities: Reshaping Government's relationship with citizens. *Governance*, *19*(2), 277–302. doi:10.1111/j.1468-0491.2006.00315.x

Ulrich, P., & Chacko, J. G. (2005). Overview of ICT policies and e-strategies: An assessment on the role of governments. *Information Technology for Development*, *11*(2), 195–197. doi:10.1002/itdj.20011

United Nations. (2008). *United Nations e-government survey 2008: From e-government to connected governance*. Retrieved September 29, 2008, from http://unpan1.un.org/intradoc/groups/public/documents/UN/UNPAN028607.pdf van Dijk, J. A. G. M., Peters, O., & Ebbers, W. (2008). Explaining the acceptance and use of government Internet services: A multivariate analysis of 2006 survey data in the Netherlands. *Government Information Quarterly, 25,* 379-399.

Weerakkody, V., Jones, S., & Olsen, E. (2007). E-government: A comparison of strategies in local authorities in the UK and Norway. *International Journal of Electronic Business*, *5*(2), 141–159. doi:10.1504/IJEB.2007.012970

Weinel, M. (2007). Primary Source Knowledge and Technical Decision-Making: Mbeki and the AZT debate. *Studies in History and Philosophy of Science*, *38*, 748–760. doi:10.1016/j.shpsa.2007.09.010

Yang, K. (2003). Neoinstitutionalism and e-government. *Social Science Computer Review*, *21*(4), 432–442. doi:10.1177/0894439303256508

ENDNOTES

1. In addition to the lack of citizen-centered input, the low use of e-government services may complicatedly result from factors such as the digital divide, no incentive offerings, the absence of marketing and promotion, and dissatisfaction with user experience (Accenture, 2004); and people are not even aware of the existence of e-services and so on.
2. The NICI has the following missions: (1) To accelerate the development of the IT industry, e-Commerce and related businesses. (2) To improve the efficiency of government services. (3) To promote Internet usage and related applications. (4) To enhance the competitiveness of Taiwan's IT industry.
3. Approximately ninety percentage or 39 participants actually attended the meeting. Only a very small portion of participants decided to leave the activity before the end of the meeting. Mortality is thus under control and acceptable.

Chapter 22
Evaluation of E-Government Services:
A Citizen-Centric Approach to Citizen E-Complaint Services

Shang-Ching Yeh
National Science and Technology Museum, Taiwan

Pin-Yu Chu
National Chengchi University, Taiwan

ABSTRACT

Do e-government services meet citizens' needs? This chapter examines the performance of e-government services from a citizen-centric perspective. This chapter, taking the Kaohsiung Citizen Electronic Complaint System (KCECS) in Taiwan as a case study, identifies satisfaction and service quality as evaluation indicators when assessing e-government services. The empirical results show that citizens perceive moderately positive satisfaction toward the e-complaint service, and that a citizen-centric approach for evaluating e-government service is desirable. Complaint resolving ability makes the most contribution to the overall satisfaction of e-complaint service, but remains the top priority for improvement of the KCECS. Some solutions are proposed to help public officials to meet citizens' needs and thus better serve citizens.

INTRODUCTION

To examine the extent to which the goals of implementing an e-government initiative or service having been achieved, and to justify its investment, performance evaluations are necessary. Among various e-government evaluation approaches, a citizen-centric or demand-side evaluation (Reddick, 2005), which is the assessment in terms of citizen' demands or needs, is highly desirable because the promise of e-government is to engage citizenry in government in a citizen-centered manner, i.e. citizen-centered e-government (Bertot & Jaeger, 2006; 2008). Furthermore, with the knowledge regarding citizen needs, it is expected that administrations will tailor e-government better to citizens (Schedler & Summermatter, 2007).

This chapter takes the Kaohsiung Citizen Electronic Complaint System (KCECS) in Taiwan, one of

DOI: 10.4018/978-1-61520-931-6.ch022

critical e-government services allowing citizens to file complaints to government officials regarding all government services or request information/services online, as an empirical example to evaluate e-government services from a citizen-centric perspective. A survey was conducted to collect demographics, characteristics, perceived service quality, and perceived satisfaction of the system's users. Determinants of perceived satisfaction are also explored for realizing the top priority for improvement of the e-service. In the following sections of this chapter, we first introduce the citizen e-complaint service (CECS), and the KCECS, as a background for this chapter. Evaluation approaches of e-government services are then reviewed for determining a suitable method for the demand-side evaluation of the KCECS. Section 4 and section 5 describe method and results of our evaluation of the KCECS. Section 6 provides some discussions, including ways to improve satisfaction of the system, and conclusion.

CITIZEN E-COMPLAINT SERVICE IN THE E-GOVERNMENT CONTEXT

Email Contact Material Worldwide

CECS with its communication vehicle being email, allowing citizens to file complaints to government officials regarding all government services or request information/services, is one of the most critical e-government services. According to West's (2008a) global e-government reports: "Improving technology utilization in electronic government around the world, 2008" witnessed eighty-eight percent of global government websites offering email contact material that allows ordinary citizens to pose questions or request services. Many government websites around the world provide citizen e-complaint services, e.g. The US Government Web, http://www.usa.gov/; Dubai Government's Department of Tourism & Commerce Marketing, U. A. E.'s Website (http://www.dubaitourism.ae/about/default.asp); and the website of the Local Government Ombudsman in the UK, an independent organization investigating complaints about councils and certain other bodies (http://www.lgo.org.uk/index.php).

The Kaohsiung Citizen Electronic Complaint System

The Kaohsiung City, with an area of 154 square kilometers and the population of 1.5 million people, is the second largest metropolis in Taiwan. To comply with the e-government policy of Taiwan, in 2003 the Kaohsiung City Government (KCG) employed customer relationship management (CRM)/citizen relationship management (CzRM) to re-design the Kaohsiung Mayor's Email Box (KMEB) as a new web-based system: the KCECS. It aims to provide an efficient communication channel between citizens and the government. The architecture of the KCECS, incorporating its functions, comprises the following segments (Chu, Yeh, & Chuang, 2008) (see Figure 1):

Citizen Access Channel

The KCG integrates all agencies' email boxes into the KCECS as a single access channel to facilitate communication with citizens. A web-based mechanism is adopted to offer a 24-hour, 365-day, boundary-free service. Citizens could therefore request the government to deliver services without the limitations of time and space. In addition, the KCECS creates a user-friendly interface by simplifying user's instructions, and provides frequently asked questions (FAQs) for citizens to make inquiries online (http://soweb.kcg.gov.tw/).

Workflow Mechanism

To efficiently handle complaints, the KCG re-engineered the complaint-handling mechanism and incorporated a responsive design for citizens.

Figure 1. The CzRM-based Kaohsiung Citizen Electronic Complaint System architecture. From "Reengineering municipality citizen electronic complaint system through citizen relationship management," by P. Y. Chu, S. C. Yeh, & M. J. Chuang, 2008. Electronic Government, An International Journal, 5(3), pp. 293.

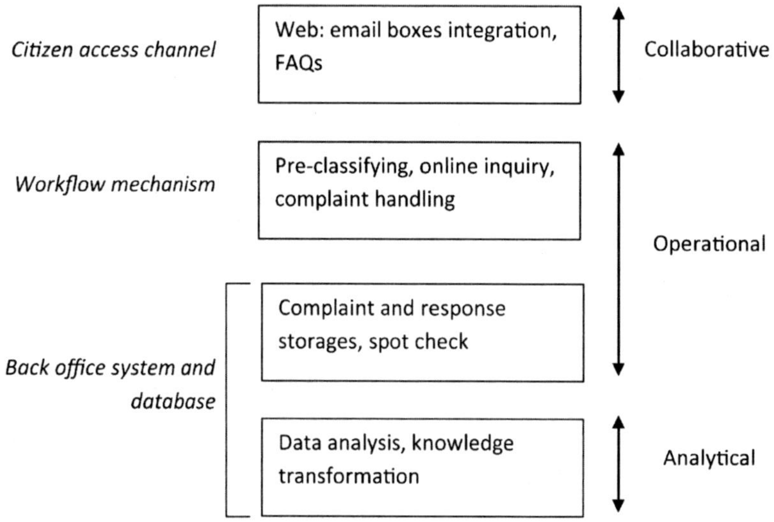

The workflow mechanism comprises information delivery and processing, which can be categorized as operational CzRM. The workflow mechanism of the KCECS is introduced in terms of core functions of the KCECS as follows.

(1) The complaint-handling mechanism: When filing a complaint, a citizen can choose a proper category for his/her complaint from the pre-classified categories to file complaint (or he/she directly files the complaint and the United Service Center will subsequently classify the complaint case). The KCECS directly sends the complaint case according to the pre-arranged staff in charge. Meanwhile, the system gives a 'case received email' with follow-up information to the complaint submitter. Once the complaint case is resolved, a "case completed email" will be sent to the complainant.

(2) Online inquiry: The "case received email" contains follow-up information, including case follow-up code and name and phone number of a responsible staff member, to the citizen for checking the handling progress of their case on-line. The citizen can therefore check the handling progress of their case on-line (http://w6.kcg.gov.tw/wm/result/result.q1.php).

(3) Satisfaction survey: The "case completed email" comprises a formal report and a satisfaction survey questionnaire to receive feedback opinions from users.

Back Office System and Database

This segment involves operational CzRM and analytical CzRM, in which the former includes storage of complaints and responses, while the latter comprises data analysis and knowledge transformation of complaint cases. The government regularly chooses completed complaint cases to check the content of the reply. The system provides statistical reports for internal control and management. Citizen satisfaction questionnaires are also analyzed to improve the KCECS.

Usage

The KCECS generates great increases in usage. According to the Kaohsiung City Government Information Management Center (2008), the monthly average cases of its preceding service, the KMEB, was around 600; while the KCECS received about 1,400~2,000 complaint cases per month from 2003 through 2007. This yields a double to triple growth in the number of using the e-complaint service. In addition, citizens complain of various public affairs. Illegal road occupation tops complaint categories, followed by buildings constructed without licenses, illegal parking, school management, public nuisance, etc.

EVALUATION APPROACHES OF E-GOVERNMENT SERVICES

While designing the KCECS, the KCG considered its evaluation. It is difficult to determine a best approach to evaluate e-government services. That is because the suitability of an evaluation approach depends on various factors such as the information system and the organizational and social context of use (Alshawi, Alahmary, & Alalwany, 2007). The assessments may vary according to the different goals and objectives of e-government services. The KCG took the following measures, which have been developed to evaluate performance of e-government, into consideration.

Financial-Oriented Assessments

The financial-oriented assessments use financial indicators, such as resources inputs, outputs or outcomes, and efficiency indicators to evaluate e-government performances. As a result, this approach is often characterized as "hard" measures, in differentiation from "soft" measures (Brudney & England, 1982). They are also thought of as "internal" measures, instead of "external" measures, because they come from a definition of efficiency/effectiveness derived and monitored by administrators (Kelly & Swindell, 2002).

Investment appraisal techniques, such as Return on Investment (ROI), Internal Rate of Return (IRR), Net Present Value (NPV), etc. (Ballantine and Stray, 1999), and cost benefit analysis (CBA) are the most commonly used methods to evaluate information system investments and e-government initiatives among traditional financial-oriented evaluation methods, which deserve the KCG's further consideration. However, the KCECS is designed to meet the need of citizens' complaint filing; the KCG didn't feel that it would be proper to perform the aforementioned techniques except for some simple efficiency indicators.

Supply-Side Evaluations

The supply-side evaluation of e-government assesses what governments offer online, which typically focuses on a description of characteristics of e-government services. For example, the United Nations' "UN e-government survey 2008" showed its member states' e-government services and their characteristics provided, including: one-stop shop, submission of online forms, personal online account, payment by card, email sign-up option, response timer frame indicated for emails/forms, etc. (United Nations, 2008). West (2008a, 2008b), following a series of annual global and the US e-government evaluation, evaluated e-government websites for the presence of various features dealing with online information, electronic service, privacy and security, etc.

The evaluation of supply side, although comprehensive in terms of studying e-government service features, does not consider the characteristics of users. It can not reflect users' demands, needs or differences in service delivery mediated by users' individual variations (Wang, Bretschneider, & Gant, 2005). Since the KCG considers the KCECS users' feedback is critical, the supply-side evaluation techniques were not employed for performance evaluation of the KCECS.

Demand-Side evaluations

The demand-side evaluations assess how users react to, and interact with, e-government services (Reddick, 2005). This perspective examines the performance of e-government in terms of users' demands or needs, i.e., a citizen-centric evaluation. It relies on users' perceptions such as satisfaction and service quality with regard to e-government services. These evaluations contrast sharply with financial-oriented assessments. The former is often categorized as "soft" or "external" measures, because they come from citizens and usually through surveys. Compared with the supply-side perspective, demand-side evaluation focuses not on what services are available on e-government sites, but on how those e-government services meet the needs of their users.

The Rationale for Choosing Demand-Side Assessment for the KCECS

The KCG decided to employ the demand-side evaluation to assess the KCECS, though some e-government evaluations mix the aforementioned techniques (financial oriented, supply-side, demand-side techniques) (e.g. DeMaio, 2002; Gupta & Jana, 2003; Irani et al., 2005; Steyaert, 2004). The rationale behind this decision is the goals of the system. They are:

1. It is an e-service that is designed for meeting citizens' needs of complaint filing;
2. It is an e-service that facilitates communication between government and citizens; and
3. It is an e-service that is much more efficient, responsive, and reliable, etc. than those preceding it.

These reasons amply justify the adoption of a citizen-centric performance evaluation for the KCECS.

When choosing the evaluation approach, one fact that the KCG has already known regarding the demand-side evaluation is that quality/service quality and satisfaction are two predominant and interchangeably used performance factors in this regard. For instance, Halaris, Magoutas, Papadomichelaki, and Mentzas (2007) examined and analyzed 36 different quality approaches concerning public sector services, e-government services, and e-services in general. They further re-classified these approaches into four layers of quality assessment for e-government services. Quality and satisfaction are two that are derived from those 36 approaches.

Service quality and satisfaction are used quite interchangeably in empirical studies, which have led to confusion regarding the two terms, though they differ in some respects. Emerging definitions in service sector literature make this distinction more clear: satisfaction results from individual and global transaction, which is transaction-specific and cumulative; whereas service quality involves a general impression of the superiority or inferiority of the service provider and the services (Bitner & Hubert, 1994) or a general attitude towards services (Bitner, 1990). Specifically, service quality is dependent on service content and service procedure when customers encounter the service provider. These include the service provider's attitude and friendliness, and the form/design of the physical environment, complicacy of the service procedure, etc. (Gronroos, 1990).

As a result, the KCG focuses on service quality and satisfaction for citizen-centric evaluation for the KCECS. The KCG examined developed instruments that have been used, such as EGOVSAT (Horan, Abhichandani, & Rayalu, 2006), WebQual (Barnes & Vidgen, 2003), eQual (previously called WebQual) (Barnes & Vidgen, 2006), E-S-QUAL and E-RecS-QUAL (Parasuraman et al., 2005). Among them, E-S-QUAL, comprising four dimensions: efficiency, fulfillment, system availability, and privacy, and E-RecS-QUAL, containing three dimensions: responsiveness, compensation, and contact, evolve from SERVQUAL (Parasuraman et al., 1988), which is designed for evaluating service quality of physical service, and e-SERVQUAL (Zeithaml, Parasuraman, & Malhotra, 2000), designed for measuring e-service quality. These instruments have been widely used and the results indicate that they are consistent and reliable scales to measure service quality (Gronroos, Heinomen, Isoniemi, & Lindholm, 2000; Kaynama & Black, 2000; Parasuraman & Grewal, 2000).

METHOD

Measures

The KCG constructed a citizen questionnaire for the KCECS's evaluation. The main focus of the questionnaire is service quality and satisfaction. As the nature of e-complaint service in the public sector is quite different from other e-services in the private or public sectors, quality measurement scales in e-service literature need to be modified. In addition, the KCG considers that too many questions in the questionnaire might annoy citizens; items for measuring service quality and satisfaction are reduced. Variables consistent with dimensions of the E-S-QUAL and E-RecS-Qual scale are used. Efficiency, fulfillment, system availability, and responsiveness represent the e-service quality of the KCECS, which are measured using four items from dimensions of Parasuraman et al.'s (2005) E-S-QUAL and E-RecS-Qual scale. Citizen satisfaction toward the service is measured using one satisfaction item representing citizen's overall evaluation of service experience (Anderson, Fornell, & Lehman, 1994; Anderson, Fornell, & Mazvancheryl, 2004; Fornell, 1992).

The KCG also collects characteristics and demographics of the KCECS users through the questionnaire. Items of user characteristics include: complaint times on the system, willingness to reuse the service, and complaint types. On the KCECS, complaint submitters decide a complaint type for their complaint case when returning the satisfaction survey. There are four kinds of complaint types. (1) Suggestion type: indicates that a complaint case is about suggesting that the government do something, such as providing more parks. (2) Inquiry type: refers to an inquiry about something. For instance, a citizen may file a complaint case inquiring about required certificates such as for applying for a marriage registration. (3) Accusation type: means complaining for the purpose of making an accusation. For example, one might accuse someone of constructing an illegal building. (4) Rights protection type: a complaint case concerning rights protection. For instance, one may complain about delays in an application for land registration in the Land Office. Demographic variables are: gender, age, education level, occupation, and years of residence in Kaohsiung City. Detailed variables used in analysis in this chapter are presented in the appendix.

Samples and Procedure

The population of the survey is citizens who had filed complaints on the KCECS. Questionnaires were accompanied by the formal report and were sent by email to those who had filed complaints. However, the KCG does not know the distribution of the population because a successfully filed complaint on the KCECS only requires the complainer's name, telephone number, and email address without demographic data. As a result, the KCG only has the questionnaire respondents' demographics, and not for all of the complainers.

RESULTS

Response Rates, Demographics, and Characteristics of the KCECS Users

Response rates

According to statistics of returned citizen satisfaction questionnaires accompanied with formal replies on the KCECS, from July 15th 2003, the launching day of the revised version of the KCECS, to Feb. 14th, 2008, there were 13,391 valid questionnaires. This gives a valid response rate of 14.2%.

Demographics

Through data collected from the survey, the KCG has a picture of the demographics of the KCECS users. More men (64%) used the KCECS than did women (see Table 1). Users between the ages of 31~40 were the largest group, accounting for forty percent of the valid surveys. The users generally enjoyed good education levels, in which 43% with college/university degree, and more than eighty percent of respondents having completed junior college or higher degrees. The majority of users served in service industry (32.8%), followed by government officials (20.5%), which include: military personnel, teachers, and public servants, manufacturing industry (13.3%), and students (10.4%) except for "other or missing". As for years of residence, users were predominantly those who had lived in Kaohsiung City for more than 31 years (33.0%), followed by 21~30 years and 11~20 years. In general, middle-aged, well-educated, male citizens, and those working in service industry as well as those with longer years of residence might comprise the predominant users of the KCECS.

The demographics of the KCECS users are similar to those of most e-government service users except for middle-aged users. Generally, people with higher education, males, and youngsters are found to be e-service intensive users. However, there is a gap between potential users and actual users of electronic government services not to say that between citizens and actual e-government service users. For example, in a survey of EU-15 countries, most of those countries illustrate a gap between potential usage and actual usage of electronic public services (Eurostat, 2005). The finding of higher middle-aged users of the KCECS contrasts with the more popular belief that younger people are more intensive users than middle-aged people. This is explained by the nature of the e-complaint service. Younger people have less interaction with government than do older people so that they complain less about government. In this regard, increasing usage of the KCECS would be also more important. To increase participation of e-government services, scholars have identified possible access to those (van Deursen, van Dijk, & Ebbers, 2006). In the context of KCECS, these accesses such as motivational access, physical access, skill access could be enhanced. These include: promoting the KCECS, in fact the KCG did nothing about this, equipping computers in public facilities, developing educational programs to the public, etc.

Characteristics

In addition to demographics, the KCG gets characteristics of the KCECS users from the survey. As shown in Table 2, 73.1% KCECS users were first time users. Most users (94.1%) stated that they will continue using the KCECS. Besides, users self-reported their complaint types. Among them, the predominant complaint type was "accusation" (46.3%), followed by "suggestion", "rights protection", and "inquiry", at 22.4%, 11.8%, and 5.7%, respectively. Another 13.9% are "other" complaint type and those without specifying any aforementioned types.

Table 1. Demographics of the Kaohsiung citizen electronic complaint system users

Variable	Frequency[a]	Valid percent
Gender		
Male	8,142	64.0
Female	4,581	36.0
Age		
20 and below	557	4.4
21-30	3,279	25.6
31-40	5,128	40.1
41-50	2,709	21.2
51-60	948	7.4
61 and above	166	1.3
Education level		
Junior high school and below	248	2.0
Senior high school	1,857	14.5
Junior college	2,968	23.3
College/university	5,488	43.0
Graduate school (master's degree)	1,883	14.8
Graduate school (PhD)	320	2.5
Occupation		
Government officials (including military personnel, teachers, and public servants)	2,612	20.5
First class industry (including agriculture, fishery, etc.)	52	0.4
Manufacturing industry	1,689	13.3
Service industry	4,177	32.8
Student	1,329	10.4
Housewife	122	1.0
Other or missing	2,748	21.6
Years of residence		
5 years and below	1,625	13.0
6-10 years	932	7.5
11-20 years	2,344	18.7
21-30 years	3,479	27.8
31 and above	4,124	33.0
Total	13,391	100.0

[a]Demographic variables not totaling 13,391 represent missing values.

Table 2. Citizens' characteristics of the Kaohsiung citizen electronic complaint system

Variable	Frequency[a]	Valid percent
Complaint times		
Once	8,853	73.1
Twice	808	6.7
Three times	1,226	10.1
Four times	491	4.1
Five times and above	736	6.1
Willingness to reuse the KCECS[b]	11,933	94.1
Complaint type		
Suggestion	2,804	22.4
Inquiry	714	5.7
Accusation	5,799	46.3
Rights protection	1,481	11.8
Other	1,740	13.9
Total	13,391	100.0

[a]Demographic variables not totaling 13,391 represent missing values.
[b]The frequency of "not willing to reuse" is 743.

Citizens' Perceived Service Quality and Satisfaction Toward the KCECS

Perceived Service Quality

Does the service quality of the KCECS meet citizens' need? Generally, the KCECS users perceived high service quality among service quality items except for "complaint resolving". Eighty-eight percent users stated that the KCECS is an effective channel for citizens to file complaints or opinions to governments (Table 3). Citizens also gave acceptable appraisal of the response manner and time efficiency of the KCECS service. The two items received 68.5% and 64.7% positive perceptions or a 3.78 and 3.87 mean scores (scaled from 5 to 1), respectively. However, the KCECS' ability in complaint-resolving left much room for improvement. Only 38.7% users had positive perceptions regarding this item, while 42.7% users gave negative evaluations. Nevertheless, it is not surprising that a complaint service often receives low appraisal due to the nature of complaint-handling. A similar e-service in Taipei City, Taiwan, the Taipei City Mayor Emailbox (TCME), got a worse appraisal of "the extent of resolving complaints" (Chen et al., 2006). In sum, the KCG knew that except for complaint resolving, citizens' perceived service quality toward the KCECS is passable. This is important because the results reveal that citizens approve of this e-service in terms of important service quality dimensions, including: system availability, responsiveness and efficiency.

Perceived Satisfaction

With respect to perceived satisfaction, citizens gave a moderate appraisal in overall evaluation toward the KCECS (Table 3). Respondents with positive perceptions (44.2%) slightly outnumbered those with negative ones (32.3%). The mean score was 3.14 (scaled from 5 to 1).

Realizing citizens perceive moderate overall satisfaction toward the KCECS, the KCG would like to know whether there is difference of per-

Table 3. Citizens' perceived service quality and satisfaction concerning the Kaohsiung citizen electronic complaint system[a]

Item	Mean	SD	Positive[b] (%)	Neutral[b] (%)	Negative[b] (%)
Perceived service quality					
Time efficiency	3.87	1.17	64.7	20.3	15.0
Response manner	3.78	1.37	68.5	15.0	16.5
Effective channel	4.46	0.90	88.4	7.0	4.6
Complaint resolving	2.87	1.47	38.7	18.6	42.7
Perceived satisfaction					
Overall evaluation	3.14	1.32	44.2	23.5	32.3

[a]Scaled from 5 to 1

[b]For better realizing citizens' perceptions about the service, respondents are divided into three groups by their perceptions (scaled from 5 to 1). Positive: score higher than 4, Neutral: score = 3, Negative: score lower than 2

ceived satisfaction among citizens' demographics and characteristics. Through analysis of variance (ANOVA), it was found (see Table 4) that (1) young people especially those ages are "20 and below" had a higher satisfaction than older people; (2) students had a higher satisfaction than other occupation groups; (3) higher education citizens, especially those having PhD degree, dissatisfied the service than other groups; and (4) those who have lived in Kaohsiung City for more than 31 years had a lower satisfaction rate toward the service than others. It is consistent that students and young people both had higher satisfaction, since a great number of younger people are students.

With regard to difference of satisfaction among characteristic, the KCG knew the following facts after performing ANOVA (Table 5). First, citizens who are willing to reuse the KCECS had a higher satisfaction than those who are not. Second, to our surprise, people with higher use rates had a lower satisfaction than first time users had. After consulting the executive officer of the KCECS, one explanation was offered: a large number of citizens tended to resend dissatisfied complaints. Finally, rights protection complaints received the lowest satisfaction, followed by accusation, suggestion, and inquiry types.

Top Priority for Improvement of the KCECS

From the above findings, the KCG already knows that the KCECS users just gave a moderate appraisal in overall evaluation to the e-service. They government also realizes that this established communication channel for filing complaints was well-recognized by citizens. However, although acceptable, there is room for improving time efficiency and responsiveness. The complaint resolving ability of the service is the worst appraisal by users. The KCG needs to know a critical question: Does service quality variables have to do with perceived satisfaction? Literature in the private sector asserts that service quality and satisfaction correlate with each other, and the sequential order of service quality preceding satisfaction outnumbered other choices (Cronin & Taylor, 1992; Parasuraman et al., 1994; Rust & Oliver, 1994; Ruyter et al., 1997). Furthermore, empirical study of e-government evaluation implicitly implies that service quality contributes to satisfaction. The ACSI E-government Satisfaction Index identifies top priority for improvement, "meaning that improvements in these areas will result in increased satisfaction" (Freed, 2008: 11).

In the case of the KCECS, bivariate correlations results (Table 6) show that all four service

Table 4. ANOVA of citizens' satisfaction among demographic variables

Variable	Group	N	Mean	SD	F value	Post Hoc Tests
Gender	Female (1)	4,501	3.2	1.3	.07	
	Male (2)	8,015	3.2	1.3		
Age	20 and below (1)	547	3.4	1.2	5.97*	(1,3), (1,4),
	21-30 (2)	3,239	3.2	1.3		(2,3)
	31-40 (3)	5,045	3.1	1.3		
	41-50 (4)	2,656	3.1	1.4		
	51-60 (5)	925	3.1	1.4		
	61 and above (6)	163	3.2	1.4		
Education level	Junior high school and below (1)	243	3.0	1.4	2.95*	(3,6); (4,6)
	Senior high school (2)	1,824	3.2	1.3		
	Junior college (3)	2,919	3.2	1.3		
	College/university (4)	5,400	3.1	1.3		
	Graduate school (master's degree) (5)	1,857	3.1	1.4		
	Graduate school (PhD) (6)	312	2.9	1.5		
Occupation	Government officers (1)	2,566	3.3	1.3	10.41*	(1,5); (3,5),
	First class industry (2)	52	3.1	1.3		(4,5); (6,5)
	Manufacturing industry (3)	1,667	3.2	1.4		
	Service industry (4)	4,110	3.1	1.3		
	Student (5)	1,311	3.4	1.2		
	Housewife (6)	120	3.0	1.3		
Years of residence	5 years and below (1)	1,593	3.2	1.3	7.42*	(1,5); (3,5),
	6-10 years (2)	912	3.1	1.3		(4,5)
	11-20 years (3)	2,311	3.2	1.3		
	21-30 years (4)	3,432	3.2	1.3		
	31 and above (5)	4,052	3.0	1.4		

* $p < .05$

quality variables significantly correlated with perceived satisfaction. Among them, Pearson correlation coefficient between satisfaction and complaint resolving was the highest (0.84), followed by that between satisfaction and response manner (0.66).

Knowing that service quality items correlate with perceived satisfaction, the next question would be: Which item of service quality contributes to perceived satisfaction most? In other word, the answer of this question tells the KCG the top priority for improvement of the KCECS. A regression analysis was then conducted. The perceived satisfaction toward the KCECS is theorized consists of two groups of variables. One group is various items/dimensions of e-complaint service quality, including: time efficiency, response manner, effective channel, and complaint resolving. The other one is demographics of citizens, which contains gender, age, education level, and years of residence. When conducting regression analysis, each demographic variable is treated as a dummy

Table 5. ANOVA of citizens' satisfaction among characteristic variables

Variable	Group	N	Mean	SD	F value	Post Hoc Tests
Willingness to reuse the KCECS	No (1)	729	1.5	0.8	1188.52*	
	Yes (2)	11,741	3.2	1.2		
Compliant times	First time (1)	8,703	3.2	1.2	299.59*	
	Second times and above (2)	3,193	2.8	1.3		
Complaint type	Suggestion (1)	2,748	3.1	1.2	27.82*	(1,2); (1,4);
	Inquiry (2)	703	3.4	1.2		(2,3); (3,4)
	Accusation (3)	5,704	3.1	1.3		
	Rights protection (4)	1,465	2.8	1.3		

* $p < .05$

variable. As a result, demographic variables were dummy-recoded for regression analysis. As shown in Table A1 (Appendix), gender was recoded such that 1 = male and 0 = female. With respect to other demographic variables, they were recoded as follows: age above 31 = 1, otherwise = 0; education level above college/university = 1, otherwise = 0; years of residence in Kaohsiung City more than 21 years = 1, otherwise = 0. The groups of variable were entered into a regression model as independent variables (scale and definition of variables see Appendix, Table A1).

From Table 7, among the service quality items, complaint resolving made the largest contribution to perceived satisfaction with the KCECS, with a standardized coefficient of 0.66. This indicates that to improve satisfaction of the KCECS, the top priority is enhancing the ability of complaint resolving. The response manner ranked as the second contributor, followed by time efficiency, and effective channel, with standardized coefficients 0.23, 0.08, 0.06, respectively. With respect to demographic variables, gender, education level, and years of residence all had effects on satisfaction. Gender positively contributed to satisfaction (coefficient 0.03), while education level and years of residence both had negative contributions (coefficients being -0.02 and -0.01, respectively). The above-mentioned indicators served as significant predictors for citizens' satisfaction in regard to the KCECS. They totally accounted for 77% total variance (adjusted R^2) (Model 2).

DISCUSSIONS AND CONCLUSION

E-government aims to make better use of information and communication technology, providing

Table 6. Bivariate correlations among items of satisfaction and service quality

Item	Satisfaction	Time efficiency	Response manner	Effective channel	Complaint resolving
Satisfaction	1				
Time efficiency	0.42**	1			
Response manner	0.66**	0.40**	1		
Effective channel	0.44**	0.32**	0.45**	1	
Complaint resolving	0.84**	0.35**	0.56**	0.37**	1

** $p < .01$

Table 7. Regression analysis predicting satisfaction of the Kaohsiung citizen electronic complaint system

Variable	Model 1	Model 2
Service quality		
Time efficiency	.08**	.08**
Response manner	.23**	.23**
Effective channel	.06**	.06**
Complaint resolving	.66**	.66**
Demographics		
Gender		.03**
Age		-.00 (-.001)
Education level		-.02**
Years of residence		-.01**
Adjusted R^2	.76	.77

**$p < .01$

government services to better serve citizens. As a result, with the idea of reinventing government (Osborne & Gaebler, 1992) and the New Public Management (e.g. Box, 1999), e-government services are designed as "citizen-centered" to meet citizens' demands and needs. The nature of e-government justifies a citizen-centric evaluation approach.

The chapter empirically tests if service quality items/dimensions affect satisfaction in e-government services. The results show that all four service quality items/dimensions, including: time efficiency, response manner, effective channel, and complaint resolving, contribute to satisfaction in the example of the KCECS. It is reasonable since empirical studies find that service quality influences satisfaction in the private sector (e.g. Cronin & Taylor, 1992; Parasuraman et al., 1994), and evidence from some empirical e-government evaluation works depicts that service quality contributes to satisfaction (e.g. Freed, 2008). The research results of this chapter empirically add support to the claim that service quality impacts on satisfaction. Among service quality items, complaint resolving is the major determinant of perceived satisfaction in e-complaint services, which is the top priority for improvement of the KCECS. The result is consistent with Hsiao et al.'s (2002) empirical study with the TCME. Researchers (Chen et al., 2006) have identified some reasons why the e-complaint system has difficulty in resolving citizen's problems; this research also proposes some solutions for each of them for continuous improvement in this area, which may result in increased satisfaction.

1. Establishing a mechanism for resolving complicated complaints

It is the street-level bureaucrats who actually resolve citizens' complaints. However, these street-level bureaucrats have less discretionary power to deal with complicated problems to satisfy citizens' requests. In order to handle this kind of complaint, mechanisms of internal communication involving coordination among departments/agencies need to be established in the short run. In the long run, an organizational reform derived from e-government should be carried out, for example the concept of the KCECS as a one-stop service center could be employed. A one-stop service center is an umbrella organization that operates on top of existing functional departments and is intended to maximize the convenience and satisfaction of users through service integration (Ho, 2002). Thus, when citizens submit complaints, the KCECS would serve as a platform for centralized handling, coordinate with functional departments and integrate responses. Citizens would not only acquire integrated service with a one-stop service, but they would also no longer need to know which department was responsible for their complaints. With the establishment of a one-stop center, the government has the opportunity to shift from a bureaucratic organization to a citizen-centered one.

However, both process reengineering and organization reengineering generate resistance from governmental employees. Civil servants are the ones that tend to lose power and authority over citizens when implementing process reengineering. The workflow is regulated, and often civil servants lose the flexibility to deal with applications. Organization reengineering generates much resistance. For example, Wagenaar et al. (2006), introducing an implementation of shared service centers (SSCs) in Netherlands, depicted the following resistance should be taken into consideration: resistance against "one fits all" (the differences among departments for organization reengineering), resistance against power concentration during implementation, resistance influencing implementation costs, knowledge drain (outflow of valuable persons), etc. Strategies suggested by scholar to minimize resistance include ensuring a right organizational climate, ensuring all stakeholders understand the reengineering, which could be achieved through education and training, etc. (Bhatnagar, 2004).

2. Developing a long range plan to resolve complaints needing longer time to resolve

We suggest that the government develops a long range plan to resolve problems such as (1) complaints involving policy adjustments or an amendment of law and (2) complaints that necessitate new budget or staff. The authors additionally recommend creating a "long term complaint cases list" on the KCECS until they have been resolved. The government should inform the users when these cases are resolved.

3. Filtering out irrational/unreasonable complaints

A user may use abusive language, make unclear statements, or submit unreasonable complaints such as a city-wide suspension of all parking fees, or a request to fire a certain staff member. The government could create a mechanism within the KCECS to filter out abuse. For unclear or unreasonable cases, a responsive response is needed.

In conclusion, citizen-centered e-government justifies its citizen-centric performance evaluation. This chapter, taking the KCECS as an example, illustrates its development and results of citizen-centric evaluation, which acts as a valuable case when conducting evaluation on e-government services. The results found in this case, including the complaint resolving ability as the top priority for improvement and the proposed solutions, help public officials to meet citizens' needs and better serve citizens when delivering e-complaint services in the public sector.

REFERENCES

Alshawi, S., Alahmary, A., & Alalwany, H. (2007). E-government evaluation factors: Citizen perspective. In *Proceedings of European and Mediterranean Conference on Information Systems 2007 (EMCIS 2007)*, June 24-26 2007, Polytechnic University of Valencia, Spain.

Anderson, E. W., Fornell, C., & Lehman, D. (1994). Customer satisfaction, market share, and profitability: Findings from Sweden. *Journal of Marketing*, *58*(July), 53–66. doi:10.2307/1252310

Anderson, E. W., Fornell, C., & Mazvancheryl, S. K. (2004). Customer satisfaction and shareholder value. *Journal of Marketing, 68*(October), 172–185. doi:10.1509/jmkg.68.4.172.42723

Ballantine, J. A., & Stray, S. J. (1999). Information systems and other capital investments: Evaluation practices compared. *Logistics and Information Management, 12*, 78–93. doi:10.1108/09576059910256286

Barnes, S. J., & Vidgen, R. (2003). Measuring web site quality improvements: A case study of the forum on strategic management knowledge exchange. *Industrial Management & Data Systems, 103*(5), 297–309. doi:10.1108/02635570310477352

Barnes, S. J., & Vidgen, R. (2006). Data triangulation and web quality metrics: A case study in e-government. *Information & Management, 43*, 767–777. doi:10.1016/j.im.2006.06.001

Bertot, J. C., & Jaeger, P. T. (2006). User-centered e-government: Challenges and benefits for government Web sites. *Government Information Quarterly, 23*(2), 163–168. doi:10.1016/j.giq.2006.02.001

Bertot, J. C., & Jaeger, P. T. (2008). The E-government paradox: Better customer service doesn't necessarily cost less. *Government Information Quarterly, 25*(2), 149–154. doi:10.1016/j.giq.2007.10.002

Bhatnagar, S. (2004). *E-government: from vision to implementation: a practical guide with case studies*. New Delhi Thousand Oaks, CA: Sage Publications.

Bitner, M. J. (1990). Evaluating service encounters: The effect of physical surroundings and employee responses. *Journal of Marketing, 54*(2), 69–82. doi:10.2307/1251871

Bitner, M. J., & Hubbert, A. R. (1994). Encounter satisfaction versus overall satisfaction versus quality: The customers' voice. In Rust, R. T., & Oliver, R. L. (Eds.), *Service quality: New directions in theory and practice* (pp. 72–94). London: Sage.

Box, R. (1999). Running government like a business: Implications for public administration theory and research. *American Review of Public Administration, 29*, 19–43. doi:10.1177/02750749922064256

Brudney, J. L., & England, R. E. (1982). Urban policy making and subjective service evaluations: Are they compatible? *Public Administration Review, 42*(2), 127–135. doi:10.2307/975534

Chen, D. Y., Huang, T. Y., & Hsiao, N. Y. (2006). Reinventing government through on-line citizen involvement in the developing world: A case study of Taipei City Mayor's E-mail Box in Taiwan. *Public Administration and Development, 26*, 409–423. doi:10.1002/pad.415

Chu, P. Y., Yeh, S. C., & Chuang, M. J. (2008). Reengineering municipality citizen electronic complaint system through citizen relationship management. *Electronic Government. International Journal (Toronto, Ont.)*, *5*(3), 288–309.

Cronin, J. J., & Taylor, S. A. (1992). Measuring service quality: A reexamination and extension. *Journal of Marketing, 56*(July), 55–68. doi:10.2307/1252296

DeMaio, C. D. (2002). *Creating a Performance-Based Electronic Government*. Retreived March 15, 2006, from http://www.performanceweb.org/research/egovernmentreport.pdf

Eurostat. (2005). E-government 2004: Internet based interaction with European business and citizens. *Statistic in focus*, 35.

Fornell, C. (1992). A national customer satisfaction barometer: The Swedish experience. *Journal of Marketing, 55*(1), 6–21. doi:10.2307/1252129

Freed, L. (2008). *American Customer Satisfaction Index: E-government Satisfaction Index*. Foresee Results. Retrieved April 3, 2009, from http://www.foreseeresults.com/Form_EgovQ32008.html

Gronroos, C. (1990). Service management and marketing: Managing the moments of truth in service competition. Lexington, MA.

Gronroos, C., Heinonen, F., Isoniemi, K., & Lindholm, M. (2000). The netoffer model: A case example from the virtual marketspace. *Management Decision*, *38*(4), 243–252. doi:10.1108/00251740010326252

Gupta, M. P., & Jana, D. (2003). E-government evaluation: A framework and case study. *Government Information Quarterly*, *20*, 365–387. doi:10.1016/j.giq.2003.08.002

Halaris, C., Magoutas, B., Papadomichelaki, X., & Mentzas, G. (2007). Classification and synthesis of quality approaches in e-government services. *Internet Research*, *17*(4), 378–401. doi:10.1108/10662240710828058

Ho, A. T. (2002). Reinventing local governments and the e-government initiative. *Public Administration Review*, *62*(4), 434–444. doi:10.1111/0033-3352.00197

Horan, T. A., Abhichandani, T., & Rayalu, R. (2006). Assessing user satisfaction of e-government services: Development and testing of quality-in-use satisfaction with Advanced Traveler Information System (ATIS). In *Proceedings of the 39th Hawaii International Conference on System Science*.

Hsiao, N. Y., Huang, T. Y., & Chen, D. Y. (2002). *Implementing electronic government in Taiwan: A case study of Taipei City Mayor's Email-box. In 2002 e-government international conference*. Seoul, Korea.

Kaohsiung City Government Information Management Center. (2008). *Kaohsiung Citizen E-Complaint System Data* (unpublished)

Kaynama, S. A., & Black, C. I. (2000). A proposal to assess the service quality of online travel agency: An exploratory study. *Journal of Professional Services Marketing*, *21*(1), 63–88. doi:10.1300/J090v21n01_05

Kelly, J. M., & Swindell, D. (2002). A multiple-indicator approach to municipal service evaluation: Correlating performance measurement and citizen satisfaction across jurisdictions. *Public Administration Review*, *62*(5), 610–621. doi:10.1111/1540-6210.00241

Mosse, B., & Whitley, E. A. (2009). Critically classifying: UK e-government website benchmarking and the recasting of the citizen as customer. *Information Systems Journal*, *19*, 149–173. doi:10.1111/j.1365-2575.2008.00299.x

Osborne, D., & Gaebler, T. (1992). *Reinventing government: How the entrepreneurial spirit is transforming the public sector*. Reading, MA: Addison-Wesley.

Parasuraman, A., & Grewal, D. (2000). The impact of technology on the Quality-Value-Loyalty chain: A research agenda. *Journal of the Academy of Marketing Science*, *28*(1), 168–174. doi:10.1177/0092070300281015

Parasuraman, A., Zeithaml, V. A., & Berry, L. L. (1988). SERVQUAL: A multiple-item scale for measuring consumer perceptions of service quality. *Journal of Retailing*, *64*(1), 12–40.

Parasuraman, A., Zeithaml, V. A., & Berry, L. L. (1994). Reassessment of expectations as a comparison standard in measuring service quality: Implications for further research. *Journal of Marketing*, *58*, 111–124. doi:10.2307/1252255

Parasuraman, A., Zeithaml, V. A., & Malhotra, A. (2005). E-S-QUAL: A multiple-item scale for assessing electronic service quality. *Journal of Service Research*, *7*(3), 213–233. doi:10.1177/1094670504271156

Reddick, C. G. (2005). Citizen interaction with e-government: From streets to servers? *Government Information Quarterly*, *22*, 38–57. doi:10.1016/j.giq.2004.10.003

Rust, R. T., & Oliver, R. L. (1994). Service quality: Insights and managerial implications from the frontier. In Rust, R. T., & Oliver, R. L. (Eds.), *Service quality: New directions in theory and practice* (pp. 1–19). London: Sage.

Ruyter, K., Bloemer, J., & Peeters, P. (1997). Merging service quality and service satisfaction: An empirical test of an integrative model. *Journal of Economic Psychology*, *18*, 387–406. doi:10.1016/S0167-4870(97)00014-7

Schedler, K., & Summermatter, L. (2007). Customer orientation in electronic government: Motives and effects. *Government Information Quarterly*, *24*, 291–311. doi:10.1016/j.giq.2006.05.005

Steyaert, J. C. (2004). Measuring the performance of electronic government services. *Information & Management*, *41*, 369–375. doi:10.1016/S0378-7206(03)00025-9

United Nations. (2008). *UN e-government survey 2008: From e-government to connected governance*. Retrieved April 25, 2008, from http://unpan1.un.org/intradoc/groups/public/documents/UN/UNPAN028607.pdf van Deursen, A., van Dijk, J., & Ebbers, W. (2006). Why e-government usage lags behind: Explaining the gap between potential and actual usage of electronic public services in the Netherlands. In M. A. Wimmer et al. (Eds.), *EGOV 2006* (pp. 269-280).

Wagenaar, R., Matthijsse, R., de Bruijn, H., van der Voort, H., & van Wendel de Joode, R. (2006). Implementation of shared service centers in public administration: Dilemmas and trade-offs. In Bekkers, V., van Duivenboden, H., & Thaens, M. (Eds.), *Information and communication technology and public innovation: Assessing the ICT-driven modernization of public administration* (pp. 141–158). Amsterdam: IOS Press.

Wang, L., Bretschneider, S., & Gant, J. (2005). Evaluating web-based e-government services with a citizen-centric approach. In *Proceedings of the 38th Hawaii International Conference on System Sciences*.

West, D. M. (2008a). *Improving technology utilization in electronic government around the world, 2008*. Retrieved April 20, 2009, from http://www.brookings.edu/~/media/Files/rc/reports/2008/0817_egovernment_west/0817_egovernment_west.pdf

West, D. M. (2008b). *State and Federal Electronic Government in the United States, 2008*. Retrieved April 20, 2009, from http://www.brookings.edu/~/media/Files/rc/reports/2008/0826_egovernment_west/0826_egovernment_west.pdf

Zeithaml, V. A., Parasuraman, A., & Malhotra, A. (2000). *A conceptual framework for understanding e-service quality: Implications for future research and managerial practice*. Working Paper. Marketing Science Institute, Cambridge, MA.

APPENDIX

Table 8. Variables used in analysis in this chapter

Variable	Scale and definition
Satisfaction	
(Overall evaluation) Overall, what is your evaluation of the complaint-handling of your complaint case?	Scaled from 5 to 1, Very satisfied (5)/very dissatisfied (1)
Service quality	
(Time efficiency) What is your perception of the time efficiency of your complaint case in the KCECS replying to you?	Scaled from 5 to 1, Formal reply received very soon (5)/ formal reply received very late (1)
(Response manner) What is your perception regarding the response manner of your complaint case?	Scaled from 5 to 1, Very friendly (5)/ very unfriendly (1)
(Effective channel) What is your perception of the KCECS as a channel for filing complaints?	Scaled from 5 to 1, Very appropriate (5)/ very inappropriate (1)
(Complaint resolving) What is your perception regarding the extent/degree of your complaint being resolved?	Scaled from 5 to 1, Completely resolved (5)/ not resolved at all (1)
Characteristics	
Complaint times	Scaled from 1 (first time user) to 5 (used four times and above)
Willingness to reuse the KCECS	Yes/no; Equals 1 if yes, 0 otherwise
Complaint type	Suggestion, inquiry, accusation, rights protection
Demographics	
Gender	Male/female; Equals 1 if male, 0 female in regression analysis
Age	20 and below, 21-30, 31-40, 41-50, 51-60, 60 and above; Equals 1 if age above 31, 0 otherwise in regression analysis
Education level	Primary school and below, junior high school, senior high school, college/university, graduate school (master's degree), graduate school (PhD); Equals 1 if education level above college/university, 0 otherwise in regression analysis
Occupation	Government officers, agriculture, manufacturing industry, service industry, student, housewife, other
Years of residence	10 and below, 11-20, 21-30, 31 and above; Equals 1 if years of residence more than 21 years, 0 otherwise in regression analysis

Chapter 23
Engaging Citizens Through Local E-Government:
an Australian Experience

Peter Shackleton
Victoria University, Australia

ABSTRACT

The early moves to e-Government in Australia were prompted by factors such as government reform, the need to reduce costs and the desire to improve the effectiveness of service delivery. Often these were the objectives of higher levels of government rather than individual councils in the local government sector. While there have been significant improvements in many areas of local e-Government, a number of local councils in Australia particularly those in rural communities are yet to have enhanced their web-based services. The chapter will report on the progress local government in Australia have made towards e-Government implementation, specifically on citizen access to electronic service delivery. The chapter provides a background to the types of electronic information and services provided by local government in Australia and recent moves in Australia to enhance citizen involvement. The research identifies many of the internal and external pressures on local government which are often different from those at higher levels of government. At the local government level, where a significant number of citizen-to-government transactions occur in Australia, e-Government can be as much a barrier as it can be an enabler for citizen access to information and services. The result for local government is often a varied and at times confused approach to e-Government.

INTRODUCTION

Throughout the last two decades, local government throughout modern Western democracies has been subject to far-reaching reform programs as part of a broader public sector reform drive (Sanderson, 2001). In the 1970s, Western economies experienced simultaneous high inflation and unemployment and the debts of governments grew for the first time since World War II (WWII). Importantly, however, as governments grappled to provide services, citizens started to question the ability of large pervasive gov-

DOI: 10.4018/978-1-61520-931-6.ch023

ernment to address social and economic problems (Feng, 2003; Sanderson, 2001). The notion of the 'welfare state' has gradually been replaced with a generic policy amongst Western governments designed to reduce the size and scope of the public sector. This has often involved attempts to reduce the cost of services yet at the same time improve the services to citizens. Since the 1990s the public sector in Australia has experienced a sustained program where many services have been privatized, or forced to compete with private providers. Governments have restructured the public sector to provide information and services that is more responsive to the needs of citizens and they have put in place a regime of management techniques with a stronger focus on performance measurement (Kloot, 1999; Sanderson, 2001).

In many respects, it is not surprising that e-Government amongst all levels of government can be seen as a natural progression of this new form of public sector 'managerialism', or New Public Management (NPM) (Hood, 1991). E-government, in varying ways, has become the vehicle upon which many of the previously none achievable objectives of NPM have been attained. According to Feng (2003), the trend towards e-Government represents a continuation of previous public sector reforms but with a substantial increased role for information and communication technologies (ICTs). Moreover, electronic government challenges the traditional relationship between public authorities and citizens; it provides the opportunity for government to rethink how it configures and provides daily services, build different and deeper relationships with the community, and devolve power and responsibility to regions and local groups (Kearns, 2001).

Much of the focus of the early e-Government implementations often centred upon transactions between identifiable customers (citizens and business enterprises) on one side, and a multitude of independent government organizations in charge of registering, issuing or collecting items or money on the other (Lenk & Traunmuller, 2002). According to Lenk and Traunmüller (2002) it is in the interest of many governments to draw attention to this side of e-Government. Many of the early e-Government policies highlighted the merits of electronic technologies by drawing attention to situations where citizens suffered inconvenience and high compliance costs in dealing with public bodies and promised better service to citizens (Multimedia Victoria, 1998).

Governments, particularly local government, are unique with respect to online activity in that they have the power to dictate rules and regulations, and the possibility to create a legal obligation (Warkentin, Green, Pavlou, & Rose, 2002). In many dealings with governments, citizens have no choice such as to submit town planning permits or pay for a garbage service, compared to the myriad of choices without obligation present in commercial electronic commerce. Moreover, electronic government in contrast to over-the-counter government services, is characterized by a number of key factors that have the potential to change the face of government to the public but require the *trust* of citizens (Warkentin et al., 2002). These include

- the extensive use of communication technology
- the impersonal nature of the online environment
- the ease by which information can be collected, processed, and used by multiple agencies
- the implicit uncertainty of using an open technological infrastructure for transactions, and
- the newness of the communication medium. (Warkentin et al., 2002)

These factors highlight both the positive and negative aspects of e-Government. While e-Government may encourage the active participation of citizens in democratic processes, it may disenfranchise those who choose not to or who are suspicious of web-based delivery. E-Government can be as much a barrier as an enabler unless governments are effective in attempting to engage with citizens. As governments increasingly turn to the electronic delivery of services, it is essential that they ensure that they are effective in achieving their desired aim and that they are able to be used universally by the citizens they target. In Australia, one of the leading countries in e-Government (United Nations, 2003), the major focus of e-Government has been on providing services at a reduced cost (SOCITM & I&DeA, 2002) which has been backed by extensive annual evaluations (2005). This is despite many other benefits that are obtainable from e-Government implementations.

This chapter examines the progress local governments in the State of Victoria, Australia have made utilizing the Internet to deliver traditional services, improve governance and enhance community contact. Through a case study of four councils, including a council where the author worked on the development and implementation of a new web system, it identifies the factors impacting on local government that determine the level, type and support for different forms of electronic service delivery and governance.

BACKGROUND TO AUSTRALIAN LOCAL GOVERNMENT

In 1901 the Australian Commonwealth Constitution established a Commonwealth government with specific powers and six independent state governments with responsibility for all those areas of authority not granted exclusively to the Commonwealth. In a variety of ways over the years the Commonwealth government progressively increased its power over the states particularly in the important area of finance. The Commonwealth government is now the only government in Australia able to levy company and income tax, excise and customs duty, and sales tax.

Local government, comprising 719 councils Australia-wide (ABS, 2002), is not recognized in the Australian Commonwealth Constitution but local councils are under the control of their respective state governments. Despite this, in the last two decades the responsibilities of councils have expanded to include services such as social and community welfare, economic development and environmental management. According to Gerritsen and Osborn (1997), over the past 25 years Australian local government has undergone extensive and continuous reform in a number of areas, "... in its structure; its powers and responsibilities; in changing patterns of public participation; the organisation of the local financial system; and in its occupational structure and management of its workforce" (Gerritsen & Osborn, 1997: 55). While many of the *First Wave* reforms left council structures relatively unchanged, the *Second Wave* reforms have significantly altered the role of local government. The result has been to increase the demands upon local government in an environment of reduced fiscal capacity and continuing restructuring, downsizing and contracting out. As part of these reforms, local governments have had to reframe their organisations to take account of the changes in and the expectations of the community, and to accommodate competition practices (DTLR, 2001; Jones, 1993; Kloot, 1999; OECD, 1996). Moreover, councils have had to continually examine their role and functions in an effort to rationalise their vast range of fragmented services while at the same time improving the quality of customer service.

Nevertheless, despite their apparent lack of independence and limited number of revenue options, Australian local governments provide an impressive array of functions and services (Figure 1). The Municipal Association of Victoria identified twenty two *core* functions undertaken by all Victorian councils (MAV, 1993) many of which relate directly to funding from the state and commonwealth government. In Australia, local councils have moved from providing just services

Figure 1. Victorian councils actual expenditure 2007/2008 (Victorian Grants Commission, 2008)

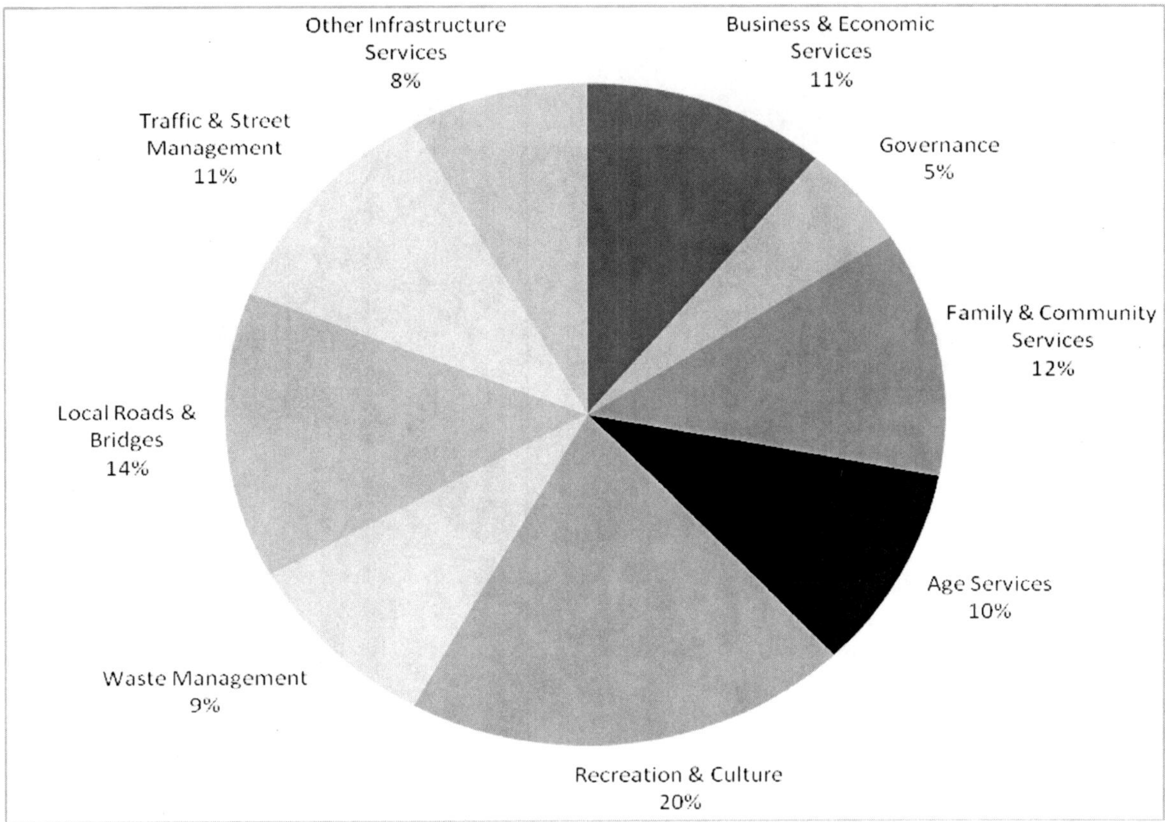

for roads, rubbish and animals to covering areas such as welfare and aged services, recreation and arts, and building and planning services The same MAV study noted that there were over one hundred smaller functions and all Victorian councils performed many of these to a greater or lesser extent depending upon the priorities and size of council, as well as where it was located.

The increased number of services is in a context where local government is still the most impoverished tier in the Australian federal system. The relative poverty of local governments in Australia is in marked contrast to the situation in many other countries such as Canada and in the United States of America, where their comprehensive local government systems were established after federation (Gerritsen & Osborn, 1997). This led Rumpf (1980) to observe that "... in these countries, local authorities are indeed third tier authorities with real powers and responsibilities".

LOCAL E-GOVERNMENT IN AUSTRALIA

The first major move by councils into e-Government came in 1999, when the Australian Commonwealth government released $45 million for funding under the Networking the Nation (DCITA, 1999) funding program specifically for local e-Government. The Municipal Association of Victoria (MAV) received $A5.77 million for the Victorian Local Government Online Service Delivery Project (VLGOSD project) in 2001 with the project to be completed by January, 2003 (MAV, 2000). The MAV coordinated e-Government initia-

Figure 2. Local government online service projects (Whitehorse Strategic Group & MAV, 2002)

tives at the local government level. They required councils to formulate strategic plans and to outline support structures before funds were allocated to individual councils (Whitehorse Strategic Group & MAV, 2002). The project identified nine areas of importance as outlined in Figure 2 - Telecommunications, Web and Intranet service delivery, Interconnected services, Payments on line, Shared services, eProcurement, Planning on line, and Graphical information systems. By the end of 2002, nearly a half of all Victorian councils had implemented some form of web content management system while a lesser number had installed payment on-line systems (Whitehorse Strategic Group & MAV, 2002).

Immediately following the VLGOSD project, citizen use of local government web sites increased. In the major case study council outlined later in this chapter, citizen use increased four-fold for some functions on the web site (Shackleton, 2006a).

With respect to funding, as local councils matured their web delivery, additional funds from both the state and commonwealth government were provided to councils and support organizations for specific projects. Often this funding has been to state Local Government Associations (LGAs) representing their respective local councils for state-wide initiatives. Alternatively competitive funds have often been won by the wealthier councils to develop a pilot initiative. Sadly much of the funding has been limited or directed to only a few councils with many smaller and rural councils left to improve engagement with citizens via the web to themselves.

LOCAL E-GOVERNMENT MATURITY, BARRIERS AND ENABLERS

While electronic government is more than just a move from a physical delivery environment to a virtual or online delivery environment, it is often a dilemma for local government in particular to ascertain which direction they should take. E-Government, particularly at the local government level, is often seen as an opportunity to improve aspects of citizen-to-government relationships and at the same time reduce costs and inconvenience on both sides of the relationship. However, many councils may not be in a position to establish a virtual counter for services, at least beyond basic information-only services. State governments have expected that more mature local e-Government will eventually change existing government processes, relationships and structures to make them less hierarchical and more responsive to community needs (SOCITM & I&DeA, 2002; United Nations, 2002). Even at the comparatively early stage in their implementation, Victorian municipal councils were often expected to move beyond service provision and to be more responsive to the needs of their communities. It is the potential of the WWW to alter the relationship with communities that has citizen-focused government or e-Democracy as a comparatively new platform in e-Government policies (CITU, 2000; Mulitmedia Victoria, 2002). Previous research has shown that this sector has been slower to adopt e-Government compared to higher levels of government (Shackleton, 2002; Shackleton, Fisher, & Dawson, 2004) yet, arguably, citizens would benefit highly from local electronic service delivery as it is the sector where they are mostly involved in over-the-counter transactions (SOCITM & I&DeA, 2002).

However, the move from a physical to an online delivery environment in the local government sector is more complex as it involves multiple types of service provision and high levels of community engagement. Moreover, within the local government sector there are huge differences in the financial standing of councils and each council may have different priorities depending upon community expectations.

Reports on the research into how local councils mature their services to citizens over time indicates that it is certainly different from that of other levels of government and varies within the sector (Shackleton, Fisher, & Dawson, 2005). Quirk's (2000) description of e-Government maturity probably best represents the implementation of e-Government amongst local councils because it emphasizes the disparate range of functions and services provided by governments at the local level. While the Quirk model outlines four progressively maturing stages with Information Giving at the lower end and Empowering Citizens as the final stage, it also marries this with different spaces of local e-Government (Figure 3).

Although the exact model depicting areas and stages of maturity may be difficult to identify, it is important to appreciate that local e-Government maturity is different from that of state and commonwealth governments (Shackleton et al., 2005).

Moreover, given the lack of independence of local government and it strong links to the community there are a range of influencing factor on e-Government maturity. For local government, the first major category of influencing factors are external factors, that is those that are beyond the control of local councils and impact on local e-Government service delivery to citizens. Previous research reveals that they may be explicit or implicit and the factors identified in the literature can be place under three broad headings: Higher levels of government policies, Priorities and Funding, Technological Advancements, and the Digital Divide (Shackleton, 2007; Shackleton et al., 2004)

A second major category of influencing factors are internal factors, that is those over which council management has substantial discretion. In some cases this may be to accept or reject some policy, or it may be to proceed in one direction versus another. In some cases the internal factors are not easily identified as they are often intertwined with the external factors. A search of the literature reveals that the internal influencing factors (either barriers, enablers, objectives or

Figure 3. e-Government for local authorities (Quirk, 2000)

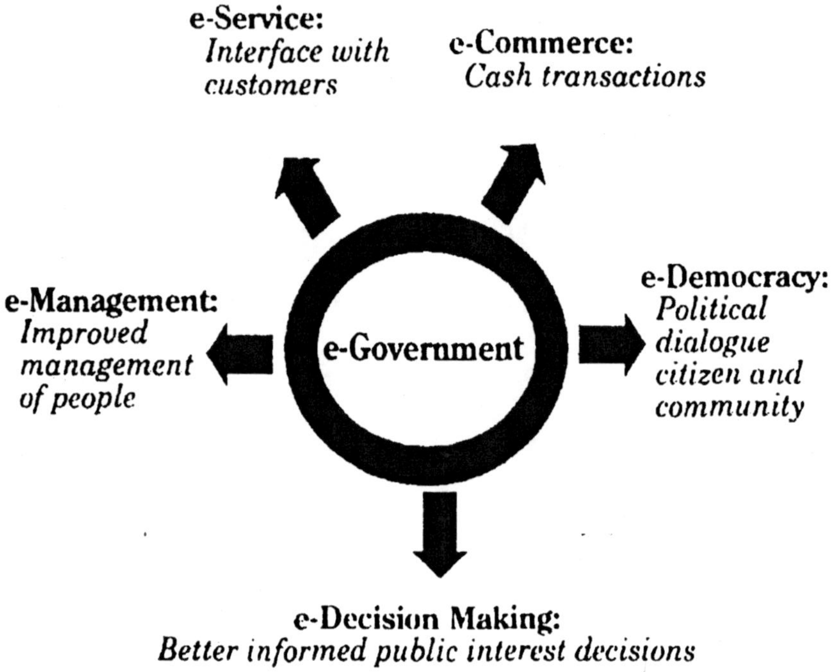

priorities) included structural and process reform (such as New Public Management reforms), and funding and resourcing issues

The remainder of the chapter reports on the research that used content analysis of local government web sites and case studies to examine the how services in the local government sector have change and the factors impacting on decisions to introduce new services to citizens.

RESEARCH METHODOLOGY

The research was broken into two broad stages. The objective of the first stage of the research was to identify content, investigate changes to content and level of maturity of different aspects of Victorian council web sites. This component of the research has spanned 6 years. The focus of the second stage was to provide qualitative data from an ethnographic case study (with interviews with key personnel in three other councils) to identify the impact of barriers and enablers to local e-Government maturity.

COUNCIL WEB SITES

A context matrix was developed and used to examine the presence of information and services and to assess the changes in the sophistication of service delivery over a three year period. Twenty of seventy nine council web sites (25%) were selected to be examined. Categories of councils were developed based on size and location. Within each category councils were randomly selected. Table 1 below shows the categories and the number of councils identified for each group. It should be noted that the time the first content analysis was conducted some Councils did not have any web presence at all.

Table 1. Sample of councils categorized by demographic and size

	Total Number of Victorian Councils				Representative Group			
	Size				Size			
	Small	Large	Total	Percentage	Small	Large	Total	Percentage
Metropolitan	2	21	23	29.6%	1	6	7	35%
Interface	4	4	8	10.2%	2	1	3	15%
Rural	43	4	47	60.2%	9	1	10	50%
Total	49	29	78	100%	13	7	20	100%

ETHNOGRAPHIC-BASED CASE STUDY

The primary objective of the study reported in this chapter is to provide rich qualitative data from an in-depth ethnographic case study to identify the factors influencing the adoption and development of e-Government initiatives and to illustrate how those factors impacted on a council's electronic service delivery strategies.

This study involved the researcher working with staff in a council (identified as OzCouncil) for over two years with an intensive period of six months, observing and interviewing council staff as they developed and implemented a web site in March 2003. Further interviews were conducted in 2004 after the launch of the web site. The council were also revisited in 2007. A strength of this interactive research methodology is that prolonged engagement in the natural setting allows the researcher to observe and record processes that would be difficult to observe by the use of other methods (Leedy, 1997). Apart from observing the process OzCouncil undertook in its moves to web development and electronic service delivery, fourteen interviews were conducted with a range of OzCouncil staff such as area and service managers, IT and Web staff, councillors and associated OzCouncil support staff. The in-depth interviews were conducted over a two-year period and were typically 45 minutes to an hour in length and explored the council's decision-making process, its web development strategy and implementation issues. Documents were collected and collated, while detailed observations were made both of formal and informal meetings and other settings. Analysis was undertaken using a detailed meta-matrix (Miles & Huberman, 1994).

The majority of the research was done in that venue although at least two interviews with staff from three other councils were undertaken to identify similarities and differences between the councils. Each of the councils chosen for the case study research were at various stages of e-Government implementation and represented different demographic parts of Victoria.

OzCouncil is located on the fringe of Melbourne. It is classified as an interface council because most of the population is concentrated in a number of large suburbs but the council must also service a sparsely populated rural constituency. Historically the community has a strong commitment to environmental protection, arts and local history and is actively involved in council governance. The council serves 20,600 households, has an annual income of $35 million, but only one full time Web developer/IT/business analyst, and a full-time Communications manager. Some IT staff are working on separate web-based projects such as GIS systems. Although comparatively small it had made significant progress in its e-Government strategy.

The other three other councils used for comparison are identified as RuralCouncil, RegionalCouncil and MetroCouncil. RuralCouncil is a small rural municipal council located in the Victorian

Mallee district. It has a basic static but dated web page. There is no IT support at the council and an Environmental Engineer works approximately 4 hours per week on web related support. Both the CEO and the Environmental Engineer are responsible for electronic service delivery and they were interviewed in this case. MetroCouncil is a metropolitan council that covers a number of affluent inner suburban areas of Melbourne. It has five Web/IT support staff incorporating business analysts, web editor, editor in the Communications section. The council has had a web page for several years and it uses a content management package and payment software. The CIO and web editor were interviewed in this case. The council has had a web page for several years and it uses a content management package and payment software. RegionalCouncil is a large regional city 200km from Melbourne. It has made significant advances in e-Participation with the introduction of web-casting of council meetings. It has 3 IT in various roles supporting and developing new systems.

WEB SITE CONTENT ANALYSIS

Over many years (Shackleton, 2002, 2006b, 2007; Shackleton, Fisher, & Dawson, 2003; Shackleton et al., 2004, 2005) a longitudinal study has investigated changes to the content of different aspects of Victorian council web sites. A context matrix was developed and used to examine the presence of and changes to information and services over a six year period. A Web site feature was given a score of '1' if it had been fully implemented, or a reduced score ('0.5') if the feature was partly implemented. The score for each feature was totalled and then divided against the total number of Web sites. As an example, if 8.5 out of 10 Web sites had implemented a particular feature, it would be given a content rating of 85% for that particular interest area.

A summary of the findings of the early research conducted in 2001 (Shackleton, 2002) and 2004 (Shackleton et al., 2005) together with the most recent analysis in 2007 is summarized in Table 2 (Shackleton, 2007). The purpose of the context matrix was to show overall maturity in broad functional areas grouped under headings as outlined in Table 2 and matching Quirk's model. While other models may be have different categories, Quirk's model reflects the different broad areas of service delivery and in particular the importance of citizen contact. It was one of the first models specifically developed for the local government sector and for that reason has been used through the study. However, additional sub-categories should probably be developed as local e-Government has matured over the years. In this research, e-Decision Making and e-Democracy were grouped together under e-Participation with e-Decision Making viewed as the first stage and e-Democracy as a more mature form of e-Participation.

E-Management

Many e-Management features such as procurement are not evident by a citizen from the web site. Many councils have Intranets and the interviews revealed that they had made significant advances in this area in recent years. Many of the core services such as finance are online and can be accesses and upgradedIt is clear from these interviews that councils have moved into areas such as document management

E-Service

This category included features that assist a resident to seek information about a product or service provided by the council. The breadth and quality of the service information has expanded significantly over the years. This matches the desire by the State government to ensure that local government services are on line as soon as possible. However, it is clear that many of the services are static in nature requiring contact with the council or providing only an application form.

Table 2. Summary of main characteristics by category in 2001 to 2007

Category & Feature	Percentage (%)				
	2001	2003	2004	2006	2007
e-Service	90%	95%	100%	100%	100%
Service details	25%	100%	100%	100%	100%
News and coming events	25%	25%	25%	90%	70%
FAQs	0%	5%	25%	80%	95%
Direct Email support	0%	20%	25%	60%	60%
Novel eServices (interactive maps, lost dogs)	0%	55%	55%	70%	75%
Service Tracking					
e-Commerce	23%	90%	95%	100%	100%
On-line payments (Rates)	0%	5%	55%	65%	65%
On-line payments (Other – pet registration, fines)	5%	70%	100%	100%	100%
Ordering facility (Downloadable Forms direct ordering, prepared forms)	5%	15%	20%	55%	60%
Email payment/ordering					
e-Participation	95%	100%	100%	100%	100%
Council Information	20%	100%	100%	100%	100%
Community information	95%	100%	100%	100%	100%
Email address (for contact with the Council)	20%	95%	100%	100%	100%
Council decision making – minutes, strategic plans	65%	95%	95%	100%	95%
Links to other organizations/businesses	0%	5%	5%	55%	50%
Community Groups/Bulletin boards/Chat Room/Broadcasting				70%	70%
Subscription service					

Services such as the ability to track the progress of a planning permit, a common over-the-counter query, is now available on some of the council sites. Recent investigation shows that most of the poorer councils still do not have these types of services. New tools such as Graphical Information Systems (GIS), increasingly common on council web sites has enabled users to seek information and support for a service product or service without having to wait until the council office opened.

E-Commerce

This section covers the transaction handling involved in placing orders and the possible payment for services and products. It also involves the payment of annual rates, regulation charges and for fines such as parking infringements. Payment facilities usually require an on-line credit card payment approval system or bank transfer. Another option is where a council provides a facility for customers to send an email or fill in a form relating to a specific service inquiry.

In 2001, the difference between the small number of sites that had an ordering facility (5%) and the larger percentage of sites that provide for on-line payment (23%) was due mainly to the payment of council rates. In 2003, the difference between the two functions closed as councils expanded their on-line payment systems to include direct payment for other services (with funding via the VLGOSD project). Recent investigations show that all sample councils have payments on line for rates (although this may be through a provider such as Australia Post) but many of the smaller councils still do not enable payment of other items such as parking tickets. Councils appear to prefer the booking of a service (such as a hall) to be undertaken via other means such as by telephone or at the main council offices.

E-Participation

This section covers features that aim to inform the resident of broad issues associated with the operation of the council and its future direction.

Items such as council minutes or strategic planning issues and newsletters are examples of this type of feature and has expanded over the two years. Other features such as links to bodies within the council region and other government services has also increased to be included on 95% of sites. Most sites in the early years offered job information through a listing of the types of employment available within the council. A more mature web site would facilitate discussions on issues through a bulletin board, organized electronic community forums, email response, and web-casting of meetings.

Many councils had placed a moderate amount of community-based material on their sites (10 – 20%) and established links to a large number of community and business organizations (65%) in 2001. In later years, this had risen considerably with most councils providing up-to-date council minutes and strategic plans on their sites. Some councils have exploited the possible interactive nature of the web and experimented with web-casting with email questions. Nevertheless, it is clear that most councils have not moved into actively engaging citizens in more informal ways such as via Web 2.0. In part this could be due to the lack of sophisticated sites in many poorer councils, a lack of staff time, or simply a decision to that the level of citizen participation is deemed to be adequate.

Summary

The analysis of the early data found a huge variation between groups of municipal councils, some having leading edge sites and others labouring to maintain a web presence. Although the difference was narrowed during the VLGOSD funding period, there appears to be an even larger variation between small rural councils and metropolitan councils in recent times.

However a limitation of this type of analysis is that it does not distinguish between the many of the different types of items within categories. Local e-Government has changed significantly over the years and thus to gain a better understanding of the differences a case study of a four municipal council was undertaken. This forms the bases of the next section.

CASE STUDY ANALYSIS

Table 2 suggests a somewhat ad hoc approach to the use of the web by local government to deliver services, provide information and gain community views. In the Australian context, however, much of the variability can be explained by the different pressures placed on local governments. The following section details the results of the case study illustrating the result those pressures have had on local government web development and electronic service delivery.

The analysis found three broad areas impacting on electronic service delivery, higher-level government policies, external factors and municipal council internal e-Government initiatives.

Higher-Level Government Priorities

The case study revealed high levels of adoption of new forms of managerial efficiency and accountability in government by local government employees. Coupled with this general trend were e-Government priorities from the state and commonwealth governments that had municipal councils reacting to what they referred to as 'new' programs. The combined result was a mixture of pressures that had municipal councils attempting to achieve improved forms of government, such as better service delivery that matched the needs of constituents, but at the same time restricted by costs, knowledge and resources. The case study revealed that the e-Government incentive programs often forced upon them by the controlling state government, enabled councils to mature their electronic service delivery but they often had to forgo another good initiative to take advantage of the offer. Moreover, another by-product of these programs was a widening of the gap between the services offered by individual councils.

The VLGOSD Project, as an example, provided funds to enable rural councils to implement specific identified initiatives. Expert assistance was provided to all councils but funding support was only available to rural councils. Ironically while this was designed to move rural councils forward with respect to electronic service delivery, metropolitan councils often gained more advantage because of their ability to implement programs. In the case study, despite the lure of $10,000 for a content management system the rural council, RuralCouncil, was unable to integrate the system given resourcing problems. MetroCouncil, which was unable to obtain funding, used the expert assistance to implement a different web content management system to support the implementation of a new web page in January, 2003.

In 2003 many more local councils had mature eCommerce functions mainly for the payment of rates but also for other charges such as dog licences and parking fines. Expensive back-end systems are required to support electronic payments and councils often lack both the money and expertise to implement and support these systems. Councils are often forced to make decisions between the implementation of fundamental eServices which is illustrated in this quote from one interviewee:

If people can pay rates over the phone then I don't see a lot of merit of pushing payment of the rates over the web. It is an easy solution for them – the quality of the transaction from the consumer point of view is no better over the web than it is over the phone. Compare that to something like [building] plans then the quality of the transaction over the phone is far inferior compared to looking at it over the web.

It is about tailoring the limited resources to get the maximum improvement in services. If you are getting a 5% improvement in putting resources into transactional stuff then I see that as marginal. Getting a 50% improvement somewhere else I see that as substantial and that is where I think resources should go ahead.

External Influences

Contact with the community is more prevalent at the local government level and the case studies revealed there was perceived community pressure within the councils to 'catch up' with other state and semi-government authorities. As an example, OzCouncil was criticized for having a low level of web-based service delivery in an article in July, 2001 in one of the large syndicated papers. Although there was no evidence to suggest extensive community pressure for electronic service delivery in any of the four councils in the case study, there was a perception that the metropolitan councils needed to have more than just a basic static web site.

The outcome of this was for councils to skew their response towards what it felt would satisfy the community at that time. In many cases, despite the obvious advantages of electronic service delivery, councils chose instead to expand into areas of governance and democracy. This is revealed in the interviews with staff and councillors who see the community as wanting more of this type of information rather than enhanced services.

Another influence on municipal councils was the state-wide council association, the Municipal Association of Victoria (MAV), of which all councils are members. The association is seen as the voice of councils on general issues and lobbies the state and commonwealth government. The MAV was seen as applying pressure to move lagging councils towards mature sites with enhanced services. 'Lighthouse' examples of progressive councils were often flagged by the association for others to follow.

The one exception to the push by the community for better electronic service delivery was in the RuralCouncil where it is viewed as a low priority amongst the council, council staff and the community. This resistance to implement electronic service delivery is despite the extensive computer usage within the community to support functions such as crop and animal management. Council services are seen as being accessible via phone queries and visits to the main town.

Internal Initiatives

While there may be pressure from a community to ensure it's council has a level of electronic service delivery similar to its neighbouring councils, it is often internal issues such as the push from staff or councillors for more flexible delivery that accelerates the process of e-Government. In part this would account for the slow transition to the web by some councils.

All of the four councils experienced some of this change in the early stages where an enthusiastic staff member championed the need for web-based service delivery and developed an initial static web page. Moving on, however, from this initial stage has often been more difficult.

At OzCouncil, the Communications Branch under the new manager was keen to establish a much more flexible web page. Extensive consultation with divisions within the council was undertaken. The page that was developed contained a large amount of rich but static information that was well organized and functionally easy to access and download. The interviews with staff reveal that they did not have a sense of ownership of the page but saw it as the domain of one area, the Communications Branch. The restrictive updating routines quickly dated the static information. A second project involved an innovative web site developed for the By Laws division was also an example of an initiative by one staff member. The difference in this case from earlier iterations within OzCouncil is that it had the support of the innovative division manager and it quickly became an achievable benchmark for the rest of the council

The IT manager at OzCouncil then engaged staff in discussion of e-Government issues, involved other divisions in new programs but more importantly he was committed to using technology to support and then change business processes. His work encouraged council staff in a range of divisions to question existing service delivery processes and look to electronic service delivery as a way of improving everyday business. Council staff were starting to question the type of material on the existing web page and the need to deliver genuine services. A staff member observed:

We need to go beyond the governance side and concentrate more on services. As a ratepayer I want to go to a web page and find out what services they can provide. Through the technology it gives me the opportunity to seek out the right people and it has confidentiality.

The metropolitan council, MetroCouncil appears to be similar although without the same level of success. Recognising the problems getting divisions to input into the web page, they eventually implemented a content management software and established 30 content editors from divisions within the council. Asked why they had not progressed as rapidly as similar councils in recent times the CIO stated:

We are about average and that is where our management here would probably prefer us to be. They don't want us to be leading edge because they don't want it to be seen that we are pouring money into fancy toys for the community. So I think they are comfortable for us to be middle of the road.

While the content management system was supported and made available to the rural council in the case study by the VLGOSD, it did not bring about significantly improved electronic service delivery. In part, this is explained by the lack of internal support for such an initiative and available resources.

Figure 4. Barriers and enablers of local government

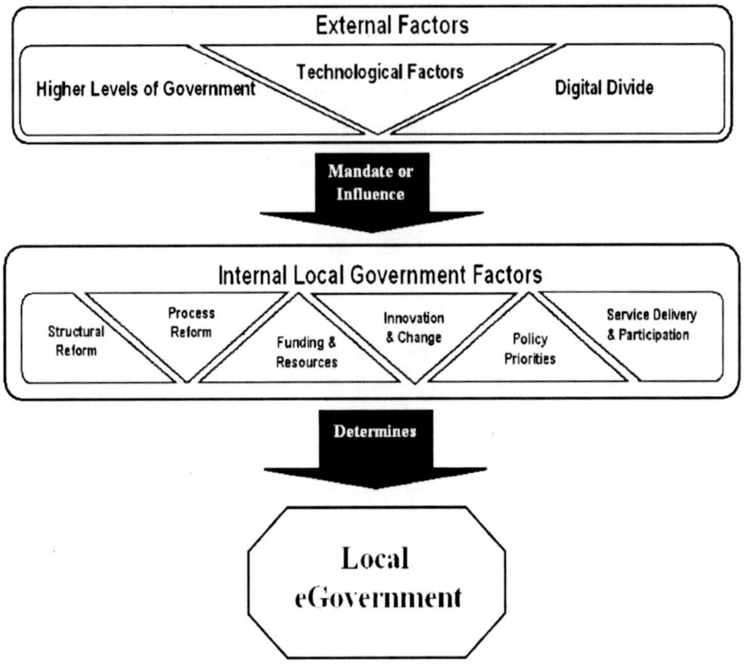

SUMMARY

A review of the literature identified the external factors that impact on electronic service delivery and citizen engagement in the local government sector (Deakins & Dillon, 2002; Dollery, Marshal, & Worthington, 2003; Feng, 2003; Hackney & Jones, 2002; Lenk & Traunmuller, 2001; OECD, 2004; Prins, 2001). The main factors identified by the OECD (2004) included legislative and regulatory barriers, budgetary barriers (both these are the responsibility of higher levels of government in Australia), technological change, and the digital divide. Additional factors identified in the research include structural reform in the sector, process reform to service delivery and the policy priorities of local councils.

These factors can be combined into a framework as shown in Figure 4.

An important aspect of this diagram to note is that many of the internal local government factors are mandated or highly influenced by higher levels of government. This means that local government often does not have any choice but to follow a path set by higher levels of government. Moreover, as the local government has very little discretionary funding, initiatives in the area of e-Government often have to wait until funds filter down from the state or commonwealth government.

The case study presented in this chapter helps to explain why local councils often have trouble engaging citizens. The research revealed that many local councils, unlike commonwealth and state departments and authorities, often have little discretionary funding particularly for e-Government. Limited funds are targeted for specific projects and any alteration to funding priorities must be justified to the community. In this environment, local governments are highly reliant on tagged external funding from State and Commonwealth grants and projects, and there will often be an expansion in local e-Government maturity even when only limited funds are available.

In addition to the external pressure from higher levels of government, the research found that local communities have brought e-Government to the fore for some local councils. This pressure incorporates both what is perceived by council staff about community expectations and real where limited evaluations have been done. In poorer rural councils the community has electronic service delivery low on the list of projects competing for scare funds while most metropolitan councils have made decisions themselves to support more than just a basic web site.

There is an emphasis in local e-Government on improving community involvement rather than hands-on specific electronic service delivery. Strong links to the community is a central tenet of local government, and the research found that municipal council staff place great emphasis on governance issues through web delivery in preference to electronic service delivery. Even at more mature levels of e-Government, municipal councils appear to emphasize governance issues before enhanced electronic service delivery.

CONCLUSION

This chapter reported on the progress local governments in Victoria have made towards citizen engagement and the factors that have influenced that progress. In Victoria local councils are subject to higher levels of accountability and are under pressure to continually improve the quality of services while reducing costs and fees to residents. Yet they have strong community links, unlike their state and commonwealth counterparts and place great emphasis on governance. The research reveals the priorities of councils in the local government sector mean that they mature in different areas and at different rates. Moreover, these are not necessarily related to the size or location of councils. While the availability of external funds and other forms of expertise have assisted local councils on their path to e-Government, many other external factors and internal initiatives have influenced the extent and direction of e-Government implementations in individual councils. However from the very beginning councils have been well situated to engage citizens through eGovernment but the type and extend of engagement will vary according to a large range of factors.

REFERENCES

ABS. (2002). *2001 Census Community Profile and Snapshot*. Canberra, Australia: Australian Bureau of Statistics.

AGIMO. (2005). *Australians' Use and Satisfaction With E-Government Services Survey*. Canberra, Australia: Australian Government Information Management Office.

CITU. (2000). *E-Government: A Strategic Framework for Public Services in the Information Age*. London: Central IT Unit, Cabinet Office.

DCITA. (1999). *Networking the Nation*. Canberra, Australia: Department of Communication, Information Technology and the Arts, Australian Commonwealth Government.

Deakins, E., & Dillon, S. M. (2002). E-government in New Zealand: the Local Authority Perspective. *International Journal of Public Sector Management*, *15*(5), 375–398. doi:10.1108/09513550210435728

Dollery, B., Marshal, N., & Worthington, A. (2003). *Reshaping Australian Local Government: Finance, Governance and Reform*. Sydney, Australia: University of New South Wales Press.

DTLR. (2001). *Strong Local Leadership - Quality Public Services*. United Kingdom: Department of Transport, Local Government and the Regions.

Feng, L. (2003). Implementing E-Government Strategy in Scotland: Current Situation and Emerging Issues. *Journal of Electronic Commerce in Organizations*, *1*(2), 44–65.

Gerritsen, R., & Osborn, D. (1997). Reform of Local Government in Australia. In Comparative Study on Local Government Reform in Japan, Australia and New Zealand (pp. 51 - 112). Sydney, Australia: Japan Local Government Centre (CLAIR).

Hackney, R., & Jones, S. (2002). *Towards E-Government in the Welsh (UK) Assembly: an Information Systems Evaluation.* Paper presented at the ISOneWorld Conference and Convention, Las Vegas, Nevada, USA.

Hood, C. (1991). A Public Management for all Seasons. *Public Administration*, *69*(Spring), 3–19. doi:10.1111/j.1467-9299.1991.tb00779.x

Jones, M. (1993). *Transforming Australian Local Government*. St Leonards, Australia: Allen and Unwin.

Kearns, I. (2001, April 27). - May 3). Wising Up About Wiring Up. *Public Finance*, 26.

Kloot, L. (1999). Performance Measurement and Accountability in Victorian Local Government. *International Journal of Public Sector Management*, *12*(7), 565–583. doi:10.1108/09513559910308039

Leedy, P. (1997). *Practical Research: Planning and Design* (6th ed.). Upper Saddle River, NJ: Merrill, Prentice Hall.

Lenk, K., & Traunmuller, R. (2001). Broadening the Concept of Electronic Government. In Prins, J. E. J. (Ed.), *Designing e-Government: On the Crossroads of Technological Innovation and Institutional Change. Hague*. Boston: Kluwer Law International.

Lenk, K., & Traunmuller, R. (2002). Preface to the Focus Theme on eGovernment. *Electronic Markets*, *12*(3), 147–148. doi:10.1080/101967802320245901

MAV. (1993). *A Guide to Performance Indicators in Local Government*. Melbourne, Australia: Municipal Association of Victoria.

MAV. (2000). *Strategic Rural & Regional Implementation Plan for the Deployment of Integrated Online Services*. Melbourne, Australia: Municipal Association of Victoria.

Miles, M. B., & Huberman, M. A. (1994). *Qualitative Data Analysis*. London: Sage.

Multimedia Victoria. (1998). *Online Government 2001 - from Vision to Reality*. Melbourne, Victoria, Australia: Department of State Development, State Government of Victoria.

Multimedia Victoria. (2002). *Putting People at the Centre: Government Innovation Working for Victorians*. Melbourne, Australia: Department of State and Regional Development.

OECD. (1996). Responsive Government: Service Quality Initiatives. Paris, France: Organisation for Economic Co-operation and Development.

OECD. (2004). *The e-Government Imperative*. Paris, France: Organisation for Economic Co-Operation and Development.

Prins, J. E. J. (Ed.). (2001). *Designing e-Government: On the Crossroads of Technological Innovation and Institutional Change*. Hague, Netherlands: Kluwer Law International.

Quirk, B. (2000). *From Managing Change to Leading Transformation*. Paper presented at the E-Government Summit, December 2000, United Kingdom.

Rumpf, P. B. (1980). *Town Hall Politics: Heidelberg's Policy Makers 1967 - 77*. Unpublished, University of Melbourne, Melbourne.

Sanderson, I. (2001). Performance Management, Evaluation and Learning in 'Modern' Local Government. *Public Administration*, *79*(2), 297–313. doi:10.1111/1467-9299.00257

Shackleton, P. (2002, December 4-6). *The Evolution of Local Government Electronic Services in Victoria.* Paper presented at the Australasian Conference on Information Systems, Melbourne, Australia.

Shackleton, P. (2006a). *Town Hall eCommerce: A Model of Web-Based Service Delivery*. Melbourne: Unpublished Unpublished, Monash University.

Shackleton, P. (2006b). *Your Dreaming: The next stage towards joined up government in Australia, Working for e-Business (We-B)*. Melbourne, Australia: School of Information Systems, Victoria Universtiy.

Shackleton, P. (2007). tGovernment: eChallenges for Australian Local Government, Working for e-Business (We-B). Melbourne, Australia: School of Information Systems, Victoria University.

Shackleton, P., Fisher, J., & Dawson, L. (2003). *E-Government Services - One Local Government's Approach.* Paper presented at the Information Systems Development, Melbourne, Australia.

Shackleton, P., Fisher, J., & Dawson, L. (2004). *Evolution of Local Government E-Services: the applicability of e-Business maturity models*. Paper presented at the HICCS'2004.

Shackleton, P., Fisher, J., & Dawson, L. (2005). *From Dog Licences to Democracy: Local Government Approaches to E-Service Delivery in Australia*. Paper presented at the Thirteenth European Conference on Information Systems, Regensberg, Germany.

SOCITM, & I&DeA. (2002). *Local E-Government Now: A Worldwide View*. Northampton, UK: Improvement & Development Agency, Society of Information Technology Management.

United Nations. (2002). *Benchmarking E-government: A Global Perspective - Assessing the Progress of the UN Member States*. New York: United Nations Division for Public Economics and Public Administration.

United Nations. (2003). *Benchmarking E-government: A Global Perspective - Assessing the Progress of the UN Member States*. New York: United Nations Division for Public Economics and Public Administration.

Victorian Grants Commission. (2008). *Victorian Grants Commission Annual Report 2007/8*. Melbourne, Victoria: State Government of Victoria.

Warkentin, M., Green, D., Pavlou, P. A., & Rose, G. M. (2002). Encouraging Citizen Adoption of e-Government by Building Trust. *Electronic Markets*, *12*(3), 157–162. doi:10.1080/101967802320245929

Whitehorse Strategic Group, & MAV. (2002). *Local Government Online Services Project Report.* Paper presented at the Online Services Demonstration Conference, Melbourne, Australia.

Chapter 24
Community Policing in India:
Transparency through E-Governance

Sudha Arlikatti
University of North Texas, USA

David Wachira
University of North Texas, USA

Sarah Gregory
University of North Texas, USA

ABSTRACT

'Community policing', a major reform in policing, broadens the police mandate beyond the traditional focus of fighting crime to addressing community problems through a personalized approach that draws citizens into the process of policing themselves. Emulating this movement, the Police Administration in numerous states of India have recently engaged in community policing through e-governance specifically tailored to meet the diverse needs of their populace. Two such case studies, eCOPS in Andhra Pradesh and Lokvani in Uttar Pradesh are discussed showing the multifold benefits of such a movement in increasing transparency, trustworthiness, and efficiency of the police administration. The chapter concludes by making a bid to foster this symbiotic digital mode of interaction between the police and citizens by introducing domain specific performance measures. Such measures will allow for easy monitoring, revising, and garnering national support to institutionalize, validate, standardize, facilitate, and promote these programs to help create a proactive all-hazards resilient citizenry for the future.

INTRODUCTION

India is one of the oldest civilizations in the world with a culture marked by a high degree of syncretism and cultural pluralism. The nation is a federal republic consisting of 28 states and seven Union Territories. The Indian peninsula has an area of 3.28 million sq kms (about 1/3 the land mass of the US), and its coastline stretches about 5,700 kms on the mainland and about 7,500 kms including the two island territories of Andaman and Nicobar. India is the world's second most populous country with an estimated population of 1.13 billion (about 1/6 of the world's population). It has a population density of approximately 340 people per square kilometer compared to the U.S. with 30 people per square kilometer (Census of India, 2001). Each state or union territory is divided into basic units of government

DOI: 10.4018/978-1-61520-931-6.ch024

and administration known as districts. There are nearly 600 districts in India and those are in turn divided into tehsils and eventually into villages. Approximately 70% of Indians reside in rural areas. However, in recent decades migration to larger cities has led to a dramatic escalation in the country's urban population thereby increasing cultural diversity. Although the constitution recognizes Hindi and English as the official language, 22 other languages are spoken abundantly, some having classical status with a number of dialects summing as high as 1,652. In addition to this linguistic heterogeneity, India is also characterized by its ethnic and religious diversity. The Indian Census (2001) has established that Hinduism accounts for 80%, Islam, accounts for 13%, about 2% of the population adheres to Christianity, Zoroastrianism and Judaism, and the rest are accounted for by other native Indian religions namely Buddhism, Jainism, and Sikhism. In 1976 constitutional law declared India as a secular nation, but even prior to this legislative proclamation the subcontinent has been distinguished by its religious secularism and cultural diversity. India is a relatively poor country, earning an estimated 2004 GDP per capita of $3,100 in the Purchasing Power Parity (CIA, 2005). Human Development Index figures indicate that it ranked 127 out of 177 countries (UNDP, 2005).

Since gaining independence from the British Raj in 1947, India has rapidly progressed through developments in information technology, the service sectors, nuclear capabilities and food exports. However, despite these impressive gains in economic investments and output, there seems to be a growing disparity between the urban rich and the rural poor due to the continued imbalances in economic and educational attainment levels of the people. Additionally, India faces pressing problems due to significant overpopulation, environmental degradation, widespread corruption, natural disasters, and, more recently, the increased threat of terrorism from political, ethnic and religious factions from within and outside the country. The unsuspecting casualties of these events are softer community targets, like women, children, the elderly, and religious and ethnic minorities. Lack of education and insufficient monetary resources make it difficult for the military and the police intelligence to mitigate against these threats, and to have a unified crime prevention strategy. Thus in recent years the Indian government has taken various legislative measures to reinforce the disaster prevention and management agencies including the police machinery and infrastructure at the national and state levels.

With technological advancements and the increasing sophistication in criminal activities, traditional anti-crime police activities are becoming increasingly difficult and less effective in India. Researchers have noted that this 'criminal cosmopolitanism' (Amarnathan 2003; Krishnamurthy 2003) has caused the Indian police to revisit their conventional policing styles. Police Administrators in numerous states of India have recently engaged in 'community policing' through e-Governance to make their functioning more transparent, quicker, and cost effective, and to empower citizens by allowing them to help the police perform non-crime functions. This chapter considers two case studies, namely *eCOPS* in the state of Andhra Pradesh and *Lokvani* in the state of Uttar Pradesh, highlighting the interactions between the police and the citizens and follows with a discussion of the challenges of sustaining them in the future. Finally, the authors conclude by making a bid for expanding community policing through e-Governance by institutionalizing it at the national level and facilitating and funding it at the state and local police levels so as to create a cadre of proactive, emergency ready, empowered community leaders, and citizens that are more disaster resilient in the future.

BACKGROUND

Indian Police Administration

The Indian Police Force was established under British rule with the enactment of the Indian Police Act in 1861. The British Parliament's purpose was to create the police function as a punitive arm of the state able to maintain law and order in the Princely states of India. As a result of those earlier times the Indian 'police' developed its reputation through intimidation and coercion and lost the trust of its citizens. Although 52 years have passed since independence from the colonial rule of the British, the Indian police continue to struggle to change this image and move towards a more inclusive collaborative policing model. India has no national police force and according to the constitution, the individual 28 state governments act as superintendent over state police forces with the Director General of Police (DGP) acting as a head of each state. States are divided into districts, which are geographical units, each typically having the strength of 1000 officers. Every district is further divided into subdivisions, which are again divided into a number of police stations depending on the geographical coverage, size of population, and crime volume. These police stations are the most important points of contact for the citizens depending upon the size and population. An Inspector or sub-inspector of Police heads a police station. Assistant sub-inspectors, Police Head Constables and Police Constables who constitute the bulk of the police force, are the staff of police stations (see Mitra and Gupta, 2008 for the State Police structure).

Traditional police goals or crime functions (Krishnamurthy 2003) in India were centered around prevention and detection of crime, crime analysis, public security, maintenance of law and order, registration of complaints, their status and follow-up, strengthening the criminal justice system through prosecution, implementation of social justice legislation, and enforcement of non-criminal codes such as background checks, passport verification, traffic control, fire and rescue services, police updates and maintaining a databases etc. More recently the emerging goals (Mitra and Gupta, 2008) or non-crime functions of the Indian police include countering cyber-crimes, anti-terrorism measures (both at home and abroad), improving intelligence collection, providing an equitable administration of law, being deployed for special security details for heads-of-state and VIPs, educational programs, help-lines, facilitation centers etc.

Paradigm Shift in Policing Style

Traditionally, as in most countries, disaster management and law enforcement agencies in India followed the dominant command and control/ military model for managing natural disasters such as hurricanes, tornadoes, tsunamis, and earthquakes and human induced disasters such as chemical spills, riots, and acts of terrorism. They utilized a defensive approach where the hazardous incident was regarded as an enemy (Dynes, 1994) and the affected citizens, as helpless bystanders incapable of rational behavior or actions. The first responders, including emergency managers, fire fighters, and police personnel, concentrated their energies on containing chaos through command and control (the 3 C's) and a closed authoritarian structure. More recently, researchers have suggested a holistic paradigm calling for a comprehensive 'vulnerability management model' (McEntire et al. 2002) or a 'community disaster impact model', which posits that humans act rationally even in disaster situations just as they do in every day life (Perry and Lindell, 2003; Lindell, Prater and Perry, 2007). Despite common myths, such as contagion and widespread panic, oftentimes people do not panic but rather make rational decisions on what to do and what protective actions to take given the available information and time (Helsloot and Ruitenberg, 2004). Generally speaking, in most cases citizens are the first to respond as they are already at the scene of the event. This model, also known as the problem-solving or collaborative model, is characterized by continuity, coordination and cooperation (the new 3 C's) and advocates the valuable contribution that citizens can make in emergency management (Dynes, 1994; Salter, 1995). Not only do citizens effectively bring themselves to safety, but their altruistic selves also help save their fellow citizens. Furthermore, fellow citizens also provide most of the initial aid as they converge to disaster locations in massive numbers to help out. Community policing mirrors the characteristics of the community disaster impact model and helps justify the paradigm shift in policing efforts around the world from a command and control to a community policing strategy.

Community Policing

The history of policing is in reality "a record of how one group of people attempts to control the behavior of others, as individuals and in groups" (Trojanowicz and Bucqueroux, 1990 pp. 59). Community policing is a major reform in policing developed in the past 30 years and changes the way police think and act. This revolutionary movement broadens the police mandate beyond the narrow focus of fighting crime to include efforts that also address fear of crime, social and physical disorder and neighborhood decay (Trojanowicz and Bucqueroux, 1990). For example, the core elements of community policing as delineated by the U.S. Department of Justice include, a) organizational elements - a wide philosophy adopted organization, decentralized decision-making and accountability, fixed geographic accountability and generalist responsibilities, utilization of volunteer resources and enhancers; b) tactical elements - enforcement of laws, proactive crime prevention and problem solving oriented; c) external elements - public involvement in community partnerships, government and other agency partnerships. Thus community-policing postulates that contemporary community problems require a new decentralized and personalized police approach that draws citizens into the process of policing. Community policing focuses on crime and social disorder by delivering police services that include aspects of traditional law enforcement, as well as prevention, problem solving, community engagement, and partnerships. Citizen participation facilitates closer cooperation between the police and the general public thereby building trust and augmenting security. Community policing transforms the police image among the general public by opening up channels of communication, which in turn provide a reservoir of intelligence and manpower.

Although the traditional crime functions (e.g. crime investigation, crime analysis, law and order, safety and security) of the police are confidential in nature with little or no direct public interface, non-crime functions (e.g. working at phone help lines and facilitation centers, as traffic control personnel, data input and management, and educational outreach) allow citizens to participate in varying capacities and is encouraged and facilitated through the 'community policing' movement around the world.

E-Governance in India

In order to provide its citizens with faster and more efficient services, the Indian government formed new strategies focused on citizen empowerment by encouraging participation and providing easy access to Information & Communication Technologies (ICT). With the setting up of the National Informatics Center in 1975, it first marked its commitment to promoting IT in managing the internal processes of various government departments (Gupta et al. 2004). In the late 90s the use of IT expanded from being used for only internal functioning of the government to a large number of initiatives targeting the rural and urban populations. The enactment of the IT Bill (2000) provided legal status to information and transactions carried out on the net (Mitra and Gupta, 2007). The ICT age has redefined governance through significant initiatives at the Central level by promoting the use of IT in managing its internal processes by drawing up a 'Minimum Agenda of e-Governance' statute. In addition, various government ministries and departments included a provision of 2 to 3 percent of their annual budgets to be expended towards IT related activities.

Researchers have noted that due to the complex and emerging nature of e-Governance and the diverse audiences it affects, no one definition or set of terms would be adequate to articulate its concepts (Mitra and Gupta, 2008). Hence some of them use e-Government as technology-led solutions. Proponents of e-Democracy, like the World Bank, profess e-Government to have the capacity to move us to the perfect form of governance that is transparent in all its operations, engages and enhances exchange of information between institutions involved in policy making, and provides easy access to government information to all its citizens. Others, taking the developmental perspective (Sen 1999) believe that in addition to empowering citizens to be proactive and participate in the running of the government, e-Government helps ensure five types of freedom: political, economic facilities, social opportunities, transparency guarantees, and protective security.

Several Indian state governments have taken various innovative steps to promote e-Governance by drawing up a roadmap for IT implementation and delivery of services to the citizens on-line. The applications implemented thus far are targeted towards providing Government-to-Business (G2B), Government-to-Citizen (G2C) and Business-to-Consumer (B2C) services with an emphasis on the use of local languages so as to reach a wider citizenry. Two such G2C initiatives that have been implemented by the Police Administration as part of their community policing strategy in the states of Andhra Pradesh and Uttar Pradesh are discussed in the following sections. However, success is not assured, as developing governments are often known for having a low tolerance towards criticism. Citizens, even when presented with the opportunities to monitor governmental action, may fail to do so out of fear or the belief that their efforts will fall on deaf ears. Many of these citizens have for years lived under the confines of corruption and government inefficiency. This is especially true for services such as those offered by the police. Transparency and citizen involvement is a process that may take years to build.

CASE STUDIES OF COMMUNITY POLICING THROUGH E-GOVERNANCE

eCOPS: Crime Reporting Database Management System in Andhra Pradesh

Andhra Pradesh (often referred to as A.P.) is a state situated on the southeastern coast of India. According to the Indian Census 2001, it is India's fourth largest state, with an area of 275,069 sq.km., and the fifth largest population, inhabited with over 75 million people (Census of India 2001). Telugu is the official language of the state spoken by 88.5% of the population. Agriculture was the chief source of income for the state's economy until the election of Chief Minister, Nara Chandrababu Naidu. Naidu holds the record of the longest serving chief minister of A.P. serving two consecutive terms from September of 1995 to May of 2004. Chadrababu represented a new breed of dynamic Indian politicians who are very well educated, charismatic, and willing to experiment. His administration was characterized by a policy tilt towards urban areas and an emphasis on economic recovery through infrastructure development, specifically Information and Communication Technology (ICT) development. He helped transform A.P.s largest city and capital, Hyderabad, into one of the ICT hubs of the country and home to Microsoft's first Research Lab outside US.

Naidu modernized the administration by computerizing a number of government operations and led initiatives like *eSeva* – through which all the utility bills and taxes could be paid at a single counter for the convenience of the citizens. He was also instrumental in the development of the new Hyderabad International Airport. During his tenure, many ports and IT parks were developed with private public partnership. On the rural front he launched schemes like *'Janmabhoomi'* (Motherland), a project that invites people to participate in developing the state (Incredible People, 2009). He created the Development of Women and Children in Rural Areas (DWCRA) groups whose mission is to provide social and economic infrastructure to the women of the state. Naidu won numerous awards including 'IT Indian of the Millennium' (India Today), Business Person of the Year Award (Economic Times). He is a member of the World Economic Forum's Dream Cabinet (1998) and declared South Asian of the Year by Time Asia magazine (1999). In recognition of his leadership and vision in the field of Information Technology, Mr.Naidu was designated as the co-chairperson of the National Task Force on Information Technology set up by the Government of India to prepare the IT road map for the future. Mr. Naidu's role in promoting Information technology for better governance has been widely recognized, both within and outside the country.

As part of his agenda for achieving excellence in community building through teamwork, he turned his attention to the Andhra Pradesh Police Department in 2002 to implement eCOPS - a crime reporting database management system. eCOPS was designed to address the growing expectations from citizens for better ethical standards, transparency, and efficiency in the police administration and to improve the image of the police department. The Police Computer Service Department and two private vendors, Sun Systems and Pioneer Systems, maintain the eCOPS database management system. The system has streamlined the work of police by reducing paperwork and helping citizens report crimes. In the past, a victim or witness reported a crime by going to the local police station with his or her jurisdiction. At the station, a duty officer would fill out a paper-based record of events known as the First Information Report (FIR). Often times this report was manipulated or the records were misplaced on purpose in exchange for a bribe.

With the eCOPS system, an individual is free to choose any police station and request the duty officer there to input the crime information directly into the system. Additionally, the individual has the freedom to access the details and monitor the progress of the case by going to any police station and requesting a report or by logging into the Andhra Pradesh Police website using an FIR number given at the time the incident was reported. This is helpful as people feel less inhibited and have fewer apprehensions associated with frequent trips to the police station, strict formality in lodging their complaints or getting updates about friends or family members. ECOPS ensures better efficiency and a quicker turn around time. To guarantee accuracy of the report, there are provisions for lodging online complaints if the details of a case were inputted incorrectly, if no progress has been made in a long time, or if one suspects fraud (Heeks, 2003). This database also assists police officers in different jurisdictions by allowing them to log in to the system and check a suspect's criminal history. Before this, the police had to rely heavily on faxes, phone calls, wiring and radioing information as a means of controlling crime. Consequently, valuable time and resources were lost due to the inefficiency of these activities. Additionally, the eCOPS system improves the efficiency and effectiveness by eliminating duplication of procedures executed during the registration process of criminal cases. The quality of information and decisions are also improved due to the integration of information systems across various police stations statewide.

The challenges of implementing eCOPS include a lack of public awareness of the eCOPS program and the continued public distrust of the police and the Internet, to securely manage such sensitive data. This insecurity concerning information placed on the Internet, as well as the public's perception of the police administration as one to be feared and mistrusted, is not easy to overcome. Additionally, there is the challenge posed by resistance from a few corrupt police officers that seek bribe and power and would not wish such a transparent system to work. The eCOPS provides little safeguards against those who wish to abuse the system by failing to use many of the facilities in the system or failing to make the public aware of the system (Heeks, 2003).

Lokvani- An Interactive Complaint Box System in Uttar Pradesh

Uttar Pradesh (often referred to as U.P.) is the 5th largest state located in the northern part of India measuring an area of 240, 928 sq.km. With a population of over 166 million people (Census of India 2001), it is India's most populous state with a population density of 689 per sq. km. (as against the national average of 312). Slightly over 80% of UP population are Hindu, and Hindi is the official language spoken here. U.P. is the second largest state economy in India with 46% of the state income accounted for by agriculture. Social development indicators like medical facilities, teacher-pupil ratio in primary schools, birth rate, death rate, infant mortality rate, literacy, per capita income, electrification of villages and per capita power consumption U.P. ranks 13th or 14th among 16 major (size and population) states of India and is considered socially backward. In terms of more demanding criteria of educational attainment on the completion of primary or secondary education, only 50% of literate males and 40% of literate females could complete the cycle of eight years of schooling involved in the primary and middle stages. Another distinguishing feature of the U.P. education system is the persistence of high level of illiteracy in the younger age group especially in rural areas. These socio-economic factors make it challenging to effect and sustain positive community changes in U.P.

To assist with crime prevention and management, police departments around the country have taken the initiative of placing complaint boxes at numerous locations around their cities to facilitate and encourage the process of receiving anonymous information from people who prefer to participate in community policing efforts and remain unidentified due to concerns of safety and security. Informants' letters are collected daily, prioritized and acted upon as quickly and efficiently as possible. *Lokvani,* or "voice of the people," is a G2C initiative started in Sitapur district of U.P. by the combined efforts of the District Administration under the leadership of District Magistrate Amod Kumar and the *National Informatics Center (NIC).* It is a community owned self-sustaining system involving online monitoring of the status of citizens' complaints and transparency in the functioning of the district administrative bodies.

Apart from the citizens and government employees, other stakeholders in this project are the service providers, Oracle and Indian Institute of Management, Lucknow that acted as consultants. Despite the extremely low literacy rate in U.P. (about 60%, below the national average) this system works because Lokvani operates on a public-private partnership model, with young, computer literate entrepreneurs owning these kiosks charging a nominal fee from citizens for helping them log into this interactive database. They are enthusiastic and motivated about being indirectly involved in local governance and policing efforts. The interactive kiosks with the site design entirely in *Hindi*, the national language of India and also the local language spoken in the state of Uttar Pradesh, has facilitated large-scale participation of the rural poor who were traditionally left out of the loop. When a complainant goes to a kiosk, the operator logs into the Lokvani site with his/her username and password with and enters the complaint in the specified format required which generates a tracking number to be passed on to the complainant for follow up/ reference. It was decided that instead of opening new kiosks, existing cyber cafes and/or computer training institutes would be granted licenses to become Lokvani Centers. This decision was taken to ensure the financial viability and the long-term sustainability of the kiosks.

All complaints logged through the Lokvani sites are sorted at the District magistrate's office by a team of police officers and marked for appropriate action and monitored closely at weekly review meetings. Furthermore, to sustain the initiative long-term, in 2006, a state-level apex society known as "Lokvani Uttar Pradesh" was created as the nodal agency responsible for coordinating and supervising the district level's functioning of Lokvani societies. By December 2007, the number of complaints received totaled 107,453 through the 700 Lokvani kiosks across the state, of which 102,648 were addressed (Shukla and Srinivasan, 2005). Following its success, in Sitapur district this initiative has been expanded by government order to other districts of U.P. as well.

Although complaint boxes are an effective method of reducing the time taken to address public grievances and to make district officials more accountable to the public at large, they come with their share of implementation challenges. Some of these include obtaining funding to purchase complaint boxes or kiosks and preventing them from being vandalized especially in rural settings. With very few computer literate educated entrepreneurs to man such a kiosk, the financial viability of setting up these at the village level is yet another hurdle. Additionally trying to locate these booths with uninterrupted supply of electricity and good Internet connectivity is imperative is a challenge in itself. All these need to be overcome in creative ways, possibly by integrating them with existing well-funded government institutions such as middle or high schools or post office. In the urban setting, choosing safe locations such as government court houses, post offices, federalized banks, public schools, college/university campuses, or ATM booths that have safety and security personnel, good infrastructure and back-up generators could be a solution.

DISCUSSIONS

The eCOPS and Lokvani case studies have shown how two states in India with differing socio-economic characteristics, styles of leadership, population size, literacy, and language have initiated the community-policing through e-Governance tailored to the needs of their people. However, success is not assured; there are deep-seated problems of mistrust and bureaucracy that would have to be overcome to help reach a wider citizenry.

Scholars studying the broad effects of e-Government (Hwang et al., 1999; Mitra 2004) have noted that it inspires change in three Windows of e-Government namely:

1. **Internal effects** (e.g. the organizational work processes, networking, horizontal connectivity and electronic data exchange between sub-units and empowering them)
2. **External effects** (e.g. accessibility, transparency, electronic service delivery, greater customer, satisfaction, and community empowerment)
3. **Acceptance effects** (e.g. employee/ managements willingness to change, overall effort, rate of progress towards achieving IT skills)

Obtaining support and validation for successful implementation at all levels of government include: overcoming bureaucratic red-tape and corruption at all levels, the lack of funding for continued IT training and certifications for police and citizens, the lack of direct rewards translating into promotions or salary bonuses for underpaid police constables to take on this training, and the lack of direct incentives or rewards that could motivate citizens to be proactive in expending personal time and effort in community building efforts with police and other government entities.

Additionally, citizens presented with electronic service delivery options and the opportunities to monitor governmental action may fail to do so out of fear or the belief that their efforts will fall on deaf ears. Many of these citizens have for years lived under the confines of corruption and government inefficiency. This is especially true for services such as those offered by the police. Transparency and citizen involvement is a process that may take years to build as a result of lack of trust between the two parties (the police administration and the citizens), derived from a persistent neglect for the concerns of citizens' personal safety by corrupt and self serving officials, undesired consequences faced by citizens for befriending the police, and organizational resistance to change within the police department. Even in situations where corruption may not be a problem, senior police officers may be unwilling to change the way they conduct their tasks, as they are worried that it would undermine the authority they traditionally have over lesser-educated subordinate officers. They may distrust the technology or face a learning curve due to the fact that many of them have only recently started using computers. Other widely cited challenges include telecommunications infrastructure constraints, lack of institutional framework support, inadequate funding, digital divide, privacy and security concerns, limited IT skills and training, lack of e-government enabling skills and training, and lack of citizen awareness and participation.

As a result of these challenges, a piece-meal approach continues to be observed in various states of India solely dependent on policy entrepreneurs like Chief Minister Chandrababu Naidu in Andhra Pradesh (eCOPS), or the pro-active leadership by certain government officials like District Magistrate Amod Kumar in Uttar Pradesh (Lokvani) or funding streams from private or international donors. With minimal accountability or oversight standards and organizational backing, these projects are certain to close down from under funding in the future. Despite these challenges, it is well worth pursuing community policing through e-Governance as it leads to lower operational costs besides the initial costs associated with setting up the hardware and software. It typically reduces paperwork and cost of storing police records for many years, thus generating higher productivity. Often scanned documents and data captured in other electronic formats makes it easier to monitor the productivity of police constables, increases accumulation of historical data on crimes investigated, resolved, and unsolved to be retrieved at a later date. In addition, it makes it easier to access data from multiple sources and platforms within districts and across states. This enhances the ability of departments and agencies to share their data and improves the decision making process at various levels of public administration.

FUTURE RESEARCH DIRECTIONS

Numerous studies have shown that regular Internet users and non-users are not identical in their needs and capacities and suggest that e-Government approaches should not be the same for everyone rather they should customized to take into account the needs of special groups (Crede and Mansell, 1998). Adopting a uniform e-Government community policing strategy across all the states in India would fail, as the dynamic nature of e-Governance is co-dependent on the demographic characteristics of the people therein. Every state has its own problems with people's work culture, infrastructure, political climate, history of law and order, multiple spoken languages and dialects, economic and educational attainment, and differing community emergencies that require special attention. Thus each state would have to prioritize its community policing efforts and decide which ones can be made more effective through the use of Information and Communication Technologies (ICT) and tailor these accordingly.

Domain Specific Performance Measures

Through their study of the Indian Police Administration's use of e-Government applications Mitra and Gupta (2008) have demonstrated that, in order to arrive at an ideal set of performance assessment measures for e-Government applications one should be domain specific (e.g. Police Administration in India) and gauge the impacts at the ground level. They contend that, "A government service provider must be able to substantiate in terms of certain context-specific parameters as to "how much" or "to what extent" or "in which way" its e-Government endeavors have helped it to better serve both external and internal customers" (p.284). They found that e-Government applications did not contribute significantly to the internal efficiency of the employees, such as the extent of police time commitment in crime investigation, analysis, reporting and arresting, the time commitment for non crime investigations, and time taken in filing prosecution documents etc. Though e-Government applications in non-crime functions were found to contribute to employee satisfaction, performance assessment measures did not indicate improvements in crime functions. For employees, these kinds of service-oriented functions and contributions were more gratifying than engaging in crime detection, investigation, or analysis. However surprisingly e-Government applications in crime function services appeared to contribute to public satisfaction more than non-crime functions. This may be due to the fact that non-crime role of police is not very well understood by the general public. People in India still associate police presence with a crime or a criminal situation.

Based on this assessment, they call for a review of the adequacy of existing crime software, especially the Crime Criminal Information System (CCIS) software used across India. The software places heavy emphasis on data thresholds, has limited analytical capabilities, and lacks the local language interface, which limits its applicability in a multi-lingual country like India. Additionally, the top-down approach of the system impedes usage at the local neighborhood police station levels. Due to these challenges, they call for a secure electronic network connection that can encourage the police employees to exchange and network horizontally and vertically thereby enhancing police efficiency in both crime and non-crime functions. The following factors emerged as most important for developing widespread police e-Governance applications:

1. Computer training
2. Availability of customized software
3. Department level support and encouragement in computer use
4. Availability of computers and peripherals
5. Court acceptance of IT work processes
6. Use of vernacular language in computer related work
7. System security
8. Clear delineation of areas of application
9. Authorization by senior officers for specific work processes

Federal Involvement to Institutionalize

In the United States, the Community Emergency Response Team (CERT) Program educates citizen volunteers about disaster preparedness from an all hazards perspective and trains them in basic disaster response skills, such as fire safety, light search and rescue, team organization, and disaster medical operations in a classroom setting and through drills and exercises. This empowers citizen members to assist others in the neighborhood and their places of work following a disaster event, especially in the event that first responders like the fire and police personnel are unavailable for help. Simpson (2001) found that direct federal involvement has helped in popularizing and sustaining this program across the country. The Federal Emergency Management Agency (FEMA) has helped bring this program to the attention of the communities by institutionalizing, validating, standardizing, facilitating, and promoting these programs. Since 1993 when this training was made available nationally by FEMA, communities in 28 States and Puerto Rico have conducted CERT training.

In India, the recently instituted National Disaster Management Authority (NDMA, 2005) can be instrumental in bringing about a similar change in attitudes by implementing community policing programs through e-governance. They can institutionalize these programs by mandating that every state and district police website include a link to their community policing programs with information on how to get trained and partner with the police in crime prevention (e.g. undercover informants) or non crime prevention activities (e.g. traffic control, natural disaster response, poverty alleviation programs). They can also create train-the-trainer courses, built on the lines of core courses offered to officials in police academies and be strengthened with topics that address "what to do" scenarios for an all-hazards approach. Additional modules can be tailored to meet the specific needs of a community (e.g. communal unrest caused by religious and caste differentials, arson, theft, flooding, etc.).

These training materials can also be uploaded on city police websites that are freely available to citizen watch groups who wish to seek training. Giving these an "official" sanctioned look will help in validating these community-policing programs and also reduce distrust in the minds of people. Listing of community policing programs across the country on a national portal with links to the achievements and best practices adopted by various neighborhoods, cities and states will further help in promoting these programs. Making video training materials available in community libraries, schools, colleges, universities and trade schools to train the younger generation of citizens will also allow citizens and police of poorer communities to share their challenges and experiences and facilitate information and resource sharing from wealthier states and organizations. Also, standardizing the content of manuals and training materials and making them available online in different languages, especially those that are spoken in India's major disaster and terrorism hotspot states (namely Hindi, Assamese, Gujarati, Marathi, Bengali, Kannada, Kashmiri and Tamil), will encourage a greater number of citizens to train and participate in community policing efforts, in order to become crime trackers/ informants and more proactive in dealing with multiple emergencies. These measures will facilitate a broader acceptance of the concept of citizen participation in disasters and emergency management by the Indian people.

CONCLUSION

'Community policing', broadens the police mandate beyond the traditional focus of fighting crime to addressing community problems through a personalized approach that draws citizens into the process of policing themselves. The Police Administration in numerous states of India have recently engaged in community policing through e-Governance specifically tailored to meet the diverse needs of their populace. The two case studies, eCOPS in Andhra Pradesh and Lokvani in Uttar Pradesh showed the multifold benefits of this movement in increasing transparency, trustworthiness, and efficiency of the police administration. Police research organizations in India like the Bureau of Police Research and Development (BPR&D) are continuously engaged in identifying indicators that help measure police performance. The use of e-Governance for policing makes it easier to: measure the time required to respond to critical incidents and complaints, identify responses that are within target time, reward the commanding police officers, monitor the percentage of citizens satisfied with the police response and actions, obtain input from citizens when dissatisfied with the status of response, and coordinate efforts between multiple jurisdictions through data sharing. Proactive community policing is based on the concept that these working partnerships between the police and the community can effectively contribute to reducing crime and promoting security through increased transparency, cooperation, and collaboration. As the Indian police administration tries to remain ahead of lawbreakers, they have to race to acquire and master modern technologies. The communities they serve can act as their working partners in helping with this and reducing crime and promoting security.

The successful implementation of community policing through e-Governance differs from country to country and the context in which they are developed and applied. Umashankar (2005) makes an appeal to seek out "champions for e-Government within the bureaucracy", who through commitment can bring about change in the style of police administration. Selecting a cadre of brilliant, motivated, educated and talented group of candidates trained in state-of-the-art computer management skills, that possess bi-lingual or multi-lingual skills, as well as traditional policing skills are necessary to meet today's demands. As they graduate from police academies, they can be given adequate exposure to field realities, and simultaneously encouraged to cultivate a synergistic partnership with the communities they serve. This new generation of computer savvy young graduates from police academies can be put in charge of bridging the digital divide that exists amongst citizens and the policing administration in a bid to increase transparency and trust. Serving as champions of community, policing through e-Governance will allow them to be amply rewarded by gaining citizens' trust and praise, and through monetary benefits (pay raise), awards, and accolades within and outside the police department ensuring job satisfaction and lowering of corruption in the long run.

Finally, strengthening community policing efforts through e-Governance can serve in not only combating the growing threat of racial and religious conflicts, riots, crime, anti-social activities, and terrorism in India, but it can also serve as an opportunity in disguise for natural hazards mitigation and management. Citizens trained as community police volunteers can be synonymous with 'Community Emergency Response Teams' (CERTs) and assist in preventing, preparing and responding to natural hazards as well. Thus, an all hazards approach to risk reduction that encourages community stakeholders to work together will be the road to sustainable development and serve in creating resilient communities of the future in India. Fostering this symbiotic digital mode of interaction between the police and citizens by introducing domain specific performance measures allows for easy monitoring and revising, and garnering national support to institutionalize, validate, standardize, facilitate, and promote these programs. Ultimately, this will help create a proactive all-hazards resilient citizenry for the future.

REFERENCES

Amarnathan, L. C. (2003). *Technological advancement: Implications for crime*. The Indian Police Journal.

Anti-corruption efforts and African economic development: Hearing before the Subcommittee on African Affairs of the Committee on Foreign Relations, United States Senate. 106th Cong., 2d Sess. (2000). Retrieved March 24, 2007, from http://frwebgate.access.gpo.gov/cgibin/getdoc.cgi?dbname=106_senate_hearings&docid=f:68756.pdf

Bhatnagar, S. (2001). Central vigilance Commission website: A bold anticorruption experiment. *World Bank*. Retrieved March 01, 2009, from http://go.worldbank.org/10T9V182Z0

Bhatnagar, S. (2001). Mandals online in Andhra Pradesh. *World Bank*. Retrieved March 01, 2002, from http://go.worldbank.org/3D3M3OG080

Bhatnagar, S. (2002, Autumn). Egovernment: Lessons from Implementation in Developing Countries. *Regional Development Dialogue*, 24.

Bhatnagar, S. (2004). *E-Government: From vision to implementation: A practical guide with case studies*. New Delhi: Sage Publications.

Bhatnagar, S., & Vyas, N. (2001). Gyandoot: Community-owned rural internet kiosks. *World Bank*. Retrieved February 24, 2009, from http://go.worldbank.org/V5YKYDSRE0

Census of India. Office of the Registrar General and Census commissioner of India. (2001). *Statistics on Demographic and Socio-Economic Characteristics*. Retrieved on September 8th, 2008 from http://www.censusindia.gov.in/Census_Data_2001/India_at_glance/glance.aspx

Central Intelligence Agency. (n.d.). *The World Factbook*. Retrieved July 29, 2009, from https://www.cia.gov/library/publications/the-world-factbook/geos/in.html

CERT. (n.d.). *Community Emergency Response Team*. Retrieved on July 15th 2009, from http://www.citizencorps.gov/cert/about.shtm

CIA. (2005).*The World Fact Book*. Retrieved on September 15th 2008, from http://www.cia.gov/cia/publications/factbook

Crede, A., & Mansell, R. (Eds.). (1998). *The importance of sustainable development ICTs in developing Countries*. Booklets I & IV, E-Journal Research. Retrieved March 01, 2009, from http://www.iicd.org/articles/IICDnews.import9

Department of Administrative Reforms and Public Grievances (DARPG). *Civil Service Awards, Government of India*. (n.d.). Retrieved on September 15th 2008 from http://darpg.gov.in/arpg-website/civilserviceday/pmsaward06-07.pdf

Dynes, R. (1994). Community Emergency Planning: False Assumptions and Inappropriate Analogies. *International Journal of Mass Emergencies and Disasters*, *12*(2), 141–158.

Gupta, M. P., & Jana, D. (2003). E-government evaluation: A framework and case study. *Government Information Quarterly*, *20*(4), 365–387. doi:10.1016/j.giq.2003.08.002

Gupta, M. P., Kumar, P., & Bhattacharya, J. (2004). *Government online: Opportunities and challenges*. New Delhi: Tata McGraw-Hill.

Heeks, R. (Ed.). (2003). *eCOPS: More open handling of criminal cases in India*. Retrieved March 29, 2009, from http://www.egov4dev.org/transparency/case/ecops.shtml

Helsloot, I., & Ruitenberg, A. (2004). Citizen Response to Disasters: a Survey of Literature and Some Practical Implications. *Journal of Contingencies and Crisis Management*, *12*(3), 98–111. doi:10.1111/j.0966-0879.2004.00440.x

Hwang, S.-D., Choi, Y., & Myeong, S.-H. (1999). Electronic Governance in South Korea, Conceptual Problems. *Government Information Quarterly*, *16*(3), 277–285. doi:10.1016/S0740-624X(99)80028-8

Krishnamurthy, S. (2003). *Preparing the Indian Police for the 21st Century*. Bangalore, India: Puliani and Puliani.

Lindell, M. K., Prater, C. S., & Perry, R. W. (2007). *Introduction to Emergency Management*. Hoboken, NJ: John Wiley and Sons.

McEntire, D., Fuller, A., Johnston, C. W., & Weber, R. (2002). A Comparison of Disaster Paradigms: The Search for a Holistic Policy Guide. *Public Administration Review*, *62*(3), 267–281. doi:10.1111/1540-6210.00178

Mitra, R. K., & Gupta, M. P. (2007). Analysis of issues of e-government in Indian Police. *Electronic Government an International Journal*, *4*, 97–125. doi:10.1504/EG.2007.012182

Mitra, R. K., & Gupta, M. P. (2008). A contextual perspective of performance assessment in eGovernment: A study of Indian Police Administration. *Government Information Quarterly*, *25*, 278–302. doi:10.1016/j.giq.2006.03.008

Morash, M., & Ford, J. K. (Eds.). (2002). *The Move to Community Policing: Making Change Happen*. Thousand Oaks, CA: Sage Publications.

Naidu, C. (2009). In *Encyclopædia Britannica*. Retrieved July 31, 2009, from Encyclopædia Britannica Online: http://www.britannica.com/EBchecked/topic/401839/Chandrababu-Naidu

National Disaster Management Authority (NDMA). *Government of India*. (n.d.). Retrieved September 5th 2008, from http://ndma.gov.in/wps/portal/NDMAPortal.

People, I. Info about the Famous People Around the World. (2009). *Biography of Chandrababu Naidu*. Retrieved on July 10th 2009 from http://profiles.incredible-people.com/chandrababu-naidu/

Perry, W. R., & Lindell, M. K. (2003). Understanding Citizen Response to Disasters with Implications for Terrorism. *Journal of Contingencies and Crisis Management*, *11*(2), 49–60. doi:10.1111/1468-5973.1102001

Salter, J. (1995). Towards a better Disaster Management Methodology. *Australian Journal of Emergency Management*, *10*(4), 8–16.

Sen, A. (1999). *Development as Freedom*. Oxford, UK: Oxford University Press.

Shukla, A., & Srinivasan, R. (2005). *Lokvani: A Case of Public-Private Partnership in e-Governance*. Retrieved on May 9th, 2009, from http://www.sitapur.nic.in/lokvani/rojgar/lokvani.pdf

Simpson, D. M. (2001). Community Emergency Response Training (CERTs), A recent History and Review. *Natural Hazards Review*, *2*(2), 54–63. doi:10.1061/(ASCE)1527-6988(2001)2:2(54)

The World Bank. (2004). *Building Blocks of Egovernment: Lessons from Developing Countries*. Retrieved on February 24, 2009, from http://www1.worldbank.org/prem/PREMNotes/premnote 91.pdf

Trojanowicz, R., Kappeler, V. E., Gaines, L. K., Bucqueroux, B., & Sluder, R. (1998). *Community Policing: A Contemporary Perspective*. Cincinnati, OH: Anderson Publishing.

Umashankar, C. (2005). Who could be the possible Champions? In *Planning e-governance in India*. Retrieved on May 9th 2009 from http://egovindia.wordpress.com/plan-egov/

United Nations Development Program (UNDP). (n.d.). *Human Development Reports*. Retrieved on September 15th 2008 from, http://hdr.undp.org/reports/global/2005/.

U.S. Department of Justice (USDOJ), Office of Community Oriented Policing Services. (n.d.). Retrieved on 15th September, 2008, from http://www.cops.usdoj.gov/Default.asp?Item=36

Compilation of References

6Perri. 2004. *E-Governance*. New York: Palgrave.

Abelson, J., Giacomini, M., Lehoux, P., & Gauvin, F.-P. (2007). Bringing the Public into Health Technology Assessment and Coverage Policy Decisions: From Principles to Practice. *Health Policy (Amsterdam)*, *82*, 37–50. doi:10.1016/j.healthpol.2006.07.009

ABS. (2002). *2001 Census Community Profile and Snapshot*. Canberra, Australia: Australian Bureau of Statistics.

Accenture. (2004). *2004 eGovernment report: High performance, maximum value*. Retrieved on January 14, 2006, from http://www.accenture.com/NR/rdonlyres/D7206199-C3D4-4CB4-A7D8-846C94287890/0/gove_egov_value.pdf

Accenture. (2005). *eGovernment Leadership: High Performance, Maximum Value*. Report published by the consulting firm Accenture.

Accenture. (2005a, January). *Driving High Performance in Government: Maximizing the Value of Public-Sector Shared Services*. Retrieved April 29, 2009, from http://www.accenture.com

Accenture. (2005b, April). *Leadership in Customer Service: New Expectations, New Experiences. The Government Executive Series*. Retrieved April 29, 2009, from http://www.accenture.com

Access America. *E-Gov*. (2001). Retrieved December 8, 2003 from http://govinfor.library.unt.edu/npr/initiati/it

Adams, P. C. (2009). *Geographies of media and communication*. Oxford, UK: Wiley-Blackwell.

Agar, M. H. (1980). *The Professional Stranger: An informal introduction to ethnography*. New York: Academic Press.

Agarwal, R., & Prasad, J. (1999). Are individual differences germane to the acceptance of new information technologies? *Journal of Decision Science*, *30*(2), 361–391. doi:10.1111/j.1540-5915.1999.tb01614.x

Ager, T., Johnson, C., & Kiernan, J. (2006). *Policy-Based Management and Sharing of Sensitive Information Among Government Agencies* (pp. 1–9). MILCOM.

Ågerfalk, P. J. (2004). *Grounding through Operationalization: Constructing Tangible Theory in IS Research.* Paper presented at the European Conference on Information Systems, Turku, Finland.

AGIMO. (2005). *Australians' Use and Satisfaction With E-Government Services Survey*. Canberra, Australia: Australian Government Information Management Office.

Aichholzer, G., & Schmitzer, R. (2000). Organizational challenges to the development of electronic government. In *Proceedings from 11th International Workshop on Database and Expert Systems Applications*, London, England (pp. 379-383).

Ainscough, T. L., Brody, R. G., & Trocchia, P. J. (2007). Identity theft and consumers' reaction to preventative technological innovations. *Psychological Reports*, *101*, 250–258. doi:10.2466/PR0.101.5.250-258

Ainsworth, S., Hardy, C., & Harley, B. (2005, August). Online consultation: e-democracy and e-resistance in the case of the development gateway. *Management Communication Quarterly*, *19*(1), 120–145. doi:10.1177/0893318905276562

Ajzen, I. (1991). The Theory of Planned Behaviour. *Organizational Behavior and Human Decision Processes*, *50*, 179–211. doi:10.1016/0749-5978(91)90020-T

Ajzen, I. (2002). Perceived Behavioral Control, Self-Efficacy, Locus of Control and the Theory of Planned Behavior. *Journal of Applied Social Psychology*, *32*, 1–20. doi:10.1111/j.1559-1816.2002.tb00236.x

Ajzen, I., & Fishbein, M. (2005). The influence of attitudes on behavior. In Albarracín, D., Johnson, B. T., & Zanna, M. P. (Eds.), *The handbook of attitudes* (pp. 173–221). Mahwah, NJ: Erlbaum.

Akesson, M., Skalen, P., & Edvardsson, B. (2008). E-government and Service Orientation: gaps between theory and practice. *International Journal of Public Sector Management*, *21*(1), 74–92. doi:10.1108/09513550810846122

Akman, I., Yazici, A., Mishra, A., & Arifoglu, A. (2005). E-Government: A Global View and an Empirical Evaluation of some Attributes of Citizens. *Government Information Quarterly*, *22*(2), 239–257. doi:10.1016/j.giq.2004.12.001

Alavi, M., & Leidner, D. (1999). Knowledge management systems: issues, challenges, and benefits. *Communications of the Association for Information Systems*, *1*, 1–28.

Alba, J., Lynch, J., Weitz, B., Janiszewski, C., Lutz, R., & Wood, S. (1997). Interactive Home Shopping: Consumer, Retailer and Manufacturer Incentives to Participate in Electronic Marketplaces. *Journal of Marketing*, *61*, 38–53. doi:10.2307/1251788

Albeda, H., & van Bijlert, J. (2001). Oude klanten verwachten inspanningen, nieuwe klanten verwachten resultaten. In van Duivenboden, H., & Lips, M. (Eds.), *Klantgericht werken in de Publieke Sector*. Utrecht: Lemma.

Aldrich, D., Bertot, J. C., & McClure, C. R. (2002). E-government: initiatives, development, and issues. *Government Information Quarterly*, *19*(4), 349–355. doi:10.1016/S0740-624X(02)00130-2

Al-Fakhri, M., Cropf, R., Higgs, G., & Kelly, P. (2008). E-Government in Saudi Arabia: Between Promise and Reality. *International Journal of Electronic Government Research*, *4*(2), 59–82.

Alford, B. (2007). *Social Networking and the Changing Face of Communication*. Retrieved May 1, 2009, from http://ezinearticles.com/?Social-Networking-And-The-Changing-Face-Of-Communication&id=843747

Allen, B. A., Paquet, G., Juillet, L., & Roy, J. (2005). E-Government as Collaborative Governance: Structural, Accountability and Cultural Reform. In Khosrow-Pour, M. (Ed.), *Practising e-Government: A Global Perspective* (pp. 1–15). Hershey, PA: Ideas Group Publishing.

Allenmang, D., Hodgson, R., & Polikoff, I. (2005). *FEA Reference Model Ontology (FEA RMO)*. GSA Osera Deliverable V1.2, February 2005.

Allison, S. F. H., Schuck, A. M., & Lersch, K. M. (2005). Exploring the crime of identity theft: Prevalence, clearance rates, and victim/offender characteristics. *Journal of Criminal Justice*, *33*, 19–29. doi:10.1016/j.jcrimjus.2004.10.007

Al-Qahtani, F. (2005). *Use of e-government in developing countries: A people centric approach focusing on Saudi Arabia as an example*. D.Sc. dissertation, The George Washington University, District of Columbia, USA.

Al-Sebie, M., Irani, Z., & Eldabi, T. (2005). Issues relating to the transaction stage of the e-government system. *Electronic Government*, *2*(4), 446–459. doi:10.1504/EG.2005.008334

Alshawi, S., Alahmary, A., & Alalwany, H. (2007). E-government evaluation factors: Citizen perspective. In *Proceedings of European and Mediterranean Conference on Information Systems 2007 (EMCIS 2007)*, June 24-26 2007, Polytechnic University of Valencia, Spain.

Altschull, J. H. (1990). *From Milton to McLuhan: The ideas behind American journalism*. New York: Longman.

Amarnathan, L. C. (2003). *Technological advancement: Implications for crime*. The Indian Police Journal.

Amoretti, F. (2007). E-Government Regimes. In Anttiroiko, A.-V., & Mälkiä, M. (Eds.), *Encyclopedia of Digital Government* (*Vol. 2*, pp. 580–587). Hershey, PA: Idea Group Reference.

Anderson, E. W., Fornell, C., & Lehman, D. (1994). Customer satisfaction, market share, and profitability: Findings from Sweden. *Journal of Marketing*, *58*(July), 53–66. doi:10.2307/1252310

Anderson, E. W., Fornell, C., & Mazvancheryl, S. K. (2004). Customer satisfaction and shareholder value. *Journal of Marketing*, *68*(October), 172–185. doi:10.1509/jmkg.68.4.172.42723

Anderson, J. M. (2003). Why We Need a New Definition of Information Security. *Computers & Security*, *22*(4), 303–313. doi:10.1016/S0167-4048(03)00407-3

Anderson, K. B. (2006). Who are the victims of identity theft? The effects of demographics. *Journal of Public Policy & Marketing*, *25*(2), 160–171. doi:10.1509/jppm.25.2.160

Anderson. (2002). *A usability analysis of selected federal government web sites*. Washington DC: Author.

Andrade, J., Ares, J., Garcia, R., Pazos, J., Rodriguez, S., & Silva, A. (2004). A Methodological Framework for Viewpoint-Oriented Conceptual Modeling. *IEEE Transactions on Software Engineering*, *30*(5), 282–294. doi:10.1109/TSE.2004.1

Angioni, M., Demontis, R., Deriu, M., De Vita, E., Lai, C., Marcialis, I., et al. (2007). DART: the distributed agent-based retrieval toolkit. In D. Sharma, L. C. Jain, D. Tran, & W. Ma (Eds.), *Proceedings of the 2007 Annual Conference on international Conference on Computer Engineering and Applications* (Gold Coast, Queensland, Australia, January 17 - 19, 2007) (pp. 425-433). Stevens Point, WI: World Scientific and Engineering Academy and Society (WSEAS).

Anthopoulos, L., & Tsoukalas, I. A. (2005). The implementation model of a Digital City. The case study of the first Digital City in Greece: e-Trikala. *Journal of E-Government*, *2*(2).

Anthopoulos, L., Siozos, P., & Tsoukalas, I. A. (2007). Applying Participatory Design and Collaboration in Digital Public Services for discovering and re-designing e-government services. *Government Information Quarterly*, *24*(2), 353–376. doi:10.1016/j.giq.2006.07.018

Anthopoulos, L., Siozos, P., Nanopoulos, A., & Tsoukalas, I. A. (2006). The Bottom-up Design of e-government. Development Methodology based on a Collaboration Environment. *e-Service Journal*, *4*(3).

Anti-corruption efforts and African economic development: Hearing before the Subcommittee on African Affairs of the Committee on Foreign Relations, United States Senate. 106th Cong., 2d Sess. (2000). Retrieved March 24, 2007, from http://frwebgate.access.gpo.gov/cgibin/getdoc.cgi?dbname=106_senate_hearings&docid=f:68756.pdf

Anttiroiko, A.-V. (2009). Government 2.0: Towards interactive and enabling e-government. In A. Kaplan, A. Balci, C. C. Aktan, & C. Dalbay (Eds.), *Advances in eGovernment & eGovernance, Selected Proceedings of the First International Conference on eGovernment and eGovernance*, 12-13 March 2009, Ankara, Turkey (Vol. 1, pp. 51-65).

Arellano-Gault, D. (2008). An organizational analysis of transparency: transparency failures as an instrument for incorporating effective transparency policies into public organizations. *Open Government*, *4*(1), 1–19.

Asubonteng, P., McCleary, K. J., & Swan, J. E. (1996). SERVQUAL revisited: a critical review of service quality. *Journal of Services Marketing*, *10*(6), 62–81. doi:10.1108/08876049610148602

Audal, J., Quincy, L., & Roman, P. (2008). Computer Crimes. *The American Criminal Law Review*, *45*, 233–264.

Australian Government. (2005). *Australians' use of and satisfaction with e-government services*. Barton, Australia: Commonwealth of Australia.

Australian Government. (2006). *Delivering Australian Government Services: Managing Multiple Channels*. Canberra: Commonwealth of Australia.

Averett, P. (2001). People: The human side of systems technology. *Journal for Quality and Participation, 24*(2), 34–37.

Backhouse, J., & Halperin, R. (2009). Approaching Interoperability for Identity Management Systems. In Rannenberg, K. (Ed.), *Identity in the Information Society: Challenges and Opportunities*. New York: Springer.

Bäckstrand, K. (2003). Civic science for sustainability: Reframing the role of experts, policy-makers and citizens in environmental governance. *Global Environmental Politics, 3*(4), 24–41. doi:10.1162/152638003322757916

Backus, M. (2001). *E-Governance and developing countries-introduction and examples*. IICD Research Report No. 3. Retrieved from http://www.ftpiicd.org/files/research/reports/report3.doc

Baker, D. L. (2009). Advancing e-government performance in the United States through enhanced usability benchmarks. *Government Information Quarterly, 26*, 75–81. doi:10.1016/j.giq.2008.01.004

Baldersheim, H., & Øgård, M. (2008). Innovatgion in e-government: Analysis of municipal web pages in Nordic countries. *Information Polity, 13*, 125–137.

Ballantine, J. A., & Stray, S. J. (1999). Information systems and other capital investments: Evaluation practices compared. *Logistics and Information Management, 12*, 78–93. doi:10.1108/09576059910256286

Ban Yue Forum. (2009, February 10). *Behind the high numbers of government sites*. Retrieved March 19, 2009, from www.henan.gov.cn/zwgk/system/2009/02/10/010118335/shtml

Bandura, A. (1977). Self-efficacy: Toward a unifying theory of behavioral change. *Japanese Psychological Review, 84*(2), 191–215. doi:10.1037/0033-295X.84.2.191

Bandura, A. (1986). *Social Foundations of Thought and Action: A social Cognitive Theory*. Englewood Cliffs, NJ: Prentice Hall.

Bandura, A. (1991). Social cognitive theory of self-regulation. *Organizational Behavior and Human Decision Processes, 50*, 248–287. doi:10.1016/0749-5978(91)90022-L

Bannister, F. (2007). The curse of the benchmark: an assessment of the validity and value of e-government comparisons. *International Review of Administrative Sciences, 73*(2), 171–188. doi:10.1177/0020852307077959

Baños, T. Y., Aquino, E., Sernas, F. D., López, Y. R., & Mendoza, R. C. (2007). EMI: a system to improve and promote the use of public transportation. In *CHI '07 Extended Abstracts on Human Factors in Computing Systems* (San Jose, CA, USA, April 28 - May 03, 2007) (2037-2042). New York: ACM. Retrieved from http://doi.acm.org/10.1145/1240866.1240946

Barclay, C. (2008). Towards an integrated measurement of IS project performance: The project performance scorecard. *Information Systems Frontiers, 10*(3), 331–345. doi:10.1007/s10796-008-9083-6

Barnes, S. J., & Vidgen, R. (2003). Measuring web site quality improvements: A case study of the forum on strategic management knowledge exchange. *Industrial Management & Data Systems, 103*(5), 297–309. doi:10.1108/02635570310477352

Barnes, S. J., & Vidgen, R. (2006). Data triangulation and web quality metrics: A case study in e-government. *Information & Management, 43*, 767–777. doi:10.1016/j.im.2006.06.001

Barnes, S. J., & Vidgen, R. (2007). Evaluating the web site of the UK Inland Revenue. *International Journal of Electronic Government Research, edit3*(1), 19-37.

Barr, S. (2007). Public less satisfied with government websites. *Washington Post*. Retrieved from http://www.washingtonpost.com/wp-dyn/content/article/2007/03/20/AR2007032001338.html.

Barzelay, M. (2001). *The New Public Management*. Berkley, CA: University of California Press.

Bates, B. R., Lynch, J. A., Bevan, J. L., & Condit, C. M. (2005). Warranted Concerns, Warranted Outlooks: A Focus Group Study of Public Understandings of Genetic Research. *Social Science & Medicine*, *60*, 331–344. doi:10.1016/j.socscimed.2004.05.012

Batini, C., Viscusi, G., & Cherubini, D. (2009). GovQual: A quality driven methodology for e-government project planning. *Government Information Quarterly*, *26*(1), 106–117. doi:10.1016/j.giq.2008.03.002

Bauer, M. (Ed.). (1997). *Resistance to New Technology: Nuclear Power, Information Technology And Biotechnology*. Cambridge, UK: Cambridge University Press.

Baum, C. H., & Di Maio, A. (2000). *Gartner's Four Phases of E-Government Model*. Retrieved July 25, 2008, from http://www.gartner.com

Baym, N. K. (1998). The Emergence of On-Line Community. In Jones, S. G. (Ed.), *Cybersociety 2.0. Revisiting Computer-Mediated Communication and Community*. London: Sage.

Beck, U. (1992). *Risk Society – Towards a New Modernity*. London: Sage.

Beck, U. Giddens. A., & Lash, S. (1994). Reflexive Modernity. Cambridge, UK: Polity Press.

Bekkers, V. (1998). *Grenzeloze overheid. Over informatisering en grensveranderingen in openbaar bestuur*. Alphen aan den Rijn: Samson.

Bekkers, V. J. J. M., & Homburg, V. M. F. (2007). The myths of e-government: looking beyond the assumptions of a new and better government. *The Information Society*, *23*(5), 373–382. doi:10.1080/01972240701572913

Bekkers, V. J. J. M., & Zouridis, S. (1999). Electronic service delivery in public administration: some trends and issues. *International Review of Administrative Sciences*, *65*(2), 183–196. doi:10.1177/0020852399652004

Bekkers, V., van Duivenboden, H., & Lips, M. (2005). ICT en Publieke dienstverlening. In Lips, M., Bekkers, V., & Zuurmond, A. (Eds.), *ICT en Openbaar Bestuur*. Utrecht: Lemma.

Belanger, F., & Carter, L. (2009). The Impact of the Digital Divide on E-Government Use. *Communications of the ACM*, *52*(4), 132–135. doi:10.1145/1498765.1498801

Belanger, F., Hiller, J., & Smith, W. (2002). Trustworthiness in electronic commerce: The role of privacy, security, and site attributes. *The Journal of Strategic Information Systems*, *11*, 245–270. doi:10.1016/S0963-8687(02)00018-5

Belkin, N. J., Brooks, H. M., & Oddy, R. N. (1982). As for information retrieval. *The Journal of Documentation*, *38*(2), 61–71. doi:10.1108/eb026722

Bellah, J. (2001). Identity theft: Ruining credit and creating criminal records. *Law & Order*, *49*(10), 222–226.

Beniger, J. (1986). *The Control Revolution: Technological and Economic Origins of the Information Society*. Cambridge, MA: Harvard University Press.

Berger, J., & Zelditch, M. Jr., (Eds.). (1993). *Theoretical research programs: Studies in the growth of theory*. Stanford, CA: Stanford UP.

Berhel, H. (2000). Digital Politics. The vote's. In The Web's potential in the political process is still lacking. *Communications of the ACM*, *43*(11), 17–22.

Berner Fachhochschule & Unisys. (2005). E-government trendbarometer. Thalwil: Unisys (Schweiz, AG).

Bertot, J. C. (2003). The multiple dimensions of the digital divide: more than the technology 'haves' and 'have nots.'. *Government Information Quarterly*, *20*(2), 185–191. doi:10.1016/S0740-624X(03)00036-4

Bertot, J. C., & Jaeger, P. T. (2006). User-centered e-government: Challenges and benefits for government Web sites. *Government Information Quarterly*, *23*, 163–168. doi:10.1016/j.giq.2006.02.001

Bertot, J. C., & Jaeger, P. T. (2008). The e-government paradox: Better customer service doesn't necessarily cost less. *Government Information Quarterly*, *25*, 149–154. doi:10.1016/j.giq.2007.10.002

Bertot, J. C., Jaeger, P. T., & McClure, C. R. (2008). *User-centered e-government services: Benefits, costs, and research needs.* Paper presented at the 9th Annual International Conference on Digital Government Research.

Bertot, J. C., Jaeger, P. T., Langa, L. A., & McClure, C. R. (2006a). Public access computing and Internet access in public libraries: The role of public libraries in e-government and emergency situations. *First Monday*, *11*(9). Retrieved from http://www.firstmonday.org/issues/issue11_9/bertot/index.html.

Bertot, J. C., Jaeger, P. T., Langa, L. A., & McClure, C. R. (2006b). Drafted: I want you to deliver e-government. *Library Journal*, *131*(13), 34–39.

Bertot, J. C., Snead, J. T., Jaeger, P. T., & McClure, C. R. (2006). Functionality, usability and accessibility: Iterative user-centered assessment strategies for digital libraries. *Performance Measurement and Metrics*, *7*(1), 17–28. doi:10.1108/14678040610654828

Betancourt, V. (2006). *E-government: An opportunity for citizen participation in the era of digital development.* Retrieved April, 14, 2009, http://www.apc.org/en/news/all/world/e-government-opportunity-citizen-participation-era.

Bevir, M., & Rhodes, R. A. W. (2003). Searching for civil society: changing patterns of governance in Britain. *Public Administration*, *81*(1), 41–62. doi:10.1111/1467-9299.00336

Bevir, M., Rhodes, R. A. W., & Weller, P. (2003). Traditions of governance: interpreting the changing role of the public sector. *Public Administration Review*, *81*(1), 1–17. doi:10.1111/1467-9299.00334

Bhatnagar, S. (2001). Central vigilance Commission website: A bold anticorruption experiment. *World Bank*. Retrieved March 01, 2009, from http://go.worldbank.org/10T9V182Z0

Bhatnagar, S. (2001). Mandals online in Andhra Pradesh. *World Bank*. Retrieved March 01, 2002, from http://go.worldbank.org/3D3M3OG080

Bhatnagar, S. (2002, Autumn). Egovernment: Lessons from Implementation in Developing Countries. *Regional Development Dialogue*, 24.

Bhatnagar, S. (2004). *E-government: from vision to implementation: a practical guide with case studies*. New Delhi Thousand Oaks, CA: Sage Publications.

Bhatnagar, S. (2007). *Impact Assessment Study of Computerized Services Delivery Projects from India and Chile.* IT@WEB Staff working Papers. Retrieved April 28, 2009, from http://www.iimahd.ernet.in/egov/documents/impact-assessment-study-wbr.pdf

Bhatnagar, S., & Vyas, N. (2001). Gyandoot: Community-owned rural internet kiosks. *World Bank*. Retrieved February 24, 2009, from http://go.worldbank.org/V5Y-KYDSRE0

Bishop, P., & Anderson, L. (2004). *E-government to e-democracy: 'High Tech' solutions to 'No Tech' problems.* A paper prepared for the Australian Electronic Governance Conference. Centre for Public Policy, University of Melbourne, Melbourne Victoria, 14th and 15th April, 2004.

Bitner, M. J. (1990). Evaluating service encounters: The effect of physical surroundings and employee responses. *Journal of Marketing*, *54*(2), 69–82. doi:10.2307/1251871

Bitner, M. J., & Hubbert, A. R. (1994). Encounter satisfaction versus overall satisfaction versus quality: The customers' voice. In Rust, R. T., & Oliver, R. L. (Eds.), *Service quality: New directions in theory and practice* (pp. 72–94). London: Sage.

Blakeley, C. J., Matsuura, J. H., & Alliance Law Group LLC. (2001). *E-government: is e-democracy inevitable?* Paper presented at Innovations for an e-Society. Challenges for Technology Assessment, Berlin, Germany, Oct 17–19, 2001

Blasi, V. (1977). The checking value in First Amendment theory. *American Bar Foundation Research Journal. American Bar Foundation*, 521–550.

Blumler, J., & Katz, E. (1974). *The uses of mass communication*. Thousand Oaks, CA: Sage.

Bolgherini, S. (2007). The Technology Trap and the Role of Political and Cultural Variables: A Critical Analysis of the E-Government Policies. *Review of Policy Research, 24*(3), 259–275. doi:10.1111/j.1541-1338.2007.00280.x

Bomil, S., & Ingoo, H. (2003). The impact of customer trust and perception of security control on the acceptance of electronic commerce. *International Journal of Electronic Commerce, 7*(3), 135–161.

Bonaccorsi, A., & Rossi, C. (2002). *Measuring and modeling Internet diffusion*. Paper presented at DRUID's Summer Conference 2002, Copenhagen.

Bonsón, E., Escobar, T., & Flores, F. (2006). Online transparency of the banking sector. *Online Information Review, 30*(6), 714–730. doi:10.1108/14684520610716180

Boonen, K., & Brand, H. (2008). *IT Governance CobiT 4.1 - A Management Guide* (3rd ed.). Amsterdam: Van Haren Publishing.

Borins, I. (2002). On the frontiers of electronic governance: A report on the United States and Canada. *International Review of Administrative Sciences, 68*, 199–211. doi:10.1177/0020852302682003

Borins, S. (2001). Public Management Innovation: Toward a Global Perspective. *American Review of Public Administration, 31*(1), 5–21. doi:10.1177/02750740122064802

Borins, S. (2002). On the frontiers of electronic governance: a report on the United States and Canada. *International Review of Administrative Science, 68*(2), 199–211. doi:10.1177/0020852302682003

Bose, R. (2002). Customer Relationship Management: key components for IT success. *Industrial Management & Data Systems, 102*(2), 89–97. doi:10.1108/02635570210419636

Bouras, C., Kastaniotis, S., & Triantafillou, V. (2000). Citizen information services using Internet technologies. In ECIS 2000, European conference on information systems, Vienna, Austria (pp. 1123–1130).

Bowman, A., & Kearney, R. C. (1988). Dimensions of State Government Capability. *The Western Political Quarterly, 41*(2), 341–362. doi:10.2307/448542

Box, R. (1999). Running government like a business: Implications for public administration theory and research. *American Review of Public Administration, 29*, 19–43. doi:10.1177/02750749922064256

Boyd, D. M., & Ellison, N. B. (2007). Social network sites: Definition, history, and scholarship. *Journal of Computer-Mediated Communication, 13*(1), 11. Retrieved May 1, 2009, from http://jcmc.indiana.edu/vol13/issue1/boyd.ellison.html

Bozeman, B. (2000). *Bureaucracy and Red Tape*. Upper Saddle River, NJ: Prentice Hall.

Breaking Barriers to eGovernment: Solution for eGovernment. (n.d.). EGovernment Unit, DG, Information Society, European Commission. Retrieved from http://www.egovbarriers.org

Breindl, Y., & Francq, P. (2008). Can Web 2.0 applications save e-democracy? A study of how new internet applications may enhance citizen participation in the political process online. *International Journal of Electronic Democracy, 1*(1), 14–31. doi:10.1504/IJED.2008.021276

Brennan, S. (2007). The Biggest Computer Programme in the World Ever! How's it going? *Journal of Information Technology, 22*, 202–211. doi:10.1057/palgrave.jit.2000104

Bretschneider, S. (2003). Information technology, e-government, and institutional change. *Public Administration Review, 63*(6), 738–741. doi:10.1111/1540-6210.00337

Brewer, G. A., Neubauer, B. J., & Geiselhart, K. (2006). Designing and implementing e-government systems: Critical implications for public administration and democracy. *Administration & Society, 38*(4), 472–499. doi:10.1177/0095399706290638

Brinkley, D. (2006). *The great deluge: Hurricane Katrina, New Orleans, and the Mississippi Gulf Coast*. New York: Harper Perennial.

British Standards Institution. (2002). *BS 6079-1:2002 Project Management: Guide to project management.*

British Standards Institution. (2003). [*Quality management systems: Guidelines for quality management in projects*.]. *BS ISO, 10006*, 2003.

Broadhurst, R. (2006). Developments in the global law enforcement of cyber-crime. *Policing: An International Journal of Police Strategies and Management, 29*(2), 408–433.

Brown, D. (2005). Electronic government and public administration. *International Review of Administrative Sciences, 71*(2), 241–254. doi:10.1177/0020852305053883

Brown, M. M. (2007). Governments Understanding E-Government Benefits: An Examination of Leading-Edge Local. *American Review of Public Administration, 37*(2), 178–197. doi:10.1177/0275074006291635

Brown, M. M., & Schelin, S. (2005). American Local Governments: Confronting the E-government Challenge. In Drüke, H. (Ed.), *Local electronic government: A comparative study*. New York: Routledge.

Browning, G. (2002). *Electronic democracy: Using the Internet to transform American politics* (2nd ed.). Medford, NJ: Cyberage Books/Information Today.

Brownson, K. (1993). Patient Handouts? We're Wasting Our Time. *RN, 56*(7), 88.

Brudney, J. L., & England, R. E. (1982). Urban policy making and subjective service evaluations: Are they compatible? *Public Administration Review, 42*(2), 127–135. doi:10.2307/975534

Brungs, A., & Jamieson, R. (2005). Identification of legal issues for computer forensics. *Information Systems Management, 22*(2), 57–66. doi:10.1201/1078/45099.22.2.20050301/87278.7

Brunner, J. (Ohio Secretary of State). (n.d.). *The Ohio Municipal, Township, and School Board Roster 2006-2007.* Columbus, OH: Ohio Secretary of State's Office.

Burgunder, L. (2007). *Legal aspects of managing technology*. Mason, OH: Cengage Learning.

Burroughs, J. M. (2009). What users want: Assessing government information preferences to drive information services. *Government Information Quarterly, 26*, 203–218. doi:10.1016/j.giq.2008.06.003

Bush, R. A. (1995 September). *Basic FidoNet(r). technical standard.* Pacific Systems Group. Retrieved June 15, 2005, from http://www.ftsc.org/download/docs/fts-0001.016

Byström, K., & Järverlin, K. (1995). Task Complexity Affects Information Seeking and Use. *Information Processing & Management, 31*(2), 191–213. doi:10.1016/0306-4573(94)00041-Z

Caiden, G. E. (2001). Dealing with Administrative Corruption. In Cooper, T. L. (Ed.), *Handbook of Administrative Ethics* (pp. 429–455). New York: Marcel Dekker.

Caiden, G. E. (2003). The burden on our backs, corruption in Latin America. En *VIII Congreso Internacional del CLAD sobre la Reforma del Estado y de la Administración Pública*, Panamá, 28-31 Oct. 2003.

Cairns, G., Wright, G., Bradfield, R., van der Heijden, K., & Burt, G. (2004). Exploring e-government futures through the application of scenario planning. *Technological Forecasting and Social Change, 71*, 217–238. doi:10.1016/S0040-1625(02)00371-2

Cambrosio, A., & Limoges, C. (1991). Controversies as Governing Process in Technology Assessment. *Technology Analysis and Strategic Management, 3*(4), 377–396. doi:10.1080/09537329108524067

Cap Gemini Ernst & Young. (2005). *Online availability of public services. How is Europe progressing?* Retrieved April 29, 2009, from http://ec.europa.eu/information_society/eeurope/2005/doc/all_about/online_5th_measurement_fv4.pdf

Carlson, J. R., & Zmud, R. W. (1994). Channel Expansion Theory: A dynamic view of media and information richness perceptions. In *Academy of Management Best Papers Proceedings 1994* (pp. 280-284). doi:10.2307/257090

Carnegie Mellon University. (2002). *Capability* Maturity *Model Integration: CMMI for Systems Engineering, Software Engineering, Integrated Product and Process Development, and Supplier Sourcing* (CMMI-SE/SW/IPPD/SS, V1.1). Carnegie Mellon University.

Carnoy, M. (2000). *Sustaining the New Economy: Work, Family, and Community in the Information Age*. Cambridge, MA, USA: Harvard University Press.

Carr, N. (2005, October 3). *The amorality of Web 2.0.* Posted to Rough Type, Nicholas Carr's blog. Retrieved June 19, 2009, from http://www.roughtype.com/archives/2005/10/the_amorality_o.php

Carrigan, R., Milton, R., & Morrow, D. (2005). *More Efficient E-Government Services for Citizens.* Computer World Honors Case Study.

Carrillo, C., de la Rosa, J. L., & Canals, A. (2007). Towards a Knowledge Economy. *International Journal of Community Currency Research*, *11*, 84–97.

Carter, L., & Belanger, F. (2003). *The Influence of Perceived Characteristics of Innovating on e-Government Adoption.* Paper presented at the First International E-Services Workshop, September, 2003.

Carter, L., & Belanger, F. (2004). Citizen Adoption of E-Government Initiatives. In *The Proceedings of the 37th Hawaiian International Conference on Systems Sciences (HICSS 04').*

Carter, L., & Belanger, F. (2004). Citizen adoption of electronic government initiatives. In *Proceedings of the 37th Hawaii International Conference on Systems Sciences,* Honolulu, HI (pp. 1-10).

Carter, L., & Belanger, F. (2004). The influence of perceived characteristics of innovating on e-government adoption. *Electronic. Journal of E-Government*, *2*(1).

Carter, L., & Belanger, F. (2005). The Utilization of E-government Services: Citizen Trust, Innovation and Acceptance Factors. *Information Systems Journal*, *15*(1), 5–25. doi:10.1111/j.1365-2575.2005.00183.x

Castells, M. (2000). *The rise of the network society: Economy, society and culture.* Oxford: Blackwell Publishing.

Castells, M. (2006). The network society. In Castells, M., & Cardoso, G. (Eds.), *The network society: From knowledge to policy.* Washington, DC: Center for Transatlantic Relations.

Castells, M. (2009). *Communication power.* Oxford, UK: Oxford University Press.

Census of India. Office of the Registrar General and Census commissioner of India. (2001). *Statistics on Demographic and Socio-Economic Characteristics.* Retrieved on September 8th, 2008 from http://www.censusindia.gov.in/Census_Data_2001/India_at_glance/glance.aspx

Census of Governments Counts 16 million State and Local Employees. (2007). Retrieved April 20, 2009, from http://www.census.gov/Press-release/www/releases/archives/employment_occupations/012797.html

Central Intelligence Agency. (n.d.). *The World Factbook.* Retrieved July 29, 2009, from https://www.cia.gov/library/publications/the-world-factbook/geos/in.html

CERT. (n.d.). *Community Emergency Response Team.* Retrieved on July 15th 2009, from http://www.citizencorps.gov/cert/about.shtm

Chadwick, A. (2001). The electronic face of government in the Internet age: Borrowing from Murray Edelman. *Information Communication and Society*, *4*(3), 435–457.

Chadwick, A. (2001). The electronic face of government in the Internet age. *Information Communication and Society*, *4*(3), 435–457.

Chadwick, A. (2003). Bring E-Democracy Back In Why It matters for Future Research on E-governance. *Social Science Computer Review*, *21*(4), 443–455. doi:10.1177/0894439303256372

Chadwick, A. (2009). Web 2.0: New challenges for the study of e-democracy in an era of informational exuberance. *I/S: A Journal of Law and Policy for the Information Society* *5*(1), 9-42.

Chadwick, A., & May, C. (2003). Interaction between states and citizens in the age of the Internet: E-government in the United States, Britain, and the European Union. *Governance*, *16*(2), 271–300. doi:10.1111/1468-0491.00216

Chai, L., & Pavlou, P. A. (2002). Customer relationship management.com. In *Proceedings of the 2002 Americans Conference in Information System*, Dallas, Texas (pp. 9-11).

Chai, L., & Pavlou, P. A. (2004). From ancient to modern: a cross cultural investigation of electronic commerce adoption in Greece and the United States. *The Journal of Enterprise Information Management*, *17*(6), 416–423. doi:10.1108/17410390410566706

Chan, H. S., & Chow, K. W. (2007). Public Management Policy and Practice in Western China: Metapolicy, Tacit Knowledge, and implications for Management Innovation Transfer. *American Review of Public Administration*, *37*(4), 479–497. doi:10.1177/0275074006297552

Chang, A., & Kannan, P. K. (2008). *Leveraging Web 2.0 in government*. New York: IBM Business of Government Foundation. Retrieved from http://www.businessofgovernment.org/main/publications/bog/chang_fall08.pdf

Chang, J., Torkzadeh, G., & Dhillon, G. (2004). Re-examining the measurement models of success for Internet commerce. *Information & Management*, *41*(4), 577–584. doi:10.1016/S0378-7206(03)00091-0

Chang, M. Y., Ching, W. C., & Chao, K. H. (2007). *The impact of perceived readiness to citizen's acceptance of e-government services*. Unpublished master's thesis: National Kaohsiung First University of Science and Technology, Yenchao, Kaohsiung, Taiwan, Republic of China.

Charih, M., & Robert, J. (2004). Government On-line in the federal government of Canada: the organizational issues. *International Review of Administrative Science*, *70*(2), 373–384. doi:10.1177/0020852304044262

Chau, P. Y. K., & Hu, P. J. H. (2001). Information technology acceptance by individual professionals: A model comparison approach. *Decision Sciences*, *32*(4), 699–719. doi:10.1111/j.1540-5915.2001.tb00978.x

Chen, D. Y., Huang, T. Y., & Hsiao, N. Y. (2006). Reinventing government through on-line citizen involvement in the developing world: A case study of Taipei City Mayor's E-mail Box in Taiwan. *Public Administration and Development*, *26*, 409–423. doi:10.1002/pad.415

Chen, H. (2002). Digital government: technologies and practices. *Decision Support Systems*, *34*, 223–227. doi:10.1016/S0167-9236(02)00118-5

Chen, H., Chen, Y., Huang, W., & Ching, R. (2006). E-government strategies in developed and developing countries: an implementation framework and case study. *Journal of Global Information Management*, *14*(1), 23–24.

Chen, K., Yen, D. C., & Huang, A. H. (2004). Media Selection To Meet Communication Context: Comparing E-Mail and Instant Messaging in an Undergraduate Population. *Communications of the Association for Information Systems*, *14*, 387–405.

Chiang, M.-H., Chen, D.-y., Huang, T.-y., Hsiao, N., & Chuanh, K.-J. (2004). *An exploratory study of utilizing ICTs to promote citizen participation in Taiwan. A Project Sponsored by the Institute for Information Industries*. Taipei, Taiwan: III.

Chile Transparente. (2008). *Estándares de Transparencia Municipal, Convenio Asociación Chilena de Municipalidades*. Retrieved April, 14, 2009, http://www.munitel.cl/eventos/otros/chiletransparente/propuestatransparencia.pdf

China Internet Network Information Center. (2008 January). *Statistical survey report on the internet development in China*. Beijing: CINIC.

China Youth Daily. (2008, December). *Survey: 85.6% visited government web sites, 61.3% were not satisfactory.* Retrieved March 19, 2009, from http://www.henan.gov.cn/zwgk/system/2008/12/16/010110657.shtml

Cho, Y. H., & Choi, B.-D. (2004). E-Government to Combat Corruption: The Case of Seoul Metropolitan Government. *International Journal of Public Administration, 27*(10), 719–735. doi:10.1081/PAD-200029114

Choo, C. W. (1998). *The Knowing Organization: How Organizations Use Information to construct Meaning, Create Knowledge, and Make Decisions.* New York: Oxford University Press.

Chu, P. Y., Yeh, S. C., & Chuang, M. J. (2008). Reengineering municipality citizen electronic complaint system through citizen relationship management. *Electronic Government. International Journal (Toronto, Ont.), 5*(3), 288–309.

CIA. (2005).*The World Fact Book.* Retrieved on September 15th 2008, from http://www.cia.gov/cia/publications/factbook

Ciborra, C. (2005). Interpreting e-government and Development: efficiency, transparency or governance at a distance? *Information Technology & People, 18*(3), 260–279. doi:10.1108/09593840510615879

Ciborra, C., & Navarra, D. (2005). Good governance, development theory, and aid policy: risks and challenges of e-government in Jordan. *Information Technology for Development, 11*(2), 141–150. doi:10.1002/itdj.20008

Cilan, C. A., Bolat, B. A., & Coskun, E. (2009). Analyzing digital divide within and between member and candidate countries of European Union. *Government Information Quarterly, 26,* 98–107. doi:10.1016/j.giq.2007.11.002

CITU. (2000). *E-Government: A Strategic Framework for Public Services in the Information Age.* London: Central IT Unit, Cabinet Office.

Clarke, R. (1994). Human identification in information systems: Management challenges and public policy issues. *Information Technology & People, 7*(4), 6-37. Retrieved March 5, 2009 from http://www.rogerclarke.com/DV/HumanID.html

Clift, S. (2002). *The Future of E-Democracy.* Democracy Online Newswire. Retrieved from http://www.e-democracy.org

Codagnone, C., & Undheim, T. A. (2008 August). Benchmarking eGovernment: tools, theory and practice. *European Journal of ePractice,* 4. Retrieved April 19, 2009, from http://www.epracticejournal.eu/document/4970.

Cohen, J. E. (2006). Citizen Satisfaction with Contacting Government on the Internet. *Information Policy, 11*(1), 51–65.

Cohen, L. (2001). Citizens and consumers in the United States in the century of mass consumption. In Daunton, M., & Hilton, M. (Eds.), *The politics of consumption: Material culture and citizenship in Europe and America.* New York: Berg.

Cohen, S., & Eimicke, W. (2002). The use of the Internet in government service delivery. In Abramson, M. A., & Means, G. E. (Eds.), *E-Government 2001* (pp. 9–43). Lanham, MD: Rowman & Littlefield Publishing, Inc.

Coleman, S. (2004). Connecting Parliament to the public via the Internet. *Information Communication and Society, 7*(1), 1–22. doi:10.1080/1369118042000208870

Compaine, B. (Ed.). (2001). *The digital divide: Facing a crisis or creating a myth.* Cambridge, MA: MIT Press.

Compeau, D. R., & Higgins, C. A. (1995). Computer self-efficacy: Development of a measure and initial test. *Management Information Systems Quarterly, 19*(2), 89–211. doi:10.2307/249688

Connolloy, R., & Bannister, F. (2008). eTax & Service Quality: The Case of the Revenue Online Service. In Proceedings of World Academy of Science, Engineering and Technology (Vol. 28).

Connolly, W. E. (1995). *Ethos of Pluralization.* Minneapolis, MN: University of Minnesota Press.

Cook, M. (2000). *What Citizens Want from E-Government*. Albany: Center for Technology in Government.

Cooper, C., & Block, R. *Disaster: Hurricane Katrina and the failure of homeland security*. New York: Times Books.

Cooper, T. L., & Yoder, D. E. (2002). Public Management Ethics: Standards in a Transnational World. *Public Integrity*, *4*(4), 333–352.

Cordella, A. (2007). E-government: towards the e-bureaucratic form? *Journal of Information Technology*, *22*, 265–274. doi:10.1057/palgrave.jit.2000105

Cortes, E., Espinosa, S., & Tari, J. (2009). E-government challenges: barriers and facilitators in Spanish City Councils. In *Connectivity and Knowledge Management in Virtual Organizations* (pp. 205–220). Hershey, PA: IGI Global.

Council for Excellence in Government. (2001). *E-government: the next American revolution*. Washington, DC: Author.

Council of the European Union. (2003). *Council Resolution on the implementation of the eEurope 2005 Action Plan*. Retrieved April 29, 2009, from http://ec.europa.eu/information_society/eeurope/2005/doc/all_about/benchmarking/resolution.doc

Coursey, D., & Killingsworth, J. (2001). Managing Web Services: Lessons from Florida. In David Garson, G. (Ed.), *Handbook of Public Information Systems* (2nd ed., pp. 331–345). New York: Marcel Dekker/CRC.

Coursey, D., & Norris, D. F. (2008). Models of E-Government: Are They Correct? An Empirical Assessment. *Public Administration Review*, *68*(3), 523–536. doi:10.1111/j.1540-6210.2008.00888.x

Coursey, D., & Norris, D. F. (2008). Models of E-government: Are They Correct? An Empirical Assessment. *Public Administration Review*, (May/June): 523–536. doi:10.1111/j.1540-6210.2008.00888.x

Courtois, M. P., & Berry, M. W. (1999). Results ranking in Web search engines. *Online*, *23*(3), 39–44.

Covington, M. J., & Sandhu, R. (2006). A usage-based authorization framework for collaborative computing systems. In *Proceedings of the Eleventh ACM Symposium on Access Control Models and Technologies* (Lake Tahoe, California, USA, June 07 - 09, 2006) (pp. 180-189). New York: ACM.

Crede, A., & Mansell, R. (Eds.). (1998). *The importance of sustainable development ICTs in developing Countries*. Booklets I & IV, E-Journal Research. Retrieved March 01, 2009, from http://www.iicd.org/articles/IICDnews.import9

Croneberger, R. Jr, & Luck, C. (1975). Defining Information and Referral Service. *Library Journal*, *100*(19), 1984–1987.

Cronin, J. J., & Taylor, S. A. (1992). Measuring service quality: A reexamination and extension. *Journal of Marketing*, *56*(July), 55–68. doi:10.2307/1252296

Cross, H. (1953). *The people's right to know: Legal access to public records and proceedings*. Morningside Heights, NY: Columbia University Press.

Crossman, G. (2007). The ID Problem. In Birch, D. (Ed.), *Digital Identity Management* (pp. 175–183). Hampshire, UK: Gower.

Cuillier, D., & Piotrowski, S. J. (2009). Internet information-seeking and its relation to support for access to government records. *Government Information Quarterly*, *26*(3), 441–449. doi:10.1016/j.giq.2009.03.001

Cullier, D., & Piotrowski, S. J. (2009). Internet information-seeking and its relation to support for access to government records. *Government Information Quarterly*, *26*, 441–449. doi:10.1016/j.giq.2009.03.001

Curwell, S., Deakin, M., Cooper, I., Paskaleva-Shapira, K., Ravetz, J., & Babicki, D. (2005). Citizens' expectations of information cities: Implications for urban planning and design. *Building Research and Information*, *33*(1), 55–66. doi:10.1080/0961321042000329422

Cyberspace Policy Research Group (CYPRG). (2001). *Web attribute Evaluation System (WAES)*. Retrieved April 14, 2004, from http://www.cyprg.arizona.edu/waes.htm

Daemen, H. H. F. M., & Thomassen, J. J. A. (1989). Afstand tussen burgers en overheid. In Hoogerwerf, A. (Ed.), *Overheidsbeleid. Alphen aan den Rijn, Nederland: Samson*.

Daft, R. L., & Lengel, R. H. (1986). Organizational Information Requirements, Media Richness and Structural Design. *Management Science*, *32*(5), 554–571. doi:10.1287/mnsc.32.5.554

Dan, V. (2000, Aug 28). *Electronic government*. Retrieved on August 28, 2000, from http://www.computerworld.com/managementtopics/ebusiness/story/0,10801,48989,00.html

Datamonitor. (2000). *P2P eCommerce information exchanges*. Datamonitor Business Report. Retrieved from http://www.datamonitor.com/industries/research/?pid=DMTC0679&type=Report

Davenport, T. H., & Prusak, L. (1998). *Working Knowledge*. Boston, MA: Harvard Business School Press.

Davenport, T. H., Harris, J. G., & Kohli, A. (2001). How do they know their customers so well? *MIT Sloan Management Review*, *42*(2), 63–73.

Davidsson, B., & Patel, R. (2003). Forskningsmetodikens grunder. Lund, Sverige: Studentlitteratur.

Davis, F. (1986). *A Technology Acceptance Model for Empirically Testing New End-User Information Systems: Theory and Results*. Ph.D. dissertation, Massachusetts Institute of Technology, Sloan School of Management, MA, USA.

Davis, F. D. (1989). Perceived Usefulness, Perceived Ease of Use and User Acceptance of Information Technology. *Management Information Systems Quarterly*, *13*(3), 318–339. doi:10.2307/249008

Davis, F., Bagozzi, R., & Warshaw, P. (1989). User Acceptance of Computer Technology: A Comparison of Two Theoretical Models. *Management Science*, *35*(8), 982–1003. doi:10.1287/mnsc.35.8.982

Davis, R. (1999). *The web of politics: The Internet's impact on the American political system*. New York: Oxford University Press.

Dawes, S. S. (2008). *An exploratory framework for future e-government research investments*. Paper presented at the 41st Hawaii International Conference on System Sciences, Hawaii.

Dawes, S. S. (2009). Governance in the digital age: A research and action framework for an uncertain future. *Government Information Quarterly*, *26*, 257–264. doi:10.1016/j.giq.2008.12.003

DCITA. (1999). *Networking the Nation*. Canberra, Australia: Department of Communication, Information Technology and the Arts, Australian Commonwealth Government.

DCMI Usage Board. (2008). *DCMI Metadata Terms*. Retrieved from http://dublincore.org/documents/dcmi-terms/

de la Rosa, J. L., Moreno, A., Rovira, M., Montaner, M., & Szymanski, B. (2009). Reward System for Completing Frequently Asked Questions. In *Proceedings of the AAAI 2009 Spring Symposium on Social Semantic Web: Where Web 2.0 meets Web 3.0, 2009*. Retrieved from http://tw.rpi.edu/portal/Reward_system_for_completing_frequently_asked_questionsDrucker, D. (2001). Knowledge mgm't revised–theory doesn't equal practice. *Internetweek, 1*(29), 60.

Deakins, E., & Dillon, S. M. (2002). E-government in New Zealand: the Local Authority Perspective. *International Journal of Public Sector Management*, *15*(5), 375–398. doi:10.1108/09513550210435728

deLeon, P. (1992). The Democratization of the Policy Sciences. *Public Administration Review*, *52*(2), 125–129. doi:10.2307/976465

Deloitte Research. (2001). *E-government's Next Generation: Transforming the Government Enterprise Through Customer Service*. New York: Deloitte Consulting.

Deloitte. (2008). *Change your world or the world will change you. The future of collaborative government and Web 2.0.* Retrieved May 1, 2009, from http://www.deloitte.com/dtt/cda/doc/content/ca_govt_web20_mar08_EN.pdf digizen.org. (2008). *What are social networking services?* Retrieved November 29, 2008, from http://www.digizen.org/socialnetworking/what.aspx

Delone, W. H., & McLean, E. R. (1992). Information systems success: The quest for the dependent variable. *Information Systems Research, 3*(1), 60–95. doi:10.1287/isre.3.1.60

Delone, W. H., & McLean, E. R. (2002). Information systems success revisited. In *Proceedings of the 35th Hawaii International Conference on System Sciences* (HICSS 02) (pp. 238-249).

Delone, W. H., & McLean, E. R. (2003). The DeLone and McLean Model of information systems success: A ten-year update. *Journal of Management Information Systems, 19*(4), 9–30.

DeMaio, C. D. (2002). *Creating a Performance-Based Electronic Government.* Retreived March 15, 2006, from http://www.performanceweb.org/research/egovernmentreport.pdf

Department of Administrative Reforms and Public Grievances (DARPG). *Civil Service Awards, Government of India.* (n.d.). Retrieved on September 15th 2008 from http://darpg.gov.in/arpg-website/civilserviceday/pmsaward06-07.pdf

Devadoss, P. R., Pan, S. L., & Huang, J. C. (2002). Structurational analysis of e-government initiatives: a case study of SCO. *Decision Support Systems, 34*(3), 253–269. doi:10.1016/S0167-9236(02)00120-3

Dimitrova, D. V., & Chen, Y.-C. (2006). Profiling the adopters of e-government information and services. *Social Science Computer Review, 24*(2), 172–188. doi:10.1177/0894439305281517

Ding, L., Finin, T., Joshi, A., & Pan, R. (2005). *Search on the Semantic Web.* IEEE Computer.

Dix, A., Levialdi, S., & Malizia, A. (2006). *Semantic halo for collaboration tagging systems* [Online]. Retrieved from http://www.sis.pitt.edu/~paws/SNCBAT06/program.html

Doctor, R., & Ankem, K. (March, 1996). *An information need and services taxonomy: For evaluating Computerized Community Information Systems.* Presented at Community Networking 96: "Bringing People Together." Retrieved February 24, 2009, from http://www.laplaza.org/about_lap/archives/cn96/doctor1.html

Dollery, B., Marshal, N., & Worthington, A. (2003). *Reshaping Australian Local Government: Finance, Governance and Reform.* Sydney, Australia: University of New South Wales Press.

Domain-b.com. (2008, October 23). *Citizen social networks may replace some government functions: Gartner.* Retrieved November 29, 2008, from http://www.domain-b.com/infotech/itnews/20081023_citizen_social_networks.html

Dong, X., Halevy, A. Y., Madhavan, J., Nemes, E., & Zhang, J. (2004). Similarity Search for Web Services. *VLDB 2004*

Donk, W. d., & Meyer, O. (1994). Beleid voor informatisering. In Zuurmond, A. (Ed.), *Inofmatisering in het openbaar bestuur. 's Gravenhage, Nederland: VUGA.*

Douglas, M. (2002 May). A tight net against terror. *Government Technology*, 46-48.

Douglas, T., & Loader, B. D. (2000). *Cybercrime: Law Enforcement, security and surveillance in the information age.* New York: Routledge, Taylor & Francis Group.

Dragulanescu, N.-G. (2002). Website quality evaluations: Criteria and tools. *The International Information & Library Review, 34*, 247–254. doi:10.1006/iilr.2002.0205

Drucker, P. (1959). Long Range Planning: Challenge to Management Science. *Management Science, 5*(3), 238–249. doi:10.1287/mnsc.5.3.238

Drucker, P. (1992). *The New Society of Organizations. Harvard Business Review Reprint 92503*. Cambridge, MA, USA: Harvard Business School Publishing.

Drüke, H. (2005). *Local Electronic Government: A Comparative Study*. New York: Routledge.

Dryzek, J. S. (1989). Policy Sciences of Democracy. *Polity*, *22*(1), 97–118. doi:10.2307/3234848

DTLR. (2001). *Strong Local Leadership - Quality Public Services*. United Kingdom: Department of Transport, Local Government and the Regions.

Dugdale, A., Daly, A., Papandrea, F., & Maley, M. (2005). Accessing e-government: challenges for citizens and organizations. *International Review of Administrative Sciences*, *71*(1), 109–188. doi:10.1177/0020852305051687

Duivenboden, H. P. M. v., & Lips, A. M. B. (2001). Klantgericht werken in de publieke sector: introductie. In H. P. M. v. Duivenboden & A. M. B. Lips (Eds.), Klantgericht werken in de publieke sector. Utrecht, Nederland: Lemma.

Dunleavy, P., Margetts, H., Bastow, S., & Tinkler, J. (2006). *Digital era governance*. Oxford, UK: Oxford University Press.

Dutton, W. H. (2007). e-Democracy: Reconfiguring Participation in Governance and Public Policy. *Journal of Korean Association for Regional Information Society*, *10*(1), 11–26.

Dwivedi, Y. K., Weerakkody, V., & Williams, M. D. (2009). Guest editorial: From implementation to adoption: Challenges to successful e-government diffusion. *Government Information Quarterly*, *26*(1), 3–4. doi:10.1016/j.giq.2008.09.001

Dye, T. (1967). *Politics, Economics, and Public Policy Outcomes in the American States*. Chicago: Rand McNally.

Dymond, K.M. (2005). A Guide to the CMMI: Interpreting the Capability Maturity Model Integration, Process Transition International Inc., 2005.

Dynes, R. (1994). Community Emergency Planning: False Assumptions and Inappropriate Analogies. *International Journal of Mass Emergencies and Disasters*, *12*(2), 141–158.

Easton, D. (1953). *The Political System: An inquiry into the state of political science*. New York: Alfred A. Knopf Publishers.

Easton, D. (1965a). *A Framework for Political Analysis*. Chicago: University of Chicago Press.

Easton, D. (1965b). *A systems analysis of political life*. Chicago: University of Chicago Press.

Ebbers, W. E., & van Dijk, J. A. G. M. (2007). Resistance and support to electronic government, building a model of innovation. *Government Information Quarterly*, *24*, 554–575. doi:10.1016/j.giq.2006.09.008

Ebbers, W. E., Pieterson, W. J., & Noordman, H. N. (2008). Electronic government: Rethinking channel management strategies. *Government Information Quarterly*, *25*, 181–201. doi:10.1016/j.giq.2006.11.003

Ebrahim, Z., Irani, Z., & Al Shawi, S. (2004). Factors influencing the adoption of e-government in public sector. *European & Mediterranean Conference on Information System*, 25-27 July 2004.

Edelman, M. (1964). *The symbolic uses of politics*. Chicago: University of Illinois Press.

Edelman, M. (1977). *Political language: Words that succeed and policies that fail*. New York: Academic Press.

Edelman, M. (1988). *Constructing the political spectacle*. Chicago: University of Chicago Press.

Edelman, M. (2001). *The politics of misinformation*. New York: Cambridge University Press. doi:10.1017/CBO9780511612640

Eggers, W. (2005). *Government 2.0: Using Technology to Improve Education, Cut Red Tape, Reduce Gridlock and Enhance Democracy*. New York: Rowman and Littlefield Publishers.

Egidius, H. (1986). Positivism-fenomenologi-hermeneutik. Lund, Sverige: Studentlitteratur.

Elmagarmid, A. K., & McIver, W. J. (2001, February). The ongoing march toward digital government. *Computer*, 32–38. doi:10.1109/2.901165

Erin Research. (2003). *Citizens First 3*. The Institue for Citizen Centred Service.

Eschenfelder, K. R., Beachboard, J. C., McClure, C. R., & Wyman, S. K. (1997). Assessing US federal government websites. *Government Information Quarterly, 14*, 173–189. doi:10.1016/S0740-624X(97)90018-6

Estabrook, L., Witt, E., & Rainie, L. (2007). *Information Searches that Solve Problems*. Retrieved July 31, 2009 from http://www.pewinternet.org/Reports/2007/Information-Searches-That-Solve-Problems.aspx

Esteves, J., & Joseph, R. C. (2008). A comprehensive framework for the assessment of e-government projects. *Government Information Quarterly, 25*(1), 118–132. doi:10.1016/j.giq.2007.04.009

European Commission. (2002). *eEurope 2005: An information society for all*, European Commission - COM 263, 2002. Retrieved April 29, 2009, from http://europa.eu.int/eeurope

European Commission. (2008). Preparing Europe's Digital [*Mid-Term Review*. Luxembourg.]. *Future*, 2010.

Eurostat. (2005). E-government 2004: Internet based interaction with European business and citizens. *Statistic in focus*, 35.

Evangelidis, A. Akomode. J., Taleb-Bendiab, A., & Taylor, M. (2002). Risk assessment & success factors for e-government in a UK Establishment. In R. Traunmueller & K. Kenk (Eds.), EGOV 2002 (LNCS 2456, pp. 395-402).

Evans, D., & Yen, D. C. (2006). E-government: evolving relationship of citizens and government, domestic, and international development. *Government Information Quarterly, 23*(2), 207–235. doi:10.1016/j.giq.2005.11.004

Evanschitzky, H., & Wunderlich, M. (2006). An Examination of Moderator Effects in the Four-Stage Model. *Journal of Service Research, 8*, 330–345. doi:10.1177/1094670506286325

Expósito, F., Mollet, R., Oliva, F., & Sanchez, J. A. (2003). *3A Un Sistema de Retención de Clientes: Análisis, Alarmas y Acciones One 2 One*. 27 Congreso Nacional de Estadística e Investigación Operativa, Lleida, April 8-11.

Eyob, E. (2004). E-government: breaking the frontiers of inefficiencies in the public sector. *Electronic Government, an International Journal, 1*(1), 107-114.

Family Educational Rights and Privacy Act (FERPA). (n.d.). Retrieved March 15, 2009 from http://www.ed.gov/policy/gen/guid/fpco/ferpa/index.html

Fang, Z. (2002). E-Government in the Digital Era: Concept, Practice, and Development. *International Journal of The Computer. The Internet and Management, 10*(2), 1–22.

Featherman, M. S., & Pavlou, P. A. (2002). Predicting E-services adoption: A perceived risk facets perspective. In *Proceedings of the eighth Americas conference on information*, Dallas.

Feinberg, L. E. (2004). FOIA, federal information policy, and information availability in a post-9/11 world. *Government Information Quarterly, 21*, 439–460. doi:10.1016/j.giq.2004.08.004

Felix, B. T., & Paul, S. (2004). Online consumer trust: a multiple-dimensional model. *Journal of Electronic Commerce in Organizations*, 40.

Feng, L. (2003). Implementing E-Government Strategy in Scotland: Current Situation and Emerging Issues. *Journal of Electronic Commerce in Organizations, 1*(2), 44–65.

Fenton, N., & Pfleeger, S. L. (1997). *Software Metrics - A Rigorous Approach*. London: International Thomson Publishing.

Fenton, R. (2004). United Kingdom adoption agency Web sites. *First Monday, 9*(2). Retrieved from http://www.firstmonday.org/issues/issue9_2/fenton/index.html.

Ferguson, D. A., & Perse, E. M. (2000). The World Wide Web as a functional alternative to television. *Journal of Broadcasting & Electronic Media, 44*(2), 155–174. doi:10.1207/s15506878jobem4402_1

Ferlie, E., Pettigrew, A., Ashburner, L., & Fitzgerald, L. (1996). *The New Public Management in Action*. Oxford, UK: Oxford University Press.

Fieldman, M. S., & Khademian, A. M. (2007). The Role of Public Management in Inclusion: Creating Communities of Participation. *Governance: An International Journal of Policy. Administration and Institution, 20*(2), 305–324.

Financial Action Task Force. (FATF). (1999). *Financial action task force on money laundering: The forty recommendations*. Paris: Organization for Economic Cooperation and Development. Retrieved April 19, 2009 from www.oecd.org/searchResult/0,2665,en_2649_201185_1_1_1_1_1,00.html

Finley, L. L. (2008). *Hawking Hits on the Information Highway: The Challenge of Online Drug Sales for Law Enforcement*. New York: Peter Lang.

Finn, K., & Detlor, B. (2002). Youth and electronic government: Towards a model of civic participation. *Quarterly Journal of Electronic Commerce, 3*(3), 191–209.

Fish, S. (1999). Mutual respect as a device of exclusion. In Macedo, S. (Ed.), *Deliberative politics: Essays on Democracy and Disagreement* (pp. 88–102). New York: Oxford University Press.

Fishbein, M., & Ajzen, I. (1975). *Belief, Attitude, Intention and Behavior: An Introduction to Theory and Research*. Reading, MA: Addison-Wesley.

Fisk, R. P., Brown, S. W., & Bitner, M. J. (1993). Tracking the evolution of the services marketing literature. *Journal of Retailing, 69*(1), 61–103. doi:10.1016/S0022-4359(05)80004-1

Fletcher, P. D. (2002). *E-file: Electronic tax administration in the United States*. Projet CEFRIO TNouve aux Mode`les de Collaborationr, re'alise' par Center for Technology in Government, Janvier 2002 1. Retrieved on June, 2004, from http://www.cefrio.qc.ca/././projets/Documents/NMC_ETA.pdf

Florini, A. (2007). *The right to know: Transparency for an open world*. New York: Columbia University Press.

Flumian, M., Coe, A., & Kernaghan, K. (2007). Transforming Service to Canadians: The Service Canada Model. *International Review of Administrative Sciences, 73*(4), 557–568. doi:10.1177/0020852307083458

Foerstel, H. (1999). *Freedom of information and the right to know: The origins and applications of the Freedom of Information Act*. Westport, CT: Greenwood Press.

Fogel, R. W. (2009). *The Impact of the Asian Miracle on the Theory of Economic Growth*. NBER Working Paper No. 14967. Cambridge, MA, USA: National Bureau of Economic Research.

Fondo Monetario Internacional (FMI). (2007). *Washington: Informe Anual 2007, Por una economía mundial para todos*. Retrieved April, 14, 2009, http://www.internationalmonetaryfund.com/external/spanish/pubs/ft/ar/2007/pdf/AR07_ESL.pdf

Fornell, C. (1992). A national customer satisfaction barometer: The Swedish experience. *Journal of Marketing, 55*(1), 6–21. doi:10.2307/1252129

Fountain, J. (2001). *Building the Virtual State: Information Technology and Institutional Change*. Washington, DC: Brookings Institution Press.

Fountain, J. E. (1999). The virtual state: Toward a Theory of Federal Bureaucracy in the 21 st Century. In Kamarck, E., & Nye, J. Jr., (Eds.), *Democracy.com? Governance in a Networked World*. Hollis, NH: Hollis Publishing.

Fountain, J. E. (2001). *Building the virtual state: information technology and institutional change*. Washington, DC: Brooking Institution Press.

Fountain, J. E. (2001). Paradoxes of Public Sector Service. *Governance: An International Journal of Policy and Administration*, *14*(1), 55–73.

Fountain, J. E. (2009). Bureaucratic reform and e-government in the United States. An institutional perspective. In Chadwick, A., & Howard, P. N. (Eds.), *Routledge handbook of Internet politics* (pp. 99–113). London, New York: Routledge.

Fraunholz, B., & Unnithan, C. (2008). Anti apathy approaches in representative democracies: e-governance and web 2.0 – facilitating citizen involvement? *International Journal of Electronic Democracy*, *1*(1), 51–84. doi:10.1504/IJED.2008.021278

Frederick, K. (2002). NFR Security. In Casey, E. (Ed.), *Handbook of Computer Crime Investigation Forensic Tools and Technology* (pp. 93–113). San Diego: Academic Press.

Freed, L. (2008). *American Customer Satisfaction Index: E-government Satisfaction Index*. Foresee Results. Retrieved April 3, 2009, from http://www.foreseeresults.com/Form_EgovQ32008.html

Freed, L. (2009). *ACSI E-government Satisfaction Index*. Retrieved from http://fcg.nbc.gov/documents/ACSI_EGov_Report_Q4_2008.pdf

Freeman, C., & Soete, L. (1997). *The economics of industrial innovation*. London: Continuum.

Fu, J. R., Chao, W. P., & Farn, C. K. (2004). Determinants of taxpayers' adoption of electronic filing methods in Taiwan: An exploratory study. *Information & Management*, *30*, 658–683.

Fu, J. R., Farn, C. K., & Chao, W. P. (2006). Acceptance of electronic tax filing: A study of taxpayer intentions. *Information & Management*, *43*, 109–126. doi:10.1016/j.im.2005.04.001

Fugini, M., & Mezzanzanica, A. (2004). *An application within the plan for e-government: the workfare portal*. Hershey, PA: Idea Group Inc.

Fukuyama, F. (1995). *Trust: The Social Virtues and the Creation of Prosperity*. New York: The Free Press.

Fung, A., & Wright, E. O. (2001). Deepening democracy: Innovations in empowered participatory governance. *Politics & Society*, *29*, 5–41. doi:10.1177/0032329201029001002

Gacek, C., Abd-Allah, A., Clark, B., & Boehm, B. (1995). *On the Definition of Software System Architecture* (Technical Report USC/CSE-95-TR-500). Los Angeles, CA, USA: University of Southern California, Center for Software Engineering.

Gandía, J. L., & Archidona, M. C. (2008). Determinants of website information by Spanish city councils. *Online Information Review*, *32*(1), 35–57. doi:10.1108/14684520810865976

Gant, J., & Gant, D. (2002). Web portal functionality and State Government E-service. In the *Proceedings of the 35th Hawaii international conference on system sciences (IEEE 2002)*.

GAO (General Accounting Office), & McClure, D. (2001). *Electronic government challenges must be addressed with effective leadership and management*. Retrieved from http://feapmo.gov/links.asp

Gareis, K., Cullen, K., & Korte, W. (2004). Putting the user at the center. Implications for the provision of online public services. In P. Cunningham & M, Cunningham (Eds.), eAdoption and the knowledge economy. Issues, applications, case studies (pp. 611-618). Amsterdam: IOS Press.

Garson, G. D. (2004). The promise of digital government. In Pavlichev, A., & Garson, G. D. (Eds.), *Digital government: Principles and best practices* (pp. 2–15). Hershey, PA: Idea Group Press.

Garson, G. D. (2006). *Public information technology and e-governance: Managing the virtual state*. Sudbury, MA: Jones & Bartlett Publishers.

Gauld, R., Gray, A., & McComb, S. (2009). How responsive is e-government? Evidence from Australia and New Zealand. *Government Information Quarterly*, *26*, 69–74. doi:10.1016/j.giq.2008.02.002

Gefen, D. (2000). E-Commerce: the role of familiarity and trust. *Omega: The International Journal of Management Science*, *28*, 725–737. doi:10.1016/S0305-0483(00)00021-9

Gefen, D., & Straub, D. W. (1997, December). Gender Differences in the Perception and Use of E-mail: An Extension to the Technology Acceptance Model. *Management Information Systems Quarterly*, 389–400. doi:10.2307/249720

Gefen, D., & Straub, D. W. (2000). Managing user trust in B2C e-services. *E-Services Quarterly*, *1*(1).

Gefen, D., Pavlou, P. A., Rise, G. M., & Warkentin, M. (2002). E-government adoption. In *Proceedings of the eighth Americas conference on information system*, Boston, MA.

German Federal Government. (2003). *BundOnline 2005. 2003 Implementation Plan*. Retrieved April 29, 2009, from http://www.en.bmi.bund.de

Gerritsen, R., & Osborn, D. (1997). Reform of Local Government in Australia. In Comparative Study on Local Government Reform in Japan, Australia and New Zealand (pp. 51 - 112). Sydney, Australia: Japan Local Government Centre (CLAIR).

Gershon, P. (2004). *Releasing Resources to the Front Line: Independent Review of Public Sector Efficiency*. London: HM Treasury. Retrieved from http://www.hm-treasury.gov.uk

Get a National Identity Card in the UAE. (2008, December 29). Retrieved April 10, 2009 from http://www.dubai.ae/en.portal

Ghere, R.K., & Young, B.A. (1998). The cyber-management environment: where technology and ingenuity meet public purpose and accountability. *Public Administration and Management: An Interactive Journal*, 3(1).

Gibson, A. N., Bertot, J. C., & McClure, C. R. (2009). *Emerging roles of public libraries as e-government providers*. Paper presented at the 42nd Hawaii International Conference on Systems Sciences.

Gibson, R., & Ward, S. (2000). A proposed framework for studying the function and effectiveness of party and candidate websites. *Social Science Computer Review*, *18*(3), 301–319. doi:10.1177/089443930001800306

Giddens, A. (1990). *The Consequences of Modernity*. Cambridge, UK: Polity Press.

Gilbert, D., Balestrini, P., & Littleboy, D. (2004). Barriers and Benefits in the adoption of E-government. *International Journal of Public Sector Management*, *17*(4/5), 286–301. doi:10.1108/09513550410539794

Gil-Garcia, J., & Martinez-Moyano, I. (2007). Understanding the evolution of e-government: The influence of systems of rules on public sector dynamics. *Government Information Quarterly*, *24*, 266–290. doi:10.1016/j.giq.2006.04.005

Gilman, S. C., & Lewis, C. W. (1996). Public Service Ethics: A Global Dialogue. *Public Administration Review*, *56*(6), 517–524. doi:10.2307/977250

Glaser, B. G., & Strauss, A. L. (1967). *The Discovery of Grounded Theory: Strategies for Qualitative Research*. New York: Aldine.

Godwin, B. (2008). *USA.gov and Web Best Practices, GSA Office of Citizen Services. Matrix of Web 2.0 Technology and Government*. Retrieved July 18, 2008, from http://www.usa.gov/webcontent/documents/Web_Technology_Matrix.pdf

Golder, S. A., & Huberman, B. A. (2006). Usage patterns of collaborative tagging systems. *Journal of Information Science*, *32*(2), 198–208. doi:10.1177/0165551506062337

Google. (2008). *Lessons learned from the 2008 campaign trail*. Washington, DC: Author.

Gorden, T. F. (2002). E-government –Introduction. *ERCIM News, Special Theme: E-government, European Research Consortium for Information and Mathematics*. Retrieved on March 4, 2009, from http://www.ercim.org/publication/Ercim_News/enw48/intro.html

Gosain, S. (2003). Issues in designing personal knowledge exchanges. *Information Technology & People*, *16*(3), 306. doi:10.1108/09593840310489403

Gouscos, D., Kalikakis, M., Legal, M., & Papadopoulou, S. (2007). A general model of performance and quality for one-stop e-government service offerings. *Government Information Quarterly, 22*(4), 860–885. doi:10.1016/j.giq.2006.07.016

Goven, J., & Langer, E. R. (2005). *Invitation to design the future: Christchurch scenario workshops on biosolids management.* Retrieved May 6, 2009, from http://www.ccc.govt.nz/wastewater/treatmentplant/InvitationToDesignTheFuture.pdf.

Grady, V. (2005). *The impact of technological change on the overall effectiveness of an organization.* D.Sc. dissertation, The George Washington University, United States – District of Columbia.

Graff, G. M. (December 2, 2007). Don't know their Yahoo from their YouTube. *Washington Post.*

Grant, G., & Chau, D. (2005). Developing a generic framework for e-government. *Journal of Global Information Management, 13*(1), 1–30.

Gray, A. (2005, November 7). Q&A: Professor Andrew Gray, editor of Public Money and Management. *eGov Monitor.* Retrieved August 10, 2008, from http://egovmonitor.com/node/3403

Gray, V. (1996). The Socioeconomic and Political Context of States. In *Politics in the American States: A Comparative Analysis* (6th ed.). Washington, DC: Congressional Quarterly Press.

Greek Information Society Observatory. (2008). *Measuring e-Europe 2005 and i2010 indices.* Retrieved April 29, 2009, from http://www.observatory.gr/ files/meletes/eEuropei2010_05-07.pdf

Greenemeier, L. (January 20, 2005). Florida Police Network Supports Post-9/11 Promises: Florida hopes to expand a data-sharing network aimed at spotting criminals or terrorists across jurisdictions. *Intelligent Enterprise.* Retrieved April 10, 2009 from http://www.intelligententerprise.com/showArticle.jhtml?articleID=57702947

Grimsley, M., & Meehan, A. (2007). e-Government information Systems: Evaluation-led design for public value and client trust. *European Journal of Information Systems, 16*, 134–148. doi:10.1057/palgrave.ejis.3000674

Gronlund, A. (2003). Emerging electronic infrastructures: exploring democratic components. *Social Science Computer Review, 21*(1), 55–72. doi:10.1177/0894439302238971

Gronroos, C. (1990). Service management and marketing: Managing the moments of truth in service competition. Lexington, MA.

Gronroos, C., Heinonen, F., Isoniemi, K., & Lindholm, M. (2000). The netoffer model: A case example from the virtual marketspace. *Management Decision, 38*(4), 243–252. doi:10.1108/00251740010326252

Grossman, L. (2006, December 13). Time's Person of the Year: You. *Time.* Retrieved May 1, 2009, from http://www.time.com/time/magazine/article/0,9171,1569514,00.html

Gundykunst, W. (1997). *Communicating with strangers: An Approach to Intercultural Communication.* New York: Random House.

Gupta, M. P., & Jana, D. (2003). E-government evaluation: A framework and case study. *Government Information Quarterly, 20*, 365–387. doi:10.1016/j.giq.2003.08.002

Gupta, M. P., Kumar, P., & Bhattacharya, J. (2004). *Government online: Opportunities and challenges.* New Delhi: Tata McGraw-Hill.

Guriting, P., & Ndubisi, N. O. (2006). Borneo online banking: evaluating customer perceptions and behavioural intention. *Management Research News, 29*(1/2), 6–15. doi:10.1108/01409170610645402

Hackney, R., & Jones, S. (2002). *Towards E-Government in the Welsh (UK) Assembly: an Information Systems Evaluation.* Paper presented at the ISOneWorld Conference and Convention, Las Vegas, Nevada, USA.

Hair, J. F., Anderson, R. E., Tatham, R. L., & Black, B. C. (1998). *Multivariate data analysis* (5th ed.). Englewood Cliffs, NJ: Prentice-Hall International.

Hair, J. F., Anderson, R. E., Tatham, R. L., & Black, W. C. (2006). *Multivariate Data Analysis* (6th ed.). Upper Saddle River, NJ: Prentice-Hall.

Halaris, C., Magoutas, B., Papadomichelaki, X., & Mentzas, G. (2007). Classification and synthesis of quality approaches in e-government services. *Internet Research, 17*(4), 378–401. doi:10.1108/10662240710828058

Halchin, L. E. (2004). Electronic government: Government capability or terrorist resource. *Government Information Quarterly, 21*, 406–419. doi:10.1016/j.giq.2004.08.002

Hall, P. (1998). *Cities in Civilization. Culture Innovation, and Urban Order.* London: Weinfeld & Nicholson.

Halpin, H., Robu, V., & Shepherd, H. (2007). The complex dynamics of collaborative tagging. In *Proceedings of the 16th international Conference on World Wide Web* (Banff, Alberta, Canada, May 08 - 12, 2007) (pp. 211-220). New York: ACM.

Hamid, H. (2007, May 10). New IRB chief on mission to improve tax compliance. *New Straits Times.* Retrieved September 26, 2008, from http://www.camtech.com.my/news_21.htm

Hammerschmid, G., & Meyer, R. E. (2005). New public management in Austria: local variation on a global theme. *Public Administration, 83*(3), 709–733. doi:10.1111/j.0033-3298.2005.00471.x

Hammond, K., Burke, R., Martin, C., & Lytinen, S. (1995). FAQ finder: a case-based approach to knowledge navigation. In *Proceedings of the 11th* [Washington, DC: IEEE Computer Society.]. *The Conference on Artificial Intelligence Applications*, (February): 20–22.

Hamner, M. (2010). Potential Barriers to Implementing E-Government in Developing Countries. In Reddick, C. (Ed.), *Politics, Democracy and E-Government: Participation and Service Delivery.* Hershey, PA: IGI Global.

Hamner, M., & Al-Qahtani, R. (2009). Enhancing the case for electronic government in developing nations: A people-centric study focused in Saudi Arabia. *Government Information Quarterly, 26*, 118–127. doi:10.1016/j.giq.2007.08.008

Handschuh, S., Volz, R., & Staab, S. (2003, September/October). Annotation for the Deep Web. *IEEE Intelligent Systems.*

Hanseth, O., & Ciborra, C. (2007). *Risk, Complexity and ICT.* Cheltenham, UK: Edward Elgar.

Haque, M. S. (2006). Modernising Government: The Way Forward – an analysis. *International Review of Administrative Sciences, 72*(3), 319–325. doi:10.1177/0020852306068007

Harris, B. (2002, August). E-government makes global progress. *Government Technology*, 22-28.

Heald, D. (2006a). Varieties of Transparency. In Hood, C., & Heald, D. (Eds.), *Transparency: The Key to Better Governance?* (pp. 25–43). Oxford, UK: Oxford University Press.

Heald, D. (2006b). Transparency as an Instrumental Value. In Hood, C., & Heald, D. (Eds.), *Transparency: The Key to Better Governance?* (pp. 59–73). Oxford, UK: Oxford University Press.

Heeks, R. (1999). *Reinventing government in the information age. International practise in IT-enabled public sector reform.* London: Routledge.

Heeks, R. (2001). Building e-governance for development: A framework for national and donor action. i-Government working paper series (paper no. 12). Institute for Development Policy and Management, University of Manchester.

Heeks, R. (2001). *Understanding e-Governance for Development (Paper No. 11). Manchester M13 9QH.* UK: University of Manchester, Institute for Development Policy and Management.

Heeks, R. (2003). *Most eGovernment-for-Development Projects Fail: How Can Risks be Reduced? (Paper No. 14). Manchester M139GH*. UK: University ofManchester, Institute for Development Policy and Management.

Heeks, R. (2004) eGovernment as a Carrier of Context (Paper No. 15). Manchester M139GH, UK: University of Manchester, Institute for Development Policy and Management.

Heeks, R. (2006). *Benchmarking eGovernment: Improving the National and International Measurement, Evaluation and Comparison of eGovernment*. iGovernment Working Paper No. 18. Manchester, UK: University of Manchester.

Heeks, R. (2006). *Understanding and measuring eGovernment: international benchmarking studies*. Paper presented at the UNDESA Workshop, E-participation and E-government: Understanding the present and creating the future, Budapest, Hungary, 12-28 July 2006.

Heeks, R. (Ed.). (2003). *eCOPS: More open handling of criminal cases in India*. Retrieved March 29, 2009, from http://www.egov4dev.org/transparency/case/ecops.shtml

Heeks, R., & Bailur, S. (2007). Analyzing e-government research: Perspectives, philosophies, theories, methods, and practice. *Government Information Quarterly, 24*, 243–265. doi:10.1016/j.giq.2006.06.005

Helsloot, I., & Ruitenberg, A. (2004). Citizen Response to Disasters: a Survey of Literature and Some Practical Implications. *Journal of Contingencies and Crisis Management, 12*(3), 98–111. doi:10.1111/j.0966-0879.2004.00440.x

Hero, R. (1998). *Faces of Inequality: Social Diversity in American Politics*. Oxford, UK: Oxford University Press.

Higgins, G. E. (2008). 5-10 Cybercrime. In J. M. Miller (Ed.), The 21st Century Criminology: A reference handbook. Thousand Oaks, CA: Sage.

Higgins, G. E. (2009). *Cybercrime: An introduction to an emerging phenomenon*. New York, NY: McGraw-Hill Companies.

Hij.gov.cn. (2008 September). *Governor's mail box*. Retrieved March 10, 2009, from http://www.hlj.gov.cn/szxx/hfxd/200811/t20081114_143012.htm

Hiler, J. S., & Belanger, F. (2001). *Privacy Strategies for Electronic Government*. Retrieved February 10 from http://www.businessofgovernment.org/main/publications/grant_reports/details/index.asp?GID=6

Hillard, R. (2000). *IEEE-Std-1471-2000 Recommended Practice for Architectural Description of Software-Intensive Systems*. Retrieved July 29, 2009 from http://www.incose.org/delvalley/Hilliard_11_14_00.pdf

Hiller, J. S., & Bélanger, F. (2001). *Privacy Strategies for Electronic Government*. Washington, DC: IBM Center for the Business of Government. Retrieved January 28, 2008, from http://www.businessofgovernment.org/pdfs/HillerReport.pdf

Hinduja, S. (2004). Perceptions of local and state law enforcement concerning the role of computer crime investigative teams. *Policing: An International Journal of Police Strategies and Management, 27*(3), 341–357. doi:10.1108/13639510410553103

Hinduja, S. (2007). Computer Crime Investigations in the United States: Leveraging Knowledge from the Past to Address the Future. *International Journal of Cyber Criminology, 1*(1), 1–26.

Hintikka, K. A. (2007). Web 2.0 – johdatus Internetin uusiin liiketoimintamahdollisuuksiin. [Web 2.0 – Introduction to New Business Opportunities of the Internet]. TIEKE – Tietoyhteiskunnan kehittämiskeskus ry:n julkaisusarja 28. Helsinki.

HIPAAcomply - The Definitive Source for Information on HIPAA Security and Privacy Compliance. (n.d.). Retrieved April 5, 2009 from http://www.hipaacomply.com

Ho, A. (2002). Reinventing local governments and the e-government initiative. *Public Administration Review, 62(4)*, 434–444. doi:10.1111/0033-3352.00197

Ho, A. T.-K., & Ni, A. Y. (2004). Explaining the adoption of e-government features: A case study of Iowa County Treasurers' offices. *American Review of Public Administration, 34*, 164–180. doi:10.1177/0275074004264355

Hoffman, D. L., Novak, T. P., & Peralta, M. (1999). Building consumer trust online. *Communications of the ACM, 42*(4), 80–85. doi:10.1145/299157.299175

Hoffman, K. M. (2007). *Government websites for special populations: Toward content-based evaluation.* Unpublished Master's Thesis: University of Maryland.

Hofstede, G. (1980). *Culture's Consequences.* Beverly Hills, CA: Sage.

Hofstede, G. (1991). *Cultures and Organizatios: Software of the Mind.* London: McGraw-Hill.

Hofstede, G. (2001). *Culture's Consequences* (2nd ed.). Thousand Oaks, CA: Sage.

Holemans, D. (1999). The Democratic Separation of Technology and Ethics—The Case of the Flemish Regulation of Genetic Engineering. *Democracy and Nature, 5*(3), 511–522.

Holliday, I., & Yep, R. (2005). E-government in China. *Public Administration and Development, 25*, 239–249. doi:10.1002/pad.361

Holt, T. J., & Bossler, A. M. (2009). Examining the Applicability of Lifestyle-Routine Activities Theory for Cybercrime Victimization. *Deviant Behavior, 30*, 1. doi:10.1080/01639620701876577

Holzer, M., & Kim, S.-T. (2004). *Digital governance in municipalities worldwide: An assessment of municipal web sites throughout the world.* National Center for Public Productivity.

Holzer, M., Manoharan, A., Shick, R., & Stowers, G. (2008). *U.S. Municipalities: E-Governance Report. The E-Governance Institute National Center for Public Performance School of Public Affairs and Administration Rutgers, the State University of New Jersey.* Campus at Newark.

Homburg, V. M. F., & Bekkers, V. J. J. M. (2005). E-government and NPM: a perfect marriage? In Bekkers, V. J. J. M., & Homburg, V. M. F. (Eds.), *The information ecology of e-government.* Amsterdam: IOS Press.

Hood, C. (1991). A Public Management for all Seasons. *Public Administration, 69*(Spring), 3–19. doi:10.1111/j.1467-9299.1991.tb00779.x

Hood, C., & Heald, D. (Eds.). (2006). *Transparency: The Key to Better Governance?*Oxford, UK: Oxford University Press.

Hood, C., & Peters, G. (2004). The Middle AGeing of New Public Management. *Journal of Public Administration: Research and Theory, 14*, 267–282. doi:10.1093/jopart/muh019

Horan, T. A., Abhichandani, T., & Rayalu, R. (2006). Assessing User Satisfaction of E-Government Services: Development and Testing of Quality-in-Use Satisfaction with Advanced Traveler Information. In *Proceedings of the 39th Hawaii International Conference on System Sciences.*

Horrigan, J. (2008). *Home broadband 2008.* Washington, DC: Pew Internet & American Life Project.

Horrigan, J. B. (2004). *How Americans get in touch with government.* Washington, DC: Pew Internet & American Life Project.

Horrigan, J. B. (2006). *Politics online.* Washington, DC: Pew Internet & American Life Project.

Horrigan, J. B., & Rainie, L. (2002). *Counting on the Internet.* Washington, DC: Pew Internet & American Life Project.

Horrigan., J.B. (2004). *How Americans get in Touch with Government*. Retrieved July 31, 2009, from http://www.pewinternet.org/Reports/2004/How-Americans-Get-in-Touch-With-Government.aspx

Horst, M., Kuttschreuter, M., & Gutteling, J. M. (2006). Perceived usefulness, personal experiences, risk perception and trust as determinants of adoption of e-government services in The Netherlands. *Computers in Human Behavior*, *23*, 1838–1852. doi:10.1016/j.chb.2005.11.003

Horst, M., Kuttschreuter, M., & Gutteling, J. M. (2007). Perceived usefulness, personal experiences, risk perception and trust as determinants of adoption of e-government services in The Netherlands. *Computers in Human Behavior*, *23*(4), 1838–1852. doi:10.1016/j.chb.2005.11.003

Howe, J. (2008). *Crowdsourcing: Why the power of the crowd is driving the future of business*. Crown Business.

Hsiao, N. Y., Huang, T. Y., & Chen, D. Y. (2002). *Implementing electronic government in Taiwan: A case study of Taipei City Mayor's Email-box. In 2002 e-government international conference*. Seoul, Korea.

Hu, Y., Xiao, J., Pang, J., & Xie, K. (2005, August 15-17). *A Research on the Appraisal Framework of E-Government Project Success*. Paper presented at ICEC Conference, Xian, China.

Huang, C. J., & Chao, M.-H. (2001). Managing WWW in public administration: Uses and misuses. *Government Information Quarterly*, *18*, 357–373. doi:10.1016/S0740-624X(01)00085-5

Huang, W., Ambra, J. D., & Bhalla, V. (2002). An empirical investigation of the Adoption of e-government in Australian Citizens: Some unexpected research Findings. *Journal of Computer Information Systems*, *43*(1), 15–22.

Hughes, O. (1994). *Public Management and Administration*. Londres: Macmillan Press Ltd.

Hunan.gov.cn. (2009, February 4). *Report on governor's mail box in the fourth quarter, 2008*. Retrieved March 19, 2009, from http://www.hunan.gov.cn/hdjl/szxx/qkfk/200902/t20090204_151543.htm

Hung, S. Y., Chang, C. M., & Yu, T. J. (2006). Determinants of the user acceptance of the e-Government services: The case of online tax filing and payment system. *Government Information Quarterly*, *23*, 97–122. doi:10.1016/j.giq.2005.11.005

Hung, S.-Y., Tnag, K.-Z., Chang, C.-M., & Ke, C.-D. (2009). User acceptance of intergovernmental services: An example of electronic document management system. *Government Information Quarterly*, *26*, 387–397. doi:10.1016/j.giq.2008.07.003

Hwang, C. S. (2000). A comparative study of tax-filing methods: Manual, Internet, and two-dimensional bar code. *Journal of Government Information*, *27*(2), 113–127. doi:10.1016/S1352-0237(00)00129-5

Hwang, S.-D., Choi, Y., & Myeong, S.-H. (1999). Electronic Governance in South Korea, Conceptual Problems. *Government Information Quarterly*, *16*(3), 277–285. doi:10.1016/S0740-624X(99)80028-8

Igbaria, M., Livari, J., & Maragahh, H. (1995). Why do individual use computer technology. A finish case study. *Information & Management*, *29*, 227–238. doi:10.1016/0378-7206(95)00031-0

INCOSE. (2009). Retrieved July 29, 2009, from http://www.incose.org/practice/whatissystemseng.aspx

Information Society DG. (2006). *i2010 Benchmarking Framework*. Retrieved April 29, 2009, from http://ec.europa.eu/information_society/eeurope/i2010/docs/benchmarking/060220_i2010_benchmarking_framework_nov_2006.doc

International Federation of Accountants (IFAC). (1993). *Managing Quality Improvements*. New York: Author.

International Project Management Association. (2009). *Project Excellence Model*. Retrieved April 29, 2009, from http://www.apm.org.uk/ProjectExcellence.asp

Irani, Z., Elliman, T., & Jackson, T. (2007). Electronic Transformation of Government in the U.K.: a research agenda. *European Journal of Information Systems, 16*, 327–335. doi:10.1057/palgrave.ejis.3000698

Irani, Z., Love, P. E. D., & Jones, S. (2008). Learning lessons from evaluating eGovernment: Reflective case experiences that support transformational government. *The Journal of Strategic Information Systems, 17*, 155–164. doi:10.1016/j.jsis.2007.12.005

IRAS. (2007). *Annual report 2007/08*. Singapore. IRB confident of collecting more than RM77 bln for assessment year 2007. (2008, September 3). *Bernama.com*. Retrieved September 26, 2008, from http://www.bernama.com/bernama/v5/newsbusiness.php?id=356860

Jaeger, P. T. (2003). The endless wire: e-government as global phenomenon. *Government Information Quarterly, 20*(4), 323–331. doi:10.1016/j.giq.2003.08.003

Jaeger, P. T. (2005). Deliberative democracy and the conceptual foundations of electronic government. *Government Information Quarterly, 22*, 702–719. doi:10.1016/j.giq.2006.01.012

Jaeger, P. T. (2006). Assessing Section 508 compliance on federal e-government websites: A multi-method, user-centered evaluation of accessibility for persons with disabilities. *Government Information Quarterly, 23*(2), 169–190. doi:10.1016/j.giq.2006.03.002

Jaeger, P. T. (2007). Information policy, information access, and democratic participation: The national and international implications of the Bush administration's information politics. *Government Information Quarterly, 24*, 840–859. doi:10.1016/j.giq.2007.01.004

Jaeger, P. T. (2008). User-centered policy evaluations of Section 508 of the Rehabilitation Act: Evaluating e-government websites for accessibility. *Journal of Disability Policy Studies, 19*(1), 24–33. doi:10.1177/1044207308315274

Jaeger, P. T., & Fleischmann, K. R. (2007). Public libraries, values, trust, and e-government. *Information Technology and Libraries, 26*(4), 35–43.

Jaeger, P. T., & Matteson, M. (2009). E-government and technology acceptance: The implementation of Section 508 guidelines for e-government websites. *Electronic Journal of E-Government, 7*(1), 87-98. Retrieved from http://www.ejeg.com/volume-7/vol7-iss1/v7-i1-art8.htm

Jaeger, P. T., & Thompson, K. M. (2003). E-government around the world: Lessons, challenges, and new directions. *Government Information Quarterly, 20*(4), 389–394. doi:10.1016/j.giq.2003.08.001

Jaeger, P. T., & Thompson, K. M. (2004). Social information behavior and the democratic process: Information poverty, normative behavior, and electronic government in the United States. *Library & Information Science Research, 26*(1), 94–107. doi:10.1016/j.lisr.2003.11.006

Jaeger, P. T., & Xie, B. (2009). Developing online community accessibility guidelines for persons with disabilities and older adults. *Journal of Disability Policy Studies, 20*, 55–63. doi:10.1177/1044207308325997

Jaeger, P. T., Langa, L. A., McClure, C. R., & Bertot, J. C. (2007). The 2004 and 2005 Gulf Coast hurricanes: Evolving roles and lessons learned for public libraries in disaster preparedness and community services. *Public Library Quarterly, 25*(3/4), 199–214. doi:10.1300/J118v25n03_17

Jaeger, P. T., Paquette, S., & Simmons, S. N. (2010). Information policy in national political campaigns: A comparison of the 2008 campaigns for President of the United States and Prime Minister of Canada. *Journal of Information Technology & Politics, 7*, 1–16. doi:10.1080/19331680903316700

Jaeger, P., & Matteson, M. (2009). e-Government and technology acceptance: the case of the implementation of section 508 guidelines for websites. *Electronic. Journal of E-Government*, 7(1), 87–98.

Jaeger, P., & Thompson, K. (2003). E-government around the world: Lessons, challenges, and future directions. *Government Information Quarterly, 20*, 389–394. doi:10.1016/j.giq.2003.08.001

Jain, A., & Patnayakuni, R. (2003). Public expectations and public scrutiny: an agenda for research in the context of e-government. In *Ninth Americas Conference on Information Systems,* Tampa, FL (pp. 811-820).

Janssen, D., Rotthier, S., & Snijkers, K. (2004). If you measure it they will score: an assessment of international eGovernment benchmarking. *Information Polity, 9*(3-4), 121–130.

Janssen, M., Gortmaker, J., & Wagenaar, R. W. (2006). Web service orchestration in public administration: challenges, roles, and growth stages. *Information Systems Management, 23*(2), 44–55. doi:10.1201/1078.10580530/45925.23.2.20060301/92673.6

Janssen, M., van der Duin, P., Wagenaar, R. W., Bicking, M., & Wimmer, M. A. (2007a). Scenario building for e-government in 2020. In *Proceedings of the 8th Annual International Digital Government Research Conference.*

Janssen, M., van der Duin, P., Wagenaar, R. W., Bicking, M., Wimmer, M. A., Dawes, S., & Petrauskas, R. (2007b). *Scenario building for e-government in 2020: Consolidating the results from regional workshops.* Paper presented at the 40th Hawaii International Conference on System Sciences, Hawaii.

Jarvenpaa, S., Tractinsky, N., Saarinen, L., & Vitale, M. (1999). Consumer trust in an Internet store: a cross-cultural validation. *Journal of Computer-Mediated Communication, 5*(2). Retrieved from http//www.ascusc.org/jcmc/vol5/issue2/jarvenpaa.html.

Jasmine, A., & Zurina, M. N. (2008). *An Application of TAM Model: Public Perception on E-Filling.* Paper presented at the e-Asia Conference, November 2008, KLCC, Malaysia.

Jasperson, J., Carter, P., & Zmud, R. (2005). A Comprehensive Conceptualization of Post-Adoptive Behaviors Associated with Information Technology Enabled Work Systems. *Management Information Systems Quarterly, 29*(3), 525–557.

Jeffres, L. W. (2007). Media technology and civic life. In Lin, C., & Atkin, D. (Eds.), *Communication technology and social change.* Mahwah, NJ: LEA.

Jensen, M. J., & Venkatesh, A. (2007). Government websites and political engagement: Facilitating citizen entry into the policy process. In B. Thönssen, et al. (Eds.), *Proceedings of TED conference on e-Government: Enhancing public administration back offices* (pp. 56-65). Linz, Austria: Trauner Verlag.

Jho, W. (2005). Challenges for e-governance: protests from civil society on the protection of privacy in e-government in Korea. *International Review of Administrative Science, 71*(1), 151–166. doi:10.1177/0020852305051690

Jijkoun, V., & de Rijke, M. (2005). Retrieving answers from frequently asked questions pages on the web. In *Proceedings of the 14th ACM international Conference on information and Knowledge Management* (Bremen, Germany, October 31 - November 05, 2005) (pp. 76-83). New York: ACM. Retrieved from http://doi.acm.org/10.1145/1099554.1099571

Johnson, C. (2004, December 17). *Policies for Federal Agency Public Websites.* Memorandum M05-04 for the Heads of Executive Departments and Agencies.

Johnson, C. (2005, December 16). *Policies for Improving Public Access to and Dissemination of Government Information and Using the Federal Enterprise Architecture Data Reference Model.* Memorandum M06-02 for the Heads of Executive Departments and Agencies.

Jones, M. (1993). *Transforming Australian Local Government.* St Leonards, Australia: Allen and Unwin.

Jones, S. G. (1998). *Cybersociety 2.0. Revisiting Computer-Mediated Communication and Community.* London: Sage.

Jones, S., Hackney, R., & Irani, Z. (2007). Towards E-government Transformation: Conceptualising "Citizen Engage". *Transforming Government: People. Process and Policy, 1*(2), 145–152.

Jonkers, H., Lankhorst, M., van Buuren, R., Hoppenbrouwers, S., Bonsangue, M., & van der Torre, L. (2004). Concepts for Modeling Enterprise Architectures. *International Journal of Cooperative Information Systems*, *13*(3), 257–287. doi:10.1142/S0218843004000985

Jorgensen, D., & Cable, S. (2002). Facing the challenges of e-government: a case study of the city of Corpus Christi, Texas. *S.A.M. Advanced Management Journal*, *67*(1), 34–45.

Jorgensen, D., & Cable, S. (2002). Facing the challenges of e-government: a case study of the city of Corpus Christi, Texas. *SAM – Advanced Management Journal*, *67*(3), 15-21.

Joseph, R. C., & Jeffers, P. I. (2009). E-Government in the Caribbean Nations. *Journal of Global Information Technology Management*, *12*(1), 52–70.

Jung, S., Harris, K., Webster, J., & Herlocker, J. L. (2004). SERF: integrating human recommendations with search. In *Proceedings of the Thirteenth ACM international Conference on information and Knowledge Management* (Washington, D.C., USA, November 08 - 13, 2004) (pp. 571-580). New York: ACM. Retrieved from http://doi.acm.org/10.1145/1031171.1031277

Justice, J. B., Melitski, J., & Smith, D. L. (2006). E-Government as an instrument of fiscal accountability and responsiveness: Do the best practitioners employ the best practices? *American Review of Public Administration*, *36*(3), 301–322. doi:10.1177/0275074005283797

Kahraman, C., Demirel, N. Ç., & Demirel, T. (2007). Prioritization of e-government strategies using a SWOT-AHP analysis: The case of Turkey. *European Journal of Information Systems*, *16*(3), 284–298. doi:10.1057/palgrave.ejis.3000679

Kakabadse, A., Kakabadse, N. K., & Kouzmin, A. (2003). Reinventing the Democratic Governance Project through Information Technology? A Growing Agenda for Debate. *Public Administration Review*, *63*(1), 44–60. doi:10.1111/1540-6210.00263

Kalakota, R., & Whinston, A. B. (1997). *Electronic Commerce*. Reading, MA: Addison-Wesley.

Kale, S. H., & Mclntyre, R. P. (1991). Distribution channel relationships in diverse cultures. *International Marketing Review*, *8*(3), 31–45. doi:10.1108/02651339110004069

Kampen, J. K., Snijkers, K., & Bouckaert, G. (2005). Public priorities concerning the development of e-government in Flanders. *Social Science Computer Review*, *23*(1), 136–139. doi:10.1177/0894439304271557

Kannabiran, G., Xavier, M., & Banumathi, T. (2008). E-Governance and ICT Enabled Rural Development in Developing Countries: Critical Lessons from RASI Project in India. *International Journal of Electronic Government Research*, *4*(3), 1–19.

Kantor, B., & Lapsley, P. (2004). *Network news transfer protocol, a proposed standard for the stream-based transmission of news*. Retrieved March 2004 from ftp://ftp.rfc-editor.org/in-notes/rfc977.txt

Kaohsiung City Government Information Management Center. (2008). *Kaohsiung Citizen E-Complaint System Data* (unpublished)

Kaplan, R. S., & Norton, D. P. (1999). *The Balanced Scorecard: Translating Strategy into Action*. Boston: Harvard Business Press.

Kappelman, L. A., Koh, C. E., Prybutok, V. R., & Sanchez, A. D. (2003). The relationship between IT for communication and e-government barriers. In *Ninth Americas Conference on Information Systems*, Tampa, FL.

Karp, H. (2000, April). Angels online: Special report. *The Reader's Digest*, 74–80.

Katz, J. E., Rice, R. E., & Aspden, P. (2001). The internet, 1995–2000: Access, civic involvement, and social interaction. *The American Behavioral Scientist*, *45*(3), 405–419.

Kaufmann, D., Kraay, A., & Mastruzzi, M. (2008, June 24). *Governance Matters VII: Aggregate and Individual Governance Indicators, 1996-2007*. World Bank Policy Research Working Paper No. 4654. Retrieved April 29, 2009, from http://ssrn.com/abstract=1148386

Kaye, B. K., & Johnson, J. (2002). Online and in the know: Uses and gratification of the Web for political information. *Journal of Broadcasting & Electronic Media*, *46*, 54–71. doi:10.1207/s15506878jobem4601_4

Kaynama, S. A., & Black, C. I. (2000). A proposal to assess the service quality of online travel agency: An exploratory study. *Journal of Professional Services Marketing*, *21*(1), 63–88. doi:10.1300/J090v21n01_05

Kearns, I. (2001, April 27). - May 3). Wising Up About Wiring Up. *Public Finance*, 26.

Keeney, R. L. (1992). *Value-Focused Thinking: A Path to Creative Decision Making*. Cambridge, MA: Harvard University Press.

Keeney, R. L. (1999). The value of Internet commerce to the customer. *Management Science*, *45*(4), 533–542. doi:10.1287/mnsc.45.4.533

Kelly P., & Stalnaker M.L. (2002). Avoiding IT Project Disasters of Counsel. *ABI/INFORM Trade & Industry*, *21*(7), 13-23.

Kelly, E. P., & Erickson, E. G. (2005). RFID tags: commercial applications v. privacy rights. *Industrial Management & Data Systems*, *105*(6), 703–713. doi:10.1108/02635570510606950

Kelly, E. P., & Erickson, G. S. (2004). Legal and privacy issues surrounding customer databases and e-merchant bankruptcies: reflection on Toysmart.com. *Industrial Management & Data Systems*, *104*(3), 209–217. doi:10.1108/02635570410525762

Kelly, J. M., & Swindell, D. (2002). A multiple-indicator approach to municipal service evaluation: Correlating performance measurement and citizen satisfaction across jurisdictions. *Public Administration Review*, *62*(5), 610–621. doi:10.1111/1540-6210.00241

Kernaghan, K., Marson, B., & Sandford, B. (2002). *The new public organization*. Toronto: Institute of Public Administration of Canada.

Kim, A. J. (2000). *Community Building on the Web: Secret Strategies for Successful Online Communities*. Englewood Cliffs, NJ: Peachpit Press.

Kim, S., Kim, H. J., & Lee, H. (2009). An institutional analysis of an e-government system for anti-corruption: The case of OPEN. *Government Information Quarterly*, *26*(1), 42–50. doi:10.1016/j.giq.2008.09.002

King, C. S., Feltey, K. M., & Susel, B. O. (1998). The question of participation: Toward authentic public participation in public administration. *Public Administration Review*, *58*(4), 317–326. doi:10.2307/977561

King, C., & Stivers, C. (1998). *Government Is Us: Public Administration in an Anti-government era*. Thousand Oaks, CA: Sage Publications.

King, D., Lee, J., Warkentin, M., & Chung, H. M. (2002). *Electronic Commerce a Managerial Perspective*. Upper Saddle River, NJ: Prentice Hall.

King, J. (2006). Democracy in the Information Age. *Australian Journal of Public Administration*, *65*(2), 16–32. doi:10.1111/j.1467-8500.2006.00479.x

King, S., & Cotterill, S. (2007). Transformational Government? The role of information technology in delivering citizen-centric local public services. *Local Government Studies*, *33*(3), 333–354. doi:10.1080/03003930701289430

Kirtley, J. E. (2006). Transparency and accountability in a time of terror: The bush administration's assault on freedom of information. *Communication Law and Policy*, *11*, 479–509. doi:10.1207/s15326926clp1104_2

Klitgaard, R. (1988). *Controlling Corruption*. Berkeley, CA: University of California Press.

Kloman, E. H. (1974). Public Participation in Technology Assessment. *Public Administration Review*, *34*(1), 52–61. doi:10.2307/974401

Kloot, L. (1999). Performance Measurement and Accountability in Victorian Local Government. *International Journal of Public Sector Management*, *12*(7), 565–583. doi:10.1108/09513559910308039

Korac-Kakabadse, A., & Korac-Kakabadse, N. (2001). Information technology's impact on the quality of democracy: Reinventing the 'democratic vessel. In Heeks, R. (Ed.), *Reinventing government in the information age* (pp. 211–228). London: Routledge.

KoreAm. (2005 August). Politics As E-Usual. The ubiquitous nature of the Internet is changing the face of South Korean politics. *KoreAm Journal*. Retrieved May 1, 2009, from http://www.koreamjournal.com/Magazine/index.php/kj/2005/august/korea_news

Kotler, P. (2000). *Marketing Management; The Millennium Edition*. Upper Saddle River, NJ: Prentice Hall.

Kovacic, Z. (2005). The impact of national culture on worldwide e-government Readiness. *Journal of Informing Science*, *8*, 143–158.

Kraemer, K., & King, J. L. (2003). *Information Technology and Administrative Reform: Will the Time After e-Government Be Different?*Irvine, CA: Centre for Research on Information Technology and Organizations.

Krishnamurthy, S. (2003). *Preparing the Indian Police for the 21st Century*. Bangalore, India: Puliani and Puliani.

Kronus, C. L., & Crowe, L. (Eds.). (1971). Libraries and neighborhood information centers. Papers presented at an institute conducted by the University of Illinois Graduate School of Library Science, October 24-27, 1971. Urbana, IL: Graduate School of Library Science.

Kroski, E. (2005). The Hive Mind: Folksonomies and userbased tagging. *Infotangle*. Retrieved December 11, 2008, from http://infotangle.blogsome.com/2005/12/07/the-hive-mind-folksonomies-and-user-based-tagging/

Kumar, V., & Venkatesan, R. (2005). Who are Multichannel Shoppers and How do They Perform? Correlates of Multichannel Shopping Behavior. *Journal of Interactive Marketing*, *19*(Spring), 44–61. doi:10.1002/dir.20034

Kunstelj, M., & Vintar, M. (2004). Evaluating the progress of e-government development: a critical analysis. *Information Polity*, *9*(3-4), 131–148.

Kunstelj, M., Jukic, T., & Vintar, M. (2007). Analysing the demand side of E-Government: what can we learn from Slovenian users? *Lecture Notes in Computer Science*, *4656*, 305–317. doi:10.1007/978-3-540-74444-3_26

Kwast, M. L., Martha, S., & Wolken, J. D. (1998). Market Definition and The Analysis of Antitrust in Banking. *Antitrust Bulletin*, *42*(4), 973–995.

La Porte, T. M., Demchak, C. C., & De Jong, M. (2002). Democracy and bureaucracy in the age of the web. Empirical findings and theoretical speculations. *Administration & Society*, *34*(4), 411–446. doi:10.1177/0095399702034004004

Lai, M. L., Sheikh Obid, S. N., & Meera, A. K. (2005). Tax practitioners and electronic filing system: An empirical analysis. *Electronic Journal of Tax Research*, *9*(1), 93-107. Retrieved 20, September 2008, from http://www.austlii.edu.au/au/journals/eJTR/2004/5.html

Landsbergen, D. (2004). Screen level bureaucracy: Databases as public records. *Government Information Quarterly*, *21*(1), 24–50. doi:10.1016/j.giq.2003.12.009

Laris, M. (January 4, 2009). O brave new world that has such avatars in it. *Washington Post.*

Larsen, E., & Rainie, L. (2002). *The rise of the e-citizen: How people use government agencies' web sites*. Washington, DC: Pew Internet & American Life Project. Retrieved from http://www.pewinternet.org/Reports/2002/The-Rise-of-the-ECitizen-How-People-Use-Government-Agencies-Web-Sites.aspx

Lau, T. Y., Aboulhoson, M., Lin, C., & Atkin, D. J. (2008). Adoption of e-government in three Latin American countries: Argentina, Brazil and Mexico. *Telecommunications Policy*, *32*(2), 88–100. doi:10.1016/j.telpol.2007.07.007

Lau, T., Fung, A., & Ji, M. (2005). E-government in China: keeping up with the Joneses? *Journal of E-Government*, *2*(4), 15–38. doi:10.1300/J399v02n04_03

Lawrence, R. Z. (1997). Is it really the economy stupid? In Nye, J. S. (Ed.), *Why people don't trust government* (pp. 111–132). Cambridge, MA: Harvard University Press.

Layne, K., & Lee, J. (2001). Developing fully functional e-government: a four stage model. *Government Information Quarterly, 18*(2), 122–136. doi:10.1016/S0740-624X(01)00066-1

Layne, K., & Lee, J. (2001). Developing fully functional e-government: a four-stage model. *Government Information Quarterly, 18*(2), 122–136. doi:10.1016/S0740-624X(01)00066-1

Lazar, J. (2005). *Web usability: A user-centered design approach.* Boston, MA: Addison-Wesley.

Lee, A. S., & Baskerville, R. L. (2003). Generalizing Generalizibility in Information Systems Research. *Information Systems Research, 14*(3), 221–243. doi:10.1287/isre.14.3.221.16560

Lee, J. K., Braynov, S., & Rao, H. R. (2005). Effects of a Public Emergency on Citizens Usage Intention toward E-Government: A Study in the Context of War in Iraq. In *Proceedings of the Eleventh Americas Conference on Information System,* Omaha, NE, USA.

Lee, J., & Soberon-Ferrer, H. (1997). Consumer vulnerability to fraud: Influencing factors. *The Journal of Consumer Affairs, 31*(1), 70–89.

Lee, M. K. O., & Turban, E. (2001). A trust model for internet shopping. *International Journal of Electronic Commerce, 6*(1), 75–91.

Leedy, P. (1997). *Practical Research: Planning and Design* (6th ed.). Upper Saddle River, NJ: Merrill, Prentice Hall.

Lee-Kelley, L., & Kolsaker, A. (2004). E-Government: the fit between supply assumptions and usage drivers. *Electronic Government, an International Journal, 1*(2), 130-140.

Leite, J., & Freeman, P. (1991). Requirements Validation through Viewpoint Resolution. *IEEE Transactions on Software Engineering, 17*(12), 1253–1269. doi:10.1109/32.106986

Lekvall, P., & Wahlbin, C. (2001). Information for Marknadsforingsbeslut. Goteborg: IHM forlag.

Lenihan, D. (2002, April). *Realigning Governance: From E-Government to E-Democracy.* Paper presented at the E-Government Working Group of OECD, Paris, France.

Lenihan, D. G. (2005). Realigning Governance: From E-Government to E-democracy. In Khosrow-Pour, M. (Ed.), *Practicing e-Government: A Global Perspective.* Hershey, PA: Idea Group Publishing.

Lenk, K., & Traunmuller, R. (2001). Broadening the Concept of Electronic Government. In Prins, J. E. J. (Ed.), *Designing e-Government: On the Crossroads of Technological Innovation and Institutional Change. Hague.* Boston: Kluwer Law International.

Lenk, K., & Traunmüller, R. (2002). Electronic Government: Where are we Heading? In Lenk, K., & Traunmüller, R. (Eds.), *Electronic government: first international conference, EGOV 2002.* New York: Springer.

Lenk, K., & Traunmuller, R. (2002). Preface to the Focus Theme on eGovernment. *Electronic Markets, 12*(3), 147–148. doi:10.1080/101967802320245901

Leoi L. S. (2007, April 19). Bold Plan For Syariah Portal. *The StarSpecial Paper,* 2

Leong, L. (2003). *Theoretical Models in IS Research and the Technology Acceptance Model (TAM).* Hershey, PA: Idea Group Inc.

Leslie, S. (2007). Government E-Payments Adoption Ranking. *The Economist Intelligence Unit Limited,* 3-11

Leventhal, L., & Barnes, J. (2008). *Usability Engineering: Process, Products, and Examples.* Upper Saddle River, NJ: Pearson Prentice Hall.

Lietaer, B. (2006). A Proposal for a Brazilian Education Complementary Currency. *International Journal of Community Currency Research, 10,* 18–23.

Liljenback, M. E. (2007). *ContextQA: Experiments in Interactive Restricted-Domain Question Answering.* MSc. in CS Thesis, San Diego University.

Lilleker, D. G. (2006). *Key concepts in political communication*. Thousand Oaks: Sage.

Lilleker, D. G., & Lees-Marshment, J. (2005). *Political marketing: A comparative perspective*. New York: Manchester University Press.

Lim, B., & Wen, H. (2003). Web services: An analysis of the technology, its benefits and implementation difficulties. *Information Systems Management*, *20*(2), 49–57. doi:10.1201/1078/43204.20.2.20030301/41470.8

Lim, E. T. K., Wee, C. T., & Pan, S. L. (2007). E-Government implementation: Balancing collaboration and control in stakeholder management. *International Journal of Electronic Government Research*, *3*(2), 1–28.

Lin, W., & Raman, W. (1998). The housing value-relevance of governmental accounting information. *Journal of Accounting and Public Policy*, *17*(2), 91–118. doi:10.1016/S0278-4254(98)10004-2

Lin, Y. (2008, December). Exposing corruption on the Internet: illusory victories? *The China Blog*. Retrieved March 31, 2009, from http://china.blogs.time.com/2008/12/31/exposing-corruption-on-the-internet-illusory-victor...

Lindell, M. K., Prater, C. S., & Perry, R. W. (2007). *Introduction to Emergency Management*. Hoboken, NJ: John Wiley and Sons.

Lips, A. M. B. (2007). E-Government Under Construction: Challenging Traditional Conceptions of Citizenship. In Nixon, P., & Koutrakou, V. (Eds.), *E-Government in Europe Rebooting the State* (pp. 33–47). London: Routledge.

Liu, A. N. N., & Walker, A. (1998). Evaluation of project outcomes. *Construction Management and Economics*, *16*(2), 209–219. doi:10.1080/014461998372493

Liu, D., Hua, X., Yang, L., Wang, M., & Zhang, H. (2009). Tag ranking. In *Proceedings of the 18th international Conference on World Wide Web* (Madrid, Spain, April 20 - 24, 2009) (pp. 351-360). New York: ACM.

Liu, J., Derzsi, Z., Raus, M., & Kipp, A. (2008). eGovernment Project Evaluation: An Integrated Framework. *Lecture Notes in Computer Science*, *5184*, 85–97. doi:10.1007/978-3-540-85204-9_8

Loei, L. S., & Hong, Y. P. (2007, April 19). Public Service: Digital Government. *Newpaper StarSpecial*.

London, S. (1994). *Electronic Democracy: A Literature Survey. Paper prepared for the Kettering Foundation*. CA: Santa Barbara.

LoPucki, L. M. (2003). Human identification theory and the identity theft problem. *Texas Law Review*, *80*(89), 89–134.

Lu, Y., He, H., Zhao, H., Meng, W., & Yu, C. (2007). *Annotating Structured Data of the Deep Web* (pp. 376–385). ICDE.

Ma, L., Chung, J., & Thorson, S. (2005). E-government in China: Bringing economic development through administrative reform. *Government Information Quarterly*, *22*(2), 20–37. doi:10.1016/j.giq.2004.10.001

Ma, W. L. (2008, December). Human flesh search-China-style anti-corruption. *ChinaStakes*. Retrieved March 31, 2009, from http://www.chinastakes.com/WatchFullArticle.aspx?articleid=937

Macintosh, A., Robson, E., Smith, E., & Whyte, A. (2003). Electronic Democracy and Young People. *Social Science Computer Review*, *21*(1), 43–54. doi:10.1177/0894439302238970

Magda, B. (2009). *Increasing the efficacy of emergency departments through systems analysis of enterprise architecture: Mitigating the impact of technological change*. Ph.D. dissertation, The George Washington University, District of Columbia, USA.

Mahler, J., & Regan, P. M. (2006). Crafting the message: Controlling content on agency Web sites. *Government Information Quarterly*, *24*, 505–521. doi:10.1016/j.giq.2006.06.008

Mahrer, H., & Krimmer, R. (2005). Towards the enhancement of e-democracy: identifying the notion of the middleman paradox. *Information Systems Journal*, *15*(1), 27–42. doi:10.1111/j.1365-2575.2005.00184.x

Maier, M. W. (2006). System and Software Architecture Reconciliation. *Systems Engineering*, *9*(2), 146–159. doi:10.1002/sys.20050

Malaysia, M. S. C. *The MSC Malaysia Flagship Applications*. (n.d.). Retrieved from http://www.msc.com.my/msc/flagships.asp

Malhotra, Y. (2002). Enabling knowledge exchanges for e-business communities. *Information Strategy*, *18*(3), 26–31.

Malhotra, Y., & Galletta, D. F. (1999). Extending the Technology Acceptance Model to account for Social Influence: Theoretical bases and empirical validation. In *Proceedings of the 32nd Hawaii International Conference on System Science*.

Management Advisory Committee. MAC. (2004). Connecting Government: Whole of Government Responses to Australian Priority Challenges. Canberra: Commonwealth of Australia.

Maniam, K. (2007). *Technology Innovations in Government Supply Chain Management Processes: A Case Study of e-Perolehan Initiative in Malaysia*. Paper presented at the 4th Asialics International Conference, Kuala Lumpur, Malaysia.

Manovich, L. (2001). *Language of the new media*. Cambridge, MA: MIT Press.

Maor, M. (2004). Feeling the Heat? Anticorruption Mechanisms in Comparative Perspective. *Governance: An International Journal of Policy. Administration and Institutions*, *17*(1), 1–28.

Marcella, A. J., & Greenfield, R. S. (2002). *Cyber Forensics: A Field Manual for Collecting, Examining, and Preserving Evidence of Computer Crimes*. Boca Raton, FL: Auerbach Publications. doi:10.1201/9781420000115

Marchionini, G., Samet, H., & Brandt, L. (2003). Digital government. *Communications of the ACM*, *46*(1), 25–27.

Margetts, H. (1999). *Information technology in government: Britain and America*. London: Routledge.

Margetts, H. (2006a). Transparency and Digital Government. In Hood, C., & Heald, D. (Eds.), *Transparency: The Key to Better Governance?* (pp. 197–207). Oxford, UK: Oxford University Press.

Margetts, H. (2006b). E-Government in Britain—A Decade On. *Parliamentary Affairs*, *59*(2), 250–265. doi:10.1093/pa/gsl003

Margetts, H. (2009). Public management change and e-government. The emergence of digital-era governance. In Chadwick, A., & Howard, P. N. (Eds.), *Routledge handbook of Internet politics* (pp. 114–127). London, New York: Routledge.

Margolis, M., & Resnick, D. (2000). *Politics as usual: The cyberspace revolution*. Thousand Oaks, CA: Sage Publications.

Marshall, C. E., Robinson, T. H., & Kwak, D. (2005). Computer Crime in a Brave New World. In Reichel, P. (Ed.), *Handbook of Transnational Crime & Justice* (pp. 114–138). Thousand Oaks, CA: Sage Publications, Inc.

Martin, P. Y., & Turner, B. A. (1986). Grounded Theory and Organizational Research. *The Journal of Applied Behavioral Science*, *22*(2), 141–157. doi:10.1177/002188638602200207

Mathieson, K. (1991). Predicting user intention: Comparing the technology acceptance model with the theory of planned behavior. *Information Systems Research*, *2*(3), 173–191. doi:10.1287/isre.2.3.173

MAV. (1993). *A Guide to Performance Indicators in Local Government*. Melbourne, Australia: Municipal Association of Victoria.

MAV. (2000). *Strategic Rural & Regional Implementation Plan for the Deployment of Integrated Online Services*. Melbourne, Australia: Municipal Association of Victoria.

Mayer, R. C., Davis, J. H., & Schoorman, F. D. (1995). An integrative model of organizational trust. *Academy of Management Review*, *20*(3), 709–734. doi:10.2307/258792

McClure, C. R., Jaeger, P. T., & Bertot, J. C. (2007). The looming infrastructure plateau?: Space, funding, connection speed, and the ability of public libraries to meet the demand for free Internet access. *First Monday*, *12*(12). Retrieved from http://www.uic.edu/htbin/cgiwrap/bin/ojs/index.php/fm/article/view/2017/1907.

McClure, D. L. (2001). *Electronic government: Challenges must me addressed with effective leadership and management*. U.S. General Accounting Office. Retrieved March 30, 2009, from http://www.gao.gov/new.items/d01959t.pdf

McEntire, D., Fuller, A., Johnston, C. W., & Weber, R. (2002). A Comparison of Disaster Paradigms: The Search for a Holistic Policy Guide. *Public Administration Review*, *62*(3), 267–281. doi:10.1111/1540-6210.00178

McKnight, D. H., & Chevancy, N. L. (2002). *What trust means in e-commerce customer relationships: An interdisciplinary conceptual typology*. Internet. J. Electronic Commerce.

McLaughlin, K., Osborne, S., & Ferlie, E. (2002). *New public management: current trends and future prospects*. London, New York: Routledge.

McLuhan, M. (1995). Media hot and cold. In McLuhan, E., & Zingrone, F. (Eds.), *The Essential McLuhan*. New York: Basic Books.

McNeal, R. S., Tolbert, C. J., Mossberger, K., & Dotterweich, L. J. (2003). Innovating in digital government in the American states. *Social Science Quarterly*, *84*(1), 52–70. doi:10.1111/1540-6237.00140

McQuade, S. C. (2006). *Understanding and Managing Cybercrime*. Boston: Pearson Education, Inc.

Mechling, J., & Booz Allen Hamilton. (2002). *Building a methodology for measuring the value of e-services*. Washington, DC: Booz Allen Hamilton.

Mehta, M. D. (1998). Virtual control and disciplining on the Internet: Electronic governmentality in the new wired world. *The Information Society*, *14*, 107–116. doi:10.1080/019722498128917

Meiklejohn, A. (1948). *Free speech and its relation to self-government*. New York: Harper.

Melitski, J. (2003). Capacity and e-government performance. *Public Performance & Management Review*, *26*(4), 376–390. doi:10.1177/1530957603026004005

MIA. (2000). *Income Tax (Amendment Bill 2000)*. Malaysian Institute of Accountants (MIA), Circular No.20, November.

Michels, A., & Meijer, A. (2008). Safeguarding Public Accountability in Horizontal Government. *Public Management Review*, *10*(2), 165–173. doi:10.1080/14719030801928490

Miles, M. B., & Huberman, M. A. (1994). *Qualitative Data Analysis*. London: Sage.

Millard, J. (2003). *ePublic services in Europe: past, present and future. Research findings and new challenges*. Final draft-paper prepared for IPTS, not published.

Millard, J. (2008 August). eGovernment measurement for policy makers. *European Journal of ePractice*, 4. Retrieved April 19, 2009 from http://www.epractice-journal.eu/document/4971

Miller, J. M., Schreck, C. J., & Tewksbury, R. (2008). *Criminological Theory: A Brief Introduction* (2nd ed.). Boston: Allyn & Bacon.

Milne, G. R., Rohm, A. J., & Bahl, S. (2004). Consumers' protection of online privacy and identity. *The Journal of Consumer Affairs*, *38*(2), 217–231.

Milward, H. B., & Snyder, O. (1996). Electronic government: linking citizens to public organizations through technology. *Journal of Public Administration: Research and Theory*, *6*(2), 261–275.

Mitchell, W. J. (1995). *City of Bits. Space, Place, and the Infobahn*. Cambridge, MA: MIT Press.

Mitra, R. K., & Gupta, M. P. (2007). Analysis of issues of e-government in Indian Police. *Electronic Government an International Journal, 4*, 97–125. doi:10.1504/EG.2007.012182

Mitra, R. K., & Gupta, M. P. (2008). A contextual perspective of performance assessment in eGovernment: A study of Indian Police Administration. *Government Information Quarterly, 25*, 278–302. doi:10.1016/j.giq.2006.03.008

Moilanen, T., & Salminen, A. (2006). *Comparative Study on the Public-service Ethics of the EU Member States. A report from the Human Resources Working Group, European Public Administration Network*. EUPAN.

Mok, K. (2002). Changing Government Role for Socio-economic Development in Hong Kong in the Twenty-first Century. *Policy Studies, 23*(2), 107–124. doi:10.1080/0144287022000011468

Moldovan, D., Paşca, M., Harabagiu, S., & Surdeanu, M. (2003). Performance issues and error analysis in an open-domain question answering system. *ACM Transactions on Information Systems, 21*(2), 133–154. Retrieved from http://doi.acm.org/10.1145/763693.763694. doi:10.1145/763693.763694

Moon, M. (2002, Jul/Aug). The evolution of e-government among municipalities: rhetoric or reality? *Public Administration Review, 62*(4), 424–433. doi:10.1111/0033-3352.00196

Moon, M. J. (2002). The evolution of e-government among municipalities: Rhetoric or reality? *Public Administration Review, 62*(4), 424–433. doi:10.1111/0033-3352.00196

Moon, M. J., & Norris, D. F. (2005). Does managerial orientation matter? The adoption of reinventing government and e-government at the municipal level. *Information Systems Journal, 15*(1), 43–60. doi:10.1111/j.1365-2575.2005.00185.x

Moon, M. J., & Welch, E. W. (2005). Same Bed, Different Dreams? A Comparative Analysis of Citizen and Bureaucrat Perspective on E-Government. *Review of Public Personnel Administration, 25*(3), 243–264. doi:10.1177/0734371X05275508

Moon, M. J., & Welch, E. W. (2005). Same bed, different dreams? A comparative analysis of citizen and bureaucrat perspectives on e-government. *Review of Public Personnel Administration, 25*(3), 243–264. doi:10.1177/0734371X05275508

Moore, G. C., & Benbasat, I. (1991). Development of an instrument to measure the perceptions of adopting an information technology innovation. *Information Systems Research, 2*(3), 192–222. doi:10.1287/isre.2.3.192

Moore, M., & Khagram, S. (2004). *On Creating Public Value: What Business Might Learn from Government about Strategic Management* (Corporate Social Responsibility Initiative Working Paper No. 3). Cambridge, MA, USA: Harvard University.

Moore, T., & Flynn, P. (2004). *Future challenges for E-Government. The changing role of multi-channel service delivery.* Discussion Paper n° 4. Australian Government Information Management Office. 2004. Retrieved September 6, 2008 from: http://www.finance.gov.au/Publications/future-challenges-for-egovernment/docs/AGIMO-FC-no4.pdf

Morash, M., & Ford, J. K. (Eds.). (2002). *The Move to Community Policing: Making Change Happen.* Thousand Oaks, CA: Sage Publications.

Moreno, A., de la Rosa, J. L., & Carrillo, C. I. (2006). WIKIFAQ: Obtaining complete FAQs. *Frontiers in Artificial Intelligence and Applications – AI Research & Development, 146*, 283-290.

Moreno, A., de la Rosa, J. L., Szymanski, B. K., & Barcenas, J. M. (2009). *Reward System for Completing FAQs.* Frontiers in Artificial Intelligence and Applications – AI Research & Development.

Moreno, E. A. (2007). Competency-based Educational Models for Electronic Governance: Implications for Inclusion and Responsiveness in the Public Service. *Journal of Public Affairs Education, 13*(1), 79–86.

Mosse, B., & Whitley, E. A. (2009). Critically classifying: UK e-government website benchmarking and the recasting of the citizen as customer. *Information Systems Journal, 19*, 149–173. doi:10.1111/j.1365-2575.2008.00299.x

Multimedia Victoria. (1998). *Online Government 2001 - from Vision to Reality*. Melbourne, Victoria, Australia: Department of State Development, State Government of Victoria.

Multimedia Victoria. (2002). *Putting People at the Centre: Government Innovation Working for Victorians*. Melbourne, Australia: Department of State and Regional Development.

Mumford, E. (1983). *Designing human systems for new technology: The ETHICS method*. Manchester, UK: Manchester Business School.

Mumford, E. (1991). Participation in system design: What can it offer? In Shackel, B., & Richardson, S. (Eds.), *Human factors for informatics usability* (pp. 267–290). Cambridge, UK: Cambridge University Press.

Musso, J. A., Weare, C., & Hale, M. C. (2000). Designing web technologies for local governance reform: Good management or good democracy? *Political Communication, 17*(1), 1–19. doi:10.1080/105846000198486

Musso, J., Weare, C., & Hale, M. (2000). Designing Web Technologies for Local Governance Reform: Good Management or Good Democracy? *Political Communication, 17*(1), 1–19. doi:10.1080/105846000198486

Naciones Unidas. (2008). *E-Government Survey 2008, From E-Government to Connected Governance*. Retrieved April, 14, 2009, from http://unpan1.un.org/intradoc/groups/public/documents/UN/UNPAN028607.pdf

Nagesh, G. (2009). Agencies used social media to manage salmonella outbreak. *Nextgov*. Retrieved from http://www.nextgov.com

Naidu, C. (2009). In *Encyclopædia Britannica*. Retrieved July 31, 2009, from Encyclopædia Britannica Online: http://www.britannica.com/EBchecked/topic/401839/Chandrababu-Naidu

Nasco, S., Kulviwat, S., Kumar, A., & Bruner, G. II. (2008). The CAT model: Extensions and moderators of dominance in technology acceptance. *Psychology and Marketing, 25*(10), 987. doi:10.1002/mar.20249

National Academy of Sciences. (2002). *Information Technology, Research, Innovation and E-government*. Washington, DC: National Academy Press.

National Computerization Agency. (2002). *E-government in Korea*. Seoul: Republic of Korea.

National Disaster Management Authority (NDMA). *Government of India*. (n.d.). Retrieved September 5th 2008, from http://ndma.gov.in/wps/portal/NDMAPortal.

National ID Card Makes Transactions at Dubai Courts Faster. (2009). Khaleej Times. Retrieved April 10, 2009 from http://www.khaleejtimes.com/DisplayArticleNew.asp?section=theuae&xfile=data/theuae/2009/march/theuae_march73.xml

National Technical University of Athens. (2008a). Implementation methodology for the study 'Improving ICT investment effectiveness in Public Administration.' *Greek Information Society Observatory*. Retrieved April 29, 2009, from http://www.observatory.gr/files/meletes/MVA_D0_gr.pdf

National Technical University of Athens. (2008b). Comparative evaluation of different stages of the ICT investment efficiency for the study Improving ICT investment effectiveness in Public Administration. *Greek Information Society Observatory*. Retrieved April 29, 2009, from http://www.observatory.gr/files/meletes/MVA_D1_gr.pdf

National Technical University of Athens. (2008c). Evaluation framework for the study 'Improving ICT investment effectiveness in Public Administration.' *Greek Information Society Observatory*. Retrieved April 29, 2009, from http://www.observatory.gr/files/meletes/MVA_D3_gr.pdf

Ndou, V. (2004). E-government for developing countries: opportunities and challenges. *Electronic Journal on Information systems in Developing countries, 18*(1), 1-24.

Needham, C. (2004). The citizen as a consumer: E-government in the United Kingdom and United States. In Gibson, R., Römmele, A., & Ward, S. (Eds.), *Electronic democracy: Mobilization, organization, and participation via new ICTs*. New York: Routledge.

Nelson, R., & Cheney, P. (1987). Training End Users: An Exploratory Study. *Management Information Systems Quarterly, 11*(4), 547–559. doi:10.2307/248985

Neslin, S. A., Grewal, D., Leghorn, R., Shankar, V., Teerling, M., & Thomas, J. S. (2006). Challenges and Opportunities in Multichannel Customer Management. *Journal of Service Research, 9*(2), 1–18. doi:10.1177/1094670506293559

Netchaeva, I. (2002). E-government and e-democracy. A comparison of opportunities in the North and South. *Gazette: the International Journal for Communication Studies, 64*(5), 467–477. doi:10.1177/17480485020640050601

Netchaeva, I. (2002). E-government and e-democracy. *Gazette: The International Journal for Communication Studies, 64*(5), 467–477. doi:10.1177/17480485020640050601

Neu, C., Anderson, R., & Bikson, T. (1999). *Sending your government a message*. Santa Monica, CA: RAND Science and Technology.

Noce, A. A., & McKeown, L. (2008). A New Benchmark for Internet Use: A Logistic Modeling of Factors Influencing Internet use in Canada, 2005. *Government Information Quarterly, 25*(3), 462–476. doi:10.1016/j.giq.2007.04.006

Nonaka, I., & Konno, N. (1998). The concept of ba: Building a foundation for knowledge creation. *California Management Review, 40*(3), 40–54.

Norris, D. F., & Moon, M. J. (2005). Advancing e-government at the grassroots: tortoise of hare? *Public Administration Review, 65*(1), 64–75. doi:10.1111/j.1540-6210.2005.00431.x

Norris, P. (2001). *Digital divide: Civic engagement, information poverty, and the Internet worldwide*. Cambridge, UK: Cambridge University Press.

Noveck, B. S. (2003). Designing deliberative democracy in cyberspace: The role of the cyber-lawyer. *Boston University Journal of Science and Technology, 9*, 1–91.

O'Brien, R. (2008, June 27). *Paying City Students Is a Wise Investment*. New America Foundation, The Baltimore Sun. Retrieved from http://www.newamerica.net/publications/articles/2008/paying_city_students_wise_investment_7445

O'Neill, O. (2006). Transparency and the Ethics of Communication. In Hood, C., & Heald, D. (Eds.), *Transparency: The Key to Better Governance?* (pp. 75–90). Oxford, UK: Oxford University Press.

O'Reilly, T. (2005, September 30). *What Is Web 2.0. Design Patterns and Business Models for the Next Generation of Software*. Retrieved May 1, 2009, from http://www.oreillynet.com/pub/a/oreilly/tim/news/2005/09/30/what-is-web-20.html

O'Shea, D., King, C. T., Greenfield, S., Shelton, E., Sullivan, L., & Taber, E. (2004). *National Benefit/Cost Analysis of Three Digit-Accessed Telephone Information and Referral Services*. Ray Marshall Centre for the Study of Human Resources, Lyndon B. Johnson School of Public Affairs, The University of Texas at Austin.

OECD. (1996). Responsive Government: Service Quality Initiatives. Paris, France: Organisation for Economic Co-operation and Development.

OECD. (2003). The E-Government imperative. Paris: OECD E-government Studies.

OECD. (2004). *The e-Government Imperative*. Paris, France: Organisation for Economic Co-Operation and Development.

OECD. (2005). E-Government for better government. Paris: OECD E-government Studies.

OECD. (2005a). *E-government for Better Government*. OECD publishing.

OECD. (2005b). *Proposed outline for Accessing E-government Benefits*. OECD publishing. Retrieved February 18, 2008, from http://webdomino1.oecd.org/COMNET/PUM/egovproweb.nsf/viewHtml/index/$FILE/GOV.PGC.EGOV.2006.1.doc

OECD. (2008). Belgium: OECD country report. Paris OECD E-government Studies.

Office of Government Commerce. The Stationary Office (2005). Managing Successful Projects with PRINCE2. London.

Office of the e-Envoy. (2008). *Modernizing government: Benchmarking electronic service delivery.* Retrieved December 2, 2008, from http://egov.alentejodigital.pt/Benchmarks/BenchmarkingESD.pdf

Ogren, I. (2000). On Principles for Model-Based Systems Engineering. *Systems Engineering, 3*(1), 38–49. doi:10.1002/(SICI)1520-6858(2000)3:1<38::AID-SYS3>3.0.CO;2-B

Olphert, W., & Damodaran, L. (2007). Citizen participation and engagement in the design of e-government services: The missing link in effective ICT design and delivery. *Journal of the Association for Information Systems, 8*(9), 491–507.

Ong, C.-S., & Wang, S.-W. (2009). Managing Citizen-Initiated Email Contacts. *Government Information Quarterly, 26*(3), 498–504. doi:10.1016/j.giq.2008.07.005

Organization for Economic Co-operation and Development (OECD). (2001b). Citizens as partners. OECD handbook on information, consultation and public participation in policy-making. France: OECD publications.

Organization for Economic Co-operation and Development (OECD). (2003a). Engaging Citizens Online for Better Policy-making, *OECD Observer, Policy Brief.* Retrieved from http://www.oecd.org/publications/Pol_brief

Organization for Economic Co-operation and Development (OECD). (2003b). Promises and problems of e-democracy. Challenges of online citizens engagement. France: OECD publications.

Orlikowski, W. (1990). CASE tools are organizational change: Investigating Incremental and Radical Changes in Systems Development. *Management Information Systems Quarterly, 17*(3), 309–340. doi:10.2307/249774

Osborne, D., & Gaebler, T. (1992). *Reinventing government: how the entrepreneurial spirit is transforming the public sector.* Reading, MA: Addison-Wesley.

Osborne, D., & Gaebler, T. (1993). Reinventing Government: How The Entrepreneurial Spirit Is Transforming The Public Sector. New York: Plume/penguin Books.

Osimo, D. (2008). Web 2.0 in Government: Why and How? JRC Scientific and Technical reports, Seville, Spain. EUR 23358 EN – 2008. European Commission.

Osvalds, G. (2001). *Definition of Enterprise Architecture-centric Models for the Systems Engineer.* Paper presented at the Eleventh Annual International Symposium of the International Council on Systems Engineering (INCOSE), Melbourne, Victoria, Australia.

Parasuraman, A. (2000). Technology readiness index (tri): A multiple item scale to measure readiness to embrace new technologies. *Journal of Service Research, 2*(4), 307–320. doi:10.1177/109467050024001

Parasuraman, A., & Grewal, D. (2000). The impact of technology on the Quality-Value-Loyalty chain: A research agenda. *Journal of the Academy of Marketing Science, 28*(1), 168–174. doi:10.1177/0092070300281015

Parasuraman, A., Zeithaml, V. A., & Berry, L. L. (1988). SERVQUAL: A multiple-item scale for measuring consumer perceptions of service quality. *Journal of Retailing, 64*(1), 12–40.

Parasuraman, A., Zeithaml, V. A., & Berry, L. L. (1994). Reassessment of expectations as a comparison standard in measuring service quality: Implications for further research. *Journal of Marketing, 58*, 111–124. doi:10.2307/1252255

Parasuraman, A., Zeithaml, V. A., & Malhotra, A. (2005). E-S-QUAL: A multiple-item scale for assessing electronic service quality. *Journal of Service Research, 7*(3), 213–233. doi:10.1177/1094670504271156

Parent, M., Vandebeek, C. A., & Gemino, A. C. (2004). *Building Citizen Trust Through e-Government.* Paper presented at the 37th Hawaii International Conference on System Sciences. Retrieved February 18, 2008, from http://csdl2.computer.org/comp/proceedings/hicss/2004/2056/05/205650119a.pdf

Parent, M., Vandebeek, C. A., & Gemino, A. C. (2005). Building Citizen Trust through E-Government. *Government Information Quarterly, 22*(4), 720–736. doi:10.1016/j.giq.2005.10.001

Pariser, E. (2008). Will he bring change.gov we can believe in? *Washington Post* (December 28, 2008), B04.

Parker, R., & Bradley, L. (2004). Bureaucracy or Post-Bureaucracy? Public Sector Organisations in a Changing Context. *The Asia Pacific Journal of Public Administration, 26*(2), 197–225.

Pauline, R. (1998). The important of trust in electronic commerce. *Internet Research: Electronic Networking Applications and Policy, 8*(4), 313–321. doi:10.1108/10662249810231050

Pavlichev, A., & Garson, G. D. (2006). Five great ideas in Public Information Technology Literature. In Rabin, J., Hildreth, W. B., & Miller, G. J. (Eds.), *Handbook of Public Administration.* Boca Raton, FL: CRC/Taylor & Francis.

Pavlou, P. A. (2001). Integrating trust in electronic commerce with the technology acceptance model – model development and validation. In *Proceedings of the 2001 Americas Conference in Information Systems*, Boston, MA, 2-5 August.

Pavlou, P. A. (2003). Consumer acceptance of electronic commerce- integrating trust and risk with the technology acceptance model. *International Journal of Electronic Commerce, 7*(3), 69–103.

Payne, A., & Frow, P. (2005). A Strategic Framework for Customer Relationship Management. *Journal of Marketing, 69*(oktober), 167-176.

Peña-López, I. (2008). Towards e-Government 2.0: Review of the 4th Internet, Law and Politics congress – Political Track. In *IV Internet, Law and Politics Congress. Social Software and Web 2.0: Legal and Political Implications.* IDP. Revista de Internet, Derecho y Politica, 7. Retrieved March 20, 2009, from http://www.uoc.edu/idp/7/dt/eng/pena.pdf

People, I. Info about the Famous People Around the World. (2009). *Biography of Chandrababu Naidu.* Retrieved on July 10th 2009 from http://profiles.incredible-people.com/chandrababu-naidu/

Peristeras, V., & Tarabanis, K. (2000). Towards an enterprise architecture for public administration using a top-down approach. *European Journal of Information Systems, 9*(4), 252–260. doi:10.1057/palgrave/ejis/3000378

Perry, W. R., & Lindell, M. K. (2003). Understanding Citizen Response to Disasters with Implications for Terrorism. *Journal of Contingencies and Crisis Management, 11*(2), 49–60. doi:10.1111/1468-5973.1102001

Peters, R., Jansen, M., & Engers, T. (2004). Measuring e-government impact: existing practices. *Sixth International Conference on Electronic Commerce*, Delft, Netherlands (pp. 480-488).

Peters, R., Janssen, M., & van Engers, T. (2005). Measuring e-government impact: existing practices and shortcomings. In *Proceedings of the 6th International Conference on Electronic Commerce, session: eGovernment services and policy track* (Copenhagen, August 22-26, 2005) (pp. 480-489). New York: ACM Press.

Pettigrew, K. (1996). Nurses' perceptions of their needs for community information. *Journal of Education for Library and Information Science, 7*(4), 351–360.

Pew Internet and American Life Project. (2007). *Latest trends.* Last accessed December 17, 2007 at http://www.pewinternet.org/trends.asp.

Phang, C. W., Li, Y., Sutanto, J., & Kankanhalli, A. (2005). Senior Citizens' Adoption of E-Government: In Quest of the Antecedents of Perceived Usefulness. In *Proceedings of the 38th Hawaii International Conference on System Science* (pp.1-8).

Phillips, D. (2009a). The value of online content. Posted to Leverwealth Blog on March 8, 2009. Retrieved April 21, 2009, from http://leverwealth.blogspot.com/2009/03/value-of-online-content.html

Phillips, D. (2009b). The real world of the Internet. Posted to Leverwealth Blog on March 19, 2009. Retrieved April 21, 2009, from http://leverwealth.blogspot.com/2009/03/real-world-of-internet.html

Pidgeon, N., & Rogers-Hayden, T. (2007). Opening up Nanotechnology Dialogue with the Publics: Risk Communication or Upstream Engagement? *Health Risk & Society*, *9*(2), 191–210. doi:10.1080/13698570701306906

Pierce, J. C., & Lovrich, N. P. (2003). Internet technology transfer and social capital. *Comparative Technology Transfer and Society*, *1*(1), 49–71. doi:10.1353/ctt.2003.0008

Pieterson, W. (2008). Kanaal Strategie [Channel Strategy]. Enschede, Nederland: Telematica Instituut.

Pieterson, W. (2009). *Channel Choice: Citizens' Channel Behavior and Public Service Channel Strategy*. Netherlands: Thesis, University of Twente.

Pieterson, W. (2009). Channel Choice; Citizens' Channel Behavior and Public Service Channel Strategy. Enschede, Nederland: University of Twente.

Pieterson, W., & Ebbers, W. (2008). The use of service channels by citizens in the Netherlands: implications for multi-channel management. *International Review of Administrative Sciences*, *74*(1), 95–110. doi:10.1177/0020852307085736

Pieterson, W., & Ebbers, W. (2008). The Use of Service Channels by Citizens in the Netherlands; implications for multi-channel management. *International Review of Administrative Sciences*, *74*(1). doi:10.1177/0020852307085736

Pieterson, W., & van Dijk, J. (2006). *Governmental Service Channel Positioning*. Paper presented at the Fifth International EGOV Conference 2006, Krakow, Poland.

Pieterson, W., & van Dijk, J. (2007). *Channel Choice Determinants; An exploration of the factors that determine the choice of a service channel in citizen initiated contacts*. Paper presented at the Proceedings of the 8th annual international conference on Digital government research: bridging disciplines & domains.

Pina, V., Torres, L., & Royo, S. (2007). Are ICTs Improving Transparency and Accountability in the EU Regional and Local Governments? An empirical study. *Public Administration*, *85*(2), 449–472. doi:10.1111/j.1467-9299.2007.00654.x

Piotrowski, S. J., & Borry, E. L. (2009). Governmental transparency and websites: The case of New Jersey municipalities. In Reddick, C. G. (Ed.), *Strategies for local e-government adoption and implementation: Comparative studies*. Hershey, PA: IGI Global.

Piotrowski, S. J., & Van Ryzin, G. G. (2007). Citizen Attitudes Toward Transparency in Local Government. *American Review of Public Administration*, *37*(3), 306–323. doi:10.1177/0275074006296777

Plouffe, C. R., Hulland, J. S., & Vanderbosch, M. (2002). Research report: Richness versus Parsimony in Modeling Technology Adoption Decisions –Understanding Merchant Adoption of a Smart Card-based Payment System. *Information Systems Research*, *13*(2), 208–222.

Polidano, C. (1999). *The New Public Management in Developing Countries* (Working Paper no. 13). Manchester M139GH, UK: University of Manchester, Institute for Development Policy and Management.

Pollard, D. (2006, September 3). *Social Networking: Still Not Meeting its Critical Promise*. Retrieved November 29, 2008, from http://blogs.salon.com/0002007/categories/businessInnovation/2006/08/14.html#a1612

Pollit, C., & Bouckaert, G. (2004). *Public management reform: a comparative analysis*. Oxford, UK: Oxford University Press.

Portable, field proven forensic system for the quick extraction and analysis of cell phones, Smartphones and PDA devices. (2009). Retrieved April 10, 2009 from http://www.cellebrite.com/

Pressman, R. (2009). *Software Engineering: A Practitioner's Approach* (7th ed.). New York: McGraw-Hill Higher Education.

Prins, J. E. (2001). *Designing e-government. On the crossroads of technological innovation and institutional change.* The Hague: Kluwer Law International.

Prins, J. E. J. (Ed.). (2001). *Designing e-Government: On the Crossroads of Technological Innovation and Institutional Change.* Hague, Netherlands: Kluwer Law International.

Programmabureau Overheidsloket 2000. (2000). *Een loket op het Internet.* Den Haag: Programmabureau Overheidsloket 2000.

Programme Management Maturity Model. (2009). *The Programme Management Web Site.* Retrieved April 29, 2009, from http://www.e-programme.com/

Project Management Institute Standard Committee (2004). *A guide to the Project Management Body of Knowledge.*

Public, A. in Waiting. (2007, July 31). *The Star Paper.* Retrieved February 20, 2008 from http://archives.thestar.com.my

Qazi, R. (2006). *Expanding the technology acceptance model (TAM), a consideration of personal computer technology use in public organizations of a developing country in South Asia, Pakistan.* D.Sc. dissertation, The George Washington University, United States – District of Columbia.

Quinn, A. C. (2003). Keeping the citizenry informed: Early congressional printing and 21st century information policy. *Government Information Quarterly, 20*(3), 281–293. doi:10.1016/S0740-624X(03)00055-8

Quinn, A. C., & Ramasubramanian, L. (2007). Information technologies and civic engagement: Perspectives from librarianship and planning. *Government Information Quarterly, 24*, 595–610. doi:10.1016/j.giq.2006.08.005

Quirk, B. (2000). *From Managing Change to Leading Transformation.* Paper presented at the E-Government Summit, December 2000, United Kingdom.

Radev, D. R., Libner, K., & Fan, W. (2002). Getting answers to natural language queries on the web. *Journal of the American Society for Information Science and Technology, 53*(5), 359–364. doi:10.1002/asi.10053

Ramayah, T., & Ignatius, J. (2005). Impact of perceived usefulness, perceived ease of use and perceived enjoyment on intention to shop online. [IJSM]. *ICFAI Journal of Management, 3*(3), 36–51.

Ramayah, T., & Jantan, M. (2003). Attitude And Intention To Use Web-Based Supply Chain Management (SCM) Among SME'S: Moderating Effect Of Self Efficacy. In *The Third International Conference on Electronic Commerce Engineering* (ICeCE2003), Hangzhou, China.

Ramayah, T., Jantan, M., Mohd Noor, M. N., & Koay, P. L. (2003). Receptiveness of Internet Banking by Malaysia Consumers: The Case of Penang. *Asian Academic of Management Journal, 8*(2), 1–29.

Ramayah, T., Siron, R., Dahlan, N., & Mohamad, O. (2002). Technology Usage Among Owners/Managers of SME's: The Role of Demographic and Motivational Variables. *The Proceedings of The 6th Annual Asian-Pacific Forum for Small Business on Small and Medium Enterprises Linkages,* Networking and Clustering, Kuala Lumpur: Malaysia.

Rask, M. (2003). The Problem of Citizens' Participation in Finnish Biotechnology Policy. *Science & Public Policy, 30*(6), 441–454. doi:10.3152/147154303781780236

Reddick, C. (2004). Empirical Models of E-Government Growth in Local Governments. *E-Service Journal, 3*(2), 59–84. doi:10.2979/ESJ.2004.3.2.59

Reddick, C. G. (2004). A two-stage model of e-government growth: Theories and empirical evidence for US cities. *Government Information Quarterly, 21*, 51–64. doi:10.1016/j.giq.2003.11.004

Reddick, C. G. (2005). Citizen interaction with e-government: From the streets to servers? *Government Information Quarterly, 22*, 38–57. doi:10.1016/j.giq.2004.10.003

Reddick, C. G. (2005a). Citizen-Initiated Contacts with Government Comparing Phones and Websites. *Journal of E-Government, 2*(1), 27–53. doi:10.1300/J399v02n01_03

Reddick, C. G. (2005b). Citizen Interaction with E-government: From the Streets to Servers. *Government Information Quarterly, 22*, 38–57. doi:10.1016/j.giq.2004.10.003

Reddick, C. G. (2005b). Citizen-initiated contacts with government: comparing phones and websites. *Journal of E-Government, 2*(1), 27–53. doi:10.1300/J399v02n01_03

Relyea, H. C. (2002). E-gov: introduction and overview. *Government Information Quarterly, 19*(1), 9–35. doi:10.1016/S0740-624X(01)00096-X

Relyea, H. C., & Halchin, L. E. (2003). Homeland security and information management. In Bogart, D. (Ed.), *The Bowker annual: Library and trade almanac 2003.* Medford, NJ: Information Today.

Reporton Cyber-stalking: A New Challenge for Law Enforcement and Industry. (1999). Retrieved March 28, 2009, from http://www.usdoj.gov/criminal/cybercrime/cyberstaling.htm

Reyes, A., O'Shea, K., Steele, J., Hansen, J. R., Jean, B. R., & Ralph, T. (2007). *Cyber Crime Investigations: Bridging the Gaps Between Security Professionals, Law Enforcement, and Prosecutors.* Rockland, MA: Syngress Publishing, Inc.

Rheingold, H. (1995). *The Virtual Community. Finding Connection in a Computerized World* (Surfing the Internet). London: Minerva. *RSS in Government.* (2008). Retrieved November 29, 2008, from http://www.rssgov.com/

Riemenschneider, C. K., Hardgrave, B. C., & Davis, F. D. (2002). Explaining Software Developer Acceptance of Methodologies: A comparison of Five Theoretical Models. *IEEE Transactions on Software Engineering, 28*(12), 1135–1145. doi:10.1109/TSE.2002.1158287

Ringeling, A. (2001). Rare klanten hoor, die klanten van de overheid. In H. P. M. van Duivenboden & A. M. B. Lips (Eds.), Klantgericht werken in de publieke sector. Utrecht, Nederland: Lemma.

Ritchie, H., & Blanck, P. (2003). The promise of the Internet for disability: A study of online services and website accessibility at centers for independent living. *Behavioral Sciences & the Law, 21*, 5–26. doi:10.1002/bsl.520

Roberts, N. (2004). Public deliberation in an age of direct citizen participation. *American Review of Public Administration, 34*, 315–353. doi:10.1177/0275074004269288

Rocheleau, B., & Wu, L. (2002). Public Versus Private Information Systems. Do they differ in important ways? A review and empirical test. *American Review of Public Administration, 32*(4), 349–397. doi:10.1177/027507402237866

Rodan, G. (1998). The internet and political control in Singapore. *Political Science Quarterly, 113*(1), 63–89. doi:10.2307/2657651

Rogers, E. (2003). *Diffusion of Innovation, Free press.* New York: Simon and Schuster.

Rogers, E. M. (1995). *Diffusion of innovations* (4th ed.). New York: The Free Press.

Rogers, E. M. (2003). *Diffusion of Innovation* (5th ed.). New York: Free Press.

Ronaghan, S. A. (2001). *Benchmarking E-Government: A Global Perspective.* New York: United Nations Division for Public Economics and Public Administration and American Society for Public Administration. Retrieved May 11, 2009, from http://www.itpolicy.gov.il/topics_egov/docs/benchmarking.pdf

Rose, M. (2004). Democrating information and communication by implementing e-government in Indonesian regional government. *The International Information & Library Review, 36*, 219–226. doi:10.1016/j.iilr.2003.11.002

Ross, K. (2007). Providing Thoughtful Feedback: Public Participation in the Regulation of Australia's First Genetically Modified Food Crop. *Science & Public Policy, 34*(3), 213–225. doi:10.3152/030234207X211500

Rotter, J. (1967). A new scale for the measurement of interpersonal trust. *Journal of Personality, 35*, 651–665. doi:10.1111/j.1467-6494.1967.tb01454.x

Rouibah, K. (2008). Social usage of instant messaging by individuals outside the workplace in Kuwait: A structural equation model. *Information Technology & People, 21*(1), 34–68. doi:10.1108/09593840810860324

Rousseau, D., Sitkin, S., Burt, R., & Comerer, C. (1998). Not so different after all: A Cross-discipline view of Trust. *Academy of Management Review, 23*(3), 393–404.

Roy, J. (2003). Introduction e-government. *Social Science Computer Review, 21*(1), 3–5. doi:10.1177/0894439302238966

Roy, R. (2006). E-service delivery and new governance capacities: 'Service Canada' as a case study. *International Journal of Services Technology and Management, 7*(3), 253–271.

Rule, J. B. (1973). *Private lives and public surveillance*. London: Allen Lane Publishers.

Rule, J., McAdam, D., Stearns, L., & Uglow, D. (1980). *The politics of privacy: Planning for personal data systems as powerful technologies*. New York: Elsevier.

Rummel, R. (1970). *Understanding factor analysis*. University of Hawaii. Retrieved March 14, 2009 from http://www.hawaii.edu/powerkills/UFA.HTM

Rumpf, P. B. (1980). *Town Hall Politics: Heidelberg's Policy Makers 1967 - 77*. Unpublished, University of Melbourne, Melbourne.

Rust, R. T., & Oliver, R. L. (1994). Service quality: Insights and managerial implications from the frontier. In Rust, R. T., & Oliver, R. L. (Eds.), *Service quality: New directions in theory and practice* (pp. 1–19). London: Sage.

Ruyter, K., Bloemer, J., & Peeters, P. (1997). Merging service quality and service satisfaction: An empirical test of an integrative model. *Journal of Economic Psychology, 18*, 387–406. doi:10.1016/S0167-4870(97)00014-7

Sæbø, Ø., Rose, J., & Flak, L. S. (2008). The shape of e-participation: Characterizing an emerging research area. *Government Information Quarterly, 25*, 400–428. doi:10.1016/j.giq.2007.04.007

Sahu, G. P., & Gupta, M. P. (2007). User's acceptance of e-government: A study of Indian Central Excise. *International Journal of Electronic Government Research, 3*(3), 1–21.

Saich, T. (2004). *Government and Politics of China*. New York: Palgrave Macmillan.

Salter, J. (1995). Towards a better Disaster Management Methodology. *Australian Journal of Emergency Management, 10*(4), 8–16.

Sanderson, I. (2001). Performance Management, Evaluation and Learning in 'Modern' Local Government. *Public Administration, 79*(2), 297–313. doi:10.1111/1467-9299.00257

Saxby, S. (2006). eGovernment is dead: Long live transformation. *Computer Law & Security Report, 22*, 1–2. doi:10.1016/j.clsr.2005.12.002

Saxena, K. B. C. (2005). Towards excellence in e-governance. *International Journal of Public Sector Management, 18*(6), 498–513. doi:10.1108/09513550510616733

Schaupp, L. C., & Carter, L. (2008) The impact of trust, risk and optimism bias on E-file adoption. *Information Systems Frontiers*. Retrieved from http://www.springerlink.com/content/e5516xp043116327/?p=a9291f0187884793951d5ae39cad254c&pi=6

Schedler, K., & Summermatter, L. (2007). Customer orientation in electronic government: Motives and effects. *Government Information Quarterly, 24*, 291–311. doi:10.1016/j.giq.2006.05.005

Scheepers, A., & Kommers, C. (1994). De overheid als dienstverlenende instelling. In Zuurmond, A., Frissen, P. H. A., Huigen, J., Snellen, I. T. M., & Tops, P. W. (Eds.), *Informatisering in het openbaar bestuur. Den Haag, Nederland: Vuga.*

Schellong, A. (2008). *Citizen Relationship Management: A Study of CRM in Government.* Berlin: Peter Lang Publishing Group.

Schellong, A., & Mans, D. (2004). *Citizens preferences towards one-stop government.* Paper presented at the The 2004 annual national conference on Digital Government research.

Schubert, P., & Hausler, U. (2001). E-government meets e-business: a portal site for startup companies in Switzerland. In *Proceedings of the 34th Hawaii International Conference on System Sciences,* Big Island, HI.

Schuler, D. (1996). *New Community Networks. Wired for Change.* New York: ACM Press.

Schuppan, T. (2009). E-Government in developing countries: Experiences from sub-Saharan Africa. *Government Information Quarterly, 26*, 118–127. doi:10.1016/j.giq.2008.01.006

Scott, J. K. (2006). E the people: Do U.S. municipal government web sites support public involvement? *Public Administration Review, 66*(3), 341–353. doi:10.1111/j.1540-6210.2006.00593.x

Seifert, J. W., & Petersen, R. E. (2002). The promise of all things E? Expectations and challenges of emergent electronic government. *Perspectives on Global Development and Technology, 1*(2), 193–212. doi:10.1163/156915002100419808

Seifert, J., & Chung, J. (2009). Using E-government to reinforce government citizen relationships: comparing government reform in the United States and China. *Social Science Computer Review, 27*(1), 3–23. doi:10.1177/0894439308316404

Sekaran, U. (2000). *Research Methods for Business.* New York: John Wiley & Sons, Inc.

Sekaran, U. (2003). *Research methods for business. A skill-building approach* (4th ed.). New York: John Wiley and Sons, Inc.

Sen, A. (1982). *Choice, Welfare, and Measurement.* Oxford, UK: Basil Blackwell.

Sen, A. (1999). *Development as Freedom.* Oxford, UK: Oxford University Press.

Shackleton, P. (2002, December 4-6). *The Evolution of Local Government Electronic Services in Victoria.* Paper presented at the Australasian Conference on Information Systems, Melbourne, Australia.

Shackleton, P. (2006a). *Town Hall eCommerce: A Model of Web-Based Service Delivery.* Melbourne: Unpublished Unpublished, Monash University.

Shackleton, P. (2006b). *Your Dreaming: The next stage towards joined up government in Australia, Working for e-Business (We-B).* Melbourne, Australia: School of Information Systems, Victoria Universtiy.

Shackleton, P. (2007). tGovernment: eChallenges for Australian Local Government, Working for e-Business (We-B). Melbourne, Australia: School of Information Systems, Victoria University.

Shackleton, P., Fisher, J., & Dawson, L. (2003). *E-Government Services - One Local Government's Approach.* Paper presented at the Information Systems Development, Melbourne, Australia.

Shackleton, P., Fisher, J., & Dawson, L. (2004). *Evolution of Local Government E-Services: the applicability of e-Business maturity models.* Paper presented at the HICCS'2004.

Shackleton, P., Fisher, J., & Dawson, L. (2005). *From Dog Licences to Democracy: Local Government Approaches to E-Service Delivery in Australia.* Paper presented at the Thirteenth European Conference on Information Systems, Regensberg, Germany.

Shah, D. V., Kwak, N., & Holbert, R. L. (2001). Connecting and disconnecting with civic life: Patterns of internet use and the production of social capital. *Political Communication, 18*(2), 141–162. doi:10.1080/105846001750322952

Shenhar, A. J., Levy, O., & Dvir, D. (1997). Mapping the dimensions of project success. *Project Management Journal, 28*(2), 5–13.

Shim, D. C., & Eom, T. H. (2008). E-Government and Anti-Corruption: Empirical Analysis of International Data. *International Journal of Public Administration, 31*(1), 298–316. doi:10.1080/01900690701590553

Shirky, C. (2003). *People on page: YASNS... Corante's Many-to-Many.* Retrieved July 21, 2007, from http://many.corante.com/archives/2003/05/12/people_on_page_yasns.php

Shoji, M. (2007). *Regional Social Networking Services (SNS) – The Current Situation and the Future Potential.* Center for Global Communications (GLOCOM), International University of Japan. February/March 2007. Retrieved May 1, 2009, from http://www.glocom.ac.jp/e/publications/Shoji_1.pdf

Shukla, A., & Srinivasan, R. (2005). *Lokvani: A Case of Public-Private Partnership in e-Governance.* Retrieved on May 9th, 2009, from http://www.sitapur.nic.in/lokvani/rojgar/lokvani.pdf

Siau, K., & Long, Y. (2005). Synthesizing e-government stage models – a meta Synthesis based on meta-ethnography approach. *Journal of Industrial Management & Data Systems, 105*(4), 443–458. doi:10.1108/02635570510592352

Siau, K., & Long, Y. (2006). Using social development lenses to understand E-government development. *Journal of Global Information Management, 14*(1), 47–62.

Simon, D. (1992). *Big brother.* East Roseville, NSW: Simon & Schuster Australia.

Simon, H. (1976). *Administrative Behavior.* New York: Free Press.

Simpson, D. M. (2001). Community Emergency Response Training (CERTs), A recent History and Review. *Natural Hazards Review, 2*(2), 54–63. doi:10.1061/(ASCE)1527-6988(2001)2:2(54)

Sindane, A. M. (2004). Public administration versus public management: parallels, divergences, convergences and who benefits? *International Review of Administrative Sciences, 70*(4), 665–672. doi:10.1177/0020852304048454

Singh, A. K., & Sahu, R. (2008). Integrating Internet, telephones, and call centers for delivering better quality e-governance to all citizens. *Government Information Quarterly, 25*, 477–490. doi:10.1016/j.giq.2007.01.001

Singh, J. (1990). Managerial culture and work related values in India. *Organization Studies, 11*, 75–101. doi:10.1177/017084069001100106

Six, P., Raab, C., & Bellamy, C. (2005). Joined-up Government and Privacy in the UK part I: Managing tensions between data protection and social policy. *Public Administration, 83*(1), 111–133. doi:10.1111/j.0033-3298.2005.00440.x

Slyke, C. V., Belanger, F., & Comunale, C. L. (2004). Factors influencing the adoption of web-based shopping: The impact of trust. *The Data Base for Advances in Information Systems, 35*(2), 32–49.

Smith, B., Fraser, B. T., & McClure, C. R. (2000). Federal information policy and access to We-based information. *Journal of Academic Librarianship, 26*, 274–281. doi:10.1016/S0099-1333(00)00128-2

Smith, C. (2001). *Invasion of your Privacy has Just Begun.* Retrieved March 15, 2009 from http://archive.newsmax.com/archives/articles/2001/3/5/220402.shtml

Smith, T. L. (1995). The resource center: Finding solutions for illiteracy. *HRFocus, 72*(2), 7.

Sneiders, E. (2002). Automated question answering using question templates that cover the conceptual model of the database. In *Proceedings of the 6th International Conference on Applications of Natural Language to Information Systems-Revised Papers* (pp. 235–239). .

Snellen, I. (2002). Electronic governance: implications for citizens, politicians and public servants. *International Review of Administrative Sciences, 68*(2), 183–198. doi:10.1177/0020852302682002

SOCITM, & I&DeA. (2002). *Local E-Government Now: A Worldwide View.* Northampton, UK: Improvement & Development Agency, Society of Information Technology Management.

Sohaimi, M. S. (2003). *The Multimedia Super Corridor (MSC) and E-government Initiatives in Malaysia. School of Global Information and Telecommunication Studies (GITS).* Waseda University.

Sombrero, G., Andersen, V., Andersen, H. H., de Gemmis, M., & Lops, P. (2008). User profiling and virtual agents: a case study on e-commerce services. *Univers. Access Inf. Soc., 7*(3), 179-194. Retrieved from http://dx.doi.org/10.1007/s10209-008-0116-1

Sonja, G. K., & Ewald, A. K. (2003). Empirical research in on-line trust: a review and critical assessment. *International Journal of Human-Computer Studies.*

Srivastava, S., & Teo, T. (2007). E-Government Payoffs: Evidence from Cross-Country Data. *Journal of Global Information Management, 15*(4), 20–40.

State Services Commission. (2006). *E-government: A vision for New Zealanders.* New Zealand. Retrieved on September 20, 2008, from http://www.e.govt.nz/about-egovt/vision.html

Sternstein, A. (2006, November 20). Web 2.0 for feds. *FederalComputerWeek.* Retrieved May 1, 2009, from http://www.fcw.com/print/12_42/news/96857-1.html

Steyaert, J. C. (2004). Measuring the performance of electronic government services. *Information & Management, 41*, 369–375. doi:10.1016/S0378-7206(03)00025-9

Stonier, T. (1983). *The Wealth of Information. A profile of the post-industrial economy.* London: Methuen.

Straub, D. (1989). Validating instruments in MIS research. *Management Information Systems Quarterly, 13*(2), 147–170. doi:10.2307/248922

Strauss, A., & Corbin, J. (1990). *Basics of Qualitative Research: Grounded Theory, Procedures, and Techniques.* Newbury Park, CA: Sage.

Streib, G., & Navarro, I. (2006). Citizen demand for interactive e-government: The case of Georgia consumer services. *American Review of Public Administration, 36*, 288–300. doi:10.1177/0275074005283371

Strickland, J. (2009) *How Web 3.0 Will Work.* HowStuffWorks. Retrieved June 19, 2009, from http://computer.howstuffworks.com/web-30.htm

Suchanek, F. M., Vojnovic, M., & Gunawardena, D. (2008). Social tags: meaning and suggestions. In *Proceeding of the 17th ACM Conference on information and Knowledge Mining* (Napa Valley, California, USA, October 26 - 30, 2008) (pp. 223-232). New York: ACM.

Swartz, N. (2004). E-government around the world. *Information Management Journal, 38*(1), 12–15.

Symonds, M. (2000). The nex revolution: a survey of government and the Internet. *The Economist,* (355), 1-34.

Tapscott, D., & Williams, A. D. (2007). *Wikinomics – How Mass Collaboration Changes Everything.* New York: Portfolio.

Tat-Kei Ho, A. (2002). Reinventing Local Governments and the E-Government Initiative. *Public Administration Review, 62*(4), 434–443. doi:10.1111/0033-3352.00197

Tayib, M., Coombs, H. G., & Ameen, J. R. M. (1999). Financial reporting by Malaysian local authorities. A study of the needs and requirements of the users of local authority financial accounts. *International Journal of Public Sector Management, 12*(2), 103–120. doi:10.1108/09513559910263453

Taylor, J. A., & Lips, A. M. B. (2008). The citizen in the information polity. *Information Polity, 13*, 139–152.

Taylor, M. C., & Saarinen, E. (1994). *Imagologies*. New York, NY: Routledge.

Taylor, R., Caeti, T., Loper, D., Fritsch, E., & Liederbach, J. (2006). *Digital crime and digital terrorism*. Upper Saddle River, NJ: Prentice Hall.

Taylor, S., & Todd, P. (1995). Assessing IT usage: The role of prior experience. *Management Information Systems Quarterly*, *19*(4), 561–571. doi:10.2307/249633

Tee, L. D. (2007, March 27). Digital Government Portal. *The Star Paper*, 24

Teerling, M. L. (2007). *Determining the Cross-Channel Effects of Informational Web Sites (doctoral dissertation Rijksuniversiteit Groningen)*. Ridderkerk, Nederland: Labyrinth Publications.

Tetlock, P., Peterson, R., & Lerner, J. (1996). Revising the Value Pluralism Model: Incorporating Social Content and Context Postulates. In C. Seligman, J. Olson, & M. Zanna (Eds.), *The Psychology of Values: The Ontario Symposium Volume 8*. Mahwah, NJ: Lawrence Erlbaum Associates, Publishers.

The Constitution of the United States of America. (n.d.). Retrieved March 20, 2009 from http://www.law.cornell.edu/constitution

The Gartner Group. (2000). *Key Issues in E-Government Strategy and Management. Research Notes, Key Issues*. Stamford, CT: The Gartner Group.

The Standish Group. (2001). Extreme Chaos. *The Standish Group*. Retrieved April 29, 2009, from http://www.standishgroup.com/sample_research

The World Bank. (2004). *Building Blocks of Egovernment: Lessons from Developing Countries*. Retrieved on February 24, 2009, from http://www1.worldbank.org/prem/PREMNotes/premnote 91.pdf

Thomas, J. C., & Streib, G. (2003). The new face of government: citizen-initiated contacts in the era of e-government. *Journal of Public Administration: Research and Theory*, *13*(1), 83–102. doi:10.1093/jpart/mug010

Thomas, J. C., & Streib, G. (2003). The new face of government: Citizen-initiated contacts in the era of e-government. *Journal of Public Administration: Research and Theory*, *13*(1), 83–102. doi:10.1093/jpart/mug010

Thomas, J. C., & Streib, G. (2005). E-democracy, e-commerce and e-research. Examining the Electronic Ties between Citizens and Governments. *Administration & Society*, *37*(3), 259–280. doi:10.1177/0095399704273212

Thompson, D. V., Rust, R. T., & Rhoda, J. (2005). The business value of e-government for small firms. *International Journal of Service Industry Management*, *16*(4), 385–407. doi:10.1108/09564230510614022

Thorson, S., Chung, J., & Ma, L. (2005). E-Government in China: Bringing economic development through administrative reform. *Government Information Quarterly*, *22*(1), 20–37. doi:10.1016/j.giq.2004.10.001

Thurow, L. C. (1997). *The Future of Capitalism*. New York: Penguin Books USA.

Titah, R., & Barki, H. (2006). E-Government adoption and acceptance: a literature review. *International Journal of Electronic Government Research*, *2*(3), 23–57.

Tolbert, C. J., & Mossberger, K. (2006). The effects of e-government on trust and confidence in government. *Public Administration Review*, *66*(3), 354–369. doi:10.1111/j.1540-6210.2006.00594.x

Tolbert, C., & McNeal, R. (2003). Unraveling the effects of the Internet on political participation. *Political Research Quarterly*, *56*(2), 175–185.

Toregas, C. (2001). The politics of e-gov: The upcoming struggle for redefining civic engagement. *National Civic Review*, *90*(3), 235–240. doi:10.1002/ncr.90304

Torkzadeh, G., & Dhillon, G. (2002). Measuring factors that influence the success of Internet commerce. *Information Systems Research*, *13*(2), 187–204. doi:10.1287/isre.13.2.187.87

Torrejón, A. M. (2004). *Ciudades Digitales Iberoamericanas. Análisis de las web de las principales capitales*. Available at: http://www.fundacionorange.es/areas/28_observatorio/pdfs/8_SPC.pdf

Torres, L., Pina, V., & Acerete, B. (2006). E-governance developments in European Union cities: Reshaping Government's relationship with citizens. *Governance, 19*(2), 277–302. doi:10.1111/j.1468-0491.2006.00315.x

Toyama, S. (2007) *Local area SNS and community building in Japan.* Communities and Action: Prato CIRN Conference 2007. Retrieved May 1, 2009, from http://www.ccnr.net/prato2007/archive/toyama%20135.pdf

Transformational Government Enabled by Technology Annual Report. (2006). *HM Government.* Retrieved August 10, 2008, from http://www.cio.gov.uk/documents/annual_report2006/trans_gov2006.pdf

Transparencia por Colombia. (2007). *Índice de transparencia municipal – itm –2005 2006.* Retrieved April, 15, 2009, http://www.transparenciacolombia.org.co/Portals/0/descargas/itm/ITM_Esquema.pdf

Transparency International. (2008). *Global Corruption Report 2008. Corruption in the Water Sector.* Cambridge, United Kingdom: University Press.

Transparency International. Spain. (2008). *Metodología utilizada en el índice de transparencia de los ayuntamientos.* Retrieved April, 20, 2009, http://www.transparencia.org.es/INDICE%20TRANSPARENCIA%20AYUNTAMIENTOS/METODOLOGÍA%20UTLIZADA%20EN%20LA%20VALORACIÓN%20DEL%20ITA.pdf

Treasury Board Secretariat. (2001, August 10). *Canada's Report on Portals.* Government of Canada.

Trevino, L. K., Webster, J., & Stein, E. W. (2000). Making Connections: Complementary Influences on Communication Media Choices, Attitudes, and Use. *Organization Science, 11*(2), 163–182. doi:10.1287/orsc.11.2.163.12510

Trojanowicz, R., Kappeler, V. E., Gaines, L. K., Bucqueroux, B., & Sluder, R. (1998). *Community Policing: A Contemporary Perspective.* Cincinnati, OH: Anderson Publishing.

Tsai, N., Choi, B., & Perry, M. (2009). Improving the process of e-government initiative: An in-depth case study of web-based GIS implementation. *Government Information Quarterly, 26,* 368–376. doi:10.1016/j.giq.2008.11.007

U.S. Department of Justice (Fraud Section-Criminal Division). (2000a). *Internet fraud.* Retrieved April 19, 2009, from http://www.internet-fraud.usdoj.gov

U.S. Department of Justice (USDOJ), Office of Community Oriented Policing Services. (n.d.). Retrieved on 15th September, 2008, from http://www.cops.usdoj.gov/Default.asp?Item=36

U.S. Department of Justice. (2000b). *Office of Justice Programs annual report to Congress Fiscal Year 1999.* Washington, DC: U.S. Department of Justice.

U.S. Office of Management and Budget. (2002). *E-government strategy: Simplified delivery of services to citizens.* Washington, DC: U.S. Government Printing Office.

Udo, G. (2001). Privacy and security concerns as major barriers for e-commerce: a survey study. *Information Management & Computer Security, 9*(4), 165–174. doi:10.1108/EUM0000000005808

UK Cabinet Office. (2000). e-government, a strategic framework for public services in the information age. *UK Cabinet Office.* Retrieved April 29, 2009, from http://archive.cabinetoffice.gov.uk/e-envoy/resources-pdfs/$file/Strategy.pdf

UK Cabinet Office. (2002). Office of the e-Envoy, e-government Interoperability Framework (e-GIF). Part two: Technical Policies and Specifications, Office of the e-Envoy. *UK Cabinet Office.* Retrieved April 29, 2009, from http://www.govtalk.gov.uk/ documents/e-GIF4Pt2_2002-04-25.pdf

Ulrich, P., & Chacko, J. G. (2005). Overview of ICT policies and e-strategies: An assessment on the role of governments. *Information Technology for Development, 11*(2), 195–197. doi:10.1002/itdj.20011

Umashankar, C. (2005). Who could be the possible Champions? In *Planning e-governance in India.* Retrieved on May 9th 2009 from http://egovindia.wordpress.com/plan-egov/

UN. (2003). *Human Development Report 2003: Millennium Development Goals: A compact among nations to end human poverty. The United Nations Development Group.* New York: Oxford University Press.

UN. (2006). Global E-government Readiness Report 2005. New York: UN.

UN. (2009). Retrieved on July 29, 2009 from http://www.un.org/esa/analysis/devplan/profile/criteria.html

United Nations Development Program (UNDP). (n.d.). *Human Development Reports.* Retrieved on September 15th 2008 from, http://hdr.undp.org/reports/global/2005/.

United Nations. (2002). *Benchmarking E-government: A Global Perspective - Assessing the Progress of the UN Member States.* New York: United Nations Division for Public Economics and Public Administration.

United Nations. (2002). *E-government at the crossroads. World Public Sector Report 2003.* New York: United Nations.

United Nations. (2003). *World Public Sector Report 2003. E-Government at the Crossroads.* New York: United Nations.

United Nations. (2008). *UN E-Government Survey – From e-government to Connected Government.* Retrieved April 29, 2009, from http://unpan1.un.org/intradoc/ groups/public/documents/UN/UNPAN028607.pdf

United Nations. (2008). *UN E-government survey 2008: From e-government to connected governance. Division for Public Administration and Development Management.* New York: United Nations.

United Nations. (2008). *UN e-government survey 2008: From e-government to connected governance.* Retrieved April 25, 2008, from http://unpan1.un.org/intradoc/groups/public/documents/UN/UNPAN028607.pdf van Deursen, A., van Dijk, J., & Ebbers, W. (2006). Why e-government usage lags behind: Explaining the gap between potential and actual usage of electronic public services in the Netherlands. In M. A. Wimmer et al. (Eds.), *EGOV 2006* (pp. 269-280).

United Nations. (2008). *United Nations e-government survey 2008: From e-government to connected governance. UN Publication ST/ESA/PAD/SER.E/112.* New York: United Nations.

United Nations. (2008). *United Nations e-government survey 2008: From e-government to connected governance.* Retrieved September 29, 2008, from http://unpan1.un.org/intradoc/groups/public/documents/UN/UNPAN028607.pdf van Dijk, J. A. G. M., Peters, O., & Ebbers, W. (2008). Explaining the acceptance and use of government Internet services: A multivariate analysis of 2006 survey data in the Netherlands. *Government Information Quarterly, 25,* 379-399.

US Federal Government. (2002). *E-Government Strategy: Simplified Delivery of Services to Citizens.* Office of Management and Budget, US Federal Government. Retrieved April 29, 2009, from http://www.firstgov.gov/Topics/ Includes/Reference/egov_strategy.pdf

van den Haak, M. J., de Jong, M. D. T., & Schellens, P. J. (2009). Evaluating municipal websites: A methodological comparison of think-aloud variants. *Government Information Quarterly, 26,* 193–202. doi:10.1016/j.giq.2007.11.003

Van Der Westhuizen, D., & Fitzgerald, E. P. (2005). Defining and measuring project success. In *the Proceedings of the European Conference on IS Management, Leadership and Governance,* 07-08 Jul 2005, Reading, United Kingdom.

van Deursen, A. J. A. M., & van Dijk, J. A. G. M. (2009). Improving digital skills for the use of online public information and services. *Government Information Quarterly*, *26*, 333–340. doi:10.1016/j.giq.2008.11.002

van Deursen, A., & Pieterson, W. (2006). *The Internet as a service channel in the Public Sector.* Paper presented at the ICA Conference, Dresden, Germany.

van Deursen, A., van Dijk, J., & Ebbers, W. (2006). Why E-Government usage lags behind: explaining the gap between potential and actual usage of electronic public services in the Netherlands. *Lecture Notes in Computer Science*, *4084*, 269–280. doi:10.1007/11823100_24

van Dijk, J. (1999). *The network society: social aspects of new media*. London: Sage.

van Dijk, J. (2005). *The deepening divide: inequality in the information Society*. London: Sage.

van Dijk, J. A. G. M. (2005). The Network Society, Social Aspects of New Media (2nd ed.). London: Thousand Oaks.

van Dijk, J. A. G. M., Peters, O., & Ebbers, W. (2007). Explaining the acceptance and use of government Internet services: A Multivariate analysis of 2006 survey data in the Netherlands. *Government Information Quarterly*, *24*, 148–164.

Van Dijk, J. A. G. M., Peters, O., & Ebbers, W. (2008). Explaining the acceptance and use of government internet services: A multivariate analysis of 2006 survey data in the Netherlands. *Government Information Quarterly*, *25*(3), 379–399. doi:10.1016/j.giq.2007.09.006

van Dijk, J., & van Deursen, A. (2006). Van Aanbod naar Vraag, Tijd voor een Perspectiefwisseling. Enschede, Nederland: Universiteit Twente.

van Dijk, J., Peters, O., & Ebbers, W. (2008). Explaining the acceptance and use of government internet services: a multivariate analysis of 2006 survey data in the Netherlands. *Government Information Quarterly*, *25*(3), 379–399. doi:10.1016/j.giq.2007.09.006

van Duivenboden, H. P. M. (2002). Responsive E-Government Services: Citizen participation in public administration. The impact of Citizen oriented public services on government and citizen. Utrecht, Nederland: Cap Gemini Ernst & Young.

Van Iwaarden, J., Van der Wiele, T., Ball, L., & Millen, R. (2003). Applying SERVQUAL to Web sites: an exploratory study. *International Journal of Quality & Reliability Management*, *20*(8), 919–935. doi:10.1108/02656710310493634

Van Loon, J. (2002). *Risk and Technological Culture: Towards A Sociology Of Virulence*. London: Routledge. doi:10.4324/9780203466384

VandenBos, G., Knapp, S., & Doe, J. (2001). Role of reference elements in the selection of resources by psychology undergraduates. [from http://jbr.org/articles.html]. *Journal of Bibliographic Research*, *5*, 117–123. Retrieved October 13, 2001.

Vargas, J. A. (2008). Politics is no longer local: It's viral. *Washington Post* (December 28, 2008), B01.

Vassilakis, C., Laskaridis, G., Lepouras, G., Rouvas, S., & Georgiadis, P. (2003). A framework for managing the lifecycle of transactional e-government services. *Journal of Telematics and Informatics*, *20*, 315–329. doi:10.1016/S0736-5853(03)00011-X

Venkatesh, V., & Davis, F. D. (2000). A Theoretical Extension of the Technology Acceptance Model (Four Longitudinal Field Studies). *Management Science*, *46*(2), 186–204. doi:10.1287/mnsc.46.2.186.11926

Venkatesh, V., & Morris, M. G. (2000). Why Don't Men Ever Stop To Ask For Direction? Gender, Social Influence, and Their Role in Technology Acceptance and Usage Behaviour. *Management Information Systems Quarterly*, *24*(1), 115–139. doi:10.2307/3250981

Venkatesh, V., Morris, M. G., & David, G. B. (2003). User acceptance of information technology: toward a unified view. *Journal of MIS Quarterly*, *27*(3), 425–478.

Venkatesh, V., Morris, M. G., Davis, G. B., & Davis, F. D. (2003). User Acceptance of Infroamtion Technology: Toward A Unified View. *Management Information Systems Quarterly, 27*(3), 425–478.

Venkatraman, V. (1994). IT-enabled business transformation: From automation to business scope redefinition. *Sloan Management Review, 35*(2), 73–87.

Verdegem, P., & Hauttekeete, L. (2008). The user at the centre of the development of one-stop government. [IJEG]. *International Journal of Electronic Governance, 1*(3), 28–274. doi:10.1504/IJEG.2008.020449

Verdegem, P., & Verleye, G. (2009). User-centered e-government in practice: a comprehensive model for measuring user satisfaction. *Government Information Quarterly, 26*(3), 487–497. doi:10.1016/j.giq.2009.03.005

Verma, K., & Sheth, A. (2007). Semantically Annotating a Web Service. *IEEE Internet Computing, 11*(2), 83–85. doi:10.1109/MIC.2007.48

Victor, G. J., Panikar, A., & Kanhere, V. K. (2007). E-government Projects–Importance of Post Completion Audits. In the *5th International Conference of e-government (ICEG, 2007)*. Retrieved April 26, 2009, from http://www.iceg.net/2007/books/1/20_308.pdf

Victorian Grants Commission. (2008). *Victorian Grants Commission Annual Report 2007/8*. Melbourne, Victoria: State Government of Victoria.

Vidrio Barón, S. B. (2009). Human-computer interaction: National culture and electronic government website usability. In Chabra, S., & Kumar, M. (Eds.), *Integrating e-business models for government solutions*. Hershey, PA: IGI Global.

Viitaniemi, V.V. (2008). Olemme aivan uudenlaisen verkkomaailman kynnyksellä. [We are on the threshold of a novel networked world]. *Kauppalehti* 11.2.2008, Debatti, 12.

Visser, P. R., Beer, M. D., Bench-Capon, T. J., Diaz, B. M., & Shave, M. J. (1999). Resolving Ontological Heterogeneity in the KRAFT Project. In T. J. Bench-Capon, G. Soda & A. M. Tjoa (Eds.), *Proceedings of the 10th international Conference on Database and Expert Systems Applications* (August 30 - September 03, 1999) (LNCS 1677, pp. 668-677). London: Springer-Verlag.

Wagenaar, R., Matthijsse, R., de Bruijn, H., van der Voort, H., & van Wendel de Joode, R. (2006). Implementation of shared service centers in public administration: Dilemmas and trade-offs. In Bekkers, V., van Duivenboden, H., & Thaens, M. (Eds.), *Information and communication technology and public innovation: Assessing the ICT-driven modernization of public administration* (pp. 141–158). Amsterdam: IOS Press.

Wagner, D. G. (1984). *The Growth of Sociological Theories*. Beverly Hills, CA: Sage.

Wagner, D., Day, R., James, T., Kozma, R., Miller, J., & Unwin, T. (2005). *Monitoring and Evaluation of ICT in Education Projects*. Washington, DC: The World Bank / The International Bank for Reconstruction and Development.

Walker, R. H., & Johnson, L. W. (2006). Why consumers use and do not use technology-enabled services. *Journal of Services Marketing, 20*(2), 125–135. doi:10.1108/08876040610657057

Wall, D. (1997). Policing the virtual community: The Internet, cyberspace and cybercrime. In Francis, P., Davies, P., & Jupp, V. (Eds.), *Policing futures: The police, law enforcement and the twenty-first century* (pp. 208–236). New York: St. Martin's.

Waller, P., Livesey, P., & Edin, K. (2001). E-government in the service of democracy. *ICA Information, 74*(5).

Wan, A. H. (2000). Opportunities to enhance a commercial web site. *Information & Management, 38*(1), 15–21. doi:10.1016/S0378-7206(00)00048-3

Wang, J., & Lochovsky, F. H. (2003). Data Extraction and Label Assignment for Web Databases. *WWW Conference, 2003.*

Wang, L., Bretschneider, S., & Gant, J. (2005). Evaluating web-based e-government services with a citizen-centric approach. In *Proceedings of the 38th Hawaii International Conference on System Sciences*.

Wang, Y. S. (2002). The adoption of electronic tax filing system: an empirical study. *Government Information Quarterly, 20*, 333–352. doi:10.1016/j.giq.2003.08.005

Wang, Y. S., Wang, Y. M., Lin, H. H., & Tang, T. I. (2003). Determinants of user acceptance of Internet banking: An empirical study. *International Journal of Service Industry Management, 14*(5), 501–519. doi:10.1108/09564230310500192

Wang, Y.-S., & Liao, Y.-W. (2008). Assessing eGovernment systems success: A validation of the DeLone and McLean model of information systems success. *Government Information Quarterly, 25*(4), 717–733. doi:10.1016/j.giq.2007.06.002

Ward, M. (1996). The effect of the Internet on political institutions. *Industrial and Corporate Change, 5*(4), 1127–1142.

Warkentin, M., Gefen, D., Pavlou, P. A., & Rose, G. M. (2002). Encouraging citizen adoption of e-government by building trust. *Electronic Markets, 12*(3), 157–162. Retrieved from http://www.electronicmarkets.org. doi:10.1080/101967802320245929

Warkentin, M., Green, D., Pavlou, P. A., & Rose, G. M. (2002). Encouraging Citizen Adoption of e-Government by Building Trust. *Electronic Markets, 12*(3), 157–162. doi:10.1080/101967802320245929

Warner, M., & Hefetz, A. (2002). Applying Market Solutions to Public Services: an assessment of efficiency, equity and voice. *Urban Affairs Review, 38*(1), 70–89. doi:10.1177/107808702401097808

Wateridge, J. (1998). How can IT/IS projects be measured for success? *International Journal of Project Management, 16*(1), 59–63. doi:10.1016/S0263-7863(97)00022-7

Watson, R., & Mundy, B. (2001). A strategic perspective of electronic democracy. *Communications of the ACM*, 44.

Weerakkody, V., Jones, S., & Olsen, E. (2007). E-government: A comparison of strategies in local authorities in the UK and Norway. *International Journal of Electronic Business, 5*(2), 141–159. doi:10.1504/IJEB.2007.012970

Weinel, M. (2007). Primary Source Knowledge and Technical Decision-Making: Mbeki and the AZT debate. *Studies in History and Philosophy of Science, 38*, 748–760. doi:10.1016/j.shpsa.2007.09.010

Weiss, T. R. (2008, June 17). Web 2.0 and City Hall: What's a local government to do? *Computerworld*. Retrieved May 1, 2009, from http://www.computerworld.com/action/article.do?command=viewArticleBasic&articleId=9099038

Welch, E. W., & Hinnant, C. C. (2002). Internet Use, Transparency, and Interactivity Effects on Trust in Government. In *Proceedings of the 36th Hawaii International Conference on System Sciences–2003*, Hawaii, USA.

Welch, E. W., Hinnant, C. C., & Moon, M. J. (2005). Linking citizen satisfaction with e-government and trust in government. *Journal of Public Administration: Research and Theory, 15*(3), 371–391. doi:10.1093/jopart/mui021

Welch, E. W., Hinnant, C. C., & Moon, M. J. (2005). Linking citizen satisfaction with e-government and trust in government. *Journal of Public Administration: Research and Theory, 15*(1), 1–21.

Wellman, B. (1997). An electronic group is virtually a social network. In Kiesler, S. (Ed.), *Cultures of the Internet*. Mahwah: Lawrence Erlbaum.

Welp, Y. (2008). América Latina en la era del gobierno electrónico. Análisis de la introducción de nuevas tecnologías para la mejora de la democracia y el gobierno. *Revista CLAD Reforma y Democracia, 41*, 42–57.

Wescott, C. (2001). E-Government in the Asia-Pacific Region. *Asian Journal of Political Science, 9*(2), 1–24. doi:10.1080/02185370108434189

West, D. (2001). E-government and the transformation of service delivery and citizen attitudes. *Public Administration Review, 64*(1), 15–27. doi:10.1111/j.1540-6210.2004.00343.x

West, D. (2003). *State and federal e-government in the United States.* Retrieved March 2, 2004, from http://www.InsidePolitics.org/DwestPubs.html

West, D. M. (2005). *Digital Government: Technology and Public Sector Performance.* Princeton, NJ: Princeton University Press.

West, D. M. (2008a). *Improving technology utilization in electronic government around the world, 2008.* Retrieved April 20, 2009, from http://www.brookings.edu/~/media/Files/rc/reports/2008/0817_egovernment_west/0817_egovernment_west.pdf

West, D. M. (2008b). *State and Federal Electronic Government in the United States, 2008.* Retrieved April 20, 2009, from http://www.brookings.edu/~/media/Files/rc/reports/2008/0826_egovernment_west/0826_egovernment_west.pdf

Westen, T. (2000). E-democracy: ready or not, here it comes. *National Civic Review, 89*(3), 217–227. doi:10.1002/ncr.89304

Westin, A. F., & Baker, M. A. (1972). *Databanks in a free society.* New York: Quadrangle Books.

Wetzker, R., Alpcan, T., Bauckhage, C., Umbrath, W., & Albayrak, S. (2007). An unsupervised hierarchical approach to document categorization. In *Proceedings of the IEEE/WIC/ACM international Conference on Web intelligence* (November 02 - 05, 2007) (pp. 482-486). Washington, DC: IEEE Computer Society.

White, C. S. (1997). Citizen participation and the internet: Prospects for civic deliberation in the Information Age. *Social Studies, 88*(1), 23–28. doi:10.1080/00377999709603741

Whitehorse Strategic Group, & MAV. (2002). *Local Government Online Services Project Report.* Paper presented at the Online Services Demonstration Conference, Melbourne, Australia.

Wikipedia. (2009). *Email spam legislation by country.* Retrieved April 19, 2009, from http://www.wikipedia.org

William, G. Z. (2003). *Business Research Method* (7th ed.). Oklahoma City, OK: South-Western.

Wilson of Dinton, L. (2006). The Contribution of Scholarship to Good Government. *British Academy Review, 9*(1), 44–47.

Wilson, C. (2008, February 22). The Wisdom of the Chaperones: Digg, Wikipedia, and the myth of Web 2.0 democracy. *Slate.* Retrieved June 19, 2009, from http://www.slate.com/id/2184487/

Wimmer, M. (2002). A European perspective towards online one-stop government: the eGov project. *Electronic Commerce Research and Applications, 1*, 92–103. doi:10.1016/S1567-4223(02)00008-X

Wimmer, M. A. (2003). E-Government services in future. Short abstract for the JANUS workshop, Brussels.

Wirth, W. (1986). Public Administration and Publics. In Kaufman, F. X., Majone, G., & Ostrom, V. (Eds.), *Guidance, Control, and Evaluation in the Public Sector.* Berlin: Walter de Gruyter.

Wolf, R., & Gordon, A. (2007). License Plate Recognition (LPR) technology: Practical and legal issues for police implementation. *Law Enforcement Executive Forum, 7*(7), 93–99.

Wong, W., & Welch, E. (2004). Does E-Government promote accountability?A comparative analysis of Website openness and government accountability. *Governance: An International Journal of Policy. Administration and Institutions, 17*(2), 275–297.

Wongtrakool, B. M. (1998). *Does paperless mean painless? Electronic tax return filing in the new millennium.* Retrieved September 25, 2008, from http://www.cyber.law.harvard.edu/is98/final_papers

World Bank. (2008). Freedom of information. Briefing paper. 'freedom of information in Pakistan: drawing on international experience'. *World Bank Workshop,* June 19, 2008.

World Bank. (2009a). Retrieved on July 29, 2009 from http://web.worldbank.org/WBSITE/EXTERNAL/DATASTATISTICS/0,contentMDK:20420458~menuPK:64133156~pagePK:64133150~piPK:64133175~theSitePK:239419,00.html

World Bank. (2009b). Retrieved on July 29, 2009 from http://web.worldbank.org/WBSITE/EXTERNAL/DATASTATISTICS/0,contentMDK:20535285~menuPK:1192694~pagePK:64133150~piPK:64133175~theSitePK:239419,00.html

Wright, S., & Street, J. (2007). Democracy, deliberation and design: The case of online discussion forums. *New Media & Society, 9*(5), 849–869. doi:10.1177/1461444807081230

Wu, I., & Chen, J. L. (2005). An Extension of Trust and TAM model with TPB in the initial adoption of on-line tax: An empirical study. *International Journal of Human-Computer Studies, 62*(6), 784–808. doi:10.1016/j.ijhcs.2005.03.003

Wu, L., Yang, L., Yu, N., & Hua, X. (2009). Learning to tag. In *Proceedings of the 18th international Conference on World Wide Web* (Madrid, Spain, April 20 - 24, 2009) (pp. 361-370). New York: ACM.

Wyld, D. (2007). *The Blogging Revolution: Government in the Age of Web 2.0. IBM Endowment for The Business of Government.* Retrieved from http://www.businessofgovernment.org/pdfs/WyldReportBlog.pdf

Xu, Z., Fu, Y., Mao, J., & Su, D. (2006). Towards the Semantic Web: Collaborative Tag Suggestions. *Workshop on Collaborative Web Tagging, WWW2006.*

Ya Ni, A., & Tat-Kei Ho, A. (2005). Challenges in e-government development: Lessons from two information kiosk projects. *Government Information Quarterly, 22*(1), 58–74. doi:10.1016/j.giq.2004.10.005

Yang, H., & Yoo, Y. (2004). It's all about attitude: revisiting the technology acceptance model. *Decision Support Systems, 38*(1), 19–31. doi:10.1016/S0167-9236(03)00062-9

Yang, K. F. (2003). Neoinstitutionalism and e-government: beyond Jane Fountain. *Social Science Computer Review, 21*(4), 432–442. doi:10.1177/0894439303256508

Yang, X. S. (2009, January). Direction of 2009 e-government development. *Saidi Net.* Retrieved March 19, 2009, from http://www.henan.gov.cn/zwgk/system/2009/01/16/010115118.shtml

Yen, D. C., & Evans, D. (2005). E-Government: An Analysis for implementation: Framework for understanding cultural and social impact. *Government Information Quarterly, 22*(3), 354–375. doi:10.1016/j.giq.2005.05.007

Yildiz, M. (2007). E-government research: Reviewing the literature, limitations, and ways forward. *Government Information Quarterly, 24*, 646–665. doi:10.1016/j.giq.2007.01.002

Yin, R. K. (1984). *Case Study Research: Design and Methods.* Thousand Oaks, CA: Sage.

Yoo, B., Naveen, D., & Lenartowicz, T. (2004, August). The Effects of Marketing Education and Individual Cultural Values on Marketing Ethics of Students. *Journal of Marketing Education, 24*, 92–103.

Yoshida, M., Shoji, M., Yamada, Y., & Minetaki, K. (2007). Analysis of Regional Social Networking Services: Community Participation and Regional Economic Revitalization in Japan. In M. Snaprud & A. Sawicka (Eds.), *T4P '07. Proceedings of the first T4P Conference*, 6 March 2008 (pp. 73-79). Retrieved May 1, 2009, from http://www.t4p.no/conference/conference/proceedings/T4P-proceedings-v5_1.pdf

Young, A. (1993). *Lessons from the East Asian NICS: A Contrarian View.* NBER Working Paper No. 4482. Cambridge, MA, USA: National Bureau of Economic Research.

Zambrano, R. (2008). E-Governance and Development: Service Deliver to Empower the Poor. *International Journal of Electronic Government Research, 4*(2), 1–13.

Zeithaml, V. A. (2002). Service excellence in electronic channels. *Managing Service Quality Journal, 12*(3), 135–139. doi:10.1108/09604520210429187

Zeithaml, V. A., Parasuraman, A., & Malhotra, A. (2000). *A conceptual framework for understanding e-service quality: Implications for future research and managerial practice*. Working Paper. Marketing Science Institute, Cambridge, MA.

Zhang, J. H. (2005). Good governance through e-governance? Assessing China's e-government strategy. *Journal of E-Government*, *2*(4), 39–71. doi:10.1300/J399v02n04_04

Zhen-Wei Qiang, C., Lanvin, B., & Minges, M. Swanson, E., Wellenius, B., Clarke, G., Halewood, N., Adamali, A., Coffey, J., & Safdar, Z. (2006). *Global trends and policies - 2006: information and communications for development*. Retrieved April 29, 2009, from http://www-wds.worldbank.org/external/default/WDSContentServer/WDSP/IB/2006/04/20/0000 12009_20060420105118/Rendered/PDF/359240PAPER0In101OFFICIAL0USE0ONLY1.pdf

Zombori, G. (2001). e + finance + crime: A report on cyber-crime and money laundering (Working document). Toronto: York University, Osgood Hall Law School, Nathanson Centre for the Study of Organized Crime and Corruption.

Zucker, L. G. (1986). Production of trust: institutional sources of economic structure, 1840-1920. *Research in Organizational Behavior*, *8*, 53–111.

Zussman, D. (2002). Alternative service delivery. In Dunn, C. (Ed.), *The handbook of Canadian public administration*. Oxford: Oxford University Press.

About the Contributors

Dr. Christopher G. Reddick is an associate professor and chair of the Department of Public Administration at the University of Texas at San Antonio. Reddick's research and teaching interests are in public administration and e-government. Reddick recently edited and authored two books—Handbook of Research on Strategies for Local E-Government Adoption and Implementation: Comparative Studies, and Homeland Security Preparedness and Information Systems: Strategies for Managing Public Policy.

* * *

Dr. Leonidas Anthopoulos studied computer science at Aristotle University of Thessaloniki, Greece. At his previous job positions, as an Expert Counselor at the Hellenic Ministry of Foreign Affairs in e-Government and e-Diplomacy areas, as an IT researcher and manager at the Research Committee of the Aristotle University of Thessaloniki (Greece), Municipality of Trikala (Greece), Administration of Secondary Education of Trikala (Greece) and Information Society S.A. (Greece), he designed and supervised multiple major IT projects. Currently, Dr Leonidas Anthopoulos is an Assistant Professor at the Project Management Department of the Technological Education Institute of Larissa, School of Business and Economics, Project Management Department (Greece). He is the author of several articles published on prestigious scientific journals, books and international conferences. His research interests concern, among others, e-Government, Enterprise Architecture, Social Networks, etc. He is also a member of evaluator committees for the Greek General Secretariat of R&D and for the Greek Information Society.

Dr. Ari-Veikko Anttiroiko is an Adjunct Professor in the Department of Regional Studies, University of Tampere, Finland. Anttiroiko's academic contributions include in a nutshell some 30 monographs, about 70 chapters and articles, and a number of conference/seminar papers. These include a special issue of IJTM on global competition of high-tech centres (IJTM, Vol. 28, Nos. 3/4/5/6, 2004) and co-edited works such as eTransformation in Governance (IGP 2004), e-City (TUP 2005), and the Encyclopedia of Digital Government (IGR 2007). He is also the editor of Electronic Government: Concepts, Methodologies, Tools, and Applications (ISR 2008), a comprehensive six-volume reference book on e-government.

Dr. Sudha Arlikatti has a Bachelor's in Architecture, Pune (1989), a Master's in City Planning, IIT Kharagpur, India (1999); and a PhD from Texas A&M University, USA (2006). She has worked as an Architect for eight years and is currently an Assistant Professor in the Department of Public Administration at the University of North Texas, Denton, Texas USA.

James Backhouse is Reader in Information Systems in the Information Systems and Innovation Group of the Department of Management at the LSE. His teaching and research focuses on the social study of information risk and security and he has publications in journals such as the Management of Information Systems Quarterly (MISQ), the European Journal of Information Systems (EJIS), and the Information Systems Journal (ISJ). He is active in standards and professional best practice, and a member of the Accreditation Committee of IISP (the Institute of Information Security Professionals). Since 2003 he has led EU-funded research at the LSE in both anti-money laundering and also in identity, security and privacy: he is a founder member of FIDIS, the 5-year EU research network of excellence. In 2007 he completed a review of ENISA, the European Network and Information Security Agency. He is the founder editor of the Springer journal Identity in the Information Society.

Dr. Martin Beer is a Principal Lecturer in the Communications and Computing Research Centre at Sheffield Hallam University. His research and teaching activities centre around the use of Multi-Agent Systems to provide more effective means of providing information and services to potential users of all types. His particular interests are currently in the use of advanced knowledge sharing techniques to allow much more focused and personalised delivery of information so that services can be provided efficiently and with minimal waste. Examples of applications where such techniques can be used effectively are in the delivery of community care, collaborative e-learning and the delivery of citizen information services.

John Carlo Bertot, Ph.D., is Professor and Director of the Center for Library and Information Innovation (http://www.liicenter.org/) in the College of Information Studies at the University of Maryland. Bertot is the Editor of Government Information Quarterly and of Library Quarterly. He has extensive research and grant management experience, having received grant funding from the Government Accountability Office, U.S. Institute of Museum and Library Services, the Bill & Melinda Gates Foundation, the American Library Association, and the Florida State Library and Archives, among others. Bertot also has conducts research in the areas of e-government and information policy, as well as public library management, technology planning, and program evaluation. His most recent book is Public Libraries and the Internet: Roles, Perspectives, and Implications (Libraries Unlimited, 2009) with Paul T. Jaeger and Charles R. McClure. Bertot currently serves as a board member of the Digital Government Society of North America, Chair of the International Standards Organization (ISO) 11620 standard working group for Library Performance Indicators, and member of the member of the American Library Association's E-government taskforce.

Dr. Manuel Pedro Rodríguez Bolívar is an Associate Professor at the Granada University (Spain). His research interests center on online financial information disclosures, the conceptual framework of accounting, the use of BSC and on environmental accounting. He is the author of articles in international journals, including the Government Information Quarterly, Public Administration and Development, Public Money & Management, International Review of Administrative Sciences and American Review of Public Administration. He has also contributed chapters to books, including one published by Kluwer Academic Publishers.

Salah Brahimi, Grey Matter International Ltd, will be a keynote speaker at the upcoming Gulf Petroleum Association annual conference. In addition, he is often invited to speak in the area of Emergency Management and Preparedness, particularly with regard to the economic impact of incidents and business continuity. Mr. Brahimi has also just received a mandate from SABIC (Saudi Arabia's Government backed petrochemicals giant) to advise on restructuring its massive private equity acquisitions special situations portfolios and to advise on foreign currency transactional policies. In January he served as the advisor to the Saudi G-20 preparatory Committee on the global financial crisis and has been involve in these issues from his time at the World Bank.

Mark K. Cassell is Associate Professor of Political Science at Kent State University where he teaches courses in public policy and administration, comparative public policy, and urban politics. His scholarship is mainly concerned with understanding public sector transformations. His work includes How Governments Privatize: The Politics of Divestment in the United States and Germany (Georgetown University Press, 2003). The book received the 2003 Charles H. Levine Award for the best book in public policy and administration. Dr. Cassell's work has also appeared in Public Administration Review, International Public Management Journal, Social Science Quarterly, and Governance: An International Journal of Policy. He currently has a book forthcoming from SUNY Press (with Susan M. Hoffmann) on mission expansion in the Federal Home Loan Bank System. Dr. Cassell holds a Ph.D., MPA, and MA in Political Science from the University of Wisconsin – Madison.

Dr. Don-yun Chen is a research fellow at the Taiwan e-Governance Research Center, which is sponsored by the Research, Development and Evaluation Committee (RDEC) of the Executive Yuan in Taiwanese central government. He is also an associate professor of Department of Public Administration, National Chengchi University, Taipei, TAIWAN. His areas of specialization are e-Governance, democratic governance, bureaucratic politics, policy analysis and management. He worked as a deputy director of Public Management Consulting Center at Shih Hsin University, a member of e-Governance committee of TASPAA (Taiwan Association for Schools of Public Administration and Affairs), policy consultant on e-government for the Taipei City Government, and a principle evaluator on e-government applications for the National Service Quality Award issued by the RDEC of the Executive Yuan.

Pin-Yu Chu is a Professor of the Department of Public Administration at National Chengchi University and the Director of Taiwan Electronic Governance Research Center, Taiwan. Dr. Chu's research interests include technology development and management, digital governance, and environment and conflict management. Her publications can be found in Government Information Quarterly, Omega, The International Journal of Management Science, Journal of Management & Organization, Public Performance and Management Review, Journal of Applied Social Psychology, International Journal of Technology Management, International Journal of Management and Decision Making, Electronic Government: An International Journal, etc. Dr. Chu teaches applied statistics, advanced research methodology, negotiation and ethics, project evaluation and decision-making, etc. She serves on the Personnel Policy Council, Central Personnel Administration of Taiwan, the Committee of Government Technology Program Review, the Review Expert Board of Higher Education Evaluation & Accreditation Council of Taiwan, the Committee of Public Advisory Panel for Taiwan Responsibility Care Association, etc.

Dr. Soon Ae Chun received her Ph.D and MBA from Rutgers University, and MS in Computer Science from SUNY Buffalo. She is currently an assistant professor of Information Systems in College of Staten Island, City University of New York. Dr Chun's research areas include Workflow Management, Information Security and Privacy, Policy-based Web Service Composition, the Semantic Web and Geospatial Database systems. Dr. Chun has served as an organization member for many conferences, including the annual conference of the digital government research, and served as reviewer for many journals and conference papers, including IEEE TSC, IEEE TKDE, IEEE Transactions of Information Technology in Biomedicine, IEEE Intelligent Systems, and International Journal of Information Security. She is a member of the IEEE Computer Society, the Association for Computing Machinery (ACM), the Association of Information Systems (AIS), and the Beta Gamma Sigma National Business Honor Society.

Magiswary Dorasamy, having earned her Bachelor of Arts in Economics from University of Malaya and a Master of Science in Information Technology from University Putra Malaysia, is currently a faculty member with the Faculty of Management, Multimedia University in Malaysia. She teaches IT subjects such as Information Systems, Management Information Systems, E-commerce and Management subjects. To date, she has had a distinguished corporate career in ICT industries and academia career spanning over 13 years and has established herself with extensive experience in research and development. She is also a member of Malaysian Economic Association (MEA) and Association of Information Systems (AIS). She has provided consultations / trainings on Technology Management in various companies such as MARTRADE and SKF Bearings Malysia. Her particular area of expertise is Information Systems. Her areas of research interest are ICT outsourcing, e-Government, and Knowledge Management Systems for Disaster Management. Her research has been accepted and published in several international and national journals including WSEAS Transactions on Systems Journal, Accountancy Business and Public Interest Journal, Journal of Public Procurement (JoPP), International Journal of Electronic Government Research (IJEGR), International Business and Economics Research Journal (IBER) and Public Sector ICT Management Review. She has also presented her works at several international and national conferences in China (2007), Turkey (2007), India (2006), Thailand (2006), Malaysia (2006, 2007. 2008), Greece (2009) and New Zealand (2009).

Yudi Fernando is currently pursuing his PhD at Universiti Sains Malaysia, Penang, Malaysia. He has an MBA from the School of Management in the same university. His research interest is on service marketing, supply chain relationships and has participated in many international conferences.

Prof. Panos Fitsilis studied computer engineering at Patras University, Greece. He received his PhD (1995) in Software Engineering. He worked, as software engineer and as business unit manager at large software development companies, and he was responsible for the development, deployment and operation of a number of prestigious IT systems for European Commission. Since 2003 he has been Professor at Technological Education Institute of Larissa, School of Business and Economics, Project Management Department. Currently, Prof. Panos Fitsilis is Head of Project Management Department and Deputy Director at Technological Research Center of Thessalia, Greece. He is the author of three books and author of many articles published on scientific journals and magazines. Further, he was member of the development team of Hellenic Standard on managerial capability of public organization, ELOT -1429. His research interests include: Project Management, Software Engineering, e-Government Systems, Business Process Reengineering, etc.

Dr. Vassilis C. Gerogiannis holds a Diploma and a PhD in Software Engineering from the University of Patras, Greece. At present, Dr. Gerogiannis is a fulltime Assistant Professor at the Project Management Department in the Technological Educational Institute (TEI) of Larissa, Greece. He is also a Lecturer at the Greek Open University and a Module Leader in a Post Graduate Program of Studies in Management Science, organized by TEI of Larissa in cooperation with the Staffordshire University, UK. Dr. Gerogiannis has been participating as a technical consultant and project manager in several EU funded R&D projects. Up to now, he has published more than 45 papers in international journals and conference proceedings. His research interests include Project Management, Software Project Management and Software Engineering.

Sarah Gregory is a senior at the University of North Texas in the College of Public Affairs and Community Service. Currently, she is working on a Bachelor of Science, majoring in Emergency Administration and Disaster Planning and minoring in Applied Anthropology.

Dr. Ruth Halperin holds a PhD in Information Systems from the London School of Economics and Political Science, where she is a Research Fellow in the Information Systems and Innovation Group of the Department of Management. Her current research interests are in information risk; security and privacy; digital identity and systems design and implementation. She is a member of the EU Network of Excellence FIDIS (Future of Identity in the Information Society) since its inception in 2004 and has published in the areas of risk perceptions, interoperable identity management systems and Profiling. Prior to joining the LSE in 2002, she was a Project Manager of a leading software development company specializing in E-learning and KM technologies.

Marvine Hamner is an Assistant Professor at George Washington University in Washington, DC, USA. Dr. Hamner is also a co-founder of a women-owned small business, LeaTech LLC. Dr. Hamner has over 20 years experience working and managing a variety of projects from research grants to multi-million dollar commercial programs and holds patents in the U.S. as well as several other countries. Dr. Hamner is an Associate Editor for the Journal of Homeland Security and Emergency Management. In addition, she reviews manuscripts for the Institute of Physics, Measurement Science and Technology Journal, Computers and Industrial Engineering, as well as Personality and Individual Differences. Dr. Hamner is currently an Associate Fellow with the American Institute of Aeronautics and Astronautics and a member of the International Association of Emergency Managers. She is a member of the MIT Club of Washington, the Women's Business Center in Washington, D.C., and the Philosophical Society of D.C.

Laurence Hauttekeete received her Ph.D in Communication Sciences from Ghent University, Belgium, in 2004. In her Ph.D she looks at tabloidisation tendencies in the Flemish press, the development of a measurement model. Her research interests include the printed and audio-visual media, media economics, new media and qualitative and quantitative research methods. She joined MICT (media and ICT) in 2005 as a senior researcher. Most of the projects she works upon are situated in a few domains: 'digitisation', 'culture and media', 'technology and youngsters/education', and 'ICT and government authorities'.

Antonio M. López Hernández, Ph. D. in Accounting, is Professor of Accounting at Granada University (Spain). His research interests center on management systems and financial information in federal and local government. He has published in journals such as International Journal of Public Sector Management, Government Information Quarterly, American Review of Public Administration, International Review of Administrative Sciences and is the author of chapters in several books, such as Innovations in Governmental Accounting (Kluwer Academic Publishers) or International Trends and Experiences in Government Accounting (Cappelen Akademisk Forlag).

George E. Higgins is an Associate Professor in the Department of Justice Administration at the University of Louisville. He received his Ph.D. in criminology from Indiana University of Pennsylvania in 2001. His most recent publications appear in Criminal Justice Studies, Deviant Behavior, Criminal Justice and Behavior, Youth and Society, and American Journal of Criminal Justice.

John Hoornbeek teaches and conducts research on public policies in the United States. He has more than twenty years of experience working in and around the local, state, and federal levels of American government. His research has appeared in both peer reviewed public policy journals and in edited books. He currently serves as director of Kent State University's (KSU) Center for Public Administration and Public Policy, and as an Assistant Professor in KSU's Department of Political Science. He earned his Bachelor's Degree at Beloit College, his Master's Degree at the University of Wisconsin – Madison, and his Doctorate at the University of Pittsburgh.

Dr. Lung-Teng Hu is a research fellow at the Taiwan e-Governance Research Center, which is sponsored by the Research, Development and Evaluation Committee (RDEC) of the Executive Yuan in Taiwanese central government. He is also an assistant professor of the Department of Public Policy and Management at Shih Hsin University in Taipei, TAIWAN. He currently serves as the vice executive director of the Transparency International's national chapter in Taiwan as well. He received his Ph.D. from the School of Public Affairs and Administration at Rutgers University at Newark, USA. His research interests include e-government and e-governance, knowledge management in the public sector, government performance measurement and management, as well as government transparency.

Tong-yi Huang received his Ph.D. from the Department of Government of the University of Texas at Austin. He is currently Associate Professor of the Department of Public Administration at National Cheng-chi University in Taipei, Taiwan. His recent research interests include deliberative democracy, e-government and bureaucracy. Professor Huang serves as a research fellow of Taiwan e-Government Research Center, on the advisory board of the Election Study Center of Cheng-chi University and Taipei University and on the executive board of Transparency International Taiwan.

Paul T. Jaeger, Ph.D., J.D., is Assistant Professor and Director of the Center for Information Policy and Electronic Government (www.cipeg.umd.edu) in the College of Information Studies at the University of Maryland. His research focuses on the ways in which law and public policy shape public access to information. Dr. Jaeger is the author of more than seventy journal articles and book chapters, along with six books. He is the Associate Editor of Library Quarterly. His research has been funded by the National Science Foundation, the Institute of Museum and Library Services, the American Library Association, and the Bill & Melinda Gates Foundation. His most recent books are Information Worlds:

Social Context, Technology, & Information Behavior in the Age of the Internet (Routledge, 2009) with Gary Burnett and Public Libraries and the Internet: Roles, Perspectives, and Implications (Libraries Unlimited, 2009) with John Carlo Bertot and Charles R. McClure.

Dr. Michael J. Jensen is a Beatriu de Pinós fellow at the Autonomous University of Barcelona Institute of Government and Public Policy (IGOP). He completed his Ph.D. at the University of California, Irvine in fall 2007 while working at the Center for Research on Information Technology and Organizations. He has since been a postdoctoral fellow in the Department of Political Science at Irvine as well as Visiting Professor at the Internet Interdisciplinary Institute at the Open University of Catalunya in Castelldefels, Spain. Dr. Jensen is currently working on the Politics and Internet in Spain (POLNET) project at IGOP where his primary interests include electronic government, electronic participation, governance practices, and political communication.

Dr. Maniam Kaliannan is an academic attached to the Universiti Teknologi MARA (UiTM), Shah Alam, Malaysia. He teaches subjects related to e-Goverment, Economics and Human Resource Management. His research work is related to e-Government and has been published in several international journals including Journal of Public Procurement (JoPP), International Journal of Business and Management (IJBM), online Journal of e-Government (IJEG), Journal of WSEAS Transactions on Business and Economics, Information Technology Journal (ITJ), International Business and Economics Research Journal (IBER) and ICT Management Review Journal. He has also presented his works at several international and national conferences and symposiums in China , Turkey (2007), Canada (2007), India (2006, 2007, 2009), Thailand (2006), Indonesia (2007), USA (2002, 2003. 2004), Greece (2009), Germany (2002), Italy (2003) and Malaysia (2002, 2003. 2006, 2007, 2008, 2009). He is currently a member of the Malaysian Economic Society and serves on the editorial board for several local and International e-Government related journals.

Dr. Ronnie L. Korosec is the Interim Associate Dean of Graduate Studies and Technology and an Associate Professor of Public Administration in the College of Health and Public Affairs at the University of Central Florida. She received her Ph.D. from the State University of New York at Binghamton, where she was a Clifford D. Clark Fellow. Her areas of interest include public policy and analysis, privatization, strategic planning and management, and state and local government issues. Dr. Korosec can be reached at rkorosec@mail.ucf.edu.

Ooh Kim Lean has an MBA from Universiti Sains Malaysia (USM). She has worked experience in manufacturing & service industry.

Chung-pin Lee is Ph.D. Candidate in the Department of Public Administration at National Chengchi University, Taiwan. He is also a Fulbright visiting researcher (August 2007- June 2008) at the Askew School of Public Administration and Policy, Florida State University. His research interests include e-government, e-democracy, citizen participation, and technology and society.

Xia Li Lollar is an associate professor at the University of Wisconsin-Whitewater. She received her Ph.D degree in political science from the University of Alabama at Tuscaloosa and a master degree of public administration from Iowa State University. Her teaching areas are public policy and administration, comparative politics and international relations. Her publications include articles on economic and political development and Internet use in China. She has also published a book titled China's Transition toward a Market economy, Civil Society and Democracy.

Kristina M. Lopez is a graduate student in the Department of Criminal Justice at the University of Texas at San Antonio. She previously served as the Managing Editor of the Journal of Criminal Justice Education and as a research assistant on a Texas Department of Criminal Justice funded evaluation of an in-prison alcohol recovery program. Currently, she is examining the effects of self-control on delinquency across Hispanic subgroups.

J. Mitchell Miller is a Professor in the Department of Criminal Justice at the University of Texas at San Antonio. The current President of the Southern Criminal Justice Association and a Fellow of Academy of Criminal Justice Sciences, his recent works include Crime & Criminals by Oxford University Press and Criminological Theory: A Brief Introduction by Prentice Hall.

Dr. Miquel Montaner, M.Sc. and Ph.D. in Computer Engineering and MBA by the University of Girona (UdG), Girona, in 1999, 2003 and 2008 respectively. His thesis focused on the application of intelligent agents to recommender systems. Part of this thesis was carried out at the Carnegie Mellon University (USA). The implementation of his thesis (the IRES/GenialChef project) was awarded with the Special Prize to the best system deployed in the Agentcities network in 2003 and the Prize to the Best University Project in the e-Tech'03. In 2003, after finishing his Ph.D., he joined Agents Inspired Technologies S.A as R+D manager. From July 2006 to June 2007, he was the business developer of the EASY transference center TECNIO-CIDEM (Government of Catalonia) at the University of Girona. From July 2007, he is working for Strategic Attention Management, S.L. as R+D manager. He currently holds a research fellowship from the Catalan Institution for Research and Advanced Studies (ICREA). He is avaible at mique@isac.cat

Ronnie Park is Information Systems (IS) Project Manager for the City of Los Angeles. While serving as an IS consultant in the field, he has been a scholar in academia. He has provided IS consulting services to various companies, such as PricewaterhouseCoopers, BlueCross, Southern California Edison and Great Western Bank. He has published e-government related papers in IEEE Computer Society and other peer-reviewed publications. He has presented his research at the Hawaii International Conference on System Sciences (HICSS, 2008), IS World (2007), Chinese Computer Association conference in Los Angeles (CCA, 2008) where he chaired the e-government sector, Korean Management Information Systems (KMIS, 2005). Dr. Park also serves as a reviewer for scholarly conferences, such as HICSS, and various publications. Dr. Park received his doctorate in IS at the Nova Southeastern University and masters degree in IS at the California State University, Los Angeles.

Carmen Caba Pérez, Ph. D. in Governmental Accounting, is Associate Professor at the Department of Accounting and Finance at the University of Almería (Spain). Her research interests are focused on the financial information disclosures on the Web (e-government), on the management system and financial information in the federal and local governments. She is author of numerous articles in national and international journals, including The International Journal of Public Sector Management, Government

Information Quarterly, International Review of Administrative Sciences, American Review of Public Administration, Public Administration and Development, Public. Also, she has written some book chapters (Kluwer Academic Publishers; Cappelen Akademisk Forlag).

Willem Pieterson works as an assistant professor in the Center for e-Government Studies at the University of Twente. He holds a PhD. Cum Laude in communication on a dissertation on channel choice decision making by citizens. He specializes in citizens' channel behavior, multi-channel management and e-Government. He has published various book chapters, conference papers and journal articles on these topics in journals such as Government Information Quarterly and the International Review of Administrative Sciences.

Dr. Murali Raman received his PhD in Management Information Systems from the School of IS & IT, Claremont Graduate University, USA. Dr. Murali is a Rhodes Scholar and a Fulbright Fellow. His other academic qualifications include an MBA from Imperial College of Science Technology and Medicine, London, an MSc in HRM from London School of Economics. Dr. Raman is currently an academician attached to Multimedia University Malaysia, where he teaches and conducts research in the area of Management Information Systems, Project Management and E-Business Models. He has published in more than fifty papers in International Journals and Conference proceedings. His corporate experience includes working with Maybank Malaysia (2 years) and Accenture Consulting (5 years) before embarking on an academic path. He has consulted with numerous companies including several based in the USA (Claremont University Consortium), Ghana (GIMPA), Singapore (AsiaOne, Kepple bank), Australia (Monash Supply Chain and Logistics Center), and Malaysia (Panasonic, OUM, RHB Bank, Intan, MAKPEM, Malaysian Association of Social Workers, CDC Consulting among others). His research interests are mainly in the area of Knowledge Management Systems and its application in an institutional context. He is currently an Associate Professor of Management Information Systems a Multimedia University. He is also a Visiting Professor at the Asia-Europe Institute (University Malaya).

T. Ramayah has an MBA from Universiti Sains Malaysia (USM). Currently, he is an Associate Professor at the School of Management in USM. He teaches main courses in research methodology and business statistics and has also conducted training courses for the local government (research methods for candidates departing overseas for higher degree, Jabatan Perkhidmatan Awam). Apart from teaching, he is an avid Researcher, especially in the areas of technology management and adoption in business and education. Thus far, he has published in several journals such as Information Development, Direct Marketing, WSEAS Transactions on Information Science & Applications, International Journal of Learning, the International Journal of Knowledge, Culture and Change Management, Asian Journal of Information Technology (AJIT), International Journal of Services and Technology Management (IJSTM), International Journal of Business Information Systems (IJBIS), etc.

Josep Lluís de la Rosa i Esteva is Associate Professor at the University of Girona (UdG) and the founding director of EASY Innova - TECNIO, and president of Strategic Attention Management S.L. He received his Ph.D. in Computer Engineering from the Autonomous University of Barcelona (UAB) in 1993, and a MBA in 2002. In 1993, he became assistant professor to the UAB, and in 1997 post-doc fellow at Laboratoire d'Architecture et d'Analyse des Systèmes (LAAS-CNRS) in Toulouse, France. His is interested in the application of intelligent agents to a variety of fields ranging from marketing and e-commerce to robotics and industrial applications. Dr. de la Rosa is a member of the Catalan Association of Artificial Intelligence ACIA (ECCAI). He is author of over one hundred scientific publications and four patents. He is now visiting Prof. Szymanski at Rensselaer Polytechnic Institute (RPI) in New York, USA, for the subject of citation auctions, an application of complementary currencies to science. He is available at peplluis@eia.udg.edu, http://eia.udg.edu/~peplluis

Mercè Rovira is visiting scientist to the University of Girona, Catalonia, Europe, and founder and former head of the I&R of the city of Girona. MSc in Management of Quality in services, and PhD candidate in Innovation in organizations, a PhD program in the University of Girona. Fulbright Scholar in USA (1993-94), specializing in Public Policy Management and Evaluation. At present, she is member of ARLab research team in the University of Girona, and project leader for knowledge transference projects (3Helix work) on Innovation in Local Administration. She is accessible to merce@isac.cat

Dr. Peter Shackleton gained his PhD in Local eGovernment from Monash University in 2006. He is currently a Senior Lecturer In Information Systems at Victoria University, Melbourne. He has over 20 years experience in teaching, consultancy and research in electronic government, programming and project management. He is a Certified Practitioner in PRINCE2 and ITIL Service Management Essentials. He has worked with the local government sector on research projects during sabbaticals. His current research has concentrated on local eGovernment service delivery maturity models.

Dr. Doaa Taha is an independent consultant in Washington, DC in the areas of Business Management and Emergency Management. Dr. Taha earned her doctorate through George Washington University's Institute for Crisis, Disaster and Risk Management. Her research in Emergency Management is highly regarded. She has several articles on Emergency Management in the area of Business Continuity and Continuity of Operations.

Dr. Kuan-Chiu Tseng is an assistant professor of the Department of Public Administration at the Tamkang University in Taipei, TAIWAN. His areas of specialization are e-Governance, government innovation, cross-boundary management and public bureaucracy. He works as a research fellow at the Taiwan e-Governance Research Center sponsored by the RDEC (Research, Development and Evaluation Committee) of the Executive Yuan.

Pieter Verdegem is a Ph.D. student and researcher at the Research Group for Media and ICT (MICT-IBBT), Ghent University (UGent) and the Interdisciplinary Institute for Broadband Technology (IBBT). His research focuses on ICT acceptance, e-government, information society, ICT policy and e-inclusion. He holds a master's degree in Communication Sciences and E-communications Studies. He is preparing a Ph.D. on government strategies particularly e-government and e-inclusion.

David Wachira is a doctoral student in Public Administration at the University of North Texas, Denton, TX. He has a B.A. in History and Political Science from the University of Mary Hardin-Baylor, Belton, TX (2005); and a M.A. in History from Tarleton State University Stephenville, TX (2008).

Janice Warner, PhD is an assistant professor at Georgian Court University, located at the New Jersey shore. Her research focuses on e-commerce – technical innovation, security and implications for society, including governments. Her doctorate from Rutgers University was in support of secure, ad-hoc collaboration. She also completed her MBA at Rutgers. Previously, she was a systems engineer with BS and MS degrees from Columbia University in Electrical Engineering. She worked with telecommunications corporations in developing their data networks as a consultant with Telcordia and Bellcore and spent two years working for Siemens in Munich, Germany. She is a member of the Association for Computing Machinery (ACM), the Beta Gamma Sigma National Business Honor Society and the Delta Mu Delta Business Honor Society.

Dr. Ross Wolf is an Assistant Professor of Criminal Justice and Research Fellow in the College of Health and Public Affairs at the University of Central Florida. His areas of research interests include police administration and training, police management, international policing, and tourism policing. Dr. Wolf has over eighteen years of experience as a law enforcement officer and has worked various assignments including Patrol, Criminal Investigations, and with a plain-clothed tactical unit. He continues to serve as a Police Academy Instructor and as Chief with the Orange County (Florida) Sheriff's Office Reserve Unit. Dr. Wolf can be reached at rwolf@mail.ucf.edu.

Shang-Ching Yeh is currently Assistant Researcher of the Division of Collections and Research at the National Science and Technology Museum, Taiwan. He is also a research fellow at the Taiwan Electronic Governance Research Center. Dr. Yeh's research interests include electronic governance, government information technology management, and digital collection. His publications have appeared in Electronic Government, An International Journal, and The Journal of Solid Waste Technology and Management.

Suhaiza Zailani graduated from Lancaster University, Lancaster, UK for MSc in Operational Research and PhD in Management Science. Currently, she is an Associate Professor attached to the School of Management, Universiti Sains Malaysia, Penang. Her teaching areas are operations management, productivity and quality control and management science. Her current areas of interest are supply chain management, benchmarking, new product development, and quality and productivity in organisations in general. She has also jointly produced many articles published in a local journal and international journal such as International Journal of Information Management, Benchmarking, Supply Chain Management: An International Journal, International Journal of Productivity and Quality Management, International Journal of Value Chain Management, International Journal of Operations and Supply Chain Management, International Journal of Services and Operations Management, etc.

Index

D

E

H

I

M

N

Q

R

S

T

U

V

W

Y

Z